ORE FROM THE PURITANS' MINE

ORE FROM THE PURITANS' MINE

The Essential Collection of Puritan Quotations

Compiled by
Dale W. Smith

Reformation Heritage Books
Grand Rapids, Michigan

Ore from the Puritans' Mine
© 2020 by Dale W. Smith

Reformation Heritage Books
2965 Leonard St. NE
Grand Rapids, MI 49525
616–977–0889
orders@heritagebooks.org
www.heritagebooks.org

Printed in the United States of America
20 21 22 23 24 25/10 9 8 7 6 5 4 3 2 1

Library of Congress Cataloging-in-Publication Data

Names: Smith, Dale W., compiler.
Title: Ore from the Puritans' mine : the essential collection of Puritan quotations / compiled by Dale W. Smith.
Description: Grand Rapids, Michigan : Reformation Heritage Books, 2020. | Includes bibliographical references and index.
Identifiers: LCCN 2020028946 (print) | LCCN 2020028947 (ebook) | ISBN 9781601787750 (hardback) | ISBN 9781601787767 (epub)
Subjects: LCSH: Puritans—Great Britain—Quotations.
Classification: LCC BX9334.3 .S65 2020 (print) | LCC BX9334.3 (ebook) | DDC 285/.9—dc23
LC record available at https://lccn.loc.gov/2020028946
LC ebook record available at https://lccn.loc.gov/2020028947

For additional Reformed literature, request a free book list from Reformation Heritage Books at the above regular or e-mail address.

For Teresa, whose character is my boon, and
for Andrew: now that I am done, let's "bring it in."

CONTENTS

FOREWORD

Have you ever wondered why preachers like Sinclair Ferguson, John MacArthur, John Piper—and thousands more not as well known—quote the Puritans so often in their preaching and teaching? Why is it that the Puritans are quoted by speakers at Reformed conferences in our day far more than any other group of writers in church history?

In an era of theological confusion and moral compromise, we can gain much by reading the Puritans. In countless areas and in various ways, the Puritans are a shining light to look back to and glean from. Though they were far from perfect and had blind spots much like every other generation, they were giants of the faith who sought to bring every part of life under the lordship of Jesus Christ.

Consequently, the Puritans excel in bringing the whole counsel of God contained in Scripture to bear upon the totality of our lives—our thinking, speaking, and acting or, as they would say it, our heads, hearts, and hands. In seamless harmony, they wed together intellectual astuteness and godly piety.

The Puritan emphasis in bringing the whole Christ to the whole man is contagious, edifying, convicting, alluring, and winsome for the true Christian. There is something gripping, something quotable, about the Puritans as they ransack Scripture and expound it in thoughts that are riveting in their word choices and metaphors, and one cannot but feel deeply the full force of the truths they convey. For example, who will not reflectively examine his own heart when reading this quotation from William Gurnall under the entry "Heart": "A sincere heart is like a clear stream in a brook: you may see to the bottom of his plots in his words and take the measure of his heart by his tongue"; or this from Ralph Robinson under the entry "Christ": "Christ is not loved at all till He be loved above all"?

The Puritan preachers were particularly zealous for Christ. They preached of the living Savior as dying men to dying people. Their rediscovery in the late

1950s and the reprinting of close to a thousand Puritan volumes since then has been a huge blessing for the church of Jesus Christ. I can honestly say that no spiritual discipline has profited me so much as to have had a steady diet of reading the Puritans for more than a half century. I always try to be reading at least one Puritan book at all times, even as I read a number of other titles from the past and present. I must admit that I usually get the most profit from the Puritan title I'm reading. Their biblical, doctrinal, experiential, and practical emphases are good for my mind, soul, will, and affections. The Puritans are masters at discipling God's children into spiritual maturity and adulthood.

These are just a few of the reasons why we are excited to publish Dale Smith's large and rich compilation of Puritan quotations. You and I are now the beneficiaries of his labor of love spanning decades, making this the most definitive, valuable, and thorough collection of Puritan quotations ever published. I, for one, feel deeply indebted to him for the substantiveness and exhaustiveness of his compilation. And I trust that as you read or peruse this volume, you will feel that everything I stated above is actually underestimating the value of reading the Puritans!

So how should you use this treasure trove of quotations? Let me provide several possible ways:

1. At the simplest level, this is a great book for quotables to use for letters, church bulletins, and filler pieces in periodicals.

2. At a slightly deeper level, open the book anywhere and start reading and meditating. You will immediately find yourself in the green pastures of God's word and Puritan wisdom.

3. At a somewhat profounder level, you would profit greatly by making this volume a daily devotional, reading one quote at a time, meditating on it, then praying about it in terms of its application to your mind and soul. Reading one subject or a portion of a page each day, with the Spirit's blessing, would be a huge boon to your soul over a period of time.

4. Fathers, you could read a few quotations or one subject at a time to your loved ones in family worship. These could serve as a rich enhancement of your family worship time — especially if you take the time to explain some of the quotations at a level that even young children could grasp.

5. At the deepest level, you could profit greatly as a pastor, teacher, parent, or student from consulting this book whenever you are preparing to deliver or write a message on a Christian subject. When you find a Puritan quotation on the subject you are studying that seems particularly

helpful, look up the original source (if possible) and read it in its context. You will usually find that the immediate context, and often the entire chapter, will shed much more scriptural light on the study you are pursuing. For this reason, I am so grateful to the compiler for providing the source and page number where each quotation can be found. This can be a tremendous help for in-depth study.

As I made my final review of this volume prior to publication, I have received untold benefit from reading it and would encourage you also to read it from beginning to end—slowly, meditatively, and prayerfully. You will not be disappointed. This, I trust, is a book that you will return to repeatedly for the rest of your life.

—Joel R. Beeke
Puritan Reformed Theological Seminary
Grand Rapids, Michigan

HOW TO USE THIS BOOK

The quotations in this book are arranged alphabetically by topic. Within the topic, they are arranged alphabetically by authors' last names. Quotations from the same author on the same topic yet drawn from more than one of an author's works are then arranged alphabetically by the first word of the work's title, excluding articles. Thus, for example, under the topic "Affliction, God's Purpose in," quotations by Thomas Watson come in this order: *The Beatitudes, The Lord's Prayer,* and *The Mischief of Sin*. A few anonymous quotes have been included. Obviously, no author's name is given, but the title of the source from which it comes is provided. These sources are listed alphabetically in the bibliography.

One of the goals of the compiler and publisher was to give readers information about the sources from which the quotations were drawn. Unique to this volume, sources are given for each quotation. Accompanying the quotation is a short form of the title of the work from which it was drawn with the page number(s). Full titles are given for works within a work (for example, Thomas Watson, *The Beatitudes,* in *Discourses*). A full citation for each source is provided in the bibliography.

A few editorial changes were made to make quotations more accessible for modern readers. British and archaic spellings were changed to modern, American spellings. Punctuation was modernized. References to Bible verses were placed in parentheses, Bible books were abbreviated according to Reformation Heritage Books preferred style, and any roman numerals for verse and chapter references were changed to arabic numerals. Any minor edits to quotations were placed in brackets to indicate word replacements or brief explanations. Nothing of substance or meaning was changed in any of the quotations.

As you read these words of the Puritans, may they bring you spiritual encouragement and growth in your knowledge of God and His word, and may this volume serve you well as a useful resource.

TO THE READER

The book you are now holding in your hand or perhaps looking at in your e-reader is a compilation, a collection of quotes. As such, it has many weaknesses. Please forgive its shortcomings and rejoice in its strengths. This is a book designed for the believer's edification more than the scholar's approval. It is offered in much the same way that the Puritan William Secker offered *The Nonsuch Professor*. He wrote, "I here present you with a piece, which is more practical than notional; more fit for a *Christian* to *live upon*, than for a *critic* to *look upon*. I hope the dregs do not lie so thick in it as to prevent your drawing clear wine from it."[1]

This selection of quotes and passages found its genesis in an invitation. At the beginning of my pastorate at The Road Church, Blue Springs, Missouri, I invited a generation of Puritan pastors, through their writings, to speak truth into my life and to form around me a cohort of men who would guide me and hold me accountable. I had some familiarity with a few of them already through reading Spurgeon's work but now have the real joy and spiritual benefit that a more thorough acquaintance with the Puritans brings. As I immersed myself in their writings, I selected certain passages and quotes that really challenged and comforted me. As the number of quotes grew, I realized that this material would be a real benefit to the believers at The Road. This motivated me to keep going, and the collection you now hold is the result of that work.

Before moving on to describe the selection process, the question must be asked, Who are the Puritans? For the purpose of this work, the Puritans are seventeenth-century English Protestants who ministered mostly in England. These were individuals who wanted to see the reformation of the English church carried out to the uttermost. They wanted all vestiges of unbiblical Roman Catholic traditions purged from the church. These were individuals who longed

---

1. William Secker, *The Nonsuch Professor* (London: Richard D. Dickinson, 1867), vi.

to see God glorified, sin mortified, and affliction sanctified. The Puritans had set themselves both to master the biblical texts and to be mastered by the text. That is to say, they studied the Bible rigorously. They applied the Bible vigorously and with great precision and zeal into every area of human existence, especially the heart.

Who were some of these individuals? I include quotations mostly from the works of Richard Baxter (1615–1691), Thomas Brooks (1608–1680), John Flavel (1628–1691), William Gurnall (1617–1679), Thomas Manton (1620–1677), John Owen (1616–1683), Richard Sibbes (1577–1635), George Swinnock (1627–1673), John Trapp (1601–1669), Ralph Venning (1621–1673), and Thomas Watson (c. 1620–1686). I do include one quote from the holy John Bradford (1510–1555), even though he is identified as a forerunner to the Puritans. Admittedly, there are others who have made their way into the text who do not fit this initial description. Puritan-minded divines from Scotland like Samuel Rutherford (1600–1661), Thomas Boston (1676–1732), and Andrew Gray (1634–1656) and English Puritans from the early eighteenth century like Matthew Henry (1662–1714) are also referenced. This collection includes material from those of differing views on the form that church government should take. Presbyterians, Independents, and Particular Baptists are represented. The one thing these individuals have in common is what bound all the Puritans together: a deep desire to live life to the glory of God.

For the most part, I exclude American Puritans like Thomas Hooker (1586–1647), John Cotton (1585–1652), and Increase Mather (1639–1723). I also exclude men who operate outside of the seventeenth century but are worthy enough to carry the mantle "Puritan." These include Jonathan Edwards (1703–1758), J. C. Ryle (1816–1900), Charles H. Spurgeon (1834–1892), and D. Martyn Lloyd-Jones (1899–1981). I also exclude the English reformers Thomas Cranmer (1489–1556), Hugh Latimer (1487–1555), and Nicholas Ridley (1500–1555).

This work reflects a tradition of collecting quotes, including I. D. E. Thomas in *A Puritan Golden Treasury* (1975) and H. J. Horn in *A Puritan Remembrancer* (1928). Their valuable work is preceded by *Oweniana* (1817), a collection of quotations by John Owen arranged by Arthur Young; *Smooth Stones* (1860), a compilation by Charles Spurgeon of quotations by Thomas Brooks; and *The Golden Book of John Owen*, edited by James Moffatt (1904). This work, *Ore from the Puritans' Mine*, is written, I imagine, in much the same spirit that motivated these other men, a desire to build the church and to introduce a generation of readers to the thought of the Puritans. The differences, which I hope are helpful, are citations that follow each quote and an annotated bibliography at the end of the book that provides the actual sources for the quotes. Also, at the end of the book is a bibliography of works recommended with resources for further reading on the Puritans. To readers who lament that they do not have access to the original materials, I say, "Lament not." Almost all the material cited in this compilation is drawn from readily available material for free through Google Books. There are just a few works that the reader will not be able to access immediately. Although there are some exceptions, I, for the most part, avoided using quotations from works included on Early English Books Online and other databases that require a fee or feature restricted access. This is not to say that I think reading the earliest versions of these works is best. On the contrary, I encourage readers who want to go deeper to purchase modernized versions of Puritan writings, like what is offered in the Puritan Treasures for Today series published by Reformation Heritage Books.

It is my sincere hope that readers will mine these materials and find themselves strengthened in their walk with the Lord. These selections reflect a pastor's heart, a preacher's ear, and, to some extent, a scholar's discipline. The very last topic to be covered in this work is "zeal." And in one of the last quotations of this last topic, Thomas Watson exhorts us: "Take heed of declining in your affections." In one sentence Watson summarizes one of the central features of Puritanism and one of the reasons this collection was compiled. Dear reader, I implore you to watch your life and doctrine closely and take heed of declining in your affections for the triune God and His truth.

Yours in what service of love I can,
Dale W. Smith

ACKNOWLEDGMENTS

"Of the making of books, there is no end," and of the listing off of those to whom I am deeply indebted, there is almost no end. I am especially grateful for the influence of the Rev. Jack Schneider. In 1983, Jack gave me two books: Loraine Boettner's *Reformed Doctrine of Predestination* and A. W. Pink's *The Sovereignty of God*. That was pretty heady stuff for a sixteen-year-old recent convert to Christianity. I loved that theology, and I really loved the God who inspired it. Jack also introduced me to Charles Haddon Spurgeon. It was through Spurgeon that I came to know and appreciate the Puritans.

There have been so many godly pastors and friends who have been a source of encouragement and joy to me through the years: Gary Clark, Barbara Austen, Tony Preston, Larry and Betty Chapman, Russell Walje, Ken Steele, Sean Lee, Tony Darnell, Spencer Ray, Trent Allen, Andy Wallis, Chris Nickerson, Wayne Tiffany, George Lank, Joe Rustin, Mark Weeks, Les McAdoo, and many others. I want to extend a special note of thanks to the church that I am currently serving as one of the pastors. The Road Church (Blue Springs, Missouri) has been such a blessing to me and to my family. We love worshiping, loving, and serving the Lord alongside all of you. I am grateful for the leadership, growing friendship, and support from the elders of The Road: Dave Cross, Roger High, Dave Schroeder, and Brian Wilson. I would be remiss not to mention my appreciation for Charles Ackmann, who serves The Road as one of its pastors. Charles has done a little bit of everything, from administrative work to preaching and teaching, from youth leadership to working with the building committee. Without his colaboring, the speed and joy with which I was able to tackle this project would not have been possible.

I want to say thank you to my wife, Teresa, and my son, Andrew. Their support, patience, and understanding are deeply appreciated. Many opportunities for family activities were set aside as I worked to finish this volume. They were good sports throughout the process. The next time you go to the zoo, I am going too! Finally, I want to say thank you to Jay Collier, Annette Gysen, and everyone at Reformation Heritage Books who brought this project across the finish line.

✦ QUOTATIONS ✦

ABILITIES

Observe and weigh well that the issue of all depends not upon the abilities of man, but upon the all-disposing hand of God. "The race is not to the swift, nor the battle to the strong; neither yet bread to the wise, nor riches to men of understanding." All our abilities are under God's providence, who puts an efficacy into man's abilities, even as He pleaseth.

♦ ISAAC AMBROSE
"The Practice of Sanctification," in *Works*, 94

ACCOUNTABILITY

No man that is in his right wits will lay open to everyone his bodily infirmities, weaknesses, diseases, ailments, and griefs, but to some near relation, bosom friend, or able physician. So no man that is in his right wits will lay open to everyone his soul infirmities, weaknesses, diseases, ailments, and griefs, but to the Lord or to some particular person that is wise, faithful, and able to contribute something to his soul's relief.

♦ THOMAS BROOKS
Privy Key of Heaven, 18

If yet Satan dogs thee, call in help and keep not the devil's counsel. The very strength of some temptations lies in the concealing of them, and the very revealing of them to some faithful friend gives the soul present ease. Satan knows this too well, and therefore, as some thieves, when they come to rob a house either gag them in it or hold a pistol to their breast, frighting them with death if they cry or speak; thus Satan, that he may the more freely rifle the soul of its peace and comfort overawes it so that it dares not disclose its temptation. "O," saith Satan, "if thy brethren or friends know such a thing by thee they will cast thee off; others will hoot at thee." Thus many a poor soul hath been kept long in its pangs by biting them in. Thou losest, Christian, a double help by keeping the devil's secret: the counsel and prayers of thy fellow brethren. And what an invaluable loss is this!

♦ WILLIAM GURNALL
Christian in Complete Armour, 68

Let not a day pass without serious communing with your own hearts. Inquire of your poor soul whether there be anything of the acting of grace in duty; anything of faith, love, humility, zeal; what answer you have of prayer; what of God you enjoy in all ordinances. In all companies inquire what progress you make heavenward and what declinings and backslidings you are guilty of, and do not bear with your hearts when they begin to be dull, indifferent, and formal.

♦ JAMES JANEWAY
Saint's Encouragement, 132–33

ACTIONS TRUER THAN WORDS

It is not the knowing, nor the talking, nor the reading man but the doing man that at last will be found the happiest man.

♦ THOMAS BROOKS
Great Gain, 12

I care not what words I hear when I see deeds. I am sure what a man doeth, he thinketh; not so always what he speaketh. Though I will not be so severe a censor that for some few evil acts I should condemn a man of false-heartedness; yet in common course of life, I need not be so foolish as not to believe rather the language of the hand than of the tongue. He that says well and doeth well is without exception commendable, but if one of these must be severed from the other, I like him well that doeth well and saith nothing.

✦ JOSEPH HALL
Meditations and Vows, 79

ADAM

Union and similitude is the ground of fellowship and communion. That union was gracious, that communion would have been glorious; for grace is the seed of glory. There was a two-fold union between Adam and God, a union of state and a union of nature: he was like God, and he was God's friend. All the creatures had some likeness to God, some engravings of His power and goodness and wisdom. But man is said to be made according to God's image: "Let us make man like unto us."

✦ HUGH BINNING
Common Principles of the Christian Religion, in Works, 1:19

"I heard thy voice in the garden" (Gen. 3:10). It is a word from without that does it. While Adam listened to his own heart, he thought fig leaves a sufficient remedy, but the voice that walked in the garden shook him out of all such fancies.

✦ JOHN BUNYAN
Riches, 144

When Adam was thrust naked out of Paradise into the cold blast of a miserable world where, from his own guilty conscience within and crosses without, he was sure to meet with trouble enough, then God gave him a word of promise, as you may observe, to fence his soul before He taught him to make coats to clothe his body (Gen. 3:15; cf. v. 21). The Lord knew how indispensably necessary a word of promise was to keep him from being made prey the second time to the devil and from being swallowed up with the dismal sight of those miseries and sorrows in which he had thrown himself and posterity; therefore, He would not suffer him to lie open to the shock of their assaults one day, but presently puts the sword of a promise into his hand, that with it he might defend and comfort his sorrowful heart in the midst of all his troubles.

✦ WILLIAM GURNALL
Christian in Complete Armour, 583–84

All were hewn out of this rock [i.e., Adam], an observation that puts us upon sundry useful considerations. It teaches us humility. As we were from Adam, so he was from the dust of the earth, and that dust from nothing. Our father was Adam, our grandfather dust, our great-grandfather nothing.

✦ WILLIAM JENKYN
Exposition upon the Epistle of Jude, 299

O, consider those fearful sins that are packed up in this one evil [i.e., Adam's sin]: (1) Fearful apostasy from God like a devil. (2) Horrible rebellion against God in joining sides with the devil and taking God's greatest enemies' part against God. (3) Woeful unbelief, in suspecting God's threats to be true. (4) Fearful blasphemy in conceiving the devil (God's enemy and man's murderer) to be more true in his temptations than God in His threatening. (5) Horrible pride, in thinking to make this sin of eating the forbidden fruit to be a step and a stair to rise higher and to be like God Himself. (6) Fearful contempt of God, making bold to rush upon the sword of the threatening secretly, not fearing the plague denounced. (7) Horrible unthankfulness, when God had given him all but one tree, and yet he must be fingering that too. (8) Horrible theft, in taking that which was none of his own. (9) Horrible idolatry, in doting upon and loving the creature more than God the Creator, who is blessed forever.

✦ THOMAS SHEPARD
Sincere Convert, 36–37

Compare the children of God with Adam in a state of innocency. Adam was a person of honor. He was the sole monarch of the world; all the creatures did vail to him as their sovereign. He was placed in the garden of Eden, which was a paradise of pleasure. He was crowned with all the contentments of the earth. Nay, more, Adam was God's lively picture; he was made in the likeness of God Himself. Yet the state of the meanest of God's children by adoption is far more excellent and honorable than the state of Adam was when he wore the robe of innocency, for Adam's condition, though it was glorious, was mutable and soon lost. Adam was a bright star, yet a falling star; but God's children by adoption are in a state unalterable. Adam had a possibility of standing, but believers have an impossibility of falling; once adopted, and ever adopted.

✦ THOMAS WATSON
The Beatitudes, in *Discourses*, 2:320

ADMONITION

Silence is consent by God's law (Lev. 5:1). And by ill silence to leave men in sin is as bad as by ill speech to draw them to sin.

✦ JOHN TRAPP
Marrow of Many Good Authors, 1046

ADOPTION

Adoption follows reconciliation, whereby the Lord accounts us sons: "Behold what manner of love the Father hath bestowed upon us, that we should be called the sons of God." The Lord accounts us just in our justification, friends in our reconciliation, sons in our adoption. Now this adoption is either begun in this life or perfected in the world to come, when we shall receive all the privileges of sons. Sanctification follows adoption: no sooner are we sons, but we receive the image of our heavenly Father in sanctification.

✦ ISAAC AMBROSE
"The Practice of Sanctification," in *Works*, 78

Adoption is the gracious sentence of God whereby He accepts the faithful for Christ's sake unto the dignity of sons.

✦ WILLIAM AMES
Marrow of Sacred Divinity, 135

Adoption is the taking of persons that are strangers and undeserving in themselves into a state and relation of sons and heirs, bringing them into a new family and condition. And such is the adoption of the sons of God: [it] is a translation of called and sanctified souls out of the family of Satan into the family of God (Col. 1:13).

✦ BARTHOLOMEW ASHWOOD
Best Treasure, 258

Now in the adoption of sanctified souls there are these…things…. [There is] a change in their state and condition; they are brought into a state of glorious privileges in respect of (1) liberty, (2) rights and interests, (3) boldness, (4) instruction, (5) correction, (6) provision, (7) protection, (8) inheritance. And by these the state of an adopted soul appears to be a glorious state.

✦ BARTHOLOMEW ASHWOOD
Best Treasure, 260

The Spirit cannot, after He hath come to the soul as a Spirit of adoption, come again as a Spirit of bondage to put the soul into his first fear—to wit, a fear of eternal damnation—because He cannot say and unsay, do and undo. As a Spirit of adoption, He told me that my sins were forgiven me and I was included in the covenant of grace, that God was my Father through

Christ, that I was under the promise of salvation, and that this calling and gift of God to me are permanent and without repentance. And do you think that after He told me this and sealed up the truth of it to my precious soul He will come to me and tell me that I am yet in my sins, under the curse of the law and the eternal wrath of God? No, no, the word of the gospel is not yea, yea; nay, nay. It is only yea and amen; it is so "as God is true" (2 Cor. 17:20).

✦ JOHN BUNYAN
Riches, 195–96

Once more, frequency and fervency in prayer will be a great evidence of your regeneration and adoption. The child when born cries, and the sinner when born again prays. Of Paul it was said as soon as he was converted, "Behold he prayeth." It is the "Spirit of adoption" that makes us cry "Abba Father." If we cannot be satisfied unless we approach God and value His favor and fellowship above all earthly things and are chiefly desirous of those blessings He never gives in wrath and, having given, never takes away again, we may conclude from our spiritual breathing our spiritual life.

✦ NATHANIEL VINCENT
Spirit of Prayer, 45

ADULTERY

Indeed, the devil tempts to it by hopes of secrecy and concealment, but though many other sins lie hid and possibly shall never come to light until that day of manifestation of all hidden things, yet [adultery] is a sin that is most usually discovered. Under the law, God appointed an extraordinary way for the discovery of it (Num. 5:13). And to this day, the providence of God doth often very strangely bring it to light, though it be a deed of darkness. The Lord hath many times brought such persons, either by terrors of conscience, temporary madness, or some other means, to be the publishers and proclaimers of their own shame.

✦ JOHN FLAVEL
"The Harlot's Face in the Scripture Glass,"
in *Navigation Spiritualized*, 181

EUCHEDIDASCALUS: What remedies have you against the temptations of adultery?

PHILEUCHES: I must meditate here:

1. that God sees me (Prov. 5:21);

2. that God can punish me (Gen. 20:3);

3. that He will punish me (2 Sam. 12:11–12);

4. that I am a member of Christ (1 Cor. 6:15);

5. that adulterers shall not inherit heaven (1 Cor. 6:9);

6. that such people seldom repent (Prov. 7:26–27);

7. that such a thing should not be done in Israel (Deut. 23:17–18);

8. that it made Solomon to commit idolatry (1 Kings 11:4);

9. that for the whorish woman, a man is brought to a morsel of bread (Prov. 6:26);

10. that I do not as I would be done to (Matt. 7:12);

11. that I wrong the church and commonwealth by obtruding to both a bastardly generation, for neither can know their true children;

12. that as by this I endanger my soul, so must I needs decay my body and when I am dead leave a blot behind me which never can be wiped out (Prov. 6:32–33).

✦ ROBERT HILL
Pathway to Piety, 1:95

Suffer not these bodies of yours to dishonor your Christ while you are upon earth. Let not those eyes be windows of lust and inlets to adultery with which you one day hope to behold your Father and your Redeemer Jesus Christ in glory.

✦ CHRISTOPHER LOVE
Heaven's Glory, 105

By wanton touches and dalliance, mental adultery is oft committed.

✦ JOHN TRAPP
Commentary on the Old and New Testaments, 1:142

ADVERSITY

A humble soul knows that to bless God in prosperity is the way to increase it, and to bless God in adversity is the way to remove it.

✦ THOMAS BROOKS
Unsearchable Riches of Christ,
in *Select Works*, 1:23–24

The wounds of mercy are better than the embraces of anger. If sickness, poverty, dishonor be in mercy, why dost thou shrink at them? Wrath in prosperity is dreadful, but mercy makes adversity comfortable.

♦ WILLIAM JENKYN
Exposition upon the Epistle of Jude, 30

Divine grace, even in the heart of weak and sinful man, is an invincible thing. Drown it in the waters of adversity, it rises more beautiful, as not being drowned in deed but only washed; throw it into the furnace of fiery trials, it comes out purer and loses nothing but the dross that our corrupt nature mixes with it.

♦ ROBERT LEIGHTON
A Commentary upon the First Epistle of Peter, in *Whole Works*, 1:61

Adversity is a condition of life which consists in the want of outward good things and presence of outward evil things, as sickness, disgrace, poverty, imprisonment, and the like.

♦ GEORGE SWINNOCK
A Christian Man's Calling, in *Works*, 2:82

ADVICE AND COUNSEL

A counselor's part is not only to give counsel but to keep counsel, to be secret and reserved. To keep your friends' secrets is religion; to keep your own is safety. For so shall you not be prevented in your designs, which will be sooner effected by a prudent disguising of your purposes, like the watermen who in rowing turn their backs to the landing place. Depend not upon human wisdom and policy, but depend on God. Choose the fittest means to your just ends and leave the success to Him.

♦ WILLIAM HIGFORD
Institutions, 66

AFFECTIONS

Labor for intenseness of affection. In meditation, prayer, or any other work, be intense. We used to say, "When the candle burns, the mouse does not nibble; but when the candle is out, then the mouse nibbles." When our hearts are warm and lively in prayer and meditation, we are free from distractions; the mouse nibbles not.

♦ WILLIAM BRIDGE
Christ and the Covenant, in *Works*, 3:150

The affections are the forcible and sensible motions of the heart, or the will, to a thing or from a thing, according as it is apprehended to be good or to be evil.

♦ WILLIAM FENNER
A Treatise of Affections, in *Works*, 2

The main work of grace is the ruling of the affections aright. It takes them off from the things here on earth and lifts them up to the things that are in heaven. When grace does convert a man, it does not take away the affections, but it rules them.

♦ WILLIAM FENNER
A Treatise of Affections, in *Works*, 22

Grace comes not to take away a man's affections, but to take them up.

✦ WILLIAM FENNER
in Horn, *Puritan Remembrancer*, 22;
Thomas, *Puritan Golden Treasury*, 89

Here be directed in a way how to enlarge your love to Godward. God's kindness has an operative virtue in it and much affects those who set their minds upon it. Naturally we have no heat of love to God in our hearts; they are frozen and cold. But as iron put into the fire soon becomes red hot, so upon a due consideration of God's mercies toward us, our affections cannot but glow with heat and be much inflamed.

✦ NEHEMIAH ROGERS
The Penitent Citizen, in *Mirrour
of Mercy*, 106

Give God thine affections, else thine actions are stillborn and have no life in them.

✦ JOHN TRAPP
*Commentary…upon…the
New Testament*, 856

AFFLICTION

A just view of afflicting incidents is altogether necessary to a Christian deportment under them, and that view is to be obtained only by faith, not by sense; for it is the light of the Word alone that represents them justly, discovering in them the work of God…. When these are perceived by the eye of faith and duly considered, we have a just view of afflicting incidents, fitted to quell the turbulent motions of corrupt affections under dismal outward appearances.

✦ THOMAS BOSTON
Crook in the Lot, 11

In comforting others who are afflicted under the sense of God's wrath, it should teach us to speak in that manner to them that they may discern what God speaks in and by us and that that comfort we desire to possess them with is a divine comfort and has its ground from God's own Word, else comfort will be but vain. Yea, we shall show ourselves but lewd and profane persons if we shall endeavor to comfort God's child by any other kind of comfort than that which proceeds from God, this being to teach them to despise God.

✦ WILLIAM BRADSHAW
Meditation of Mans Mortalitie, 65

What is affliction? Affliction is all that is contrary to one's will; thereby God eats out the core of our wills. Whensoever therefore you meet with any affliction, pray over it and beg that God would eat out the core of your wills thereby; and the more the core of your wills is eaten out, the more willing will you be to suffer for the name of Jesus Christ.

✦ WILLIAM BRIDGE
Seasonable Truths in Evil Times,
in *Works*, 3:342

Shall we bind God to give us a reason of His doings, who is King of kings and Lord of lords and whose will is the true reason and only rule of justice? If the general grounds and reasons that

God hath laid down in His Word, why He afflicts His people—namely, for their profit (Heb. 12:10); for the purging away of their sins (Isa. 1:25); for the reforming of their lives (Ps. 119:67, 71); and for the saving of their souls (1 Cor. 11:32)—should work them to be silent and satisfied under all their afflictions; though God should never satisfy their curiosity in giving them an account of some more hidden causes which may lie secret in the abyss of His eternal knowledge and infallible will.

✦ THOMAS BROOKS
Mute Christian, 79

Let not men and women pore too much on their afflictions—that is, busy their thoughts too much to look down into their afflictions. You shall have many people that all their thoughts are taken up about what their crosses and afflictions are; they are altogether thinking and speaking of them. It is just with them as with a child that hath a sore about him; his finger is always upon the sore. And so men and women, their thoughts are always on their afflictions. When they awake in the night, their thoughts are on their afflictions, and when they converse with others—nay, it may be when they are praying to God—they are thinking of their afflictions. Oh! No marvel though you live a discontented life if your thoughts be always poring upon such things. You should rather labor to have your thoughts on those things that may comfort you.

✦ JEREMIAH BURROUGHS
Rare Jewel, 82

Materially, all afflictions belong to the covenant of works, but by the cross of Christ they are transferred to the new covenant. They are thereby made healthful, as the tree that Moses cast into the waters took away their bitterness, which some think was a type of this. Afflictions are bitter, and men murmur at them as the Israelites at the bitter waters. But the cross of Christ makes them wholesome waters; they are like salt to the sacrifices (Lev. 2:13). They consume men's corrupting humors.

✦ ALEXANDER CARMICHAEL
Believer's Mortification of Sin, 54

Afflicted Hannah was large and long in prayer, insomuch that Eli, observing her moving her lips so long, said, "How long wilt thou be drunken?" When David's spirit is so hard placed, then does he pour out a complaint. And when so persecuted and reproached, then is employed in little else but praying. And this argues that some spiritual principles are within, that such griefs and ails enlarge their hearts which naturally rather contract the spirits of men and silence them, as in hypocrites which are then straitened. Bonds of afflictions are bonds to their spirits; they cry not when God binds them. But afflictions sanctified to the saints make them more abound in prayer.

✦ THOMAS COBBET
Gospel Incense, 394

Affliction is a gift of love even as faith is. It's grace as well to bleed for as to believe in Christ. It may be fair overhead when and while foul under foot.

In a bad way a man may have good weather. A fair sky and a filthy way may consist. The shepherd may pipe, though the dog bark. Build upon it, ye suffering saints!

✦ JOHN DURANT
Sips of Sweetness, 150

We are sure of this, that God intends His church no hurt. True indeed, take a single affliction and it will seem to hurt…but view the whole frame, and you will see how one wheel turns about another (like the wheels of a watch), which (though they have cross and contrary motions) all conspire and work together for good (Rom. 8:28).

✦ RICHARD GILPIN
Temple Rebuilt, 15

This waiting on God for deliverance in an afflicted state consists much in a holy silence: "Truly my soul waiteth upon God; from him cometh my salvation"; or, as the Hebrew, "My soul is silent" (Ps. 62:1). It is a great mercy in an affliction to have our bodily senses so as not to lie raving, but still and quiet; much more to have the heart silent and patient. And we find the heart is as soon heated into a distemper as the head. Now what the sponge is to the cannon when hot with often shooting, hope is to the soul in multiplied afflictions; it cools the spirit and meekens it so that it doth not break out into distempered thoughts or words against God.

✦ WILLIAM GURNALL
Christian in Complete Armour, 524

Truly, none of our temporals (whether crosses or enjoyments), considered in themselves abstractedly, are either a curse or a mercy. They are only as the covering to the book. It is what is written in them that must resolve us whether they be a mercy or not. Is it an affliction that lies on thee? If thou canst find it comes from love and ends in grace and holiness, it is a mercy, though it be bitter to thy taste. Is it an enjoyment? If love doth not send it and grace end it, it is a curse, though sweet to thy sense.

✦ WILLIAM GURNALL
Christian in Complete Armour, 733

How have I borne my afflictions? When providence has crossed me and frowned on me, what frame have I been in repining or repenting? Have I submitted to the will of God in my afflictions and accepted the punishment of my iniquity, or have I not striven with my Maker and quarreled with His disposals? When mine own foolishness has perverted my way, has not my heart fretted against the Lord? What good have I gotten to my soul by my afflictions? What inward gain by outward losses? Has my heart been more humbled and weaned from the world? Or have I not been hardened under the rod and trespassed yet more against the Lord?

✦ MATTHEW HENRY
The Communicant's Companion, in
Miscellaneous Writings, 208

Thou hast comforted us in all our tribulation, hast considered our trouble and known our souls in adversity, and showed us thy marvelous kindness, as in a strong city. When afflictions have abounded, consolations have much more abounded. Though no affliction for the present has been joyous, but grievous; nevertheless, afterward it has yielded the peaceable fruit of righteousness and hath proved to be for our profit, that we might be partakers of Thy holiness. We have had reason to say that it was good for us we were afflicted, that we might learn Your commandments; for before we were afflicted we went astray, but afterward have kept your word.

✦ MATTHEW HENRY
Method for Prayer, 114–15

EUCHEDIDASCALUS: What remedies have you against impatience in affliction?

PHILEUCHES: I must meditate
1. That naked I came into this world, and naked I must return again (Job 1:21).
2. I must remember the afflictions of Job and what end God made of them (James 5:11).
3. That the patient abiding of the righteous shall be gladness (Prov. 10:28).
4. That God hath a stroke in affliction (2 Sam. 16:10).
5. That they are nothing to the joys of heaven (2 Cor. 4:17).
6. That I have deserved more.
7. That they will tend to my good.
8. That in this world we must have tribulations.
9. That murmuring is a sign of a bad child.
10. Christ said, "Not My will, but Thine be done."
11. Many of God's servants have endured more.
12. That God's children have been ready to suffer.

✦ ROBERT HILL
Pathway to Piety, 1:99

As it is the duty of God's children to prepare for affliction before it comes, so is it to improve affliction when it does come. If we do not prepare for it, we shall be surprised by it; and if we do not improve it, we are likely to increase it. He who would prepare for affliction must beforehand resign all to God, strengthen his graces, store up promises, clear up evidences, recall experiences, and search out sins. And he who would improve affliction must by its means labor to see sin more and more in its filthiness so as to mortify it; the heart in its deceitfulness so as to watch over it; the world in its emptiness so as to be crucified to it; grace in its amiableness so as to prize it; God in His holiness so as to fear Him; and heaven in its desirableness so as to long after it. Be wanting, then, in neither respect, for he who takes more care to avoid afflictions than to be fitted for them or is more solicitous to be delivered from them than to be bettered by them is likely to come soonest into them and to live longest under them.

✦ T. S., *Aids to the Divine Life*, 114–15

Afflictions are a negative, if we speak properly, even as sin is. And whenever we are afflicted in any kind, we are emptied of some created good, as poverty is nothing but the absence of riches; sickness, the want of ease, of order, of health in the constitution; restraint is the loss of liberty.... It appears, then, that in a time of affliction God is emptying us of creature enjoyments, for indeed affliction itself is little or nothing else but such an emptying or deprivation. And that then the emptiness of the creature doth most appear, I suppose all will grant.

✦ SAMUEL SHAW
Voice of One Crying in the Wilderness, 78

David says, "My times are in thy hand" (Ps. 31:15). If our times were in our own hand, we would have deliverance too soon; if they were in our enemy's hand, we should have deliverance too late; but my times are in Thy hand, and God's time is ever best.... Everything is beautiful in its season; when the mercy is ripe, we shall have it. It is true we are now between the hammer and the anvil, but do not cast away your anchor; God sees when the mercy will be in season. When His people are low enough and the enemy high enough, then appears the church's morning star. Let God alone to His time. "My soul waiteth for the Lord" (Ps. 130:6). Good reason God should have the timing of our mercies: "I the Lord will hasten it in His time." Deliverance may tarry beyond our time, but it will not tarry beyond God's time.

✦ THOMAS WATSON
Gleanings, 58–59

AFFLICTION, COMFORTING OTHERS IN

By temptations the Lord will make you the more serviceable and useful to others. None so fit and able to relieve tempted souls, to sympathize with tempted souls, to succor tempted souls, to counsel tempted souls, to pity tempted souls, to support tempted souls, to bear with tempted souls, and to comfort tempted souls as those who have been in the school of temptations.

✦ THOMAS BROOKS
Mute Christian, 185

There is little to be expected from man till deeply plunged [into affliction].... He cannot pity others till experience hath taught him.... He will not be serviceable till afflictions have humbled and broken him.... He knows not how to comfort others till [he] himself hath been wounded and healed. But when he hath learned by experience, he can make his own bandage serve another man and comfort him in the same affliction with the same consolation.

✦ ROBERT HARRIS
David's Comfort at Ziklag, 7

AFFLICTION: COMPARED TO GOD'S MERCIES

A humble heart looks upon small mercies as great mercies, and great afflictions as small afflictions, and small afflictions as no afflictions, and therefore sits mute and quiet under all. Do but keep humble, and you will keep silent before the Lord. Pride kicks and flings and frets, but a humble man hath still his hand upon his mouth. Everything on this side of hell is mercy—much mercy, rich mercy—to a humble soul, and therefore he holds his peace.

♦ THOMAS BROOKS
Mute Christian, 245

It is a speech of Luther; saith he, "The sea of God's mercies should swallow up all our particular afflictions." Name any affliction that is upon thee, there is a sea of mercy to swallow it up. If you pour a pail full of water on the floor of your house, it makes a great show; but if you throw it into the sea, there is no appearance of it. So afflictions, considered in themselves, we think are very great; but let them be considered with the sea of God's mercies we do enjoy, then they are not so much. They are nothing in comparison.

♦ JEREMIAH BURROUGHS
Rare Jewel, 77

AFFLICTION, GOD'S FATHERLY

There is no surer token of God's fatherly love and care than to be corrected with some cross as oft as we commit any sinful crime. Affliction, therefore, is a seal of adoption, no sign of reprobation; for the purest corn is cleanest fanned, the finest gold is oftest tried, the sweetest grape is hardest pressed, and the truest Christian heaviest crossed.

♦ LEWIS BAYLY
Practice of Piety, 273

Afflictions were the rod of God's anger; they are now the gentle medicines of a tender father. God heretofore afflicted for sin; now God afflicts men from sin.... "Before I was afflicted," saith David, "I went astray, but now have I learned to keep thy law: therefore," saith he, "it is good for me that I have been afflicted" in this regard because of prevention. If you will but carry it clearly without carping or a spirit that seeks contention and quarrelling, you never need to stumble at such a position as this; for afflictions are the smiles of God, as gracious as the choicest embraces.

♦ TOBIAS CRISP
Christ Alone Exalted, 1:48

The apostle makes this free submission to the disposure of God's afflicting hand to evidence a son's spirit: "If ye endure chastening, God dealeth with you as with sons" (Heb. 12:7). Observe, he doth not say, "If you be chastened," but "If you endure chastening." Naked suffering does not prove sonship, but to endure it so as not to sink in our courage or shrink from under the burden God lays on but readily to offer our shoulder to it and patiently carry it, looking with a cheerful eye at the reward when we come; not to throw it off, but to have it taken off by that hand which laid it on does (all which the word imports). This shows a childlike spirit, and the evidence thereof must needs be a comfortable companion to the soul, especially at such a time when that sophister of hell uses the afflictions which lie upon us as an argument to disprove our relation to God. Now to have this answer to stop the liar's mouth at hand: "Satan, if I be not a child, how could I so readily submit to the Lord's family discipline?" This is no small mercy.

✦ WILLIAM GURNALL
Christian in Complete Armour, 407

Your afflictions smell of the children's care. The children of the house are so nurtured, and suffering is no new life; it is but the rent of the sons. Bastards have not so much of the rent. Stay and wait on till Christ loose the knot that fasteneth His cross on your back, for He is coming to deliver. This school of suffering is a preparation for the King's higher house. O happy and blessed death, that golden bridge laid over by Christ my Lord between time's clay banks and heaven's shore!

✦ SAMUEL RUTHERFORD
Garden of Spices, 88

AFFLICTION, GOD'S PURPOSE IN

Affliction is a winged chariot that mounts up the soul toward heaven; nor do we ever so rightly understand God's majesty as when we are not able to stand under our own misery.

✦ THOMAS ADAMS
"The Sinner's Mourning-Habit,"
in *Works*, 1:49

The truth is, the crook in the lot [i.e., affliction] is the great engine of providence for making men appear in their true colors, discovering both their ill

and their good; and if the grace of God be in them, it will bring it out and cause it to display itself.

✦ THOMAS BOSTON
Crook in the Lot, 45

Iron, till it be thoroughly heated, is incapable to be wrought; so God sees good to cast some men into the furnace of affliction and then beats them on His anvil into what frame He pleases.

✦ ANNE BRADSTREET
Meditation 31, in Works, 54

As of all blessings, those are the greatest where grace and comfort are joined together; so where sin and affliction are twisted together, of all afflictions they are the most afflictive.

✦ WILLIAM BRIDGE
Lifting Up, 128

Now all the afflictions of the saints are but their medicine, prescribed and given them by the hand of their Father.

✦ WILLIAM BRIDGE
Lifting Up, 194

Affliction is God's soap. Before a godly man enters into afflictions, his very graces are mixed with sin. His faith is mixed and dirtied with unbelief and doubtings, his humility with pride, his zeal with lukewarmness. But now, by his tribulation, his garments and robes are made white and washed, and he shall be of a more royal spirit and be clothed with robes.

✦ WILLIAM BRIDGE
Lifting Up, 208

Afflictions are a golden key by which the Lord opens the rich treasures of His Word to His people's souls.

✦ THOMAS BROOKS
Mute Christian, iv

Why must Christians be mute and silent under the greatest afflictions, the saddest providences, and sharpest trials that they meet with in this world? I answer…that they may the better hear and understand the voice of the rod. As the Word hath a voice, the Spirit a voice, and conscience a voice, so the rod hath a voice. Afflictions are the rod of God's anger, the rod of His displeasure, and His rod of revenge. He gives a commission to this rod to awaken His people, to reform His people, or else to revenge the quarrel of His covenant on them, if they will not hear the rod and kiss the rod and sit mute and silent under the rod. "The LORD's voice crieth unto the city, and the man of wisdom shall see thy name: hear ye the rod, and who hath appointed it" (Mic. 6:9). God's rods are not mutes; they are all vocal. They are speaking as well as smiting; every twig hath a voice.

✦ THOMAS BROOKS
Mute Christian, 58–59

Afflictions are but our Father's goldsmiths who are working to add pearls to our crowns.

✦ THOMAS BROOKS
Precious Remedies, 93

Afflictions are God's furnaces to purge out the dross of our sins, God's files to pare off our spiritual rust, God's fans to winnow out our chaff. In prosperity we gather much soil, but adversity purges and purifies us.

✦ EDMUND CALAMY
Godly Man's Ark, 9

Affliction is God's forge wherein He softens the iron heart.

✦ THOMAS CASE
Correction, Instruction, 87

Behold I show you a mystery! Sin brought affliction into the world, and God makes affliction to carry sin out of the world.

✦ THOMAS CASE
Correction, Instruction, 106

The truth is, the Word and the rod teach the same lessons. The rod many times is but the Word's remembrancer; and therefore, as the rod quickens the Word, so the Word will revive and sanctify the teachings of the rod. They mutually help to set on one another with deeper impressions.

✦ THOMAS CASE
Correction, Instruction, 136–37

Wicked men in affliction are like iron, which while in the fire it melts, but after it hath been a while out, it grows stiff again.

✦ SAMUEL CLARK
Saint's Nosegay, 83

As two pieces of iron cannot be soundly soldered together but by beating and heating them both together in the fire, so neither can Christ and His brethren be so nearly united and fast affected but by fellowship in His sufferings.

✦ SAMUEL CLARK
Saint's Nosegay, 107

Afflictions in themselves are tokens of God's anger, curses rather than blessings; but yet when God by His wonderful power, drawing light even out of darkness, shall turn them to our good to the increase of grace and sanctification in us, then are they undoubted badges of our blessedness.

✦ DANIEL DYKE
"The School of Affliction,"
in *Two Treatises*, 338

A Christian must not expect two heavens; it is enough if he possesses one. We must not travel to heaven through a bed of roses. It is not much though we go to heaven in a fiery chariot, having afflictions and calamities our companions all along the way.

✦ ANDREW GRAY
The Spiritual Warfare, in *Works*, 388

The day of affliction makes discovery of much evil to be in the heart that was not seen before. Affliction shakes and exposes the creature; if any sediment be at the bottom, it will appear then.... It is impossible for a naughty heart to think well of an afflicting God.... Sharp afflictions are to the soul as a driving rain to the house; we know not that there are such crannies and holes in the house till we see it drop down here and there. Thus, we perceive not how unmortified this corruption, not how weak that grace is, till we are thus searched and made more fully to know what is in our hearts by such trials.

✦ WILLIAM GURNALL
Christian in Complete Armour, 174–75

When [God] afflicts [His people], it is for the trial of their faith (1 Peter 1:7). Afflictions, they are God's spade and mattock by which He digs into His people's hearts to find out this gold of faith; not but that He inquires for other graces also, but this is named for all as the chief, which found, all the other will soon appear.

✦ WILLIAM GURNALL
Christian in Complete Armour, 432

The afflictions of the saints are not judgments, but corrections or trials; they are God's discipline to mortify sin or His means to discover grace and to prove our faith, love, patience, sincerity, and constancy. Well, then, behave thyself as one under trial; let nothing be discovered in thee but what is good and gracious.

✦ THOMAS MANTON
Practical Exposition on the Epistle of James, 6

God hath two hedges that the Scripture takes notice of: The hedge of His protection that you read of in Job 1:10: "Hast not thou made an hedge about him, and about his house, and about all that he hath on every side?" The hedge of affliction that you read of here: "I will hedge up thy way with thorns" (Hos. 2:6–7). Now the Lord makes great use of both these hedges. The hedge of God's protection, that is to keep His people from danger. The hedge of affliction, that is to stop them that wander. The hedge of protection is to keep them in God's way. The hedge of affliction is to keep them out of sin's way. The hedge of protection is to keep them from suffering. The hedge of affliction is to keep them from sinning and to put them upon returning.

✦ MATTHEW MEAD
"The Power of Grace," in
Name in Heaven, 104–5

How many souls have reason to say, "If the Lord had not ploughed me with afflictions and dunged me with reproaches, what barren ground had I been? How had I wandered if the Lord had not sent His dogs to fetch me to the fold? I had been cast away if I had not been cast down." The Lord often writes angry epistles to His children, yet observe still at the bottom of the letter He subscribes, "Your loving Father." Again, "I form the light, and create darkness" (Isa. 45:7). Sin is man's creature, and afflictions are God's creatures; every affliction bears the image of its Maker, and God is not ashamed of His own handiwork. Sinful man is the meritorious, but providence is the efficient cause of evils. Man is the cause of moral evils, God of penal evils in the city (Amos 3:6).

✦ FRANCIS RAWORTH
On Jacob's Ladder, 21

O, what owe I to the file, to the hammer, to the furnace of my Lord Jesus! Grace tried is better than grace, and it is more than grace; it is glory in its infancy. Who knows the truth of grace without a trial?

✦ SAMUEL RUTHERFORD
Garden of Spices, 151–52

The dross of my cross gathers a scum of fears in the fire: doubting, impatience, unbelief, accusations of providence as sleeping and as not regarding my sorrow. But my goldsmith, Christ, was pleased to take off the scum and burn it in the fire. And, blessed be my Refiner, He hath made the metal better and furnished new supply of grace to cause me to hold out weight, and I hope He hath not lost one grain-weight by burning His servant.

✦ SAMUEL RUTHERFORD
Garden of Spices, 153

All God's afflictions are to remove impediments of grace: "By this," saith Isaiah, "shall the iniquity of Jacob be purged; and this is all the fruit, to take away his sin." All the ploughing is but to kill weeds and to fit the ground for seed.

✦ HENRY SCUDDER
Christian's Daily Walk, 199

A saint is inwardly pious when he is not outwardly prosperous. The sharper the medicine is, the sounder the patient is for its operation. The higher the flood swells on earth, the nearer the ark mounts to heaven. God can strike straight strokes with crooked sticks.

✦ WILLIAM SECKER
Nonsuch Professor, 43

What is so sweet a good as Christ? And what is so great an evil as lust? Sin has brought many a believer into suffering, and suffering has instrumentally kept many a believer out of sin. It is better to be preserved in brine than to rot in honey. The bitterest medicine is to be preferred by all wise men before the sweetest poison. In the same fire wherein the dross is consumed, the precious gold is refined.

✦ WILLIAM SECKER
Nonsuch Professor, 58

God loves His people when He strikes them as well as when He strokes them. God brings His people into various afflictions that they may know what is in their hearts toward Him and what is in His heart toward them. Being afflicted does often reveal hypocrites, yet being afflicted is no revealing of a hypocrite.

✦ RALPH VENNING
Canaan's Flowings, 13

Jonah was sent into the whale's belly to make his sermon for Nineveh.

✦ THOMAS WATSON
in Horn, Puritan Remembrancer, 20

God had one son without sin, but no son without stripes.

✦ THOMAS WATSON
The Beatitudes, in Discourses, 2:323

Afflictions are said to be sent us to make us do God's will.… The rod has this voice, "Be doers of God's will." Affliction is called a furnace. The furnace melts the metal, and then it is cast into a new mold. God's furnace is to melt us and mold us into obedience.

✦ THOMAS WATSON
Lord's Prayer, 153

Sin not only brings us low but it embitters affliction. Sin puts teeth into the cross. Guilt makes affliction heavy. A little water is heavy in a lead vessel, and a little affliction is heavy in a guilty conscience.

✦ THOMAS WATSON
Mischief of Sin, 7

God's rod is a pencil to draw Christ's image more distinctly on us. It is good there should be symmetry between the Head and the members. To be part of Christ's mystical body, we must be like Him: "He was a man of sorrows and acquainted with grief." Hence, it is good to be like Christ, though it be by sufferings.

✦ THOMAS WATSON
Puritan Gems, 4

AFFLICTION: NOT INTRINSICALLY EVIL

The least sin is worse than the greatest affliction.

✦ WILLIAM BRIDGE
Lifting Up, 68

O Christians! Under your greatest troubles lieth your greatest treasures. Afflictions are good, but not pleasant; sin is pleasant, but not good. But there is more evil in a drop of corruption than there is in the sea of afflictions. God by affliction separates the sin He hates so dearly from the soul He loves so dearly. By the greatest affliction God teacheth us the greatest instruction, and a believer, when he lies under that hand that doth afflict him, lies in the heart that doth affect him.

✦ WILLIAM DYER
Christ's Famous Titles, 112

Afflictions in themselves are evil (Amos 2:6), very bitter, and unpleasant (see Heb. 12:11). Yet they are not morally and intrinsically evil, as sin is; for if so, the holy God would never own it for His own act, as He doth (Mic. 3:2), but also disclaimeth sin (James 1:3). Besides, if it were so evil, it could in no case, or respect, be the object of our election and desire, as in some cases it ought to be (Heb. 11:25). But it is evil, as it is the fruit of sin, and grievous unto sense (Heb. 12:11). But though it be thus brackish and unpleasant in itself, yet passing through Christ and the covenant, it loses that ungrateful property, and unpleasant in the fruits and effects thereof unto believers (Heb. 12:11).

✦ JOHN FLAVEL
Navigation Spiritualized, 69

If affliction were intrinsically evil, it could in no respect be the object of our desire, which sometimes it is and may be. We are to choose affliction rather than sin — yea, the greatest affliction before the least sin. Moses chose affliction with the people of God rather than the pleasures of sin for a season. We are bid to rejoice when we fall into diverse temptations — that is, afflictions.

✦ WILLIAM GURNALL
Christian in Complete Armour, 174

There are some things good but not pleasant, as sorrow and affliction. Sin is pleasant but unprofitable, and sorrow is profitable but unpleasant. By affliction the Lord separates the sin that He hates from the soul that He loves. He does not always ordain it to take your spirit out of your flesh, but your flesh out of your spirit. It is not sent to take down the tabernacle of nature, but to rear up the temple of grace within you. As waters are purest when they are in motion, so saints are generally holiest when in affliction.

✦ WILLIAM SECKER
Nonsuch Professor, 7

AFFLICTION, RIGHT USE OF

Divine rebukes on men's earthly interests help them to a discovery of those sins that procure them (Deut. 31:17). Afflictions are Christ's clay and spittle to open His people's eyes and to bring them to see those evils that have brought those deaths upon their comforts and breed those worms that have destroyed their substance. Times of correction are times of instruction (Job 36:8–9). When Jacob's sons were cut short of their provisions, reduced to great distress, and plunged in sore dangers, then they thought upon their sin and wrong done to their brother Joseph (Gen. 42:21).

✦ BARTHOLOMEW ASHWOOD
Heavenly Trade, 328

As my greatest, so my daily business is also with God. He purposely leaves me under daily wants and necessities and the daily assaults of enemies and surprise of afflictions, that I may be daily driven to Him. He loves to hear from me. He would have me to be no stranger with Him.

✦ RICHARD BAXTER
Converse with God in Solitude, 93

Consider what a work [i.e., affliction] of [God's] it is, how it is a convincing work, for bringing sin to remembrance; a correcting work, to chastise you for your follies; a preventing work, to hedge you up from courses of sin you would otherwise be apt to run into; a trying work, to discover your state, your graces, and corruptions; a weaning work, to wean you from the world and fit you for heaven.

✦ THOMAS BOSTON
Crook in the Lot, 85

God's children afflicted count piety, religion, and the fear of God their greatest beauty and ornament; yea, by afflictions God is wont to bring them to a higher estimation of these graces and a purer use of His ordinances than formerly they had. And then may we well deem that our afflictions have done good on us when they have brought us into a further measure of liking, and high esteem of spiritual graces, and a greater conformity unto God in them.

✦ WILLIAM BRADSHAW
Meditation of Mans Mortalitie, 72

As the only way to have an outward blessing is to be content to go without it, so the only way to have a spiritual or outward affliction removed is to be contented that it should be continued, if God and Christ will have it so.

✦ WILLIAM BRIDGE
Lifting Up, 64

Afflictions are but as a dark entry into our Father's house; they are but as a dirty lane to a royal palace.

✦ THOMAS BROOKS
Smooth Stones, 156

That is the main thing that brings the quiet of heart and helps against discontentedness in a gracious heart. I say, the desire and care that thy soul hath to sanctify God's name in an affliction, it is that that quiets the soul.

✦ JEREMIAH BURROUGHS
Rare Jewel, 16

It is the great mistake and folly of men that they make more haste to get their afflictions removed than sanctified.

✦ THOMAS CASE
Correction, Instruction, 122

Sanctified afflictions are great promotions and are far better for the Christian than all the silver and gold in the world, seeing that the trial of our faith is much more precious than that of gold which perishes.

✦ JOHN DOD AND PHILIP HENRY
Gleanings of Heavenly Wisdom, 14

[One] kind of lesson taught by affliction is to those already converted. And these lessons are of two sorts: (1) concerning the right manner of bearing affliction; (2) concerning the right profit and holy use of afflictions. These lessons are proper to the converted, it being impossible for a man unconverted to leave either of them.

✦ DANIEL DYKE
"The School of Affliction,"
in *Two Treatises*, 345

In all the troubles and afflictions that befall you, eye Jesus Christ and set your hearts to the study of these four things in affliction. Study His sovereignty and dominion, for He creates and forms them. They rise not out of the dust nor do they befall you casually, but He raises them up and gives them their commission…. Study the wisdom of Christ in the contrivance of your troubles. His wisdom shines out many ways in them…. Study the tenderness and compassions of Christ over His afflicted people. Oh, think if the devil had but the mixing of my cup how much more bitter would he make it! There would not be one drop of mercy in it, but here is much mercy mixed with my troubles…. Study the love of Christ to thy soul in affliction. "As many as I love, I rebuke and chasten" (Rev. 3:19). This is the device of love, to recover thee to thy God and prevent thy ruin. Oh, what an advantage would it be thus to study Christ in all your evils that befall you!

✦ JOHN FLAVEL
Fountain of Life, 159–60

Sanctified afflictions discover the emptiness and vanity of the creature.

✦ JOHN FLAVEL
Navigation Spiritualized, 70

Let [sincerity] teach us not to fear affliction, but hypocrisy. Believe it, friends, affliction is a harmless thing to a sincere soul; it cannot be so great as to make it inconsistent with his joy and comfort.

✦ WILLIAM GURNALL
Christian in Complete Armour, 290

Affliction is like the shepherd's dog, to bark at and bring us in.

✦ THOMAS JOLLIE
Heavenly-Mindedness, in Slate,
Select Nonconformists' Remains, 227

There are two great evils, one of which does generally seize on men under their afflictions and keep them from a due management of them. Either men despise the Lord's correction or sink under it. (1) Men despise it. They account that which befalls them to be a light or common thing. They take no notice of God in it; they can shift with it well enough. (2) Men faint and sink under their trials and afflictions. The first despises the assistance of the Holy Ghost through pride of heart; the latter refuse it through dejectedness of spirit and sink under the weight of their troubles.

✦ JOHN OWEN
Golden Book, 202–3

Glory follows afflictions not as the day follows night, but as the spring follows winter. Winter prepares the earth for spring; so do afflictions, sanctified, prepare the soul for glory.

✦ RICHARD SIBBES
*Divine Meditations and Holy
Contemplations*, 21

Afflictions make a divorce between the soul and sin. It is not a small thing that will work sin out of the soul; it must be the spirit of burning, the fire of afflictions sanctified. Heaven is for holiness, and all that is contrary to holiness affliction works out and so fits the soul for further and perfect communion with God.

✦ RICHARD SIBBES
Divine Meditations and Holy Contemplations, 22

AMBITION

An ambitious man is the greatest enemy to himself of any in the world besides, for he still torments himself with hopes and desires and cares, which he might avoid if he would remit of the height of his thoughts and live quietly. My only ambition shall be to rest in God's favor on earth and to be a saint in heaven.

✦ JOSEPH HALL
Meditations and Vows, 16

An ambitious man undermines all others; if an enemy stands to resist him, he will make his way even through blood. He will also tread on his friends to get to honor. A soul that is graciously ambitious considers what stands in his way and hates father and mother—nay, his own life; pulls out the right eye; even cuts off his right hand and offers violence to everything that stands betwixt him and his God.

✦ RICHARD SIBBES
Divine Meditations and Holy Contemplations, 93

Ambition…is for aiming at things out of the tradesman's sphere, making him restless and uneasy in his present condition because his mind is too high for his calling or his success unequal to his desires, and the shoe is uneasy because the foot is swelled…. Persons, indeed, may allowably endeavor to raise themselves as far as the sober improvement of their time and capacities will admit of, but those desires and pursuits are certainly criminal that render them discontented and unthankful for their present enjoyments, which obstruct the love and duty they owe to God and their neighbor.

✦ RICHARD STEELE
Religious Tradesman, 169

Ambition is boundless, rides without reins, builds itself on the ruins of others, and cares not to swim to its design, though in a sea of blood.

✦ JOHN TRAPP
Commentary on the Old and New Testaments, 1:45

Another meditates how to satisfy his ambition: "Honor me before the people" (1 Sam. 15:30). Alas, what is honor but a meteor in the air—a torch lighted by the breath of people, with the least puff blown out! How many live to see their names buried before them.

✦ THOMAS WATSON
A Christian on the Mount,
in *Discourses*, 1:263

That suffering will not make men blessed when they suffer out of sinister respects, to be cried up as the head of a party or to keep up a faction. The apostle implies that a man may give his body to be burned, yet go to hell (1 Cor. 13:3). Ambitious men may sacrifice their lives to purchase fame; these are the devil's martyrs.

✦ THOMAS WATSON
The Beatitudes, in *Discourses*, 2:358

ANGELS

There is no worshiping of angels, and yet we must not throw away the comfortable doctrine of angels.

♦ ISAAC AMBROSE
*Ministration of, and Communion
with Angels, 5*

We may wonder at this: that the angels should thus minister to man after his fall, which they never did before. In that collation betwixt Innocent Adam, Second Adam, Renewed Adam, and Old Adam, it is said that the angels did neither minister unto nor keep the first Adam before the fall because he was in no danger; only they loved him. The angels, indeed, ministered unto Christ, the Second Adam, and loved Him, but did not keep Him…. Christ is the head of angels, and therefore He is not kept by them. The angels now minister to the Renewed Adam—yea, they love him and keep him—and yet this argues not any prerogative that the saints have above Christ but rather their weakness and wants, that they have need of the angels to preserve them, as young children stand in need of nurses to wait on them. But as for Old Adam, or wicked reprobates, the angels neither minister to them nor love them nor keep them in respect of any special and particular keeping.

♦ ISAAC AMBROSE
*Ministration of, and Communion
with Angels, 39–40*

The promise of angel protection, as all temporal promises, runs with this tacit reservation and condition, always provided that God in His infinite wisdom, for reasons best known to Himself, does not judge the contrary more conducing to His glory and our inward good. We know Job was afflicted that he might be tried, and the Lord doth sometimes suspend the protection of His angels that we may the more depend on Himself.

♦ ISAAC AMBROSE
*Ministration of, and Communion
with Angels, 61*

Angels are exact and careful observers and eyewitnesses of our behavior and deportment in the public ordinances. To this end were the curtains of the tabernacle pictured: full of cherubim to signify that about our solemn meetings, whole troops of angels take notice of our behavior. Surely, if this were considered, we should be very serious in God's worship. Yea, how spiritual and heavenly should we be if our hearts were but fixed on these glorious angels?

♦ ISAAC AMBROSE
*Ministration of, and Communion
with Angels, 100*

Shall the Lord Himself be your protector and charge His angels with you for such a time as this, and will you not trust in the Lord [Ps. 91:11–12]? It is recorded of Alexander [the Great], that being in great danger and to fight next day with his enemies, he slept very soundly the night before, and he being asked the reason thereof, said, "Parmenio wakes," meaning a great and faithful captain of his; "Parmenio wakes," says he. The angels are called watchmen; they watch and are faithful; therefore you may be secure, quiet, and at rest.

♦ WILLIAM BRIDGE
Righteous Man's Habitation, 104

For I have been in my preaching, especially when I have been engaged in the doctrine of life by Christ without works, as if an angel of God had stood at my back to encourage me. Oh! It hath been with such power and heavenly evidence on my own soul while I have been laboring to unfold it, to demonstrate it, and to fasten on the consciences of others that I could not be contented with saying, "I believe and am sure"; I thought I was more than sure (if it is lawful to express myself) that those things which then I asserted were true.

♦ JOHN BUNYAN
Grace Abounding, 110

Let those that hope to live with the angels in heaven learn to live like the angels on earth in holiness, activity, and ready obedience.

♦ JOHN FLAVEL
Golden Gems, 54

Concerning angels, it is true that they and ministers are fellow servants (Rev. 22:9), but yet ministers have various prerogatives above them.

1. Angels rejoice at the conversion of a sinner (Luke 15:10), but by the ministry of prophets, sinners are converted unto God (Acts 26:18).

2. An angel was sent to Cornelius to advise him whither to go to be instructed, but a minister instructed him in the way of life (Acts 10:6, 34).

3. Was the word of reconciliation ever committed to angels? To ministers it is committed (2 Cor. 5:18). It is observable that the embassage of ministers is not simply a message, but the gospel—the gladsome tidings of salvation by Jesus Christ into which the angels themselves do desire to look, as the apostle Peter expresses (1 Peter 1:12). The Lord hath also committed to His ministers the administration of the sacraments, which are the seals of His covenant, whereby all His precious promises are ratified and confirmed unto us.

♦ THOMAS GOUGE
Riches Increased by Giving, 80

Where the Scripture hath no tongue we need not have ears, but must content ourselves with a learned ignorance, lest we fall into the sin of those angel worshipers (Col. 2:18).

♦ JOHN TRAPP
Marrow of Many Good Authors, 1067

The angels are called ministering spirits; they are willing to minister for the good of the saints. Hence some observe, it is said, Lazarus was carried by the angels, in the plural, not by one angel—as if the angels had been ambitious to carry Lazarus and every one strived that should have a part.

♦ THOMAS WATSON
The Christian's Charter of Privileges,
in *Discourses*, 1:36

[The saints] shall sit nearer the throne than the angels. The angels are noble and sublime spirits, but by virtue of our marriage union, Christ having taken our flesh and the knot being tied between the divine and human nature in the virgin's womb, we shall be ennobled with greater honor than the angels. The angels are Christ's friends but not His spouse; this honor have all His saints. As the saints' robes in glory shall be brighter than the angels' (theirs being only the righteousness of creatures, but these having upon them the righteousness of God), so their dignity shall be greater. O infinite! Here we are prisoners at bar, but there favorites at court. The saints shall sit down in glory above the angels.

✦ THOMAS WATSON
The Christian's Charter of Privileges,
in *Discourses,* 1:40

The highest angels take care of the lowest saints. Are they not all ministering spirits?

✦ THOMAS WATSON
Puritan Gems, 14

ANGER

There is a just and lawful anger, for it is said, "Be ye angry, and sin not." We may be angry where God is angry, as Jacob, Moses, Nehemiah, and Jeremiah were. But their anger was holy, temperate, and short.

✦ ISAAC AMBROSE
Christian Warrior, 116

Whether our anger be carnal or spiritual may be thus discerned: if it hinder not but quicken our holy exercise of prayer and other religious duties; if it interrupt not our meditations nor withdraw us from performing our duty to the party offended, neither make us peevish to others, it's spiritual, not carnal.

✦ EZEKIEL CULVERWELL
Time Well Spent, 11

Thou a Christian and carry hellfire about thee! How can it be? When we see a child furious and revengeful who comes of merciful parents, we...say we wonder of whom he got his currish, churlish disposition; his father and mother were not so. Who learns thee, O Christian, to be so revengeful and unmerciful? Thou hast it not of thy heavenly Father, I am sure.

✦ WILLIAM GURNALL
Christian in Complete Armour, 371

Thus, to be angry at nothing but sin is the way not to sin in anger.

✦ MATTHEW HENRY
Gems, 19

It is the great duty of all Christians to put off anger. It unfits for duty. A little jogging puts a clock or watch out of frame, so a little passion the heart. A man cannot wrestle with God and wrangle with his neighbor at the same time. Short sins often cost us long and sad sorrow. An angry man is like one in a crowd that hath sore bile; every one thrusts him and troubles him." With the froward thou wilt shew thys[elf] froward," a dreadful scripture to a peevish, froward man. Those that are too merry when pleased are commonly too angry when crossed. Blessed Lord, subdue this lust [i.e., anger] in my heart; I am very weak there. Lord, there strengthen me, turn the stream of my anger [against] self and sin. O how doth my anger at men make God angry at me! Lord, pardon in Christ.

✦ PHILIP HENRY
Diaries and Letters, 61

Anger should not be destroyed, but sanctified. Be angry with the tempter, the devil, who stirs up thy brother to wrong thee, and be not like the furious dog who bites the stone thrown and meddles not with the hand that threw it. The man is to be pitied. Satan threw this stone at thee; he instigated thy brother's passion.

✦ WILLIAM JENKYN
Exposition upon the Epistle of Jude, 285

There is a necessary, holy anger that is the whetstone of fortitude and zeal. So it is said, Lot's righteous soul was vexed (2 Peter 2:7). So Christ Himself, He looked round about Him with anger (Mark 3:5). So "Moses's anger waxed hot" (Ex. 32:19). This is but an advised motion of the will guided by the rules of reason. Certainly, they are angry and sin not who are angry at nothing but sin. It is good when every passion serves the interests of religion. However, let me tell you, this being a fierce and strong motion of the spirit, it must be used with great advice and caution.

✦ THOMAS MANTON
Practical Exposition on the Epistle of James, 58–59

Anger may kindle in the breast of a wise man, but rests only in the bosom of a fool.

✦ HENRY SCOUGAL
"Indispensable Duty of Loving Our Enemies," in *Works*, 101

Anger should not be a burning coal from Satan's furnace, but a blazing coal from God's altar. It should resemble fire in straw, which is as easily quenched as suddenly kindled. He who would be angry and not sin must be angry at nothing but sin. Let not the sun go down upon your wrath, neither give place to the devil. He that carries passions to bed with him will find the devil creep between the sheets.

✦ WILLIAM SECKER
Nonsuch Professor, 94

Anger is a short madness; whensoever it displaces reason, it is sinful.

✦ JOHN TRAPP
Commentary on the Old and New Testaments, 1:603

Anger is a tender virtue and such as by reason of our unskillfulness may be easily corrupted and made dangerous. He that in his anger would not sin must not be angry at anything but sin.

✦ JOHN TRAPP
Marrow of Many Good Authors, 1070

Many there are that suffer the sun not only to go down upon their anger, but to run his whole race—yes, many races—ere they can be reconciled, whereby their anger becomes inveterate and turns into malice, for anger and malice differ but in age.

✦ JOHN TRAPP
Marrow of Many Good Authors, 1071

APOSTASY

That man's beginning was in hypocrisy whose end is in apostasy. Indifference in religion is the next step to apostasy from religion. Oh! Do not make him a stone of stumbling that God hath made a stone for building.

✦ WILLIAM DYER
Christ's Famous Titles, 73

Whoever fell into heresy or into apostasy or into despair before he fell from prayer, the preservative of the soul?

✦ HENRY SMITH
"The Ladder of Peace," in *Sermons,* 116

The truth has no such pestilent persecutors as apostates; [the] sweetest wine makes [the] sourest vinegar.

✦ JOHN TRAPP
*Commentary…upon…the
New Testament,* 317

'Tis to be feared that they who leave the saints of God will not cleave to the God of saints.

✦ RALPH VENNING
Canaan's Flowings, 16

Thus, unbelief and atheism prevailing, the livery of religion is presently thrown off, and all former violence for heaven ceases. Infidelity is the mother of apostacy.

✦ THOMAS WATSON
*Christian Soldier, or, Heaven
Taken by Storm,* 103

APOSTLES

Had it been published by a voice from heaven that twelve poor men taken out of boats and creeks without any help of learning should conquer the world to the cross, it might have been thought an illusion against all the reason of men, yet we know it was undertaken and accomplished by them. They published this doctrine in Jerusalem and quickly spread it over the greatest part of the world. Folly outwitted wisdom and weakness overpowered strength. The conquest of the cast by Alexander was not so admirable as the enterprise of these poor men.

✦ STEPHEN CHARNOCK
*Discourses upon the Existence
and Attributes of God,* 440

APPEARANCES

Many sinners who seem so jocund in our eyes have not such merry lives as you think. A book may be fairly bound and gilt, yet have sad stories written within it. Sinners will not tell us all the secret rebukes that conscience from the Word gives them. If you will judge of Herod by the jollity of his feast, you may think he wanted no joy; but at another time we see that John's ghost walked in his conscience. And so does the Word haunt many a one who to us appears to lay nothing to heart; in the midst of their laughter their heart is sad. You see the lightning in their face but hear not the thunder that rumbles in their conscience.

✦ WILLIAM GURNALL
Christian in Complete Armour, 572

ARMINIANISM

Man naturally would be a god to him-self, though by clambering so high he got his fall; and whatever doctrine nourishes a good opinion of man in his own eye, this is acceptable to him. And this has spawned another fry of dangerous errors—the Pelagian and semi-Pelagian—which set nature upon its own legs and persuade man he can go alone to Christ, or at least with a little external help of a hand to lead or argument to excite, without any creating work in the soul. O! We can-not conceive how glib such stuff goes down. If one workman should tell you that your house is rotten and must be pulled down and all new materials pre-pared, sad [that] another should say, "No such matter. Such a beam is good, and such a spar may stand; a little cost will serve the turn." It were no won-der that you should listen to him that would put you to least cost and trouble. The faithful servants of Christ tell sin-ners from the Word that man in his natural state is corrupt and rotten, that nothing of the old frame will serve, and there must needs be all new.

✦ WILLIAM GURNALL
Christian in Complete Armour, 53

ASSURANCE

The feeling of sin does not annihilate the assurance of salvation. We feel the ache of a finger more sensibly than the health of the whole body, yet is the health of the whole body far more than the ache of a finger. Sanctification is itself, though joined with some im-perfection.

✦ THOMAS ADAMS
Exposition upon…Second…Peter, 118

Grace comes into the soul as the morn-ing sun into the world: there is first a dawning, then a mean light, and at last the sun in his excellent brightness. In a Christian life there is *professio, profectio, perfectio*. A profession of the name of Christ wrought in our conversion [is] not the husk of religion, but the sap: "A pure heart, a good conscience, and faith unfeigned." Next, there is a *profection*, or going forward in grace, "working up our salvation in fear and trembling." Last, a *perfection*, or full assurance, that we are "sealed up to the day of redemption."

✦ THOMAS ADAMS
"Heaven Made Sure," in *Sermons*, 106

Reason's arm is too short to reach the jewel of assurance.

✦ THOMAS BROOKS
in Horn, *Puritan Remembrancer*, 17

Bitterly did Mary weep when Jesus stood by her, she not knowing it. Tears filled Hagar's eyes and despairs drew the blood of her heart when the well was fast by her and she was not aware of it. 'Tis often so through their own fault, and long so with God's recon-ciled ones. They have their pardon and their pass for heaven sealed in heaven, but not knowing so much, their con-sciences write and sign their mittimus to hell and so make the greatest part of their breath be spent in sighs. Horrid robbery—to God of praise, to souls of peace, and of usefulness in the world!

O, Christian, this remember: want of assurance made by negligence is a sin whose name ought to be Legion, for it is a thousand strong.

✦ DANIEL BURGESS
Man's Whole Duty, 52–53

Assurance saith, "I believe my sins are pardoned through Christ"; faith's language is, "I believe on Christ for the pardon of them."

✦ WILLIAM GURNALL
in Horn, *Puritan Remembrancer,* 17

Assurance encourages us in our combat; it delivers us not from it. We may have peace with God when we have none from the assaults of Satan.

✦ JOHN OWEN
Golden Book, 227

Doubtings, fears, temptations, if not ordinarily prevailing, are consistent with gospel assurance. Though the devil's power be limited in reference unto the saints, yet his hands are not tied. Though he cannot prevail against them, yet he can assault them; and although there be not an evil heart of unbelief in believers, yet there will still be unbelief in their hearts.

✦ JOHN OWEN
Practical Exposition of the 130th Psalm,
in *Oweniana,* 172

The rule is believe not either your deceitful heart nor the devil when they tell you either that you are in a state of salvation or in a state of damnation; but believe the Scripture, what it saith in either.

You may know when these persuasions come from your deceitful heart or from the devil thus: (1) If the means to persuade you either be from false grounds or from misapplication of true grounds. (2) If the conclusions inferred from either persuasion be to keep you in a sinful course and to keep you or to drive you from God, as if you need not be so strict in godliness, or that now it is in vain or too late to turn and seek unto God, then it is from Satan and from a deceitful heart, and you must not believe them. But if these persuasions be from a right application of true grounds and do produce these good effects, to drive you to God in praise or prayer and unto a care to please God, they are from His gracious Spirit.

✦ HENRY SCUDDER
Christian's Daily Walk, 271

It is faith and adherence to Christ and His promises which, even in fears and doubts, must be the cable we must hold by lest we make shipwreck of all when we are assaulted with our greatest temptations, for then many times our assurance leaves us to the mercy of the winds and seas, as mariners speak. If you have faith, though you have little or no feeling, your salvation is yet sure in truth, though not in your own apprehension. When both can be had it is best, for then you gain most strength and most comfort, giving you cheerfulness in all your troubles; but the power and grace of the Lord Jesus Christ and faith in His naked word and promise is that to which you must trust.

✦ HENRY SCUDDER
Christian's Daily Walk, 346–47

The want of assurance: Many are ignorant, unskillful, and negligent in the great work of self-examination. Many have but very low degrees of grace; the handwriting of God's Spirit on their hearts is in so very small a character that they are not able to read it. Too many are loose and careless in their walk. Not a few are overrun with melancholy and have dismal apprehensions of their state, though a judicious stander-by may perceive the goodness of it. The dark side of the lantern is toward themselves, and though others behold the grace of God in them as a burning and a shining light, yet the persons themselves cannot discern it. And in this gloomy state they conclude if they should die, they should be banished from the presence of Christ, and under these apprehensions, death is such a thing as strikes terror and confusion into every corner of their souls.
✦ NATHANIEL TAYLOR
Funeral Sermon [on Luke 12:40], 20

The strength of sin which is the law being taken away, sin itself is the less dreadful; the saint is already freed from sin, though he be not as yet free from sinning. He can therefore rejoice in his spirit, though sin (an ill neighbor) dwells in the flesh. For he has more good in Christ for him than there is evil in sin against him; and God is more pleased with him for Christ's sake than He was displeased with him for sin's sake.
✦ RALPH VENNING
"Triumph of Assurance," in
Orthodox Paradoxes, 27

ATHEISM/ATHEISTS

Atheism is the fruit that grows out of the blossom of discontent.
✦ SIMEON ASHE
Primitive Divinity, 102

I am apt to think that if there be any head atheism, it proceeds from heart atheism. But certain it is that when men have blotted out all sense of God upon their mind, sense of sin must needs be gone too. No doubt it is from the prevalence of atheism in these days that some have denied any real difference between good and evil.
✦ ALEXANDER CARMICHAEL
Believer's Mortification of Sin, 79

Evil works are a dust stirred up by an atheistical breath.
✦ STEPHEN CHARNOCK
Discourses upon the Existence
and Attributes of God, 2

[The fool] wished there were not any [gods] and sometimes hoped there were none at all. He could not raze out the notion of a deity in his mind, but he neglected fixing the sense of God in his heart and made it too much his business to deface and blot out those characters of God in his soul which had been left under the ruins of original nature. Men may have atheistical hearts without atheistical heads. Their reasons may defend the notion of a deity, while their hearts are empty of affection to the deity.
✦ STEPHEN CHARNOCK
Discourses upon the Existence
and Attributes of God, 46

There is a generation of men that seems to have crept out of hell who bid open defiance to whatever is sacred; who set their mouths against heaven and laugh at the notions of God and eternity; who make the great fundamental truths of our religion to be no better than fables invented to abuse and keep in awe men of easy belief; that take up things on trust and never examine them to the bottom. In a word, who censure all those for credulous fools that are not of their mind and as very atheists as themselves.

✦ JOHN CONANT
Sermon 3 on John 17:3, in
Sermons, 100–101

There is no man so confirmed and established in faith that hath not still some remainders of unbelief and atheism in his heart. The seeds of atheism are in every man by nature since the fall, and they can never be totally destroyed as long as we live in this world. 'Tis only death that perfectly frees us from them.

✦ JOHN CONANT
Sermon 3 on John 17:3,
in Sermons, 102

Are there not a sort of atheistical seamen who own not providence at all, either in the raising of these horrid tempests or in their marvelous preservation in them, but look on all as coming in a natural way and their escape to be only by good fortune and chance? How wonderful a thing is it in the eyes of all considering men that providence should take any notice of them in a way of favor that so wickedly disown it and so directly disoblige it? How can you possibly shut your eyes against such clear light and stop your ears against such loud and plain language whereby the power and goodness of God proclaim themselves to you in these providences!

✦ JOHN FLAVEL
"Seaman in a Storm," in
Navigation Spiritualized, 267

Atheism needs not be planted; you do enough to make your children such if you do not endeavor to plant religion in their minds. The very neglect of the gardener to sow and dress his garden gives advantage enough to the weeds to come up. This is the difference between religion and atheism: religion doth not grow without planting, but will die even where it is planted without watering; atheism, irreligion, and profaneness are weeds that will grow without setting, but they will not die without plucking up.

✦ WILLIAM GURNALL
Christian in Complete Armour, 115

Some will ask if I think that any, where the gospel is preached, neglect prayer on this account [i.e., atheism]? I do, and which is more, I think there are worse atheists to be found under the meridian light of the gospel than in the darkest nook in America. As weeds grow rankest in richest grounds and fruits ripest in hottest climates, so do sins grow to the greatest height where the gospel sun climbs highest.

✦ WILLIAM GURNALL
Christian in Complete Armour, 634

Those are the greatest enemies to religion that are not most irreligious. Atheists, though in themselves they be the worst, yet are seldom found hot persecutors of others, whereas those who in some one fundamental point be heretical are commonly most violent in oppositions. One hurts by secret infection; the other, by open resistance. One is careless of all truth; the other, vehement for some untruth. An atheist is worthy of more hatred; a heretic, of more fear; both, of avoidance.

✦ JOSEPH HALL
Holy Observations, in
Select Tracts, 323–24

Chrysostom speaks of a certain [man] that came unto him and told him, "I would become a Christian, but there is such variety of sects among you that I cannot anchor upon anything as certain in your religion." Certainly nothing begets atheism so much as this. Men have suspected the gospel because there have been such differences and strife; it makes them doubt of all to see distinct factions making the word of God…pliable to so many several purposes. Therefore, now a universal unity would much vindicate and recover the glory of Christ out of the hands of such a scandal.

✦ THOMAS MANTON
Meate Out of the Eater, 11

One principle contended for as rational and true, which, if admitted, will insensibly seduce the mind unto and justify a practice ending in atheism, is more to be feared than ten thousand jests and scoffs against religion.

✦ JOHN OWEN
Golden Book, 223

ATONEMENT

In the creation the Lord made man like Himself, but in the redemption He made Himself like man.

✦ JOHN BOYS
in Horn, *Puritan Remembrancer,* 129

When the Lord Jesus Christ offered up Himself a sacrifice unto God the Father and had our sins laid upon Him, He did give more perfect satisfaction unto divine justice for our sins than if you and I and all of us had been damned in hell unto all eternity. For a creditor is more satisfied if his debt be paid him all down at once than if it be paid by the week; a poor man that cannot pay all down will pay a groat a week or sixpence a week, but it is more satisfaction to the creditor to have all paid at once. Should we have been all damned, we should have been but paying the debt a little, and a little, and a little; but when Christ paid it, He paid it all down to God the Father…. And therefore the Lord is infinitely more satisfied by the satisfaction that Christ made upon the cross for our sins than if all we had gone to hell and been damned to all eternity. Oh! What a glorious and blessed satisfaction did this our High Priest make unto God the Father!

✦ WILLIAM BRIDGE
On Christ's Priestly Office, in
Works, 1:12–13

Sin is altogether black and abominable, but by the admirable wisdom of God, He hath drawn out of the dreadful darkness of sin the saving beams of His mercy and displayed His grace in the incarnation and passion of His Son for the atonement of sin.

✦ STEPHEN CHARNOCK
Discourses upon the Existence and Attributes of God, 346

As Christ is the primary object of faith, so Christ as crucified. Not Christ in His personal excellencies; so He is the object rather of our love than faith. But as bleeding, and that to death, under the hand of divine justice for to make an atonement by God's own appointment for the sins of the world.

✦ WILLIAM GURNALL
Christian in Complete Armour, 426

BACKSLIDING

I know you are not ignorant "that strait is the gate, and narrow is the way that leadeth unto life, and few there be that find it." And will you yet do as the most and decline the way of strictness, and holy self-denial, and give the flesh the reins? What, when God, that cannot lie, has said, "If you live after the flesh, you shall die"? Do you not know that you do in vain name the name of the Lord Jesus Christ, except you depart from iniquity?

✦ JOSEPH ALLEINE
Letter 34, "To a Backsliding Fellow-Student," May 18, 1664, in *Christian Letters,* 130

In the winter there's little visible difference between the living and the dead tree; neither is there betwixt a saint and a sinner in time of desertion and temptation. God's children may be led captive by sin and brought into bondage by their lusts (Rom. 7:23), and then 'tis hard to say how unlike they are to them that never knew God. And therefore, Christian, judge not thyself by thy changeable frames if thou dost not repent of thy change [i.e., conversion], thy leaving thy old courses and choosing God and grace (2 Cor. 7:10). If thou dost not approve of any sin or secretly love thy filthy ways (Rom. 7:15, 20); if thy heart be discontented with thy state of backsliding and longs after a return to thy resting place, then thou art gracious (Ps. 14:7; Jer. 31:18). If thou does find a war betwixt thy members and thy mind, the law of the Spirit of life warring against the law of sin and death, thy state is good (Rom. 7:21–23; Gal. 5:17).

✦ BARTHOLOMEW ASHWOOD
Best Treasure, 150

When persons are prejudiced against the means of recovery; hate them that rebuke them in the gate (Amos 5:10); shun the light and cannot endure those that would reclaim them from the error of their way (John 3:19); their hearts rise against any attempts to reduce them (Amos 7:10); cannot bear them that are good; slight and hate the people of God they formerly loved, avoiding their company; jeer and reproach those ministers, people, and ways they once took pleasure in, this shows a dangerous state.

Such a person's condition seems desperate and not far from the chambers of death. O you that are fallen back in religion! Get your hearts affected with it. Do you begin to decay? You know not where it will end. Are you gone back? 'Tis questionable whether ever you may return, and then what will your latter end be? Your last state will be worse than your first, and if twice dead, you will be plucked up by the roots; if after showers and dressings you decay, your end will be to be burned.

✦ BARTHOLOMEW ASHWOOD
Heavenly Trade, 341–42

When you are heartless and dull under the ordinances of God and Scripture hath little life or sweetness to you, and you are almost indifferent whether you call upon God in secret or no; and whether you go to the congregation and hear the word and join in God's praises and communion of the saints, and you have no relish in holy conference or any ordinance, but do them merely almost for custom or merely to satisfy your consciences, and not for any great need you feel of them or good you find by them; this shows for certain you want some more of the rod and spur; your hearts are not sufficiently broken and awakened, but God must take you in hand again.

✦ RICHARD BAXTER
Baxteriana, 95

Did the disciples thus forsake Christ, and yet were all recovered at last? Then, though believers are not privileged from backslidings, yet they are secured from final apostasy and ruin. The new creature may be sick, but it cannot die. Saints may fall, but they shall rise again (Mic. 7:8). The highest flood of natural zeal and resolution may ebb and be wholly dried up, but saving grace is "a well of water springing up into everlasting life" (John 4:14). God's unchangeable election, the frame and constitution of the new covenant, the meritorious and prevalent intercession of Jesus Christ do give the believer abundant security against the danger of a total and final apostasy.

✦ JOHN FLAVEL
Fountain of Life, 275–76

Weariness makes way for wandering.

✦ THOMAS MANTON
in Horn, *Puritan Remembrancer*, 110

The subtlety and deceitfulness of indwelling sin, Satan, and the world; the fallacious reasonings of deceitful principles, extenuating duties, aggravating difficulties, and suggesting false rules of profession are the principal causes of backsliding.

✦ JOHN OWEN
On the Hebrews, in *Oweniana*, 51

BAPTISM

We largely acknowledge that many learned and holy men, whom we much honor, do differ from us in the points of baptism, yet we must not let go any truth of God for their sakes. And we doubt not but the time is drawing nigh when God will cause the light of His holy word so to shine forth that all remaining darkness on the minds of the Lord's people shall vanish away, and then Zion's builders shall no more take a stone for a corner nor a stone for a foundation of Babylon's rubbish.

✦ PHILIP CARY
"To the Reader," in *Solemn Call*, x

Anabaptist: None ought to be baptized but those that profess faith and repentance, and consequently, no children ought to be christened.

Refutation: The children of such parents as profess the Christian religion and are members of the visible church, [since] they are comprised within God's covenant made to the faithful children of Abraham and their seed, may and ought to receive the seal of that covenant, which was circumcision under the law but now is baptism, which I prove.

✦ DANIEL FEATLEY
Dippers Dipt, 29

I cannot but love all who have the image of my heavenly Father stamped upon their souls. 'Tis not your opinion of paedobaptism (though an error) that shall alienate my heart from you nor restrain that catholic love that should run in all the veins of everyone that is born of God, though I am an enemy to your opinion and practice in that case, yet a dear lover of your persons and precious souls. And I have so much charity to believe that 'tis through ignorance you err in that matter and that

God has for some wise ends hid the truth of His holy ordinance of gospel baptism at present from you and do hope, did you see otherwise, you would practice otherwise: "Charity…thinketh no evil," etc. (1 Corinthians 13).

✦ BENJAMIN KEACH
Light Broke Forth in Wales, iii

BIBLE (See THE SCRIPTURES)

BLASPHEMY

As for the sin against the Holy Ghost, he never sins against the Holy Ghost that fears he has sinned against the Holy Ghost.

✦ WILLIAM BRIDGE
Lifting Up, 162

When a man does, speaks, or thinks anything derogatory to the holy nature or works of God with an intent to reproach Him or His ways, this properly is blasphemy.

✦ WILLIAM GURNALL
Christian in Complete Armour, 491

BLESSINGS

Some are not made better by God's gifts; yea, many are made worse. Give Saul a kingdom, and he will tyrannize; give Nabal good cheer, and he will be drunk; give Judas an apostleship, and he will sell his Master for money. But if God gives all to us, let us give something to Him. What shall I give Him? Not only my goods but myself.

✦ THOMAS ADAMS
Exposition upon…Second…Peter, 37

If your estate be small, yet God can bless a little. It is not how much money we have, but how much blessing.

✦ SIMEON ASHE
Primitive Divinity, 56

God gives thee many blessings, lest through want, being His child, thou shouldst despair; and He sends thee some crosses, lest by too much prosperity, playing the fool, thou shouldst presume.

✦ LEWIS BAYLY
Practice of Piety, 120

Common and ordinary blessings once lost and found again become extraordinary.

✦ WILLIAM BRIDGE
Lifting Up, 32

As there is a curse wrapped up in the best things [God] gives the wicked, so there is a blessing wrapped up in the worst things He brings upon His own. As there is a curse wrapped up in a wicked man's health, so there is a blessing wrapped up in a godly man's sickness. As there is a curse wrapped up in a wicked man's strength, so there is a blessing wrapped up in a godly man's weakness. As there is a curse wrapped up in a wicked man's wealth, so there is a blessing wrapped up in a godly man's wants. As there is a curse wrapped up in a wicked man's honor, so there is a blessing wrapped up in a godly man's reproach. As there is a curse wrapped up in all a wicked man's mercies, so there is a blessing wrapped up in all a godly man's crosses, losses, and changes.

✦ THOMAS BROOKS
Mute Christian, 93

Great blessings that are won with prayer are worn with thankfulness.

✦ SAMUEL CLARK
Saint's Nosegay, 95

Believe me, the gleanings of a Christian are better than the vintage of a reprobate. "A little that a righteous man hath is better than the riches of many wicked."

✦ ANDREW GRAY
"Spiritual Contentment," in *Works*, 398

When the father gives his child the whole orchard, it were folly to question whether he gives him this apple or that in it. All things are yours, and ye are Christ's (1 Cor. 3:22–23). The reconciled soul hath a right to all; the whole world is his. But as a father, though he settles a fair estate on his child yet lets him hold no more in his own hand than he can well manage, so God gives believers a right to all the comforts of this life, but proportions so much out to them for their actual use as His infinite wisdom sees meet, so that he that hath less than another in his present possession ought to impute it not to any want of love or care in God, but to the wisdom both of His love and care that gives stock as we have grace to work it out. We pour the wine according as the cup is; that which but fills one would be half lost if poured into a less.

✦ WILLIAM GURNALL
Christian in Complete Armour, 371

Temporal blessings are chiefly to be desired for the sake of spiritual. The traveler desires a horse not for itself so much as for the convenience of the journey he has to go. Thus, the Christian, when praying for temporal things, should desire them as helps in his way and passage to heaven.

✦ WILLIAM GURNALL
Christian in Complete Armour, 718

A little coming from the heart of God is better than a great deal from His hand only. Better to be an heir of one promise than to possess the whole world by common providence.

✦ RALPH ROBINSON
Christ All and in All, 331

We should keep a register in our minds of all the eminent blessings and deliverances we have met with; some whereof have been so conveyed that we might clearly perceive they were not the issues of chance, but the gracious effects of the divine favor and the signal returns of our prayers.

✦ HENRY SCOUGAL
Life of God in the Soul of Man, 112

A thankful heart for all God's blessings is the greatest of all blessings. Some men's blessings are turned into curses, and some men's curses are turned into blessings. Seeing it pleases the Lord to bless us, and that without cause given Him, how much should it please us to bless Him who hath given us so much cause to bless Him.

✦ RALPH VENNING
Canaan's Flowings, 19

Prayer will turn curses into blessings. Afflictions are part of the curse inflicted because of sin, but prayer alters the nature of them. For the sanctification of them being desired and granted, they work together for the good of them that feel them. Afflictions yield the "peaceable fruits of righteousness to them that are exercised thereby," says the apostle. On the other hand, where prayer is not, blessings are a snare, and the good things which are received work together for the harm and ruin of those that enjoy them.

✦ NATHANIEL VINCENT
Spirit of Prayer, 38

Temporal blessings are the fruit of prayer when they are not only asked of God but for God, that they may be employed in His service and to His praise…. When we desire some estate, that we may do good with it and honor the Lord with our substance; when we desire health and strength, that we may be the more useful and serve our generation according to the will of God, and what we desired is bestowed, surely prayer is heard. Temporal blessings are the fruit of prayer when they are asked with a humble and holy submission and not asked as the principal things. When we pray for daily bread and the meat that perishes in such a measure as the Lord sees good to deal out unto us but our greatest hunger and thirst is after higher things, even that meat which endures to everlasting life and the waters of that fountain which is always flowing and yet ever full. Temporal blessings are the fruit of prayer when they prove as cords to draw the heart nearer to God and effectually engage unto obedience.

✦ NATHANIEL VINCENT
Spirit of Prayer, 104–5

BOASTING

I confess the proverb is true, "The greatest talkers are not always the greatest doers." But it is true also he is seldom a great doer who hath nothing to say. There is a speaking which is our doing; there is a speaking in a way of boasting to magnify and set up ourselves—beware of that. And there is a speaking to the use of edifying to build up our brethren.
✦ RICHARD ALLEINE
Heaven Opened, 99

Man by nature is a vainglorious creature, apt to boast and brag of the sins that he is free of but unwilling to confess the sins he is guilty of (Job 31:33). There are no men so prone to conceal their own wickedness as those that are most forward to proclaim their own goodness.
✦ THOMAS BROOKS
Cabinet of Choice Jewels, 235

He that falls into sin is a man; that grieves at it is a saint; that boasts of it is a devil.
✦ THOMAS FULLER
Holy and Profane States, 189

Least doers are great boasters.
✦ WILLIAM GURNALL
Christian in Complete Armour, 449

BODY, EARTHLY

[Drunkenness] is a sin by which thou greatly wrongest and abusest thine own body. The body is the soul's instrument; it is as the tools are to a skillful artificer. This lust both dulls and spoils it so that 'tis utterly unfit for any service of Him that made it. Thy body is a curious piece not made by a word of command, as other creatures, but by a word of counsel: "I am fearfully and wonderfully made" and curiously wrought (Ps. 139:14); or...like a garment richly embroidered. Look how many members, so many wonders. There are miracles enough, saith one, betwixt head and foot to fill a volume. There is, saith another, such curious workmanship in the eye that, upon the first sight of it, some atheists have been forced to acknowledge a God.
✦ JOHN FLAVEL
"A Sober Consideration of the Sin of Drunkenness," in *Navigation Spiritualized*, 151

God is Lord of my body also and therefore challenges as well reverent gesture as inward devotion. I will ever in my prayers either stand as a servant before my Master or kneel as a subject to my Prince.
✦ JOSEPH HALL
Meditations and Vows, 44

Though the soul be made willing and forward by a divine principle implanted in it, yet the body remains a body, a weak and sluggish instrument, and so it will be while it is animal; it will go down into the dust a weak body (1 Cor. 15:43). What man ever had a more willing and cheerful heart than Moses, the friend of God? Yet his hands were heavy and ready to hang down (Ex. 17:12). Shall I instance in the excellent duties of preaching and of hearing: The spirits of the most spiritual preacher are soon exhausted; the tongue of the learned is ready to cleave to the roof of his mouth; the head is seized with dizziness, the heart with pantings, and the knees with trembling. And as to hearers, the ears of the most devout are often assailed with heaviness, the eyes with sleepiness, and the whole body in a short time with weakness.

✦ SAMUEL SHAW
Voice of One Crying in the Wilderness, 102

Take heed of pampering the body, of treating it too gently and delicately. Deny it nothing that may fit it for the service of God and your own souls, and allow it no more than may do that. Thy pampering is…unseemly. What! Make a darling of that which keeps us from our Lord; carry it gently and delicately and tenderly toward that which, while we carry about with us, we cannot be happy!… [Thy pampering is] injurious. If you bring up this servant delicately from a child, you shall have him become your son at length—yea, your master.

✦ SAMUEL SHAW
Voice of One Crying in the Wilderness, 124

A distempered body may have a healthy soul.

✦ GEORGE SWINNOCK
in Horn, *Puritan Remembrancer*, 329

BODY, GLORIFIED

Activity, agility, lightness, nimbleness, and speed in motion may also be implied in this spiritualness of the body. Not dull, slow, heavy-molded as now, but in agility and activity more like to spirits. Hence, easily made to ascend to meet the Lord in the air (1 Thess. 4:17). And afterward to go up with Him to the third heaven and able, no doubt, in a very little time (though not properly in an instant) to move through those vast spaces and distances of those heavenly mansions and from one quarter of the celestial world to another.

✦ JONATHAN MITCHEL
Discourse of the Glory, 49

God fits our souls here to possess a glorious body after; and He will fit the body for a glorious soul. So both shall be glorious—a glorious soul and a glorious body. He hath "wrought us" for the same. If a man therefore find the beginning of the new creature, that it is begun to be wrought in him, he may know that he shall partake of this glory of the body because he is "wrought" for it [see 2 Cor. 5:1–5].

✦ RICHARD SIBBES
"The Redemption of Bodies,"
in *Complete Works*, 5:171

[Glorified bodies] shall be agile and nimble. The bodies of the saints on earth are heavy and weary in their motion, but in heaven there shall be no elementary gravity hindering. But our bodies being refined shall be swift and facile in their motion and made fit to ascend, as the body of [Elijah]. This is the apostle's meaning when he calls it a spiritual body—that is, not only a body tunable and made fit to serve God without weariness but a body that can move swiftly from one place to another. In this life the body is a great hindrance to the soul in its operation: "The spirit is willing, but the flesh is weak." The soul may bring its action against the body; when the soul would fly up to Christ, the body as a leaden lump keeps it down, but there is a time coming when it shall be otherwise. Here the body is a clog; in heaven it shall be a wing.

✦ THOMAS WATSON
The Christian's Charter of Privileges,
in *Discourses,* 1:79

The bodies of the saints shall be immortal. Here our bodies are still dying. It is improper to ask when we shall die, but rather when we shall make an end of dying: first, the infancy dies, then the childhood, then youth, then old age, and then we make an end of dying. It is not only the running out of the last sand in the glass that spends it but all the sands that run out before. Death is a worm that is ever feeding at the root of our gourds, but in heaven "our mortal shall put on immortality."

✦ THOMAS WATSON
The Christian's Charter of Privileges,
in *Discourses,* 1:82–83

BONDAGE

How great is the sin and misery of those who continue in bondage to sin and Satan and refuse the government of Christ! Satan writes his laws in the blood of his subjects, grinds them with cruel oppression, wears them out with bondage to diverse lusts, and rewards

their service with everlasting misery. And yet how few are weary of it and willing to come over to Christ!

✦ JOHN FLAVEL
Fountain of Life, 146

There is no real bondage but what is either from or for sin.

✦ VAVASOR POWELL
in Thomas, *Puritan Golden Treasury,* 40

It is the greatest bondage in the world to have most freedom in ill.

✦ RICHARD SIBBES
in Horn, *Puritan Remembrancer,* 140

BOOKS

He that loveth a book will never want a faithful friend, a wholesome counselor, a cheerful companion, an effectual comforter. By study, by reading, by thinking one may innocently divert and pleasantly entertain himself; as in all weathers, so in all fortunes.

✦ ISAAC BARROW
"Of Industry in Our Particular Calling,
as Scholars," in *Sermons,* 331

The reading of books—what is it, but conversing with the wisest men of all ages and all countries who thereby communicate to us their most deliberate thoughts, choicest notions, and best inventions, couched in good expression and digested in exact method?

✦ ISAAC BARROW
"Of Industry in Our Particular Calling,
as Scholars," in *Sermons,* 332

Make careful choice of the books which you read. Let the Holy Scriptures ever have the pre-eminence; and next [to] them the solid, lively, heavenly treatises which best expound and apply the Scriptures; and next [to] those the credible histories, especially of the church, and tractates upon inferior sciences and arts. But take heed of the poison of the writings of false teachers, which would corrupt your understandings, and of vain romances, playbooks, and false stories, which may bewitch your fantasies and corrupt your hearts.

✦ RICHARD BAXTER
A Christian Directory, in
Practical Works, 2:150

Vocal preaching has the preeminence in moving the affections and being diversified according to the state of the congregations which attend it; this way the milk comes warmest from the breast. But books have the advantage in many other respects: you may read an able preacher when you have but a mean one to hear. Every congregation cannot hear the most judicious or powerful preachers, but every single person may read the books of the most powerful and judicious. Preachers may be silenced or banished, when books may be at hand. Books may be kept at a smaller charge than preachers. We may choose books which treat of that very subject which we desire to hear of, but we cannot choose what subject the preacher shall treat of. Books we may have at hand every day and hour, when we can have sermons but seldom and at set times. If sermons be forgotten, they are gone. But a book we may read over and over until we remember it, and, if we forget it, may again peruse it at our pleasure or at our leisure. So that good books are a very great mercy to the world.

✦ RICHARD BAXTER
A Christian Directory, in
Practical Works, 2:151

See that besides the Bible, they have some profitable moving books in every family. If they have none, persuade them to buy some of a low price. If they are not able, either give them or procure for them such as are likely to be of the greatest use to them. Engage them to read in the evening, when they have leisure, but especially on the Lord's Day; and by all means persuade them to teach their children to read.

✦ RICHARD BAXTER
Reformed Pastor, 45

What excellent helps do our libraries afford, where we have such a variety of wise, silent companions whenever we please!

✦ RICHARD BAXTER
Reformed Pastor, 131

A minister must be furnished with books as good helps to further his study, and these of all sorts. First, for humanities, of the several arts of ethics, politics, economics, natural philosophy, such as have written of trees, herbs, beasts, of husbandry, geography, histories of Jewish customs, of their weights and measures, and what other matter the learned have written of for the Scriptures especially.

✦ RICHARD BERNARD
Faithful Shepherd, 38

[Read] commentaries of orthodox writers, all which will help thee in understanding the text. They will more confirm thy judgment, seeing others to agree in that which thou has conceived thyself; they, by occasion of words, may put into thy mind what of thyself thou canst not dream of.... By these thou mayest, as it were, talk with and ask the judgment of the greatest divines of the world of any Scripture they write of, they yet living and speaking to us by their labors, as Calvin, Peter Martyr, Musculus, and others.

✦ RICHARD BERNARD
Faithful Shepherd, 40

Luther would often say he had rather that all his books should be burned than that they should be a means to hinder persons from studying the Scripture.

✦ THOMAS BROOKS
Smooth Stones, 51

Presently after this, I changed my condition into a married state, and my mercy was to light upon a wife whose father and mother were counted godly. This woman and I, though we came together as poor as poor might be (not having so much household stuff as a dish or spoon betwixt us both), yet this she had for her part, *The Plain Man's Pathway to Heaven* [by Arthur Dent] and *The Practice of Piety* [by Lewis Bayly], which her father had left her when he died. In these two books I sometimes read, wherein I found some things that were somewhat pleasing to me (but all this while I met with no conviction).

✦ JOHN BUNYAN
Grace Abounding, 14–15

Let your study be furnished not with many, but with choice books.

✦ EDMUND CALAMY
Saints' Memorials, 38

An index is the bag and baggage of a book, of more use than honor; even such who vehemently slight it, secretly using it, if not for need for speed of what they desire to find.

✦ THOMAS FULLER
Wise Words and Quaint Counsels, 141

I care not so much in anything for multitude as for choice. Books and friends, I will not have many; I would rather seriously converse with a few than wander among many.

✦ JOSEPH HALL
Meditations and Vows, 87

His sermons, wherein nothing could be more remote from ramble, [Dr. William Bates] constantly delivered from his memory. And hath sometime told me, with an amicable freedom, that he partly did it to teach some that were younger to preach without notes. His learning and acquired knowledge of things, usually reckoned to be within that compass, were a vast treasure. He had lived a long, studious life; an earnest gatherer and, as the phrase is, a devourer of books. With which he had so great an acquaintance, and they that were acquainted with him so well knew it, that one who was for the dignity of his station and the eminency of his endowments as great a pillar and as excellent an ornament of the church as ally it has had for many an age, has been known to say that were he to collect a library, he would as soon consult Dr. Bates as any man he knew. He was, indeed, himself a living one.

✦ JOHN HOWE
"A Funeral Sermon on the Death of Dr. William Bates," in *Works*, 984

To cure this evil frame [i.e., excessive mirth and spiritually unprofitable behavior at funerals], we have thought good to propound that which we find to be the wish of the generality of pious persons—namely, that books of this nature [i.e., that focus the mind on eternity] may be given at burials instead of rings, gloves, biscuits, wine, etc. (either to persons invited or to such godly poor people as may be thought most convenient who are not able to buy them), as their last legacy. And the relations of the deceased may have a small abridgment of his or her life and character printed in two or three leaves to bind up with the books for a small charge, and what number they think most convenient to dispose of for the benefit of the living, being their last act of charity to the poor.

✦ EDWARD PEARSE
Great Concern, 7

I have read of one of the ancients, noted for his singular piety and eminent holiness, who being asked what books he made his companions and used most, he answered that it was his practice every day to read over a book that had

three leaves—one red, a second black, a third white. In the red he used to read and meditate on the bloody passion of Christ; in the black, the darkness and damnation of hell; in the white, the light and glory of heaven, whereby he gained more in the way of practical godliness than by any other study. I would here add a fourth leaf to this book—namely, this opening day [i.e., judgment day]—and commend the reading of it to everyone that would be then ready.

✦ HENRY PENDLEBURY
Books Opened, in *Invisible Realities*, 203

Seeing such books as have been mentioned should be read, it follows that men should therefore as their ability will permit have such books in their houses. Those who cannot purchase them should provide the best that may be obtained at a cheaper price by the help of their faithful and learned teachers—namely, sound and plain catechisms and godly sermons and treatises concerning faith and repentance. These should be viewed as another kind of household instrument, such as cards [i.e., a device for processing wool] and tables and similar things, without which the house is thought to be naked.

✦ RICHARD ROGERS
Holy Helps for a Godly Life, 152

Seeing that [people] should read books which are fit for building them up in godliness, they must not spend their time in reading filthy, lewd, and wanton books nor books needless nor unprofitable, nor superstitious pamphlets, nor Niccolò Machiavelli's blasphemies, nor the subtle devices and deceitful dreams and errors of the Church of Rome—except they be able for their sound judgment to discern them, so that they may be better able to detest and give others warning of them.

✦ RICHARD ROGERS
Holy Helps for a Godly Life, 153

Speech requires presence; writings have their use in absence. Sermons are as showers of rain that water for the instant; books are as snow that lies longer on the earth. These may preach when the author cannot and, which is more, when he is not.

✦ SAMUEL WARD
"The Happiness of Practice," in
Sermons and Treatises, 161

Books are the children of the brain.

✦ THOMAS WATSON
Great Gain of Godliness, vii

Get good books into your houses. When you have not the spring near to you, then get water into your cistern. So when you have not that wholesome preaching that you desire, good books are cisterns that hold the waters of life in them to refresh you.

✦ THOMAS WATSON
"Mr. Watson's Afternoon Sermon, August 17, 1662," in Calamy, *Farewell Sermons*, 244

Books are a memory without us, and memory is a book within us.

✦ HEZEKIAH WOODWARD
Treatise of Prayer, 11

BREVITY OF LIFE

What being we have is but of a short duration in regard of our life in this world. Our life is in a constant change and flux; we remain not the same an entire day. Youth quickly succeeds childhood, and age as speedily treads upon the heels of youth. There is a continual defluxion of minutes, as there is of sands in a glass. [A person] is as a watch wound up at the beginning of his life, and from that time is running down, till he comes to the bottom; some part of our lives is cut off every day, every minute. Life is but a moment: what is past cannot be recalled; what is future cannot be ensured.

✦ STEPHEN CHARNOCK
*Discourses upon the Existence and
Attributes of God*, 191

Who makes the lease? The tenant or the landlord? Or dost thou forget thou farmest thy life and art not an owner? This is the device of Satan to make you delay, whereas a present expectation of the evil day would not let you sit still unprepared. Oh, why do you let your souls from their work, make them idle and rest from their burdens, by telling them of long life while death chops in upon you unawares?

✦ WILLIAM GURNALL
Christian in Complete Armour, 179

BUSINESS, INTEGRITY IN

We can easily understand the sin of them who spend their precious time at taverns and alehouses. But who thinks himself a sinner while he is busy with his yarnman or other chapman? Yet who liveth and thus sinneth not? Who asks himself at night, *Have I saved or gained nothing this day by a lying tongue? Have I spoke no evil words in making my bargains?* A man may trade as well as drink himself to hell; lying will bring one into the lake that burns with fire and brimstone as well as swearing and cursing.

◆ JOHN COLLINGES
Weaver's Pocket-book, 33

In buying and selling this may be a good rule to guide us: to do as we would be done unto. For example, when we sell, consider we whether knowing the marketable price and goodness of the thing, we would gladly give so much as we demand. If we would not, we deal not justly. So in buying, but herein take we heed that our hearts deceive us not, whereto we be very prone.

◆ EZEKIEL CULVERWELL
Time Well Spent, 31–32

In buying and selling, this is a sure rule: to be sure our neighbor gains by us.

◆ EZEKIEL CULVERWELL
Time Well Spent, 32

CALLING OF GOD

God's call is not like man's. Man's call always presupposes abilities; God's call sometimes brings them.

◆ WILLIAM BRIDGE
Lifting Up, 222

CAREER: SOME HELPS IN CHOOSING

Let due consideration be used. It is highly absurd to fix upon such a weighty affair as a condition for life without the serious exercise of reason and thought.... Let faithful, judicious persons be consulted, especially of the same calling.... Choose such a calling and place as may not be dangerous to the mind.... Let the divine providence be acknowledged by earnest supplications for direction and assistance.... In concurrence with the foregoing directions, let the person's inclination be consulted, which, if it is strongly and reasonably fixed on any particular calling, is one method whereby we receive the direction of providence and a good step to a proper choice.

◆ RICHARD STEELE
Religious Tradesman, 32–36

CARNAL (See THE WORLD/WORLDLINESS)

CATECHISM

And I must say that I think it is a much easier matter to compose and preach a good sermon than to deal rightly with an ignorant man for his instruction in the principles of religion. This work [i.e., the catechism] will try the abilities and tempers of ministers; it will show the difference between one man and another more than pulpit preaching can do.

◆ RICHARD BAXTER
Reformed Pastor, 78

Experience shows how that little profit comes by preaching where catechizing is neglected. Many there are who teach twice or three times in a week and yet see less fruit of many years labor by not catechizing with all than some reap in one year who perform both together. This manner of catechizing is to be performed by propounding questions and the people answering to them. This plain and simple kind is the best and will bring the most profit, though it seem childish and be to many tedious.

♦ RICHARD BERNARD
Faithful Shepherd, 9

I advise that [the catechism] may be gone through in a family constantly, once a month.... Let it be once or twice distinctly read over, and that by parts, so much only at a time as is allotted for one day.... When you first begin to examine your family, let them answer only out of the book and after you have once or twice gone over the whole catechism within the book and that you perceive their understandings to be somewhat enlightened. Then, and not till then, let them be required to answer without book.

♦ THOMAS LYE
Assemblies Shorter Catechism, 3

The doctrine which shows the way unto everlasting life and happiness is commonly termed theology, or divinity; and the familiar declaration of the principles thereof (for the use especially of the ignorant) is called catechizing (Heb. 5:12–14)—namely, a teaching by voice and repetition of the grounds of the Christian religion (Acts 18:25–26; 1 Cor. 14:19; Gal. 5:6), and this both at home by the master of the house and in the church likewise by the minister. At home especially because houses are the nurseries of the church.

♦ JAMES USSHER
Body of Divinity, 2

CHARACTER

A man is what indeed he is in his family and among his relations. He that is a bad child can never be a good Christian. Either bring testimonies of your godliness from your relations, or it may be well suspected to be no better than counterfeit. Never talk of your obedience to God whilst your disobedience to the just commands of your parents gives you the lie.

♦ JOHN FLAVEL
Fountain of Life, 310–11

A man is known by his custom and the course of his endeavors what is his business. If a man be constantly, easily, and frequently carried away to sin, it discovers a habit of soul and the temper of his heart. Meadows may be overflowed, but marsh ground is drowned with the return of every tide. A child of God may be carried away and act contrary to the bent and inclination of the new nature, but when men are drowned and overcome with the return of every temptation and carried away, it argues a habit of sin.

♦ THOMAS MANTON
in Bertram, *Homiletic Encyclopaedia,* 269

CHASTISEMENT

I shall take chastisements here in the utmost latitude for all kinds and degrees of sufferings, whether from God or man or Satan; whether sufferings for sin or sufferings for righteousness' sake.

✦ THOMAS CASE
Correction, Instruction, 2–3

By chastisements God doth teach us how to prize our outward mercies and comforts more and yet to dote upon them less — to be more thankful for them and yet less ensnared by them.

✦ THOMAS CASE
Correction, Instruction, 8

By chastisement man is made more attentive unto God. In prosperity the world makes such a noise in a man's ears that God cannot be heard. "He speaks indeed once and twice" again and again very often, "yet man perceives it not." He is so busy in the crowd of worldly affairs that God is not heeded.

✦ THOMAS CASE
Correction, Instruction, 88

The lessons themselves which God teacheth his people…are sympathy, moderation, self-denial, humility, self-knowledge, prayer, the Scriptures, evidences for heaven, evil of sin, communion with God, exercise of grace, life of faith, self-diffidence, knowledge of God, duties of suffering, privilege of suffering, the one thing necessary, time redemption, the sufferings of Christ, and the value of heaven. Behold Christians! To be taught of God when chastised by Him is a blessedness compounded of twenty several precious ingredients.

✦ THOMAS CASE
Correction, Instruction, 90

Better be pruned to grow than cut up to burn.

✦ JOHN TRAPP
Commentary…upon…the New Testament, 494

CHEERFULNESS

A Christian of a right temper should be ever cheerful in God: "Serve the Lord with gladness" (Ps. 100:2). A sign the oil of grace hath been poured into the heart is when the oil of gladness shines in the countenance. Cheerfulness credits religion. How can the discontented person be cheerful? Discontent is a dogged sullen humor; because we have not what we desire, God shall not have a good word or look from us.

✦ SIMEON ASHE
Primitive Divinity, 125

Now they [i.e., an unbelieving world] will believe it is good news indeed the gospel brings when they can read it in your cheerful lives; but when they observe Christians sad with this cup of salvation in their hands, truly they suspect the wine in it is not as good as the preachers commend it to them for. Should man see all who trade to the Indies come home poorer than they went, it would be hard to persuade others to venture thither, for all the golden mountains said to be there.

✦ WILLIAM GURNALL
Christian in Complete Armour, 351

It is required that we suffer in imitation of Christ, as making Him our example. We are not to take up the cross, but with design to follow Christ. "Take up the cross" is but half the command; "take up the cross and follow" is the whole command. And we are to suffer willingly and cheerfully, or we are the most unlike Jesus Christ in our sufferings of any persons in the world. Christ was willing and cheerful.

✦ JOHN OWEN
"Discourse 12 on Phil. 3:10," in
Twenty-Five Discourses, 160

Sense of pardon is the true ground of spiritual joy. Christ's usual receipt for working of comfort is this: "Be of good cheer; thy sins be forgiven thee" (Matt. 9:2).

✦ RALPH ROBINSON
Christ All and in All, 311

The heart must be kept courageous and strong and lively, like an instrument which is tuned to tune all the rest, or else every grief will make thee impatient. In Deuteronomy 30:9 it is said that God rejoices to do us good, and therefore in Deuteronomy 28 the Jews are reproved because they rejoiced not in the service of God. As He loveth a cheerful giver, so He loveth a cheerful server and a cheerful preacher and a cheerful hearer and a cheerful worshiper; and therefore David saith, "Let us sing unto the LORD" (Ps. 95:1), showing, as it were, the tune which delights God's ears.

✦ HENRY SMITH
"The Ladder of Peace," in *Sermons*, 115

To suffer as Christians is to suffer with cheerfulness. Patience is a bearing the cross; cheerfulness is a taking up the cross. Christ suffered for us cheerfully; His death was a freewill offering (Luke 12:50).

✦ THOMAS WATSON
The Beatitudes, in *Discourses*, 2:360

Cheerfulness is like music to the soul. It excites to duty. It oils the wheels of the affections. Cheerfulness makes service come off with delight, and we are never carried so swift in religion as upon the wings of delight. Melancholy takes off our chariot wheels, and then we drive on heavily.

✦ THOMAS WATSON
"The One Thing Necessary," in
Discourses, 1:377

CHILDREN

Our fathers [i.e., ministers] being Christ's immediate and, if I may so say, domestic servants, it is to be supposed that they were always doing their Master's work and strictly observing all those pious, wise, and good laws that He set before them, by which means we had a better example of virtue and goodness than other Christians usually have. So that we cannot pretend to follow our fathers' steps except we walk in the narrow path that leads to bliss. And besides, our fathers being authorized and required to administer the means of grace and salvation to Christ's flock, we who were bred up under them have always had the opportunity of enjoying the said means, having, from our infancy, been trained up and exercised continually in them. And therefore, unless they have their due effect upon us, we shall be much more inexcusable than they who enjoy them only now and then.

✦ WILLIAM BEVERIDGE
"A Sermon Preached before the Sons of the Clergy," in *Thesaurus Theologious*, 204

Subjection and obedience [to your parents] is not absolute and universal. God has not divested Himself of His own authority to clothe a parent with it. Your obedience to them must be in the Lord—that is, in such things as they require you to do in the Lord's authority. In things consonant to that divine and holy will to which they, as well as you, must be subject; and therein you must obey them. Yea, even the wickedness of a parent exempts not from obedience where His command is not so. Nor, on the other side, must the holiness of a parent sway you where his commands and God's are opposite.

✦ JOHN FLAVEL
Fountain of Life, 307

So must the son please him that begot him, that he displease not Him that created him.

✦ THOMAS FULLER
in Thomas, *Puritan Golden Treasury*, 43

Remember the advantages of your being thus related to holy parents. For temporal blessings, Ishmael, Solomon, Rehoboam, and others are instances of the kindness of God to children upon the account of their fathers. But you stand fairest for spiritual and eternal blessings: you are children of the covenant and members of the visible church of Christ, the blessing of Abraham ("I will be thy God"), which reached unto his seed, being now come upon us Gentiles (Gal. 3:14). You have many helps to serious godliness which others have not. You have many hindrances removed which make it more difficult for others who descend from wicked parents and live in ignorant, irreligious families. You have more knowledge of God and Christ, of sin and duty. And usually the spirit of grace begins more early with such children and follows them with more calls, offers, invitations, strivings, convictions and leaves them not till they are profligate, desperate, and resolved in wickedness, whereof Ishmael, a scoffer; Esau, a profane person; and the Jewish nation, who filled up the measure of their iniquity by rejecting and murdering the Lord of glory, are eminent examples.

✦ JOHN SHOWER
Family Religion, 109–10

Three things children receive of their parents: life, maintenance, and instruction. For these three they owe other three; for life they owe love; for maintenance they owe obedience; for instruction they owe reverence. For life, they must be loved as fathers; for maintenance, they must be obeyed as masters; for instruction, they must be reverenced as tutors.

✦ HENRY SMITH
"The Affinity of the Faithful,"
in *Sermons*, 207

Before we teach parents to love their children, they had need be taught not to love them too much, for David's darling was David's traitor. And this is the manner of God—when a man begins to set anything in God's room and love it above Him which gave it, either to take it away or to take him away before he provoke Him too much. Therefore, if parents would have their children live, they must take heed not to love them too much, for the Giver is offended when the gift is more esteemed than He.

✦ HENRY SMITH
"A Preparative to Marriage," in *Works*, 1:35

Obedience to parents is shown in subscribing to their commands. A child should be the parents' echo: when the father speaks, the child should echo back obedience.

✦ THOMAS WATSON
Body of Practical Divinity, 301

CHRIST/JESUS

Herein our Phoenix rose from His ashes, our Eagle renewed His feathers, the First Begotten of the dead was born from the womb of the earth. Christ, like the sun eclipsed by the moon, got Himself out by His resurrection; and as the sun by the moon, He was darkened by them to whom He gave light. His death did justify us; His resurrection did justify His death. He buried the law with Himself, and both with honor. He raised up the gospel with Himself, and both with glory. His resurrection was the first stone of the foundation: "In Christ shall all be made alive" (1 Cor. 15:22); and the last stone of the roof, for God assures us He shall come to judgment by this token—that He raised Him up from the dead (Acts 17:31). Satan danced on His grave for joy. When he had Him there once, he thought Him sure enough, but He rose again and trampled on the devil's throne with triumph.

✦ THOMAS ADAMS
Exposition upon...Second...Peter, 476

Wilt thou have Jesus for thy husband? Understand before thou answer. The taking of Christ for thy husband implies intimate union, ingenuous subjection, total dependence. (1) Intimate union: by choosing and accepting Him for thine and resigning and giving up thyself to Him for His own to live with Him in the dearest conjugal affection forever. (2) Ingenuous subjection: by a free and cheerful putting thyself under Him as thy Lord whom thou wilt obey and be subject to in all things. The wife must be subject to her husband, yet not as a slave by constraint but freely and by consent. (3) Total dependence: holding him as thy head, expecting nothing, owning nothing but what descends upon thee from Him; depending on Him for all things—the bearing of thy debts, thy discharge from thy bonds, and thy whole provision for a livelihood and maintenance. Consider, then, what sayest thou? Doth thine heart choose and accept and resign up itself unto Christ? Dost thou choose Him as a husband?

✦ RICHARD ALLEINE
Heaven Opened, 312

Only Christ is the sun and center of all divine revealed truths. We can preach nothing else as the object of our faith, as the necessary element of your soul's salvation, which doth not some way or other either meet in Christ or refer to Christ. Only Christ is the whole of man's happiness, the sun to enlighten him, the physician to heal him, the wall of fire to defend him, the friend to comfort him, the pearl to enrich him, the ark to support him, the rock to sustain him under the heaviest pressures, "as an hiding place from the wind, and a covert from the tempest; as rivers of water in a dry place, as the shadow of a great rock in a weary land" (Isa. 32:2). Only Christ is that ladder between earth and heaven, the Mediator between God and man, a mystery which the angels of heaven desire to pry and peep and look into (1 Peter 1:12).

✦ ISAAC AMBROSE
Looking unto Jesus, 10–11

We have shown already that [Christ's] treasures are bottomless, boundless, unfathomable, inexhaustible, never to be wasted or spent. O soul, come to Christ as such a one. Measure not Christ's gold by thy bushel nor His plenty by thy poverty. Think not thy debts too great for Christ to pay because thou knowest not where to get money of thy own. Think not thy straits too many for Him to relieve.

✦ BARTHOLOMEW ASHWOOD
Best Treasure, 364

Believers, have all your expectations from Christ: "My soul, wait thou only upon God; for my expectation is from him" (Ps. 62:5). If the Lord Jesus be so rich, then He is able to maintain you and supply all your wants. There's bread enough in His house to feed you, light enough in Him to guide you, comfort enough to cheer you, blood enough to pardon you, righteousness enough to justify you, grace enough to sanctify you, strength enough to bear and support you, treasures enough to satisfy and requite you. Hence 'tis He calls His people to look to Him and be saved (Isa. 45:22). And on this belief the saints resolved to wait and look for Him (Isa. 8:17). O Christians! Expect all you need from Christ. His sufficiency to help you and His willingness to supply you are arguments enough for your expectation. Why should you look to creatures more than to the Creator?

✦ BARTHOLOMEW ASHWOOD
Best Treasure, 411

As Jesus Christ is the Lord Treasurer of all our graces, so He is the Lord Keeper of all our comforts. And therefore when God is pleased to give any comfort to you, go to Jesus Christ and say, "Lord, keep my comforts for me, keep my evidences for me, keep my assurance for me." You must not only depend upon Christ for graces but for comforts, and as well for the keeping as for the getting of them. As you have any spiritual comfort from Christ, spend all for Christ; for though in temporal things the way to have little is to spend much, yet in spiritual things, the more you spend the more you have.

✦ WILLIAM BRIDGE
Lifting Up, 46

Beloved, there is a twofold righteousness in Christ. First, there is His essential and personal righteousness as God. Now this essential personal righteousness of Christ cannot be imputed to us. But then there is, secondly, His mediatory righteousness; that is that righteousness which He wrought for us as mediator whereby He did subject Himself to the precepts, to the penalties, commands, and curses, answering both God's vindictive and rewarding justice. This is communicated to us and made ours by virtue of which we stand justified in God's sight. The mediatory righteousness of Christ is the matter of our justification.

✦ THOMAS BROOKS
Cabinet of Choice Jewels, 347

When Caesar gave one a great reward, "this," said he, "is too great a gift for me to receive"; but, says Caesar, "it is not too great a gift for me to give." So though the least gift that Christ gives, in one sense, is too much for us to receive, yet the greatest gifts are not too great for Christ to give.

✦ THOMAS BROOKS
Smooth Stones, 33

The Lord Jesus has as great and as large an interest in the weakest saints as He has in the strongest. He has the interest of a friend, and the interest of a father, and the interest of a head, and the interest of a husband, and

therefore, though saints be weak—yea, though they be very weak—He overlooks their weakness and keeps a fixed eye upon their graces.

✦ THOMAS BROOKS
Smooth Stones, 155

Riches always imply two things: abundance, and abundance of such things as be of worth. Now in the Lord Jesus Christ are the greatest riches, the best riches, the choicest riches. In Christ are riches of justification (Titus 2:14); in Christ are riches of sanctification (Phil. 4:12–13); in Christ are riches of consolation (2 Cor. 12:9); and in Christ are riches of glorification (1 Peter 1:11).

✦ THOMAS BROOKS
Unsearchable Riches of Christ,
in *Select Works*, 1:2

Christ was never so joyful in all His life that we read of as when His sufferings grew near. Then He takes the sacrament of His body and blood into His own hands and with thanksgiving bestows it among His disciples. Then He sings a hymn, then He rejoices, then He comes with a "Lo, I come." O the heart—the great heart—that Jesus had for us to do us good! He did it with all the desire of His soul.

✦ JOHN BUNYAN
Riches, 103

When a man shall not only design me a purse of gold but shall venture his life to bring it to me, this is grace indeed. But, alas, what are a thousand such short comparisons to the unsearchable love of Christ?

✦ JOHN BUNYAN
Riches, 103

Did [Christ] make His soul an offering for sin to procure men a liberty of sinning? Or was Christ crucified that the body of sin might remain unmortified—yea, get ground and be the more rampant upon it? Is this your kindness to your Friend, to be so in love with His enemies, the spear and the nails that pierced Him, that you will spend and be spent for the service of your lusts? He died that those He died for might live. Live to whom? Not to themselves, but to Him that died for them.

✦ ELISHA COLES
Practical Discourse of God's
Sovereignty, 149

Faith and holiness are great things indeed and highly to be valued. Yet, let me say that even these and all other good things laid together will be but a very little heap to that grace which put us into Christ, the honor and privilege of union with Him, and the price He hath paid for our ransom: "Herein is love," that God "sent his Son to be the propitiation for our sins" (1 John 4:10).

✦ ELISHA COLES
Practical Discourse of God's
Sovereignty, 155

Oh! Christ's riches are so many, they cannot be numbered; they are so precious, they cannot be valued; so great, they cannot be measured. Oh, the infinite riches of our King! Christ is a mine of gold which we must dig till we find heaven.

✦ WILLIAM DYER
Christ's Famous Titles, 51

Poor Christian, be not dejected because thou seest thyself outstripped and excelled by so many in other parts of knowledge; if thou know Jesus Christ, thou knowest enough to comfort and save thy soul. Many learned philosophers are now in hell, and many illiterate Christians in heaven.

✦ JOHN FLAVEL
Fountain of Life, 6

Christ's sitting down at God's right hand in heaven notes the advancement of Christ's human nature to the highest honor, even to be the object of adoration to angels and men. For it is properly His human nature that is the subject of all this honor and advancement, and being advanced to the right hand of Majesty, it is become an object of worship and adoration. Not simply as it is flesh and blood, but as it is personally united to the second person and enthroned in the supreme glory of heaven. Oh, here is the mystery, that flesh and blood should ever be advanced to the highest throne of Majesty, and being there installed in that glory, we may now direct our worship to him as God-man.

✦ JOHN FLAVEL
Fountain of Life, 420

[Christ] is ordained to be judge. Judgment is the act of the whole, undivided Trinity. The Father and Spirit judge, as well as Christ, in respect of authority and consent; but it is the act of Christ in respect of visible management and execution.

✦ JOHN FLAVEL
Fountain of Life, 426–27

Jesus Christ is a comprehensive mercy, including all other mercies in Himself: He is the tree of life; all other mercies are but the fruits growing on Him. He is the Sun of Righteousness, and whatever comfort, spiritual or natural, refreshes your souls or bodies is but a beam from that sun, a stream from that fountain. If then God part with Christ to you and for you, He will not withhold other mercies. He will not give the whole tree and deny an apple; bestow the fountain itself and deny you the streams. All spiritual mercies are in Him and given with Him: "Blessed be the God and Father of our Lord Jesus Christ, who hath blessed us with all spiritual blessings in heavenly places in Christ" (Eph. 1:3). All temporals are in Him and given with Him (Matt. 6:33); they are additional to that great mercy.

✦ JOHN FLAVEL
Sacramental Meditations, 122

THE CALL

Come, my Way, my Truth, my Life!
Such a Way as gives us breath,
Such a Truth as ends all strife,
Such a Life as killeth death.

Come, my Light, my Feast, my
Strength!
Such a Light as shows a feast,
Such a Feast as mends in length,
Such a Strength as makes His guest.

Come, my Joy, my Love, my Heart!
Such a Joy as none can move,
Such a Love as none can part,
Such a Heart as joys in love.

✦ GEORGE HERBERT
Poems, 161

[Jesus] is a faithful friend, and none that ever had to do with Him can say anything to the contrary. He never forgot any business that any of His friends desired Him to do for them; He never neglected it or did it by halves. Where did any of them come to Him to reveal some secret loathsome distemper to Him that He reproached them with it? To which of them did He promise a heaven and put them off with this world? When this pilot undertakes to steer their course, their vessel shall never split upon the rock, run upon the sands, or spring a leak so as to sink in the seas. To be sure, He will see them safe in their harbor.

✦ JAMES JANEWAY
Heaven upon Earth, 102

Christ is a prophet, priest, and king, and all as mediator; without any one of these offices the work of salvation could not have been completed. As a priest He redeems us; as a prophet He instructs us; as a king He sanctifies and saves us. Therefore the apostle says, He is made to us of God, wisdom, righteousness, sanctification, and redemption (1 Cor. 1:30). Righteousness and redemption flow from Him as a priest; wisdom as a prophet; sanctification as a king. Now many embrace Christ as a priest, but yet they own Him not as a king and prophet; they like to share in His righteousness, but not to partake of His holiness. They would be redeemed by Him, but they would not submit to Him. They would be saved by His blood but not submit to His power. Many love the privileges of the gospel but not the duties of the gospel. These are but almost Christians, notwithstanding their close with Christ, for it is upon their own terms but not upon God's.

✦ MATTHEW MEAD
Almost Christian Discovered, 191–92

The truth of it is, that person who is firmly satisfied and heartily pleased that this way of the death of Christ for the salvation of sinners by the forgiveness of sin is the way whereby God is and will be glorified—I say that person is a true believer. Now let not your assent be only to this thing, that it is true, that Christ came into the world to save sinners; but to this, that this is the way whereby God is and will be glorified. He will be glorified in pardoning such guilty creatures as we are, in imputing righteousness to such sinners as we are. He is glorified in laying all our iniquities on Christ. By this way, His righteousness, His love, grace, and wisdom are all manifested; this is God's being glorified.

✦ JOHN OWEN
Discourse 19 on Gal. 2:20, in
Twenty-Five Discourses, 224

See here the greatness of Christ's grace! One would think that He should have been wholly taken up with the dishonor of His present condition, with the sense of His Father's desertion, with the foresight of His approaching sufferings. And yet behold, when He is wholly possessed of weakness, He is yet at leisure for a work of power. The righteous justice of His God

and the unjust cruelty of his enemies were not able to drive Him from the remembrance or exercise of His mercy. He that came to suffer all these things for man does in the midst of His sufferings remember man, honoring the scorns and buffets of His judgment with the conversion of a fallen apostle [i.e., Peter] and the nails and ignominies of His cross with the conversion of a reviling thief.

✦ EDWARD REYNOLDS
*Meditations on the Fall and Rising
of St. Peter*, 54–55

Christ is not loved at all till He be loved above all.

✦ RALPH ROBINSON
Christ All and in All, 6

A member of Christ, however poor in outward riches, is the richest man in the world, for he doth possess Christ, who is a stone of invaluable worth. If you knew a man had an estate worth all the precious stones in the world, you would account him a very rich man. A believer hath one precious stone in his possession of greater worth than all the stones which now are or ever were in the world. When other men boast of their jewels, you boast of your Christ; or tell you what rich, sparkling diamonds they have, you bring out this precious stone and lay it before them. When you hear others speaking of the costly foundation of their houses, you think what a glorious foundation your souls are built upon. He that wants Christ is the truly poor man, whatever he enjoys. He is rich, we say, whom

God loves; he is rich that inherits Christ. If thou hadst thy house full of diamonds, thou wouldst judge thyself a wealthy man. If Christ be thine, thou hast much more.

✦ RALPH ROBINSON
Christ All and in All, 263

The doctrine which Christ preached and which by His appointment is published is very glorious, yet it is an occasion of offense to the world. The Arians are offended at the doctrine of His divine nature; the Manichees at His humanity; the Socinians at His satisfaction; the Papists at justification by faith alone; the Pelagians and Arminians at His doctrine of nullifying the power of nature in things supernatural. The antinomians stumble at His ratification of the moral law, etc. The Pharisees were offended at His doctrine against tradition (Matt. 15:11–12). But to come to particulars: the strictness of His doctrine is a stumbling block to many; it condemns not only actual sin but the very sinful risings of corruption in the heart.

✦ RALPH ROBINSON
Christ All and in All, 270

O that the heaven, and the heaven of heavens were paper, and the sea ink, and the multitude of mountains pens of brass, and I able to write my dearest, my loveliest, my sweetest, my matchless, and my most unequaled and marvelous Well Beloved! Woe is me, I cannot set Him out to men and angels! I am put to my wit's end how to

get His name made great. How sweet is Christ's back! O, what there is in His face! Those that see His face, how are they able to get their eye plucked off Him again!

✦ SAMUEL RUTHERFORD
Garden of Spices, 41

If you win Christ, though not in the sweet and pleasant way you would have Him, it is enough. For the Well Beloved comes not our way; He must choose His way Himself. He cuts off your love to the creature that you might learn that God only is the right owner of your love, sorrow, loss, sadness, death, or the worst things that are.

✦ SAMUEL RUTHERFORD
Prison Sayings, 37

If we knew the glory of our elder Brother in heaven, we should long to be there to see Him. We children think the earth a fair garden, but compared with the garden of the Lord it is but wild, cold, barren ground. All things are fading that are here; it is our happiness to make sure of Christ.

✦ SAMUEL RUTHERFORD
Prison Sayings, 53–54

When I was in meditation, I saw when Christ was present, all blessings were present; as where any were without Christ present, there all sorrows were. Hence I saw how little of Christ was present in me. I saw I did not cease to be and live of myself, that Christ might be and live in me. I saw that Christ was to do, counsel, direct, and that I should be wholly diffident of myself and careful for this that He might be all to me; hence I blessed Christ for showing me this and mourned for the want of it.

✦ THOMAS SHEPARD
Meditations and Spiritual Experiences, 40

We are weak, but we are His; we are deformed, but yet carry His image upon us. A father looks not so much at the blemishes of his child as at his own nature in him; so Christ finds matter of love from that which is His own in us. He sees His own nature in us. We are diseased, but yet His members. Whoever neglected his own members because they were sick or weak? None ever hated his own flesh. Can the head forget the members? Can Christ forget Himself? We are His fullness, as He is ours.

✦ RICHARD SIBBES
Bruised Reed and Smoking Flax, 107

Let us not look so much who are our enemies as who is our Judge and Captain, nor what they threaten but what He promises; we have more for us than against us. What coward would not fight when he is sure of victory? None are here overcome but those that will not fight. Therefore, when any base fainting seizes upon us, let us lay the blame where it is to be laid.

✦ RICHARD SIBBES
Bruised Reed and Smoking Flax, 195–96

The very beholding of Christ is a transforming sight. The Spirit that makes us new creatures and stirs us up to behold this servant—it is a transforming beholding. If we look upon Him with the eye of faith, it will make us like Christ; for the gospel is a mirror, and such a mirror that when we look into it and see ourselves interested in it, we are changed from glory to glory (2 Cor. 3:18). A man cannot look upon the love of God and of Christ in the gospel, but it will change him to be like God and Christ. For how can we see Christ and God in Christ, but we shall see how God hates sin, and this will transform us to hate it as God doth, who hated it so that it could not be expiated but with the blood of Christ, God-man. So, seeing the holiness of God in it, it will transform us to be holy.

✦ RICHARD SIBBES
"A Description of Christ," in
Complete Works, 1:14

We must always take heed of coming to God in our own persons or worthiness, but in all things only look to God in Christ. If we would look to God as a Father, we must see Him to be Christ's Father first. If we desire to see ourselves acquitted from our sins, let us first look at Christ risen for our justification; if we think of glorification in heaven, let us look up to Christ as glorified; and when we consider of any spiritual blessing, consider it in Christ first. All the promises are made to Christ; He takes them first from God the Father and gives them to us by His Holy Spirit. The first fullness is in God, and He empties Himself into Christ. "And of his fullness we all receive grace."

✦ RICHARD SIBBES
*Divine Meditations and Holy
Contemplations*, 98–99

Alas! Many have the Bible and use it but little; and many use it amiss because they know not its right name. It is well and warrantably, from its contents, called in its title page in all languages and translations the Old and New Testament of our Lord and Savior Jesus Christ. But how few, in reading this title, mind the use and virtue of the blood of Jesus, which turned the covenant of God's grace into the testament of Christ and thereby sealed and confirmed all the good words and good things in that covenant? It was a happy word we find in [Foxe's] *Book of Martyrs* that some in the dawning of the light of the gospel in this land used, in calling the New Testament (a great rarity in those days), "the blood of Christ." You never rightly read the gospel, nor do you understand the design of it, nor rightly believe one promise in it till in heart you can say, "This gospel is the only charter of my salvation, sealed with the blood of my only Savior."

✦ ROBERT TRAILL
Sermon 3, in Sixteen Sermons on the Lord's Prayer, for His People, 47

We should give [Christ] the glory that is due to Him; to believe that the willingness to save is greater in the Savior than [the] willingness to be saved is in the sinner. For Christ's goodwill to save is the cause of any desire of salvation in any: "Thy people shall be willing in the day of thy power" (Ps. 110:3). When He hath a mind to save, He doth work this willingness in men to be saved by Him.

✦ ROBERT TRAILL
Sermon 3, in Sixteen Sermons on the Lord's Prayer, for His People, 53

Christ is the most bountiful physician. Other patients do enrich their physicians, but here the physician doth enrich the patient. Christ prefers all His patients. He doth not only cure them but crown them (Rev. 2:10). Christ doth not only raise from the bed but to the throne; He gives the sick man not only health but heaven.

✦ THOMAS WATSON
Gleanings, 19–20

Is [Christ] the captain of salvation? See what a blessed army He has listed under His banner of love, and they have followed Him through all the dangers of life and time under His conduct. These are the chosen, the called, the faithful. They have sustained many a sharp conflict, many a dreadful battle, and they are at last made more than conquerors through Him that has loved them. They attribute all their victories to the wisdom, the goodness, and the power of their divine leader and even stand amazed at their own success against such mighty adversaries. But they fought under the banner, conduct, and influence of the Prince of Life, the King of Righteousness, who is always victorious and has a crown in His hand for every conqueror.

✦ ISAAC WATTS
Devout Meditations, 176–77

Whatsoever Satan or conscience say, do not conclude against thyself. Christ shall have the last word. He is judge of quick and dead and must pronounce the final sentence. His blood speaks reconciliation (1 Cor. 1:20), cleansing

(1 John 1:7), purchase (Acts 20:28), redemption (1 Peter 1:18–19), purging (Heb. 9:14, 18), remission (Eph. 1:7), liberty (Heb. 10:19), justification (Rom. 5:9), nighness to God (Eph. 2:18). Not a drop of this blood shall be lost.

✦ THOMAS WILCOX
Choice Drop of Honey, 16

CHRIST, ASCENSION OF

A heart ascendant is the best evidence of your interest in Christ's ascension.

✦ JOHN FLAVEL
Fountain of Life, 414

Having now dispatched that great work on earth for them, [Christ] hastens to heaven as fast as He can to do another. And though He knew He had business yet to do upon earth that would hold Him forty days longer, yet to show that His heart was longing and eagerly desirous to be at work for them in heaven, He speaks in the present tense and tells them, "I ascend"; and He expresses His joy to be not only that He goes to His Father but also that He goes to their Father to be an advocate with Him for them.

✦ THOMAS GOODWIN
Heart of Christ in Heaven, 27

[Christ's] glorious ascension is our stepping-stone to heaven; it is our ladder by which we ascend after Him whither He is gone. Well indeed might He say to His disciples, "It is expedient for you that I go away," and this in many ways and upon many accounts.

Because of His ascension we have the gate opened, the way cleared, mansions prepared, an inheritance, a crown, and a kingdom in safe keeping. By His ascension to glory, we have an advocate in heaven, a descent of heavenly blessings, a pledge of our ascension, and an assurance of our welcome there.

✦ HENRY PENDLEBURY
"The Design of Christ's Ascension," in *Slate, Select Nonconformists' Remains*, 359

Think of the privileges and advantages that come to you by His ascending to heaven and remaining there for you; they are so many I can only mention a few. They that have Christ in heaven for them have a right to Him now He is there and to all the benefits which believers can receive on earth resulting from His passion, ascension, and intercession. In these few words I have told you of greater privileges that you are invested with than if I could have told you of an unquestionable right to all the crowns and great things of the present world, for they are all very nothings to an interest in Christ. You have liberty to go to heaven upon all occasions.... You may go to heaven with your prayers at any time.... You may go out of any place.... Christians, through Christ, may go to God at any time and lay all their matters before "him that is able to do exceeding abundantly above all that we ask or think" (Eph. 3:20). We have always an advocate ready to solicit our business in heaven.

✦ HENRY PENDLEBURY
"The Design of Christ's Ascension," in *Slate, Select Nonconformists' Remains*, 375

CHRIST, CROSS OF

[Christ] despatched [i.e., transacted] more work in those thirty-three years wherein He lived—yea, in those three hours wherein he suffered—than ever was or will be done by all creatures to eternity. It was a good six days' work when the world was made, and He had a principal hand in that, neither has He been idle since; "I and my Father work hitherto," says Christ (John 5:17). But that three hours' work upon the cross was more than all the other. Eternity will not have more done in it than virtually was done in those three hours.

✦ THOMAS GOODWIN
Of Christ the Mediator, in Works, 5:103

Let the bands of [Christ's] love draw our hearts, for…He could have broken all these cords, as Samson did those with which he was bound; but the cords of love bound Him as well as the cords of our sins. It was these cords fastened Him to the cross more than the nails—yea, and bound Him there more than our sins did, or else He would never have suffered Himself to be bound.

✦ THOMAS GOODWIN
Of Christ the Mediator, in Works, 5:229

No sinner will come near to Christ unless he be drawn, and to be drawn is to be made willing to come unto Him and to follow Him in chains of love. Christ draws none to Him, whether they will or no; but He casts on their minds, hearts, and wills the cords of His grace and love, working in them powerfully, working on them kindly, to cause them to choose Him, to come to Him, and to follow Him. "Draw me; we will run after thee." The great principal and fountain from whence the drawing efficacy and power of grace doth proceed is from the lifting up of Christ. Drawing grace is manifested in and drawing love proceeds from the sufferings of Jesus Christ on the cross.

✦ JOHN OWEN
*Discourse 15 on John 12:32, in
Twenty-Five Discourses,* 189

The shame of the cross was as much as the blood of the cross; His name was crucified before His body. The sharp arrows of reproach that the world did shoot at Christ went deeper into His heart than the spear.

✦ THOMAS WATSON
Art of Divine Contentment, 72

CHRIST, INCARNATION OF

Why [Christ] was born of a woman, not of a man? Because the Lord would do a new thing upon the earth…. For one of mankind to be made of another, without a woman, was no new thing, for so was Eve made of Adam long since. And for a man to be made without woman or man is older, for so was Adam. And for one to be made of man and woman is almost as old and much more common; we see it daily. There is no new in these. Yet there was one way left, and that was new indeed: for one to be made of a woman without a man was never done before. And this was as miraculous as any of the other.

✦ WILLIAM AUSTIN
*Certain Devout, Godly, and
Learned Meditations,* 11

The Son of God became the Son of man that we, the sons of men, might become the sons of God; and all this He did to save the nations.

✦ WILLIAM DYER
Christ's Famous Titles, 15

Yea, to express the depth of His humility, He was made in the likeness of men. O how did Christ abase Himself in taking flesh! It was more humility in Christ to humble Himself to the womb than to the cross. It was not so much for flesh to suffer but for God to be made flesh—this was the wonder of humility.

✦ THOMAS WATSON
The Christian's Charter of Privileges,
in *Discourses*, 1:128

CHRIST, INTERCESSION OF

The Lord Jesus waits in heaven to receive your prayers. 'Tis His business and work in glory to pursue your advantages, and therefore He expects to hear from you (Heb. 9:24). As an agent that expects to hear from his client and receive intimation about his condition; as a friend in a foreign country that is hearkening for letters from his friend, Christ in heaven desires to hear from His people on earth. Not that He is ignorant of them or needs to be put in remembrance, but this way are His graces in them exercised, their love and duty maintained, and Himself glorified: "Therefore will the LORD wait, that he may be gracious" (Isa. 30:18). In the original it is, "He longs and, as it were, greedily and enlargedly

desires an occasion to be gracious; He waits in heaven to be put in remembrance to do His people good."

✦ BARTHOLOMEW ASHWOOD
Best Treasure, 130–31

Sometimes, the guilt of renewed infirmities or decays doth renew distrust and make us shrink, and we are like the child in the mother's arms that fears when he loses his hold, as if his safety were more in his hold of her than in her hold of him. Weak duties have weak expectations of success. In this case, what an excellent remedy has faith in looking to the perpetual intercession of Christ. Is He praying for us in the heavens, and shall we not be bold to pray and expect an answer? O remember that He is not weak when we are weak.

✦ RICHARD BAXTER
A Christian Directory, in
Practical Works, 2:186

Prayers and supplications, earnest prayers out of affection, should be poured out even for them that cannot or do not pray for themselves. Wherefore are we taught to pray but that we may be the mouth of others? And since an intercessor is given to us above, how are we bound to be intercessors for others below.

✦ HUGH BINNING
"An Essay upon Christian Love,"
in *Several Sermons*, 201

If once pardoned, thou will be always pardoned. For the first pardon Christ paid His blood; for the continuance He does but plead His blood, and we cannot be without a pardon till Christ be without a plea.

✦ STEPHEN CHARNOCK
"The Pardon of Sin," in *Choice Works*, 212

His love and care were manifested in the choice of mercies for them. He does not pray for health, honor, long life, riches…but for their preservation from sin, spiritual joy in God, sanctification, and eternal glory. No mercies but the very best in God's treasury will content Him for His people; the rest He is content should be dispensed promiscuously by providence. But these He will settle as a heritage upon His children.

✦ JOHN FLAVEL
Fountain of Life, 188

That blood which [Christ] offered with tears and strong cries on the cross, where He likewise interceded, the same blood He continues virtually to offer up with prayers in the heavens and makes atonement by both, only with this difference: on earth, though He interceded, yet He more eminently offered up Himself; in heaven He more eminently intercedes and does but present that offering.

✦ THOMAS GOODWIN
"Christ Set Forth," in *Works*, 4:58

Suppose a king's son should get out of a besieged city where he had left his wife and children, whom he loves as his own soul, and these all ready to die by sword or famine if supply came not the sooner. Could this prince, when he arrived at his father's house, please himself with the delights of the court and forget the distress of his family? Or rather would he not come post to his father, having their cries and groans always in his ears, and before he eat or drink do his errand to his father and entreat him, if ever he loved him, that he would send all the force of his kingdom to raise the siege rather than any of his dear relations should perish?

✦ WILLIAM GURNALL
Christian in Complete Armour, 17

CHRIST, LOVE OF

[Christ] knew both your weight and your worth, your natural unfitness for Him, and averseness to the match. He also knew what it must cost Him to make you both meet and willing and that it was so stupendous a work that all the hosts of heaven would have broken under. He further knew that after all He should do and suffer for you, you could not advantage Him in the least; only He should have the satisfaction to have made you happy against your unrenewed will, and yet He declined it not. He came "leaping upon the mountains and skipping over the hills" of death and difficulties, as longing for and delighting to be in that work. He was straitened until it was accomplished. Such was the intenseness of His love to you! And a great deal ado He had with your wills before you were brought to be willing. And for all this He only expects you will carry it worthy of so great a lover and such manner of love, which is, in effect, but to accept of and continue in His love and be willing He should save you freely and own this love of His as the immediate fountain whence your happiness is derived.

✦ ELISHA COLES
Practical Discourse, 153

The general love of Christ is scattered and branched unto all the creatures in the world, but His special love, His exceeding great and rich love, is only settled upon His church. Now, if you ask me what Christ's distinguishing love is, I shall name it and but name it to you. It is pardoning love…redeeming love, calling love, justifying love, adopting love, sanctifying love, glorifying love. This, I say, is a particular love. Christ's love is not only sweeter than wine but better than life. He is most lovely; He is altogether lovely. Christ is nothing but love to those who are His love.

✦ WILLIAM DYER
Christ's Famous Titles, 32

Love, love—I mean Christ's love—is the hottest coal that ever I felt. O, but the smoke of it is hot; cast all the salt sea on it, it will flame! Hell cannot quench it; many, many waters will not quench love. Christ is turned over to His poor prisoner in a mass and globe of love. I wonder that He should waste so much love upon such a waster as I am; but He is no waster, but abundant in mercy. Free grace is an unknown thing. This world hath heard but a bare name of Christ, and no more. There are infinite plies in His love that the saints will never attain to unfold.

✦ SAMUEL RUTHERFORD
Garden of Spices, 113

CHRIST, PASSIVE AND ACTIVE OBEDIENCE OF

This twofold obedience of Christ stands opposed to a twofold obligation that fallen man is under: the one to do what God requires, the other to suffer what He hath threatened for disobedience. Suitably to this double obligation, Christ comes under the commandment of the law to fulfill it actively (Matt. 3:15) and under the malediction of the law to satisfy it passively. And whereas it is objected by some, if He fulfilled the whole law for us by His active, what need then of His passive obedience? We reply, great need, because both these make up that one, entire, and complete obedience by which God is satisfied and we justified. The whole obedience of Christ, both active and passive, makes up one entire perfect obedience.

✦ JOHN FLAVEL
Fountain of Life, 126

There are two things, say divines, in justification: (1) Remission of sin, and this is from Christ's passive obedience: "Remission of sins through his blood; and much more being now justified by his blood—i.e., from our sins—we shall be saved from wrath through him." (2) The imputation of righteousness, and this is from Christ's active obedience; and here He is called "the Lord our Righteousness," and we "the righteousness of God in him" (2 Cor. 5:21). And again, Christ's active obedience was necessary to qualify Him for His passive. For had He not been holy and obedient in His life, He must in His death have offered for His own sins, as well as the people's, which must not be imagined.

✦ OBADIAH GREW
Sinner's Justification, 26

CHRIST, PRIESTHOOD OF

Since Christ is an intercessor, I infer that believers should not rest at the cross for comfort; justification they should look for there, but being justified by His blood, they should ascend up after Him to His throne. At the cross you will see Him in His sorrows and humiliations, in His tears and blood; but follow Him to where He is now, and then you shall see Him in His robes—in His priestly robes and with His golden girdle about Him. There you shall see Him wearing the breastplate of judgment and with all your names written upon His heart. Then you shall perceive that the whole family in heaven and earth is named of Him and how He prevails with God the Father of mercies for you. Stand still awhile and listen—yea, enter with boldness unto the holiest and see your Jesus as He now appears in the presence of God for you, what work He makes against the devil and sin and death and hell for you. Ah, it is brave following of Jesus Christ to the holiest. The veil is rent; you may see with open face as in a glass the glory of the Lord.

✦ JOHN BUNYAN
Riches, 127

His sanctifying Himself imports the extraordinariness of His person, for it speaks Him to be both priest, sacrifice, and altar all in one—a thing unheard of in the world before, so that His name might well be called Wonderful. "I sanctify Myself": I sanctify, according to both natures; "Myself"—that is, My human nature, which was the sacrifice upon the altar of My divine nature, for it is the altar that sanctifies the gift. As the three offices never met in one person before, so these three things never met in one priest before.

✦ JOHN FLAVEL
Fountain of Life, 55

The priesthood of Christ under the gospel excels Aaron's in respect of word:

1. [Aaron] was to enter into the holy place
2. to appear before God;
3. to hear the sins of the people (Ex. 28:38);
4. to make an atonement (Lev. 16:32);
5. to judge of uncleanness (Lev. 13:2);
6. to offer incense (Lev. 16:17–18);
7. to determine controversies (Deut. 17:8);
8. to bless the people, and many other things which Jesus Christ infinitely excels in.

✦ BENJAMIN KEACH AND
THOMAS DELAUNE
Tropologia, book 3:530

The priesthood of Christ under the gospel excels Aaron's in respect of... office:

1. Christ is entered into the true holy place, *sanctum sanctorum*, the holy of holies, heaven itself.

2. He appears really before God for us, being set down on the right hand of the majesty on high.

3. He hath, as the great Antitype, borne our sins in His own body upon the tree.

4. He hath made a complete and perfect atonement.

5. He judges our uncleanness, both of the heart as well as of the flesh.

6. He resolves all our doubts, ends controversies, speaks peace to the disconsolate, a word in season to him that is weary.

7. He offers incense: "And there was given unto him much incense, that he should offer it with the prayers of all saints" (Rev. 8:3).

8. He gives down all blessings: "Him hath God sent to bless you in turning away every one of you from his iniquities."

♦ BENJAMIN KEACH AND
THOMAS DELAUNE
Tropologia, book 3:530

CHRIST, RESURRECTION OF

[Easter] is the Sabbath of the new world, our passover from everlasting death to life, our true jubilee, the first day of our week, and the chief in our calendar. Herein our Phoenix rose from His ashes, our Eagle renewed His feathers, the First Begotten of the dead was born from the womb of the earth. Christ, like the sun eclipsed by the moon, got Himself out by His resurrection; and as the sun by the moon, He was darkened by them to whom He gave light. His death did justify us; His resurrection did justify His death. He buried the law with Himself, and both with honor; He raised up the gospel with Himself, and both with glory.

♦ THOMAS ADAMS
in Bertram, *Homiletic Encyclopaedia*, 732

Consider how impossible it is in itself that so many men [i.e., the apostles and early witnesses to the resurrection of Christ] should agree together to deceive the world, and that for nothing, and at the rate of their own undoing and death. And that they should all agree in the same narratives and doctrines so unanimously, and that none of these should ever confess the deceit and disgrace the rest. All things well considered, this will appear not only a moral but a natural impossibility.

♦ RICHARD BAXTER
A Christian Directory, in
Practical Works, 2:501

Although Christ's obedience in His life and His death past do alone afford the whole matter of our justification and make up the sum of that price paid for us,...so as faith may see a fullness of worth and merit therein to discharge the debt; yet faith has a comfortable sign and evidence to confirm itself in the belief of this from Christ's resurrection after His death. It may fully satisfy our faith that God Himself is satisfied and that He reckons the debt as paid.

✦ THOMAS GOODWIN
"Christ Set Forth," in *Works*, 4:25

Christ did not rise from the dead as a private person but as the public head of the church, and the head being raised, the rest of the body shall not always lie in the grave. Christ's rising is a pledge of our resurrection (2 Cor. 4:14).

✦ THOMAS WATSON
Body of Practical Divinity, 204

CHRIST, SUFFERINGS OF

That [Christ] the God of life was put to death. That He who is one with the Father should cry out of misery, "My God, my God, why hast thou forsaken me?" That He who had the keys of hell and death at His girdle should lie in the sepulcher of another, having in His lifetime nowhere to lay his head nor after death to lay His body. That that head before which the angels cast down their crowns should be crowned with thorns, and those eyes purer than the sun put out by the darkness of death. Those ears, which hear nothing but hallelujahs of saints and angels, to hear the blasphemies of the multitude. That face that was fairer than the sons of men to be spit on by those beastly wretched Jews. That mouth and tongue "that spake as never man spake" accused for blasphemy. Those hands that freely swayed the scepter of heaven and those "feet like unto fine

brass" nailed to the cross for man's sins.... Oh! How should the consideration of this stir up the soul against it and induce the soul to fly from it and to use all holy means whereby sin may be subdued and destroyed.

✦ THOMAS BROOKS
Precious Remedies, 25–26

The burden of sufferings and provocations which Christ supported was very great, for on Him met all sorts and kinds of trouble at once, and those in their highest degrees and fullest strength. Troubles in His soul, and these were the soul of His troubles. He "began to be sore amazed, and to be very heavy" (Mark 14:33). The wrath of an infinite God beat Him down to the dust.

✦ JOHN FLAVEL
Fountain of Life, 281

He suffered in His soul; yea, the sufferings of His soul were the very soul of His sufferings. He felt in His inner man the exquisite torments and inexpressible anguish of the wrath of God.

✦ JOHN FLAVEL
Sacramental Meditations, 111

He suffered everything that was required to repair and make up the glory of God. Better you and I and all the world should perish than God should be damaged in His glory. It is a truth, and I hope God will bring all our hearts to say, Christ hath suffered to make up that. The obedience that was in the sufferings of Christ brought more glory unto God than the disobedience of Adam, who was the original of the apostasy of the whole creation from God, brought dishonor unto Him. That which seemed to reflect great dishonor upon God was that all His creatures should as one man fall off by apostacy from Him. God will have His honor repaired, and it is done by the obedience of Christ much more.

✦ JOHN OWEN
Discourse 8, in *Twenty-Five Discourses*, 127

Christ died for our preferment; He suffered that we might reign. He hung on the cross that we might sit on the throne; His crucifixion is our coronation.

✦ THOMAS WATSON
Puritan Gems, 16–17

CHRIST: THE SUM OF SCRIPTURE

This blessed Christ is the sole paragon of our joy, the fountain of life, the foundation of all blessedness. The sum of the whole Bible, prophesied, typified, prefigured, exhibited, demonstrated, to be found in every leaf, almost in every line—the Scriptures being but as it were the swaddling bands of the child Jesus. Abraham, Moses, Joshua, Samson, David were all renowned, yet are but meant on the by. Christ is the main, the center whither all these lines are referred. They were all His forerunners to prepare His way; it is fit that many harbingers and heralds should go before so great a prince. Only John Baptist was that phosphorus, or morning star, to signify the sun's approaching. The world was never worthy of Him, especially not so early; He was too rich a jewel to be exposed at the first opening of the shop. Therefore, He was wrapped up in those obscure shadows—the tree of life, Noah's ark, Jacob's ladder; therefore called the "expectation of nations," longed and looked for more than health to the sick or life to the dying.

✦ THOMAS ADAMS
Meditations upon the Creed, in *Works*, 3:224

This Jesus Christ is the center…of the whole Scripture. The sum of divinity is the Scripture; the sum of the Scripture is the gospel; the sum of the gospel is Jesus Christ.

✦ THOMAS ADAMS
"*Semper Idem*, or, The Immutable Mercy of Jesus Christ," in *Works*, 3:2

Christ is the scope of the Scripture.

✦ RICHARD SIBBES
in Horn, *Puritan Remembrancer*, 1

CHRISTIANITY

Certainly Christianity is nothing else but an imitation of the divine nature, a reducing of a man's self to the image of God, in which he was created in righteousness and true holiness. A Christian's whole life should be but a visible representation of Christ.

✦ THOMAS BROOKS
Privy Key of Heaven, 12

The general nature and necessity of Christ's priesthood...shows the incomparable excellency of the Christian religion above all other religions known to or professed in the world. What other religions seek, the Christian religion alone finds, even a solid foundation for true peace and settlement of conscience. While the Jew seeks it in vain in the law, the Mohammedan in his external and ridiculous observances, and the Papist in his own merits, the believer only finds it in the blood of this great sacrifice. This, and nothing less than this, can pacify a distressed conscience laboring under the weight of its own guilt. Conscience demands no less to satisfy it than God demands to satisfy Him. The grand inquest of conscience is, Is God satisfied? If He be satisfied, I am satisfied.

✦ JOHN FLAVEL
Fountain of Life, 100

CHRISTIAN LIBERTY

Christian liberty is a spiritual liberty, freeing the true Christian from the servitude of sin and from all other yokes of spiritual bondage wherewith sin had entangled us. Neither is Christian liberty only privative, as being a freedom and immunity from bondage, as though this were all, that by it we are not servants; but as appears by [John 8:36], it is also positive, as being a liberty, power, right, and interest to the privileges of God's children, who are also heirs of God and coheirs with Christ.

✦ GEORGE DOWNAME
Christian's Freedom, 10

The second [use of the doctrine of Christian liberty] is the conscience of our manifold wants and imperfections in those duties which we do perform. For how can a man be persuaded that God, to whom no creature being compared is pure, will allow of his imperfect and stained obedience? And if he be not persuaded that his service is acceptable unto God, with what heart can he perform it? The doctrine therefore of Christian liberty assures our consciences that we are freed from the law's exaction of perfect obedience to the acceptation of our actions; that God, covering our imperfections as an indulgent father with the perfect righteousness and obedience of Christ, imputes not our wants unto us but accepts of the truth of our will and desire for the deed and our sincere endeavor for the perfect performance. And therefore a Christian may, in respect of this liberty, with comfort and cheerfulness perform obedience according to the measure of grace received, being assured that our defective and stained obedience will be accepted of God through the mediation and intercession of Jesus Christ.

✦ GEORGE DOWNAME
Christian's Freedom, 128–29

Liberty is the Diana of our times. O what apologies are made for some suspicious practices: long hair; gaudy, garish apparel; spotted faces; naked breasts! These have been called to the bar in former times and censured by sober and solid Christians as things at least suspicious and of no good report, but now they have hit on a more favorable jury that find them not guilty; yea, many are so fond of them that they think Christian liberty is wronged in their censure. Professors are so far from a holy jealousy that should make them watch their hearts, lest they go too far, that they stretch their consciences to come up to the full length of their tether, as if he were the brave Christian that could come nearest the pit of sin and not fall in.

✦ WILLIAM GURNALL
Christian in Complete Armour, 306

CHRISTIANS

Great men love to see great spirits in their children, and the great God loves to see a great spirit in His children. We are one spirit with God and with Christ and one spirit with the Holy Ghost; therefore, we should have a spirit that might manifest the glory of the Father, Son, and Holy Ghost in our spirits. That is the spirit of a Christian indeed. The spirit of a Christian should be a lion-like spirit. As Jesus Christ is the Lion of the tribe of Judah (so He is called), so we should manifest somewhat of the lion-like spirit of Jesus Christ. He manifested His lion-like spirit in passing through all afflictions and troubles whatsoever without any murmuring against God.

✦ JEREMIAH BURROUGHS
Rare Jewel, 56

Believers are like letters of gold engraven on the very heart of Christ.

✦ WILLIAM DYER
Christ's Famous Titles, 34

They that are indeed lovers of God are united by that their hearts meet in Him, as in one center; they cannot but love one another. Where a godly man sees his Father's image, he is forced to love it. He loves those whom he perceives godly so as to delight in them because that image is in them; and those that appear destitute of it, he loves them so as to wish them partakers of that image. And this is all for God: he loves *amicum in Deo, et inimicum propter Deum*; that is, He loves a friend in God, and an enemy for God. And as the Christian's love is pure in its cause, so in its effects and exercise. His society and converse with any tend mainly to this: that he may mutually help and be helped in the knowledge and love of God. He desires most that he and his brethren may jointly mind their journey heavenward and further one another in their way to the full enjoyment of God. And this is truly the love of a pure heart, which both begins and ends in God.

✦ ROBERT LEIGHTON
A Commentary upon the First Epistle of Peter, in Whole Works, 1:147

The main of a Christian's duty lies in these two things—patience in suffering and avoidance of sin.

✦ ROBERT LEIGHTON
Spiritual Truths, 106

Grace is little at the first. There are several ages in Christians: some babes, some young men. Grace is as a grain of mustard seed (Matt. 17:20). Nothing so little as grace at first, and nothing more glorious afterward. Things of greatest perfection are longest in coming to their growth.

✦ RICHARD SIBBES
Bruised Reed and Smoking Flax, 36–37

It may be observed that the aged seem not to grow, at least not to be so zealous as many young Christians. But the reason is because there is in young Christians a greater strength of natural parts and more lively affections, and these make a great appearance. But aged men grow in spiritual strength and are more refined; their knowledge is more clear, their actions more pure, their zeal more seraphic and not mingled with wildfire. Therefore, though aged Christians be not carried with a high and full stream, yet they become, through grace, more stable and judicious, more heavenly-minded and mortified; they continually grow deeper in humility by a clearer fight of their own corruptions and daily sins and rise higher toward heaven on the wings of faith and holy love.

✦ RICHARD SIBBES
Divine Meditations and Holy Contemplations, 119

[Christians] are indeed in the world but not of it, for they are called out of the world by (1) Christ's separation: "I have chosen you out of the world" (John 15:19); (2) Christ's interdiction: "Love not the world, neither the things that are in the world" (1 John 2:15); (3) Christ's operation: "The world is crucified unto me, and I unto the world" (Gal. 6:14).

✦ THOMAS TAYLOR
Pilgrim's Profession, 27

Christians should be walking Bibles.

✦ THOMAS WATSON
Bible and the Closet, 40

THE CHURCH

For the church is a company of men that are called (1 Cor. 1:24; 10:32), both Jews and Greeks, to the Jews, to the Greeks, and to the church of God. But because the end of calling is faith, and the work of faith is engrafting into Christ, and this union with Christ does bring with it communion with Christ. Hence it is defined, in the very same sense, a company of believers, a company of those who are in Christ, a company of those that have communion with Christ.

✦ WILLIAM AMES
Marrow of Sacred Divinity, 152

A church is a company of those who are called (and this call must be answered or else it is nothing) to the visible profession of faith in Christ and obedience unto Christ, according to the gospel.

✦ GILES FIRMIN
Sober Reply, 14

No church in this world can be free from all faults. Even Ephesus, the best of the seven, had somewhat amiss in it. As long as there be spots in the moon, it is vain to expect anything spotless under it. The earnest of perfection, which is sincerity, may be received in this life, but the full payment thereof must be expected in another. Such as fancy a possibility of a perfect church here must not only mold a new form but make a new matter, cause frailty to be firm, folly to be wise, flesh to be Spirit, men to be angels, saints being too little in this life as full of their infirmities.

✦ THOMAS FULLER
"The Fear of Losing the Old Light,"
in *Pulpit Sparks*, 160

As the church was the great thing which God in the creation of the world had an eye upon as a means of glorifying Himself, so is it likewise the main object of providence. Had it not been for this, He would not have created the world (Eph. 3:9–10). We have two things asserted by the apostle: (1) that all things were created by Jesus Christ, who is the Mediator and Savior of His church, and consequently, all this was done in reference to the great design of His church (I understand the place to speak of the creation of the world, as John 1:3, and not of the work of redemption, though I know many expound it so); (2) That He appointed His church to be the great means of displaying to men and angels that wonderful variety of wisdom which is more to be seen in it than in all the creation besides.

✦ RICHARD GILPIN
Temple Rebuilt, 14

We may follow the Lamb safely wherever He goes. Now God does not, for corruptions of doctrine that are remote from the foundation or of worship in things ritual and of an inferior nature, cast off a church and withdraw His presence from it; neither ought we. Indeed, if the foundation of doctrine be destroyed and the worship become idolatrous, in that case God goes before us and calls all the faithful after Him to come out from the communion of such a church. But where corruptions in a church are of the former nature and such laws be not imposed by the church in their communion with it as bring a necessity of approving things unlawful, the sin is not in holding communion with it but in withdrawing from it. Many things may be tolerated for maintaining peace and unity and enjoying the worship of God when it is not in our power to redress them. Neither does our presence at the ordinance carry a consent with it of all that is there done. Whoever said that all who are present in an assembly, by it show their consent to every impertinent phrase in the minister's prayer, corrupt gloss, or false interpretation he makes of any text!

✦ WILLIAM GURNALL
Christian in Complete Armour, 699

The church comes out of Christ's side in the sleep of His death.

✦ WILLIAM JENKYN
in Thomas, *Puritan Golden Treasury*, 53

We see in a jeweler's shop that as there are pearls and diamonds and other precious stones, so there are files, cutting instruments, and many sharp tools for their polishing. And while they are in the workhouse, they are continual neighbors to them and come often under them. The church is God's jewelry, His workhouse, where His jewels are polishing for His palace and house. And those He especially esteems and means to make most resplendent, He hath oftenest His tools upon them.

✦ ROBERT LEIGHTON
Spiritual Truths, 108

The church is the garden of God, the doctrine is the flowers of this garden, discipline is the hedge.

✦ CHRISTOPHER LOVE
Zealous Christian, 9

Many may be members of the church of Christ and yet not members of Christ, the head of the church. There was a mixed multitude came up with the church of Israel out of Egypt; they joined themselves to the Israelites, owned their God, left their own country, and yet in heart were Egyptians notwithstanding. All are not Israel that are of Israel (Rom. 9:6). The church in all ages hath had unsound members: Cain had communion with Abel, Ishmael dwelt in the same house with Isaac, Judas was in fellowship with the apostles, and so was Demas with the rest of the disciples. There will be some bran in the finest meal; the drawnet of the gospel catches bad fish as well as good. The tares and the wheat grow together, and it will be so till the harvest.

✦ MATTHEW MEAD
Almost Christian Discovered, 72–73

What is the church for? There are two great ends why Christ did institute a particular church, and they were to express the two great graces and duties that He requires of us. The first end was that his saints together might jointly profess their faith in Him and obedience to Him. And we have no other way of doing it: He hath tied us up to this.... The next great end was that we might have a direct exercise of His other great command and of that other great duty, of love to believers.

✦ JOHN OWEN
"Exposition upon Psalm 130,"
in *Golden Book*, 109

To be a member of the true church is one thing, and to be a true member of the church is another thing.

✦ JOHN PENRY
Defence, 13

The church of Christ is a common hospital wherein all are in some measure sick of some spiritual disease or other, that we should all have ground of exercising mutually the spirit of wisdom and meekness.

✦ RICHARD SIBBES
Bruised Reed and Smoking Flax, 63

Certainly when we undervalue mercy, especially so great a one as the communion of saints is, commonly the Lord takes it away from us till we learn to prize it to the full value. Consider well therefore the heinousness of this sin, which that you may the better conceive. First, consider it is against God's express precept, charging us not to forsake the assemblies of the saints (Heb. 10:20, 25). Again, it is against our own greatest good and spiritual solace, for by discommunicating and excommunicating ourselves from that blessed society, we deprive ourselves of the benefit of their holy conference, their godly instructions, their divine consolations, brotherly admonitions, and charitable reprehensions, and what an inestimable loss is this? Neither can we partake such profit by their prayers as otherwise we might, for as the soul in the natural body conveys life and strength to every member, as they are compacted and joined together and not as dissevered, so Christ conveys spiritual life and vigor to Christians, not as they are disjoined from but as they are united to the mystical body, the church.

✦ RICHARD SIBBES
Memoir, in *Complete Works,* 1:cxv

If the church be a burning bush, it will not be consumed because God is in it.

✦ GEORGE SWINNOCK
"Pastor's Farewell," in *Works,* 4:87

So is it with the Christian [pilgrim]: his mind is not where his body is. And if he cannot get home in the body as soon as he desires, yet in his spirit he will mind heaven and heavenly things.

He will get as near home as he can. If he cannot get into the city, he will be sure to get into the suburbs, the church of God. If he cannot get suddenly into that Jerusalem which is above, he will get into the Jerusalem which is from above. And where his person cannot be for the time, his conversation and meditation shall be in heaven, for where his treasure is, there will his heart be also.

✦ THOMAS TAYLOR
Pilgrim's Profession, 66–67

CHURCH AND STATE

Repentance for every known sin, but repentance especially for sins in the matter of religion, the present epidemical disease of this land which threatens changes and armies of sorrows; so it pleases the Lord to give more than a taste of the bitter fruits of bad church government and a sad representation of the face of the kingdom if every man should be left to preach, profess, and print what he will. O that my people had harkened unto me and Israel had walked in my ways!

✦ ALEXANDER HENDERSON
preface to *Sermon Preached*

There be three things in England which give us hope and promise deliverance. First, your frequent and continued fasting and humiliation. Secondly, your entering into a solemn covenant with God for obtaining mercy. Thirdly, your begun reformation and the course you have taken for persecuting the same, "that whatsoever is commanded by the God of heaven may be diligently done for the house of the God of heaven." If these three be performed in truth, you may expect a blessing: true humiliation, covenanting with God, and reformation are the harbingers of peace and happiness. But when they are not in truth, the hypocrisy threatens more than the performance promises.

♦ ALEXANDER HENDERSON
Sermon Preached, 5

CHURCH DISCIPLINE

The accusations of none, not even the best in the church, should be taken without proof. A minister should never make himself a party before he has sufficient evidence of the case. It is better to let many vicious persons go unpunished and without censure when we want full evidence against them than to censure one unjustly, which we may easily do if we go upon bold presumptions alone. And that will bring upon a pastor the scandal of partiality and unrighteous dealing, which will make all his reproofs and censures become contemptible.

♦ RICHARD BAXTER
Reformed Pastor, 108–9

The neglect of discipline has a strong tendency to the deluding of souls by making men think that they are Christians when they are not because they are not separated from such as are, and by making scandalous sinners think their sin tolerable because it is so tolerated by the pastors of the church. We hereby corrupt Christianity itself in the eyes of the world and do our part to make them believe that to be a Christian is only to be of such or such an opinion, and that the Christian religion requires holiness no more than the false religions of the world.

♦ RICHARD BAXTER
Reformed Pastor, 124

Against all that I have said in behalf of discipline you will plead, "Our people are not ready for it; they will not yet bear it." But is not the meaning of this that you will not bear the trouble and hatred which it will occasion? I beseech you, in order that you may make a comfortable account to the Chief Shepherd and that you may not be found unfaithful in the house of God, that you do not shrink from duty because of the trouble that may attend it.

♦ RICHARD BAXTER
Reformed Pastor, 125

I think it is my duty to choose rather to join with those who refuse to admit into the Communion with them such as are openly vicious and profane than with those who, being under an unhappy obligation to administer the Lord's Supper to all in office and to transfer the trial of all suspensions to the bishop's court, cannot possibly use so strict a discipline. Not that I think I am ever the worse for bad people's joining with me in the Lord's Supper, but perhaps they are the worse for my joining with them; and I would not be accessory to the hardening of them in their impieties. I do not expect to meet with any society of Christians perfectly pure on this side heaven. There are spots, I know, in our feasts of charity; but I must prefer those who appear to me either to be more pure from the mixture of corrupt members, or at least more solicitous and desirous to be so and capable of being so by their own constitution.

✦ MATTHEW HENRY
"The Lay-Man's Reasons for His Joining in Stated Communion with a Congregation of Moderate Dissenters," in *Miscellaneous Writings*, 638

Of secret things the church judges not, but…scandalous acts, being faults against the church, cannot be remitted by the minister alone. The offense being public, so was the confession and acknowledgment to be public, as the apostle saith of the incestuous Corinthian that his punishment "was inflicted of many" (2 Cor. 2:6). And he bids Timothy, "Them that sin rebuke before all" (1 Tim. 5:20), which Aquinas refers to ecclesiastical discipline. Now this was to be done partly for the sinner's sake, that he might be brought to the more shame and conviction, and partly because of them without, that the community of the faithful might not be represented as an ulcerous, filthy body and the church not be thought a receptacle of sin, but a school of holiness; and therefore, as Paul shook off the viper, so these were to be cast out and not received again, but upon solemn acknowledgment.

✦ THOMAS MANTON
Practical Exposition on the Epistle of James, 207–8

No censures are to be excessive, much less church censures, whose end is chiefly medicinal, they being (as [Augustine] speaks of the corrections of God) *castigationes emendatoria, non interfectoria*—chastisements to procure amendment, not to work ruin.

✦ WILLIAM SPURSTOWE
Wiles of Satan, 2–3

CIVIL DISOBEDIENCE

When the commands of authority run cross to the commands of God, the commands of God must be obeyed, though the greatest authority under heaven should be displeased and enraged. God never gave the greatest authority in the world any authority to act contrary to His commands. Disobedience to unlawful commands is no disobedience.

✦ THOMAS BROOKS
Cabinet of Choice Jewels, 119–20

CIVIL WAR, ENGLISH

Thus many in our times stand still; they plead ignorance.… They will be of no side.… They know not what to do.… One saith one thing, and another saith another thing; the king commands one thing, and the parliament another.… To go against the king, is it not rebellion? And so they stand still because they plead ignorance and their consciences are not informed. It hath been the work of diverse ministers that have hazarded themselves in this to open to you the counsel of God and to set your consciences at liberty. Diverse things I have spoken in this place, but certainly men do blind their own eyes and are willing to stand still, to plead ignorance, after so much light revealed. It is strange that any rational man should speak of rebellion now, when we know that the king himself sent aid to the Rochellers [i.e., French Huguenots rebelling against the French crown] and that, we know, in the case of their liberties and religion; they took up arms to defend themselves against their own king, and he sent help to them. Surely he did not himself take them to be rebels.

✦ JEREMIAH BURROUGHS
"Saint's Duty in Time of Extremity,"
in *Rare Jewel*, 87

We desire nothing but the maintenance of our liberty and of our religion.

✦ JEREMIAH BURROUGHS
"Saint's Duty in Time of Extremity,"
in *Rare Jewel*, 87

Suppose blood should be shed. Beloved, God hath such mercy for England that shall pay for all the blood of His saints that shall be shed.... Every drop of the blood of His people is very precious, and the adversaries shall be accountable for every drop. God will value it, and there shall be a valuable consideration given for every drop of blood; and the more difficulties we have in obtaining that mercy God is about to give us, the mercy shall be the greater: "O thou afflicted, tossed with tempest... I will lay thy stones with fair colours, and lay thy foundations with sapphires" (Isa. 54:11).

✦ JEREMIAH BURROUGHS
"Saint's Duty in Time of Extremity,"
in *Rare Jewel*, 95–96

At the beginning of the Civil War, when many persons, being affrighted because of the soldiers, came to [John Dod], he encouraged them by observing that if a house were full of rods, the child need not fear, none of them being able to move without his father's hand. And, he added, the Lord is a loving Father—estate and life and all are at His disposal.

✦ JOHN DOD AND PHILIP HENRY
Gleanings of Heavenly Wisdom, 29

CLASS DISTINCTIONS

In the entertaining of any such [gentlemen], be not put out of yourself; speak freely, and always remember that they are but men. And for being gentlemen, it puts no distance between you, for you have part in nobleness of birth. Though some have place before you, yet you may be in their company. And this I say to you, not to make you proud or conceited of yourself, but that you should know yourself and so not to be put out of yourself when you are in better company than ordinary. For I have seen many, when they come into good company, lose themselves. Surely they have too high esteem of man, for they can go boldly to God and lose themselves before men. Remember, therefore, when you are with them that you are but with those who are such as yourself, though some wiser and more honorable.

✦ BRILLIANA HARLEY
to her son Edward, January 19, 1638,
in *Letters*, 21–22

God is no accepter of persons. All men naturally pity the poor, whether their cause be right or wrong, and condemn the rich ere their cause be discussed. God doth not so. His commiseration is not so great as to save all the poor nor His austerity so great as to condemn all the rich. Though He be a friend to the poor, yet is He not an enemy to the rich. Though the poor more commonly find His ear open, yet is He not hard to be entreated by the rich and wealthy.

✦ FRANCIS TAYLOR
God's Glory in Man's Happiness, 91–92

CLOTHING

The [Rabbi's] rule is, Clothe thy wife above thy estate, thy children according to thy estate, and thyself beneath thy estate.

✦ SAMUEL CLARK
Saint's Nosegay, 158

Clothes are for necessity: warm clothes for health, cleanly for decency, lasting for thrift, and rich for magnificence. Now there may be a fault in their number, if too various; making, if too vain; matter, if too costly; and mind of the wearer, if he takes pride therein.... He that is proud of the rustling of his silks, like a madman, laughs at the rattling of his fetters. For, indeed, clothes ought to be our remembrancers of our lost innocency. Besides, why should any brag of what's but borrowed?

✦ THOMAS FULLER
Holy and Profane States, 197–99

COMFORT

Be it remembered that the first and chief ground of our comfort is that Christ as a priest offered himself as a sacrifice to His Father for us. The guilty soul flies first to Christ crucified, made a curse for us. Thence it is that Christ has a right to govern us; thence it is that He gives us His Spirit as our guide to lead us home.

✦ RICHARD SIBBES
Bruised Reed and Smoking Flax, 135

Question: How may they be comforted who bewail their want of growth and weep that they cannot find the kingdom of grace increase?

Answer 1: To see and bewail our decay in grace argues not only the life of grace but growth. 'Tis a sign a man recovers and gets strength when he feels his weakness; it is a step forward in grace to see our imperfections....

Answer 2: If a Christian does not increase in one grace he may in another. If not in knowledge, he may in humility. If a tree doth not grow so much in the branches, it may in the root; to grow downward in the root is a good growth.

Answer 3: A Christian may grow less in affection when he grows more in judgment. As a musician when he is old, his fingers are stiff and not so nimble at the lute as they were, but he plays with more art and judgment than before; so a Christian may not have so much affection in duty as at the first conversion, but he is more solid in religion and more settled in his judgment than he was before.

♦ THOMAS WATSON
Body of Practical Divinity, 434

COMMUNION
(See *THE LORD'S SUPPER*)

COMMUNION WITH GOD

It is a great mistake among many tender Christians to think that they have no communion with God but when they find God raising the springs of joy and comfort in their souls; when they find the sensible presence of God cheering, refreshing, and enlarging of them in their closets. Then they are willing to grant that they have had sweet communion with God in their closets, but if He breaks their hearts for sin, if He meets with them and makes His power and His presence manifest in debasing and casting down their souls upon the sight and sense of their strong corruptions and imperfections, how unwilling are they to believe that they have had any communication with God? Well, friends, remember this once for all, that a Christian may have as real communion with God in a heart-humbling way as he can have in a heart-comforting way; a Christian may have as choice communion with God when his eyes are full of tears as he can have when his heart is full of joy.

♦ THOMAS BROOKS
Privy Key of Heaven, 184

The more any man improves his grace, the clearer, sweeter, fuller, and richer is his enjoyment of God here. There is no man in all the world who has such enjoyment of God as that man has who most improves his graces. It is not he that knows most, nor he that hears most, nor yet he that talks most but he that exercises grace most that has most communion with God, that has the clearest visions of God, that has the sweetest discoveries and manifestations of God.

♦ THOMAS BROOKS
The Unsearchable Riches of Christ,
in *Select Works*, 1:186

Make God your choice and not your necessity, and labor to maintain such constant converse with Him that when you die, you may change your place only but not your company.

♦ THOMAS CASE
Correction, Instruction, 117

Christ and the soul may be at supper within and thou not so much as see one dish go in or hear the music that sounds so sweetly in the Christian's ears. Perhaps thou thinkest he wants peace because he doth not hang out a sign in his countenance of the joy and peace he hath within. Alas, poor wretch! May not the saint have a peaceful conscience, with a solemn—yea, sad—countenance, as well as thou and thy companions have a sorrowful heart when there is nothing but fair weather in your faces?

♦ WILLIAM GURNALL
Christian in Complete Armour, 380

If therefore we would maintain our acquaintance with God, we must often and daily visit Him; frequent His house and ordinances; be frequent in reading, hearing, praying; converse with Him by holy meditations and soliloquies; invite Him home to us; importune Him to visit our hearts with His Spirit. As we do by our other friends—we often visit them and invite them to visit us, assuring them that our house and anything that we have is at their service—thus must we deal with God, and this is the way to maintain communion and acquaintance with Him.

✦ MATTHEW NEWCOMEN
Best Acquaintance, 92–93

As we cannot live a moment out of God, so neither ought we to live a moment without God in the world. We ought continually to endeavor to walk in subservience to and converse with God; yea, and as far as may be, in a feeling converse with Him too.

✦ SAMUEL SHAW
Voice of One Crying in the Wilderness, 30

I saw my blessedness did not chiefly lie in receiving good and comfort from God and in God, but in holding forth the glory of God and His virtues. For 'tis, I saw, an amazing, glorious object to see God in a creature—God speaking and acting. The deity not being the creature, yet turned into it, filling of it, and shining through it; to be covered with God as with a cloud or as a glass lantern, to have His beams penetrate through it. Nothing is good but God, and I am no further good than as I hold forth God.... Hereupon I found my heart more sweetly drawn to close with God thus as my end and to place my happiness in it, and also I saw it was my misery to hold forth sin and Satan and self in my course; and I saw one of those two things I must do. Now because my soul wanted pleasure, I purposed thus to hold forth God and did hope it should be my pleasure so to do, as it would be my pain to do otherwise.

✦ THOMAS SHEPARD
Meditations and Spiritual Experiences, 84

Take a man that makes riches his treasure, and he enlarges his desires as hell and is not satisfied; and a man that desires pleasures cries always as the horse-leech's daughter, "Give, give" [Prov. 30:15]. Let him glut himself today and he is hungry tomorrow. Why? Because it is his chief good. So take a man whose chief good is laid up in God: though he has glorious incomes from God, he is still calling for more and more—more grace from Him, more communion with Him, more consolation from the Spirit of God. Why? It is his chief good. The Spirit says "come, and the bride says come."

✦ WILLIAM STRONG
Heavenly Treasure, 30–31

That which is the aim of a man's heart, that he makes use of all things to obtain, makes all things else in the world serviceable and subordinate thereunto. If the bent of the heart be set on God, he cares for riches no further than that he may honor God with his substance (Prov. 3:9). He looks on ordinances, but ordinances no further than in them he may enjoy communion with God—nay, the Lord Jesus Christ Himself as mediator. No other way desires him, then, as he may come to God by Him, "for we come unto God by Christ." Therefore, he makes use of everything to bring him to that where the bent of his soul is.

✦ WILLIAM STRONG
Heavenly Treasure, 298–99

COMPLAINING

Those that are of a fretful spirit will always find something to quarrel with. When we complain without cause, it is just with God to give us cause to complain.

✦ MATTHEW HENRY
Gems, 28

Holy complaint may agree with patient submission to God's will; but though we may complain to God, we must not complain of God.

✦ THOMAS WATSON
Lord's Prayer, 166

CONFERENCE

Whatever incomes you receive from God into your own souls be free in dispersing to others. I mean in a way of holy discourse and conference. Dispersing and communicating is the best way to thriving. "There is that scattereth, and yet increaseth; and there is

that withholdeth…but it tendeth to poverty" (Prov. 11:24). 'Tis true with respect to spirituals as well as to temporals. There are none that grow more rich toward God than those, who by bringing forth what they have received, labor to make others rich also. Give the holy fire within you a vent, and it will burn the clearer. Keep not your religion to yourselves; let your full cup run over, let your lips drop as the honeycomb, let your mouth be a well of life, and your lips feed many (Prov. 10:11). Build up one another in the most holy faith; provoke one another to love and to good works.

✦ RICHARD ALLEINE
Companion for Prayer, 5

What are we in our societies! To how little profit do we meet! How little heat do we get; yea, how much do we lose at our brethren's fires. We serve often but to damp and cool each other's spirits, as if it might be no longer said, "Woe to him that is alone," but "Woe be to him that is in company; alone he is more warm."

✦ RICHARD ALLEINE
Heaven Opened, 222–23

Many are the advantages attending this lovely conduct [i.e., conference]: the various devices of Satan to entangle and perplex the minds of believers are exposed; the influence of earthly things on the mind is confessed and mutually lamented before the Lord; the frequent deliverances the saints experience in times of trouble are recorded to the manifest honor of their great Deliverer;

the faithfulness of a covenant God in answering prayer and honoring them that honor Him is abundantly testified; the power of the cross of Christ to crucify sin in the heart is declared; the usefulness and suitableness of the preached word is acknowledged; love is increased; faith is strengthened; hope is enlarged; and a foretaste of heaven itself is often experienced on earth. Even when the people come together with their hearts comparatively cold, reciprocal and free communication is often like the striking together of a cold flint and cold steel, and there comes out fire, as saith the wise man, "Iron sharpeneth iron; so a man sharpeneth the countenance of his friend" (Prov. 27:17).

✦ SIMEON ASHE
Primitive Divinity, 211

Confer [the shepherds in Luke 2] did, and the substance of their conference was an exhortation: "Let us go." We may here make them again our example. Let us confer, for there is no time lost by such conference. Such conference in itself is a part of the journey.

✦ WILLIAM AUSTIN
Certain Devout, Godly, and Learned Meditations, 35

But those who conscientiously employ [the Lord's Day] in duties proper to it—in prayer and hearing and reading the Scriptures and spiritual books; in holy conference, whereby light and heat is mutually communicated among the saints; and in the meditation of eternal things, whereby faith removes

the veil and looks into the sanctuary of life and glory. As Moses by conversing with God in the mount came down with a shining countenance, so a divine luster will appear in their conversations in the following week.

✦ WILLIAM BATES
Spiritual Perfection Unfolded and Enforced, in *Whole Works*, 2:508

Let your holy conference with others be much about the glorious excellencies, works, and mercies of the Lord in way of praise and admiration. This is indeed to speak to edification and as the "oracles of God."

✦ RICHARD BAXTER
A Christian Directory, in *Practical Works*, 2:446

Your fruitful conference is a needful help to the ministerial work. When the preacher hath publicly delivered the word of God to the assembly, if you would so far second him as in your daily converse to set it home on the hearts of those that you have opportunity to discourse with, how great an assistance would it be to his success! Though he must teach them publicly and from house to house (Acts 20:20), yet is it not possible for him to be so frequent and familiar in daily conference with all the ignorant of the place as those that are still with them may be. You are many, and he is but one and can be but in one place at once. Your business bringeth you into their company when he cannot be there. O happy is that minister who hath such a people who will daily preach over the matter of his sermons in their private conference with one another.

✦ RICHARD BAXTER
A Christian Directory, in
Practical Works, 6:250

In some respects, private instruction has the preference to preaching. What other argument need we than our own experience? I seldom deal with men on this great business in private serious conference, but they go away with some seeming convictions and promises of new obedience and sometimes with a deep remorse and affecting sense of their condition. Yea, I have found (and I doubt not but you have experienced the same) that an ignorant sot, who for a long time had been an unprofitable hearer, has got more knowledge and remorse of conscience in half an hour's close conversation than he did by ten years' public preaching.

✦ RICHARD BAXTER
Reformed Pastor, 90–91

Let thy eternal rest be the subject of thy frequent serious discourse, especially with those that can speak from their hearts and are seasoned themselves with a heavenly nature. It is pity Christians should ever meet together without some talk of their meeting in heaven, or of the way to it, before they part. It is pity so much time is spent in vain conversation and useless disputes, and not a serious word of heaven among them. Methinks we should meet together on purpose to warm our spirits with discoursing of our rest. To hear a Christian set forth that blessed,

glorious state with life and power from the promises of the gospel methinks should make us say, "Did not our hearts burn within us, while he opened to us the Scriptures?"

✦ RICHARD BAXTER
Saint's Everlasting Rest, 216

Wicked men can be delighted in talking together of their wickedness, and should not Christians then be delighted in talking of Christ? And the heirs of heaven in talking of their inheritance? This may make our hearts revive, as it did Jacob's to hear the message that called him to Goshen and to see the chariots that should bring him to Joseph. O that we were furnished with skill and resolution to turn the stream of men's common discourse to these more sublime and precious things!

✦ RICHARD BAXTER
Saint's Everlasting Rest, 216

[The hypocrite's] conference will be cold and careless and for the most part about unnecessary and curious arguments, as whether we shall know one another in heaven or not; whether hell be in the air, in the earth, or where it is...all tending to controversy and mere vanity.

✦ PAUL BAYNES
Commentary upon...Ephesians, 138

We may well perceive what great reason there is that we should account this to be one of those private exercises whereby we should sanctify the Sabbath and keep it holy as we are commanded; unto which we must adjoin as another part of God's service and a most excellent help of our infirmities the conferring and talking with others of that which we have in the Word read or heard, especially seeing both it is commended unto us in the Scripture and also by experience we shall find the profit of it to be so great to ourselves and others.

✦ NICHOLAS BOWND
Doctrine of the Sabbath, 210–11

The Jews have a proverb that two dry sticks put to a green one would kindle it. The best way to be in a flame Godward, Christward, heavenward, and holinessward is to be among the dry sticks, the kindled coals, the saints; for as live coals kindle those that are dead, so lively Christians will heat and enliven those that are dead Godward, Christward, heavenward, and holinessward. "As iron sharpens iron, so doth the face of man his friend." Men's wits, talents, and gifts and industry commonly grow more strong, vigorous, and quick by friendly conference and communion.

✦ THOMAS BROOKS
Apples of Gold, 208–9

I came where there were three or four poor women sitting at a door in the sun talking about the things of God.... Their talk was about a new birth, the work of God in their hearts, as also how they were convinced of their miserable state by nature. They talked how God had visited their souls with His love in the Lord Jesus and with what words and promises they have been refreshed, comforted, and supported

against the temptations of the devil. Moreover, they reasoned of the suggestions and temptations of Satan in particular and told to each other by what means they had been afflicted and how they were borne up under his assaults. They also discoursed of their own wretchedness of heart and of their unbelief and did contemn, slight, and abhor their own righteousness as filthy and insufficient to do them any good. And methought they spake with such pleasantness of Scripture language and with such appearance of grace in all they said that they were to me as if they had found a new world.

✦ JOHN BUNYAN
Grace Abounding, 21–22

Although the Lord hath a special blessing to the public ministry of His word, yet we must not tie His wisdom to the ordinary means either of begetting or increasing our faith. But if any shall at any time have more effectual feelings by private conference, let him neither contemn nor neglect the public ministry, but with all holy and humble thankfulness yield this sovereignty to the Lord, that He is to dispose His gifts when, to whom, by whom, and where it pleases Him.

✦ EZEKIEL CULVERWELL
Time Well Spent, 225–26

We must use the help of holy conferences—instructing, exhorting, admonishing, counseling, and comforting one another—that we may be further edified in our holy faith. For as sticks scattered asunder will hardly keep fire but if they be laid together will quickly grow to a great flame, so if we single ourselves from one another and admit no communion by religious conferences, we shall quickly cool and quench the fire of the Spirit. But if we meet together and exercise ourselves in holy conferences, we shall hereby stir up God's graces in us. We shall, like unto knives whetted one upon another, sharpen our gifts and set an edge on our desires to the performance of all good duties. We shall pile up our graces one on another, and with these bellows of conference blow upon them until they grow to a great flame.

♦ JOHN DOWNAME
Christian Warfare, 1165

Converse with the saints that have the Spirit of God in them. They that would learn a foreign language associate with men of the country whose natural tongue it is. Wouldst thou have God and learn to speak heaven's language? Associate with those who by reason of their heavenly nature will be speaking of the things of God. It is true, they cannot propagate their spiritual nature; but it is as true that the Spirit of God may make the gracious discourses which they breathe forth the means of quickening thee. While thou art with such, thou walkest in the Spirit's company.

♦ WILLIAM GURNALL
Christian in Complete Armour, 761

Thou mayest be accessory to the quenching of the Spirit in others because thou hinderest the exercise of those graces in them which would have been drawn forth in prayer for

thee hadst thou acquainted them with thy condition. By opening thy wants or desires to thy brethren, thou feedest the spirit of prayer in them, as they have new matter administered to work upon. By acquainting them with the merciful providences of God to thee, thou prickest a song of praise for them. How many groans and sighs should God in prayer have had from thy neighboring saints hadst thou not hid thy temptations and afflictions from their knowledge! What peals of joy and thankfulness would they have rung hadst thou not concealed thy mercies from them!

♦ WILLIAM GURNALL
Christian in Complete Armour, 789

[Believers] may meet together to confer one with another (Luke 24:14).

♦ THOMAS HALL
Pulpit Guarded, 2

Omit not private duties and stir up yourself to exercise yourself in holy conference; beg of God to give you a delight in speaking and thinking of those things which are your eternal treasure. I many times think godly conference is as much neglected by God's children as any duty. I am confident you will [in] no ways neglect the opportunity of profiting in the ways of learning, and I pray God prosper your endeavors.

♦ BRILLIANA HARLEY
to her son Edward,
October 18, 1639, *Letters*, 65

God hath given diverse gifts: as in the ministry, some have a more excellent gift of conference, some of prayer, some of exhortation, some in opening of a text...and all for the good of the church.

✦ ELNATHAN PARR
An Exposition upon the Epistle to the Romans, in Workes, 206

This meeting together of the members of the body of Christ and their mutual conference brings with it an exceeding great consolation and joy, for the Lord hath promised to send that Comforter, the Holy Spirit, to these meetings of the saints. And Christ says in Matthew 18:20, "Where two or three are gathered together in my name, there will I be in the midst of them." If thou despisest these holy meetings and disdainest thou the holy conference, I denounce to thee in the name of Christ, thou shalt never find a solid joy or consolation. Many there are who contemn the meetings of the faithful and the assemblies of the saints and disdain the means of grace, godly speeches and conferences, and yet will dream to themselves that the Holy Spirit will dwell in their souls and that they will find joy and consolation. But the end will prove that their corrupt and false hearts have deceived them.

✦ ROBERT ROLLOCK
"Of the Resurrection of Christ,"
in *Select Works*, 2:484

Religious company brings fire to our graces to kindle them when they are freezing, but irreligious company brings water to quench them when they are flaming.

✦ WILLIAM SECKER
Nonsuch Professor, 54

Let the word preached or read be as a voice from heaven talking with you. Let your conference be a comment upon that word. Let meditation be as a kind of bringing down God into your souls, and prayer as a raising up of your souls unto God, nothing but faith and love put into praises.

✦ SAMUEL SHAW
Voice of One Crying in the Wilderness, 169

If men can find no comfort and yet set themselves to teach and encourage weaker Christians, by way of reflection they receive frequently great comfort themselves. So doth God reward this duty of mutual discourse; that those things we did not so fully understand before by discourse we come to know and relish far better. This should teach us to love and often engage in holy conference, for besides the good we do to others, we shall be profited ourselves.

✦ RICHARD SIBBES
Divine Meditations and Holy Contemplations, 77

None in sincerity frequently promote holy conference but are great gainers thereby. Many ask questions and are inquisitive to know, but not that they might practice. This is a proud desire to taste of the tree of knowledge. But the desire of Christians is to know more that they might more diligently seek Christ and obey His voice.

✦ RICHARD SIBBES
Divine Meditations and Holy Contemplations, 132–33

By good company, pious souls have been confirmed. Whilst Latimer and Ridley lived, they kept up Cranmer by intercourse of letters. Christian conference is a great help to perseverance. The staff of bonds was the Jews' beauty and safety (Zech. 11:14). Company causeth courage; the beams of joy are the hotter for reflection.... The very countenance of a good man makes us cheerful; our sight of him is reviving to us.

✦ GEORGE SWINNOCK
The Christian Man's Calling,
in *Works*, 2:337

"As iron sharpens iron." Rub one file against another, and though before they were dull and blunt, they both become thereby bright and sharp. So, friends that are heavy and backward and overrun with rust for want of use, by mutual conference and communion they become lively, quick, and keen about spiritual things. Christian society, like rubbing iron against iron, takes away that rust which made them so dull and inactive and sets a spiritual edge upon them.

✦ GEORGE SWINNOCK
The Christian Man's Calling,
in *Works*, 2:339

It was the practice of the monks to meet together once in a week and to acquaint each other with their temptations, the means of resistance, and the issue thereof. I believe if Christians were more open-hearted in declaring to one another the state of their souls, their experiences in point of loss or gain in spirituals, and sense of God's favor or anger...it would much tend not only to the honor of God but also to the defeating of our great enemy and our own mutual advantage.

✦ GEORGE SWINNOCK
The Christian Man's Calling,
in *Works*, 2:349

[Nathanael Vincent] has been noted for this: that he was very ready upon all occasions to start some holy and serious discourse, a thing that is grown almost out of fashion among the professors of this age. When we meet together, we talk of news, of worldly affairs; it may be of the sins and miscarriages of our brethren. We can spend whole hours together and hardly drop one word of God or Christ or heaven all the while. But hardly any company could he come into, but he was like an open box of precious ointment. He would leave some sweet perfume, some heavenly discourse behind him.

✦ NATHANIEL TAYLOR
Funeral Sermon [on Luke 12:40], 26

Great is the benefit of conference and private admonition.

✦ JOHN TRAPP
Commentary on the Old and New Testaments, 1:502

Holy conference and good discourse is like the best wine that moves aright — and that is directly up to Christ, which as it awakens others and with God's blessing may be a well and tree of life to them. So, as speech in nature, it's a sign and evidence of life in us; and that that life is Christ, which is thus busily and constantly employed in speaking of Christ to His praise and our own and others' benefit.

✦ ANTHONY TUCKNEY
Sermon 40, in *Forty Sermons*, 664

Holy conference is very edifying. The apostle bids us edify one another (Eph. 4:29). And how more than this way? Good conference enlightens the mind when it is ignorant; settles it when it is wavering. A good life adorns religion; good discourse propagates it.

✦ THOMAS WATSON
Christian Soldier, or, Heaven Taken by Storm, 70

You that are the people of God, do you often associate together: "Those who feared the LORD spoke to one another" (Mal. 3:16). Christ's doves should flock together; one Christian will help to heat another. A single coal of juniper will soon die, but many coals put together will keep life in one another. Conference sometimes may do as much good as preaching. One Christian by good discourse drops holy oil upon another; that makes the lamp of his grace to shine the brighter.

✦ THOMAS WATSON
Godly Man's Picture, 239

Put this great duty [i.e., conference] into practice. Imitate these holy ones in [Malachi 3:16]: they "spake often to one another." Jerome thinks they spoke something in defense of the providence of God; they vindicated God in His dealings and exhorted one another not to be discouraged at the virulent speeches of the wicked, but still to hold on a course of piety. Thus, Christians, when you meet, give one another's souls a visit, drop your knowledge, impart your experiences to each other (Ps. 66:16). Samson having found honey did not only eat of it himself but carried it to his father and mother (Judg. 14:9). Have you tasted the honey of the Word? Let others have a taste with you.

✦ THOMAS WATSON
Great Gain of Godliness, 68

When you meet, speak one to another of the promises. The promises are the support of the faith, the springs of joy, the saints' royal charter. Are you citizens of heaven and yet do not speak of your charter? Speak of the preciousness of Christ: He is beauty and love; He has laid down His blood as the price of your redemption. Have you a friend who has redeemed you and never speak of Him? Speak one to another of sin, what a deadly evil it is, how it has infected your virgin nature and turned it into a lesser hell. Speak of the beauty of holiness, which is the soul's embroidery, filling it with such an oriental splendor as makes God and the angels fall in love with it. The graces are the sacred "characters and impressions of the divine nature" [John of Damascus]. Speak one to another of your souls; inquire whether they are in health. Speak about death and eternity: Can you belong to heaven and not speak of your country? Speak to one another of the times, wherein God is the great sufferer; let your hearts bleed for His dishonors. Thus, you see, here is matter enough for holy conference.

✦ THOMAS WATSON
Great Gain of Godliness, 69–70

CONFESSION

As true, penitential confession is full, so it is sincere; it is cordial; it is not a feigned nor a formal nor a mere verbal confession, but an affectionate confession; it is a confession that has the mind, the heart, the soul, as well as the lip in it. The penitent man's confession springs from inward impressions of grace upon his soul; he feels what he confesses, and his affections go along with his confessions. The poor publican smote upon his breast and confessed (Job 42:6; Ezra 9:6; Pss. 38:4; 51:11; Isa. 26:8–9; Jer. 18:19–20; Luke 18:13). Look as the sick man opens his disease to the physician feelingly, affectionately, and as the client opens his case to his lawyer feelingly, affectionately; so the penitent opens his case, his heart, to God, feelingly, affectionately. Cold, careless, verbal, formal, customary confessions are no small abominations in the eye of God (Jer. 12:2). Such men's confessions will be their condemnations at last; their tongues will one day accuse and

denounce themselves. Though confession to men is a work of the voice, yet confession to God must be the voice of the heart.

✦ THOMAS BROOKS
Cabinet of Choice Jewels, 236

He that does not forsake his sin as well as confess it forsakes the benefit of his confession. And indeed, there is no real confession of sin where there is no real forsaking of sin; it is not enough for us to confess the sins we have committed, but we must peremptorily resolve against committing again the sins we have confessed; we must desire as freely to forego our sins as we do desire God to forgive us our sins. Confession of sin is a spiritual vomit; now you know a man that is burdened in his stomach is heartily willing to be rid of that load on his stomach that doth oppress nature. And so a man that is real in his confession of sin is as heartily willing to be rid of his sin that lies as a load upon his conscience as any sick man can be heartily willing to be rid of that load that lies upon his stomach.

✦ THOMAS BROOKS
Cabinet of Choice Jewels, 248–49

Now this...acknowledging [i.e., confession] must have sundry properties: 1. It must proceed from the hatred of sin. Take heed of confessing sins in jesting or boasting; it is as in a vomit casting out things enemies to the stomach. 2. With faith in the promises of mercy in Christ, otherwise despair will assault. 3. From a settled judgment...that [we] ourselves are sinners. 4. According to the things we are rebuked of by the word, as it was with David toward Nathan, not taking exception against his charge. 5. Frankly, not by compulsion but of our own accord. 6. Without excuse or lessening our fault, nay rather with exaggerating. 7. Without delay.

✦ GEORGE ESTEY
Certain Godly and Learned Expositions, 12

Confession is an act of mortification; it is, as it were, the vomit of the soul. It breeds a dislike of the sweetest morsels when they are cast up in loathsome ejections. Sin is sweet in commission, but bitter in the remembrance. God's children find that their hatred is never more keen and exasperated against sin than in confessing.

✦ THOMAS MANTON
Practical Exposition on the Epistle of James, 206

Because sin has put out our eyes, we vainly imagine that it hath put out God's. Because we behold not what He does in heaven for us, we think that He sees not what we do on earth against Him. Men care not what they do when they believe that God sees not what is done. They slay the widow and the stranger and murder the fatherless. They say, "The Lord shall not see, neither shall the God of Jacob regard it." The adulterer waits for the twilight." His sin gets up when the sun goes down. The time of darkness pays most tribute to the prince of darkness. There are many that blush to confess their faults who never blush to commit them.

✦ WILLIAM SECKER
Nonsuch Professor, 141–42

No man was ever kept out of God's kingdom for his confessed badness; many are for their supposed goodness.

✦ JOHN TRAPP
Commentary...upon...the New Testament, 945

CONFLICT

Alluding to the controversies of those times, [Philip Henry] said, "It is not so much our difference of opinion that doth us the mischief as the mismanagement of that difference."

✦ PHILIP HENRY
Life and Sayings, 7

CONSCIENCE

If conscience, which is the eye of the soul, be covered with a film of ignorance; if it be bleared with the false glitterings of the world; if it totally neglects its office or makes but a cold application of saving terrors that may control the licentious appetites; if it be disregarded when it suggests and excites to our duty, the sinner is hardened and settled in his lost state. Now prosperity foments the sensual affections that obscure the light of conscience, that corrupt its judgment, that smother and suppress its dictates, or despise and slight them that 'tis powerless, though constituted God's deputy to order our lives.

✦ WILLIAM BATES
Danger of Prosperity, 68–69

A dead conscience and a dissolute life are inseparable. And how many that are surrounded with the celestial beams of the gospel are as impure and impenitent as those in the black night of paganism? They stand at the entrance of the bottomless pit yet do not smell the brimstone that enrages the fire there. The flames of their lusts have seared their consciences to a desperate degree of hardness and insensibility.

✦ WILLIAM BATES
Danger of Prosperity, 75

The books of God's omniscience and man's conscience shall then be opened, and then secret sins shall be as legible in the forehead as if they were written with the most glittering sunbeams upon a wall of crystal. All men's secret sins are printed in heaven, and God will at last read them aloud in the ears of all the world (1 Cor. 4:5).

✦ THOMAS BROOKS
Privy Key of Heaven, 215–16

There is yet another witness for the condemning transgressors of these laws, and that is conscience: "Their consciences also bearing witness," says the apostle. Conscience is a thousand witnesses. Conscience! It will cry amen to every word that the great God doth speak against thee. Conscience is a terrible accuser; it will hold pace with the witness of God as to the truth of evidence to a hair's breadth. The witness of conscience, it is of great authority; it commands guilt and fastens it on every soul which it accuses.

✦ JOHN BUNYAN
Riches, 63

The first step to the cure of a wounded conscience is for thee to know the grace of God, especially the grace of God as to justification.

✦ JOHN BUNYAN
Riches, 88–89

Erroneous times may unsettle truth, but the conscience of a good man is firm.

✦ EDMUND CALAMY
Saints' Memorials, 30

I cannot but from hence first observe the mighty power of conscience awakened to the fear of sinning against God. Men of no conscience may make a jeer of it; none knows the power of it but he that feels it. It turns a prison into a delectable garden, a scorching flame into a bed of roses. And no wonder that it doth so, for what is it but God's vice-regent in the little world of man? God's interpreter to every soul.

✦ JOHN COLLINGES
Weaver's Pocket-book, 140

Consider God's goodness and good will toward men.... He has given you preachers, both inward and outward. By outward preachers, I mean the ministers of Christ, who beseech you and entreat you, for Christ's sake, to be reconciled to God and make your peace with Him. By inward preachers, I mean your own conscience that judges you and checks you and reproves you for your sins and abominations.

✦ WILLIAM DYER
Christ's Famous Titles, 92

We see God coming down in flesh and so intimately uniting our flesh to Himself that it hath no proper subsistence of its own, but is united with the divine person. Hence it is easy to imagine what worth and value must be in that blood and how eternal love, springing forth triumphantly from it, flourishes into pardon, grace, and peace. Here is a way in which the sinner may see justice and mercy kissing each other, and the latter exercised freely without prejudice to the former. All other consciences through the world lie either in a deep sleep in the devil's arms or else are rolling, seasick, upon the waves of their own fears and dismal presages. Oh, happy are they that have dropped anchor on this ground and not only know they have peace but why they have it.

✦ JOHN FLAVEL
Fountain of Life, 39–40

We are but stewards, and stewards must give an account in order whereto there must be a great audit day. And what need we seek evidence of this truth further than our own conscience? Lo, it is a truth engraven legibly upon every man's own breast. Every one hath a kind of little tribunal in his own conscience which both accuses and excuses for good and evil, which it could never do were there not a future judgment, of which it is now conscious to itself. In this court, records are now kept of all we do, even of our secret actions and thoughts, which never yet took air. But if no judgment, what need of records? Nor let any imagine that this may be but the fruit of education and discourse—that we have heard of such things and so are scared by them. For if so, how comes it to obtain so universally? Who could be the author of such a common deception?

✦ JOHN FLAVEL
Fountain of Life, 428–29

Conscience is the seat of guilt. It is like a burning glass, so it contracts the beams of the threatenings, twists them together, and reflects them on the soul until it smoke, scorch, and flame.

✦ JOHN FLAVEL
Navigation Spiritualized, 91

This one comfort of a quiet mind doth wonderfully cure and comfortably assuage all other griefs whatsoever. For if our assistance were as an host of armed soldiers; if our friends were the princes and the governors of the earth; if our possessions were as large as between the east and the west; if our meat were as manna from heaven; if our apparel were as costly as the ephod of Aaron; if every day were as glorious as the day of Christ's resurrection; yet if our minds be appalled with the judgments of God, these things would little comfort us.

✦ RICHARD GREENHAM
Paramuthion, 9

You must know conscience is a faculty that is corrupted as much as any other by nature and is very often made use of by Satan to deceive both good and bad, godly and ungodly. Many that know their consciences, they say, speak peace to them will be found merely cheated and gulled when the books shall be opened; no such discharge will then be found entered in the book of the word as conscience hath put into their hand. And many gracious souls who passed their days in a continual fear of their spiritual state and were kept chained in the dark dungeon of a troublesome conscience shall then be acquitted and have their action against Satan for false imprisonment and accusing their consciences to the disturbing their peace.

✦ WILLIAM GURNALL
Christian in Complete Armour, 253

Conscience demands as much to satisfy it as God Himself does to satisfy Him for the wrong the creature has done Him. Nothing can take off conscience from accusing but that which takes off God from threatening. Conscience is God's sergeant, which He employs to arrest the sinner.

✦ WILLIAM GURNALL
Christian in Complete Armour, 375

He that hath a blind conscience which sees nothing, a dead conscience that feels nothing, and a dumb conscience that says nothing is in as miserable condition as a man can be in on this side hell.

✦ PHILIP HENRY
Life and Sayings, 10

The voice of conscience, rightly informed by the Scripture, is the voice of God Himself. It is God speaking in a man and whispering to a man's very heart. As Moses was the interpreter betwixt God and the Israelites, so conscience is the interpreter betwixt God and us.

✦ EZEKIEL HOPKINS
"The Nature of Presumptuous Sins,"
in *Select Works*, 380

Blotting out implies that our transgressions are written down. And written they are in a twofold book: The one is in the book of God's remembrance, which He blots out when He justifies a sinner. The other is the book of our own consciences, which He blots out when He gives us peace and assurance. And oftentimes these follow one upon the other. When God blots His remembrance book in heaven, that blot diffuses and spreads itself even to the book of conscience and blots out all that is written there also.

✦ EZEKIEL HOPKINS
"Of Pardon and Forgiveness of Sin,"
in *Select Works*, 494

[The conscience] discovers to us what is sin and what is duty and the reward that is entailed upon both. And thus it gives in its verdict according to that light that shines into it. If it hath only the twilight of nature to illustrate it, as the heathens had no other, then it can pass judgment only upon natural duties and unnatural sins. Thus, the consciences of heathens, through some remainders of original knowledge, informed them that worship was due to God and justice to men and that all impieties against God and all injuries against men should, in the end, be severely punished. But if conscience enjoys the superadded light of Scripture, it judges then of those duties and those sins that could only be known by divine revelation. Hence it is that conscience is enabled to form such a proposition as this: "He that believeth shall be saved. He that believeth not shall be damned." This proposition it forms not from natural light, but from the superinduced light of Scripture.

✦ EZEKIEL HOPKINS
"Of the Nature, Corruption, and Renewing of the Conscience," in *Select Works*, 276

This is conscience: that faithful register in every man's bosom that writes down the actions, discourses, and cogitations of every hour and minute.

✦ EZEKIEL HOPKINS
"Of the Nature, Corruption, and Renewing of the Conscience," in *Select Works*, 277

Every quiet conscience is not a clear conscience. Some are lulled asleep in security, and their consciences are quiet merely because they are insensible. It may be they have so harassed and wasted their consciences by dreadful sins, so often mortally wounded them, that now they have not strength enough to become quarrelsome and troublesome; and this they call peace.

✦ EZEKIEL HOPKINS
"Of the Nature, Corruption, and Renewing of the Conscience," in *Select Works*, 282

As every quiet conscience is not a clear conscience, so every troubled conscience is not an evil conscience.... For the most part it is seen that those that have the best consciences are most troubled, at least for a time, until the Holy Ghost persuades them of the love of God and of the pardon of their sins. It is the greatest fault of a tender conscience that it misinterprets everything against itself, and oftentimes, when God rejoices over it, it apprehends He frowns upon it, mistaking the firing of a bonfire for the firing of a beacon and giving an alarm when they should proclaim peace and joy. Many times it is so with them that have tender consciences.

✦ EZEKIEL HOPKINS
"Of the Nature, Corruption, and Renewing of the Conscience," in *Select Works*, 283

There is the book of conscience, in which is exactly written all our actions, thoughts, words, and deeds, according to this book of conscience. And what is therein written will then proceed in judgment, and every man's conscience shall be his own judge. Saith God, "What hast thou done? How hast thou lived in the world?"

"Why thus and thus have I lived," saith conscience. Conscience will then speak the truth.

✦ ANDREW JONES
Black Book of Conscience, 4

A tormenting and condemning conscience, who can endure? Oh there is no resisting of conscience. It is God's vice-regent in the soul. When conscience speaks threatening language to many of such and such sins, they seek to turn conscience out of doors, but because they cannot possibly do this, they strive to stop his mouth by running willfully into sin, like men that desperately give up their souls to the devil and so make shipwreck of faith, conscience, soul, and all forever. And then follows (as we have seen by woeful experience) self-stabbing, self-hanging, drowning, poisoning, or some such like cursed end.

✦ ANDREW JONES
Black Book of Conscience, 10

O ye great ones of the world who live in pleasure, remember that there is a conscience, that there is a God, and that thou hast a precious and immortal soul, which if thy conscience witness against shall be thrown into hell. You that eat the fat and sweet of the earth and drink wine in bowls and clothe yourselves in silks, remember this: that conscience takes notice of all thy ways—of the pride of thy heart, of the vanity of thy life—and sets it all down in his black book. You that like the harlot in Proverbs 7 cry, "Let us take our fill of love and pleasure," consider that all these things must have an end; when all is done the bell must toll, and you all must dance after death's pipe who are now singing and swinging yourselves in worldly pleasures and delights.

✦ ANDREW JONES
Black Book of Conscience, 11

Some [consciences] are quiet because there is no grace to oppose corruption. The old man is quiet enough if he may have what he will. The devil is as quiet as another creature if he be let alone to rule all as he [pleases]. There is peace, peace, and yet no peace. Have you never heard of that? "They shall cry, peace, peace," and yet no peace, no favor with God, but wrath burning and judgment at the door. Peace may be in a sinner's mouth and wrath in God's mouth; peace may be in a sinner's heart and wrath in God's heart—yea, when wrath is in God's hand and ready to cut him off.

✦ NICHOLAS LOCKYER
Balm for England, 161

Conscience must be satisfied with something; therefore men usually please themselves with so much of obedience as is least contrary to their interests and inclinations and have not an entire uniform respect to the whole law. As if a servant should think himself dutiful when he goes to a feast or a fair when his master bids him, when in the meantime he declines errands of less trouble but of more service; whereas in such matters he does not obey his master's will, but his own inclination. So in commands easy and compliant with our own humors and designs, we do not so much serve God as our own interests, and there is more of design than of duty and religion in such actions; and therefore they lose their reward with God.

✦ THOMAS MANTON
Practical Exposition on the Epistle of James, 91

Conscience is a shrewd remembrancer; it writes when it does not speak. Many times for the present it is silent and seems to take no notice of those circumstances of guilt, but they are all registered and produced at the last day.

✦ THOMAS MANTON
Practical Exposition on the
Epistle of James, 183

Conscience is the territory or dominion of God in man which He hath so reserved to Himself that no human power can possibly enter into it or dispose of it in any wise.

✦ JOHN OWEN
Golden Book, 240

The false peace and evil quiet of conscience doth arise from these three causes: (1) from gross ignorance of the danger wherein a man lives because of sin, whence follows a blind conscience; (2) from groundless security and presumption that all shall be well with him, notwithstanding that he knows he hath sinned and knows that sin is damnable, whence he hath a deluded conscience; (3) from obstinacy, through delight and custom in sin, whence cometh hardness and insensibility of heart, which is a seared conscience.

✦ HENRY SCUDDER
Christian's Daily Walk, 272

Keep therefore the conscience tender by all means: (1) by hearkening readily to the voice of the word; (2) by a careful survey of your ways daily; (3) by keeping the conscience soft with godly sorrow for sin; (4) by hearkening to the voice of conscience admonishing and checking for sin.

✦ HENRY SCUDDER
Christian's Daily Walk, 289

From God's register, or notary, which is in every man, I mean the conscience of man, which tells them there is a God. And although they silence it sometimes, yet in time of thunder or some great plague, as Pharaoh, or at the day of death when they are near God's tribunal, then they acknowledge Him clearly. The fearful terrors of conscience prove [that there is a God], which, like a bailiff, arrests men for their debts; ergo, there is some creditor to set it on. Sometimes like a hangman it torments men; ergo, there is some strange judge that gave it that command.

✦ THOMAS SHEPARD
Sincere Convert, 16

But the sincere Christian that allows himself in no sin delights to commune with his own soul and when he is debating things with his own conscience esteems himself in good company. He had rather God's deputy, conscience, should admonish him to contrition than that God Himself should do it to his confusion.

✦ GEORGE SWINNOCK
The Christian Man's Calling,
in *Works*, 2:452

Every man has a domestical chaplain within his own bosom that preaches over the sermon to him again.

✦ JOHN TRAPP
Commentary… upon… the New Testament, 276

We must watch over our consciences, that they perform their office faithfully. Their office is to observe and condemn every miscarriage, to urge unto a more spiritual manner of praying, and to be restless and unquiet if prayer be omitted on any slight pretense or the "male in the flock be not offered, but a corrupt thing." A tender conscience is a blessing that can never be sufficiently valued. This will cause the best to be given unto God; this will not be satisfied till God approves and commends. And what a heaven follows upon prayer when the Lord Himself and His officer conscience are both pleased! But if we grow unwatchful over our consciences and suffer them to fall asleep and become seared, a thousand faults in prayer will be winked at—nay, we shall be but little reproached for the total omission of it.

✦ NATHANIEL VINCENT
Spirit of Prayer, 96

The authority which the Lord allows to conscience is great, and its office is of a large extent. Conscience is a witness and a judge of the evil which we do, of the good which we refuse to do, and likewise observes when we are careful of our duty. As a judge, it acquits or condemns, according as we are either good or faithful or evil

and slothful servants. As a monitor, it tells us beforehand of our duty, and as we would avoid its accusations and reproaches, we should not venture upon any sin which it cries out against nor neglect prayer or any other duty which it charges us to perform, as we would answer it before God.

✦ NATHANIEL VINCENT
Spirit of Prayer, 98–99

In the understanding part [the conscience] is a judge, determining and prescribing, absolving and condemning *de jure*. In the memory it is a register, a recorder, and witness testifying *de facto*. In the will and affections, a jailor and executioner punishing and rewarding.

✦ SAMUEL WARD
"Balm from Gilead to Recover Conscience," in Sermons and Treatises, 97

Conscience is God's echo, and sometimes it is so shrill and clamorous that the sinner cannot endure the noise, but silences conscience; and at last by often sinning, conscience begins to be sleepy and seared.

✦ THOMAS WATSON
The Christian's Charter of Privileges, in Discourses, 1:95

Conscience is like a looking glass. If it be foul and dusty, you can see nothing in it; but wipe away the dust, and you may see your face in it clearly. There is a time coming when God will wipe off the dust from the glass of a man's conscience, and he shall see his sins clearly represented.

✦ THOMAS WATSON
The Christian's Charter of Privileges, in Discourses, 1:95

There is a time when the Spirit hath done striving. There are certain spring-tides of the Spirit, and these being neglected, possibly we may never see another tide come in. When conscience hath done speaking, usually the Spirit hath done striving.

✦ THOMAS WATSON
"The One Thing Necessary,"
in *Discourses*, 1:374

CONTENT BUT UNSATISFIED

A true Christian is a wonder; he is the most contented and yet the least satisfied. He is contented with a morsel of bread and a little water in the cruse, yet never satisfied with a little grace. He doth pant and breathe after more.

✦ SIMEON ASHE
Primitive Divinity, 154

One that is contented in a Christian way, it may be said of him that he is the most contented man in the world and yet the most unsatisfied man in the world; these two together must needs be mysterious: I say "a contented man," as he is the most contented, so he is the most unsatisfied of any man in the world. You never learned the mystery of contentment except it may be said of you that as you are the most contented man so you are the most unsatisfied man in the world. You will say, how is that? A man that hath learned the art of contentment is the most contented with any low condition that he hath in the world, and yet he cannot be satisfied with the enjoyment of all the world, and yet he is contented if he hath but a

crust, but bread and water—that is, if God disposes of him for the things of the world to have but bread and water for his present condition, he can be satisfied with God's dispose in that.

✦ JEREMIAH BURROUGHS
Rare Jewel, 20

CONTENTMENT

[Contentment] is a sweet temper of spirit whereby a Christian carries himself in an equal poise in every condition. The nature of this will appear more clear in these three general rules: (1) Contentment is a divine thing. It becomes ours not by acquisition, but infusion. It is a slip taken off from the tree of life and planted by the Spirit of God in the soul; it is a fruit that grows not in the garden of philosophy, but is of a heavenly birth.... (2) Contentment is an intrinsical thing. It lies within a man—not in the bark, but the root. Contentment hath both its fountain and stream in the soul. The beam hath not its light from the air. The beams of comfort which a contented man hath do not arise from foreign comforts, but from within.... (3) Contentment is an habitual thing. It shines with a fixed light in the firmament of the soul. Contentment doth not appear only now and then, as some stars which are seen but seldom; it is a settled temper of the heart.

One action doth not denominate it.

✦ SIMEON ASHE
Primitive Divinity, 37–39

Contentment, though it be not properly a grace—it is rather a disposition of mind—yet in it there is a happy temperature and mixture of all the graces. It is a most precious compound which is made up of faith, patience, meekness, humility, and love, which are the ingredients put into it.

✦ SIMEON ASHE
Primitive Divinity, 89

The way for a Christian to be contented is not by raising his estate higher, but by bringing his spirit lower; not by making his barns wider, but his heart narrower. One man, a whole lordship or manor will not content him; another is satisfied with a few acres of land. What is the difference? The one studies to satisfy curiosity, the other necessity. The one thinks what he may have; the other thinks what he may spare.

✦ SIMEON ASHE
Primitive Divinity, 187

Christian contentment is that sweet, inward, quiet, gracious frame of spirit, freely submitting to and taking complacency in God's wise and fatherly dispose in every condition.

✦ JEREMIAH BURROUGHS
Rare Jewel, 12

Contentment is a soul business: first, it is inward; secondly, quiet; thirdly, it is a quiet frame of spirit. It is a grace that spreads itself through the whole soul.

✦ JEREMIAH BURROUGHS
Rare Jewel, 14

That soul that is capable of God can be filled with nothing else but God.

✦ JEREMIAH BURROUGHS
Rare Jewel, 20

If you would get a contented life, do not grip too much of the world; do not take in more of the business of the world than God calls you to. Be not greedy of taking in a great deal of the world, for if a man will go among thorns when he may go in a plainer way, there is not reason that this man should complain that he is pricked with them. Thou goest among thorns. Is it thy way? Must you of necessity go among them? Then it is another matter. But if thou wilt electively choose that way when thou mayest go another, then thou hast no cause to complain. So for men and women that will put themselves upon things of the world that they need not, then no marvel though they be pricked and meet with that that doth disquiet them. For such is the nature of all things here in the world, that everything hath some prick or other in it.

✦ JEREMIAH BURROUGHS
Rare Jewel, 80

We have better things than a cup of water to refresh and delight us when we are thirsty, and yet are not pleased. Oh, that this complaint of Christ on the cross, "I thirst," were but believingly considered; it would make you bless God for what ye now despise and beget contentment in you for the meanest mercies and most common favors in this world. Did the Lord of all things cry, "I thirst" and had nothing in His extremity to comfort Him? And dost thou, who hast a thousand times over forfeited all temporal as well as spiritual mercies, contemn and slight the good creatures of God? What! Despise a cup of water, who deserves nothing but a cup of wrath from the hand of the Lord! Oh, lay it to heart and hence learn contentment with anything.

✦ JOHN FLAVEL
Fountain of Life, 343

Contentment is a willing submission of ours to God's will in all conditions. I say "willing," for if it be patience perforce, what reward have you?... In all conditions, patient in adversity, humble in prosperity, thankful in both; looking neither above our estates with the ambitious man to have it higher, nor beyond it with the covetous man to spread it broader, nor besides it with the envious man, repining at the estate of others; but directly on the portion God hath given us, and fully satisfied with the same.

✦ THOMAS FULLER
"A Sermon of Contentment,"
in *Pulpit Sparks*, 215–16

Contentment consists not in adding more fuel but in taking away some fire—not in multiplying of wealth but in subtracting men's desires. Worldly riches, like nuts, tear many clothes in getting them; spoil many teeth in cracking them; but fill no belly with eating them, obstructing only the stomach with toughness and filling the guts with windiness. Yea, our souls may

sooner surfeit than be satisfied with earthly things. He that at first thought ten thousand pounds too much for any one man will afterward think ten millions too little for himself.

✦ THOMAS FULLER
Wise Words and Quaint Counsels, 89

We may say, if a Christian made the world but his servant, a little would content him; but if once he make the world his master and lord of his affections, then his desires will be infinite and cannot at all be satisfied.

✦ ANDREW GRAY
"Spiritual Contentment," in *Works*, 382

We conceive it is so excellent a grace, this grace of contentment, that it is indeed a compound of these five graces: faith, humility, patience, hope, and mortification. In a manner, contentment is the result of all these exercising themselves in one; and except these be in a most vigorous exercise, absolute contentment is not easily to be attained.

✦ ANDREW GRAY
"Spiritual Contentment," in *Works*, 394

Such a commander is contentation [i.e., contentment], that wheresoever she sets foot, an hundred blessings wait upon her. In every disease she is a physician; in every strife she is a lawyer; in every doubt she is a preacher; in every grief she is a comforter.

✦ HENRY SMITH
"The Benefit of Contentation,"
in *Three Sermons*, 15

Get a humble spirit if you would have a contented one. Pride causes men to be unthankful for their mercies and impatient under their crosses, but afflictions are easily borne and benefits are ever gratefully acknowledged by the mind that is truly humble under a sense of its defects.

✦ RICHARD STEELE
Religious Tradesman, 133

A contented man cannot be a poor man, especially if a godly man. For why? The Father, that Ancient of Days, fills his memory; the Son, the wisdom of the Father, fills his understanding; the Holy Ghost, the Comforter, fills his will. And so he must needs have all that thus has the Haver of All.

✦ JOHN TRAPP
Commentary…upon…the New Testament, 718

Here is the difference between a holy complaint and a discontented complaint: in the one we complain to God, and in the other we complain of God.

✦ THOMAS WATSON
Art of Divine Contentment, 28

CONTROVERSY

That as in the burning of some wet fuel we cannot see the fire for the smoke, so the light of the Scriptures is dusked by the vapors of controversies. Whilst green wits range abroad into the woods and thickets of schoolmen, that wild forest of polemical divinity, they cannot escape unscratched. Those briers and brambles pluck off the wool of the sheep. They that love such intricate and perplexed walks had need of iron shoes, for they tread upon thorns.

✦ THOMAS ADAMS
Exposition upon…Second…Peter, 790

I never cared to meddle with things that were controverted and in dispute among the saints, especially things of the lowest nature; yet it pleased me much to contend with great earnestness for the word of faith and the remission of sins by the death and sufferings of Jesus. But I say, as to other things, I would let them alone because I saw they engendered strife and because that they neither in doing nor in leaving undone did commend us to God to be His. Besides, I saw my work before me did run into another channel, even to carry an awakening word; to that therefore I did stick and adhere.

✦ JOHN BUNYAN
Grace Abounding, 110–11

[Henry Newcome] was not for novel, undigested speculations. He studiously declined controversy at all times, but especially in the pulpits. Nor did he make it his business to reflect upon the different parties among Protestants. Instead of that, he endeavored, with all his strength, to declare divine truths with so convincing an evidence and to enforce his exhortations with such irresistible arguments and with such poignant expressions as might leave the hearers under strong convictions concerning the necessity of holiness.

✦ JOHN CHORLTON
Glorious Reward, 29

CONVERSION

Conversion…lies in the thorough change both of the heart and life.
✦ JOSEPH ALLEINE
Alarm to the Unconverted, 30

The author [of conversion], it is the Spirit of God; and therefore it is called the sanctification of the Spirit (2 Thess. 2:13) and the renewing of the Holy Ghost (Titus 3:5), yet not excluding the other persons in the Trinity. For the apostle teacheth us to bless the Father of our Lord Jesus Christ, for that He hath begotten us again (1 Peter 1:3), and Christ is said to give repentance to Israel (Acts 5:31) and is called the everlasting Father (Isa. 9:6), and we His seed and the children which God hath given Him (Isa. 53:10). O blessed birth! Seven cities contended for the birth of Homer, but the whole Trinity fathers the new creature. Yet is this work principally ascribed to the Holy Ghost, and so we are said to be born of the Spirit (John 3:8). So then it is a work above man's power.
✦ JOSEPH ALLEINE
Alarm to the Unconverted, 30

Endeavor to get a right knowledge of God and the chief of Christian religion. 'Tis ignorance that is the first impediment that keeps us from God, and it is knowledge must be the first means to bring us to Him. To sacrifice to an unknown God was indeed the Athenian [mode of worship], but is no true Christian worship. No, we must either first know the God we ought to serve, or we can never serve the God that we are to know (1 Chron. 28:9). Light was the first thing God made in the creation of the world, and 'tis the first thing He doth in the conversion of a soul to Himself, without which 'tis as impossible for us to turn to God as it is to be converted and not converted at the same time; for our true knowledge of God is one, yea, and the first part of our turning to Him.
✦ WILLIAM BEVERIDGE
Thesaurus Theologious, 4:146

Possibly a man may see a greater beauty in the things of the world after conversion than ever he saw before. As now, in the case of the law. While a man is in the state of nature, then he is under the law; but when a man is converted and drawn to Christ, then he is free from the law. And then when he is freed from the law, he sees a greater excellency in the law than ever he saw before conversion; for then says he, "Now I see that the commandment is holy, just, and good." Indeed, as to the point of justification, he sees a greater emptiness in the law than ever he did before; but as to the point of rule of life, he sees a greater beauty in the law than ever he did before…. Though as to the matter of satisfaction, his soul cannot be satisfied. He sees less in the world than ever he did before; yet as to the matter of Christ's purchase, a man after his conversion may see a greater beauty in the things of the world than ever he did before.
✦ WILLIAM BRIDGE
The Spiritual Life, in Works, 1:315

Mercy may receive him that we have doomed to hell, and justice may take hold on him whom we have judged to be bound up in the bundle of life. We, like Joseph, are for setting of Manasseh before Ephraim; but God, like Jacob, puts his hands across and lays His right hand upon the worst man's head and His left hand upon the best (Genesis 48), to the amazement and wonderment even of the best of men.
✦ JOHN BUNYAN
Riches, 28

Conversion is a creation work which, though done by degrees, must be gone through with, and that by Him who laid the foundation, or all the foregoing parts, as conviction, etc., will molder and come to nothing. As when Adam was to be made the Lord first prepares the earth, then molds it in such a form, and then "breathes into him the breath of life," else that lump had never been a "living soul," so, in the new creation, the Lord works, and goes on to work, and leaves it not until He hath set it going. He doth not only cause the light to shine into darkness but gives withal a suitable understanding (1 John 5:20), a faculty connatural with the object, as without which the darkness would never comprehend it (John 1:5). Ezekiel might have prophesied till doomsday ere those dry bones would have lived if the Lord Himself had not caused breath to enter into them.
✦ ELISHA COLES
Practical Discourse, 203

First, God by His word and Spirit enlighteneth the understanding of a sinner truly to conceive the doctrine of man's misery and of his full recovery by Christ. Secondly, by the same means He works in his heart both such sound sorrow for his misery and fervent desire after Christ the remedy that he can never be at quiet till he enjoy Christ. Thirdly, God so manifesteth His love in freely offering Christ with His benefits unto him, a poor sinner lost, that thereby He draws him in such wise to give credit unto God herein, that he gladly accepts of Christ offered unto Him. These three works of God, whosoever finds to have been truly wrought in himself may thereby know certainly that he hath true faith, and therefore sound conversion.
✦ CLEMENT COTTON
None but Christ, 76–77

For any man to make the way of God working with him to be the way to which He will tie up all others is little better than high tyranny. God hath not tied up Himself to one way. Why must yours be the only way? Yet this I have observed in some ministers (men of great spirits and parts) who in their preaching (may I not say also in printing?) have pressed upon people that particular way they found God came to them in. Because God did handle them thus, therefore He must do so with all. "One man is not a fair copy," saith Mr. Shepherd, and this is very true. God takes a man of a high lofty spirit and batters him with such or such workings. Must the same be found in all others?
✦ GILES FIRMIN
Real Christian, 17

A rule: Never did God declare against self or call a man to deny himself in that which did hinder his own salvation and happiness, lying in union and communion with God by Christ.

✦ GILES FIRMIN
Real Christian, 209

The real Christian closes with and embraces Christ freely. Forced matches are like never to do well, nor will Christ force any; the sound believer gives his consent freely and willingly. A contract, or match, made up by fears and scares is no true one. There are indeed many times fears and scares in the preparatory legal work, which do more properly tend to loosen the soul from its lusts and idols from which he is called. But to choose Christ merely out of fear and because I am scared with hellish horrors, as if Christ were not worthy the choosing or regarding, were it not for these which I dread and lie in danger of, this choice or embracing of Christ will not hold.

✦ GILES FIRMIN
Real Christian, 245

Conversion work went out slowly in Christ's days; it was quicker in Peter's time than ever since, three thousand souls converted at a sermon. Now three thousand sermons hardly convert one soul.

✦ WILLIAM GREENHILL
Exposition of the Prophet Ezekiel, 818

I know there is very great variety in the way and manner of conversion, and to some, especially if it be in their tender years, grace may be instilled and dropped in, as it were, insensibly. But this I may confidently say, that whatsoever be the way of working it, there will be a wide and apparent difference betwixt friendship with God and the condition of nature, which is enmity against Him. Do not flatter yourselves so long as your minds remain carnal, ardent in love to the world and cold in love to God, "lovers of pleasure more than of God" (as the apostle speaks); you are His enemies, for with Him there is no neutrality.

✦ ROBERT LEIGHTON
Spiritual Truths, 150

The altogether Christian closes with and accepts of Christ upon gospel terms. True union makes a true Christian. Many close with Christ, but it is upon their own terms; they take Him and own Him, but not as God offers Him. The terms upon which God in the gospel offers Christ are that we shall accept of a broken Christ with a broken heart, and yet a whole Christ with a whole heart—a broken Christ with a broken heart as a witness of our humility; a whole Christ with the whole heart as a witness of our sincerity. A broken Christ respects His suffering for sin; a broken heart respects our sense of sin. A whole Christ includes all His offices; a whole heart includes all our faculties.

When God converts a soul, He comes into it with a cloud. I know nothing in this world I would be more jealous of in my ministry than of speaking anything on conversion or regeneration that I had not experienced of myself. I would not bind others by any experience of my own unless it be confirmed by a general rule, for one man may have an experience that another hath not. But yet I think this I can say that God generally takes possession of souls in a cloud. That is, there is some darkness upon them; they cannot tell what their state is. Sometimes they have hopes, and sometimes fears; sometimes they think things are well, and sometimes they are cast down again. This is the way whereby God generally enters into all souls. These things may be in part where God does not come, but seldom have I heard of any that have come unto God but that God first took possession of them in a cloud.

✦ JOHN OWEN
Golden Book, 142–43

The conversion of the soul is supposed to be as considerable a work, if not a greater, than the creation, for in the creation God had no adversary. The light did not say, "I will not be created"; the earth did not say, "I will not be formed." But in the new creation, sinners labor to prevent (as much as in them lies) the conception of grace, take down antidotes against salvation, and study how to defeat the Spirit of God and make its works abortive. God, when He comes, finds the house not only empty of grace but filled with lusts and the strong man up in arms; not a milk-white paper, but He finds the devil to have been scribbling and the world to have been scribbling. Angels may knock at the door of a sinner's heart, but God only can open it. The body is not so much at the command of the soul as the soul is at the command of God. "Without me ye can do nothing" (John 15). The Lord opened the heart of Lydia. Man's heart is God's lock, and not man's wisdom; but the Spirit of the Lord is the key that must unlock it.

✦ FRANCIS RAWORTH
On Jacob's Ladder, 9–10

True conversion and repentance doth consist of a true and thorough change of the whole man, whereby not only some actions are changed but first and chiefly the whole frame and disposition of the heart is changed and set aright toward God from evil to good as well as from darkness to light. And whereas man is naturally earthly-minded and maketh himself his utmost end, so that either he only mindeth earthly things or, if he mind heavenly things, it is in an earthly manner and to an earthly end, as did Jehu. If this man has truly repented and be indeed converted, he becometh heavenly-minded; he maketh God and His glory his chief and highest end, insomuch that when he hath cause to mind earthly things, his will and desire is to mind them in a heavenly manner and to a heavenly end.

✦ HENRY SCUDDER
Christian's Daily Walk, 286

What is conversion? It's the change of a man's treasure, of a man's chief good. Till thou change thy chief good, it's in vain to complain of the disorders of thy heart; therefore, every unregenerate man may hence see the absolute necessity of conversion.

✦ WILLIAM STRONG
Heavenly Treasure, 384–85

CONVICTION

Conviction follows illumination.... There cannot be conviction without light. The Spirit is a practical teacher.

✦ GILES FIRMIN
Real Christian, 45

The Holy Ghost speaks so to man as to make man know his distance. He speaks so as to make him know Him that speaks to be God, and him that is spoken to is but man. God speaks so as to make man admire, tremble, stoop. Man is a conceited creature and yet of no reach.

✦ NICHOLAS LOCKYER
Balm for England, 54

Sound and deep conviction tends to solid consolation.

✦ ADAM MARTINDALE
Life, 43

You will say, "Suppose I am at any time under conviction. How shall I know whether my convictions be only from a natural conscience or whether they be from the Spirit of God?"... There is a great difference between conviction which is natural and that which is spiritual, that which is common and that which is saving. Yea, such is the difference that though a man hath ever so much of the former, yet if he be without the latter, he is but almost a Christian, and therefore we have great reason to inquire more after this spiritual conviction. For spiritual conviction is an essential part of sound conversion; conversion begins here. True conversion begins in convictions, and true convictions end in conversion.

✦ MATTHEW MEAD
Almost Christian Discovered, 158–64

COURTSHIP

He which will know all his wife's qualities before he be married to her must see her eating and walking and working and playing and talking and laughing and chiding, or else he shall have less with her than he looked for or more than he wished for.

✦ HENRY SMITH
"Preparative to Marriage," in *Works*, 1:18

COVENANT OF WORKS

NOMISTA: But, sir, you know the word *covenant* signifies a mutual promise, bargain, and obligation betwixt two parties. Now, though it is implied that God promised man to give him life if he obeyed, yet we read not that man promised to be obedient.

EVANGELISTA: I pray take notice that God does not always tie man to verbal expressions but doth often contract the covenant in real impressions in the heart and frame of the creature, and this was the manner of covenanting with man at the first. For God had furnished his soul with an understanding mind, whereby he might discern good from evil and right from wrong; and not only so, but also in his will was most great uprightness (Eccl. 7:29), and his instrumental parts were orderly framed to obedience. The truth is, God did engrave in man's soul wisdom and knowledge of His will and works, and integrity in the whole soul, and such a fitness in all the powers thereof that neither the mind did conceive, nor the heart desire, nor the body put in execution anything but that which was acceptable to God, so that man, endued with these qualities, was able to serve God perfectly.

✦ EDWARD FISHER
Marrow of Modern Divinity, 10

NOMISTA: But yet I cannot but marvel that God, in making the covenant with man, did make mention of no other commandment than that of the forbidden fruit.

EVANGELISTA: Do not marvel at it, for by that one species of sin the whole genus, or kind, is shown as the same law, being more clearly unfolded doth express (Deut. 28:26; Gal. 3:10). And indeed, in that one commandment the whole worship of God did consist as obedience, honor, love, confidence, and religious fear, together with the outward abstinence from sin and reverend respect to the voice of God. Yea, herein also consisted his love and so his whole duty to his neighbor so that, as a learned writer says, Adam heard

as much (of the law) in the garden as Israel did at Sinai, but only in fewer words and without thunder.

✦ EDWARD FISHER
Marrow of Modern Divinity, 11

The covenant of works which God made with Adam, and in him with all mankind, was in some respects a covenant of grace, for God was not bound to promise man eternal felicity upon his perfect obedience, but might have required it by virtue of His sovereignty and dominion. But since man's apostasy and impossibility thereby of attaining happiness by his own works, God hath been pleased to accept of the perfect obedience of Jesus Christ on the behalf of the believing, penitent Christian, which act of infinite grace being revealed in the gospel, it is most fitly called the word of His grace.

✦ GEORGE SWINNOCK
"The Pastor's Farewell," in *Works*, 4:61

COVENANT OF WORKS: COMPARED TO COVENANT OF GRACE

To preach the law, in order to Christ; to labor to make men that lie in their spiritual lethargies to know and feel their disease, that they may see the need of and embrace the blessed Physician—is not this rational? I think all men naturally stand under a covenant of works, and to make men know what that state is, I think, is very requisite if ever we would make them feel the necessity and know the worth of a covenant of grace; yet I know not how it comes about. Of late years this kind of preaching is laid by. When I consider the people, then I can see their reasons why they love it not; but when I think of the ministry, I know not why ministers should so gratify the corruptions of people. So the law were rightly preached, I never knew it offend any godly and judicious Christian.

✦ GILES FIRMIN
Real Christian, 51

There is a covenant of nature, or law covenant [i.e., covenant of works], which God made with innocent Adam, and the condition of this was perfect obedience of the person that claimed happiness by it. This is not the condition now required, and he that stands groping at this door in hope to enter into life by it shall not only find it nailed up and no entrance to be had but also deprives himself of any benefit of that true door which stands open and by which all pass that get thither: "Whosoever of you are justified by the law; ye are fallen from grace" (Gal. 5:4). You must therefore inquire what the other covenant is. It is a covenant of grace, as the other was of nature—of reconciliation between God and man, as the other was a covenant to preserve those friends who had never fallen out. Now the requisites of this covenant are repentance and faith (see John 3:36; Acts 2:38; 5:31; 20:21; Gal. 5:5). Labor, therefore, to give a firm assent to the truth of these promises and hold it as an inviolable principle, that whoever sincerely repents of his sins and with a faith unfeigned receives Christ to be

his Lord and Savior; this is the person that hath the word and oath of a God that cannot possibly lie for the pardon of his sins and salvation of his soul.

✦ WILLIAM GURNALL
Christian in Complete Armour, 547–48

You will say, "Who are now under the covenant of works?" There is a vulgar prejudice abroad which supposes that the first covenant was repealed and disannulled upon the fall and that God now deals with us upon new terms, as if the covenant of grace wholly shut out the former contract, wherein they think Adam only was concerned. But this is a gross mistake because it was made not only with Adam but with all his seed. And every natural man, whilst natural, whilst merely a son of Adam, is obliged to the tenor of it. The form of the law runs universally: "Cursed is every one that"...(Gal. 3:10), which rule allows no exception but that of free grace and interest in Christ.

✦ THOMAS MANTON
Practical Exposition on the Epistle of James, 99

There are two questions of very great importance which we should every one of us often put to ourselves: What am I? and Where am I? What am I? Am I a child of God or not? Am I sincere in religion, or am I only a hypocrite under a profession? Where am I? Am I yet in a natural state, or in a state of grace? Am I yet in the old root, in old Adam, or am I in the root of Christ Jesus? Am I in the covenant of works, that ministers only wrath and death? Or am I in the covenant of grace, that ministers life and peace?

✦ MATTHEW MEAD
Almost Christian Discovered, 186

It will prove a special help to know distinctly the difference between the covenant of works and the covenant of grace—between Moses and Christ. Moses without all mercy breaks all bruised reeds and quenches all smoking flax. For the law requires (1) personal, (2) perpetual, (3) perfect obedience, (4) and from a perfect heart, and that under a most terrible curse and gives no strength—a severe task master, like Pharaoh, requiring the whole tale and yet giving no straw. Christ comes with blessing after blessing even upon those whom Moses had cursed and with healing balm for those wounds which Moses had made.

✦ RICHARD SIBBES
Bruised Reed and Smoking Flax, 67–68

COVETOUSNESS

Rich in miseries, miserable in riches. Other sinners that have forfeited heaven yet receive some pleasure on earth. But the covetous deprives himself of this world, and God will deprive him of the world to come, so he enjoys neither. Is not this a curse?

✦ THOMAS ADAMS
Exposition upon…Second…Peter, 498

[The covetous man] is an ill harvest man, for he is all at the rake, nothing at the pitchfork. The devil is a slave to God, the world to the devil, the covetous man to the world; he is a slave to the devil's slave, so that his servant is like to have a good office. He foolishly buries his soul in his chest of silver when his body must be buried in the mold of corruption. When the fisher offers to catch him with the net of the gospel, he strikes into the mud of avarice and will not be taken.

✦ THOMAS ADAMS
"The Soul's Sickness," in *Sermons*, 217

Because men believe not providence, therefore they do so greedily scrape and hoard. They do not believe any reward for charity; therefore they will part with nothing.

✦ ISAAC BARROW
in Bertram, *Homiletic Encyclopaedia*, 68

Drunkenness and covetousness do much resemble one another, for the more a man drinks, the more he thirsts; and the more he has, still the more he covets. And for their effects, besides other, both of them have the power of transforming a man into a beast—and, of all other beasts, into a swine. The former is evident to sense; the other, though more obscure, is no more questionable. The covetous man in two things plainly resembles a swine: that he ever roots in the earth, not so much as looking toward heaven; that he never doth good till his death. In desiring, my rule shall be necessity of nature or estate; in having, I will account that my good which doeth me good.

✦ JOSEPH HALL
Meditations and Vows, 26–27

When we ourselves and all other vices are old, then covetousness alone is young and at his best age. This vice loves to dwell in an old, ruinous cottage.... A young man might plead the uncertainty of his estate and doubt of his future need, but an old man sees his set period before him. Since this humor is so necessarily annexed to this age, I will turn it the right way and nourish it in myself. The older I grow, the more covetous I will be—but of the riches not of the world I am leaving, but of the world I am entering into. It is good coveting, what I may have and cannot leave behind me.
✦ JOSEPH HALL
Meditations and Vows, 176–77

Gracious souls, though they still covet more of God, never covet more than God.
✦ MATTHEW HENRY
Gems, 91

If covetousness reigns in the heart, commonly all compassion is banished from it.
✦ MATTHEW HENRY
Gems, 138

Covetousness may be defined to be a sinful desire of getting or keeping money or wealth inordinately.
✦ JOHN PRESTON
"A Remedy against Covetousness," in
Four Godly and Learned Treatises, 30

This affection [i.e., covetousness] is said to be inordinate in these four respects. First, when as we seek it by measure more than we should. Secondly, when we seek it by means that

we should not. Thirdly, when we seek it for wrong ends. Fourthly, when we seek it in a wrong manner.
✦ JOHN PRESTON
"A Remedy against Covetousness," in
Four Godly and Learned Treatises, 31

Covetousness is an uncontentedness, or a desire of having much, arising from an uncontentedness with a man's condition. It is an uncontentedness with or a desire of having abundance out of a discontentedness with a man's present estate, though he might by lawful means mend or better it.
✦ SYDRACH SIMPSON
"On Covetousness," in *Two Books*, 218–19

A man may be said to have a desire after much or abundance two ways. Either when as he desires to have that which he hath not, and in that respect it may be a poor man's fin, as well as the rich. Or else when a man is content with that which he hath but is not willing to lay it forth as God assigns him. When he would have that whereof he is possessed and not part with it or lay it out to such uses which God assigns him. Mark it: though a man counts he hath enough and desires no more, yet if he be not willing to part with that which he hath when God commands him, he is covetous.
✦ SYDRACH SIMPSON
"On Covetousness," in *Two Books*, 220

Because when we preach we know not whether we shall preach again, my care is to choose fit and proper texts to speak that which I would speak and that which is necessary for you to hear. Therefore, thinking with myself what doctrine were fittest for you, I sought for a text which speaks against covetousness, which I may call the Londoners' sin. Although God hath given you more than others, which should turn covetousness into thankfulness, yet as the ivy grows with the oak, so covetousness hath grown with riches.

✦ HENRY SMITH
"The Benefit of Contentation,"
in *Sermons*, 193

"If riches increase, set not your heart upon them" (Ps. 62:10). If you want riches, set not your hearts upon them. Take heed of that, for the nearer a man comes to enjoy them, the more his heart goes out unto them. And therefore covetous men, the richer they are, the more miserably they scrape and gape after riches. And the reason is this: because the nearer a man's love comes to the thing beloved, the swifter it moves after it, and with the greater earnestness.

✦ WILLIAM STRONG
Heavenly Treasure, 348

You may as soon fill a bag with wisdom, a chest with virtue, or a circle with a triangle as the heart of man with anything here below.

✦ JOHN TRAPP
*A Commentary…upon…the
New Testament*, 39

It is a subtle sin, a sin that many do not so well discern in themselves, as some have the scurvy yet do not know it. This sin can dress itself in the attire of virtue. It is called the "cloak of covetousness" (1 Thess. 2:5). Covetousness

is a sin that wears a cloak; it cloaks itself under the name of frugality and good husbandry. It hath many pleas and excuses for itself—more than any other sin, as the providing for one's family. The more subtle the sin is, the less discernible.

✦ THOMAS WATSON
Body of Practical Divinity, 334

Lay aside covetousness. Covetousness is not only getting worldly gain unjustly, but loving it inordinately. This is a great hindrance to the preached word. The seed which fell among thorns was choked. The covetous man is thinking on the world when he is hearing; his heart is in his shop. "They sit before thee as my people, and they hear thy words…but their heart goes after their covetousness" (Ezek. 33:31).

✦ THOMAS WATSON
Gleanings, 95

COWARDICE

When Ahab said to [Elijah], "Art thou he that troubleth Israel?" "No," saith he, "it is thou and thy father's house that troubleth Israel." And then he comes and gets the priests of Baal together, and gets fire from heaven to consume the sacrifice, and destroys all the priests of Baal, and gets rain from heaven to rain upon the earth. What an excellent spirit had Elijah in the eighteenth chapter [of 1 Kings]! Yet in the nineteenth chapter, Jezebel did but threaten Elijah, and he takes him to his heels and runs away at the threatening of wicked Jezebel, though he had such a brave spirit in the former chapter. So is it truly with many men; at sometimes their courage makes their adversaries afraid, and at other times their cowardice makes their friends ashamed. Many have been so; they have been a terror to their adversaries one day and a shame to their friends another day.

✦ JEREMIAH BURROUGHS
"The Saint's Duty in Times of
Extremity," in *Rare Jewel*, 92

I think it manhood to play the coward and take shelter by the side of Christ. Thus I am not only saved from my enemies but I obtain the victory.

✦ SAMUEL RUTHERFORD
Prison Sayings, 41

Now, pray, tell me where your hazards are. Where is the man that for the truths of God and the interests of Christ will hazard the loss of his estate, the loss of friends, the spoiling of his goods? Where be the men that be apt thus to hazard anything? The truth is, love turns cowardice into courage.

✦ WILLIAM STRONG
Heavenly Treasure, 360

Take heed of cowardliness. He must needs be evil who is afraid to be good.

✦ THOMAS WATSON
Godly Man's Picture, 189

CREATION

The whole creation is a poem, every species a stanza and every individual creature a verse in it. The creation presents us with a prospect of the wisdom of God, as a poem doth the reader with the wit and fancy of the composer. By

wisdom He created the earth (Prov. 3:19) and stretched out the heavens by discretion (Jer. 10:12). There is not anything so mean, so small, but glitters with a beam of divine skill.

✦ STEPHEN CHARNOCK
Selections, 84

The heavens…by their unwearied and perpetual motion ride in a circuit about the earth and compass it every day since the one and the other had a being, without cessation or intermission. How great a work must it appear to be to any man that shall take it into his serious consideration; and how convincing an argument that there is a supreme, most wise, and powerful Being that hath made these things and given such laws to them as that they cannot but keep their stations and remain where the Author of their being hath placed them and go on in that course He hath appointed for them!

✦ JOHN CONANT
Sermon 4 on John 17:3, in
Sermons, 140–41

The Lord made as well the least worm on earth as the most glorious angel in heaven, and it costeth the Lord as many words to make a worm as to make an angel, for all was done with a word. It is no disgrace for the Lord to walk up and down by His providence and overlook all His creatures; the baseness of any creature no more defiles God than a dunghill vapor infects the sunbeams. God is great in the greatest creatures, and He is great in the smallest creatures. It is to be feared that those that at present question providence upon the same account may ere long deny the creation. But the Lord can no more be absent from His creatures than cease to be their Creator—nay, than cease to be (Ps. 147:9). According to the old observation, God is present in heaven by His glory, in His church by His Spirit, in hell by His justice, in the earth by His providence, though it be not full, for God is everywhere in His essence.

♦ FRANCIS RAWORTH
On Jacob's Ladder, 8

God is the Father of lights; therefore must needs see. It is His own argument:"He that planted the ear, shall he not hear? he that formed the eye, shall he not see?" (Ps. 94:9). He that makes a watch knows all the pins and wheels in it, and though these wheels move cross one to another, he knows the true and perfect motion of the watch and the spring that sets these wheels going. "He that formed the eye, shall he not see?" Man may be compared to a spiritual watch. The affections are the wheels; the heart is the spring. The motion of this watch is false; the heart is deceitful. But God that made this watch knows the true motion of it (be it never so false) and the spring that sets the wheels going. God knows us better than we know ourselves. He is as Ezekiel's wheels, full of eyes; and, as Augustine saith, He is all eye.

♦ THOMAS WATSON
"God's Anatomy upon Man's Heart,"
in *Discourses*, 1:152–53

CROSS (See CHRIST, CROSS OF)

DEATH

We walk in this world as a man in a field of snow; all the way appears smooth, yet cannot we be sure of any step. All are like actors on a stage; some have one part, and some another. Death is still busy among us. Here drops one of the players. We bury him with sorrow, and to our scene again. Then falls another—yea all, one after another—till death be left alone upon the stage. Death is that damp which puts out all the dim lights of vanity. Yet man is easier to believe that all the world shall die than to suspect himself.

♦ THOMAS ADAMS
Exposition upon…Second…Peter, 342

Death takes away difference between king and beggar and tumbles both the knight and the pawn into one bag.

♦ THOMAS ADAMS
in Horn, *Puritan Remembrancer*, 147

I find not one in ten of the most obstinate, scornful wretches in the parish but when they come to die will humble themselves, confess their faults, seem penitent, and promise, if they should recover, to reform their lives. With what resolution will the worst of them seem to cast away their sins, exclaim against their follies and the vanities of the world when they see that death is in earnest with them! I confess it is very common for persons at such a season to be frightened into ineffectual purposes, but not so common to be converted to fixed resolutions. Yet there are some exceptions.

✦ RICHARD BAXTER
Reformed Pastor, 47–48

What is this life but a smoke, a vapor, a shadow, a warfare, a bubble of water, a word, grass, a flower? Thou shalt die is most certain, but of the time no man can tell when. The longer in this life thou dost remain, the more thou sinnest, which will turn to thy more pain. By cogitation of death our minds be often in manner oppressed with darkness because we do but remember the night of the body, forgetting the light of the mind and of the resurrection. Thereto remember the good things that after this life shall ensue without wavering in certainty of faith, and so shall the passage of death be more desired.

✦ JOHN BRADFORD
"Meditation of Death," in
John Bradford, 145

With troubled heart and
trembling hand I write,
The heavens have chang'd to
sorrow my delight.
How oft with disappointment
have I met,
When I on fading things
my hopes have set?

Experience might 'fore this have
made me wife,
To value things according to
their price:
Was ever stable joy yet found below?
Or perfect bliss without mixture
of woe.

I knew she [i.e., Bradstreet's
granddaughter] was but as a
withering flower,
That's here today, perhaps gone
in an hour;
Like as a bubble, or the brittle glass,
Or like a shadow turning as it was.

More fool than I to look on that
was lent,
As is mine own, when thus
impermanent.

Farewell, dear child, thou ne'er
shall come to me,
But yet a while, and I shall go to thee;
Meantime my throbbing heart's
cheer'd up with this
Thou with thy Saviour art in
endless bliss.

✦ ANNE BRADSTREET
"In Memory of My Dear Grand-child,"
in *Works*, 405–6

The serious thoughts of death may do that for you which neither friends, counsel, example, prayers, sermons, tears have done to this very day. Well, remember this: to labor not to die is labor in vain, and to put this day far from you and to live without fear of death is to die living. Death seizes on old men and lays wait for the youngest. Death is oftentimes as near to the young man's back as it is to the old man's face.

✦ THOMAS BROOKS
Apples of Gold, 147

Death is not…the death of the man, but the death of his sin. When Sampson died, the Philistines died together with him; so, when a believer dies, be it by the pestilence or any other disease, his sin dies with him. As death came in by sin, so sin goes out by death.

✦ THOMAS BROOKS
Heavenly Cordial, 78

Death is our birthday; we say falsely when we call death the last day. For it is indeed the beginning of an everlasting day, and is there any grievance in that? Death is the funeral of our vices and the resurrection of our graces. Death was the daughter of sin, and in death shall that be fulfilled: "The daughter shall destroy the mother." We shall never more be infected with sin nor troubled with ill natures.

✦ NICHOLAS BYFIELD
Cure of the Fear of Death, 37

We are manifestly mistaken concerning death. For the last gasp is not death. To live is to die. For how much we lived, so much we die; every step of life is a step of death. He that hath lived half his days is dead the half of himself. Death gets first our infancy, then our youth, and so forward. All that thou hast lived is dead.

✦ NICHOLAS BYFIELD
Cure of the Fear of Death, 127

Death mine enemy shall then set me free from the devil's temptation, the world's enticements, the outrage of men, the arrows of the Almighty, and the lustings of mine own flesh—all which have all my days stung my soul and battered my body. My soul! Take courage unto this last encounter.

✦ ZACHARY CROFTON
Defence against the Dread of Death, 25–26

If there certainly be such an eternal state into which souls pass immediately after death, how great a change then doth death make upon every man and woman! Oh, what a serious thing is it to die! It is your passage out of the swift river of time into the boundless and bottomless ocean of eternity. You that now converse with sensible objects, with men and women like yourselves, enter then into the world of spirits. You that now see the continual revolutions of days and nights, passing away one after another, will then be fixed in a perpetual now. Oh, what a serious thing is death!

✦ JOHN FLAVEL
Fountain of Life, 318

Oh then let not believers stand in fear of the grave. He that hath one foot in heaven need not fear to put the other into the grave.

✦ JOHN FLAVEL
Fountain of Life, 376

A grave with Christ is a comfortable place.

✦ JOHN FLAVEL
Fountain of Life, 378

There is also a lawful contempt of death. We freely grant it, that in two cases a believer may contemn it. First, when it is propounded to them in a temptation on purpose to scare them from Christ and duty, then they should slight it as in Revelation 12:11. They loved not their lives to the death. Secondly, when the natural evil of death is set in competition with the enjoyment of God in glory, then a believer should despise it, as Christ is said to do

(Heb. 12:2), though His was a shameful death. But upon all other accounts and considerations, it is the height of stupidity and security to despise it.

♦ JOHN FLAVEL
"The Seamen's Catechism," in
Navigation Spiritualized, 206–7

Lord, be pleased to shake my clay cottage before Thou throw it down. May it totter awhile before it doth tumble. Let me be summoned before I am surprised. Deliver me from sudden death—not from sudden death in respect of itself, for I care not how short my passage be, so it be safe. Never any weary traveler complained that he came too soon to his journey's end. But let it not be sudden in respect of me. Make me always ready to receive death. Thus, no guest comes unawares to him who keeps a constant table.

♦ THOMAS FULLER
Good Thoughts, 24–25

It is not long since Elijah ran on foot and Ahab rode in his chariot; but now Elijah, he hath a chariot—a chariot of fire and horses of fire—a bright, a glorious, and shining chariot, a company of blessed angels to carry him into the holy and highest heavens. Let Ahab ride now; Elijah shall ride at the last. God's people shall have their chariots one day as well as others.

♦ ALEXANDER GROSSE
Deaths Deliverance, 28

For the day of death to the body is, as one saith, the birthday of eternity to the soul.

♦ ALEXANDER GROSSE
Deaths Deliverance, 36

Thou art young; thou canst not therefore say thou shalt not die as yet. Alas! Measure the coffins in the churchyard and thou wilt find some of thy length. Young and old are within the reach of death's scythe. Old men, indeed, go to death; their age calls for it. But young men cannot hinder death's coming unto them.

♦ WILLIAM GURNALL
Christian in Complete Armour, 767–68

Think, there is but one common road to all flesh…and the commonness of an evil makes it less fearful. What worlds of men are gone before us—yea, how many thousands out of one field! How many crowns and scepters lie piled up at the gates of death which their owners have left there as spoils to the conqueror! Have we been at so many graves and so often seen ourselves die in our friends, and do we shrink when our course cometh? Imagine you alone were exempted from the common law of mankind or were condemned to Methuselah's age; assure yourself, death is not now so fearful as your life would then be wearisome.

♦ JOSEPH HALL
Select Devotional Works, 247–48

She prayed again for all the church that she stood related to, that God would bring them all triumphing to glory. "Oh, friends," said she, "look well to the inward part, search every corner." When she perceived some to be weeping about her, she said, "Oh, weep not for me, for I rejoice, and Christ rejoices in me; weep for yourselves. Oh sirs, begin betimes. There is God's early, and man's. God's is presently; man's is at death or in old age or distress. Oh, seek God now presently and take this from me: begin with God, and He will end with you."

✦ JAMES JANEWAY
"Account of Some of the Death-Bed
Experiences of Mrs. B.," in *Saint's
Encouragement*, 146–47

When faith and love, which parted
    from thee never,
Had ripened thy just soul to dwell
    with God,
Meekly thou didst resign this
    earthy load
Of death, called life, which us
    from life doth sever.

Thy works, and alms, and all thy
    good endeavor,
Stayed not behind, nor in the
    grave were trod;
But, as Faith pointed with her
    golden rod,
Followed thee up to joy and
    bliss forever.

Love led them on; and Faith, who
    knew them best
Thy handmaids, clad them o'er
    with purple beams
And azure wings, that up they
    flew so drest,
And speak the truth of thee on
    glorious themes
Before the Judge; who thenceforth
    bid thee rest,
And drink thy fill of pure immortal
    streams.

✦ JOHN MILTON
sonnet 14, in *Complete
Poetical Works*, 543

Let thine heart and tongue be still employed in prayer to the Lord: first, for patience in thy trouble; secondly, for comfort in thine affliction; thirdly, for strength in His mercy; fourthly, for deliverance at His pleasure. Yea, endeavor even to die praying when thou art in the depth of miseries; and at the gates of death there is a depth of God's mercy which is ready to hear and help thee. Misery must call upon mercy.

✦ WILLIAM PERKINS
in Richard Rogers, *Garden of
Spirituall Flowers*, 24–25

The old cannot live long; the young may die very quickly.

✦ JOHN RAINOLDS
in Horn, *Puritan Remembrancer*, 241

Your child is not sent away but only sent before, like unto a star which, going out of our sight, doth not die and vanish but shineth in another hemisphere; you see her not, yet she doth shine in another country. If her glass were but a short hour, what she wanteth of time that she hath gotten of eternity; and you have to rejoice that you have now some furniture up in heaven. Build your nest upon no tree here, for you see God hath sold the forest to death; and every tree whereupon you would rest is ready to be cut down, to the end that we might fly and mount up and build upon the Rock and dwell in the holes of the Rock.

✦ SAMUEL RUTHERFORD
Garden of Spices, 198

Against this arrest there is no bail.

✦ GEORGE SWINNOCK
in Thomas, *Puritan Golden Treasury*, 69

For my own part, on mature deliberation, I don't think it a desirable thing for a good man who is ready to be worn away like a stone, by a long and continual dropping. May my house and soul be in order, and then the sooner it quits this vile body and leaves this wretched world, if in the twinkling of an eye, so much the better. To which there is but one circumstance more, which I should desire may be added, that I may die preaching the everlasting gospel or administering the Lord's Supper. May my taper be blown out in the sanctuary, and may I presently pass in an instant from serving the church militant here on earth to join with the church triumphant in heaven. But we must not be our own choosers, and to be sure God will dispose all things in the best manner for them that are His.

✦ NATHANIEL TAYLOR
Funeral Sermon [on Luke 12:40], 8

Death is a believer's ferryman to ferry him over to the land of rest; it opens the portal into heaven.... The day of a Christian's death is the birthday of his heavenly life; it is his ascension day to glory; it is his marriage day with Jesus Christ. After his funeral begins his marriage. Well then might Solomon say, "Better is the day of a man's death than the day of his birth."

✦ THOMAS WATSON
The Christian's Charter of Privileges,
in *Discourses*, 1:30

Death is a triumphant chariot to carry every child of God to his Father's mansion house.

✦ THOMAS WATSON
Lord's Prayer, 25

Thee we adore, eternal name!
And humbly own to Thee,
How feeble is our mortal frame,
What dying worms are we!

Our wasting lives grow shorter still,
As years and days increase;
And every beating pulse we tell,
Leaves but the number less.

Infinite joy or endless woe,
Attends on every breath;
And yet how unconcerned we go,
Just on the brink of death!

Waken, O Lord, our drowsy sense.
To walk this dangerous road;
And if our souls are hurried hence,
May they ascend to God!

✦ ISAAC WATTS
Devout Meditations, 159

DEATH: THE DESIRE OF THE GODLY

If believers are immediately with God after their dissolution, then it is their duty to long for that dissolution and cast many a longing look toward heaven. So did Paul: "I desire to be dissolved, and to be with Christ, which is far better." The advantages of this exchange are unspeakable: you have gold for brass; wine for water; substance for shadow; solid glory for very vanity. Oh! If the dust of this earth were but once blown out of your eyes that you might see the divine glory, how weary would you be to live, how willing to die!

✦JOHN FLAVEL
Fountain of Life, 322

Preserve in thyself a willingness to die. I mean a well-grounded, real willingness, not slavish or constrained through impatience under sufferings or discontent in an unwelcome condition, but sincere, from a longing after Jesus Christ, to enjoy Him in the full fruit of His redemption. This was Paul's temper (Phil. 1:21). There is indeed in every man naturally an averseness from death, being the dissolution of his frame, and an evil of punishment, and the grace of regeneration does not wholly take it away but only keeps it within due boundaries and raises up in the soul a supernatural desire of blessedness with Christ in heaven and a willingness to submit to death in order to the attaining thereof. Get thy heart wrought to this frame and hold it up.

✦ELKANAH WALES
Mount Ebal Levelled, 254–55

The apostle doth not say having a desire to die, but "to depart." What a wicked man fears, a godly man hopes for. "I desire," says Paul, "to depart"; a sinner cries, "I am loath to depart." David calls death a going out of the world (Ps. 39:13). A wicked man doth not go out, but is dragged out. If a wicked man were put to his choice, he would never come where God is but would choose the serpent's curse to eat dust (Gen.

3:14), but not to return to dust. A soul enlivened with grace looks upon the world as a wilderness wherein are fiery serpents, and he desires to get out of this wilderness. Simeon, having taken Christ in his arms, cries out, "Lord, now lettest thou thy servant depart in peace" (Luke 2:29). He that has taken Christ into the arms of his faith will sing Simeon's song: "Lord, let thy servant depart." The bird desires to go out of the cage though it be made of gold.

✦THOMAS WATSON
Gleanings, 116–17

DEATH: DYING IN THE LORD

Death is indeed a curse to sinners, but the course of nature unto saints; the direful executioner of God's wrath and law to all who die in their sin, but a messenger of divine favor to all who die in the Lord; a harbinger of peace to all who walk in uprightness; a grim porter to fetch home to their Father's mansions all that are God's children. Death is indeed a dismal doom on the sons of the first Adam, but the discharge of all sin, sorrow, pain, and travail to all the sons of the second Adam.

✦ZACHARY CROFTON
Defence against the Dread of Death, 33–34

Death will be your very good physician; it will cure all your diseases, end all your miseries, set you free from all troubles. And therefore as the people came readily to Bethesda to be healed of their infirmities, as we come cheerfully to the physician, so should we to the grave. For what is death to the people of God? What is it to them to die?

✦ ALEXANDER GROSSE
Deaths Deliverance, 35

To die in the Lord is to die in the faith of Christ, whom He sent into the world for the redemption thereof (John 3), which is done when four things are observed. First, if the sick man in his sickness call unto his remembrance what he hath done all his lifetime against the first and second table of the Lord's commandments; the second, if upon his examination he find his brother and neighbor hurt by him in goods or fame, he study unfeignedly to satisfy him as near as he can again in both; the third, that the sick man acknowledge unto the Lord as much as he hath offended against the commandments of the first table, with a detestation of them all; the fourth, that he ask of God, for the death of Christ, remission of them all.

✦ JOHN HOOPER
Early Writings, 563

It was a noble speech of good Dr. Preston when he lay a-dying and full of Christian confidence and comfort, "I shall change my place, but not my company." The meaning was that he had so acquainted himself with God here upon earth and had so much conversed with Him, that now that he was to die, his company should still be the same after death that it was in life.

✦ MATTHEW NEWCOMEN
Best Acquaintance, 69

DEATH: DYING WELL

Let us all lay hold on well-doing that we may have comfort in well-dying. We desire to shut up our last scene of life with..."Lord, into Thy hands I commend my spirit." Behold, while we live God says to us..."Man, into thy hands I commend My Spirit." As we use God's Spirit in life, God will use our spirit at death. If we open the doors of our hearts to His Spirit, He will open the doors of heaven to our spirit.

✦ THOMAS ADAMS
"The Soul's Refuge," in *Works*, 3:37

O my soul, look for death hourly, long for it greatly, prepare for it carefully, meet and welcome it joyfully, for it is Christ's part to direct His spouse, the soul, to Him, and thy friend that comes to set thee at liberty from thy sins, discharge thee from thy prison, dismiss thee from thy debts, and bring thee at once to enjoy all thy desires.

✦ ANONYMOUS
Life, 62–63

Well, young men, remember this: the frequent, the serious thoughts of death will prevent many a sin. It will arm you against many temptations. It will secure you from many afflictions. It will keep you from doting on the world. It will make you do much in a little time. It will make death easy when it comes, and it will make you look out betimes for a kingdom that shakes not, for riches that corrupt not, and glory that fadeth not away.

Therefore, do not—oh, do not—put the day of death far from you!
✦ THOMAS BROOKS
Apples of Gold, 148–49

It is the forgetfulness of death that makes life sinful and death terrible (Ps. 90:12; Lam. 1:9). And we should begin this exercise of meditation betimes. "Remember now thy Creator in the days of thy youth" (Eccl. 12:1).
✦ NICHOLAS BYFIELD
Cure of the Fear of Death, 186

[Death], among others, ought often to be thought on, to have all things ready for our departure out of this wretched world. And therefore not only to set our outward estate in order (which natural wise men do) for the good and peace of our posterity but especially to set our spiritual state in such a readiness that we may with continual care and comfort wait for our change and our Savior's second coming; and withal to leave to our posterity some testimony of God's fatherly dealing with us and fidelity in performing His promise to us, the seed of faithful parents, that our posterity may be hereby stirred up to serve the Lord God of their fathers.
✦ EZEKIEL CULVERWELL
Time Well Spent, 64–65

Think not so much what death is as from whom he comes and for what. We receive even homely messengers from great persons, not without respect to their masters. And what matters it who he be, so that he bring us good news? What news can be better than this, that God sends for you to take possession of a kingdom? Let them fear death who know him but as a messenger sent from hell, whom their conscience accuseth of a life willfully filthy and binds over secretly to condemnation. We know whither we are going and whom we have believed; let us pass on cheerfully through these black gates unto our glory.... Know that our improvidence only adds terror unto death. Think of death, and you shall not fear it. Do you not see that even bears and tigers seem not terrible to those that live with them? How have we seen their keepers sport with them when the beholders durst scarce trust their chain! Be acquainted with death; though he look grim upon you at first, you shall find him (yea, you shall make him) a good companion. Familiarity cannot stand with fear.
✦ JOSEPH HALL
Select Devotional Works, 248

A little before [Philip Henry's] sickness and death, one asked him how he did. He answered, "I find the chips fly off apace; the tree will be down shortly." And he was often used to say, "It is a serious thing to die, and to die is a work by itself."
✦ PHILIP HENRY
Life and Sayings, 9

Nothing makes a deathbed so uneasy and hard as a life spent in the service of sin and lust; nothing makes a deathbed so soft and sweet as a life spent in the service of God and Christ.
✦ MATTHEW MEAD
Almost Christian Discovered, 232

Inure yourself by little and little to die, before you come to that point that you must needs die. He that leaves the world before the world leaves him gives death the hand, like a welcome messenger, and departs in peace.

✦ WILLIAM PERKINS
in Richard Rogers, *Garden of Spirituall Flowers*, 23–24

Walking with God will make death sweet. It was Augustus's wish that he might have a quiet easy death, without much pain. If anything makes our pillow easy at death, it will be this: that we have walked with God in our generation. Do we think walking with God can do us any hurt? Did we ever hear any cry out upon their deathbed that they have been too holy, that they have prayed too much or walked with God too much? No, that which hath cut them to the heart hath been this: that they have walked no more closely with God. They have wrung their hands and torn their hair to think that they have been so bewitched with the pleasures of the world. Close walking with God will make our enemy death to be at peace with us.

✦ THOMAS WATSON
Godly Man's Picture, 164

The eminently useful have more manifest grounds for a comfortable death than others can expect. Death makes a great discovery of the true value of things; whatever renders this safe and easy we ought highly to esteem.

✦ DANIEL WILLIAMS
Excellency of a Publick Spirit, 51

DEATH: MADE EASIER

How then can that heart get to glory that is nailed down to the world and things below? Be daily loosening your hearts from the world, estates, houses, lands, trades, friends, relations, and everything below, for you may not have time to get them off without loss when death comes. You must leave them all shortly, and you know not how soon, to go to better friends and interests. These have been snares and spears to your souls, and have given you many a wound, and still hinder your speeding to glory, and why should you be loath to part with them? O Christians! If you are willing to be with Christ, you will give your hearts warning to be gone from these tabernacles and to take their leave of this world daily.

✦ BARTHOLOMEW ASHWOOD
Heavenly Trade, 462–63

If God have blessed thee with any competent state of wealth, make thy will in thy health time. It will neither put thee farther from thy goods nor hasten thee sooner to thy death, but it will be a greater ease to thy mind in freeing thee from a great trouble when thou shalt have most need of quiet. For when thy house is set in order, thou shalt be better enabled to set thy soul in order and to dispose of thy journey toward God. If thou hast children, give to every one of them a portion, according to thy ability in thy lifetime, that thy life may seem an ease and not a yoke to them; yet so give, as that thy children may be still beholden unto thee and not thou unto them. But if thou keep all in thy

hands whilst thou live, they may thank death and not thee for the portion that thou leave them.
♦ LEWIS BAYLY
Practice of Piety, 268–69

It was the saying of an eminent minister on his deathbed that he had much peace and quietness not so much from a greater measure of grace than other Christians had or from any immediate witness of the Spirit, but because he had a more clear understanding of the covenant of grace than many others, having studied it and preached it so many years as he had done. Doubtless, had Christians a more clear and full understanding of the covenant of grace, they would live more holily, serviceably, humbly, fruitfully, comfortably, and sweetly than they do, and they would die more willingly, readily, and cheerfully than many—may I not say most—Christians do.
♦ THOMAS BROOKS
Cabinet of Choice Jewels, 96

A godly man shall have the greatest benefit of his piety and graces when he draws nearest to his death.
♦ ROBERT CLEAVER
AND JOHN DOD
Plain and Familiar Exposition, 79

Preparation for death, whereof every affliction is a messenger or harbinger, and therefore when afflictions come, we have warning given us of death's approach and so are justly occasioned to renew our preparation for the entertainment of him. This use the apostle Paul made of his afflictions (1 Corinthians 15), when by them he learned to die daily. For besides that they put us in mind of our mortality, they themselves, being little kinds of death, make death seem less grievous unto us.
♦ DANIEL DYKE
"The School of Affliction," in
Two Treatises, 364

Did Christ meet death with such a heavy heart? Let the hearts of Christians be the lighter for this when they come to die. The bitterness of death was all squeezed into Christ's cup. He was made to drink up the very dregs of it, that so our death might be the sweeter to us. Alas! There is nothing now left in death that is frightful or troublesome beside the pain of dissolution, that natural evil of it.
♦ JOHN FLAVEL
Fountain of Life, 212

He that lives well cannot choose but die well, for if he die suddenly, yet he dies not unpreparedly; if by leisure, the conscience of his well-led life makes his death more comfortable. But it is seldom seen that he which lives ill dies well, for the conscience of his former evils, his present pain, and the expectation and fear of greater so take up his heart that he cannot seek God. And now it is just with God not to be sought or not to be found because He sought to him in his lifetime and was repulsed. Whereas, therefore, there are usually two main cares of good men: to live well and die well. I will have but this one, to live well.
♦ JOSEPH HALL
Meditations and Vows, 30–31

I thank thee, O heavenly Father, for the many advantages of sickness to weaken the power of sin; to humble my pride and cure my worldliness and sensuality; to reduce me from wandering; to empty me of self-conceit; to awaken the consideration of death and judgment; to impress the thoughts of the vanity of this world and the eternity of the next; to assist me to mortify the flesh, to rule my passions, to exercise patience and quicken me in prayer and try my faith and love and excite my diligence to redeem time and convince me of the worth and uncertainty of it; and thereby promote my preparations for my final change.

✦ JOHN SHOWER
Serious Reflections, 86

In well settling your worldly estates — do this in the time of health, that it may be your last will; yours, and not the will of those that are about you who otherwise may be practicing upon you when you are sick and weak in body and mind too. The neglecting or the not doing this to their own full satisfaction has caused very great uneasiness of mind in many when they have been suddenly within the near views of death. We need not to have these worldly matters to distract and decompose us when we have much weightier affairs, enough to take up all the little remainder of our time and our most serious thoughts.

✦ NATHANIEL TAYLOR
Funeral Sermon [on Luke 12:40], 18

When a saint comes to die, his greatest grief is that he hath done no more for God, and his greatest joy is that God hath done so much for him.

✦ RALPH VENNING
Canaan's Flowings, 44

Sickness is but a harbinger to bespeak lodging for death.

✦ THOMAS WATSON
in Horn, *Puritan Remembrancer*, 326

If anything makes our pillow easy at death, it will be that we have endeavored to do God's will on earth. Did you ever hear any cry out on their deathbed that they have done God's will too much? No!

✦ THOMAS WATSON
Lord's Prayer, 155

DEATH: PROVIDES PERSPECTIVE

When we lose a neighbor, a friend, a brother, we weep and howl and lament as if, with Rachel, we could never be comforted; but the body once interred and the funeral ceremonies ended, if we do not stay to inquire for some legacies, we run back with all possible haste to our former sins and turpitudes, as if there had been no such matter. Alas, that the farthest end of all our thoughts should be the thought of our ends!

✦ THOMAS ADAMS
Exposition upon…Second…Peter, 667

My brethren, our days are short, our work is great, our sun's a-setting, death is hasting to put a period to all our works. Or howsoever, if we be not dissolved, we must be changed, and how soon none of us can tell. Only this we know: it will be done in the twinkling of an eye. So that we cannot promise ourselves to live one moment longer than just we see ourselves alive. I cannot promise myself to speak this sentence out to you, neither can you promise yourselves to hear this sentence out from me; for before I have spoken or you have heard these words, we may all be standing in another world before the judgment seat of Christ. And thus do we all stand upon the very brink of eternity, ready every moment to launch into it.

✦ WILLIAM BEVERIDGE
Thesaurus Theologious, 4:190

To silence and quiet your souls under the afflicting hand of God, dwell much upon the brevity, or shortness, of man's life. This present life is not life, but a motion, a journey toward life.... Thou hast but a day to live, and perhaps thou mayest be now in the twelfth hour of that day. Therefore, hold out faith and patience; thy troubles and thy life will shortly end together. Therefore hold thy peace: thy grave is going to be made, thy sun is near setting, death begins to call thee off the stage of this world, death stands at thy back, thou must shortly sail forth upon the ocean of eternity. Though thou hast a great deal of work to do, a God to honor, a Christ to close with, a soul to save, a race to run, a crown to win, a hell to escape, a pardon to beg, a heaven to make sure, yet thou hast but a little time to do it in. Thou hast one foot in the grave. Thou art even a-going ashore

on eternity, and wilt thou now cry out of thy afflictions?

✦ THOMAS BROOKS
Mute Christian, 248–49

Rouse your heart to diligence. If a man have much to write and is almost at the end of his paper, he will put much matter in a little room.

✦ JOHN FLAVEL
Golden Gems, 104

Though death shut all men's eyes, yet the approach of death opens them oft to see more of themselves than ever before.

✦ WILLIAM GREENHILL
Exposition of the Prophet Ezekiel, 616

God will have us ignorant of the day of our death that we might be ready every day. We are but tenants at will and know not how soon our great Lord and landlord may eject us.

✦ ANDREW JONES
Dying Man's Last Sermon, 11

Whenever I see the funeral of another, let me think thus with myself: Why might not I have been that man or woman that is now carried to the grave?

✦ JOHN SHOWER
Serious Reflections, 77

Are the years of my life but few, and they hastening to a period? And may this be my last? Let me not then greedily covet riches and abundance and waste my little time to scrape together large provisions for many years to come when I have no assurance to see the end of this. Is it becoming such a belief to toil from day to day, that I may lay up that which I must so soon leave? As if I were to spend an eternity here on earth and in the meanwhile neglect the one thing necessary. Am I not upon the shore of eternity? May not the next tide carry me off? And shall I spend my whole life in diversions from the main business of it? Have I nothing else to do but to gather shells (if they were pearls, the absurdity were still the same) and pile them up in heaps, till I am snatched away past all recovery?

✦ JOHN SHOWER
Serious Reflections, 98

Meditate upon the uncertainty of time. We have no lease, but may be turned out the next hour. There are so many casualties that it is a wonder if life be not cut off by untimely death. How soon may God seal us a lease of ejectment? Our grave may be digged before night. Today we may lie upon a pillow of down; tomorrow we may be laid upon a pillow of dust.

✦ THOMAS WATSON
A Christian on the Mount,
in *Discourses*, 1:225

We are not born angels. Die we must; therefore, we had need carry always a death's head about us. The basilisk, if it sees a man first, it kills him; but if he sees it first, it doth him no hurt. The basilisk death, if it sees us first before we see it, it is dangerous; but if we see it first by meditating upon it, it doth us no hurt. Study death; often walk among the tombs. It is the thoughts of death beforehand that must do us good. In a dark night, one torch carried

before a man is worth many torches carried after him. One serious thought of death beforehand, one tear shed for sin before death is worth a thousand shed after, when it is too late.

✦ THOMAS WATSON
The Christian's Charter of Privileges,
in *Discourses*, 1:32

Hast thou seen the vanity of man as a mortal, dying creature? It is an easy matter to say, alas, "We must all die"; but hast thou felt the penetrating force of this truth, and does it influence thy whole conduct? Art thou not still at every turn putting thy confidence in one creature or another whose breath is in his nostrils and whose death disappoints thy hope? Or hast thou removed thy dependence from all creatures to God and fixed thy hope in Him that lives forever? O blessed effect of the meditation of death!

✦ ISAAC WATTS
Devout Meditations, 124–25

DEATH, TERROR OF

Death is said to be the king of terrors; and this is the terror of death, after that the judgment. All these, the impress of God upon their hearts, the wonders of God in the world, the vengeance of God executed on sin, the sense of guilt, and of a judgment to come do preach to the consciences of sinners that "it is a fearful thing to fall into the hands of the living God."

✦ RICHARD ALLEINE
Heaven Opened, 180

Beloved, you know death is strong; it is the king of terrors and the terror of kings. It subdues all sorts of people: high and low, rich and poor, old and young, good and bad; the greatest monarchs, kings, and emperors have been thrown down by death. Where did ever that man dwell that was too strong for death? If strength could have resisted it, then Samson had missed it. Could greatness have overlooked it, Nebuchadnezzar had escaped it. Could beauty have outfaced it, then Absalom had never met it. Could riches have bribed it, Dives [Luke 16:19–31] had avoided it. But, alas! None of these were hardy enough for death.

✦ WILLIAM DYER
Christ's Famous Titles, 41

Our graves would not be so sweet and comfortable to us when we come to lie down in them if Jesus had not lain there before us and for us. Death is a dragon, the grave its den—a place of dread and terror. But Christ goes into its den, there grapples with it, and forever overcomes it; disarms it of all its terror and not only makes it cease to be inimical but to become exceeding beneficial to the saints—a bed of rest and a perfumed bed. They do but go into Christ's bed, where He lay before them.

✦ JOHN FLAVEL
Fountain of Life, 370

Even death itself brings a terror with it that nothing can conquer but faith—I mean conquer duly. He is not crowned that doth not overcome by faith. It is only to be done through the death of Christ. He delivered them who through fear of death were in bondage all their days. There is no deliverance that is true and real from a bondage frame of spirit to death but by faith in Christ.

✦ JOHN OWEN
"Discourse 3 on 1 Cor. 10:16,"
in *Twenty-Five Discourses*, 35

DEFECTS: PHYSICAL

Natural crookedness or want of beauty and defects are not the creature's fault, but the Creator's pleasure; and therefore he that finds fault with them finds fault with God.

✦ RALPH VENNING
Canaan's Flowings, 46

DELIGHT IN GOD

Behold Him in the infinite perfections of His being: His omnipotence, omniscience, and His goodness; His holiness, eternity, immutability, etc. And as your eye delights in an excellent picture or comely buildings or fields or gardens not because they are yours, but because they are a delectable object to the eye, so let your minds delight themselves in God considered in Himself, as the only object of highest delight.

✦ RICHARD BAXTER
Baxteriana, 154

Diligently labor, that God and holiness may be thy chief delight. And this holy delight may be the ordinary temperament of thy religion.

✦ RICHARD BAXTER
A Christian Directory, in
Practical Works, 2:408

Rightly understand what delight in God it is that you must seek and exercise. It is not a mere sensitive delight, which is exercised about the objects of sense or fancy and is common to beasts with men; nor is it the delights of immediate intuition of God, such as the blessed have in heaven; nor is it an enthusiastic delight, consisting in irrational raptures and joys, of which we can give no account of the reason. Nor is it a delight inconsistent with sorrow and fear, when they are duties; but it is the solid, rational complacency of the soul in God and holiness, arising from the apprehensions of that in Him, which is justly delectable to us. And it is such as, in estimation of its object and inward complacency and gladness though not in passionate joy or mirth, must excel our delight in temporal pleasure and must be the end of all our humiliations and other inferior duties.

✦ RICHARD BAXTER
A Christian Directory, in
Practical Works, 2:408–9

The benefits which follow our delight in God (besides the sweetness of it) are unspeakable: (1) Delight in God will prove that thou knowest Him and loves Him and that thou art prepared for His kingdom, for all that truly delight in Him shall enjoy Him. (2) Prosperity, which is but the small addition of earthly things, will not easily corrupt thee or transport thee. (3) Adversity, which is the withholding of earthly delights, will not much grieve thee or easily deject thee. (4) Thou wilt receive more profit by a sermon or good book or conference which thou delight in than others that delight not in them will do in many. (5) All thy service will be sweet to thyself and acceptable to God. If thou delight in Him, He doth certainly delight in thee. Thou hast a continual feast with thee which may sweeten all the crosses of thy life and afford thee greater joy than thy sorrow is in thy saddest case. (6) When you delight in God, your creature delight will be sanctified to you and warrantable in its proper place, which in others is idolatrous, or corrupt.

✦ RICHARD BAXTER
A Christian Directory, in
Practical Works, 2:415–16

That, therefore, which we are to understand ourselves called to, under the name of delighting in God, is the keeping of our souls open to divine influences and communications—thirsting after them, praying and waiting for them, endeavoring to improve them and cooperate with them, and to stir up ourselves to such exercises of religion as are most suitable to our present state, together with an allowing and applying ourselves to stay and taste, in our progress and course, the sweetness and delightfulness of those communications and operations whereof we have any present experience.

✦ JOHN HOWE
Treatise of Delighting in God, 100

Delight in religion crowns all our services. Therefore, David counsels his son Solomon not only to serve God but to serve Him "with a willing mind" (1 Chron. 28:9). Delight in duty is better than duty itself, as it is worse for a man to delight in sin than to commit it because there is more of the will in sin. So delight in duty is to be preferred before duty: "O how love I thy law" (Ps. 119:97)! It is not how much we do, but how much we love. Hypocrites may obey God's law, but the saints love His law; this carries away the garland.

✦ THOMAS WATSON
"The Saint's Spiritual Delight,"
in *Discourses*, 1:190

Delight in God's service makes us resemble the angels in heaven. They serve God with cheerfulness; as soon as God speaks the word, they are ambitious to obey. How are they ravished with delight while they are praising God! In heaven we shall be as the angels; spiritual delight would make us like them here. To serve God by constraint is to be like the devil. All the devils in hell obey God, but it is against their will; they yield a passive obedience. But service which comes off with delight is angelical. This is that we pray for, that "God's will may be done on earth as it is in heaven." Is it not done with delight there?

✦ THOMAS WATSON
"The Saint's Spiritual Delight,"
in *Discourses*, 1:192

DEPRAVITY

There was a holy man that rarely heard of other men's crimson sins, but he usually bedewed the place with his tears, considering that the seeds of those very sins were in his own nature.

In thy nature thou hast that which would lead thee, with the Pharisees, to oppose Christ; and, with Judas, to betray Christ; and, with Pilate, to condemn Christ; and, with the soldiers, to crucify Christ. Oh! What a monster wouldst thou prove should God but leave thee to act suitably to that sinful and woeful nature of thine.

✦ THOMAS BROOKS
Smooth Stones, 41

DEPRESSION/MELANCHOLY

Judge not of so great a cause in a time of melancholy, when fears and confusions make you unfit. But in such a case as that, as also whenever Satan would disturb your settled faith or tempt you at his pleasure to be still new questioning resolved cases and discerned truths, abhor his suggestions and give them no entertainment in your thoughts, but cast them back into the tempter's face. There is not one melancholy person of a multitude but is violently assaulted with temptations to blasphemy and unbelief when they have but half the use of reason and no composedness of mind to debate such controversies with the devil. It is not fit for them in this incapacity to hearken to any of those suggestions which draw them to dispute the foundations of their faith, but to cast them away with resolute abhorrence.

✦ RICHARD BAXTER
A Christian Directory, in
Practical Works, 2:508

Usually other causes go before this disease of melancholy (except in some bodies naturally prone to it), and therefore before I speak of the cure of it, I will briefly touch them. And one of the most common causes is sinful impatience, discontents and cares proceeding from a sinful love of some bodily interest and from a want of sufficient submission to the will of God, and trust in Him, and taking heaven for a satisfying portion. I must necessarily use all these words to show the true nature of this complicated disease of souls. The "ands" tell you that it is a conjunction of many sins, which in themselves are of no small malignity; and were they the predominant bent and habit of heart and life, they would be the signs of a graceless state. But while they are hated and overcome not grace, but our heavenly portion is more esteemed, chosen, and sought than earthly prosperity, the mercy of God through Christ doth pardon it and will at last deliver us from all.

✦ RICHARD BAXTER
Preservatives against Melancholy, 28–29

Melancholy is a dark and dusky humor which disturbs both soul and body, and the cure of it belongs rather to the physician than to the divine. It is a most pestilent humor where it abounds; one calls it the devil's bath. It is a humor that unfits a man for all sorts of services, but especially those that concern his soul, his spiritual estate, his everlasting condition. The melancholy person tires the physician, grieves the minister, wounds relations, and makes

sport for the devil. There are five sorts of persons that the devil makes his ass to ride in triumph upon—namely, the ignorant person, the unbelieving person, the proud person, the hypocritical person, and the melancholy person. Melancholy is a disease that works strange passions, strange imaginations, and strange conclusions. It unmans a man; it makes a man call good evil and evil good, sweet bitter and bitter sweet, light darkness and darkness light. The distemper of the body oftentimes causeth distemper of the soul, for the soul follows the temper of the body.

✦ THOMAS BROOKS
Cabinet of Choice Jewels, 83–84

There are times of desertion when graces are not visible. In darkness we can neither see black nor white. In times of great dejection and discouragement, the work of a Christian is not to try, but believe: "Let him trust in the name of the LORD, and stay upon his God" (Isa. 50:10). It is most seasonable to encourage the soul to acts of faith and to reflect upon the absolute promises rather than conditional. The absolute promises were intended by God as attractives and encouragements to such distressed souls. There is a time when the soul is apt to slumber and to be surprised with a careless security; then it is good to awake it by a serious trial. To a close carnal spirit an absolute promise is as poison; to a dejected spirit, as cheering wine. When the soul lies under fear and sense of guilt, it is unable to judge; therefore, examination only increases the trouble. But again, when the heart is drowsy and careless, trial is most seasonable, and it is best to reflect upon the conditional promises, that we may look after the qualifications expressed in them ere we take comfort.

✦ THOMAS MANTON
Practical Exposition on the Epistle of James, 109

If melancholy be the cause of the sadness of thy thoughts, then physics and exercise may be requisite for thy body (to remove and prevent the cause thereof) as well as cheerful exercitation for the mind. Melancholy is Satan's chariot in which he rides and triumphs over sad-thinking souls.

✦ EDWARD REYNER
Precepts for Christian Practice, 314

In melancholy distempers, especially when there is guilt on the soul, we can find no comfort in wife, children, friends, estate, etc. It is a pitiful state when body, soul, and conscience all are distempered, but even now let a Christian look to God's nature and promises. Though he cannot live by sight, yet let him live much by faith.

✦ RICHARD SIBBES
Divine Meditations and Holy Contemplations, 88

DESERTION

I am sure of this: that God loves to see the workings of all our graces, our faith and love especially. There are some graces that do not open nor show themselves but in the sunshining day of God's presence. When the sun shines, the marigold opens. When the sun shines, the fish that lay at the bottom of the water in a cloudy day swim at the top of the water and are seen. In the sun-shining day of God's presence, then, our thankfulness, our joy, our assurance float and are to be seen upon the top of the water. But there are other graces that are best seen when God withdraws and when God is absent—faith in God and love to God especially.

✦ WILLIAM BRIDGE
Christ and the Covenant, in *Works*, 3:164

Divine desertion, generally considered, is God's withdrawing Himself from any, not as to His essence, for that fills heaven and earth and constantly remains the same; but it is the withdrawment of His favor, grace, and love. When these are gone, God is said to be gone. And this is done two ways: either absolutely and wholly or respectively, and only as to manifestation. In the first sense, devils are forsaken of God. They once were in His favor and love, but they have utterly and finally lost it. God is so withdrawn from them as that He will never take them into favor anymore. In the other sense He sometimes forsakes His dearest children; that is, He removes all sweet manifestations of His favor and love for a time.

✦ JOHN FLAVEL
Fountain of Life, 328

When God hides His face from His child, His heart may be toward him, as Joseph when he spake roughly to his brethren and made them believe he would take them for spies, still his heart was toward them, and he was as full of love as he could hold; he was fain to go aside and weep. So, God is full of love to His children, even when He seems to look strange. And as Moses, his mother, when she put her child into the ark of bulrushes and went away a little from it, yet still her eye was toward it. "The babe wept"; aye, and the mother wept too. So God, when He goes aside as if He had forsaken His children, yet He is full of sympathy and love toward them. God may change His countenance but not break His covenant. It is one thing for God to desert, another thing to disinherit (Hos. 11:8).

✦ THOMAS WATSON
The Beatitudes, in *Discourses*, 2:327–28

DESPAIR

Despair is hope stark dead; presumption is hope stark mad. This enrages it, the other strangles it.

✦ THOMAS ADAMS
*Exposition upon…Second…
Peter*, 437

All other sins may be carried away and buried in oblivion, but despair is a rejection of pardoning mercy. Judas sinned more grievously by despairing of mercy than by betraying his Master, and Cain sinned more by thinking his sins to be more than God could pardon than by killing his brother. Despair is the sin of hell.

✦ ISAAC AMBROSE
Christian Warrior, 47

Blessed be God, who has made it my duty to hope for His salvation. Hope is the ease—yea, the life—of our hearts that else would break—yea, die within us. Despair is no small part of hell. God cherishes hope, as He is the lover of souls. Satan, our enemy, cherishes despair when his way of blind presumption fails.

✦ RICHARD BAXTER
Baxteriana, 233

If the good ye desire appear impossible, that stirs up despair. Despair is the excess or extremity of fear or a casting away of confidence and hope.

✦ EDWARD REYNER
Precepts for Christian Practice, 387

We know it is the pride of Satan to imitate God; as God magnifies His power in bringing strength out of weakness, so doth the devil labor to gain the glory of a strong enemy by the ruinating of a great saint with the temptation of a weak sex. Nor is he herein more apish than cunning, for the end of the devil's conflicts is the despair of his enemy. He gets Judas to betray his master that he may after get him to hang himself. And he hath the same end in Peter's denial which he had in Judas's treason. Now what is there that can more draw a man to despair than an apprehension of greatness in his sin? And what fall greater than to be foiled by a question put by a maid? What could more aggravate Peter's sin than that the voice of a maid should be stronger to overcome him than the faith in a Jesus to sustain him? The devil tempts us that he may draw us unto sin, but he tempts us by weak instruments that he may draw us unto despair.

✦ EDWARD REYNOLDS
*Meditations on the Fall and
Rising of St. Peter*, 27–28

Despair cuts the sinews of endeavor.

✦ THOMAS WATSON
in Horn, *Puritan Remembrancer*, 154

Despair…affronts God, undervalues Christ's blood, damns the soul. "They said, There is no hope: but we will walk after our own devices, and we will every one do the imagination of his evil heart" (Jer. 18:12). This is the language of despair: There is no hope. I had as good follow my sins still and be damned for something. Despair presents God to the soul as a judge clad in the garments of vengeance (Isa. 59:17). Judas's despair was in some sense worse than his treason. Despair destroys repentance, for the proper ground of repentance is mercy.

✦ THOMAS WATSON
The Beatitudes, in *Discourses*, 2:113

DEVIL (See also SATAN)

Though the devil be the greatest scholar in the world, and though he have more learning than all the men in the world, yet there are many thousand secrets and mysteries in the gospel of grace that he knows not really, spiritually, feelingly, efficaciously, powerfully, thoroughly, and savingly.

✦ THOMAS BROOKS
Privy Key of Heaven, 46

The hell of devils belongs to [God's] authority. They have cast themselves out of the arms of His grace into the furnace of His justice. They have by their revolt forfeited the treasure of His goodness but cannot exempt themselves from the scepter of His dominion. When they would not own Him as a Lord Father, they are under Him as a Lord Judge. They are cast out of His affection but not freed from His yoke. He rules over the good angels as His subjects, over the evil ones as His rebels.

✦ STEPHEN CHARNOCK
Selections, 186–87

Adam's fall was the devil's masterpiece; to bring men into his own condemnation is the trophy he glories in.

✦ ELISHA COLES
Practical Discourse, 201

"Behold, the devil shall cast some of you into prison, that ye may be tried; and ye shall have tribulation ten days" (Rev. 2:10). Here are four remarkable limitations upon Satan and his agents in reference to the people of God: a limitation as to the persons—not all, but some; a limitation of the punishment—a prison, not a grave, not hell; a limitation upon them as to the end—for trial, not ruin; and lastly, as to the duration—not as long as they please, but ten days.

✦ JOHN FLAVEL
Navigation Spiritualized, 74

The devil's empire is confined to place as well as time: he is the ruler of this lower world, not of the heavenly. The highest the devil can go is the air, called the prince thereof, as being the utmost marches of his empire; he hath nothing to do with the upper world. Heaven fears no devil, and therefore its gates stand always open.

◆ WILLIAM GURNALL
Christian in Complete Armour, 104

THE DEVIL:

My words, I see, no place at all can find
Within the center of thy evil mind;
I'll leave thee therefore with my
    dreadful curse,
Which is as bad as hell, nay it is worse
Than all the plagues of the infernal
    lake;
And let all those who love me
    vengeance take
Upon so vile a wretch; and though I do
Forsake thee now, within a day or two
I'll come again, and will thy soul
    torment
'Til thou of thy repentance shalt
    repent.

THE YOUTH:

O Lord, I praise Thee for that glorious
    power,
Which helped my soul in such a
    needful hour
Of strong assaults from the vile
    wicked one;
Thou helpest me to resist him, and
    he's gone.
Therefore, dear God, be pleased to
    inflame

My heart with grace to magnify thy
    name:
And when he comes again,
    O then be near,
And let thy truth also for me appear.
Though I am young and weak,
    I shall thereby
Not fear the assaults of any enemy.
Come, speak, O truth, wilt thou
    be on my side,
'Tis in thy strength still I very
    much confide.
Though I am feeble, thou art mighty
    strong;
And whilst for me, there's none
    can do me wrong.

◆ BENJAMIN KEACH
War with the Devil, 84–85

DILIGENCE / INDUSTRY

By *industry* we understand a serious and steady application of mind joined with a vigorous exercise of our active faculties in prosecution of any reasonable, honest, useful design, in order to the accomplishment or attainment of some considerable good; as, for instance, a merchant is industrious who continues intent and active in driving on his trade for acquiring wealth; a soldier is industrious who is watchful for occasion and earnest in action toward obtaining the victory; and a scholar is industrious who doth assiduously bend his mind to study for getting knowledge.

◆ ISAAC BARROW
"Of Industry in General,"
in *Sermons*, 244

Industry doth beget ease by procuring good habits and facility of acting things expedient for us to do. By taking pains today, we shall need less pains tomorrow; and by continuing the exercise, within awhile we shall need no pains at all, but perform the most difficult tasks of duty or of benefit to us with perfect ease—yea, commonly with great pleasure. What sluggish people account hard and irksome (as to rise early, to hold close to study or business, to bear some hardship) will be natural and sweet, as proceeding from another nature raised in us by use. Industry doth breed assurance and courage, needful for the undertaking and prosecution of all necessary business or for the performance of all duties incumbent on us.

✦ ISAAC BARROW
"Of Industry in General,"
in *Sermons*, 267

One asking what was the best compost to manure land, it was answered, the dust of the master's feet.

✦ THOMAS FULLER
in Horn, *Puritan Remembrancer*, 204

The…antidote against the wiles of Satan is diligence and industry in your calling. The bird while it is flying is safe, but when it sits and perches upon a tree, it becomes an object for any instruments wherewith to shoot it and destroy it. And so a Christian, when he is busy in his calling, is in a great measure safe from temptations, but when he becomes idle and doth not busy himself in that station God hath set him in, he becomes fit ground and soil for Satan to sow any temptation and lust in. Idleness exposes the soul to all its spiritual enemies, and whereas it is the devil's business to tempt us, it is an idle man's business to tempt the devil.

✦ WILLIAM SPURSTOWE
Wiles of Satan, 106

Diligence, as it relates to trade, is a habitual employment of our bodily and mental powers about our proper callings in a just and happy medium between idleness, supineness, and trifling curiosity on the one hand and slavish drudging and immoderate care on the other.

✦ RICHARD STEELE
Religious Tradesman, 81

DISCERNMENT

A Christian in all his ways must have three guides: truth, charity, wisdom—truth to go before him; charity and wisdom on either hand. If any of the three be absent, he walks amiss. I have seen some do hurt by following a truth uncharitably; and others, while they would salve up an error with love, have failed in their wisdom and offended against justice. A charitable untruth and an uncharitable truth, an unwise managing of truth or love are all to be carefully avoided of him that would go with a right foot in the narrow way.

✦ JOSEPH HALL
"Holy Observations," in
Select Tracts, 317

There is gold in ore which God and His Spirit in us can distinguish. A carnal man's heart is like a dungeon wherein is nothing to be seen but horror and confusion. This light makes us judicious and humble upon clearer sight of God's purity and our own uncleanness and makes us able to discern the work of the Spirit in another.

✦ RICHARD SIBBES
Bruised Reed and Smoking Flax, 73

DISCIPLESHIP

You have heard much of Christ. Have you learned Christ? The Jews, as one saith, carried Christ in their Bibles but not in their hearts (Romans 14). Their sound went into all the earth (Rom. 10:18). The prophets and apostles were as trumpets whose sound went abroad into the world, yet many thousands who heard the noise of these trumpets had not learned Christ. They have not all obeyed (v. 16). A man may know much of Christ and yet not learn Christ. The devils knew Christ (Matt. 8:29). A man may preach Christ and yet not learn Christ, as Judas. A man may profess Christ and yet not learn Christ. There are many professors in the world that Christ will profess against (Matt. 7:22–23). What is it then to learn Christ? To learn Christ is to be made like Christ when the divine characters of His holiness are engraven upon our hearts.

✦ SIMEON ASHE
Primitive Divinity, 21

Whosoever will take Christ truly must take as well His yoke as His crown; as well His sufferings as His salvation; as well His grace as His mercy; as well His Spirit to lead as His blood to redeem.

✦ SAMUEL CLARK
Saint's Nosegay, 103–4

They who will not wear Christ's yoke will much less bear His burden.

✦ WILLIAM GURNALL
in Horn, *Puritan Remembrancer*, 126

Some commands of God, as those which are inward, are contrary to our affections; others, as those which enforce duties external, are contrary to our interests. But we must take Christ's yoke (Matt. 11:29). A main thing to be looked at in our first applications to God is this: Are we willing to give up ourselves to the will of God without reservation? Can I subject all without any hesitancy and reluctance of thought to the obedience of Christ (2 Cor. 10:5)?

✦ THOMAS MANTON
Practical Exposition on the Epistle of James, 160

Christians are to take up a double yoke—the yoke of evangelical command and the yoke of the cross that accompanies them. In both, subjection is requisite—in the one, subjection to Christ's authority commanding; in the other, subjection to His providence ordering. And that Christians may be subject to both, they must look to the great pattern and learn meekness and humility from Him.

✦ EDWARD POLHILL
Armatura Dei, 151

Christ requires nothing but for your good. And ask but your own souls why you are not in love with the ways of Christ and with the counsels and commands of Jesus Christ, and you are notable to give an answer, for 'tis only Satan's suggestions to make you think the yoke of Christ to be uneasy. He accuses Christ to you that he may never want whereof to accuse you before God night and day, and will you hearken to his delusions? Will you willingly bear the yoke of the world, the yoke of your lusts, the yoke of Satan and only refuse the yoke of Christ? What hath the Lord Jesus Christ deserved at your hands that you should be under anyone's command and only refuse to be under the command of Jesus Christ?

✦ JEREMIAH WHITAKER
Christians Great Design on Earth, 37–38

DISCIPLINE

God corrects with the same love that He crowns me. God is now training me up for heaven; He carves me to make me a polished pillar fit to stand in the heavenly mansion.

✦ SIMEON ASHE
Primitive Divinity, 166–67

DISCONTENT

Every man is complaining that his estate is no better, though he seldom complains that his heart is no better. One man commends this kind of life, another commends that; one man thinks a country life best, another a city life. The soldier thinks it best to be a merchant, and the merchant to be a soldier. Men can be content to be anything but what God will have them.

✦ SIMEON ASHE
Primitive Divinity, 47

Remember, in every loss there is only a suffering, but in every discontent there is a sin; and one sin is worse than a thousand sufferings. What! Because some of my revenues are gone, shall I part with some of my righteousness? Shall my faith and patience go too? Because I do not possess an estate, shall I not therefore possess my own spirit? O, learn to be content!

✦ SIMEON ASHE
Primitive Divinity, 58

Discontent, arising from disrespect, savors too much of pride; a humble Christian hath a lower opinion of himself than others can have of him. He that is taken up about the thoughts of his sins and how he hath provoked God, he cries out as Agur: "I am more brutish than any man" (Prov. 30:2) and therefore is contented, though he be set "among the dogs of my flock" (Job 30:1). Though he be low in the thoughts of others, yet he is thankful that he is not laid in "the lowest hell" (Ps. 86:13). A proud man sets a high value upon himself and is angry with others because they will not come up to his price. Take heed of pride.

✦ SIMEON ASHE
Primitive Divinity, 71–72

Discontent is nothing else but the echo of unbelief, and remember, distrust is worse than distress.

✦ SIMEON ASHE
Primitive Divinity, 124

Discontent is a spider that sucks the poison of unthankfulness out of the sweetest flower of God's blessings, and, by a devilish chemistry, extracts dross out of the most refined gold. The discontented person thinks everything he does for God too much, and everything God does for him too little. Oh, what a sin is unthankfulness!

✦ SIMEON ASHE
Primitive Divinity, 126

A carnal heart—because there is nothing but filthiness, a filthy stink in himself, nothing but vileness and baseness within him—upon this it is that he seeks his contentment elsewhere. And as it is with a vessel that is full of liquor, if you strike upon it, it will make no great noise, but if it be empty, then it makes a great noise. So it is with the heart—a heart that is full of grace and goodness within, such a one will bear a great many strokes and never make any noise; but an empty heart, if that be struck, that will make a noise. Those men and women that are so much complaining and always whining, it is a sign that there is an emptiness in their hearts; but if their hearts were filled with grace, they would not make such a noise as now they do.

✦ JEREMIAH BURROUGHS
Rare Jewel, 32

There is a great deal of folly in discontentedness, for it makes our affliction a great deal worse than otherwise it would be. It no way removes our affliction—nay, while they do continue they are a great deal the worse and

heavier, for a discontented heart is a proud heart, and a proud heart will not pull down his sails when there come a tempest and storm. If a mariner when a tempest and storm come should be froward and would not pull down his sails but is discontented with the storm, is his condition the better because he is discontented and will not pull down his sails? Will this help him? Just so, it is for all the world with a discontented heart. A discontented heart is a proud heart, and he out of his pride is troubled with his affliction and is not contented with God's dispose, and so he will not pull down his spirit at all and make it bow to God in this condition in which God hath brought him.

✦ JEREMIAH BURROUGHS
Rare Jewel, 60–61

Take heed of discontent. It was the devil's sin that threw him out of heaven. Ever since which, this restless spirit loves to fish in troubled waters.

✦ JOHN TRAPP
Commentary…upon…the New Testament, 481

Discontent keeps a man from enjoying what he doth possess. A drop or two of vinegar will sour a whole glass of wine. Comfort depends upon contentment. It is not trouble that troubles, but discontent. It is not the water without the ship but the water that gets within the leak which sinks it. It is not outward afflictions that can make the life of a Christian sad; a contented mind would sail above these waters. But when there is a leak of discontent open and trouble gets into the heart, then it is disquieted and sinks.

✦THOMAS WATSON
Gleanings, 37–38

Discontent is when a man is not angry at his sins, but at his condition. This is different from patience. Discontent is the daughter of pride.

✦THOMAS WATSON
Godly Man's Picture, 106

DISCOURAGEMENT

If you would not be discouraged in any condition, then never make your comforts depend on your condition nor be in love with any condition for itself. Let not your condition itself be the cause or ground of your encouragements.

✦WILLIAM BRIDGE
Lifting Up, 62

Remember the promise: God will give the Holy Spirit unto them that ask Him (Luke 11:1[3]). He will give such a supply of grace that ye shall be enabled to withstand any temptation; therefore, if you would grow strong, take heed of discouragements and let one Christian take heed of discouraging of another Christian by any speech, action, or behavior, and let ministers take heed of discouraging of their flocks. For it is the property of false prophets to discourage the people from God.

✦JOHN PRESTON
"The Saints' Spiritual Strength,"
in *Remaines*, 124

DISCOURSE AND DISPUTE

Discourse not to cavil but to convince or to be convinced. Many discourse and dispute more for faction than satisfaction and hence come so many fractions.

✦RALPH VENNING
Mysteries and Revelations, 19

DISEASE

It's most meet in the time of a contagious sickness that there be one minister to teach the whole and another to visit the sick, and that by choice of the people. If people admonished will not take this order, a godly pastor may in wisdom to his power provide for both, speaking to the infected afar off. If any danger come, he is free.

✦EZEKIEL CULVERWELL
Time Well Spent, 299

DIVINITY (STUDY OF THEOLOGY)

Read such books as contain the essential principles of religion, and treat of them in the most plain, affectionate, and practical manner, tending to deep impressions, renovation of the soul, and spiritual experience, without which you will want the essential qualifications for your future work. The art of theology without the power, consisting of holy life, light, and love, is the very constitution of the hypocrite.

✦RICHARD BAXTER
"Hints of Advice to Students,"
in *Reformed Pastor*, 233

Three noble ends divinity propounds to her followers: the first and greatest, God's glory; the second, next to that, man's own contentment here and salvation hereafter; the last like to the former, the edification and conversion of our neighbors. In the attainment of these is a Christian's perfection and happiness, none whereof bare theory shall ever more than come near. All three practice, joined thereto, fully apprehends.

✦ SAMUEL WARD
"The Happiness of Practice," in
Sermons and Treatises, 165

Of all men I hold them fools that bend their studies to divinity, not intending to be doers as well as students and preachers; not much wiser, such as will be professors of religion and not practitioners.

✦ SAMUEL WARD
"The Happiness of Practice," in
Sermons and Treatises, 166

DIVISIONS

It's too commonly seen even among dear friends, and those also true Christians, that in much talking even about good things there fall out diversities of opinions, which commonly (if great care and conscience be not had) breed contrary reasonings, in which most offend by stiffness in maintaining thereof. And hard it is not to let slip some inconsiderate speech, which if it be ill taken makes breach of love and falling out many times when no ill was meant.

✦ EZEKIEL CULVERWELL
Time Well Spent, 50–51

God hath armed the beasts with teeth and claws, but man with reason and judgment. To smite with the hand is beneath a man, and to smite with the tongue beneath a Christian…and yet how often is it found that Christians are guilty of both. The controversies between them degenerate into carnal strife and debates and are no more religious but personal.

✦ THOMAS MANTON
Meate out of the Eater, 36

O! That we did consider that though Paul and Peter be in heaven, yet that there are neither Paulians nor Peterians in heaven, that Christ is not a Calvinist in the Calvinists or a Lutheran in the Lutherans, but in those that are believers amongst both Christ is all in all. God must scourge this folly from us; His children are wrangling, and we may expect that either He should separate or correct us. O Lord, if man's apostate were Thy apostate, and man's heretic Thy heretic, and man's reprobate always Thy reprobate, election to eternal life would prove but a fable, and all the world would be damned.

✦ FRANCIS RAWORTH
On Jacob's Ladder, vi

This is a foul fault in any, but especially in ministers, who must see, said Luther, that those three dogs follow them not into the pulpit: pride, covetousness, and contentiousness. A quarrelsome person is like a cock of the kind, ever bloody with the blood of others and himself. And divisions are Satan's powder plot to blow up religion.

✦ JOHN TRAPP
*Commentary…upon…the New
Testament,* 687

Seedsmen sow not in a storm.

✦ JOHN TRAPP
in Horn, *Puritan Remembrancer,* 287

DOCTRINAL CURIOSITIES

Beware of curiosity. He is half gone into error that vainly covets novelties and listens after every newfangled opinion.

✦ WILLIAM GURNALL
Christian in Complete Armour, 215

Curious questions and vain speculations are like a plume of feathers which some will give anything for, and some will give nothing for. Paul rebuked them which troubled their heads about genealogies. How would he reprove men and women of our days if he did see how they busy their heads about vain questions, tracing upon the pinnacles where they may fall while they might walk upon the pavement without danger? Some have a great deal more desire to learn where hell is than to know any way how they may escape it; to hear what God did purpose before the world began rather than to learn what He will do when the world is ended; to understand whether they shall know one another in heaven than to know whether they belong to heaven. This rock hath made many

shipwrecks, that men search mysteries before they know principles.

✦ HENRY SMITH
"A Looking-Glass for Christians,"
in *Sermons,* 130–31

When the question was asked, How many angels might stand upon a needle's point at once? The answer was that it was but a needless point to stand upon. Let not us stand upon such needless points of curiosity, to the breach of Christian charity.

✦ EDWARD WILLAN
"An Exhortation to Christian
Charity," in *Six Sermons,* 17

DOCTRINE

Examine with humble diligence what in hearing appeared to you as doubtful. Suspect your own understandings more than your minister's, but lean not rashly on your own or idolatrously on his. If error be in his doctrine, it turns to poison in thy soul. Wherefore do not swallow what thou dost suspect. The most noble hearers try all doctrine by the Holy Scriptures.

✦ DANIEL BURGESS
Rules and Directions, 14

Those that are all in exhortation, no whit in doctrine, are like to them that snuff the candle but pour not in oil. Again, those that are all in doctrine, nothing in exhortation, drown the wick in oil but light it not, making it fit for use if it had fire put to it, but, as it is, rather capable of good than profitable in present. Doctrine without exhortation makes men all brain, no heart; exhortation without doctrine makes the heart full, leaves the brain empty. Both together make a man. One makes a man wise, the other good. One serves that we may know our duty; the other, that we may perform it. I will labor in both, but I know not in whether more. Men cannot practice unless they know; and they know in vain if they practice not.

✦JOSEPH HALL
Meditations and Vows, 151

To retain and maintain the ancient catholic and apostolic faith:…

(1) Strive for a well-grounded knowledge. He that embraces the truth he knows not why will leave it he knows not how. The ship that is not well ballasted may soon be overturned…. Let that which hath been heard by you be assented to upon good grounds, and then it will abide with you. (2) Keep the mind lowly. Ignorance is a sponge to suck in, and pride is a bawd to vent error. None more likely to fall than he that proudly leans to his own understanding; nor are any hearers more foolishly fickle than they that think themselves wiser than their teachers. (3) Love the truth affectionately. "Hold fast," saith St. Paul to Timothy, "that which thou hast heard of me in faith and love." These are the two hands by which we both receive and retain

what we hear. Love is the best key to open the heart for receiving God's word and the strongest lock to keep it in when we have received it…. (4) Practice what you have heard. He that digests the word by obedience retains it by perseverance. St. Paul saith of them who put away a good conscience that they made shipwreck of their faith (1 Tim. 1:21). (5) "Be strong in the Lord, and in the power of His might."

✦NATHANIEL HARDY
First General Epistle of St. John, 349

Doctrine is but the drawing of the bow; application is the hitting of the mark. How many are wise in generals, but vain…in their practical inferences (Rom. 1:21–22)! Generals remain in notion and speculation; particular things work. We are only to give you doctrine and the necessary uses and inferences; you are to make application. Whenever you hear, let the light of every truth be reflected upon your own souls; never leave till you have gained the heart to a sense of duty and a resolution for duty.

✦THOMAS MANTON
Practical Exposition on the
Epistle of James, 159

DOUBT

The weak Christian's doubting is like the wavering of a ship at anchor; he is moved yet not removed from his hold on Christ.

✦WILLIAM GURNALL
Christian in Complete Armour, 473

There be in spiritual doubtings two things: there is a solicitous care of the soul concerning its own estate and a diligent inquiry into it, and that is laudable, being a true work of the Spirit of God; but the other thing in them is perplexity and distrust arising from darkness and weakness in the soul. Where there is a great deal of smoke and no clear flame, it argues much moisture in the matter, yet it witnesses certainly that there is fire there; and, therefore, dubious questioning of a man concerning himself is a much better evidence than that senseless deadness which most take for believing. Men that know nothing in sciences have no doubts. He never truly believed who was not made first sensible and convinced of unbelief.

✦ ROBERT LEIGHTON
Spiritual Truths, 72–73

The devil sometimes tempts believers to sin, and that causes them to doubt; and sometimes tempts them to doubt, and that causes them to sin.

✦ RALPH VENNING
Canaan's Flowings, 49

DRUNKENNESS

While the wine is in thy hand, thou art a man; when it is in thy head, thou art become a beast. The drunkard cries to his fellow, "Do me reason," but the drink answers, "I will leave thee no reason; scarce so much as a beast, for they will drink no more than they need." Diogenes being urged to drink immoderately cast the drink on the ground. Being reproved for that loss,

he answered, "If I had drunk it, I had lost both the drink and myself."

✦ THOMAS ADAMS
Exposition upon…Second…Peter, 75

Wine tempers the heart like wax for the devil's impression.

✦ THOMAS ADAMS
in Horn, *Puritan Remembrancer,* 165

A drunkard is the annoyance of modesty, the spoiler of civility, the destruction of reason, the brewer's agent, the alehouse benefactor, his wife's sorrow, his children's trouble, his own shame, his neighbors' scoff, a walking swill bowl, the picture of a beast, and a monster of a man.

✦ JOHN DOD
Sermon on Malt, 6–7; also in
Brook, *Lives of the Puritans,* 3:6

Take heed and beware of the detestable sin of drunkenness, which is a beastly sin, a voluntary madness, a sin that unmans thee and makes thee like the beasts that perish; yea, sets thee below the brute beasts, which will not drink to excess.

✦ JOHN FLAVEL
"A Sober Consideration of the Sin
of Drunkenness," in *Navigation
Spiritualized,* 146

Hence one aptly calls [drunkenness] "the devil's bridle," by which he turns the sinner which way he pleases; he that is overcome by it can overcome no other sin.

✦ JOHN FLAVEL
"A Sober Consideration of the Sin
of Drunkenness," in *Navigation
Spiritualized,* 157

I had rather be a sober heathen than a drunken Christian, a chaste heathen than an unclean believer.

✦ WILLIAM GURNALL
Christian in Complete Armour, 485

What one sin more mangles and defaces God's image and man's beauty than this? How doth it dam up the head and spirits with mud? Blow the cheeks with wind? Fill the eyes and nose with fire? Lade the hands and legs with water? Plague, in short, the whole man with the diseases of a horse, the belly of a cow, the head of an ass...and turn him into a very walking dunghill?

✦ ROBERT HARRIS
Drunkard's Cup, 10

Our aim should be God's glory, but many drink to this end: that they may the easier forget God, forget Him in His threats which stick in their souls after sermon; forget Him in His judgments, which have taken hold of some of their companions. They drink to the end they may drown conscience and put off all thoughts of death and judgment; to the end they may harten [i.e., encourage] and harden themselves against all the messages of God and make themselves both to know and move at God's own words, as in this prophesy we find afterward. How many a man's heart can tell him that this hath been one of his special errands to the cup?

✦ ROBERT HARRIS
Drunkard's Cup, 21

[Drunkenness] turns grace into wantonness and medicine into disease; it makes the body, which should be the temple of the Holy Ghost, the very cellar of Bacchus.

✦ EDWARD MARBURY
Commentarie...upon...Habakkuk, 306

In Barnwell, near to Cambridge, one at the sign of the plough, a lusty young man with two of his neighbors and one woman in their company agreed to drink a barrel of strong beer. They drunk up the vessel. Three of them died within four and twenty hours; the fourth hardly escaped after great sickness. This I have under a justice of peace's hand, near dwelling, besides the common fame.

A butcher in Haslingfield, hearing the minister inveigh against drunkenness, being at his cups in the alehouse, fell a-jesting and scoffing at the minister and his sermons. As he was drinking, the drink, or something in the cup, quackled him, stuck so in his throat that he could not get it up nor down, but strangled him presently.

✦ SAMUEL WARD
"Woe to Drunkards," in *Sermons and Treatises*, 153

There is no sin which does more deface God's image than drunkenness; it disguises a person and does even unman him. Drunkenness makes him have the throat of a fish, the belly of a swine, and the head of an ass. Drunkenness is the shame of nature, the extinguisher of reason, the shipwreck of chastity, and the murder of conscience. Drunkenness is hurtful for the body; the cup kills more than the cannon.

✦ THOMAS WATSON
Body of Practical Divinity, 613

DUTY

It is highly perilous to rest in duties and go no further, for the duties of religion are only means to an end. Many deluded souls, when they attend on the means of grace and go through a round of duties, quiet their conscience and feel satisfied that the work is now done and that all is safe. By this they trust to what they themselves have done instead of going on through divine ordinances to rest on what Christ has done by His obedience unto death. Those who rest in duties instead of resting on Christ are building on the sand instead of on the rock. Like Lot's wife, they go out of Sodom yet never go in to Zoar, but perish by the way. See the danger of resting on duties. We must go through duties to Christ Himself. We must rest nowhere short of Him.

✦ ISAAC AMBROSE
Christian Warrior, 62–63

When the soul sees his wound and his sin ready to condemn him, it thinks by duties or some such like matters to succor itself, and it begins to say, "My hearing and my prayer—will not these save me?" Thus, the soul in conclusion rests on duties. I will not say but these duties are all good, honorable, and comfortable, yet they are not God, but the ordinances of God. It is the nature of a sinful heart to make the means as meritorious to salvation. A man that sees his drunkenness and his base contempt of God vows to take up a new course and cries, "No more drunkenness, no more scoffing at those that go to hear the word"; and then he thinks,

"What can I do more? To heaven I must go." All this is but a man's self. Christ, who is the substance of all, is forgotten, and therefore the poor soul famishes with hunger.... So though you boast of praying and hearing and fasting and of your alms, if none of these bring you to or settle you on Christ, you shall die, though your works were as the works of an angel.

✦ ISAAC AMBROSE
"The Doctrine of Regeneration,"
in *Works*, 50–51

It is a sign that a man rests in his duties if he gain no evangelical righteousness by duties—that is, if he prize not, desire not, delight not in union with the Lord Jesus Christ. Hence a child of God asks himself after sermon, after prayer, after sacrament, "What have I gained of Christ? Have I got more knowledge of Christ? More admiring of the Lord Jesus Christ? Have my affections been raised, my graces acted, my soul refreshed with the delights of Christ?" On the contrary, a carnal heart that rests in his duties asks only, "What have I done?"

✦ ISAAC AMBROSE
"The Practice of Sanctification,"
in *Works*, 81–82

I smell wherein lies the venom of [the antinomian]. He has free grace bestowed on him which has freed him from all duties of obedience to the Lord, so that what he does is only out of free love; for he thinks to be tied by way of duty will not stand with his free grace. But I say again, we trust in no duty as causes of our salvation, but we obey and do these duties as the way to salvation. Neither did they ever hear those worthy divines, whom they vilify with the terms of "legal teachers," press any duties to merit salvation for the doing of them; but let the sons of Belial [i.e., the antinomians] know that if they slight their duties to the law of God, they may purchase damnation by it. Neither can there be any salvation for that man till he humble himself and freely yield to the commanding power of the law of God and count it his duty to give all the power of body and soul in obedience to it.

✦ THOMAS BAKEWELL
Short View of the Antinomian Errours, 33

Duties can never have too much diligence used about them or too little confidence placed in them; they are good helps but bad saviors. It is necessary we do them, but it is dangerous to rely upon them.

✦ THOMAS BROOKS
Cabinet of Choice Jewels, 363

Secret duties shall have open rewards.

✦ THOMAS BROOKS
Privy Key of Heaven, 19

If a man be not interested in Christ, he may perish with "Our Father" in his mouth. It is as natural to a man to rest in his duties as it is for to rest in his bed.

✦ THOMAS BROOKS
Privy Key of Heaven, 165

The dove made use of her wings to flee to the ark; so does a humble soul of his duties to flee to Christ. Though the dove did use her wings, yet she did not trust in her wings but in the ark; so though a humble soul does use duties, yet he does not trust in his duties but in his Jesus.

✦ THOMAS BROOKS
Unsearchable Riches of Christ, in
Select Works, 1:10

No duty can be performed without wrestling! The Christian needs his sword as much as his trowel.

✦ WILLIAM GURNALL
Christian in Complete Armour, 78

Let me ask you, Christian, what you have found in the observation of thy own heart to be the fruit that has grown from such delays? Has neglect of duty at one time fitted thee for it at another? I believe not. Sloth is not cured with sleep, nor laziness with idleness. If our leg be numbed we walk, and so it wears off. Satan knows if you play the truant today, you will be the more loath to go to school tomorrow.

✦ WILLIAM GURNALL
Christian in Complete Armour, 637

Can one sin be a good argument for committing another? Thou hast fallen into sin in the day. Wilt thou not, therefore, pray at night? Surely it were better to beg of God forgiveness of this and more grace, that thou mayest not do the like tomorrow. Neglect of duty is not the way to help thee out of the pit thou art in, nor keep thee from falling into another. Take heed thou run not further into temptation.

✦ WILLIAM GURNALL
Christian in Complete Armour, 638

Bare words will not discharge or satisfy duty. Good words are good in themselves and become a Christian mouth, but they must not be rested in. Some cannot go so far in profession as good words, religious conference, and holy discourse. Words argue that you have a knowledge of duty, and bare words that you want a heart for it. That a few charitable words are not enough. Some men's words are fierce and cruel; others love in word and in tongue (1 John 3:18), but this is not enough. Words are cheap; compliments cost nothing. And will you serve God with that which cost nothing? Words are but a cold kind of pity. The stomach is not filled with words, but meat; nor is the back clothed with good wishes.

✦ THOMAS MANTON
Practical Exposition on the
Epistle of James, 103

Duty will either make us weary of the world, or the world will make us weary of duty. The children of God have experience of the one, and hypocrites of the other.

✦ THOMAS MANTON
Practical Exposition on the
Epistle of James, 153

A natural man prides himself in his duties; if he be much in duty, then he is much lifted up under duty. So did the Pharisee: "God, I thank thee that I am not as other men are." And why? Where lay the difference? For "I fast twice in the week; I give tithes of all that I possess" (Luke 18). But a gracious heart, a renewed conscience, when his duties are at highest, then his

heart is at lowest. Thus it was with the apostle Paul. He was much in service "in season and out of season," preaching the Lord Jesus with all boldness and earnestness and yet very humble in a sense of his own unworthiness under all: I "am not worthy to be called an apostle" (1 Cor. 15:9).

✦ MATTHEW MEAD
Almost Christian Discovered, 146

The altogether Christian is much in duty and yet much above duty: much in duty in regard of performances, much above duty in regard of dependence; much in duty by obeying, but much above duty by believing. He lives in his obedience, but he doth not live upon obedience, but upon Christ and His righteousness. The almost Christian fails in this: he is much in duty, but not above it, but rests in it; he works for rest, and he rests in his works. He cannot come to believe and obey too. If he believes, then he thinks there is no need of obedience, and so he casts off that; if he be much in obedience, then he casts off believing and thinks there is no need of that.

✦ MATTHEW MEAD
Almost Christian Discovered, 197

If a man shall cast away his clothes, leave his food, and decline the means of preserving heat and life, he must needs grow cold if he be not quickly killed. If a man reads not, meditates not, prays not, hears not, or is negligent and formal herein, he must needs, like a dying man, grow cold. It much depends upon the lively performance of holy duties that you keep your heart warm or that you decay in your fervor by carelessness in the means. Meditation will mind you of this and put you upon mending it in time.

✦ NATHANAEL RANEW
Solitude Improved by Divine Meditation, 76

A desire to get and keep communion with God. This is one end for which holy duties are appointed, that by them God and the soul may come together. And this hath been the end which holy men have propounded to themselves in holy duties: "Thy face, LORD, will I seek" (Ps. 27:8). Thus it was with David: "When shall I come and appear before God?" (Ps. 42:2); and "To see thy power and thy glory, so as I have seen thee in the sanctuary" (Ps. 63:2). Now when a person can in the uprightness of soul say that his end in coming to duties, public and private, is because he would see Him whom his soul loveth and therefore is not satisfied with a duty if he meet not with God in it, he may then comfortably conclude, from the performing of duties, a principle of grace in his heart.

✦ RALPH ROBINSON
Christ All and in All, 108

Duties are ours; events are the Lord's. When our faith goeth to meddle with events and to hold a court—if I may so speak—upon God's providence and beginneth to say, "How wilt Thou do this and that?" we lose ground. We have nothing to do there. It is our part to let the Almighty exercise His own office and steer His own helm.

✦ SAMUEL RUTHERFORD
Garden of Spices, 161

The great duty of a saint is to trust in God's word, to keep in His way, and to submit to His will. And these are duties which promote each other, for he who rightly believes what God says will carefully observe what He commands and quietly rest in what He does. Though there may be darkness in God's providences, he will see light in God's promises, and feel comfort in his duty.

✦ T. S.
Aids to the Divine Life, 86

The severities of a holy life and that constant watch which we are obliged to keep over our hearts and ways are very troublesome to those who are only ruled and acted by an external law and have no law in their minds inclining them to the performance of their duty. But where divine love possesses the soul, it stands as sentinel to keep out everything that may offend the Beloved and doth disdainfully repulse those temptations which assault it. It complies cheerfully not only with explicit commands but with the most secret notices of the Beloved's pleasure and is ingenious in discovering what will be most grateful and acceptable unto Him. It makes mortification and self-denial change their harsh and dreadful names and become easy, sweet, and delightful things.

✦ HENRY SCOUGAL
Life of God in the Soul of Man, 53–54

Though [God] has not tied Himself to means, yet He has tied us to the use of them; and we have never more reason to expect the divine assistance than when we are doing our utmost endeavors.

✦ HENRY SCOUGAL
Life of God in the Soul of Man, 76

Duties are but dry pits, though never so curiously wrought till Christ fill them. Reader, I would neither have you be idle in the means, nor make an idol of the means. Though it be the mariner's duty to weigh his anchor and spread his sails, yet he cannot make his voyage until the winds blow.... Duties can never have too much of our diligence or too little of our confidence.

✦ WILLIAM SECKER
Nonsuch Professor, 102–3

Another singular principle by which a Christian should walk is this: that duties can never have too much attention paid to them or too little confidence placed in them.

✦ WILLIAM SECKER
Nonsuch Professor, 167

It is our bounden duty to live in obedience, but it will prove our utter ruin to live on obedience. Heaven is either the gift of mercy or the reward of duty. If the latter, Christ is dead in vain; but if the former, we boast in vain. Fear not, little flock; for it is your Father's good pleasure to give you the kingdom. Thus, we see that heaven is not the product of man's labor but the token of God's good pleasure.

✦ WILLIAM SECKER
Nonsuch Professor, 172

Duties—these are also ways of converse with God, such as confession, petition, thanksgiving, conference, singing, meditation, observation. In all which, God impresses something of Himself upon the soul and draws answerable affections of the soul unto Himself, as might appear in the particular explication of them.

✦ SAMUEL SHAW
Voice of One Crying in the Wilderness, 35

Satan's wile is when he cannot hinder from duty, then he endeavors to spoil them; he will excite to duties, but to do them unseasonably. It is the commendation of a duty when it is done in season: The blessed man "bringeth forth his fruit in his season" (Psalm 1). Now when he cannot put out the candle, he will make it sparkle and flair, as in Martha (Luke 10:40–41); or he will turn affection the wrong way. The Jews were zealous for the law, and he stirs up that against the gospel. Saul had a conscience of serving God (1 Sam. 13:12), and he forced him to offer sacrifice. The Corinthians were at first too remiss toward the incestuous Corinthian; after, too severe. He sees some heat, and he drives it on too much. He will make us tyrannize in some service, and some duties he will make tyrants unto us. His aim is by marrying religion and tyranny to discourage men from religion.

✦ WILLIAM SPURSTOWE
Wiles of Satan, 81

Let us…learn to be in duty in respect of performance and yet out of duty in respect of dependence.

✦ JOHN TRAPP
*Commentary…upon…the
New Testament*, 450

To do God's will acceptably is to do it willingly. Delight in duty is better than duty itself.

✦ THOMAS WATSON
Lord's Prayer, 160

Prayer, meditation, and divine conference, are *vehicula anime* [means of conveyance for the soul] and elevate the soul and revive thy drooping spirit. They add a miraculous rigor and alacrity amid all the crosses and discomforts in the world. If then thou wouldst retain thy joy, take heed of remissness and negligence in duties.

✦ HENRY WILKINSON
"Joy in the Lord," in *Three Decades
of Sermons*, 182

Take away these [spiritual duties], you starve the soul. They are as necessary as meat and drink for the body. If you keep not time and touch with God in a constant, conscientious performance of duties, it's evident you have no care of your souls. The soul hath need of all duties, prayer, reading, hearing, meditation, conference—these are *pabula anime* [food for the soul] and *anime vehicula* [means of conveyance for the soul]; they wing the soul and make it soar aloft. As you love your souls, neglect not spiritual duties.

✦ HENRY WILKINSON
"The Dignity of the Soule," in
Three Decades of Sermons, 240

EFFECTUAL CALLING

You must distinguish, first, of the church—that there is a church visible and a church invisible, which is the mystical body of Christ. And you are to know that there be many in the church visible which are not of the church invisible; many in the house of God which be servants and not sons. Secondly, of calling—that there is an outward calling by the word, which is common to all in the church, of which it is said, "Many be called and few chosen." And there is an inward and effectual calling, according to God's purpose, of which it is said, "Whom he elected, he called."

✦ GEORGE DOWNAME
Christian's Freedom, 18

Effectual calling is the first gathering of men unto Christ, the first making of men to come to Christ, the first putting of a man into the estate of grace. It is the very portal to religion, the very entry into eternal life; it is the first bringing of a man to partake of the Lord Jesus Christ and to have fellowship with Him.

✦ WILLIAM FENNER
"Treatise of Effectual Calling,"
in *Works*, 20

This calling is by the grace of God. As He graciously appeared to the patriarchs, offered better things to them, and moved upon them by His Spirit, so He allures them that they can say: "Immediately I conferred not with flesh and blood." It is grace that draws you to Him and draws you after Him. He constrains His people by a holy violence; being merciful to them, He catcheth hold of them, as He did of lingering Lot. Such is our infirmity, and such a hold the world hath of us, that "the lord said unto the servant, Go out into the highways and hedges, and compel them to come in, that my house may be filled" (Luke 14:23).

✦ THOMAS JOLLIE
Treatise on Heavenly-Mindedness, in Slate,
Select Nonconformists' Remains, 215

When the Lord Himself speaks by this His Spirit to a man, selecting and calling him out of the lost world, he can no more disobey than Abraham did when the Lord spoke to him after an extraordinary manner to depart from his own country and kindred. Abraham departed as the Lord had spoken to him (Gen. 12:4). There is a secret but very powerful virtue in a word or look or touch of this Spirit upon the soul, by which it is forced not with a harsh but a pleasing violence and cannot choose but follow it, not unlike that of Elijah's mantle upon Elisha. How easily did the disciples forsake their callings and their dwellings to follow Christ! The Spirit of God draws a man out of the world by a sanctified light sent into his mind.

✦ ROBERT LEIGHTON
A Commentary upon the First Epistle of Peter, in *Whole Works*, 1:16–17

"The voice of the LORD is powerful" and "full of majesty" (Ps. 29:4). If He speaks once to the heart, it cannot choose but follow Him and yet most willingly chooses that. The workings

of grace (as oil, to which it is often compared) do insensibly and silently penetrate and sink into the soul and dilate themselves through it. That word of His own calling disentangles the heart from all its nets, as it did the disciples from theirs, to follow Christ. That call which brought St. Matthew presently from his receipt of custom puts off the heart from all its customs and receipts too; makes it reject gains and pleasures and all that hinders it to go after Christ. And it is a call that touches the soul, so as the touch of Elijah's mantle that made Elisha follow him.

✦ ROBERT LEIGHTON
A Commentary upon the First Epistle of Peter, in *Whole Works*, 1:250

There is a twofold call of God.... There is an internal call of God. Now this call is a special work of the Spirit by the ministry of the word, whereby a man is brought out of a state of nature into a state of grace; "out of darkness into light," from being a "vessel of wrath" to be made an "heir of life." I grant that whoever is under this call of God is called effectually and savingly, called to be a Christian indeed. "Every man therefore that hath heard, and hath learned of the Father, cometh unto me" (John 6:45). There is a call of God which a man may have, and yet not be this call; there is an external call of God which is by the ministry of the word. Now every man that lives under the preaching of the gospel is thus called; God calls every soul of you to repent and lay a sure foundation for heaven and salvation by the word you hear (Matt. 22:9).

✦ MATTHEW MEAD
Almost Christian Discovered, 101–2

If you would know whether your names are written in heaven, satisfy yourselves in this: that the call of God hath took effectual hold of your hearts. Hath it brought your souls off from everything below Christ wholly to follow Christ? It is said when Christ called Peter and Andrew, they presently "left their nets, and followed him" (Matt. 4:18–20). Every man hath his nets, somewhat that his soul is entangled in, till the call of God take hold of him. Can you now, with Peter, when God calls, lay aside your nets to follow Him?

✦ MATTHEW MEAD
Name in Heaven, 51

God's effectual calling is that whereby God calleth out of darkness into His admirable light, from the power of Satan unto God, in Christ Jesus, those whom He knew from eternity and predestinated unto life of His mere favor, by the promulgation of the covenant of grace, or preaching of the gospel. Such, also, as be called by the same grace of God answer and believe in Him through Jesus Christ. This answer is of faith, which is in very truth the condition of the promise which is in the covenant of grace. Wherefore our effectual calling doth consist of the promise of the covenant (which is under condition of faith) and in faith also, which is nothing else but the fulfilling of the condition.

Therefore, there be two parts of our effectual calling. The first is the outward calling of such as are predestinate unto life, from darkness unto light, and that of God's mere grace; and that, I say, by the publication of the covenant of grace, or preaching of the gospel. The latter part is their inward faith, wrought in them by the same grace and Spirit of God whereby they are converted from Satan unto God; for I cannot see how this second part of our effectual calling can differ from faith itself.

✦ ROBERT ROLLOCK
"A Treatise of Our Effectual Calling,"
in *Select Works*, 1:29–30

ELECT/ELECTION

Our election passively is God's actively. God's eternal purpose [is] to reconcile us. But how should this be made sure unto our hearts without their believing and considering that God has eternal purposes about that matter?

✦ DANIEL BURGESS
Man's Whole Duty, 76

The doctrine of election contains the whole sum and scope of the gospel, and our minds, if honestly subdued to the doctrine of God's sovereignty, cannot be employed about a more excellent subject. It is called the foundation of God not only because of the supereminency of it but as a foundation of His laying, which God Himself is the author of and He alone, and the basis whereof is Himself. It is that foundation which stands sure and keeps all them sure who stand upon it. Election is the pitching of everlasting love, or the good pleasure of God choosing and decreeing to eternal life. It is the great charter of heaven—God's special and free-grace deed of gift to His chosen ones, made over in trust unto Jesus Christ for their use and benefit.

◆ ELISHA COLES
Practical Discourse, 57–58

Election is absolute. In this are two things of great import—irrevocableness and independency. The decree is irrevocable on God's part, and independent as to human performances. The Lord will not go back from His purpose to save His people, nor shall their unworthiness or averseness make void or hinder His most gracious intendment. And hence those various expressions of the same thing—namely, predestinate, ordain, prepare, appoint—have nothing subjoined that is like a conditional. There is, indeed, a kind of conditions, or rather qualifications, that must and always do precede the final completement of election, as "repentance towards God, and faith towards our Lord Jesus Christ," which, therefore, may be called conditionals of salvation, but not so to election.

◆ ELISHA COLES
Practical Discourse, 67

Heaven was made at the beginning of the world, but election was before.

◆ ELISHA COLES
Practical Discourse, 75

To derive election from any root besides the good pleasure of God is to frustrate the principal end of man's salvation—namely, "the glory of [God's] grace" (Eph. 1:6; [see also] 2:7). This attribute, of all the rest, He will not have eclipsed nor entrenched upon. It is so divinely sacred as not to admit the least human touch, for which very cause, the Lord hath so contrived that blessed design and plot of His glory, that all boasting is excluded; and "no flesh should glory in his presence" (1 Cor. 1:29). But if anything in the creature be entitled to the causality of election, flesh will glory; and, instead of excluding man's boasting, grace itself will be excluded (Rom. 11:6), which is far from a glorifying of it.

◆ ELISHA COLES
Practical Discourse, 88–89

[*Objection*]: [Election] must needs make men very remiss and loose in the service of God. *Answer*: A strange assertion, that the assurance of God's love should make men careless in serving Him! They that so judge can never be overdiligent to "make their calling and election sure." Christ knew that the angels had charge over Him and that He should not dash His foot against a stone, yet was nevertheless careful of His own preservation. Paul was sure of the crown of righteousness, and yet as diligent in beating down his body and strained as hard in running his race as any of those who lay the stress of salvation upon their works.

◆ ELISHA COLES
Practical Discourse, 96

[Election] being a doctrine of so great importance, be not indifferent about it. Put yourself on the trial touching your interest in it and bring forth your evidences for it. Observe what are the properties of God's elect, and see if they stand on your side.

✦ ELISHA COLES
Practical Discourse, 111

Election...draws with it even all that is tendent to the saints' actual investiture with glory. The apostle, therefore, linketh eternity past with eternity to come. He makes election and glorification the two extreme points of the compass; calling and justification, which are parts intermediate, he founds upon the first in order to the last and gives you their set course in Romans 8:29–30: "Whom he did foreknow, he also did predestinate." To what? "To be conformed to the image of his Son...[and] whom he did predestinate, them he also called." And what did He call them to? He called them to holiness, to glory, and virtue (2 Peter 1:3). And "whom he called, them he also justified...and... glorified" (Rom. 8:30). These also do belong to the same persons, and that by virtue of the decree; and no one of them did ever go alone.

✦ ELISHA COLES
Practical Discourse, 193–94

The counsel of God concerning election is secret. The minister knows not who are the objects of it and therefore must preach to all, according to his commission. The Lord deals in this as in the matter of lots. Saul was foreappointed to be king, yet all Israel must come together and lots must be cast on the whole nation, as if the person were yet undesigned (1 Sam. 9:16; 10:20–21). The falling of the lot was wholly contingent as to men; another might have been taken as well as he it fell upon. But the Lord disposed it and casts it on the right person (Prov. 16:33). So, touching the gospel: it is sent to a place where, perhaps, but one or very few elect persons are, and those only shall be taken by it; and yet it must be published to the whole city promiscuously. But the Holy Ghost, "who knoweth the deep things of God," brings it to the hearts of those for whom it is prepared and there it fixeth, which the jailer, Lydia, and other examples make evident.

✦ ELISHA COLES
Practical Discourse, 224

[*Question*]: Are any other redeemed by Christ effectually called, justified, adopted, sanctified, and saved, but the elect only?

[*Answer*]: No (John 6:64–65; 8:47; 10:26; 17:9; Rom. 8:28; 1 John 2:19). Well then, do not the Papists, Quakers, Socinians, and Arminians err, who maintain that all men, even reprobates, are redeemed by Christ and that many reprobates are effectually called, justified, and adopted? Yes. By what reasons are they confuted? First, from the golden chain which cannot he loosed mentioned by the apostle Paul. "Whom he did predestinate, them he also called; and whom he called, them he also justified; and whom he justified, them he also glorified" (Rom. 8:30). Secondly, because those, and those only, believe whom God hath ordained to life eternal (Acts 13:48).

✦ DAVID DICKSON
Truth's Victory over Error, 60

Election, I say, is expressed to us by all that God means to bestow upon us actually to eternity, forever and ever, which He "hath prepared for them that love him"; so the phrase is (1 Cor. 2:9). And verse 12: "We have received…the Spirit which is of God; that we might know the things that are freely given to us of God"—that is, given us when He first set His heart upon us. My brethren, when God first began to love you, He gave you all that He ever meant to give you in the lump, and eternity of time is that in which He is retailing of it out.

✦ THOMAS GOODWIN
"An Exposition of the Second Chapter
of the Epistle to the Ephesians,"
in *Works*, 2:167

Election indeed is first in order of divine acting—God chooses before we believe, yet faith is first in our acting—we must believe before we can know we be elected; yea, by believing we know it. The husbandman knows it is spring by the sprouting of the grass, though he hath no [astronomy] to know the position of the heavens; thou mayest know thou art elect as surely by a work of grace in thee as if thou hadst stood by God's elbow when He writ thy name in the Book of Life. It had been presumption for David to have thought he should have been king till Samuel anointed him, but then none at all. When thou believest first and closes with Christ, then is the Spirit of God sent to anoint thee to the kingdom of heaven; this is that holy oil which is poured upon none but heirs of glory. And it is no presumption to read what God's gracious purpose was toward thee of old, when He prints those His thoughts and makes them legible in thy effectual calling.

✦ WILLIAM GURNALL
Christian in Complete Armour, 65

God did choose some rather than others out of His mere good pleasure. There was no cause, motive, or condition in the party chosen moving the Lord to choose Him and pass by others. But whereas God might have utterly rejected all, of His free grace and mercy He had compassion on some. Thus, the apostle teacheth that he did predestinate us according to the good pleasure of His will, to the praise of the glory of His grace (Eph. 1:5). If He had chosen some (as Peter, for example) because He foresaw they would be good and die in the faith and had refused others (as Judas) because He foresaw they would be wicked and obstinate despisers of His gospel, this had not been an act of grace; it had not set forth the glory of that attribute but rather of His distributive justice. But that which God mainly intended in this free choice was the praise of the glory of His grace, that man should find nothing to admire or boast in but in the rich grace of God.

✦ WILLIAM LYFORD
Plain Man's Senses, 168–69

The decree of election stands upon an unchangeable foundation—to wit, that Rock of ages, Jesus Christ, the same yesterday, today, and forever (Heb. 13:8). As the first Adam was the foundation stone in the decree of creation, so the second Adam, even Jesus, is the foundation stone in the decree of election. God hath blessed us in Him, yea, and we shall be blessed; He hath chosen us in Him, pardoned us in Him, sealed us in Him, built us up and completed us in Him, "according to His own purpose and grace, which was given us in Christ Jesus before the world began" (2 Tim. 1:9). All those acts of grace are said to be in Christ.

◆ CHRISTOPHER NESS
Antidote against Arminianism, 17

The Scripture expressly states that only a few are chosen, though many be called (Matt. 20:16). It is only a little flock (Luke 12:32) and but one of a city and two of a family that are brought to Zion (Jer. 3:14). "I have chosen you out of the world," saith Christ (John 15:19), and the Lord calls Paul a chosen vessel unto him (Acts 9:15; 22:14). How ill it sounds in the ears of a gospel spirit to say that Pharaoh and Judas were elected as well as Paul and Barnabas, and that Simon Magus was elected as well as Simon Peter—all which, a general election, which is the Arminian hypothesis, most necessarily asserts. How can these "reprobate silver" pieces be, in a gospel sense, termed chosen vessels, as Paul was, to know God's will and see the just One (Acts 22:14)?

◆ CHRISTOPHER NESS
Antidote against Arminianism, 32

It is true that God, before the foundation of the world, fully determined with Himself whom to choose to salvation by grace, to which also He ordained them, and whom to pass by and leave in their sins, for which He determined in His just wrath to condemn them. But who these be is a secret which even the elect themselves cannot know until they be effectually called—nay, nor being called, until by some experience and proofs of their faith and holiness, they do understand the witness of the Spirit, which testifies to their spirits that they are the children of God and do make their calling and election, which was always sure in God, sure to themselves.

◆ HENRY SCUDDER
Christian's Daily Walk, 307

We make our election sure by making our calling sure: "God hath chosen you to salvation through sanctification." By the streams we come at last to the fountain. If we find the stream of sanctification running in our souls, we may by this come to the springhead of election. I do not look up into the secret of God's purpose, yet I may know I am elected by the shining of sanctifying grace in my soul. Whosoever he be that can find the word of God transcribed and copied out into his heart may undeniably conclude he is elected of God.

◆ THOMAS WATSON
Puritan Gems, 30–31

ELECTION AND ADOPTION

We cannot enjoy Him unless we resemble Him, nor take any pleasure in Him if we were with Him without something of likeness to Him. Holiness fits us for communion with God. We can have no evidence of our election and adoption without it. Conformity to God in purity is the fruit of electing love: "He hath chosen us... that we should be holy" (Eph. 1:4). The goodness of the fruit evidences the nature of the root. This is the seal that assures us the patent is the authentic grant of the Prince.

✦ STEPHEN CHARNOCK
Discourses upon the Existence and Attributes of God, 532

ELECTION AND PREDESTINATION

Question 19: But to what purpose will all my endeavors to come to Christ be, unless I be elected? All will be to no purpose.

Answer: True, if thou be not elected, thou canst not obtain Him or happiness by Him. But yet that is no discouragement to strive. For in thy unconverted state, thy election or non-election is a secret to thee. The only way to make it sure is by striving and giving all diligence in the way of duty (2 Peter 1:10). And if you ponder the text well, you will find that election is not only made sure in the way of diligence and striving but calling is put before it and

lies in order to it. First secure thy effectual calling, and then thine election.

JOHN FLAVEL
"The Seamen's Catechism," in
Navigation Spiritualized, 217–18

[Predestination] is a doctrine that tells no man in particular who is elected or who is rejected; we cannot tell who are reprobates—nay, no man can know himself to be a reprobate, for his sins are not above God's grace. God can change his heart, even when he is breathing out curses and threatenings against the name of Christ, as He did Paul's. God is above thy naughty heart, and He can change it at the ninth or eleventh or at the last hour of the day. No man can know himself to be a reprobate, and therefore we preach the gospel to men as sinners, not as elect or reprobate, to all sinners without exception, to the greatest of sinners. We bid them come unto Christ, and He will refresh and heal them. We challenge all the world to name any one man or woman that ever repented in vain or fought the Lord in vain; and therefore to shut the door of grace and mercy against thyself, which we set wide open upon a conceit that the gospel will do thee no good if thou be a reprobate, is a grievous temptation of the devil, the enemy of thy salvation.

✦ WILLIAM LYFORD
Plain Man's Senses, 174–75

It was a good saying, I think, of the blessed martyr Bradford: "No man should go to the university of predestination till he be well trained up in the grammar school of faith and repentance." If this or the like method be neglected, no good can but much hurt will ensue. God's decrees are some way like the mount that must not be touched; but you must first worship at a distance and then make a reverent and awful approach. This is not only holy ground, but it is unsearchable by us. Now know that though electing love hath no cause nor ground for it without God Himself, yet it hath great and noble fruits; and in the decree of the end, salvation, there is a wise design of fit means and ways to compass this end: "But we are bound to give thanks alway to God for you, brethren beloved of the Lord, because God hath from the beginning chosen you to salvation, through sanctification of the Spirit and belief of the truth" (2 Thess. 2:13).

✦ ROBERT TRAILL
Sermon 2, in *Sixteen Sermons on the Lord's Prayer, for His People*, 34–35

EMOTION

Neither do thou measure thy faith by thy present feeling of God's favor, for thy soul is sometimes sick, sometimes in a swound, and so may judge amiss of thine estate, but measure thou thy faith by thy true apprehending of God's love in Christ, which may be when there is no feeling. It is one thing...not to feel faith in the time of thy first conversion and of temptation; another thing...not to be willing to believe or to feel faith.

✦ HANNIBAL GAMMON
God's Just Desertion of the Unjust, 27

ENEMY

If we love an enemy, we shall wish his welfare and rejoice in it and be unfeignedly sorry for any disaster that befalls him; so far shall we be from rejoicing in his misfortunes. And certainly, had we a right sense of things, we should be more troubled for the harm which our enemy does to his own soul by wronging us than for the prejudice we sustain by him. Our compassion toward him would diminish, if not altogether swallow up the resentment of what we suffer from him.

✦ HENRY SCOUGAL
"Indispensable Duty of Loving Our Enemies," in *Works*, 103–4

It is far better to have the ungodly man's enmity than his society. By the former, he is most hateful, but by the latter, he is most hurtful. A religious man in the company of wicked men is like a green branch among dry and burning brands; they can sooner kindle him than he can quench them.

✦ WILLIAM SECKER
Nonsuch Professor, 52

It is unnatural to hate them that love us, and it is supernatural to love them that hate us.

✦ WILLIAM SECKER
The Nonsuch Professor, 93

To render evil for evil is brutish; to render evil for good is devilish; to render good for evil is Christian.

✦ THOMAS WATSON
The Beatitudes, in *Discourses*, 2:153

ENVY

This sin [i.e., envy] does so prevail that it is difficult to get two ministers to live together in love and quietness unanimously to carry on the work of God. Unless one of them be greatly inferior to the other and content to be so esteemed and to be governed by him, they are contending for precedency, envying each other's interest and behaving with strangeness and jealousy toward one another to the shame of their profession and the injury of their congregations. Nay, so great is the pride of some ministers that when they might have an equal assistant to further the work of God, they had rather take all the burden upon themselves, though more than they can bear, than that any should share with them in their honor or lest they should diminish their own interest in the people.

♦ RICHARD BAXTER
Reformed Pastor, 163–64

Mr. Badman's envy was so rank and strong that if it at any time turned its head against a man, it would hardly ever be pulled in again. He would watch over that man to do him mischief, as the cat watches over the mouse to destroy it; yea, he would wait seven years, but he would have an opportunity to hurt him, and when he had it, he would make him feel the weight of his envy. This envy is the very father and mother of a great many hideous and prodigious wickednesses. It both begets them and also nourishes them up till they come to their cursed maturity in the bosom of him that entertains them.

♦ JOHN BUNYAN
Riches, 51

Such [hypocrites] secretly envy the luster of the gifts and graces of such as go beyond them and cannot abide to be outshined. If thou love grace as such, thou wilt love it wherever it is most pure and shines most brightly. The Pharisees, hating Christ for this, discovered what they were.

♦ ALEXANDER CARMICHAEL
"An Essay on Hypocrisy," in
Believer's Mortification of Sin, 221

Envy is a denial of providence.

♦ STEPHEN CHARNOCK
in Horn, *Puritan Remembrancer*, 93

There is great diversity between love and envy, for he that loveth taketh himself to be benefited in the benefit of him whom he loveth, himself to be praised in the praises of that man whom he liketh. The envious man, on the contrary part, thinketh that [when] another man is praised, [he] in the self-same is dispraised, that another cannot be profited but that in the same he is hindered, and therefore stormeth when anything is attributed to another, as if in that deed something had been taken from himself. Thus, in all things the envious man deals as if it were a stranger from the other; the loving man as if he were not diverse, but one with the other and a very part and member of the same. Let us therefore keep ourselves far from this envy, the truest token that can be of the absence of charity.

✦ JOHN KNEWSTUB
Lectures, 187

[Envy] is a sin that breaks both tables at once. It begins in discontent with God and ends in injury to man. It is the root of hatred against godliness. They that are at the bottom of the hill fret at those that are at the top, and men malign what they will not imitate. Wicked men would have all upon the same level.

✦ THOMAS MANTON
Practical Exposition on the
Epistle of James, 155

There is little of the Spirit of God where there is such an envious spirit. Grace stands in conformity to God, and therefore it is expressed by a participation of the divine nature (2 Peter 1:4). Grace is nothing else but an introduction of the virtues of God into the soul. Now God delights in giving more grace, and therefore such as are not communicative and diffusive of their good to others, or are all for an enclosure of blessings, or cannot rejoice in the parts [i.e., gifts], services, or excellences of others have nothing at all or very little of the nature of God in them.

✦ THOMAS MANTON
Practical Exposition on the
Epistle of James, 156

Envy: when men indulge an envious disposition at the prosperity of others. "There is one," says discontent, "less deserving than I in more credit; another less diligent but more successful. There

are others who live without care or pains, and yet riches flow in upon them, and they have all that heart can wish." Sure the world is very unequally divided that we must have labor and disappointment, and they wealth and ease. "See," says envy, "what a fine house, what rich furniture, what a flowing trade, and the like, such and such enjoy." And what is all this to thee? "Is thine eye evil because God is good?" A little more modesty would teach you that the Governor of the universe knows best where to bestow His gifts. Alas! He sees that thy neighbor's high estate and thy high spirit would undo thee. He knows what is fittest both for him and thee, and therefore be content to be at His disposal.

✦ RICHARD STEELE
Religious Tradesman, 170

This sin [i.e., envy] was to be found not only in women which envied others that exceeded them in beauty of body, in clothes, and dressing, and such like toys but also in men, who envied them who were of the same trade, which had better houses and shops, more custom and wealth than themselves. Yea, this envying was to be found among many ministers who envied others that had better parts and more learning, greater applause, and more auditors than themselves. There was a spirit among us which lusted to envy (James 4:5), which, besides the great torment that it brings to the spirit where it reigns, is a very great provocation to the Lord.

✦ THOMAS VINCENT
God's Terrible Voice in the City, 154

ESCHATOLOGY

Augustine desired to have seen three things before he died: First, Rome in her glory and purity. Secondly, Paul in the pulpit preaching. Thirdly, Christ in the flesh upon earth. Cato, the heathen, repented himself of three things: First, that ever he spent a day idle. Secondly, that ever he revealed his secrets to a woman. Thirdly, that ever he went by water when he might have gone by land. Thales gave thanks for three things: First, that he was endued with reason and was not a beast. Secondly, that he was a man and not a woman. Thirdly, that he was a Grecian and not a barbarian. And I, poor I, desire to see three things before I die: First, Babylon's ruin. Secondly, Christ's reigning. Thirdly, Satan's binding.

✦ WILLIAM DYER
Christ's Famous Titles, 22

A dear friend of mine (now I hope with God) was much troubled with an impertinent and importunate fellow, desirous to tell him his fortune. "For things to come," said my friend, "I desire not to know them but am contented to attend divine providence. "Tell me, if you can, some remarkable passages of my life past." But the cunning man was nothing for the preter[ite] tense (where his falsehood might be discovered), but all for the future, counting himself therein without the reach of confutation. There are in our age a generation of people who are the best of prophets and worst of historians; Daniel and the Revelation are as easy to them as the Ten Commandments and the Lord's Prayer. They pretend exactly to know the time of Christ's actual reign on earth; of the ruin of the Romish antichrist; yea, of the day of judgment itself. But these oracles are struck quite dumb if demanded anything concerning the time past: about the coming of the children of Israel out of Egypt and Babylon, the original increase and ruin of the four monarchies. Of these and the like they can give no more account than the child in the cradle. They are all for things to come, but have gotten (through a great cold of ignorance) such a crick in their neck, they cannot look backward on what was behind them.

✦ THOMAS FULLER
Good Thoughts, 297–98

The dream of setting up an outward, glorious, visible kingdom of Christ, which He must bear rule in and over the world, be it in Germany or in England, is but an ungrounded presumption. The Jews not called, antichrist not destroyed, the nations of the world generally wrapped up in idolatry and false worship, little dreaming of their deliverance—will the Lord Christ leave the world in this state and set up His kingdom here on a molehill?

✦ JOHN OWEN
Golden Book, 231

That the time of this great opening [of God's books] is uncertain. The opening is certain, but the time when is unseen. There have some indeed undertaken to foretell the time. In the primitive days and while the apostles were yet alive, there were some that pretended revelations or visions from the Spirit, declaring this day to be then near (2 Thess. 2:2). And since, many have presumed to foretell the year whose predictions time hath already confuted. Aventinus shows that about the year 1062, the credulous people were so deluded by such ridiculous predictions that there was a general expectation of the great day of judgment as then just upon them.... There are some who told us that the year 1675, others that the year 1680, others that 1688, others that 1695, and some tell us that 1700 will put an end to the world and open the great opening day. But our Savior asserts that it is an unknown day (Matt. 24:36; Mark 13:32).

✦ HENRY PENDLEBURY
Books Opened, in *Invisible Realities*, 189–90

I might add here, as a cause of the security of some, the presumptuous confidences of future events which belong only to God to foreknow, which some have taken upon them so absolutely to determine as if they had looked into the book of God's decrees or had an infallible revelation from Him of what should come to pass. O, the good days that some have looked for upon presumption of what they had no ground for! Great expectations many had of the fall of antichrist and Babylon in the year 1666 and other events, limiting times, which God hath not clearly revealed, which is an entrenching upon God's prerogative, and I believe a greater provocation than such persons are aware of. This may be one reason why London is

fallen instead of Babylon in this year of such expectation and presumption.

✦ THOMAS VINCENT
God's Terrible Voice in the City, 156–57

ETERNAL SECURITY (See PERSEVERANCE OF THE SAINTS)

ETERNITY

A Christian in the holy assemblies and in his reading, learning, prayer, conference is laying up for everlasting, when the worldling in the market, in the field, or shop is making provision for a few days or hours. Thou gloriest in thy riches and preeminence now, but how long wilt thou do so?

✦ RICHARD BAXTER
Baxteriana, 236–37

Suppose a bird was to come once in a thousand years to some vast mountain of sand and carry away in her bill one sand in a thousand years. O what a vast time would it be ere this immortal bird, after that rate, had recovered the mountain, and yet in time this might be done, for there would be still some diminution. But in eternity there can be none. There be things in time which are not competent to eternity. In time there is a succession: one generation, year, and day passeth and another comes; but eternity is a fixed now. In time there is a diminution and wasting; the more is past, the less is to come. But it is not so in eternity.

✦ JOHN FLAVEL
Navigation Spiritualized, 25

There is no wrinkle on the brow of eternity.

✦ THOMAS MANTON
in Horn, *Puritan Remembrancer*, 7

It is highly reasonable that we begin now to be that which we expect to be forever, to learn that way of living in which we hope to live to all eternity.

✦ SAMUEL SHAW
Voice of One Crying in the Wilderness, 171

EVANGELISM

There are two pools wherein the net should be set. [The first place is] in the public assemblies of the Lord's people. There it was that Lydia's heart was opened. The pool of ordinances sometimes is made healing water to souls pining away in their iniquity. The second place to set a net is in private conference. Many times the Lord is pleased to bless this for the good of souls.

✦ THOMAS BOSTON
Art of Man-Fishing, 42–43

We have toiled all day, all the days of our lives, and have caught nothing. The net of the gospel hath been always spread out, and not scarce one soul taken in it. We read Acts 2:40 that at a sermon of St. Peter's, three thousand souls were converted to the Lord, but now we may hear three thousand sermons preached, and scarce one soul brought to heaven. Men are altogether of Gallio's mind (Acts 18:17). They care not for these things. Never was there since the days of Adam so much

means of grace and salvation as now. Have we not line upon line, precept upon precept, sermon upon sermon, mercy upon mercy, and yet all will not do; men stop their ears.

✦ ARTHUR DENT
Plain Man's Plain Path-way, 13

It is the duty of all the sons and daughters of Adam who hear the gospel preached and Christ offered to them to believe in or receive Christ, be they prepared or not prepared. I say, it is the duty incumbent upon them all.

✦ GILES FIRMIN
Real Christian, 2

But what is it to go to Christ?… To go to Christ is to embrace Him in His person and offices and to rest entirely and closely upon Him for pardon of sin and eternal life, being deeply sensible of the want and worth of Him. "As many as received him, to them gave he power to become the sons of God, even to them that believe on his name" (John 1:12).

✦ JOHN FLAVEL
"Seamen's Catechism," in
Navigation Spiritualized, 212

For though brotherly kindness be to the saints, yet love (2 Peter 1:7) reaches to all. Near and far off, strangers, enemies within and without the pale of the church, Turks [i.e., Muslims], and pagans—we must pray for them and do them any good if they come in our way, as the Samaritan did to the Jew (Luke 10).

✦ JOHN ROGERS
Treatise of Love, 42

Now followeth to speak of the persons whom we ought to love; and they are all men upon the face of the earth, good and bad, without or within the pale of the church. Our love must stretch itself to any of them. They are our neighbor, whom we are bidden to love as ourselves, as we may see in the parable of the Samaritan. These we ought to do good to if they need and we be able, and for these we must pray. For though we must not pray for the salvation of all men because we know it's contrary to the revealed will of God that all should be saved, yet we ought to pray for every particular person that we know or can see because we know not (whatsoever he be now) but he may belong to God.
✦ JOHN ROGERS
Treatise of Love, 108–9

EVIL COMPANY

It is not so much your loose companions that are your tempters to evil as the devil in and by them. When Peter tried to persuade his Master to avoid sufferings, Christ rebuked the evil spirit that spoke in Peter and said, "Get thee behind me, Satan." Peter was set to work by Satan; therefore Christ calls him by the name of Satan. Those wicked men are instruments in the hand of Satan who propose carnal comforts as a cure for spiritual wounds.
✦ ISAAC AMBROSE
Christian Warrior, 60

Evil company, commonly termed goodfellows, but indeed the devil's chief instruments to hinder a wretched sinner from repentance and piety. The first sign of God's favor to a sinner is to give him grace to forsake evil companions.
✦ LEWIS BAYLY
Practice of Piety, 90

Do you want peace and comfort and quietude of soul? Take heed how you walk with doubting company; take heed how you walk with those that are full of fears and doubtings. As one drunkard makes another, and one swearer begets another, and one opposer of godliness draws on another, and one adulterer makes another, so one doubting Christian makes another.
✦ WILLIAM BRIDGE
Lifting Up, 26

Sinful examples are very enticing and encouraging; many have found it so to their eternal undoing. Those that have no ears to hear what you say have many eyes to see what you do. Bad princes make bad subjects, bad masters make bad servants, bad parents make bad children, and bad husbands make bad wives. It is easier for the bad to corrupt the good than for the good to convert the bad. It is easier to run down the hill with company than to run up the hill alone.
✦ THOMAS BROOKS
Apples of Gold, 273

Clothes and company do oftentimes tell tales in a mute but significant language.
✦ THOMAS BROOKS
Smooth Stones, 103

Christian…said to his brother, "I told you how it would happen. Your words and his lusts could not agree. He had rather leave your company than reform his life. But he is gone, as I said. Let him go; the loss is no man's but his own. He has saved us the trouble of going from him, for he continuing, as I suppose he will do, as he is, he would have been but a blot in our company. Besides, the apostle says, 'From such withdraw thyself.'"

✦ JOHN BUNYAN
Pilgrim's Progress, 80

There is a secret and bewitching power in profane company to poison and pervert even the best disposition, sin being of a contagious nature—more infectious than the plague—and the soul much more catching of the contagion of sin than the body of an infectious disease. It is a thing of great difficulty ordinarily and intimately to converse with wicked men and not to be tainted with their sins.

✦ THOMAS GOUGE
The Young Man's Guide, in *Works*, 377

How will young men put themselves on any company, any society? At first being delighted with evil company, then with the evil of the company.

✦ JOHN OWEN
Golden Book, 228

Beware we…of their companies; avoid we as much as may be both conversation and conference with the wicked. Their heads are forges of wicked wiles; they are plentifully furnished with [a] store of stratagems and have mischievous fetches to bring their purposes to pass. Of receiving harm we stand in great peril; of effecting good there is small hope.

✦ NEHEMIAH ROGERS
"The Watchful Shepherd," in
True Convert, 101

The godly are more frequently corrupted by the evil deportment of the worldling than the worldling is refined by the chaste conversation of the godly.

✦ WILLIAM SECKER
Nonsuch Professor, 52–53

The sixth bar in the way to salvation is evil company. They will take us off our work. The sweet waters lose their freshness when they run into the salt; Christians lose their freshness and savoriness among the wicked. Christ's doves will be sullied by lying among these pots. Sinful company is like the water in a smith's forge which quenches the iron be it ever so hot; such cool good affections.

✦ THOMAS WATSON
"The One Thing Necessary,"
in *Discourses*, 1:379

EVIL THOUGHTS

It is not what thoughts are in your hearts and pass through them as what lodging they have that doth difference your repentance. Many good thoughts…may pass as strangers through a bad man's heart, and so likewise multitudes of vain thoughts may make a thoroughfare of a believer's heart and disturb him in good duties by knockings and interruptions and breakings in upon the heart of a good man; but still they lodge not there—are not fostered, harbored.

✦ THOMAS GOODWIN
"The Vanity of Thoughts," in
Works, 3:509–10

The Christian's heart is of that color which his most abiding, constant thoughts dye it into. Transient, fleeting thoughts, be they comfortable or sad, do not much work upon the soul or alter its temper into joy or sorrow. Neither poison kills, nor food nourishes that does not stay in the body; no, then the affliction soaks into the heart and embitters the Christian's spirit into perplexing fears and disconsolate dejections when his thoughts lie steeping in his sorrows from day to day.

✦ WILLIAM GURNALL
Christian in Complete Armour, 617

Evil thoughts are continually arising out of our hearts, as sparks out of a furnace. Sin keeps house with us whether we will or not. The best saint alive is troubled with inmates; though he forsakes his sins, yet his sins will not forsake him.

✦ THOMAS WATSON
The Christian's Charter of Privileges,
in *Discourses*, 1:27

EXAMPLE

Precepts instruct us what things are our duty, but examples assure us that they are possible. They resemble a clear stream wherein we may not only discover our spots but wash them off. When we see men like ourselves, who

are united to frail flesh and in the same condition with us to command their passions, to overcome the most glorious and glittering temptations, we are encouraged in our spiritual warfare.

✦ WILLIAM BATES
in Bertram, *Homiletic
Encyclopaedia*, 323

Example is the most powerful rhetoric.

✦ THOMAS BROOKS
in Horn, *Puritan Remembrancer*, 50

Old Testament examples are New Testament instructions.

✦ JOHN OWEN
Golden Book, 221; also in Thomas,
Puritan Golden Treasury, 96

Man is a creature that is led more by patterns than by precepts.

✦ GEORGE SWINNOCK
in Thomas, *Puritan Golden Treasury*, 95

EXCESS

He wrestles with a body of flesh. This to the Christian in duty is as the beast to the traveler; he cannot go his journey without it, and much ado to go with it. If the flesh be kept high and lusty, then it is wanton and will not obey; if low, then it is weak and soon tires. Thus the Christian rids but little ground because he must go his weak body's pace. He wrestles with a body of sin as well as of flesh; this mutters and murmurs when the soul is taking up any duty.

✦ WILLIAM GURNALL
Christian in Complete Armour, 78

EXPECTATIONS

Remember that all men are so selfish that their expectations will be higher than you are able to satisfy. They will not consider your hindrances, or avocations, or what you do for others, but most of them look to have as much to themselves as if you had nobody else to mind but them. Many and many a time when I have had an hour or a day to spend, a multitude have every one expected that I should have spent it with them. When I visit one, there are ten offended that I am not visiting them at the same hour. When I am discoursing with one, many more are offended that I am not speaking to them all at once. If those that I speak to account me courteous, and humble, and respectful, those that I could not speak to, or but in a word, account me discourteous and morose. How many have censured me because I have not allowed them the time which God and conscience commanded me to spend upon greater and more necessary work!

✦ RICHARD BAXTER
A Christian Directory, in
Practical Works, 2:560

Expectation, in a weak mind, makes an evil greater and a good less. But in a resolved mind, it digests an evil before it come and makes a future good long before present. I will expect the worst because it may come; the best because I know it will come.

✦ JOSEPH HALL
Meditations and Vows, 9

EXPERIENCE

It pleases God at times to give to His people high enjoyment of spiritual things, such as clear views of Christ, manifestations of His love, a sense of pardon, and assurance of hope, with peace and joy. The devil often makes these privileges occasions of pride, and this pride soon drives God away: "For he will know the proud afar off." High enjoyment seldom lasts long. This is well for us, for had we always a heavenly feast our corrupt hearts would be puffed up with pride.

✦ ISAAC AMBROSE
Christian Warrior, 112

'Tis a common observation that those discourses that savor most of inward experience are more influential and warming than those that are more scholastic, wanting that experience; for what comes from the heart reaches it.

✦ ANONYMOUS
Stated Christian Conference, 23

They have most of Christ and are the best Christians who have their corruptions most mortified. Value this more than talking, more than a plausible way of praying—yea, more than raptures.

✦ ALEXANDER CARMICHAEL
Believer's Mortification of Sin, 37–38

This experience we have of the powers of religion in our souls is that only which fixes a man's spirit in the ways of godliness. It made the Hebrews take joyfully the spoiling of their goods; no arguments or temptations can wrest truth out of the hand of experience....

For want of this, many professors turn aside from truth in the hour of trial. Oh, brethren, labor to feel the influences of religion upon your very hearts.... This will settle you better than all arguments in the world can do. By this the ways of God are more endeared to men than by any other way in the world. When your hearts have once felt it, you will never forsake it.

✦ JOHN FLAVEL
Sacramental Meditations, 34–35

Experiences, saith Parisiensis, are like crutches which do indeed help a lame man to go, but they do not make the lame man sound or strong; food and physic must do that. And therefore, Christian, labor to lean more on the promise and less on sensible expressions of God's love, whether it be in the present feeling or past experiences of it. I would not take you off from improving those but leaning on these, and limiting the actings of our faith to these.

✦ WILLIAM GURNALL
Christian in Complete Armour, 467

I speak with the experience of many saints and, I hope, according to Scripture if I say there is a communication of the Spirit of God which is sometimes let out to some of His people that is somewhat besides, if not beyond, that witnessing of a sonship spoken of before. It is a glorious divine manifestation of God unto the soul, shedding abroad God's love in the heart. It is a thing better felt than spoken of. It is no audible voice, but it is a flash of glory filling the soul with God, as He is life,

light, love, and liberty countervailing that audible voice, "O men, greatly beloved," putting a man in a transport with this on his heart: "It is good to be here."

✦ WILLIAM GUTHRIE
Christian's Great Interest, 196–98

There is a third knowledge of God, and that is a knowledge of experience. In Scripture phrase, men are said to know those things that they have experience of and not to know those things they have had no experience of. And this experimental knowledge is in Scripture in special manner called acquaintance. It is said of the Lord Christ that He was a man of sorrows and acquainted with grief. That is, He felt and tasted and had experience of griefs and sorrows of all kinds.

✦ MATTHEW NEWCOMEN
Best Acquaintance, 12–13

Among the various ways of God's teaching, experience is one of the chiefest, for that is the inward sense and feeling of what is outwardly read and heard, and the spiritual and powerful enjoyment of what is believed. Experience is a copy written by the Spirit of God upon the hearts of believers. It is one of faith's handmaids and attendants, and hope's usher (Rom. 5:3).

✦ VAVASOR POWELL
*Spirituall Experiences of
Sundry Beleevers, ii–iii*

Carefully observe and call to mind the many and sweet experiences you have of God's love and favor. The more plentiful our apprehension is of God's love to us, the more will our hearts be enlarged to love him again. "Whoso is wise, and will observe these things, even they shall understand the loving-kindness of the LORD" (Ps.107:43). Hence it was that David did so gather upon God when he was to encounter with Goliath (1 Sam. 17:36) and at other times (Ps. 61:2–3; 63:7; 71:5–6, 20; 22:21; 27:9–10). Experience being so great a prop of faith, it must needs be a special means to increase love.

✦ NEHEMIAH ROGERS
The Penitent Citizen, in
Mirrour of Mercy, 101

FAILINGS

When we see wherein we have failed in any part of our daily practice, we are not to make slight account thereof or favor ourselves therein, but labor speedily to recover, lest we grow hardened and incurable.

✦ EZEKIEL CULVERWELL
Time Well Spent, 106

FAITH

Faith is generally an acknowledgment and assent to the truth (James 2:19). It is either common to all: such is an historical faith which is in the devils themselves, and temporary faith that will always keep the warm side of the hedge, never windward. Christ is little beholden to that faith, and that faith shall be little beholden to Christ.

✦ THOMAS ADAMS
Meditations upon the Creed,
in *Works,* 3:86

Faith is a resting of the heart on God as on the author of life and eternal salvation. That is to say that by Him we may be freed from all evil and obtain all good.

✦ WILLIAM AMES
Marrow of Sacred Divinity, 5

Faith is the soul's ear.

✦ JOHN BOYS
in Horn, *Puritan Remembrancer,* 106

Properly, according to Scripture phrase, trusting in God is the recumbency, or the reliance, of the soul upon God in Christ for some good thing that lies out of sight.

✦ WILLIAM BRIDGE
Lifting Up, 263

Consider these few following things as some helps to your faith: (1) that God never leads His people into any great mercy but first He puts the sentence of death upon all means that tend unto it; (2) that it is a great sin to limit God's mercy, as well as limit His power; (3) that when the Lord has given a promise to His people, He does then sometimes try whether they will trust to His naked word or no; (4) that God oftentimes fulfills one promise by denying another; (5) that when we see nothing but what is contrary unto our help, then is Christ's time to help.

✦ WILLIAM BRIDGE
Lifting Up, 281–82

A man may want the feeling of his faith and cry and call again and again for it, and yet nevertheless have true and sound faith; for the feeling of and mourning for the want of faith and the earnest and constant desire of it is an infallible sign of faith. For this is a sure rule, that so long as one feels himself sick, he is not dead; and the high estimation of faith, joined with a vehement desire of it, is a singular evidence that there is a sound and lively root of faith in our hearts.

✦ THOMAS BROOKS
Cabinet of Choice Jewels, 34

If thou wouldst be silent and quiet under the saddest providences and sorest trials, then keep up faith in continual exercise. Now faith in the exercise of it will quiet and silence the soul, thus: (1) by bringing the soul to sit down satisfied in the naked enjoyments of God; (2) by drying up the springs of pride, self-love, impatience, murmuring, unbelief, and the carnal delights of this world; (3) by presenting to the soul greater, sweeter, and better things in Christ than any this world doth afford (Phil. 3:7–8); (4) by lessening the soul's esteem of all outward vanities. Do but keep up the exercise of faith, and thou wilt keep silent before the Lord. No man so mute as he whose faith is still busy about invisible objects.

✦ THOMAS BROOKS
Mute Christian, 244

Faith has an influence upon all other graces. It is like a silver thread that runs through a chain of pearls; it puts strength and vivacity into all other graces.

✦ THOMAS BROOKS
Smooth Stones, 26

Faith cannot be lost, but assurance may; therefore, assurance is not faith.

✦ THOMAS BROOKS
in Horn, *Puritan Remembrancer*, 17

I never heard a presumptuous man in my life say that he was afraid that he presumed, but I have heard many an honest, humble soul say that they have been afraid that their faith has been presumptive.

✦ JOHN BUNYAN
Riches, 192

Faith will suck sweetness out of God's rod, but unbelief can find no comfort in His greatest mercies. Faith makes great burdens light, but unbelief makes light ones intolerably heavy. Faith helps us when we are down, but unbelief throws us down when we are up. Unbelief may be called the white devil, for it oftentimes, in its mischievous doing in the soul, shows as if it was an angel of light; yea, it acts like a counselor of heaven.

✦ JOHN BUNYAN
Riches, 290

Ye have seen now what Abraham did [i.e., sacrifice Isaac by faith]; "go ye and do likewise." Take hold of God's sovereignty as your own, engaged by a covenant of grace, and so to be exerted for your good. Faith gives a propriety in any attribute it looks upon and draws out the virtues thereof for itself. And therefore, whatever difficulties are in your way, be not disheartened by them, but call in this sovereign power by faith to your help. Remember the ready subjection which all creatures do pay to His word, by which alone (without

creatures' service) He can level the mountains and make crooked things straight; restrain, alter, invert, and turn upside down the very course of nature, so that which is death in itself shall be life to you.
✦ ELISHA COLES
Practical Discourse, 37–38

Abraham was justified by works before men, but before God it was the righteousness of Christ wherein, by faith, he shrouded himself. Faith justifies the person, and works justify his faith, both to himself and other men.
✦ ELISHA COLES
Practical Discourse, 125

Faith is your spiritual optic which shows you things of greatest moment and not otherwise visible; even chariots and horsemen of fire are not discernible without it. If temptations from the world do endanger you, turn your faith that way, and through it view and consider how shallow and short-lived the pleasures of it are and how momentary your sufferings. Then look at the world to come—the glory of it and your interest in it and how much your crown will be brightened by the trials you have passed under here, and dwell on the contemplation of it.
✦ ELISHA COLES
Practical Discourse, 296

The way to increase faith is to apply to ourselves God's promise in His word and sacraments by hearing the word, praying, meditation, conference, and the like.
✦ EZEKIEL CULVERWELL
Time Well Spent, 107

Faith in Christ, then, is the receiving of Christ as He is offered in the gospel, and so resting upon Him alone for life and salvation.
✦ GILES FIRMIN
Real Christian, 203

Faith is a true glass that represents all those [Jesus's] sufferings and agonies to the life. It presents them not as a fiction or idle tale, but as a true and faithful narrative.
✦ JOHN FLAVEL
Fountain of Life, 244

'Tis just matter of wonder and astonishment that ever one spark of faith was kindled in such a heart as thine is, a heart which had no predisposition or inclination in the least to believe. Yea, it was not *rasa tabula*, like clean paper, void of any impression of faith, but filled with contrary impressions to it so that 'tis marvelous that ever your hearts received the stamp or impression of faith on them. It was wonderful that that fire should fall from heaven and burn upon the altar when Elijah had laid the wood in order upon it, but much more when he poured so much water upon it as not only wet all the wood but filled the trenches (1 Kings 18:33). Just so was the case of thy soul, reader, when God came to kindle faith there.
✦ JOHN FLAVEL
Sacramental Meditations, 130

Justifying faith is not a naked assent to the truths of the gospel.... Assent to the truth of the word is but an act of the understanding which reprobates and devils may exercise. But justifying faith is a compounded habit and hath its seat both in the understanding and will and therefore called a believing with the heart (Rom. 10:10)—yea, a believing with all the heart: "Philip said, If thou believest with all thine heart, thou mayest" (Acts 8:37). It takes in all the powers of the soul.

✦ WILLIAM GURNALL
Christian in Complete Armour, 424–25

Everyone that assents to the truth of what the Scripture saith of Christ doth not believe on Christ. No, this believing on Christ implies a union of the soul to Christ and fiduciary recumbency on Christ. Therefore, we are bid to take hold of Christ (who is there called God's strength, as elsewhere His arm), that we may make peace with God, and we shall make peace with Him (Isa. 27:5). It is not the sight of a man's arm stretched out to a man in the water will save him from drowning, but the taking hold of it.

✦ WILLIAM GURNALL
Christian in Complete Armour, 427

True faith on the promise works obedience to the command.

✦ WILLIAM GURNALL
Christian in Complete Armour, 446

The more able to wait long for answers to our desires and prayers, the stronger faith is. Weak faith is all for the present; if it hath not presently its desires answered, then it grows jealous, lays down sad conclusions against itself— his prayer was not heard, or he is not one God loves, and the like.... But

strong faith, that can trade with God for time—yea, wait God's leisure: "He that believeth shall not make haste" (Isa. 28:16). He knows his money is in a good hand, and he is not over-quick to call for it home, knowing well that the longest voyages have the richest returns.

✦ WILLIAM GURNALL
Christian in Complete Armour, 468

When, therefore, Satan sets forth the believer's sins in battle array against him and confronts him with their greatness, then faith runs under the shelter of this rock. Surely, saith faith, my Savior is infinitely greater than my greatest sins. I should impeach the wisdom of God to think otherwise, who knew what a heavy burden He had to lay upon His shoulders and was fully satisfied of His strength to bear it. He that refused sacrifice and burnt offering because of their insufficiency would not have called Him had He not been all-sufficient for the work. Indeed, here lies the weight of the whole building: a weak faith may save, but a weak Savior cannot. Faith hath Christ to plead for it, but Christ hath none to plead for Him. Faith leans on Christ's arm, but Christ stood upon His own legs. And if He had sunk under the burden of our sins, He had been past the reach of any creature in heaven or earth to help Him up.

✦ WILLIAM GURNALL
Christian in Complete Armour, 501

Faith is a certain persuasion wrought in the heart of man of the truth of all God's promises; and a confident application of them is made to the believer, both which are wrought in the believer by the Spirit of God.

✦ EDWARD MARBURY
Commentarie…upon…Habakkuk, 198

Faith may dance because Christ sings.

✦ SAMUEL RUTHERFORD
Garden of Spices, 162

The point to be observed is how glorious a thing it is to God firmly to believe and rest upon His word. I know not whether by any one duty God reap more honor than from this of believing. His power, His truth, His goodness, His mercy—attributes that the Lord counts most glorious to Himself and desires rather to be acknowledged among men; by believing we acknowledge. Yea, if there be any other office and duty whereby God's glory is published and occasionally acknowledged by others, from faith it issues; profession, patience, love, mercy, or if there be any other virtue by exercise whereof men are excited to glorify God, from faith they all flow, as from their fountain.

✦ WILLIAM SCLATER
Exposition with Notes, 161

Where there is no confidence in God, there will be no continuance with God. When the wind of faith ceases to fill the sails, the ship of obedience ceases to plough the seas.

✦ WILLIAM SECKER
Nonsuch Professor, 41

As the strongest faith may be shaken, so the weakest where truth is, is so far rooted that it will prevail. Weakness with watchfulness will stand out when strength with too much confidence fails. Weakness with acknowledging of it is the fittest seat and subject for God to perfect His strength in, for consciousness of our infirmities drives us out of ourselves to Him in whom our strength lies.

✦ RICHARD SIBBES
Bruised Reed and Smoking Flax, 156

When we believe the truth of all that is revealed in the Holy Scriptures, this is not the faith which doth privilege us in sonship; the devils believe all the articles in the creed. It is not the bare knowledge of a medicine or believing the sovereign virtue of it will cure one that is ill. This general faith, so much cried up by some, will not save; this a man may have and yet not love God. He may believe that God will come to judge the quick and the dead and hate Him, as the prisoner believeth the judge's coming to the assizes and abhors the thoughts of him. Take heed of resting in a general faith; you may have this and be no better than devils.

✦ THOMAS WATSON
The Beatitudes, in *Discourses*, 2:299

Faith is the golden clasp that knits us to Christ.

✦ THOMAS WATSON
"A Christian on Earth Still in Heaven," in *Discourses*, 1:280

Faith is full of good works. It believes as if it did not work, and it works as if it did not believe.

✦ THOMAS WATSON
Lord's Prayer, 69

Faith shows the believer better things than the world can show: it gives a sight of Christ and glory; it gives a prospect of heaven. As the mariner in a dark night climbs to the top of the mast and cries out, "I see a star!" so faith climbs up above sense and reason into heaven and sees Christ, that bright Morning Star.

✦ THOMAS WATSON
Puritan Gems, 45

A living faith is ever a loving faith, and a loving faith is ever a doing faith.

✦ EDWARD WILLAN
"An Exhortation to Christian Charity," in *Six Sermons,* 13

FAITH, LIVING BY

To live by faith is, by faith in Christ, to possess the whole Word of God as our own in all states and conditions, resting quietly upon His gracious and faithful promise and yielding ourselves unto His good pleasure in sincere, universal, and constant obedience. Or to live by faith is to feed upon the several promises of God made in His Word and to apply them to our own selves, according to our needs, and so to uphold, comfort, and encourage ourselves against all temptations and unto every good duty.

✦ ISAAC AMBROSE
"The Practice of Sanctification," in *Works,* 107

Now faith does bring forth obedience in a threefold respect: (1) as it doth apprehend Christ, who is the fountain of life and the spring of all power to do well; (2) as it receives and rests in those arguments which God has propounded to us in Scripture to persuade obedience—namely, by promises and threatenings; [and] (3) as it has power to obtain all grace, and so that grace whereby obedience is performed.

✦ WILLIAM AMES
Marrow of Sacred Divinity, 218

Sense, while it seems to help, renders the work of faith more difficult by doubling it. A man must first believe the insufficiency of what he seeth before he can believe the all-sufficiency of him that is invisible: "We look not at the things which are seen, but at the things which are not seen." It is harder to live by faith in abundance than in want. The soul is a step nearer living upon God when it hath nothing to live upon but God.

✦ THOMAS CASE
Correction, Instruction, 28

Faith uses means but trusts God; obediently closes with the providence of means but sweetly leaves the providence of success to God.

✦ THOMAS CASE
Correction, Instruction, 38

Use lawful and fair means for accomplishing and bringing about thy lawful designs, but let thy main trust be on God. Do thy duty and commit thyself and thy affairs to Him in quietness of heart. For a man to say he trusts in

God and yet neglects to do his duty, this is but to mock God.... Faith uses means but trusts in God alone.

✦ SAMUEL CRADOCK
Knowledge and Practice,
part 2, chap. 5, 69

Should you see a man in a ship throw himself overboard into the sea, you might at first think him out of his wits; but if a little while after you should see him stand safe on the shore and the ship swallowed up of the waves, you would then think he took the wisest course. Faith sees the world and all the pleasures of sin sinking; there is a leak in them which the wit of man cannot stop. Now, is it not better to swim by faith through a sea of trouble and get safe to heaven at last than to sit in the lap of sinful pleasures till we drown in hell's gulf?

✦ WILLIAM GURNALL
Christian in Complete Armour, 480

[Faith] breaks the force of opposite propensions. If the world stands in the way of duty, faith overcometh the world (1 John 5:4), partly by bringing Christ into the combat, partly by spiritual replies and arguments. Reason tells us we must be for ourselves; faith tells us we must be for God. Reason saith, "If I take this course, I shall undo myself." Faith, by looking within the veil, sees it is the only way to save all (2 Cor. 4:15–18). Reason presents the treasures in Egypt, and faith the recompense of the reward. From hence are those bickerings and counter-buffs which a believer feels sometimes within himself.

✦ THOMAS MANTON
Practical Exposition on the
Epistle of James, 112

Ah, my beloved, there is no comfort to be compared to the comfort of believing, no life to be compared to the life of faith. We may talk of comfort, but till we come to live by faith we shall never taste of comfort. It is the only Christian life. Sense makes a beast, reason makes a man, but faith makes a Christian. We are no farther Christians than as we can live upon Christ in all conditions.

✦ MATTHEW MEAD
"The Power of Grace," in
Name in Heaven, 114

FAITH: THE PREEMINENT GRACE

Our heavenly King is pleased with all our graces: hot zeal and cool patience please Him; cheerful thankfulness and weeping repentance please Him; charity in the height and humility in the dust please Him. But none of them are welcome to Him without faith, as nothing can please Him without Christ. There is none that dares venture into His presence without faith; she is that Esther to which God holds out His golden scepter. Adorn thy soul with this grace.

✦ THOMAS ADAMS
Exposition upon…Second…Peter, 838

Faith is the mother grace, the root grace, the grace that has all others in the bowels of it, and that from which all others flow.

✦ JOHN BUNYAN
Riches, 290

Faith, of all graces, is the chief and chiefly to be labored for. There is a precedency, or preeminence, peculiar to this above all other; it is among graces as the sun is among the planets or as Solomon's virtuous woman among the daughters (Prov. 31:29). Though every grace hath done virtuously, yet thou, O faith, excel them all. The apostle, indeed, gives the precedency to love and sets faith on the lower hand (1 Cor. 13:13).… It is true, love is the grace that shall triumph in heaven, but it is faith, not love, which is the conquering grace here on earth.… In a word, it is love that unites God and glorified saints together in heaven, but it was faith that first united them to Christ while they were on earth: "That Christ may dwell in your hearts by faith" (Eph. 3:17).

✦ WILLIAM GURNALL
Christian in Complete Armour, 431

Faith quickens our graces. The Spirit of God infuses all the seeds and habits, but faith is the fountain of all the acts of grace. It is as the spring in the watch that moves the wheels; not a grace stirs till faith set it a work.

✦ THOMAS WATSON
The Christian's Charter of Privileges,
in *Discourses*, 1:112

FAITH: RELATIONSHIP TO HOPE

Hope is the offspring and refreshment of faith; 'tis begotten by faith, and, says one, "As a good child relieves its father faith in time of need." Hope is an expectation, faith a persuasion. Faith eyes the promise; hope the thing promised as sure, though future, which comforts the soul under the present want of desired mercy.

✦ BARTHOLOMEW ASHWOOD
Heavenly Trade, 180

Faith looks to Christ as dead, buried, and ascended; and hope to His second coming. Faith looks to Him for justification; hope for glory. Faith fights for doctrine; hope for a reward. Faith for what is in the Bible; hope for what is in heaven. Faith purifies the heart from bad principles; hope from bad manners (2 Peter 3:11, 14). Faith sets hope at work; hope sets patience at work. Faith says to hope, "Look for what is promised"; hope says to faith, "So I do, and will wait for it too." Faith looks through the word of God in Christ; hope looks through faith, beyond the world, to glory.

✦ JOHN BUNYAN
Riches, 294

A Christian, indeed, is comforted by faith, but not satisfied; or if satisfied, it is in point of security, not of desire, because here we are absent from the Lord, and walk by faith, not by sight. Hope, though it keep life in the soul, yet it is not able to fill it; he longs and thinks every day a year till he be at home. They that walk by faith cannot be quiet till they be in the sight of those things which they believe.

✦ THOMAS CASE
Correction, Instruction, 66

There are two graces which Christ uses above any other to fill the soul with joy—faith and hope—because these two fetch all their wine of joy without door. Faith tells the soul what Christ hath done for it and so comforts it; hope revives the soul with the news of what Christ will do. Both draw at one tap—Christ and His promise.

✦ WILLIAM GURNALL
Christian in Complete Armour, 524

The difference of these two graces, faith and hope, is so small that the one is often taken for the other in Scripture. It is but a different aspect of the same confidence, faith apprehending the infallible truth of those divine promises of which hope doth assuredly expect the accomplishment, and that is their truth, so that this immediately results from the other. This is the anchor fixed within the veil which keeps the soul firm against all the tossings on these swelling seas and the winds and tempests that arise upon them. The firmest thing in this inferior world is a believing soul. Faith establishes the heart on Jesus Christ, and hope lifts it up, being on that rock, over the head of all intervenient dangers, crosses, and temptations and sees the glory and happiness that follow after them.

✦ ROBERT LEIGHTON
A Commentary upon the First Epistle of Peter, in Whole Works, 1:105–6

Faith looks to the Word promising; hope to the things promised in the Word.

✦ RICHARD SIBBES
in Horn, Puritan Remembrancer, 52

Faith and hope are two sisters: they bear a resemblance to each other, yet differ thus—faith looks at the certainty of the promise, hope at the excellency of the promise.

✦ THOMAS WATSON
Puritan Gems, 49

FAITH: RELATIONSHIP TO LOVE

You may easily see your stability, strength, and growth does consist. (1) It does not most, or much, consist in speculations or less useful truths. (2) It does not consist in the mere heat of affections, for zeal may be misguided and do hurt and may prove sometimes but a mere natural or distempered sinful passion. (3) It consists not in mere fears, or purposes, that you are frightened into against your wills. (4) Nor does it consist in the common gifts of grace or nature. (5) Nor yet in running into groundless singularities and unusual strains. But, in a word, it consists in holy love kindled by effectual faith. When a firmly believing soul is fullest of the love of God and Christ and holiness, this is the most confirmed state of soul; and in this your chiefest growth consists.

✦ RICHARD BAXTER
Baxteriana, 99–100

Faith works by love. It is not henceforth the fear of wrath but the sense of Christ's love in delivering from wrath that both curbs the unregenerate part and carries to higher acts of obedience than fear is capable of, although at times all sorts of motives may be needful to keep us going; and the Lord, for exercise of our graces and other holy ends, may let the dearest of His children long conflict with their fears, under which He yet supports them and brings them forth like gold at last.

✦ ELISHA COLES
Practical Discourse, 270

Love is the affection that governs this royal fort of man's heart: we give our hearts to them we give our love. And indeed, thus it is that faith brings the heart over into subjection and obedience to God by putting it under a law of love: faith which worketh by love (Gal. 5:6). First, faith works love, and then it works by it. As first the workman sets an edge on his tools and then he carves and cuts with them, so faith sharpens the soul's love to God and then acts by it.

✦ WILLIAM GURNALL
Christian in Complete Armour, 447

The more…love is in thy walking [i.e., obedience], the stronger thy faith is. Faith works by love, and therefore its strength or weakness may be discovered by the strength or weakness of that love it puts forth in the Christian's actings. The strength of a man's arm that draws a bow is seen by the force [of] the arrow which he shoots flies

with. And certainly the strength of our faith may be known by the force that our love mounts to God with. It is impossible that weak faith (which is unable to draw the promise as a strong faith can) should leave such a forcible impression on the heart to love God as the stronger faith doth. If, therefore, thy heart be strongly carried out from love to God to abandon sin, perform duty, and exert acts of obedience to His command, know thy place and take it with humble thankfulness; thou art a graduate in the art of believing.

✦ WILLIAM GURNALL
Christian in Complete Armour, 469

FAITH: RELATIONSHIP TO WORKS

There is fruitfulness [in faith]. It is not barren, for "faith without works is dead" (James 2:20). Nudifidians are nullifidians. We will never take her for a true lady that has not her gentleman usher before, and her servants following after. If you see not repentance going before faith nor works attending on her, know it is not she.

✦ THOMAS ADAMS
Exposition upon…Second…Peter, 8

True faith is a jewel, rare and precious, and not so common as nominal, careless Christians think. "What," say they, "are we not all believers; will you make infidels of all that are not saints? Are none Christians but those that live so strictly?" Answer: I know they are not infidels by profession, but what they are indeed and what God will take them for you may soon perceive by comparing the description of faith with the inscription legible on their lives.

✦ RICHARD BAXTER
Baxteriana, 66–67

Faith justifies the person, and works justify his faith.

✦ ELISHA COLES
in Horn, *Puritan Remembrancer*, 271

We teach that God, having sworn that to those whom He justifies, He will give grace to worship Him in holiness and righteousness. No man can be assured of his justification without obedience, that sanctification being the end of our election, calling, redemption, and regeneration; it is a necessary consequent of saving grace. We teach and profess that howsoever good works do not concur with faith unto the act of justification as a cause thereof, yet they concur in the party justified as necessary fruits of faith and testimonies of justification. And as we teach with Paul that faith alone doth justify, so, with James, that the faith which is alone doth not justify.

✦ GEORGE DOWNAME
Christian's Freedom, 69

The end then both of hearing and knowing is doing. It is the badge of our profession, the pledge of our election, the assurance of our effectual vocation, the fruit of our justification, a special part of our sanctification, and the highway to our eternal salvation. Faith, without it, being but a vain speculation; and hope but a vain presumption; and charity but a vain ostentation.

✦ GEORGE HAKEWILL
King David's Vow for Reformation, 45

Till faith have fastened us to Christ, neither persons nor performances can be acceptable. Good works go not before but follow justification. We are not justified by doing works, but being justified, we then do good (Eph. 2:8–10).

✦ WILLIAM JENKYN
Exposition upon the Epistle of Jude, 224

Believers must see that they honor and justify their faith by works. Never content yourselves with an empty profession. Profession shows to what party we addict ourselves, but holiness shows we addict ourselves to God.

✦ THOMAS MANTON
Practical Exposition on the Epistle of James, 108

It is no wrong to good works to give faith the upper hand, which goes hand in hand with Christ. Good works are not separated from faith; only faith challenges its seniority. Faith believes as if it did not work, and it works as if it did not believe…. Faith is that spouselike grace which marries Christ, and good works are the children which faith bears.

✦ THOMAS WATSON
The Christian's Charter of Privileges,
in *Discourses*, 1:116

We shall not be saved without working, yet not for our working.

✦ THOMAS WATSON
"The One Thing Necessary,"
in *Discourses*, 1:368

THE FALL

There are five things we lost in our fall: (1) Our holy image, and became vile. (2) Our sonship, and became slaves. (3) Our friendship, and became enemies. (4) Our communion, and became strangers. (5) Our glory, and became miserable. Christians see an utter inability and insufficiency in themselves and in all other creatures to deliver them out of their fallen estate.

✦ THOMAS BROOKS
Cabinet of Choice Jewels, 46

There are three main defects in man since the fall. There is ignorance and blindness. There is rebellion in the will and affections. And in regard of his condition, by reason of the sins of nature and life, a subjection to a cursed estate, to the wrath of God and eternal damnation. Now, answerable to these three grand ills, whosoever shall be ordained a savior must provide proportionable remedies for these.

✦ RICHARD SIBBES
"A Description of Christ," in
Complete Works, 1:16

FALSE DOCTRINE AND ERROR

There is difference betwixt error, schism, and heresy. Error is when one holds a wrong opinion alone; schism, when many consent in their opinion; heresy runs further and contends to root out the truth. Error offends, but separates not; schism offends and separates; heresy offends, separates, and rages.... Error is weak, schism strong, heresy obstinate. Error goes out and often comes in again; schism comes not in, but makes a new church; heresy makes not a new church, but no church. Error untiles the house, schism pulls down the walls, but heresy overturns the foundation. Error is as a child, schism a wild stripling, heresy an old dotard. Error will hear reason, schism will wrangle against it, heresy will defy it. Error is a member blistered, schism a member festered, heresy a member cut off. He that returns quickly from error is not a schismatic; he that returns from schism is not a heretic. Error is reproved and pitied, schism is reproved and punished, heresy is reproved and excommunicated. Schism is in the same faith; heresy makes another faith. Though they may be thus distinguished, yet without God's preventing grace, one will run into another.

✦ THOMAS ADAMS
Exposition upon...Second...Peter, 211

Error is a spiritual bastard. The devil is the father, and pride the mother. You never knew an erroneous man, but he was a proud man. Now it is good that such men should be laid open to the intent, first, that God's righteous judgments upon them may be adored (2 Thess. 2:12). Secondly, that others who are free be not infected.

✦ SIMEON ASHE
Primitive Divinity, 77

Error needs a great deal of defending to keep it from sinking into oblivion, a great deal of equivocation to hide its certain and natural consequences from being detected by honest inquiry, and a great deal of learning and rhetoric to plead its cause. But in order to embrace truth, we need only light to see it by and a heart to love it.

✦ SIMEON ASHE
Primitive Divinity, 202

[Error] has its origin from the devil, who was a liar from the beginning and the father thereof (John 8:44). And spreaders of corrupt doctrine have special influence on the upholding and spreading of his kingdom. It is even as murder, adultery, witchcraft; and seeing it is so ranked by the apostle (Gal. 5:19–20), can it be but scandalous?

✦ JAMES DURHAM
Treatise concerning Scandal, 140

I must tell you that I never yet knew the man that had but one error. If the devil can but draw you into one, he'll quickly lead you into more, as in logic grant but one absurdity, and a hundred will follow. He that saith yea to the devil in a little shall not say nay when he pleases. He that tumbles down the hill of error will never leave tumbling till he come to the bottom.

✦ THOMAS HALL
Pulpit Guarded, xviii

One error is a bridge to another.

✦ WILLIAM JENKYN
in Horn, *Puritan Remembrancer*, 13

They abuse their souls that poison their souls; error is a sweet poison. Ignatius calls it the invention of the devil. A man may as well damn his soul by error as vice and may as soon

go to hell for a drunken opinion as for a drunken life.

✦ THOMAS WATSON
The Beatitudes, in *Discourses*, 2:410

FALSE TEACHERS

[Nathanael Vincent] had a great zeal against bold intruders into the work of the ministry. And I hope you that are his people will herein resemble him; turn away from those men, and do not so much as vouchsafe them the hearing. These vermin begin to swarm among us and disturb us by their hideous noise not in corners or chambers but in our very pulpits and are like to prove an Egyptian plague to us. If these illiterate antinomian usurpers are not speedily and effectually discountenanced by ministers and people too, they who are already the blemish of Nonconformity will quickly prove the total ruin of it.

✦ NATHANIEL TAYLOR
Funeral Sermon [on Luke 12:40], 25

FALSEHOOD

It is easy to tell one lie, hard to tell but one lie.

✦ THOMAS FULLER
in Thomas, *Puritan Golden Treasury*, 108

Lie not to one another. No, not in jest, lest you go to hell in earnest.

✦ JOHN TRAPP
A Commentary...upon...the New Testament, 798

FAMILY

The next observable performance of providence which must be heedfully…weighed is the designation of the stock and family out of which we should spring and rise. And truly this is of special consideration, both as to our temporal and eternal good, for whether the families in which we grew up were great or small in Israel, whether our parents were of higher or lower class and rank among men; yet if they were such as feared God and wrought righteousness, if they took any care to educate you righteously and trained you up "in the nurture and admonition of the Lord," you are bound to reckon it among your chief mercies, that you descended from such parents, for from this spring a double stream of mercy rises to you: temporal and external mercies to your outward man…. But especially take notice what a stream of spiritual blessings and mercies flows from this providence to the inner man. Oh, it is no common mercy to descend from pious parents; some of us do not only owe our natural life to them, as instruments of our being, but our spiritual and eternal life also.

♦ JOHN FLAVEL
Divine Conduct, 52–53

[Philip Henry] would often say, "We are that really, which we are relatively. It is not so much what we are at church as what we are in our families."

♦ PHILIP HENRY
Life and Sayings, 8

It is a thing of much concernment, the right ordering of families; for all other societies, civil and religious, are made up of these. Villages and cities and churches and commonwealths and kingdoms are but a collection of families, and therefore, such as these are, for the most part, such must the whole societies predominantly be. One particular house is but a very small part of a kingdom, yet the wickedness and lewdness of that house, be it but of the meanest in it of servants one or more, and though it seem but a small thing, yet goes in to make up that heap of sin which provokes the wrath of God and draws on public calamity. And this particularly, when it declines into disorder, proves a public evil.

♦ ROBERT LEIGHTON
A Commentary upon the First Epistle of Peter, in *Whole Works,* 1:318

Look what the roots are in the family; such will the fruit be in the church and commonwealth.

♦ JOHN OWEN
Golden Book, 208

Families are the seminaries both of church and state, and therefore, as you desire the church may be pure and the state righteous, look well unto your families and let religion flourish in them. Reformation indeed must begin at persons, and if everyone would mend one, all would be reformed. But from persons it must proceed to houses, and if these were but once leavened with godliness, what holy cities and what a happy nation would there be.

♦ NATHANIEL VINCENT
Spirit of Prayer, 66

FAMILY WORSHIP

He that has set up Christ in his heart will be sure to study to set Him up in his house. Let every family with you be a Christian church (1 Cor. 16:19), every house a house of prayer; let every householder say with Joshua, "I and my house will serve the Lord" (Josh. 24:15) and resolve with David, "I will walk within my house with a perfect heart" (Ps. 101:2).

✦JOSEPH ALLEINE
Alarm to the Unconverted, 231

Be not content to live where religion dies. "Salute the brethren…and Nymphas, and the church which is in his house" (Col. 4:15). The house of the godly is a little church; the house of the wicked a little hell (Prov. 7:27).

✦SIMEON ASHE
Primitive Divinity, 152

Pretend not necessity against this duty, for it is but unwillingness or negligence that makes men remiss in family worship. The lively and constant performance of family duties is a principal means to keep up the power and interest of godliness in the world, all which decays when these grow dead, slight, and formal. Those families wherein this service of God is performed are, as it were, little churches—yea, even a kind of paradise upon earth.

✦WILLIAM GEARING
Sacred Diary, 71

If God be the founder, the owner, the governor, and benefactor of families; if such little societies be of His appointment and do both need and receive daily mercies from Him, it is but fit He should be worshiped and owned every day in particular families. Before the giving of the law to Moses, how was God worshiped but in families? Family worship was the first kind of social worship.

✦JOHN SHOWER
Family Religion, 35–36

FASTING

Fasting which tames the body, without humility, makes proud the mind.

✦JOHN BOYS
in Horn, *Puritan Remembrancer,* 125

Fasting is a moderate use and taking of meat and drink lest the flesh should, by abundance and too much of it, rebel and overcome the spirit. And this fast, either it is continually or at certain times used. Continually, when as a Christian man moderately feedeth his body with thanksgiving for necessary nutriment, and not for to abound or surfeit. This fasting and abstinence the scripture calleth sobriety (1 Peter 5).

The fast done at certain times is also either private or public. Private when any man, considering and weighing his own infirmities, bindeth himself from meats and drinks to tame and overcome the vehement and lascivious inclinations thereof to the obedience and rule of the Spirit (1 Cor. 7).

A public fast is, when for a public and common calamity, trouble, or adversity, the magistrates command a solemn and public abstinence and fast. But in both these fasts there must be used a circumspect and godly diligence, lest in the abuse of fasting we offend and provoke the ire and displeasure of God the more against us.

✦ JOHN HOOPER
Early Writings, 538–39

For the mortification of any distemper so rooted in the nature of a man unto all other ways and means already named or further to be insisted on, there is one expedient peculiarly suited. This is that of the apostle: "I keep under my body, and bring it into subjection" (1 Cor. 9:27). The bringing of the very body into subjection is an ordinance of God, tending unto the mortification of sin. This gives check unto the natural root of the distemper and withers it by taking away its fatness of soil. Perhaps because the Papists (men ignorant of the righteousness of Christ, the work of His Spirit, and whole business in hand) have laid the whole weight and stress of mortification in voluntary services and penances, leading to the subjection of the body, not knowing indeed the true nature of sin nor mortification, it may on the other side be a temptation to some to neglect some means of humiliation which by God Himself are owned and appointed. The bringing of the body into subjection in the case insisted on by cutting short the natural appetite, by fasting, watching, and the like, is doubtless acceptable to God.

✦ JOHN OWEN
On Mortification of Sin, in
Oweniana, 233

The fast…of which I am now to treat is a religious fast, which is sanctifying a day to the Lord by a willing abstinence from meat and drink, from delights and worldly labors, that the whole man may be more thoroughly humbled before God and more fervent in prayer. This fast hath two parts: the one, outward—the chastening the body; the other, inward—the afflicting of the soul, under which are contained all those religious acts which concern the setting of the heart right toward God and the seeking help of God for those things for which the fast is intended.

✦ HENRY SCUDDER
Christian's Daily Walk, 83

FEAR OF GOD

[The fear of God] is further heightened by His judgments, which He executes on the earth. The judgments of God are God revealing Himself from heaven against the ungodliness and unrighteousness of men, and do then strike most terror (1) when He smites suddenly and makes quick work with sinners, as when Herod was smote by an angel of God, Nadab and Abihu consumed by fire from God immediately upon their sin. Sudden strokes shake secure hearts. (2) When He executes strange judgments, makes a new thing; as in the case of Korah and his company, He made the earth to open her mouth upon them and swallow them up; so, He made the flies, and the frogs, and the lice…to be the executioners of His wrath on Pharaoh.

(3) When He executes great wrath for little sins, as men account them, as in the case of Uzzah, whom He struck dead for but touching the ark when it shook. (4) When He exercises great severity on His own, on those that are near Him. If He spares not His sons, what will He do with His enemies! "If these things be done on the green tree, what shall be done on the dry!"

✦ RICHARD ALLEINE
Heaven Opened, 179

To fear God is to have the awe of God abiding upon the heart, to be under a sense of the majesty and glory of the Lord shining forth in all His attributes, especially in His holiness and omniscience; the glory of His holiness, and the sense of such a holy eye upon the soul strikes it with dread and consternation. This is expressed in Scripture by sanctifying the Lord in the heart. "I will be sanctified in them that come nigh me" (Lev. 10:3). "Sanctify the LORD of hosts himself; and let him be your fear, and let him be your dread" (Isa. 8:13).

✦ RICHARD ALLEINE
Heaven Opened, 183

HOPEFUL: I do believe, as you say, that fear tends much to men's good and to make them right at their beginning to go on pilgrimage.

CHRISTIAN: Without all doubt it doth, if it be right; for so says the word, "The fear of the Lord is the beginning of wisdom."

HOPEFUL: How will you describe right fear?

CHRISTIAN: True or right fear is discovered by three things: (1) by its rise — it is caused by saving convictions for sin; (2) it drives the soul to lay fast hold of Christ for salvation; (3) it begets and continues in the soul a great reverence of God, His word, and ways, keeping it tender and making it afraid to turn from them to the right hand or to the left to anything that may dishonor God, break its peace, grieve the Spirit, or cause the enemy to speak reproachfully.

✦ JOHN BUNYAN
Pilgrim's Progress, 138–39

When the fear of God is strong in your heart, then the fear of man ceases. When the dictator ruled at Rome, then all other officers ceased; and when this fear of God rules, all other fears will be hushed.

✦ WILLIAM GREENHILL
Exposition of the Prophet Ezekiel, 91

We fear man so much because we fear God so little. One fear cures another.

✦ WILLIAM GURNALL
Christian in Complete Armour, 813

Pray what is meant by the fear of the Lord?… Reverential fear and awe of the majesty of God, from a right apprehension of His greatness and holiness; so Proverbs 1:7: "The fear of the LORD is the beginning of knowledge"; that is, God being rightly known and the soul thereby duly overawed. A man had never any wisdom till this entered into his soul.

✦ WILLIAM STRONG
Heavenly Treasure, 19–20

Fear of God is a leading grace; it is the first seed God sows in the heart. When a Christian can say little of faith and perhaps nothing of assurance, yet he dares not deny but he fears God. God is so great that he is afraid of displeasing Him and so good that he is afraid of losing Him.

✦ THOMAS WATSON
Great Gain of Godliness, 13

FELLOWSHIP

Social religion is the nurse of all the graces of the Holy Spirit in the souls of believers.

✦ SIMEON ASHE
Primitive Divinity, 206

Love God in His saints and delightfully converse with Christ in them while thou hast opportunity. But remember thou livest not upon them or on their love, but upon God. And therefore desire their company but for His; and if thou hast His, be content if thou hast not theirs. He wants not man that enjoys God.

✦ RICHARD BAXTER
Converse with God in Solitude, 87

[The believer] falls in with the holiest person as his dearest acquaintance. If there be a saint in the town where he lives, he will find him out, and this shall be the man he will associate with. And in his conversation with these and all else, his chief work is for heaven; his heavenly principle within inclines him to it. Now this alarms hell: What, not contented to go to heaven himself, but by his holy example, gracious speeches, sweet counsels, seasonable reproofs

will be trading with others and labor to carry them along with him also? This brings the lion fell and mad out of his den; such, to be sure, shall find the devil in their way to oppose them.

✦ WILLIAM GURNALL
Christian in Complete Armour, 154

To [the word, meditation, and prayer] join fellowship and communion with the saints thou livest among. No wonder to hear a house is robbed that stands far from neighbors. He that walks in communion of saints, he travels in company; he dwells in a city where one house keeps up another to which Jerusalem is compared. It is observable concerning the house in whose ruins Job's children were entombed that a wind came from the wilderness and smote the four corners of it; it seems it stood alone. The devil knows what he does in hindering this great ordinance of communion of saints; in doing this he hinders the progress of grace—yea, brings that which Christians have into a declining, wasting state.

✦ WILLIAM GURNALL
Christian in Complete Armour, 171

Many coals make a good fire, and that is a part of the communion of saints.

✦ SAMUEL RUTHERFORD
Letters, 162

When, therefore, you meet with those that fear God, improve the communion of saints not only by communicating in natural and temporal good things as you are able and as there is need, but especially in the communion of things spiritual, edifying yourselves in your most holy faith by holy speech and conference and (in due time and place) in reading the Holy Scriptures and good books and by prayer and singing of psalms together.

✦ HENRY SCUDDER
Christian's Daily Walk, 167

He that travels alone is easily made a prey.... "One man is no man." Even counties that have been large have drawn themselves into associations for mutual and common defense.

✦ GEORGE SWINNOCK
The Christian Man's Calling,
in *Works*, 2:331

If you would be pure, walk with them that are pure; as the communion of saints is in our creed, so it should be in our company (Prov. 13:20)."He that walketh with wise men shall be wise"; and he that walketh with the pure shall be pure. The saints are like a bed of spices; by intermixing ourselves with them we shall partake of their savoriness. Association begets assimilation; sometimes God blesses good society to the conversion of others.

✦ THOMAS WATSON
The Beatitudes, in *Discourses*, 2:262

A godly man is a lover of the saints. The best way to discern grace in one-self is to love grace in others: "We know that we have passed from death to life, because we love the brethren" (1 John 3:14). What is religion but reli-gation, a knitting together of hearts; faith knits us to God, and love knits us one to another.

✦ THOMAS WATSON
Godly Man's Picture, 124

No discourse is so pleasant. Next to the songs of angels, the pious con-ference of holy men is the sweetest melody our ears can be entertained with; other things comparatively sound harsh to the things of God. Neither at the instant affect the ear with that pleasure nor afterwards leave it in that composure.

✦ EDWARD WEST
"How Must We Govern Our Tongues?,"
in Annesley, *Morning Exercises
at Cripplegate*, 2:441

FLATTERY

Flattery is the very spring and mother of all impiety; it blows the trumpet and draws poor souls into rebellion against God.... It puts persons upon neglect-ing, undervaluing, contemning the means of grace; it puts men upon abas-ing God, slighting Christ, and vexing the Spirit; it unmans a man, it makes him call black white, and white black; it makes a man change pearls for pebbles and gold for gilded counters; it makes a man judge himself wise when he is foolish; knowing, when he is ignorant; holy, when he is profane; free, when he is a prisoner; rich, when he is poor; high, when he is low; full, when he is empty; happy, when he is miserable. Ah! Take heed of flatterers; they are the very worst of sinners. They are left of God, blinded by Satan, hardened in sin, and ripened for hell.

✦ THOMAS BROOKS
Apples of Gold, 153–54

Say we be blamed for rudeness and incivility. Better it is that we hazard our reputation this way than purchase the reputation of fair behavior by speechless sufferance or smoothing flattery, sewing pillows where we should quilt thorns.

✦ NEHEMIAH ROGERS
The Penitent Citizen, in *Mirrour of Mercy*, 24

FLESH

The flesh is a worse enemy than the devil; it is a bosom traitor. An enemy within is worse. If there were no devil to tempt, the flesh would be another Eve to tempt to the forbidden fruit. Oh, take heed of giving way to it! Whence is all our discontent, but from the fleshly part? The flesh puts us upon the immoderate pursuit of the world; it consults for ease and plenty, and, if it be not satisfied, then discontents begin to arise. Oh, let it not have the reins! Martyr the flesh.

✦ SIMEON ASHE
Primitive Divinity, 192

"Confidence in the flesh": That is in external privileges which yet profit not those that rest in them. An empty title yields but an empty comfort at last. God cares for no retainers that only wear His livery but serve themselves. A man may go to hell with baptismal water on his face; yea, the sooner for his abused privileges.

✦ JOHN TRAPP
Commentary…upon…the New Testament, 783

FOOLS

I observe three seasons where a wise man differs not from a fool; in his infancy, in sleep, and in silence. For in the two former, we are all fools; and in silence, all are wise. In the two former yet, there may be concealment of folly. But the tongue is a blab; there cannot be any kind of folly, either simple or wicked, in the heart but the tongue will bewray it. He cannot be wise that speaks much or without sense or out of season nor be known for a fool that says nothing. It is a great misery to be a fool, but this is yet greater, that a man cannot be a fool but he must show it.

✦ JOSEPH HALL
Meditations and Vows, 183–84

If all fools wore white caps, we should seem a flock of geese.

✦ GEORGE HERBERT
comp., *Witts Recreations*, proverb 513

Nothing is a more evident acknowledged character of a fool than upon every slight occasion to be in a transport. To be much taken with empty things betokens an empty spirit. It is a part of manly fortitude to have a soul so fenced against foreign impressions as little to be moved with things that have little in them; to keep our passions under a strict and steady command, that they be easily retractable and taught to obey; not to move till severe reason have audited the matter and pronounced the occasion just and valuable.

✦ JOHN HOWE
The Vanity of Man as Mortal, in *Works*, 285

Fools are ever futuring.
◆ WILLIAM JENKYN
in Horn, *Puritan Remembrancer*, 174; and
Thomas, *Puritan Golden Treasury*, 110

None but fools oppose faithful reprovers, and who are such that if the truth be told them will not be pleased, and if they be pleased, the truth is not told them.
◆ WILLIAM JENKYN
Exposition upon the Epistle of Jude, 353

He is two fools that is wise in his own eyes.
◆ JOHN TRAPP
in Horn, *Puritan Remembrancer*, 211

FORBEARANCE

Oh, how sweet is the music when saints join thus in concert! And how harsh is the sound of jarring strings! A mutual yielding and forbearance is no small help to our peace and safety. There is a story of two goats which may excellently illustrate the benefit of this duty. They both met on a narrow bridge under which a very deep and fierce stream did glide; there was no going blindly back, neither could they pass forward for the narrowness of the bridge. Now had they fought for their passage, they had been certain both to perish. This therefore they did: they agreed that the one should lie down and the other go over him, and by this means both their lives were preserved. While Christians are fighting like some small chickens, they are a prey to kites and other ravenous creatures: In quietness shall be their strength

(Isa. 30:15) is true in this, as well as other senses.
◆ GEORGE SWINNOCK
The Christian Man's Calling,
in *Works*, 2:370

FORGIVENESS

Will you rob God of His almightiness in pardoning? You say your sin is great, but is it infinite? Is not God alone infinite? Is your sin as big as God, as big as Christ? Is Jesus Christ only a mediator for small sins?
◆ WILLIAM BRIDGE
Lifting Up, 74

Forgiveness is according to the riches of God's grace, wherein He has abounded toward us in all wisdom and prudence. Grace can continue to pardon, favor, and save—from falls, in falls, and out of falls. Grace can comfort, relieve, and help those that have hurt themselves; and grace can bring the unworthy to glory. This the law cannot do; this man cannot do; this angels cannot do; this God cannot do, but only by the riches of His grace through the redemption that is in Christ Jesus.
◆ JOHN BUNYAN
Riches, 77

Injuries should be wrote in dust, but kindnesses in marble.
◆ EDMUND CALAMY
Saints' Memorials, 40

Forgiveness is God's gracious discharge of a believing, penitent sinner from the guilt of all his sin, for Christ's sake.
◆ JOHN FLAVEL
Fountain of Life, 296

Christian forgiveness is not an injurious giving up of our rights and properties to the pleasure of everyone that hath a mind to invade them. No, these we may lawfully defend and preserve and are bound so to do; though, if we cannot defend them legally, we must not avenge our wrongs unchristianly. This is not Christian forgiveness. But then, positively, it is a Christian lenity, or gentleness of mind, not retaining but freely passing by the injuries done to us in obedience to the command of God. It is a lenity, or gentleness, of mind. The grace of God calms the tumultuous passions, corrects our sour spirits, and makes them benign, gentle, and easy to be entreated: "The fruit of the Spirit is love, joy, peace, longsuffering, gentleness," etc. (Gal. 5:22). This gracious lenity inclines the Christian to pass by injuries—so to pass them by as neither to retain them revengefully in the mind or requite them when we have opportunity with the hand. Yea, and that freely, not by constraint, because we cannot avenge ourselves but willingly. We abhor to do it when we can. So that as a carnal heart thinks revenge its glory, the gracious heart is content that forgiveness should be his glory.

✦ JOHN FLAVEL
Fountain of Life, 300

As to the point of justification, our inherent righteousness must be denied and rejected, as well as our sins: "All our righteousnesses are as filthy rags"; and this holy Paul knew well when he sought "to be found in Christ, not having his own righteousness." The meat that Jacob provided for his father, Isaac, was good and pleased him well, yet he got not the blessing by this, but by being found in his elder brother's garment: "He smelled the smell of his garment and blessed him." So though the precious graces and holy duties and holy lives of believers and holy men are well pleasing to God, yet it is not for these that God doth bless them with forgiveness of sin, but because they are in their elder Brother's garment, in the righteousness of Christ put upon them.

✦ OBADIAH GREW
Sinner's Justification, 29–30

When you are tempted to take ill that goodness and patience of God to sinners, consider: (1) Can this be right, to differ from His mind in anything? Is it not our only wisdom and ever safe rule to think as He thinks and will as He wills? And I pray you, does He not hate sin more than you do? Is not His interest in punishing it deeper than yours? And if you be zealous for His interest, as you pretend, then be so with Him and in His way; for starting from that, sure you are wrong. Consider: (2) Did He not wait for thee? What had become of thee if longsuffering had not subserved His purpose of further mercy, of free pardon to thee? And why wilt thou not always allow that to which thou art so much obliged? Wouldst thou have the bridge cut because thou art so far over? Sure thou wilt not own so gross a thought. Therefore, esteem thy God still the more thou seest of His longsuffering to sinners and learn for Him and with Him to bear and wait.

> ✦ ROBERT LEIGHTON
> *Spiritual Truths*, 296–97

There are no excellencies of God's nature that are more expressive of divine goodness, loveliness, and beauty than those are of mercy, grace, long-suffering, and patience; and therefore there is nothing that so requires our likeness unto Him in our conformity unto His image as in these—namely, mercy, grace, and readiness to forgive. And the contrary frame in any He doth of all things most abhor: "They shall have judgment without mercy who showed no mercy." And therefore, it is certain that God will be glorified in the manifestation of these properties of His nature. These properties can be no otherwise exercised and consequently no otherwise known, but only in and by the pardon of sin, which puts it beyond all question that there is forgiveness with God. God will not lose the glory of these, His excellencies; He will be revealed in them, He will be known by them, He will be glorified for them, which He could not be if there were not forgiveness with Him, so that here comes in not only the truth but the necessity of forgiveness also.

> ✦ JOHN OWEN
> "Practical Exposition of the
> 130th Psalm," *Oweniana*, 101–2

If we could sin more than He could pardon, then we might have some reason to despair.

> ✦ RICHARD SIBBES
> *Soul's Conflict*, 208

Pardon of sin never comes alone; whom God pardons He sanctifies, adopts, crowns.

> ✦ THOMAS WATSON
> *Puritan Gems*, 102

When a man seriously weighs within himself the glory and purity of that Majesty which sin hath offended, the preciousness of that soul which sin hath polluted, the loss of that happiness which sin hath endangered, the greatness of that torment which sin hath deserved—all this laid together must surely make sin burdensome and induce sinners most earnestly to seek for pardoning mercy.

> ✦ THOMAS WATSON
> *Puritan Gems*, 103

FORMALITY

Take heed of formality and resting in a mere outward performance of religious services. Learn to distinguish between Religion-the-end and Religion-the-means. Religion-the-end is to attain a gracious frame of spirit, to enjoy God, to fear Him, love Him, and have our natures conformed unto Him. Religion-the-means is to perform such religious duties and services as God hath appointed for the attaining of this end. Now if we rest in the means—that is, in a bare performance of religious duties—without desiring to enjoy God in them or laboring to get our hearts into a better frame by them and aiming at those higher ends to which they were appointed, our services are rather a mocking of God.

> ✦ SAMUEL CRADOCK
> *Knowledge and Practice*, xxxviii

FORTUNE

If the absolute will of God be the universal cause of all things, then no event can fall beyond or beside God's will. And fortune (in the world's sense thereof) is but the devil's blasphemous spit upon divine providence.

✦ CHRISTOPHER NESS
Antidote against Arminianism, 25

FRIENDSHIP

Such unfortunate and apostate times are we fallen into that to uphold God's honor is held uncivil tartness. Such men are saucy, and such sauce is too sharp for proud and vicious stomachs. This dissolves the knot of friendship. Let it; better a holy discord than a profane concord. Care not for that mirth which must grieve the Holy Ghost; disclaim that peace which must be at war with Christ.

✦ THOMAS ADAMS
Exposition upon…Second…Peter, 79

Selfishness is the great enemy of all societies, of all fidelity and friendship.… He that is prevailingly selfish was never a real friend to any. He has always some interest of his own which his friends must needs contradict or are insufficient to satisfy. His houses, lands, or money; his children, reputation, or something which he calls his own will frequently be the matter of contention; and for the sake of these things which are so near to him, he will cast off his nearest friend. Contract no special friendship with a selfish man.

Put no confidence in him, whatever friendship he may profess. He is so confined to himself that he has no true love to spare for others. If he seem to love a friend it is not as a friend but as a servant, or at best as a benefactor. He loves you for himself, as he loves his money, his horse, or house—because you may be serviceable to him. When you have no more capacity to serve him, he has no more love for you.

✦ RICHARD BAXTER
Converse with God in Solitude, 40–41

How often have I found that human friendship is a sweet addition to our woe, a beloved calamity, an affliction which nature will not be without! Not because nature loves evil nor is wholly deceived in its choice, for there is good in friendship and delight in holy love, but because the good which is here accompanied with so much evil is the beginning of a more high and durable friendship and points us to the blessed society and converse which we shall have with Christ in the heavenly Jerusalem.

✦ RICHARD BAXTER
Converse with God in Solitude, 85

Friendship must be cemented by piety. A wicked man can be no true friend.

✦ RICHARD BAXTER
Reformed Pastor, 173

A true friend is neither known in prosperity nor hid in adversity.

✦ THOMAS BROOKS
Cabinet of Choice Jewels, 199

A sincere Christian prays his friends to search him, and he prays soul-searching ministers to search him; but, above all, he begs hard of God to search him: "Search me, O God."

♦ THOMAS BROOKS
Cabinet of Choice Jewels, 320

Man is made to be a friend, and apt for friendly offices. He that is not friendly is not worthy to have a friend; and he that has a friend and does not show himself friendly is not worthy to be accounted a man. Friendship is a kind of life, without which there is no comfort of a man's life. Christian friendship ties such a knot that great Alexander cannot cut. Summer friends I value not, but winter friends are worth their weight in gold.

♦ THOMAS BROOKS
Great Gain, 145–46

Christ is (1) a universal friend; (2) an omnipotent friend, an almighty friend. He is no less than thirty times called almighty in the book of Job; He can do above all expressions and beyond aft apprehensions. (3) He is an omniscient friend; (4) an omnipresent friend; (5) an indeficient friend; (6) an independent friend; (7) an unchangeable friend; (8) a watchful friend; (9) a tender and compassionate friend. (10) He is a close and faithful friend. And therefore He cannot but open and unbosom Himself to all His bosom friends. To be reserved and close is against the very law of friendship. Faithful friends are very free in imparting their thoughts, their minds, and their secrets one to another. A real friend accounts nothing worth knowing, unless he makes it known to his friends.

♦ THOMAS BROOKS
Privy Key of Heaven, 42

A friend, an unfeigned well-willer which bears Christian affection unto him whom he loves, is nearer than a brother, is more faithful and constant in ministering help and comfort than an ordinary kinsman or mere natural brother. It is in vain for him to expect constant kindness from others which is careless to perform duties to others.

♦ ROBERT CLEAVER AND
JOHN DOD
Plain and Familiar Exposition, 30–31

Rash, unadvised friendship seldom proves sound or lasting. A hasty friend and a slow enemy are accounted alike dangerous. Yea, how oft does rash, hasty friendship degenerate into downright enmity and hatred?

♦ THEOPHILUS GALE
Theophilie, 11

A true friend is not born every day. It is best to be courteous to all; entire with few. So may we, perhaps, have less cause of joy—I am sure, less occasion of sorrow.

♦ JOSEPH HALL
Meditations and Vows, 74

The best mirror is an old friend.

♦ GEORGE HERBERT
comp., *Witts Recreations*, proverb 296

True friendship will value a great advantage of another's before a small one of our own.

♦ ADAM MARTINDALE
Life, 218

True friendship and acquaintance stands not in bare words and complemental visits, but in real communication of offices and benefits. So here, converse and acquaintance with God stands in our improving God and our interest in Him, so as to acquaint Him with all our secrets, so as to impart unto Him all our griefs and fears, so as to rely upon Him to guide us in all our ways and to supply all our wants. This [very thing] God looks we should do and takes it unkindly when we do otherwise, as a true friend that is willing and able to help his friend takes it unkindly if he go to any other, thinks himself either distrusted or slighted, and it is almost a matter of falling out between them.

✦ MATTHEW NEWCOMEN
Best Acquaintance, 24–25

Dead stones in an arch uphold one another, and shall not living? It is the work of an angel to comfort—nay, it is the office of the Holy Ghost to be a comforter not only immediately but by breathing comfort into our hearts together with the comfortable words of others. Thus, one friend becomes an angel—nay, a God to another, and there is a sweet sight of God in the face of a friend.

✦ RICHARD SIBBES
Soul's Conflict, 131

He loves his friend best who hates his lusts most.

✦ GEORGE SWINNOCK
in Horn, *Puritan Remembrancer*, 259

A true friend is another self.

✦ GEORGE SWINNOCK
The Christian Man's Calling,
in *Works*, 2:273

He can be no true friend to thee that is a friend to thy faults, and thou canst be no friend to thyself if thou be an enemy to him that tells thee of thy faults. Wilt thou like him the worse that would have thee be better?

✦ RALPH VENNING
Canaan's Flowing, 76

Grace teaches good nature. We are to be civil to the worst, but not twist into a cord of friendship; that were to be brethren in iniquity: "Have no fellowship with the unfruitful works of darkness" (Eph. 5:11).... We must not so far have peace with others as to endanger ourselves. If a man hath the plague, we will be helpful to him and send him our best recipes, but we are careful not to have too much of his company or suck in his infectious breath. So we may be peaceable toward all—nay, helpful: pray for them, counsel them, relieve them. But let us take heed of too much familiarity, lest we suck in their infection. In short, we must so make peace with men that we do not break our peace with conscience: "Follow peace...and holiness" (Heb. 12:14). We must not purchase peace with the loss of holiness.

✦ THOMAS WATSON
The Beatitudes, in *Discourses*, 2:278

FRUGALITY

Be careful to prevent all superfluities in your expenses. As diligence in your calling, so frugality in your spending is a special means for the practice of charity. "Frugality," saith Justin, "is the mother of virtue." I am sure it is the foundation and supporter of charity, for let a man's estate be ever so great, yet if there be not frugality used in the management thereof, there will be but little found for works of charity. And on the other side, though a man's estate be but mean and low in the world, yet if there be frugality used in the management of it, there will always be something for charitable uses. As therefore thou desire to be charitable, be careful to prevent all unnecessary expenses.

+ THOMAS GOUGE
"A Sermon on Good Works," in
Riches Increased by Giving, 133–34

He is not a covetous man who lays up something providentially, but he is a covetous man who gives out nothing willingly. He is as prudent a man who sometimes distributes discreetly as he who accumulates hastily. Men frequently discover more wisdom in laying out than in laying up. Reader, the hope of living long on earth should not make you covetous, but the prospect of living long in heaven should make you bounteous. Though the sun of charity rise at home, yet it should always set abroad.

+ WILLIAM SECKER
Nonsuch Professor, 66

GIFTS

The more our gifts and graces are exercised, the more they are strengthened and increased. All acts strengthen habits.

+ THOMAS BROOKS
Smooth Stones, 203

Joseph's coat made him finer than his brethren, but this caused all his trouble. This set the archers a-shooting their arrows into his side. Thus, great gifts lift a saint up a little higher in the eyes of men, but it occasions many temptations which thou meet not with [those who] are kept low. What with envy from their brethren, malice from Satan, and pride in their own hearts, I dare say none find so hard a work to go to heaven as such.

+ WILLIAM GURNALL
Christian in Complete Armour, 138

Want of use causeth disability; and custom, perfection. Those that have not used to pray in their closet cannot pray in public but coldly and in form. He that discontinues meditation shall be long in recovering, whereas the man inured to these exercises, who is not dressed till he have prayed nor hath supped till he have meditated, doth both these well and with ease. He that intermits good duties incurs a double loss of the blessing that follows good, of the faculty of doing it.

+ JOSEPH HALL
"Holy Observations," in
Select Tracts, 326

So if you feed not the soul diligently and use not the means constantly, you will breed weakness in the soul, and the more secure and remiss you are in the performance of holy duties, the weaker you are. It may be you think it will not weaken you to neglect private prayer, but omit it once, and it will make you careless, and the more you neglect, the more unfit and undisposed you will find yourselves. So you may think you may profane one Sabbath, neglecting therein the duties required and serving not God, but your own lusts. But beloved, it will make you secure; the more a man doth in this kind the more he may do. For this is true in every art: every act begets a habit, and a habit brings custom. So it is as true in good things: the beginning of good brings many particular good things, and therefore if you can but get your hearts in a frame of grace, you will find a supply of grace because Christ says, "Whosoever has, to him more shall be given." He that hath grace and is careful in the use of the means by God's appointment, he shall thrive in holiness.

✦ JOHN PRESTON
"The Saints' Spiritual Strength,"
in *Remaines*, 110–11

GIVING

Most men are too tenacious of their interests to be dead to them. Close hands argue cleaving hearts to the world. Alas, with what reluctancy do men that have the abundance of this world's goods lay them out again for God! How hard is it to draw any proportions of charity from them that have this world's goods?

✦ BARTHOLOMEW ASHWOOD
Heavenly Trade, 81

A compassionate heart and a helping hand will gather by expending. Such giving is getting; such bounty is the most compendious way to plenty. Whereupon the wise man adds, "There is that scattereth, and yet increaseth; there is that withholdeth more than is meet, but it tendeth to poverty" (Prov. 11:24). Who is he here that scatters? Not he that wastes his estate upon his throat, his back, and his belly, or with the prodigal upon harlots; but he that casteth his bread upon the waters, as the expression is (Eccl. 11:1). He that disperseth and giveth to the poor (Ps. 112:9). This is the scatterer in that text. And what of him? Is he wasted? Is he impoverished? Behold, quite the contrary! The man is grown rich—he is increased by scattering.

✦ THOMAS GOUGE
Riches Increased by Giving, 13

It is observed that they are the richest merchants and citizens who trade boldly, whereas they who are fearful to adventure their goods have but small returns. In like manner it is found by experience that such Christians as are most forward to supply the wants of the poor, boldly adventuring their goods upon the waters, do most of all thrive and prosper in the world. Why, then, will any man be so unwise as to lose his riches for fear of losing them? And not rather seem to lose them that he may in truth find them? These earthly things are assuredly lost by keeping and kept by well bestowing them.

✦ THOMAS GOUGE
Riches Increased by Giving, 51

In 2 Corinthians 8:2, the apostle, boasting of the Macedonian Christians and of the riches of their liberality, tells us that they first gave themselves to the Lord (v. 5). He that will not give himself to the Lord is like to give but little else. And if he should give all that he had, and only withhold himself, God will not accept nor reward it. God will have nothing of thee if He may not have thy heart.

✦ THOMAS GOUGE
Riches Increased by Giving, 56

My meaning is that you so give all to the Lord as to resolve to dispose of your whole estate to such persons and purposes as God orders and appoints you. The Lord would have you live and maintain yourself and provide for your family soberly, according to your rank and degree (some extraordinary cases being excepted). But still you must allow no more to yourself nor no less to those in need than is according to the will and good pleasure of the Lord.

✦ THOMAS GOUGE
Riches Increased by Giving, 58

Give out proportionably to what God hath given unto you (1 Cor. 16:2). The apostle advises the Corinthians to give as God hath prospered them. Rich men therefore ought to be rich in good works, for God expects fruit answerable to the seed which He sows. Hath

he abounded to you in this world's goods? You ought thereupon to be abundant in good works toward others. Your pounds are expected where the widow's mites are accepted.

✦ THOMAS GOUGE
Riches Increased by Giving, 64

I shall not value his prayers at all, be he never so earnest and frequent in them, who gives not alms according to his ability.

✦ JOHN OWEN
Golden Book, 210

Some observe that the most barren grounds are nearest to the richest mines. It is too often true in a spiritual sense that those whom God hath made the most fruitful in estates are most barren in good works. It is too generally true that the rich spend their substance wantonly, while the poor give their alms willingly. A penny comes with more difficulty out of a bag that is pressing full than a shilling out of a purse that is half empty.

✦ WILLIAM SECKER
Nonsuch Professor, 67

They are fools that fear to lose their wealth by giving, but fear not to lose themselves by keeping it.

✦ JOHN TRAPP
in Horn, *Puritan Remembrancer*, 127

Mr. Bradford [the martyr] counted that hour lost wherein he did not some good with his tongue, pen, or purse.

✦ JOHN TRAPP
Marrow of Many Good Authors,
in *Commentary…upon…the
New Testament*, 1051

He that detains a penny from the poor puts a plague into his own purse.

✦ RALPH VENNING
in Calamy et al., *Saints'*
Memorials, 131

The way to lay up is to lay out. Other parts of your estate you leave behind, but that which is given to Christ's poor is hoarded up in heaven. That is a blessed kind of giving, which, though it makes the purse the lighter, makes the crown the heavier. You shall have good security: "He that hath pity upon the poor lendeth unto the LORD; and that which he hath given will he pay him again" (Prov. 19:17). You shall be paid with overplus. For a wedge of gold which you have parted with, you shall have a weight of glory. For a cup of cold water, you shall have rivers of pleasure which run at God's right hand forevermore. The interest comes to infinitely more than the principal.

✦ THOMAS WATSON
Gleanings, 26

GLORIFICATION

Glorification is a real transmutation of a man from misery or the punishment of sin unto happiness eternal (Rom. 8:30).

✦ WILLIAM AMES
Marrow of Sacred Divinity, 146

The first degree of this glorification begun is the apprehension and sense of the love of God shining forth in Christ upon the communion which the faithful have with Him (Rom. 5:5), the love of God issued abroad in our hearts by the Holy Spirit which is given to us.

✦ WILLIAM AMES
Marrow of Sacred Divinity, 147

Perfect glorification is in the taking away of all imperfection from soul and body and communication of all perfection. This is granted to the soul immediately after the separation of it from the body (2 Cor. 5:2; Phil. 1:23; Heb. 12:23). But it is not ordinarily granted to the soul and body jointly before that last day, wherein all the faithful shall be perfected together in Christ (Eph. 4:13; Phil. 3:20–21).

✦ WILLIAM AMES
Marrow of Sacred Divinity, 150

GLUTTONY

Gluttony is the bane of the body. For many more perish by intemperance than by violence, by surfeiting than by suffering.

✦ JOHN TRAPP
Marrow of Many Good Authors,
in *Commentary ... upon ... the*
New Testament, 1042

Many a man's table is a snare to him.... They serve not the Lord Jesus Christ that serve their own bellies (Rom. 16:18). How can they, when their kitchen is their shrine, their cook their priest, their table their altar, and their belly their god.

✦ JOHN TRAPP
Marrow of Many Good Authors,
in *Commentary ... upon ... the*
New Testament, 1043

GOD

God is an essence spiritual, simple, infinite, most holy. (1) An essence subsisting in Himself and by Himself, not receiving it from any other; all other things subsist in Him and by Him: "in him we live, move, and have our being." (2) Spiritual: He hath not a body nor any parts of a body, but is a spirit invisible, indivisible. (3) Simple: we are all compounded; God is without composition of matter, form, or parts. (4) Infinite: and that in respect [1] of time, without beginning or ending; [2] of place, excluded nowhere, included nowhere; within all places, without all places. (5) Most holy; His wisdom, goodness, mercy, love are infinite.

♦ THOMAS ADAMS
Meditations upon the Creed,
in *Works*, 3:97

The will of God is eternal because He does not begin to will what before He would not nor ceases to will that which before He willed.

♦ WILLIAM AMES
Marrow of Sacred Divinity, 16

He is not only the all-wise but the all-powerful God, the Lord Almighty. As there is nothing that He can but He will do for us, so there is nothing that He will but He can do for us. This is our one friend; as He is wiser, so is He stronger than all our enemies. This, our best friend, is more potent than our worst foe. He is more able to do us good than all our foes are to do us harm; nay, they can do nothing at all — much less do any harm to us — unless they receive power from Him to do it. The devil himself is in God's chain and cannot go one link beyond His leave, so that there is no affliction that any of our enemies can bring us into, but still this our friend is able to deliver us out of it. If we be in want, He can supply us; if we be in danger, He can deliver us.

♦ WILLIAM BEVERIDGE
Thesaurus Theologious, 4:21

It is a necessary and rational truth that the Lord doth thus carry on His great salvations for His own greater glory, for His people's greater benefit, and for His enemies' greater confusion. Therefore, it is not out of want either of power or wisdom but out of a transcendency of both that He doth order His deliverances in such a manner.

♦ JOHN BOND
Salvation in a Mystery, 28

I have found much sweetness in communion with God, especially at the sacrament of the Lord's Supper, in prayer and meditation, hearing the word faithfully and seriously preached, and in preaching it myself. When the candle of the Lord shines on my tabernacle, then was it a sweet exercise to my soul.

♦ THOMAS BOSTON
Art of Man-Fishing, 55

Will you consider a little what an excellent transcendent portion God is? (1) He is a present portion.... (2) God is an immense portion.... (3) God is an all-sufficient portion. (4) God is a pure and unmixed portion.... He hath nothing in Him but goodness. (5) God is a glorious, a happy, and a blessed portion.... (6) God is a...portion peculiar to His people. (7) God is a universal portion...that includes all other portions. (8) God is a safe portion...that none can rob a believer of. (9) God is a suitable portion.... (10) God is an incomprehensible portion. (11) God is an inexhaustible portion.... (12) God is a soul-satisfying portion.... (13) God is a permanent portion...an everlasting portion. (14) And lastly, God is an incomparable portion.... Nothing can make that man miserable that has God for his portion, nor nothing can make that man happy that hath not God for his portion.

✦ THOMAS BROOKS
London's Lamentations, 225–26

Jacob is reproved for his curious inquiring, or asking after, the angel's name [Gen. 32:29], which is a clear argument or demonstration of his majesty and glory, God being above all notion and name. God is a supersubstantial substance, an understanding not to be understood. One being asked what God was answered that he must be God Himself before he could know God fully. We are as well able to comprehend the sea in a cockleshell as we are able to comprehend the Almighty.

✦ THOMAS BROOKS
Privy Key of Heaven, 28

God's presence is renewing, transforming, seasoning, sanctifying, commanding, sweetening, and lightening to the soul. Nothing like it in all the world.

His presence supplies all wants, heals all maladies, saves from all dangers—is life in death, heaven in hell, all in all.

✦ JOHN BUNYAN
Riches, 33

Objection: But if a sufficiency of means to repent and believe be not afforded to all, how shall God be just in punishing for neglects?

Answer: The justice of God will not need our salving, especially by a balm of our making. Whether He judge or justify, He is just in what he doeth, though purblind reason sees not how. His judgments are a great deep, not to be fathomed by human comprehension. In sounding at sea, will it follow that there is no bottom because your line will not reach it? God dealt not so, in respect of means, with any nation as with Israel; and the men going with Paul to Damascus, the Lord would not give them to see His face nor to hear His voice, both which He vouchsafed to Paul. And yet He needs no vindication or apology for punishing their unbelief: They that "have sinned without law will also perish without law" (Rom. 2:12).

✦ ELISHA COLES
Practical Discourse, 220

The prediction, or foretelling, of future things of a casual and contingent nature, which no reason of men or angels could foresee in their causes, is another argument to prove the existence of God. We have many instances of such predictions in Scripture where also we have an account of the events exactly corresponding with the predictions.

✦ JOHN CONANT
Sermon 6 on John 17:3,
in *Sermons*, 210

Beloved, when our miseries are at the greatest, [God's] help is at the nearest. Man's extremity is God's opportunity.

✦ WILLIAM DYER
Christ's Famous Titles, 34

Is God's honor to be preferred before our eternal salvation? These two cannot stand in opposition. The more we seek God's honor, the more we help forward our salvation and the more we seek our salvation aright, the more we advance God's honor.

✦ WILLIAM GOUGE
Guide to Goe to God, 39

Man's will and weakness cannot hinder the efficacy and execution of God's decree. The prophet's [i.e., Ezekiel's] spirit was against this work; he refused, sat still seven days together, and would have frustrated God's intentions if he could, but it was decreed in heaven: that decree was efficacious, His will must be brought off, and he must be the man to execute God's pleasure in a prophetical way to the house of Israel. Jonah departs, will prejudice God's design concerning Nineveh; but the Lord knew how to humble him, to fetch him back, being fled, and to make him instrumental to his ends, notwithstanding his willfulness and weakness. "He commanded, and it stood fast"; and "The counsel of the LORD stands

forever" (Ps. 33:9, 11). Let there be contrary counsels, wills, commands; they stand not.

✦ WILLIAM GREENHILL
Exposition of the Prophet Ezekiel, 109

How can God stoop lower than to come and dwell with a poor, humble soul, which is more than if He had said such a one should dwell with Him? For a beggar to live at court is not so much as the king to dwell with him in his cottage. Yet this promise is ushered in with the most magnificent titles: "Thus saith the high and lofty One that inhabiteth eternity, whose name is Holy; I dwell in the high and holy place, with him also that is of a contrite and humble spirit" (Isa. 57:15).

✦ WILLIAM GURNALL
Christian in Complete Armour, 112

That God who bids us be most tender of His lambs is much more tender of them Himself. Observable is that place, 1 John 2:12–14. There are three ranks of saints—fathers, young men, little children—and the Spirit of God chiefly shows His tender care of them as by mentioning them first (v. 12), so by leaving the sweet promise of pardoning mercy in their lap and bosom rather than either of the other: "I write unto you, little children, because your sins are forgiven you for his name's sake." But are not the fathers' sins and the young men's also forgiven? Yes, who doubts it? But he doth not so particularly apply it to them as to these because these, from a sense of their own failings, out of which the other were more grown, were more prone to dispute against this promise in their own bosoms. Yea, he doth not only in plain terms tell them their sins are forgiven but meets with the secret objection which comes from their trembling hearts in opposition to this good news, taken from their own vileness and unworthiness, and stops its mouth with this: "Forgiven for my name's sake," a greater name than the name of their biggest sin, which discourages them from believing.

✦ WILLIAM GURNALL
Christian in Complete Armour, 235

The highest created throne that God can sit in is the soul of a believer.

✦ WILLIAM GURNALL
Christian in Complete Armour, 350

Some, by way of subjection, stooping to [God]; angels and saints, they worship Him, acknowledging His highness by denying their own but setting up His will as their supreme law and excellency, cast down their crowns; and veiling their glory, they cover their face and make His glory the object of their admiration.

✦ THOMAS HODGES
Glimpse of God's Glory, 6

Foreknowledge…is His eternal and unchangeable love; and that thus He chooses some and rejects others is for that great end, to manifest and magnify His mercy and justice. But why He appointed this man for the one and that man for the other made Peter a vessel of this mercy and Judas of wrath;

this is even so because it seemed good to Him. This, if it be harsh, yet is apostolic doctrine. "Hath not the potter," saith St. Paul, "power over the same lump, to make one vessel unto honor and another unto dishonor?"

✦ ROBERT LEIGHTON
A Commentary upon the First Epistle of Peter, in *Whole Works*, 1:20

God can by no means be looked upon as the direct author of [sin] or the proper cause of that obliquity which is in the actions of the creatures; for His providence is conversant about sin without sin, as a sunbeam rests upon a dunghill without being stained by it.

✦ THOMAS MANTON
Practical Exposition on the Epistle of James, 35

The divine jealousy will not brook a rival. God delights in this honor of being the sole author of all our good and therefore cannot endure that we should give it to another. When God was about to work miracles by Moses's hand, He first made it leprous (Ex. 4:6).

✦ THOMAS MANTON
Practical Exposition on the Epistle of James, 45

The relation of sons is a communicative relation; the relation of a servant is not so. A master doth not impart all his mind nor disclose his secrets to his servant; he lays upon him his commands but doth not betrust him with his secrets. So saith our Lord Christ: "Henceforth I call you not servants; for the servant knoweth not what his lord doeth" (John 15:15). But a father will disclose and communicate his heart to his child; he will tell all his mind and will and counsels to his son.

◆ MATTHEW MEAD
Name in Heaven, 40–41

If we maintain then the glory of God, let us speak in His own language or be forever silent. That is glorious in Him which He ascribes unto Himself. Our inventions, though never so splendid in our own eyes, are unto Him an abomination; a striving to pull Him down from His eternal excellency, to make Him altogether like unto us. God would never allow that the will of the creature should be the measure of His honor.

◆ JOHN OWEN
*Death of Death in the
Death of Christ*, ix

There are two things required unto those thoughts which we have of God: (1) That we take delight in them. The remembrance of God delights and refreshes the hearts of His saints and stirs them up to thankfulness (Ps. 30:4).... That God is what He is, is the matter of their chiefest joy. (2) That they be accompanied with godly fear and reverence. It is unimaginable how the subtle disquisitions and disputes of men about the nature, properties, and counsels of God have been corrupted, rendered sapless and useless, by vain curiosity and striving for an artificial accuracy in the expansion of men's apprehensions. When the wits and minds of men are engaged in such thoughts, "God is not in all their

thoughts," even when all their thoughts are concerning Him.

◆ JOHN OWEN
"Spiritual Mindedness," in
Golden Book, 177–78

We are apt to frame notions of God according to what we find in our own disposition, to fancy a God like unto ourselves. And therefore we cannot eye an afflicting God, but we presently conclude an angry God, as though the eternal and pure Being were subject to passions and changes as we are. These apprehensions being once entertained, the soul becomes unhinged and almost afraid to behold the face of Love itself, but flies and hides itself, as Adam in the garden.

◆ SAMUEL SHAW
*Voice of One Crying in the
Wilderness*, 71

Now these three things are in a treasure: that which a man loves most and sets the highest price upon and that to which his heart doth retire and seek supply from in all his wants; and every man must be supplied out of his treasure, that I will tell you. Take a rich man when he comes to die, riches avail not in the day of wrath. Therefore God only is the saint's treasure and chief good; he lays up treasure in heaven and this treasure is God.

◆ WILLIAM STRONG
Heavenly Treasure, 139

Jonah runs from his business. God sends him to Nineveh; he will go to Tarshish. Here was plain rebellion against his sovereign. One would have expected that the jealous God should have given him a traitor's wages and when he was at sea have suffered the ocean of waters to have swallowed up his body and the ocean of fire and wrath his soul. But lo, He cannot permit His Jonah to perish; He will rather whip him to his work than let him wander to his ruin. But how gentle is the rod! God cannot forget the love of a father, though Jonah forget the duty of a child, but will rather work a miracle and make the devourer his savior than Jonah shall miscarry.

✦ GEORGE SWINNOCK
The Christian Man's Calling,
in *Works,* 2:367

[God's] being is an independent being; He is by Himself as well as from and for Himself. None ever in heaven or earth contributed the least toward the maintenance or continuance of His being; neither the creatures' goodness nor their goods do Him the least good.

✦ GEORGE SWINNOCK
The Incomparableness of God,
in *Works,* 4:389

God is a simple being. In this I take simplicity not as opposed to wisdom, for in Him are all the treasures of wisdom and knowledge (Col. 2:9), but as simplicity is opposed to mixture and composition. Thus, there is a simplicity in the gospel (2 Cor. 12:3). So anything, the more simple it is, the more excellent it is. God is a most pure, simple, unmixed, indivisible essence; He is incapable of the least composition and therefore of the least division. He is one most pure, one without all

parts, members, accidents, and qualities. Whatsoever is in Him is Himself, His very being.

✦ GEORGE SWINNOCK
The Incomparableness of God,
in *Works,* 4:397

God does not do many things that He can, but He does all things that He will. He can do more than He will. He cannot do what is sinful; He cannot lie (Titus 1:2); He cannot deny Himself (1 Tim. 2:13). He cannot do that which implies a contradiction. He cannot make Himself a creature or make a creature a god because the doing of these things speaks weakness and imperfection, but whatsoever speaks power or perfection, that He can do.

✦ GEORGE SWINNOCK
The Incomparableness of God,
in *Works,* 4:434

This knowledge [of God] must needs be a sanctifying knowledge because it renders sin abominable, the world contemptible, God honorable, and the soul the more humble.

✦ GEORGE SWINNOCK
The Incomparableness of God,
in *Works,* 4:483

GOD, ALMIGHTY

Is [the Lord] not an overmatch for all His enemies? Is not one Almighty more than many mighties? Does His presence stand for nothing with us? If God be for us, who can be against us?

✦ JOHN FLAVEL
Saint Indeed, 104

Question: What are we to conceive by this, that God is almighty?

Answer: By this, that God is almighty we are to conceive that God needs not anything; that He can do everything which is neither wicked nor unequal; that He does whatsoever He pleases and is one of whom, by whom, and for whom are all things.

✦ JOHN NORTON
Catechistical Guide, 32

GOD, ATTRIBUTES OF

There is a full manifestation of the attributes of God in Jesus Christ, the Mediator of the new covenant. These attributes that were never manifested before, mercy and longsuffering, are revealed in Him; and these that were manifested before shine more brightly through Christ.

✦ PATRICK GILLESPIE
Ark of the Covenant Opened, 166

Love in the creature commands all the other affections, sets all the powers of the whole man on work; thus, in God, love sets all His other attributes on work. When God once pitched His thoughts on doing good to lost man, then wisdom fell on projecting the way, almighty power that undertook to raise the fabric according to wisdom's model. All are ready to effect what God saith He likes.

✦ WILLIAM GURNALL
Christian in Complete Armour, 15

Love is the only attribute which God hath acted to the utmost. We have never seen the utmost of His power, what God can do, but we have seen the utmost of His love: He hath found a ransom for lost souls (Job 33:24).

✦ MATTHEW MEAD
Name in Heaven, 30

Those [communicable] attributes are all one in God. His justice is His mercy, and His wisdom is His patience, and His knowledge is His faithfulness, and His mercy is His justice, etc. Though they are distinguished in regard of their objects and in regard of our apprehensions of them and in regard of their effects, yet they are all one in themselves, and this flows from the former head because they are the essence of God, and His essence is a pure, undivided being.

✦ GEORGE SWINNOCK
Incomparableness of God, in
Works, 4:423

GOD, ETERNITY OF

God is of an eternal duration. The eternity of God is the foundation of the stability of the covenant, the great comfort of a Christian.

✦ STEPHEN CHARNOCK
*Discourses upon the Existence and
Attributes of God,* 174

Eternity is a perpetual duration which hath neither beginning nor end; time hath both. Those things we say are in time that have beginning grow up by degrees, have succession of parts; eternity is contrary to time and is therefore a permanent and immutable state, a perfect possession of life without any variation. It comprehends in itself all years, all ages, all periods of ages; it never begins; it endures after every duration of time and never ceases; it doth as much outrun time as it went before the beginning of it. Time supposes something before it, but there can be nothing before eternity; it were not then eternity. Time hath a continual succession; the former time passes away and another succeeds; the last year is not this year, nor this year the next. We must conceive of eternity contrary to the notion of time; as the nature of time consists in the succession of parts, so the nature of eternity in an infinite, immutable duration. Eternity and time differ as the sea and rivers. The sea never changes place and is always one water, but the rivers glide along and are swallowed up in the sea. So is time by eternity.

♦ STEPHEN CHARNOCK
Discourses upon the Existence and Attributes of God, 175

It is not proper to say of [God] He was, for none of His duration is ever past with Him; or He shall be, for none of His duration is ever to come. But He is; His full eternity is always present. Hence His name is I Am (Ex. 3:14), not I Was or Shall Be. And Christ tells the Jews, "Before Abraham was, I am" (John 8:58). It seems false grammar, but it is the most proper true divinity.

♦ GEORGE SWINNOCK
Incomparableness of God,
in Works, 4:395

GOD, FAITHFULNESS OF

Man's faith may fail him sometimes, but God's faithfulness never fails Him (Ps. 89:33). God will not suffer His faithfulness to fail.

♦ WILLIAM GREENHILL
Exposition of the Prophet Ezekiel, 535

One great part of justice consists in a faithful and punctual performance of promises. He is a just man that keeps his word. And can God be a just God if He doth not? The word is gone out of His mouth that He will forgive such. Yea, He is willing to be accounted just or unjust by us as He makes performance thereof. See where He pledges His attribute upon this very account: "If we confess our sins, he is faithful and just to forgive us our sins, and to cleanse us from all unrighteousness" (1 John 1:9). He doth not say "merciful" but "just," as the attribute which we fear most should vote against us; this, He would have us know, is bound for the performance of the promise. It was mercy in God to make the promise, but justice to perform what mercy hath promised.

♦ WILLIAM GURNALL
Christian in Complete Armour, 504

GOD, GLORY OF

You see Christ Himself begs for this [i.e., His own glorification (John 17:5)] at God's hand. None can violently invade this glory or break into those heavenly mansions whether God will or no; all heavenly glory is with

God, who is therefore called the God of glory, or glorious, not only because He is glorious in Himself but because He is the bountiful author and dispenser of all glory, as the sun is the fountain of all light.

✦ ANTHONY BURGESS
Sermon 26: "Of Heavenly Glory," in
CXLV Expository Sermons, 144

The love to God's glory should be preferred before ours; we are to desire His glory principally, and our salvation as subordinate. Oh then let the profane and wicked men of the world tremble at their death when their night approaches, for how can thou look for glory who never did pray for it? How can thou think to be partaker of it who wasn't very much in seeking after it?

✦ ANTHONY BURGESS
Sermon 26: "Of Heavenly Glory," in
CXLV Expository Sermons, 146

As the sun, which would shine in its own brightness and glory though all the world were blind or did willfully shut their eyes against it, so God will ever be most glorious, let men be ever so obstinate or rebellious. Yea, God will have glory by reprobates, though it be nothing to their ease; and though He be not glorified of them, yet He will glorify Himself in them.

✦ NEHEMIAH ROGERS
in Thomas, *Puritan Golden
Treasury*, 120

GOD, GOODNESS OF

God is all good; there is none good but one, that is God. God is essentially good, goodness in the abstract. He is infinitely excellent; He is all perfection. In this one attribute all the rest of the attributes of God are included, and this in each of them. However, the Scriptures speaking to our capacities describe God and His glorious attributes in several and distinct notions, yet in each one all are included; each one is infinite, and infinite perfection is essentially all perfection. God is originally good, the fountain and pattern of all that moral good which is in the creatures. He is bountiful and gracious, ready to do them good. And He is the felicitating end, or the blessedness of the soul.

✦ RICHARD ALLEINE
Heaven Opened, 153

God only is immutably good. Other things may be perpetually good by supernatural power, but not immutably good in their own nature. Other things are not so good, but they may be bad; God is so good that He cannot be bad.

✦ STEPHEN CHARNOCK
Selections, 30

[God] doth not only forbear but also doth men good. His goodness toward them is positive as well as privative. He upholds them in their beings, protects them in their goings, supports them by His power, supplies them by His providence, as well as forbears them by His patience. His enemies are hungry, He feeds them; they are thirsty, He gives them drink. He gives them that corn and wine and oil which they bestow on Baal. He bestows on them those mercies with which they fight against Him. He blesses them with life, health, strength, food, raiment, sleep, reason, friends, peace, liberty, riches, honors, the gospel, sermons, Sabbaths, offers of pardon and life whilst they persist in their provocations against Him.

✦ GEORGE SWINNOCK
The Christian Man's Calling,
in *Works,* 2:476

GOD, HOLINESS OF

The holiness of God and the honor of God call aloud upon all Christians to avoid the suspicion of sin. God is so essentially holy; so universally holy; so transcendently holy; so superlatively holy; so originally, radically, and fundamentally holy; He is so independently holy; so unchangeably, constantly, and exemplarily holy that He cannot but hate and abhor the very appearance of evil. Look, as apparent sin stirs up the judicial anger of God against sinners, so the appearance of sin stirs up the fatherly anger of God against saints. A gracious heart knows that God is "of purer eyes than to behold evil" (Hab. 1:13), and therefore He keeps at a distance from the appearance of iniquity. Of all men in the world none honors God at so high a rate as those that keep most aloof from the appearance of evil.

✦ THOMAS BROOKS
Cabinet of Choice Jewels, 125

The notion of a God cannot be entertained without separating from Him whatsoever is impure and bespotting both in His essence and actions, though we conceive Him infinite in majesty, infinite in essence, eternal in duration, mighty in power, and wise and immutable in His counsels, merciful in His proceedings with men, and whatsoever other perfections may dignify so sovereign a being. Yet if we conceive Him destitute of this excellent perfection and imagine Him possessed with the least contagion of evil, we make Him but an infinite monster and sully all those perfections we ascribed to Him before; we rather own Him a devil than a God. It is a contradiction to be God and to be darkness or to have one mote of darkness mixed with His light.

✦ STEPHEN CHARNOCK
Selections, 129

It is a high demonstration of [God's] excellency that He cannot deny Himself; that is, He cannot do anything that is in the least degree contrary to His holy nature, nothing that needs to be retracted or to alter His mind about it. His will is the rule of righteousness, and righteousness is the rule of His will. The saints of old were perfectly of this mind: "Shall not the Judge of all the earth do right?" (Gen. 18:25).

✦ ELISHA COLES
Practical Discourse, 46

GOD, IMMUTABILITY OF

What our God hath been at any time to His distressed, endangered people, that He is and will be without alteration. For He is a strong, stable, ever-standing, unmoveable, immutable refuge to secure and safeguard them who are His by peculiar covenant.

♦ SIMEON ASHE
Best Refuge, 24

If God were changeable, He were not infinite and almighty. All change ends in addition or diminution. If anything be added, He was not infinite before; if anything be diminished, He is not infinite after. All change implies bounds and limits to that which is changed, but God is infinite; "His greatness is unsearchable." We can add number to number without any end and can conceive an infinite number, yet the greatness of God is beyond all our conceptions.

♦ STEPHEN CHARNOCK
Discourses upon the Existence and Attributes of God, 211

The Lord is unchangeable in holiness and glory. He is a sun that shines always with equal brightness. God, and all that is in God, is unchangeable; for this is an attribute which, like a silken string through a chain of pearl, runs through all the rest: "His mercy is everlasting; and his truth endureth to all generations" (Ps. 100:5). So His strength (Isa. 26:4), and therefore He is called the Rock of ages.... He may change His sentence, the outward threatening or promise, but not His inward decree. He may will a change but not change His will. So His love is immutable; His heart is the same to us in the diversity of outward conditions. We are changed in estate and opinion, but God is not changed.... Our safety lies in God's immutability; we cannot perish utterly because He cannot change.

♦ THOMAS MANTON
Practical Exposition on the Epistles of James, 46

GOD: JUDGMENT IN HARDENING MEN

God is said to harden men when He removes not from them the incentives to sin, curbs not those principles which are ready to comply with those incentives, withdraws the common assistances of His grace, concurs not with counsels and admonitions to make them effectual, flashes not in the convincing light which He darted upon them before. If hardness follows upon God's withholding His softening grace, it is not by any positive act of God but from the natural hardness of man.

♦ STEPHEN CHARNOCK
Selections, 155

The most tremendous judgment of God in this world is the hardening of the hearts of men.

♦ JOHN OWEN
Golden Book, 212

GOD, LOVE OF

Doth your love toward God hold the same course that His love hath done toward you? All that God hath done or will do for His chosen is the product of electing love. Does all your obedience arise from love? And does this love of yours grow out of His? Is His electing love the root of it? Is all that you do toward God in a way of gratitude and duty and with design to glorify His grace? And when the Lord seems to go from you, do you follow the harder after Him, as He for a long time followed you, waiting that He might be gracious unto you? This is truly a God-like love, the eminency whereof lies in this, that He loved us when enemies to Him and loved us into a likeness to Himself, answerable whereto we should love Him, even while our fears may apprehend Him to be our enemy; and through the power of His love secretly working in our hearts, go on to love Him until the glory of the Lord be risen upon us. You could not thus love God if He had not loved you first (1 John 4:19).

✦ ELISHA COLES
Practical Discourse, 112

It is a special consideration to enhance the love of God in giving Christ, that in giving Him He gave the richest jewel in His cabinet, a mercy of the greatest worth and most inestimable value. Heaven itself is not so valuable and precious as Christ is: "Whom have I in heaven but thee?" (Ps. 73:25). Oh, what a fair One! What an only One! What an excellent, lovely One is Christ! Put the beauty of ten thousand paradises like the garden of Eden into one; put all trees, all flowers, all smells, all colors, all tastes, all joys, all sweetness, all loveliness in one. Oh, what a fair and excellent thing would that be! And yet it should be less to that fair and dearest well-beloved Christ than one drop of rain to the whole seas, rivers, lakes, and fountains of ten thousand earths. Now for God to bestow the mercy of mercies, the most precious thing in heaven or earth, upon poor sinners, and as great, as lovely, as excellent as His Son was, yet not to account Him too good to bestow upon us, what manner of love is this!

✦ JOHN FLAVEL
Fountain of Life, 28–29

This is the glory of love, the most orient pearl in the crown of it. It is not mercenary nor self-ended nor deserved (Eph. 1:4), but as a spring or fountain it freely vents or pours out itself upon its own account. And what ingenuous, truly noble, heavenly descended heart can hold out against the power of this love?... Its constancy and unchangeableness is another star of eminent magnitude in the heaven of love. It is not a fading, a wavering, an altering thing, but abides forever.... It may be eclipsed and obscured, as to its beams and influence for a season, but changed, turned away, it cannot be. And this consideration of it renders it to the souls of the saints inestimably precious. The very thought of it is marrow to their bones and health to their souls and makes them cry out to all that is within them to love the Lord and to live unto Him.

✦ JOHN OWEN
The Perseverance of the Saints,
in Golden Book, 125

A godly man weeps sometimes out of the sense of God's love. Gold is the finest and most solid of all the metals, yet is soonest melted with the fire. Gracious hearts, which are golden hearts, are the soonest melted into tears by the fire of God's love.

✦ THOMAS WATSON
Godly Man's Picture, 49

GOD, MERCIES OF

The best God will always take the best time to hand out mercies to His people; there is no mercy so fair, so ripe, so lovely, so beautiful as that which God gives out in His own time. Therefore, hold thy peace; though God delays thee, yet be silent, for there is no possibility of taking a mercy out of God's hand till the mercy be ripe for us, and we ripe for the mercy (Eccl. 3:11).

✦ THOMAS BROOKS
Mute Christian, 224

God shows more mercy in saving some when He might have condemned all than justice in judging many when He might have saved none.

✦ SAMUEL CLARK
Saint's Nosegay, 67

Where God multiplies His mercies and men multiply their sins, there God will multiply their miseries.

✦ SAMUEL CLARK
Saint's Nosegay, 67

How good is God to deny us mercies in mercy.

✦ WILLIAM JENKYN
in Horn, Puritan Remembrancer, 16

There is nothing doth so kindly work repentance as the right apprehension of the mercy and love of God. The beams of that love are more powerful to melt the heart than all the flames of Mount Sinai, all the threatenings and terrors of the law. Sin is the root of our misery, and therefore it is the proper work of this mercy to rescue the soul from it, both from the guilt and the power of it at once.

✦ ROBERT LEIGHTON
A Commentary upon the First Epistle
of Peter, in Whole Works, 1:263

God is incomparable in His mercy. Mercy is an attribute of God whereby He pities and relieves His creature in misery. It is an attribute which relates to the creature only. God knows Himself and loves Himself and glorifies Himself, but He is not merciful to Himself. It is an attribute that relates to the creature in misery. Justice seeks a worthy object, grace is exercised toward an unworthy object, but mercy looks out for a needy, an indigent object.

✦ GEORGE SWINNOCK
Incomparableness of God, in Works, 4:417

GOD, OMNIPRESENCE OF

God is an infinite and immense being whose center is everywhere and whose circumference is nowhere. Now if God be omnipresent, then wheresoever we are, God is present with us. If we are in prison alone, with Joseph, God is present with us there; or if we are in exile alone, with David, God is present with us there; or if we are alone in our closets, God is present with us there. God sees us in secret; therefore let us seek His face in secret.

♦ THOMAS BROOKS
Privy Key of Heaven, 55

As eternity is the perfection whereby [God] has neither beginning nor end, immutability is the perfection whereby He has neither increase nor diminution; so immensity, or omnipresence, is that whereby he has neither bounds nor limitation. As He is in all time yet so as to be above time, so is He in all places yet so as to be above limitation by any place. It was a good expression of a heathen to illustrate this, "that God is a sphere or circle whose center is everywhere, and circumference nowhere."

♦ STEPHEN CHARNOCK
Discourses upon the Existence and Attributes of God, 233

He is an all-seeing God. He knows what possibly can or may be known; approve thyself therefore to this God only in all thy ways. It is no matter what men say, censure, or think of thee. It is no matter what thy fellow actors on this stage of the world imagine. God is the great spectator that beholds thee in every place. God is thy spy and takes complete notice of all the actions of thy life, and they are in print in heaven, which that great spectator and judge will open at the great day and read aloud in the ears of all the world. Fear to sin, therefore, in secret unless thou canst find out some dark hole where the eye of God cannot discern thee. Mourn for thy secret neglect of holy duties, mourn for thy secret hypocrisy, whoredom, profaneness, and, with shame in thy face, come before this God for pardon and mercy. Admire and wonder at His patience, that having seen thee, hath not damned thee.

♦ THOMAS SHEPARD
Sincere Convert, 22–23

GOD, OMNISCIENCE OF

If God did not know all future things, He would be mutable in His knowledge. If He did not know all things that ever were or are to be, there would be upon the appearance of every new object an addition of light to His understanding and therefore such a change in Him as every new knowledge causes in the mind of a man or as the sun works in the world upon its rising every morning, scattering the darkness that was upon the face of the earth. If He did not know them before they came, He would gain a knowledge by them when they came to pass which He had not before they were effected; His knowledge would be new according to the newness of the objects and multiplied according to the multitude of the objects. If God did know things to come as perfectly as He knew things present and past, but knew those certainly and the others doubtfully and conjecturally, He would suffer some change and acquire some perfection in His knowledge when those future things should cease to be future and become present; for He would know it more perfectly when it were present than He did when it was future, and so there would be a change from imperfection to a perfection. But God is every way immutable.

✦ STEPHEN CHARNOCK
Discourses upon the Existence and Attributes of God, 279

The [weaver's] shuttle passes not up and down for nothing. All our thoughts, words, and actions are of an abiding nature; thousands of them slip our memory, but none of them escape the book of the divine Omniscience. "In thy book," saith David, "all my members are written" (Ps. 139:16); and again, "Thou tellest my wanderings, put my tears in thy bottle, are they not in thy book?" It is as true concerning all our actions: Are they not in God's books?

✦ JOHN COLLINGES
Weaver's Pocket-book, 59

God is nearer to us than we are to ourselves and knows our thoughts long before, as a gardener knows what flowers he shall have at spring because he knows the roots.

✦ JOHN TRAPP
Commentary…upon…the New Testament, 436

GOD, PATIENCE OF

[God] would have none to perish that are His, but all to repent and to be saved. He instructs that He may not threaten; He threatens that He may not smite; He smites that He may not destroy; yea, and sometimes He destroys temporally that He may not destroy eternally.

✦ WILLIAM ATTERSOLL
"The Conversion of Nineveh,"
in *Three Treatises*, 6–7

If the prince had an enemy got into one of his towns, he doth not send them provision but lays close siege to the place and doth what he can to starve them. But the great God that could in a moment destroy all His enemies bears with them and is at daily cost to maintain them. Well may He command us to bless them that curse us who Himself does good to the evil and unthankful. But think not, sinners, that you shall escape thus; God's mill goes slow but grinds small. The more admirable His patience and bounty now are, the more dreadful and insupportable will that fury be which arises out of His abused goodness. There is nothing smoother than the sea, yet when stirred into a tempest, nothing rages more. There is nothing so sweet as the patience and goodness of God and nothing so terrible as His wrath when it takes fire.

✦ WILLIAM GURNALL
Christian in Complete Armour, 740–41

How slow God is to anger. He was longer in destroying Jericho than in making the world.

✦ THOMAS WATSON
Gleanings, 133

GOD, WISDOM OF

By wisdom, I mean that attribute in God whereby He orders and manages whatsoever He takes in hand by the best means, in the best manner, and to the best end that possibly can be imagined, so that it is impossible for us or, I may say, for Himself too to find out better means to make use of, a better way to go in, or a better end to aim at than Himself makes use of, goes in, and aims at in everything that ever did or ever shall come from Him.

✦ WILLIAM BEVERIDGE
Thesaurus Theologious, 3:28

How comfortable is it to think that our distresses, as well as our deliverances, are the fruits of infinite wisdom! Nothing is done by Him too soon or too slow, but in the true point of time, with all its due circumstances, most conveniently for His glory and our good. How wise is God to bring the glory of our salvation out of the depths of a seeming ruin and make the evils of affliction subservient to the good of the afflicted!

✦ STEPHEN CHARNOCK
Selections, 126

The wisdom of God: there was great and infinite wisdom showed in creating the world and ruling it by His wise providence, but what is that to the wisdom that is showed in Christ? The wisdom that reconciled justice and mercy, the wisdom that punished sin and pardoned the sinner? How wonderful and unsearchable is that wisdom that by the fall of man raised him to a greater height of happiness than ever he had before?

✦ PATRICK GILLESPIE
Ark of the Covenant Opened, 166

God is wise to conceal the succors He intends in the several changes of thy life, that so He may draw thy heart into an entire dependence on His faithful promise. Thus, to try the metal of Abraham's faith, He let him go on till his hand was stretched forth, and then He comes to his rescue. Christ sends His disciples to sea but stays behind Himself on a design to try their faith and show His love. Comfort thyself, therefore, with this: though thou cannot see thy God in the way, yet thou shalt find Him in the end.

✦ WILLIAM GURNALL
Christian in Complete Armour, 65

God will not only be admired by His saints in glory for His love in their salvation but for His wisdom in the way to it. The love of God in saving them will be the sweet draft at the marriage feast, and the rare wisdom of God in effecting this as the curious workmanship with which the cup shall be enameled.

✦ WILLIAM GURNALL
Christian in Complete Armour, 75

Meditate on the wisdom of God. He is called "the only wise God" (1 Tim. 1:17). His wisdom shines forth in the works of providence: He sits at the helm guiding all things regularly and harmoniously; He brings light out of darkness; He can strike a straight stroke by a crooked stick; He can make use of the injustice of men to do that which is just. He is infinitely wise. He breaks us by afflictions and upon these broken pieces of the ship brings us safe to shore. Meditate on the wisdom of God.

✦ THOMAS WATSON
A Christian on the Mount,
in *Discourses,* 1:206

GOD, WITHDRAWAL OF

By God's withdrawing from His people, He prevents His people's withdrawing from Him; and so by an affliction He prevents sin. For God to withdraw from me is but my affliction, but for me to withdraw from God, that is my sin. And therefore it were better for me that God should withdraw a thousand times from me than that I should once withdraw from God (Heb. 10:38–39). God therefore forsakes us that we may not forsake our God. God sometimes hides Himself that we may cleave the closer to Him and hang the faster upon Him.

✦ THOMAS BROOKS
Mute Christian, 198

By divine withdrawings, the soul is put upon hanging upon a naked God, a naked Christ, a naked promise. Now the soul is put upon the highest and the purest acts of faith (Isa. 63:15–16)—namely, to cleave to God, to hang upon God, and to carry it sweetly and obediently toward God—though He frowns, though He chides, though He strikes, yea, though He kills (Job 13:15).

✦ THOMAS BROOKS
Mute Christian, 204

My Lord and Savior, whom I do love unfeignedly and above all other things, having in my sense and feeling withdrawn Himself from me, I fought earnestly and labored to recover my comfort in by serious meditations and trial of mine own heart and crying unto Him upon my bed in the night, when I was most free from all other distractions.

✦ ARTHUR HILDERSHAM
Canticles, 30–31

Sin separates and hides His face not only from a people that profess His name but even from a soul that really bears His name stamped upon it. Though He will not fully and forever cut off such a soul, yet in part and for a time sin may—yea, to be sure it will separate and hide the face of God from it. Their daily inevitable frailties do not this, but either a course of careless walking and many little unlawful liberties taken to themselves that will rise and gather as a cloud and hide the face of God; or some one gross sin, especially if often reiterated, will prove as a firm stone wall or rather as a brazen wall, built up by their own hands betwixt them and heaven and will not be so easily dissolved or broken down. And yet till that be, the light of His countenance, who is the life of the soul, will be eclipsed and withheld from it.

✦ ROBERT LEIGHTON
"The Goodness of God, and the Wickedness of Man" in *Sermons*, 206

There may be a time when God will not be found, but no time wherein He must not be trusted.

✦ THOMAS LYE
in Horn, *Puritan Remembrancer*, 60

How sad and strange soever thy condition may seem to be, thou art not the first nor art like to be the last of the friends and saints of God whose condition this hath been or may be. Read but over the book of the Psalms. How often do you find there the saints complaining of God's hiding His face from them; casting them out, casting them off, forsaking, forgetting them; shutting out their prayers, and the like? Now this may be some comfort to thee, as it is to a man that is in a wilderness, to find the tract and footsteps of men that have gone that way before.

✦ MATTHEW NEWCOMEN
Best Acquaintance, 107–8

When God seems to be turning a man into a desolate and ruinous heap, yet even then is He building and preparing him to be a more excellent structure. The gardener digs up his garden, pulls up his fences, takes up his plants, and, to the eye, seems to make a pleasant place as a waste. But we know he is about to mend it, not to mar; to plant it better and not to destroy it. So God is

present even in desertions, and though He seem to annihilate or to reduce His new creation into a confused chaos, yet it is to repair its ruins and to make it more beautiful and more strong.

✦ JOSEPH SYMONDS
Case and Cure of a Deserted Soul, 9

GODLINESS

Religion is one continued work which allows of no intermission but has its work every day and in everything; break but one link of this golden chain of godliness, and it weakens the whole. O the slothfulness of Christians at this day in their soul businesses! Every day is filled up with neglects: neglect of prayer, neglect of reading, meditation, conference, heart-watching, grace-cherishing work; forget this duty, pass by another, cold, sleight, formal in all. This spoils the prosperity of souls.

✦ BARTHOLOMEW ASHWOOD
Heavenly Trade, 345–46

A godly life is a seal to sound doctrine.

✦ RICHARD BERNARD
Faithful Shepherd, 93

True godliness is that which breeds the quarrel between God's children and the wicked.

✦ JOHN DOD
in Horn, *Puritan Remembrancer*, 8

Have you the power of godliness, or a form of it only? There be many that do but trifle in religion and play about the skirts and borders of it, spending their time about jejune and barren controversies. But as to the power of religion and the life of godliness which consist in communion with God, and as to duties and ordinances which promote holiness and mortify their lusts, they concern not themselves about these things. But surely "the kingdom of God is not in word, but in power" (1 Cor. 4:20). It is not meat and drink (that is, dry disputes about meats and drinks) "but righteousness, and peace, and joy in the Holy Ghost. For he that in these things serveth Christ is acceptable to God, and approved of men" (Rom. 14:17–18). Oh, I am afraid when the great host of professors shall be tried by these rules, they will shrink up into a little handful, as Gideon's host did.

✦ JOHN FLAVEL
Fountain of Life, 147–48

Paul saith, "Godliness with contentment, is great gain." It is by faith that a Christian enjoys God, it is by love that he enjoys his neighbor, and by contentment that he enjoys himself.

✦ ANDREW GRAY
"Spiritual Contentment," in
Works, 389

As the gospel is a mystery of godliness, it enables [Christians] to do as strange things as they believe: to live by another's spirit, to act from another's strength, to live to another's will, and aim at another's glory. They live by the Spirit of Christ, act with His strength, are determined by His will, and aim at His glory. It makes them so gentle that a child may lead them to anything that is good, yet so stout that fire shall not frighten them into sin. They can love their enemies and yet, for Christ's sake, can hate father and mother. It makes them diligent in their worldly calling, yet enables them to contemn the riches they have obtained by God's blessing on their labor. They are taught by it that all things are theirs, yet they dare not take a pin from the wicked by force or fraud. It makes them so humble as to prefer everyone above themselves yet so to value their own condition that the poorest among them would not change his estate with the greatest monarch of the world. It makes them thank God for health and for sickness also, to rejoice when exalted and not to repine when made low. They can pray for life and at the same time desire to die!

✦ WILLIAM GURNALL
Christian in Complete Armour, 800

Godliness, as to his inward and more hidden parts and power, is a holy conformity to the sacred and divine principles which natural men understand not. True godliness consists in the light of supernatural truths and life of grace, God manifesting Himself in the light of those glorious principles and working the life of supernatural grace in the soul by the Holy Ghost. It consists in the saving and experimental knowledge of God and Jesus Christ, in having all the evil qualities of the soul removed and heavenly habits infused in their room; or in a gracious conformity, disposition, and affection of the heart to God, cleaving to all truths made known to us, finding the powerful influences of the gospel and Spirit of Christ upon us, whereby our souls are brought into the image and likeness of His death and resurrection.

✦ BENJAMIN KEACH
Travels of True Godliness, 9–10

This is true godliness: it is not a bare living up to the natural principles of morality nor a simple knowledge of the letter of the Word or a historical, notional, or dogmatical knowledge of the sacred gospel and the precepts thereof; but in a faithful living up to the supernatural principles of grace and the gospel, discharging our duties with as much readiness and faithfulness toward God as toward man, so that our conscience may be kept void of offense toward both (Acts 24:16). It consists in forsaking of every sin and not only to leave it but to loathe it as the greatest evil and to cleave to God in sincerity of heart, valuing Him above all who is the chiefest good and, from a principle of divine love, willingly subjecting to all His laws and appointments.

✦ BENJAMIN KEACH
Travels of True Godliness, 9–10

Riches make bate [i.e., frantic], but godliness makes peace; riches breed covetousness, but godliness brings contentation; riches make men unwilling to die, but godliness makes men ready to die; riches often hurt the owner, but godliness profits the owner and others. Therefore, only godliness hath this honor, to be called great riches.

✦ HENRY SMITH
"The Benefit of Contentation,"
in *Sermons*, 197

He grieves truly that weeps without a witness; so it may be said of godliness, he is sincere in his godliness who is godly in secret.

✦ GEORGE SWINNOCK
The Christian Man's Calling,
in *Works*, 2:411

A godly man does bear God's name and image; godliness is Godlikeness. 'Tis one thing to profess God, another thing to resemble Him.

✦ THOMAS WATSON
Godly Man's Picture, 26

GOOD WORKS

Naked faith is no faith. Let us not be solifidians, as the Papists call us, lest we be nullifidians, as they are. Faith is of Rachel's humor: "Give me children, or else I die." The want of good works makes faith sick; evil works kill her outright. Good deeds are such things that no man is saved for them nor without them.

✦ THOMAS ADAMS
Exposition upon…Second…Peter, 63

Divine knowledge makes us understand the gospel, but it is divine grace which makes us live according to the gospel. Therefore, what you want in great learning supply with good living. I love preaching, and I love practicing; and I had rather hear one sermon in a day and do three good works than hear three sermons in a day and do never a good work else.

✦ THOMAS ADAMS
*Exposition upon…Second…
Peter*, 786

The end must be as noble as the means, or else a man may be undone for all his doings. A man's most glorious actions will at last be found to be but glorious sins if he hath made himself, and not the glory of God, the end of those actions.

✦ THOMAS BROOKS
Privy Key of Heaven, 198

The heart that is fullest of good works has in it the least room for Satan's temptations.

✦ JOHN BUNYAN
Riches, 209

Good works have diverse good uses and ends, and good reasons there are for God's ordaining them to be walked in without supposing our walking in them to be the ground, condition, or motive of our election, as (1) to testify our love to God, of which we have no such evidence, as the keeping of His commandments (2 John 6); (2) to show forth His virtues whose offspring we profess ourselves to be: "That ye may be"—that is, that ye may appear and approve yourselves to be—"the children of your Father which is in heaven" (Matt. 5:45); (3) to convince those without that they, by our good conversation, may be won over and learn to do well, or else be compelled to glorify God in the day of visitation; (4) for encouragement and example to weaker Christians, who are yet children in the good ways of God and are more aptly led by example than precept; (5) that by having our senses exercised about holy things, we might become more holy and so more capable of communion with God here, and meetened [i.e., prepared] for our heavenly inheritance; (6) good works are a part of election, and the elect are as absolutely ordained to them as to salvation itself (John 15:16).

✦ ELISHA COLES
Practical Discourse, 92

I observe the weaver carrying his silk and his yarns to the twisters; they bring several threads into one. Methinks, I cannot but reflect, what twisting there must be too in the Christian's trade. First, there must be a twisting in every good and spiritual action: (1) a true principal; (2) a right manner of performance; (3) a true end must be all twisted together or the action is but *splendidum peccatum* [i.e., splendid sin], as Augustine was wont to call the moral actions of heathens. The end must be the glory of God; the principal must be love to God; for the manner it must be done in faith. Where these three are twisted together, the action is truly good and spiritual.

✦ JOHN COLLINGES
Weaver's Pocket-book, 37

To encourage himself and others to works of charity, [Philip Henry] would say, "He is no fool who parts with that which he cannot keep when he is sure to be recompensed with that which he cannot lose."

✦ PHILIP HENRY
Life and Sayings, 7

We place religion much in our accustomed performances in coming to church, hearing and repeating of sermons, and praying at home, keeping a round of such and such duties. The "way of God's commandments" is more in doing than in discourse. In many, religion evaporates itself too much out by the tongue, while it appears too little in their ways.

✦ ROBERT LEIGHTON
Spiritual Truths, 228

Works are an evidence of true faith. Graces are not dead, useless habits; they will have some effects and operations when they are weakest and in their infancy. It is said of Paul as soon as he was regenerate, "Behold, he prayeth" (Acts 9:11). Newborn children will cry, at least before they are able to go. This is the evidence by which we must judge, and this is the evidence by which Christ will judge.

✦ THOMAS MANTON
*Practical Exposition on the
Epistle of James*, 104

Works ratify the Spirit's witness. The apostle saith, then it was fulfilled—that is, [it was] seen that Abraham was a believer indeed, according to the testimony of God. The Spirit assures us sometimes by expressions, speaking to us by some inward whisper and voice; sometimes by impressions, implanting gracious dispositions—as it were, writing His mind to us. It is well when both are sensible, and with the witness of the Spirit we have that of water (1 John 5:8). To look after works is the best way to prevent delusion; here is no deceit, as in flashy joys. Fanatic spirits are often deceived by sudden flashes of comfort. Works being a more sensible and constant pledge of the Spirit beget a more solid joy.

✦ THOMAS MANTON
*Practical Exposition on the
Epistle of James*, 113

God lays His charge, His solemn charge, upon us to be much in works of mercy. Now if God should charge the rocks, they would send forth water; if the stones, they would become bread; if the ravens, they would feed Elias [i.e., Elijah]; if the quails, they would victual the camp; if the clouds, they would rain down food from heaven upon His poor people. Shall we then be more rocky than rocks? More ravenous than ravens? More senseless than birds? More empty than clouds?

✦ JOHN TRAPP
Marrow of Many Good Authors, 1051

GOSPEL

Now the word of the gospel and the work of the Spirit always go together—not that God is tied to any means, but that He ties Himself to the means. Hence the gospel is called the power of God to salvation because the power of God ordinarily, and in common course, appears therein. The waters of life and salvation run only in the channel of the gospel.

✦ ISAAC AMBROSE
*"The Doctrine of Regeneration,"
in Works*, 62

All gospel mourning flows from believing.
✦ THOMAS BROOKS
in Horn, *Puritan Remembrancer*, 82

Brown bread with the gospel is good fare.
✦ JOHN DOD
Worthy Sayings, n.p.; John Dod and Philip Henry, *Gleanings of Heavenly Wisdom*, 18

Gospel comfort springs from a gospel root, which is Christ.
✦ WILLIAM GURNALL
Christian in Complete Armour, 147

The gospel presents us with the articles of peace, which God graciously offers to treat, and conclude an inviolable peace upon with rebellious man. In it we have the whole method which God laid in His own thoughts from eternity of reconciling poor sinners to Himself. The gospel, what is it but God's heart in print? The precious promises of the gospel, what are they but heaven's court rolls translated into the creature's language?
✦ WILLIAM GURNALL
Christian in Complete Armour, 354

Gospel truth is the only root whereon gospel holiness will grow.
✦ JOHN OWEN
Golden Book, 137

A man may want liberty and yet be happy, as Joseph was. A man may want peace and yet be happy, as David was. A man may want children and yet be blessed, as Job was. A man may want plenty and yet be full of comfort, as

Micaiah was. But he that wants the gospel wants everything that should do him good. A throne without the gospel is but the devil's dungeon. Wealth without the gospel is fuel for hell. Advancement without the gospel is but a going high to have the greater fall.
✦ JOHN OWEN
Golden Book, 219

No softening like gospel-softening; no hardening like gospel-hardening.
✦ GEORGE SWINNOCK
in Horn, *Puritan Remembrancer*, 42

GOSSIP

A credulous man is akin to a fool; he believes all that is told him, and this often doth create differences. As it is a sin to be a tale-bearer, so it is a folly to be a tale-believer. A wise man will not take a report at the first bound but will sift and examine it before he gives credit to it.
✦ THOMAS WATSON
The Beatitudes, in *Discourses*, 2:287

GOVERNMENT

Without justice, great commonwealths are but great troops of robbers.
✦ JOHN OWEN
in Horn, *Puritan Remembrancer*, 34

GRACE

If you cry louder for comfort than for grace, your soul is in a bad state. Then say, "Lord, if my heart is not sufficiently broken, break it still more; if my wounds are not thoroughly searched,

lance them still deeper; if there be any wickedness in me, search me, Lord, and try me, till my heart is right with God."
✦ ISAAC AMBROSE
Christian Warrior, 59

Grace is beyond gifts. Thou comparest thy grace with another's gifts; there is a vast difference. Grace without gifts is infinitely better than gifts without grace. In religion the vitals are best; gifts are extrinsical, and wicked men are sometimes under the common influence of the Spirit. But grace is a more distinguishing work and is a jewel hung only upon the righteous. Hast thou, the seed of God, the holy anointing? Be content.
✦ SIMEON ASHE
Primitive Divinity, 82

True grace loves examination. It loves to examine and to be examined, for it is sincere, and sincerity is much in examination.... True grace is much engaged in the work of humiliation; it grows in a waterish place. It is much engaged in humiliation.... True grace, though weak, works according to the proportion of its own weakness. It staggers at the promise, yet it goes to the promise; it doubts of Christ's love, yet it runs to Christ; it stumbles, yet it keeps its way.... True grace is willing to learn of others.... True grace is very sensible of its own weakness.
✦ WILLIAM BRIDGE
Lifting Up, 100–101

There is no such way to attain to greater measures of grace as for a man to live up to that little grace he has.
✦ THOMAS BROOKS
Smooth Stones, 15

He who lives up to a little light shall have more light; he who lives up to a little knowledge shall have more knowledge; he who lives up to a little faith shall have more faith; and he who lives up to a little love shall have more love. Verily, the main reason why men are such babes and shrubs in grace is because they do not live up to their attainments.
✦ THOMAS BROOKS
Smooth Stones, 135

It is free grace in redemption that is to be glorified, but something of your own would lessen your need of Christ and lower your esteem of His grace. Nay, it would be a means to keep you from Him, as farms and oxen did those full guests from the wedding supper. Consider further: no man was ever accepted of Christ for what he brought to Him. They are best welcome that bring nothing and yet expect all things. What did you give to Christ, or what did you for Him, or even can, that might move Him to die for you?
✦ ELISHA COLES
Practical Discourse, 176

I knew a man who, when he came under convictions, endeavored with all his might to stifle them. His convictions grew stronger, and he hardened himself against them. He saw their tendency but was so opposite to it that he resolved, in express terms, he would not be a Puritan, whatever came of it. To the church he must go, his master would have it so. But this was his wont—to loll over the seat with his fingers in both his ears. Here general or conditional grace was surely nonplussed. But a chosen vessel must not be so lost. Now steps in electing grace, and by a casual slip of his elbows drew out the stoppers and sent in a word from the pulpit, which, like fire from heaven, melted his heart and cast it in a new mold. Surely in this the Lord did not wait for the man's compliance or improvements; His word was not originated thence nor dependent thereon.

✦ ELISHA COLES
Practical Discourse, 210

Greater things are expected from [believers] than from other men. See that you turn not all this grace into wantonness. Think not because Christ hath done so much for you, you may sit still, much less indulge yourselves in sin, because Christ offered up such an excellent sacrifice for the expiation of it. No, though Christ came to be a curse, He did not come to be a cloak for your sins.

✦ JOHN FLAVEL
Fountain of Life, 436

Be well versed in Christ's righteousness as founded on free grace, and you will find it a good nurse to obedience and a godly life. The taste of free grace makes a man of a free spirit in serving Christ and suffering for Him. If you would enlarge a straightened heart, get a taste of free grace. This brings all into tune in a Christian's spiritual motion. As Jonathan's tasting of that honey quickened his sight, so quickening will the taste of the free grace of God in Christ be to your minds in duties incumbent on you.

✦ OBADIAH GREW
Sinner's Justification, 47

Grace is of a stirring nature and not such a dead thing, like an image, which you may lock up in a chest, and none shall know what God you worship. No, grace will show itself; it will walk with you in all places and companies; it will buy with you and sell for you; it will have a hand in all your enterprises; it will comfort you when you are sincere and faithful for God, and it will complain and chide you when you are otherwise. Go to, stop its mouth and heaven shall hear its voice; it will groan, mourn, and strive even as a living man when you would smother him. I will as soon believe the man to be alive that lies peaceably as he is nailed up in his coffin, without strife or bustle, as that thou hast grace and never exercise it in any act of spiritual life.

✦ WILLIAM GURNALL
Christian in Complete Armour, 44

Those spiritual blessings which are intrinsical to the saint's happiness are to be prayed for with boundless desires. Not "Give me thus much grace, and I will trouble thee for no more"; no, God gives a little grace not to stop our mouth but to open it wider.... He that knows the true worth of grace thinks he hath never enough till satisfied with it in glory.

✦ WILLIAM GURNALL
Christian in Complete Armour, 719

Nature may teach a man to loathe sin in others, but 'tis only grace that teacheth us to abhor sin in ourselves.

✦ JOHN HART
Christ's First Sermon, 15

Good nature: Many people are naturally ingenuous, kind, free, bountiful. But this is not grace.... Good nature is born with us; grace is not.

Civil behavior: We may be easily mistaken in taking this for grace.

External profession: Such as worship God with His people in all ordinances we judge with charity; God only with infallibility.

To be of a party: This is not grace. Some of old said, "I am of Paul; I of Apollos," etc., but Paul calls them all carnal.

Knowledge in the things of God, and of our souls, and of the Scriptures: A man may have his head full of knowledge and not have a grain of grace....

Conviction: A man may have a convinced conscience, and yet no grace.... A man may go to hell loaded with convictions.

Good purposes and promises: These are like buds and blossoms which oftentimes a frosty night nips and they die.

Reformation is not grace. A man may leave off old sins and do some duties and yet be a stranger to the good work.

✦ PHILIP HENRY
Remains, 13–14

I speak of a subjective grace inherent in us whereby a real change is made in our lives and natures. And, in brief, you may take this description of subjective, or inherent, grace: it is a supernatural habit immediately infused into the soul by the Holy Ghost, residing in every power and faculty of the soul as a principle of holy and spiritual operation. And there is a fivefold change wrought by it: upon the judgment, or the direct understanding, by informing and enlightening it; upon the conscience in the reflex understanding by awakening and pacifying it; upon the affections by spiritualizing them; upon the will by converting it; upon the life and conversation by reforming it. This fivefold change is wrought upon the whole soul by the true and sanctifying grace.

✦ EZEKIEL HOPKINS
The Almost Christian Discovered,
in *Select Works*, 222

Grace is not of an equal extent to nature: grace is not native, but donative; not by generation, but by regeneration. It is from the Father of spirits, not fathers of our flesh. Who can bring a clean thing out of filthiness? The new birth is "not of blood, nor of the will of the flesh, nor of the will of man" (John 1:13).

✦ WILLIAM JENKYN
Exposition upon the Epistle of Jude, 14

Divine grace, even in the heart of weak and sinful man, is an invincible thing. Drown it in the waters of adversity, it rises more beautiful, as not being drowned indeed but only washed;

throw it into the furnace of fiery trials, it comes out purer and loses nothing but the dross which our corrupt nature mixes with it.

✦ ROBERT LEIGHTON
A Commentary upon the First Epistle of Peter, in Whole Works, 1:61

Grace doth not pluck up by the roots and wholly destroy the natural passions of the mind because they are distempered by sin! That were an extreme remedy to cure by killing and heal by cutting off; no, but it corrects the distemper in them. It dries not up this main stream of love but purifies it from the mud which it is full of in its wrong course or turns it into its right channel, by which it may run into happiness and empty itself into the ocean of goodness. The Holy Spirit turns the love of the soul toward God in Christ, for in that way only can it apprehend His love. So then Jesus Christ is the first object of this divine love; He is *medium unionis,* through whom God conveys the sense of His love to the soul and receives back its love to Himself.

✦ ROBERT LEIGHTON
A Commentary upon the First Epistle of Peter, in Whole Works, 1:74

The kingdom of grace yields "joy unspeakable" (1 Peter 1:8), though not glory unspeakable. We have "songs in the house of [our] pilgrimage" (Ps. 119:54). God will have us to enter upon our possession by degrees: joy enters into us before we enter into our Master's joy. We have first the daystar, then the sun. What a good Master

do we serve that gives us a part of our wages ere we have done our work! While we are sowing we have peace, the conscience and contentment of a good action.

✦ THOMAS MANTON
Practical Exposition on the Epistle of James, 144

It is beyond the power of the greatest gifts to change the heart; a man may preach like an apostle, pray like an angel, and yet may have the heart of a devil. It is grace only can change the heart. The greatest gifts cannot change it, but the least grace can. Gifts may make a man a scholar, but grace makes a man a believer.

✦ MATTHEW MEAD
Almost Christian Discovered, 31–32

Many men are changed in a moral sense, and one may say they are become new men, but they are in heart and nature the same men still. They are not changed in a spiritual and supernatural sense, and therefore it cannot be said of them they are become new creatures. Restraining grace may cause a moral change, but it is renewing grace that must cause a saving change. Now many are under restraining grace, and so changed morally, that are not under the power of renewing grace, and so changed savingly.

✦ MATTHEW MEAD
Almost Christian Discovered, 80

Grace not only makes a man more a man, but it also makes him more than a man. The primitive Christians were the best of men. None were more lowly in their dispositions or more lovely in their conversation. Noah was a just man and perfect in his generation. He was not a sinner among saints, but he was a saint among sinners. Who would have looked for so fair a bird in so foul a nest? Though he once acted as the sons of men do, yet he was numbered with the sons of God. A field of wheat may be good and yet have a weed in it. A saint is not free from sin — that is his burden; a saint is not free to sin — that is his blessing.

✦ WILLIAM SECKER
Nonsuch Professor, 5

These riches [i.e., grace] make a man wise; wisdom is the best possession. Other riches cannot make one wise. A man may have a full purse and an empty brain. Many a rich heir, though he lives till he become of age, yet he never comes to years of discretion. But these riches of grace have power to make a man wise. "The fear of the LORD is the beginning of wisdom" (Ps. 111:10). The saints are compared to wise virgins (Matthew 25). Grace makes a man wise to know Satan's devices and subtleties (2 Cor. 2:11); it makes him wise unto salvation (2 Tim. 3:15). Grace gives the serpent's eye in the dove's head.

✦ THOMAS WATSON
The Beatitudes, in *Discourses*, 2:461

The meditation of the excellency of grace would make us earnest in the pursuit after it. We dig for gold in the mine, we sweat for it in the furnace. Did we meditate on the worth of grace,

we would dig in the mine of ordinances for it. What sweating and wrestling in prayer? We would put on a modest boldness and not take a denial.

✦ THOMAS WATSON
A Christian on the Mount,
in *Discourses*, 1:219

Grace is Christ's portrait drawn on the soul.

✦ THOMAS WATSON
Puritan Gems, 60

God's children have various degrees of grace: some are little children who only feed upon the milk of the gospel; others are young men grown to maturity; others are fathers who are ready to take their degree in glory. Each has the vitality of godliness. The Scriptures speak both of the cedar and of the bruised reed: each is a plant of God's creation—each of His care; so the weakest plant in God's garden of the church is equally regarded by Him with the strongest. God can read the work of His Spirit on the soul which has received the dimmest impression.

THOMAS WATSON
Puritan Gems, 62

GRACE, GROWTH IN

Though no man shall be rewarded for his works, yet God will at last measure out happiness and blessedness to His people according to their service, faithfulness, diligence, and work in this world. Grace is glory in the bud, and glory is grace at the full. Glory is nothing else but a bright constellation of graces, happiness nothing but the quintessence of holiness. Grace and glory differ in degree, not in kind. Grace and glory differ very little: the one is the seed, the other is the flower. Grace is glory militant, and glory is grace triumphant; and a man may as well plead for equal degrees of grace in this world as he may plead for equal degrees of glory in the other world. Surely the more grace here, the more glory hereafter; and the more work Christians do on earth, the more glory they shall have in heaven.

✦ THOMAS BROOKS
Apples of Gold, 120–21

Our growth in grace doth in nothing more show itself than in our continual care to please God in all things, for they that seldom look to their ways how they [might] please God show they least love God.

✦ EZEKIEL CULVERWELL
Time Well Spent, 173

Grace is glory militant, and glory is grace triumphant; grace is glory begun, and glory is grace made perfect. Grace is the first degree of glory; glory is the highest degree of grace. Grace is the seed, glory is the flower; grace is the ring, glory is the sparkling diamond in the ring; grace is the glorious infant, and glory is the perfect man of grace; grace is the spring, glory is the harvest. The soul of man is the cabinet, the grace of God is the jewel; Christ will throw away the cabinet where He finds not the jewel. He that restored us in His image will restore us to His image.

✦ WILLIAM DYER
Christ's Famous Titles, 81

Grace tried is better than grace and more than grace. It is glory in its infancy. Who knows the truth of grace without a trial? And how soon would faith freeze without a cross! Bear your cross therefore with joy.

✦ JOHN FLAVEL
Fountain of Life, 256

As the seed, though little in itself, yet hath in it virtually the bigness and height of a grown tree, toward which it is putting forth with more and more strength of nature as it grows; so in the very first principle of grace planted at conversion there is perfection of grace contained, in a sense—that is, a disposition putting the creature forth in desires and endeavors after that perfection to which God hath appointed him in Christ Jesus.... "For the LORD God is a sun and a shield: the LORD will give grace and glory: no good thing will he withhold from them that walk uprightly" (Ps. 84:11). Mark that "grace and glory"—that is, grace unto glory. He will still be adding more grace to that thou hast till thy grace on earth commences glory in heaven.

✦ WILLIAM GURNALL
Christian in Complete Armour, 336

I put down here a certain note whereby the gifts of God may be discerned—namely, that they grow up and increase as the grain of mustard seed to a great tree and bear fruit answerably. The grace in the heart is like the grain of mustard seed in two things: first, it is small to see at the beginning; secondly, after it is cast into the ground of the heart, it increases speedily and spreads itself. Therefore, if a man at the first have but some little feeling of his wants, some weak and faint desire, some small obedience, he must not let this spark of grace go out, but these motions of the Spirit must be increased by the use of the word, sacraments, and prayer; and they must daily be flirted up by meditation, endeavoring, striving, asking, seeking, knocking. The master delivering his talents to his servants saith to them, "Occupy 'til I come, and not hide them in the earth."

✦ WILLIAM PERKINS
Grain of Mustard Seed, 18–19

As some cannot hear of a curious flower but they will have it in their garden, so a Christian cannot hear of any grace but he will labor to obtain it.

✦ RICHARD SIBBES
in Bertram, *Homiletic Encyclopaedia*, 431

It is a greater work of God to bring men to grace than, being in the state of grace, to bring them to glory, because sin is far more distant from grace than grace is from glory.

✦ JOHN TRAPP
A Commentary…upon…the New Testament, 629

That saint that grows in grace grows more a man and more than a man.

✦ RALPH VENNING
in Calamy et al., *Saints' Memorials*, 125

The life of grace is to fight with our spiritual enemies; the life of glory is we shall have no enemies to fight with.

✦ JEREMIAH WHITAKER
Christians Great Design on Earth, 28

GREAT EJECTION OF 1662

Whether it be not better to glorify God by a prison (if that you fear should come upon you) than to be an offense and stumbling block by sitting still? Consider, we beseech you, what are we for but our Maker's ends? What are we good for, for what do we serve, but only for His pleasure? Better we had no being than not to be for Him; better we were without liberty than that it should not serve Him. What a small thing is riches or poverty, sickness or health, liberty or bonds, unless in order to His glory? Let us but live in the power of this acknowledged principle, that it is our business and blessedness to glorify God, and all will be set at rights. If that be true, then that is the best condition wherein we may best glorify God, and the happiness of every estate is to be esteemed according to the order and reference that it hath to this end. Now then, let God glorify Himself in us, and it cannot but be well.

✦ JOSEPH ALLEINE
Call to Archippus, 15–16

Ply the throne of grace. "Give God no rest, till he make Jerusalem a praise in the earth." And as our silence should make you speak the more to God, so also the more and oftener one unto another in holy conference, "to provoke to love and to good works." And I beseech you, brethren, pray for us. Whatever God may do with us or whithersoever we may be driven, we shall carry you in our hearts. And when and while we remember ourselves to

God, we shall never forget you, but present you and your souls' concernments daily unto God at the throne of grace in our prayers.

♦ ANONYMOUS
England's Remembrancer, 43

If any think they have no need of ministers, having God's written word at hand to consult with (which we assert to be a perfect rule), I would answer such in the words of the Rev. Mr. D. Williams: "What God threatens as the sorest judgment, these contend for as a privilege—namely, that God should remove the churches' candlestick by taking away its teachers which gave light and no longer hold the stars in His right hand for the people's benefit.

Then was not that a sad and dark day...[in] 1662 when so many hundred lights were put out together? Posterity will scarce believe...that they were incendiaries when they look into the writings that many of them have left behind. Was there no loss of such men, as Mr. R. Baxter, Dr. Manton, Dr. Goodwin, Dr. Tuckney, Dr. Owen, Dr. Bates, Mr. Howe, Mr. Edmund Calamy, Mr. Caryl, Dr. Wilkinson, Dr. Jacomb, Mr. A. Pool, Mr. Mead, Mr. Dav. Clarkson, Mr. Flavel, Mr. Charnock, Mr. Cradock, Mr. Watson, Mr. Sam. Clark, Mr. Richard and Mr. Joseph Allein, Mr. Hickman, Mr. Corbet, Mr. J. Otefield, Mr. Haywood, Mr. Doolittle, Mr. Vincent, Mr. Janeway, Dr. Collins, Mr. Hammond, Mr. Talents, Mr. Firmin, Mr. Case, Mr. Mayo,

Mr. Newcome, Mr. Steel, Mr. Slater, Mr. Gouge, Mr. Sylvester, &c.

♦ JOHN BARRET
Funeral Sermon, 11–12

That black day [of the Great Ejection] was not forgotten though twenty-one years ago; we did therefore take occasion then to humble our souls and seek the Lord together in remembrance of that sad stroke not yet revoked.

♦ THOMAS JOLLY
Note Book, 55

I am apt to think I could do anything for this loving congregation, only I cannot sin. But since, beloved, there is a sentence gone out against us...this is the last day that is prefixed to us to preach. I shall now speak to you (God assisting me) if my passion will give me leave, just as if I would speak if I were immediately to die.

♦ THOMAS LYE
sermon, August 17, 1662, in
Calamy, *Farewell Sermons*, 282

Time may come (bear with the expression) you may have little but cold dishes to feed upon. In a time of scarcity, when there is little corn to be reaped, it is some comfort to have it in the barn or storehouse. The corn of Joseph laid up in years of plenty helped to preserve himself and the whole family—yea, all the land of Egypt. And if you be careful to remember how you have received and heard, you may be able to feed yourselves and others in a time of scarcity of spiritual opportunities, if for your and others' sins God should bring it on you. Let me therefore leave the counsel in the text with you: Go to the old store. Feed on cold meat when you may want warm. Warm it again on your hearts by meditation and a practical remembrance of the word.

◆ JOHN WHITLOCK
in *England's Remembrancer*, 23

If doctrines come to be preached that tend to the beating down the power of godliness or practice of holiness; or that prejudice the free grace of God in election or justification, crying up conditional decrees upon foresight of faith or works or perseverance; or advancing works in the business of justification; or such doctrines as advance the power of nature, the freedom of man's will, [or] assert that true believers may finally and totally fall from grace, the remembrance of what you have received and heard with the experience of the work of God in your own hearts (you who are saints) will antidote you against and help you to confute these and such like false doctrines.

◆ JOHN WHITLOCK
in *England's Remembrancer*, 25

GREAT FIRE OF LONDON (1666)

A serious commemoration of God's judgments is a thing that is highly pleasing to the Lord. God delights as much in the glory of His justice as He does in the glory of His mercy or grace. Now when we commemorate His judgments, we glorify His justice that has inflicted them. Severe judgments contribute much to the enlightening

of men's understandings, and to the awakening of their consciences, and the reforming of their lives and to work men to judge them and justify the Lord. And therefore it highly concerns you to keep up the remembrance of London, desolation by fire, always fresh and flourishing in your souls. Smart judgments are teaching things. All God's rods have a voice.

◆ THOMAS BROOKS
London's Lamentations, 182

Let me a little inquire if this has been the fruit of your personal or family afflictions or of the sore astonishing judgments of God upon this place. You have seen many houses and streets burned down in fewer days than they were hundreds of years in building. You have seen riches that were many years in gathering scattered or maybe in a few hours consumed. And the Lord knows how many have lost their souls and forfeited eternal happiness to build and furnish and gather that which a few moments pulled down, scattered, and consumed. And yet when you have but a little intermission and breathing time, are you not as eagerly at it again?… Have the dismal looks and outcries of those days mortified your carnal mirth? Have you learned righteousness? Have ye made your new dwellings Bethels? Ye have seen or heard of but a few years ago, many as delicate persons as yourselves whose carcasses were carried out in dung carts and thrown into pits, heaps upon heaps. And will ye yet please and pamper such carcasses? Will you gather and patch up, as it were, their rags to adorn your bodies with? Ah! The ashes of London and the dust of those dead bodies shall be witnesses against the present inhabitants.

✦ ALEXANDER CARMICHAEL
Believer's Mortification of Sin, 123–24

If London's sins be greater now than before the pestilence or before the fire, what wonder if greater judgments from God come? If God shall give you up into the hands of bloody papists, it will be worse than fire or pestilence in David's reckoning, as we see by his choice; and yet better have fallen into the hands of the Philistines or Ammonites or any enemies David had than into the hands of anti-Christian butchers.

✦ ALEXANDER CARMICHAEL
Believer's Mortification of Sin, 126

Now water's useless: and the next
    intent
Is, by great ruins, greater to prevent.
By hooks and mines, next houses
    level'd lie,
In hope, the flames may for mere
    hunger die.

But all in vain: those ruins prove a
    stile,
O'er which the fire strides, to the
    standing pile.
Yea, where its actual contact is denied,
Like mischiefs from inflamed air
    betide.

Here, ruinous cracks; there, doleful
    shrieks do sound:

And those, that danger should unite,
    confound.
False fears suggested, common aid,
    distracts;
While each his cabin voids, the
    vessels, wracked:
Their emptied houses to the flames
    they yield;
And change the city for the open field.

✦ SIMON FORD
Conflagration of London, 8,
lines 51–64

At least we must be allowed to observe that the fire happened not six months after the commencing of the Five Mile Act, by which they who but a little before were turned out of their churches, were barbarously turned out of their houses and not suffered to live within five miles of any corporation or of the places where they had been ministers. It was the observation of a wise and good man at that time "that as it was in mercy to many of the ministers, that they were removed out of the city, before that desolating judgment came."

✦ MATTHEW HENRY
"Commemoration of the Fire of London,"
in *Miscellaneous Writings,* 625

September 2 [, 1666]. A lamentable fire began in London in a baker's house in Pudding Lane behind the King's Head Tavern in New Fish Street, which continued burning till Thursday following, laying waste that famous and beautiful city, except a very small remnant of it, in its own rubbish. The use I would desire to make of this sad providence is as followeth:

(1) To get my heart deeply affected with it and with sin the cause of it, the nation's sin, the sin of London, my own sin.

(2) To weep with those that weep and to mourn with those that mourn, as being myself also in the body. How many thousand families that have not where to lay their head!

(3) To see herein as in a glass what a pitiful portion is a portion in this world, and how far it must needs be from making a man happy, seeing in one moment it makes to itself wings and flies away.

(4) To bless God for His wakeful eye of providence over my house and goods continually from morning to evening and from evening to morning again.

(5) What a terrible day will it be when all the world shall be on fire and the elements shall melt with fervent heat the earth also, and all the works that are therein shall be burned up!

(6) Was there not mercy in it to poor, silenced ministers, that they were banished out of the city before this sweeping judgment came upon it, and is not the case somewhat like that of Lot fetched out of Sodom (Gen. 19:15–16)?

◆ PHILIP HENRY
Diaries and Letters, 192–93

Let London seriously consider whether her gospel privileges were not her best defense against temporal calamities and whether, since her slighting, abuse, and forfeiture and God's seizure and stripping her so much of these, she hath not been laid naked to those heavy strokes of extraordinary judgments which she has lately received.

◆ THOMAS VINCENT
God's Terrible Voice in the City, 26

GRIEF

O who will give me tears?
　　Come, all ye springs,
Dwell in my head and eyes;
　　come, clouds and rain;
My grief hath need of all the
　　wat'ry things
That nature hath produc'd:
　　let ev'ry vein
Suck up a river to supply mine eyes,
My weary weeping eyes, too dry for me,
Unless they get new conduits,
　　new supplies,
To bear them out, and with my
　　state agree.

What are two shallow fords,
　　two little spouts
Of a less world? The greater is
　　but small,
A narrow cupboard for my griefs
　　and doubts,
Which want provision in the midst
　　of all.

Verses, ye are too fine a thing,
　　too wise,
For my rough sorrows; cease,
　　be dumb and mute,
Give up your feet and running to
　　mine eyes

And keep your measures for some
  lover's lute,
Whose grief allows him music and
  a rhyme;
For mine excludes both measure,
  tune, and time:
Alas, my God!
       ✦ GEORGE HERBERT
            Poems, 169

GUIDANCE

Take God into thy counsel; heaven
overlooks hell. God at any time can
tell thee what plots are hatching there
against thee.
       ✦ WILLIAM GURNALL
    Christian in Complete Armour, 43

HAPPINESS

The universal principle of carnal persons is to be happy here. Their eyes are
ever engaged upon and their desires
ever thirsting after sensual satisfaction: "Who will show us any good?"
And by consequence their main care is
to obtain and secure temporal things,
the materials of their happiness. The
supernatural principle of a saint is to
please God and enjoy His favor. As
men believe they love, and as they love
they live.
       ✦ WILLIAM BATES
      Danger of Prosperity, 106

God is the chief good—good so as
nothing is but Himself. He is in Himself most happy. Yea, all good and all
true happiness are only to be found
in God, as that which is essential to
His nature, nor is there any good or
any happiness in or with any creature
or thing but what is communicated
to it by God. God is the only desirable good; nothing without Him is
worthy of our hearts. Right thoughts
of God are able to ravish the heart.
How much more happy is the man
that has interest in God. God alone is
able by Himself to put the soul into a
more blessed, comfortable, and happy
condition than can the whole world—
yea, and more than if all the created
happiness of all the angels of heaven
did dwell in one man's bosom. I cannot tell what to say. I am drowned. The
life, the glory, the blessedness, the soul-
satisfying goodness that is in God are
beyond all expression.
       ✦ JOHN BUNYAN
            Riches, 23

Wherefore to seek our happiness anywhere but in love, its very element, is
to leave the waters and go fish in the
woods.
       ✦ DANIEL BURGESS
      Man's Whole Duty, 3

Behold on what sure foundations his
happiness is built whose soul is possessed with divine love, whose will is
transformed into the will of God, and
whose greatest desire is that his Maker
should be pleased. Oh the peace, the
rest, the satisfaction that attends such
a temper of mind!
       ✦ HENRY SCOUGAL
    Life of God in the Soul of Man, 50

HEART

The heart—this of all foes is the most subtle and crafty. "The heart is deceitful above all things and desperately wicked." Then "keep thine heart with all diligence, for out of it are the issues of life." Indeed, the heart is the chief monarch of this little world, man, which rules and commands all other parts. It is the main wheel of the machine, which sets all the rest of the wheels going. It is the fountain of all our thoughts, words, and actions. As the heart is, so is the whole man.

♦ ISAAC AMBROSE
Christian Warrior, 37–38

Other things may be the worse for breaking, yet a heart is never at the best till it be broken.

♦ RICHARD BAKER
in Horn, *Puritan Remembrancer*, 102

Only resign [thy heart] to Him, and do but consent that thy heart be His and entirely and absolutely His, and He will take it and use it as His own. It is His own by title. Let it be also so by thy consent. If God have it not, who shall have it? Shall the world or pride or fleshly lust?… Do they bid more for thy heart than God will give thee? He will give thee His Son and His Spirit and image and the forgiveness of all thy sins. If the greatest gain or honor or pleasure will win it and purchase it, He will have it.

♦ RICHARD BAXTER
A Christian Directory, in
Practical Works, 2:393–94

So a man that hath a watch and understands the use of every wheel and pin, if it goes amiss, he will presently find out the cause of it; but one that hath no skill in a watch, when it goes amiss, he knows not what the matter is and therefore cannot mend it. So indeed, our hearts are as a watch, and there are many wheels and windings and turnings there, and we should labor to know our hearts well, that when they are out of tune we may know what the matter is.

♦ JEREMIAH BURROUGHS
Rare Jewel, 40

Fear and mistrust of our false hearts is painful but safe; presumption of our case to be good is pleasant but dangerous.

♦ EZEKIEL CULVERWELL
Time Well Spent, 137

As for his heart, all the kings and potentates in the world—nay, all the angels in heaven—cannot subdue the heart of a poor sinner; and this is the glory of Christ, that He can do this. Heart-work is God's work. The great heartmaker must be the great heartbreaker; none can do it but He.

♦ WILLIAM DYER
Christ's Famous Titles, 52

Heart sorrow is gospel sorrow: "They were pricked in their heart" (Acts 2:37). And Peter, like an honest surgeon, will not keep these bleeding patients longer in pain with their wounds open but presently claps on the healing plaster of the gospel: "Believe in the Lord Jesus." Now a prick to the heart is more than a wound to the conscience. The heart is the seat of life.

✦ WILLIAM GURNALL
Christian in Complete Armour, 61

A gracious heart pursues earthly things with a holy indifference, saving the violence and zeal of his spirit for the things of heaven. He uses the former as if he used them not, with a kind of nonattendance; his head and heart are taken up with higher matters: how he may please God, thrive in his pace, enjoy more intimate communion with Christ in His ordinances; in these he spreads all his sails, plies all his oars, strains every part and power. Thus, we find David upon his full speed: "My soul pressed hard after thee" (Psalm 63). And before the ark we find him dancing with all his might. Now a carnal heart is clean contrary: his zeal is for the world and his indifference in the things of God. He prays as if he did not pray.… He sweats in his shop but chills and grows cold in his closet. Oh, how hard to pulley him up to a duty of God's worship or to get him out to an ordinance! No weather shall keep him from the market; rain, blow, or snow, he goes thither; but if the church path be but a little wet or the air somewhat cold, it is apology enough for him if his pew be empty.

✦ WILLIAM GURNALL
Christian in Complete Armour, 157

A sincere heart is like a clear stream in a brook: you may see to the bottom of his plots in his words and take the measure of his heart by his tongue.

✦ WILLIAM GURNALL
Christian in Complete Armour, 256

Hide the word in thy heart. This was David's preservative: "Thy word have I hid in my heart, that I might not sin against thee" (Ps. 119:11). It was not the Bible in his hand to read it, not the word on his tongue to speak of it nor in his head to get a notional knowledge of it, but the hiding it in his heart that he found effectual against sin. It is not meat in the dish but taken into the stomach that nourishes; not physic in the glass but taken into the body that purges. Now, *heart* in Scripture, though it be used for all the faculties of the soul, yet principally for the conscience and the affections.

✦ WILLIAM GURNALL
Christian in Complete Armour, 611

David had sat many months under the lectures of the law, unhumbled for his complicated sin, but Nathan is sent to preach a rehearsal sermon to him of the many mercies that God had graced him with, and while those coals are pouring on his head, his heart dissolves presently (2 Sam. 12:13). The frost is seldom quite out of the earth till the sun hath gotten some power in the spring to dissolve its bands. Neither will hardness of heart be removed until the soul be thoroughly warmed with the sense of God's mercies.

✦ WILLIAM GURNALL
Christian in Complete Armour, 712

There must be solid mortification of the heart or else you can never come to walk in these paths; you may as soon expect that a man lame with the extremity of the gout (who cannot endure to put his foot to the ground), that this man should run as that a heart laden and captivated with lusts, with sinful diseases and fetters, should walk in a righteous path. For he hath no principle of righteous motions in him—nay, his principles strongly and prevalently incline him to crooked paths.

✦ OBADIAH SEDGWICK
Shepherd of Israel, 158

The heart of a Christian is Christ's garden, and His graces are as so many sweet spices and flowers, which His Spirit blowing upon makes them to send forth a sweet savor. Therefore, keep the soul open for entertainment of the Holy Ghost, for He will bring in continually fresh forces to subdue corruption, and this most of all on the Lord's Day.

✦ RICHARD SIBBES
Bruised Reed and Smoking Flax, 120

Knowledge and affection mutually help one another; it is good to keep up our affections of love and delight by all sweet inducements and divine encouragements, for what the heart likes best the mind studies most. Those that can bring their hearts to delight in Christ know most of His ways.

✦ RICHARD SIBBES
Bruised Reed and Smoking Flax, 165

[God] marks how I speak and how you hear and how we pray in this place; and if it come not from the heart, He repels it as fast as it goes up, like the smoke which climbs toward heaven but never comes there. Man thinks when he has the gift, he has the heart too; but God,

when He has the gift, calls for the heart still (Ps. 73:1). The Pharisee's prayer, the harlot's vow, the traitor's kiss, the sacrifice of Cain, the feast of Jezebel, the oblations of Ananias, the tears of Esau are nothing to Him, but still He cries, "Bring thy heart or bring nothing."

✦ HENRY SMITH
"The Christian's Sacrifice,"
in *Sermons*, 250

God hath placed us here in this world as husbandmen to plough upon the fallow of our hearts, as laborers to work in the vineyard, as travelers to seek a country, as soldiers to fight the battle of the Lord against the flesh, the world, and the devil.

✦ HENRY SMITH
"The Sinful Man's Search,"
in *Sermons*, 223

Perhaps you give to God your feet to carry you to sermons; you give Him your hands to work or fight for Him; you give Him your tongue to discourse of Him. But have you given Him your heart? Does that cleave to Him, long and pant after Him, sigh for Him, live only in Him?

✦ PETER STERRY
Rise, Race, and Royalty of the Kingdom, 32

[The Christian] believes that none knows the heart but God, and yet he meets with many saints who can tell him his heart.

✦ RALPH VENNING
Orthodox Paradoxes, 19

Heart work is hard work, and it is so hard that most have let it alone; they have been discouraged with the difficulty.

The opposition of Satan and lust to this work hath been so strong that they have been quickly overpowered upon their first attempts and endeavors after a change and rectifying of the disorders which they have perceived.

Heart work is secret work. Many have employed themselves in the more open work of religion, few have taken pains with their hearts in secret; many take heed to their tongues what they speak, and before whom; to their hands, what they do; to their feet, whither they go. But few take heed to their hearts; murder, adultery, theft, and the like sins have been committed in the heart by many who would have been afraid and ashamed of the outward acts.

✦ THOMAS VINCENT
God's Terrible Voice in the City, 112

Godliness is an intrinsical thing; it lies chiefly in the heart. "Circumcision is that of the heart" (Rom. 2:29). The dew lies on the leaf; the sap is hid in the root. The moralist's religion is all in the leaf; it consists only in externals. But godliness is a holy sap which is radicated in the soul.

✦ THOMAS WATSON
Godly Man's Picture, 8

A godly man's heart is the library to hold the word of God.

✦ THOMAS WATSON
Godly Man's Picture, 53

The spirits of the wine are best; so is the spiritual part of duty: "Making melody in your heart to the Lord" (Eph. 5:19). It is the heart makes the music; the spiritualizing of duty gives life to it. Without this, it is dead praying, dead hearing, and dead things are not pleasing; a dead flower has no beauty.

✦ THOMAS WATSON
Godly Man's Picture, 149

HEART, KEEPING THE

Sin is the turning away of the heart from God. The great thing in all the world which God respects and requires as His own is the heart. "My son, give me thine heart." "Keep thy heart with all diligence" (Prov. 4:23).

✦ RICHARD ALLEINE
Heaven Opened, 189

Keep your hearts with all keeping. Let nothing have entertainment there which would abridge your liberty of conversing with God. Fill not those hearts with worldly vanities which are made, and new made, to be the habitation of God. Desire not the company which would diminish your heavenly acquaintance and correspondence. Be not unfriendly nor self-sufficient and self-conceited, but beware, lest under the ingenuous title of a friend—a special, prudent, faithful friend—you should entertain an idol or an enemy to your love of God or a competitor with your highest and best friend.

✦ RICHARD BAXTER
Converse with God in Solitude, 121

By "keeping the heart," understand the diligent and constant use and improvement of all holy means and duties to preserve the soul from sin and maintain its sweet and free communion with God.

✦ JOHN FLAVEL
Keeping the Heart, 2

Be intimately acquainted with thy own heart, and thou wilt the better know his design against thee who takes his method of tempting from the inclination and posture of thy heart. As a general walks about the city and views it well and then raises his batteries where he has the greatest advantage, so doth Satan compass and consider the Christian in every part before he tempts.

✦ WILLIAM GURNALL
Christian in Complete Armour, 56

Keep a strict eye over thy own heart in thy daily walking; hypocrisy is a weed with which the best soil is so tainted that it needs daily care and dressing to keep it under.

✦ WILLIAM GURNALL
Christian in Complete Armour, 272

I doubt not but that you are diligent in the way in which you are to store yourself with knowledge, for this is your harvest in which you must gather the fruits which bear; after, you may bring out to your own and others' profit. It is a sorrowful repentance to repent for the loss of that which we cannot recall, which many men do in sorrowing over their lost time. But above all, my dear Ned, keep your heart close with your God. O let it be your resolution and practice in your life rather to die than sin against your gracious and holy God. We have so gracious a God that nothing can put a distance between Him and our souls but sin; watch therefore against that enemy.

✦ BRILLIANA HARLEY
to her son Edward, November
1639, *Letters*, 71

There is nothing in the life but what was first in the heart. "Strife in your hearts." "Out of the heart proceed evil thoughts, murders, adulteries, fornications, thefts, false witness, blasphemies" (Matt. 15:19). There is the source of sin and the fountain of folly. As the seeds of all creatures were in the chaos, so of all sins in the heart. Well, then, look to the heart; keep that clean if you would have the life free from disorder and distempers. "Keep thy heart with all diligence; for out of it are the issues of life" (Prov. 4:23).

✦ THOMAS MANTON
*Practical Exposition on the
Epistle of James*, 134

The believer being thus sanctified and changed must give all diligence to keep his heart in that estate afterward and endeavor to practice the godly life in his particular actions — that is, deny all ungodliness in his behavior and worldly lusts in his heart. And contrarily live soberly himself in moderating his affections in all lawful liberties, righteously toward men, in giving everyone their due and holily toward God in worshiping and serving Him only, in which things stands our true repentance.

✦ RICHARD ROGERS
Garden of Spirituall Flowers, 13

HEAVEN

Heaven is a state of perfect holiness and of a continual love and praise to God, and the wicked have no heart to this. The imperfect love and praise and holiness which are here to be attained they have no mind of, much less of that which is so much greater. The joys of heaven are of so pure and spiritual a nature that the heart of the wicked cannot desire them.

✦ RICHARD BAXTER
Call to the Unconverted, 83

If you would [live in heaven], you know that there is no sinning, no worldly mind, no pride, no passion, no fleshly lust or pleasures there. Oh, did you but see and hear one hour how those blessed spirits are taken up in loving and magnifying the glorious God in purity and holiness and how far they are from sin, it would make you loathe sin ever after and look on sinners as on men in Bedlam wallowing naked in their dung. Especially, to think that you hope yourselves to live forever like those holy spirits, and therefore sin doth ill beseem you.

✦ RICHARD BAXTER
A Christian Directory, in
Practical Works, 2:253

It is by our success in mortification that we make our access to and fitness for heaven. Can ye love and cherish sin here and think to hate it in heaven? Ye mistake heaven if ye think it stands so much in freedom from trouble as in freedom from sin. And indeed, the successful practice of mortification will

clear more what heaven is to you than all your studies and speculative contemplations of it.

✦ ALEXANDER CARMICHAEL
Believer's Mortification of Sin, 43

Afflictions make heaven appear as heaven indeed. To the weary, it is rest. To the banished, home. To the scorned and reproached, glory. To the captive, liberty. To the soldier, conquest; and to the conqueror, it is a crown of life, of righteousness and of glory. To the hungry, it is hidden manna. To the thirsty, the fountain of life. To the grieved, fullness of joy. And to the mourner, pleasures forevermore. In a word, to them that have lain upon the dunghill and kept their integrity, it is a throne on which they shall sit and reign with Christ forever and ever.

✦ THOMAS CASE
Correction, Instruction, 65

You may go to heaven without health, without wealth, without honor, without pleasure, without friends, without learning, but you can never go to heaven without Christ.

✦ WILLIAM DYER
Christ's Famous Titles, 19

The delight and pleasure resulting from the observation of providence are exceedingly great, and it will doubtless be a part of our entertainment in heaven to view, with transporting delight, how the designs and methods were laid to bring us thither. And what will be a part of our blessedness in heaven may be well allowed to be a prime ingredient in our heaven upon earth. To search for pleasure among the due observations of providence is to search for water in the ocean, for providence does not only ultimately design to bring you to heaven but as intermediate thereunto to bring, by this means, much of heaven into your souls in the way thither. How great a pleasure is it to discern how the most wise God is providentially steering all to the port of His own praise and His people's happiness while the whole world is busily employed in managing the sails and tugging at the oars, with quite an opposite design and purpose!

✦ JOHN FLAVEL
Divine Conduct, 4–5

The saints in heaven shall be like the angels in their alacrity, love, and constancy to serve God; and the damned, like the devils in sin as well as punishment.

✦ WILLIAM GURNALL
Christian in Complete Armour, 128

Let thy hope of heaven conquer thy fear of death. Why shouldst thou be afraid to die who hopest to live by dying? Is the apprentice afraid of the day when his time will be out? He that runs a race, of coming too soon to his goal? The pilot troubled when he sees his harbor? Death is all this to thee! Thy indenture expires and thy jubilee is come; thy race is run, and the crown won, and is sure to drop on thy head when thy soul goes out of thy body. Thy voyage, how troublesome soever it was in its sailing, is now happily finished, and death doth but land thy soul on the shore of eternity at thy heavenly Father's door, never to be put to sea more.

✦ WILLIAM GURNALL
Gleanings, 133

How can they look for heaven when they die that thought it not worth their minding while they lived?

✦ JAMES JANEWAY
in Calamy et al., *Saints' Memorials*, 225

Heaven is reserved for heaven.

✦ JAMES JANEWAY
in Horn, *Puritan Remembrancer*, 346

Heaven is a freedom from all evil both of sin and suffering, so that a name in heaven entitles us to a blessed redemption from all evil. There is no sin there. Grace weakens sin, but it is glory that abolishes it. Old Adam shall there be put off, never be put on again. The Lord Christ will present His church in that day, "faultless before the presence of his glory with exceeding joy" (Jude 24). There is no affliction there. Sin and sorrow came in together, and they shall go out together.

✦ MATTHEW MEAD
Name in Heaven, 74

Especially the affection and grace of love…shall be enlarged and flourish [in heaven]: love to God and to His saints, the perfume of that will fill heaven. Heaven is the place of love — that is, the head grace there, always acting, never failing.

✦ JONATHAN MITCHEL
Discourse of the Glory, 43

[In heaven] God will be enjoyed by His people in a communion forever, not in a single separate way but in conjunction and society (Matt. 8:11), and that communion will be a help to their enjoyment of God, a way and means of their communion with God. When we speak of our immediate communion with God in heaven, we are not to understand it absolutely, that there shall be no mediums between us and the transcendent majesty of God; for there will be the human nature of Christ and the communion of saints who, in a celestial way and manner, will be helpful and useful one to another to convey much of God to one another. But immediate compared with what we have here, and so as these inferior instituted means and helps and glasses that we have here shall be laid aside, but the communion of saints will be in its perfection and fullest excellency in the church triumphant. And love, holiness, and communicativeness, which is the life of communion, then will flourish (1 Cor. 13:8). You must there enjoy Christ your Head not alone, but in fellowship with all His mystical body.

✦ JONATHAN MITCHEL
Discourse of the Glory, 50

O sirs, how should saints be set on going for heaven, where they shall see no war nor hunger of bread! O think of it. There you shall see no lusts to entice, no devil to tempt, no world to seduce, no afflictions to load, no labors to weary, no cares to perplex, no losses to vex, no evils to exercise and disquiet. All these things that are now seen shall

then be unseen things forever. Saints now in heaven are seeing none of them, shall never see any of them again forever.

✦ HENRY PENDLEBURY
Invisible Realities, 109–10

No one shall be kept out of heaven but such as love the world better than heaven.

✦ HENRY SMITH
in Horn, *Puritan Remembrancer*, 63

"Of this blest man [i.e., Richard Sibbes], let this just praise be given,

Heaven was in him, before he was in heaven.

✦ IZAAK WALTON
in Richard Sibbes,
Complete Works, 1:xx

In this blessed inheritance there is nothing but glory. There is the King of glory, there are the vessels of glory, there are the thrones of glory, there is the weight of glory, there are the crowns of glory, there is the kingdom of glory, there is the brightness of glory. This is a purchase worth getting.

✦ THOMAS WATSON
The Christian's Charter of Privileges,
in *Discourses*, 1:50

Eternity is the highest link of the saint's happiness; the soul of a believer shall be forever bathing itself in the pure and pleasant fountain of bliss. The lamp of glory shall be ever burning, never wasting. As there is no intermission in the joys of heaven, so no expiration. When once God hath set His plants in the celestial paradise, He will never pluck them up anymore; He will never transplant them. Never will Christ lose any member of this body; you may sooner separate light from the sun than a glorified saint from Jesus Christ. O eternity, eternity, what a spring will that be that shall have no autumn. What a day that shall have no night!

✦ THOMAS WATSON
The Christian's Charter of Privileges,
in *Discourses,* 1:54

HEAVEN: CONTRASTED WITH HELL

What thoughts shall we have when, sitting in the bosom of [Christ] whom our souls love, we shall see the greatest part of the world tormented in that flame! The tortures of that lake will sweeten those rivers of pleasures in which we shall eternally bathe our souls. That dismal place shall be as a beauty spot to make our glory more glorious.

✦ DAVID CLARKSON
"The Love of Christ," in
Practical Works, 3:11

In heaven there is all life and no dying. In hell is all death and no life. In earth there is both living and dying, which, as it is betwixt both, so it prepares for both. So that he which here below dies to sin doth after live in heaven, and contrarily, he that lives in sin upon earth dies in hell afterward. What if I have no part of joy here below, but still succession of afflictions? The wicked have no part in heaven, and yet they enjoy the earth with pleasure. I would not change portions with them. I

rejoice that seeing I cannot have both, yet I have the better. O Lord, let me pass both my deaths here upon earth. I care not how I live or die, so I may have nothing but life to look for in another world.

✦ JOSEPH HALL
Meditations and Vows, 156–57

Hell is full of purposes, heaven of performances.

✦ JOHN ROGERS
in Horn, *Puritan Remembrancer,* 113

HELL

It pleased God to cast the book of John Bunyan into my hands called *The Groans of the Damn'd,* which did much terrify me in his saying, "that tho' a soul were in hell ten thousand times ten thousand years, he would never be the nearer the coming out than he would be the first day that he went in, because it is for eternity."

✦ ANONYMOUS TESTIMONY
in Charles Doe, *Collection of Experience,* 11

"Depart from me, ye cursed, into everlasting fire, prepared for the devil and his angels." *Depart from me:* There is a separation from all joy and happiness. *Ye cursed:* There is a black and direful excommunication. *Into fire:* There is the cruelty of pain. *Everlasting:* There is the perpetuity of punishment. *Prepared for the devil and his angels:* Here are thy tormenting and tormented companions. O terrible sentence from which the condemned cannot escape, which being pronounced, cannot possibly be withstood. Against which a man cannot except and from which a man can nowhere appeal, so that to the damned, nothing remains but torments which know neither ease of pain nor end of time!

✦ LEWIS BAYLY
Practice of Piety, 42

What if God will that His people should have a taste of hell in this life, that so they may be sensible of and very thankful for their deliverance from hell and the wrath to come? There are three things in hell: torment of body, horror of conscience, loss of God. By our pains and torments, gouts and stone, we think of the torments of hell, or may think. By the horror of conscience that we meet withal, we may think of the horror of conscience there. And by God's withdrawing and God's departing from us here, we may think of the loss of God forever there.

✦ WILLIAM BRIDGE
Seasonable Truths in Evil Times,
in *Works*, 3:163–64

The best way to prevent this hell of hells is to give God the cream and flower of your youth, your strength, your time, your talent. Death may suddenly and unexpectedly seize on you; you have no lease of your lives. Youth is as fickle as old age; the young man may find graves enough of his length in burial places. As green wood and old logs meet in one fire, so young sinners and old sinners meet in one hell and burn together.

✦ THOMAS BROOKS
Apples of Gold, 53

To think often of hell is the way to be preserved from falling into hell. Oh, that you would often consider the bitterness of the damneds' torments and of the pitilessness of their torments and of the diversity, the easelessness, the remedilessness of their torments! The sinner's delight here is momentary; that which torments hereafter is perpetual. When as sinners in hell, dost thou think, O young man, that another Christ shall be found to die for them or that the same Christ shall be crucified again for them or that another gospel shall be preached to them? Surely not.

✦ THOMAS BROOKS
Apples of Gold, 170–71

God never yet sent any man to hell for sin to whom sin has commonly been the greatest hell in this world. God has but one hell, and that is for those to whom sin has been commonly a heaven in this world. That man that hates sin and that daily enters his protest against sin — that man shall never be made miserable by sin hereafter.

✦ THOMAS BROOKS
Cabinet of Choice Jewels, 202

A man may endure to touch the fire with a short touch, and away; but to dwell with everlasting burnings, that is fearful. Oh then, what is dwelling with them and in them forever and ever? We used to say, "Light burdens carried far are heavy." What then will it be to bear that burden, that guilt, that the law and the justice and the wrath of God will lay upon the lost soul forever? Now tell the stars, now tell the drops of the sea, and now tell the blades of grass that are spread upon the face of all the earth if thou canst; and yet sooner mayest thou do this than count the thousands of millions of thousands of years that a damned soul shall lie in hell! Suppose every star that is now in the firmament was to burn by himself one by one, a thousand years apiece. Would it not be a long while before the last of them was burned out? And yet sooner might that be done than the damned soul be at the end of punishment.

✦ JOHN BUNYAN
Riches, 466

O sinners, consider when you are sinning, you are dancing about the mouth of hell. If the Lord should but snap in sunder the slender thread of your lives, you would presently fall into hell. Men think the pleasures of sin very sweet; the Lord knows they are bitterness in the latter end.

✦ ARTHUR DENT
Plain Man's Plain Path-way, 18

Many have declared that all the torments in the world are nothing to the wrath of God upon the conscience. What is the worm that never dies but the efficacy of a guilty conscience? This worm feeds upon and gnaws the very inwards, the tender and most sensible part of man, and is the principal part of hell's horror.

✦ JOHN FLAVEL
Fountain of Life, 342

None sink so far into hell as those that come nearest heaven, because they fall from the greatest height. As it aggravates the torments of damned souls

in this respect above devils, they had a cord of mercy thrown out to them, which devils had not; so by how much God by His Spirit waits on, pleads with, and by both gains on a soul more than others, by so much such a one, if he perish, will find hell the hotter; these add to his sin, and the remembrance of his sin in hell thus accented will add to his torment. None will have such a sad parting from Christ as those who went halfway with Him and then left Him.

✦ WILLIAM GURNALL
Christian in Complete Armour, 34

Could the damned forget the way they went into hell, how oft the Spirit of God was wooing, and how far they were overcome by the conviction of it—in a word, how many turns and returns there were in their journey forward and backward, what possibilities—yea, probabilities—they had for heaven when on earth. Were but some hand so kind as to blot these tormenting passages out of their memories, it would ease them wonderfully.

✦ WILLIAM GURNALL
Christian in Complete Armour, 75

Satan labors to put off the sinner with delays. Floating, flitting thoughts of repenting he fears not; he can give sinners leave to talk what they will do so he can beg time and by his art keep such thoughts from coming to a head and ripening into a perfect resolution. Few are in hell but thought of repenting.

✦ WILLIAM GURNALL
Christian in Complete Armour, 111

Many among us, I think, would be content if there were such a law that might tie up ministers' mouths from scaring them with their sins and the miseries that attend their unreconciled state. The most are more careful to run from the discourse of their misery than to get out of the danger of it, are more offended with the talk of hell than troubled for that sinful state that shall bring them thither.

✦ WILLIAM GURNALL
Christian in Complete Armour, 365

They say smelling of the earth is healthful for the body and taking in the scent of this sulphurous pit, by frequent meditation, cannot but be as wholesome for the soul. O Christian, be sometimes walking in the company of those scriptures which set out the state of the damned in hell and their exquisite torments. This is the true house of mourning, and the going into it by serious meditation is a sovereign means to make the living lay it to heart; and laying it to heart, there is the less fear that thou wilt throw thyself by thy impenitency into this uncomfortable place who art offered so fair a mansion in heaven through faith and repentance.

✦ WILLIAM GURNALL
Christian in Complete Armour, 607

The damned in hell are under easeless and endless sufferings because they would have sinned always if they could have lived always. Wicked men would have no end of their lives here; they would live forever that they might sin forever. Therefore the Lord giveth them a life, not such a one as they would have but such a one as they deserve to have, which is indeed a death forever; wicked men shall die eternally for sin because they would have lived eternally in sin.

✦ JOHN HART
Christ's Last Sermon, 12

O soul, the things thou now seest, even the finest and fairest and fullest of them, are but things that many a man has had who is now in hell, and things that many have who must never come to heaven. Is it a fine house that thine eye is on? Many a one has dwelt in a fine house who is now dwelling in darkness. Is it fine clothes thou lookest at, how thou mayest go gallant and be all in the mode? Why, alas, many that have been clothed in purple and fine linen and decked with all manner of ornaments are now naked in rivers of fire and brimstone. Is it great possessions thou art looking at—houses, lands, treasures? Why many a one hath laid house to house and field to field and heap to heap that now lack a drop of water.

✦ HENRY PENDLEBURY
Invisible Realities, 81

The punishment of hell will be extreme. The souls of the wicked shall be filled with anguish, as full as they can hold. Their capacity will be larger, and they will be filled up to the height of their capacity, and their bodies also will have the most exquisite pain it is possible for them to endure; their sense of pain will be quicker, and their strength to endure pain greater, and their pain will be in the utmost extremity. Some pains of the body here are not very acute, and some troubles of mind may well enough be borne, but any disease in extremity is very irksome. The pain of the head or the tooth in extremity; the gout, stone, cholic in extremity, especially the troubles of the mind in extremity, will make a man weary of his life. But to have every part afflicted in extremity, and the uttermost extremity, and that beyond our own capacity, or conception, this will be very dreadful.

✦ THOMAS VINCENT
Christ's Sudden and Certain Appearance to Judgment, 177–78

When the fire was in London, I believe few of you could take much sleep for divers nights together. When the fire was burning in your streets and burning down your houses, you could not sleep in your houses lest the fire should have burned your persons too. And when the fire of lust is within you and burning within you; when the fire of God's anger is kindled above you and burning over you; and the fire of hell, so dreadful and unextinguishable, is burning beneath you; and you are hanging over the burning lake by a twine-thread, which, ere long, will untwine of itself and may, ere you are aware, and suddenly, be cut or snapped asunder, and then you must drop into the midst of flames. Can you sleep under the guilt and power of sin when you are in such danger? Awake! Sinners, awake!

✦ THOMAS VINCENT
God's Terrible Voice in the City, 172

Here thou shrinkest to think of the gout, colic, stone, or strangury; shiver to hear of the strappado, the rack, or the lawn [i.e., forms of torture]. How then wilt thou bear universal tortures in all the parts of thy body—exquisite anguish and pains such as of which the pangs of childbirth, burnings of material fire and brimstone, gnawings of chest worms, drinks of gall and wormwood are but shadows? And to which they are all but sports and flea bitings, even to the torments thy body shall suffer for its sins against the Creator.

✦ SAMUEL WARD
"The Life of Faith in Death," in
Sermons and Treatises, 60

Hell is full of hard hearts; there is not one soft heart there. There is weeping there, but no softness.

✦ THOMAS WATSON
The Beatitudes, in *Discourses,* 2:102

But it may be objected, if there be any material fire in hell, it will consume the bodies there. I answer, it shall burn without consuming, as Moses's bush did (Ex. 3:2). The power of God silences all disputes. If God by His infinite power could make the fire of the three children not to consume, cannot He make the fire of hell burn and not consume?

✦ THOMAS WATSON
A Christian on the Mount,
in *Discourses,* 1:229

Eternity is the hell of hell; the loss of the soul is irreparable. If all the angels in heaven should go to make a purse, they could not make up this loss. When a sinner is in hell, shall another

Christ be found to die for him? Or will the same Christ be crucified again? Oh no, they are everlasting burnings.

✦ THOMAS WATSON
The Christian's Charter of Privileges,
in *Discourses,* 1:101

The loss of gospel opportunities will be the hell of hell. When a sinner shall at the last day think with himself, "O what might I have been! I might have been as rich as the angels, as rich as heaven could make me. I had a season to work in, but I lost it." This, this will be as a vulture gnawing upon him; this will enhance and accent his misery.

✦ THOMAS WATSON
"The One Thing Necessary,"
in *Discourses,* 1:374

I need not say that it is the most foulest opinion that can be harbored (some impute it unto Origen), and Augustine, he abundantly confutes it; but it needs no great confutation—the very naming of it is a refutation, that all men, after they had been tormented in hell, should at last come out of hell and be freed from eternal death and be partakers of this eternal life. Certainly, there the worm never dies and the fire never goes out; our Savior oft repeats it. And there are abundance of arguments to prove that death to be eternal, but I must omit them. The Scriptures are clear to evince this error; therefore, believe this—that eternal life is not so universal as natural life.

✦ JEREMIAH WHITAKER
Christians Great Design on Earth, 24

To lie in woe and undergo
the direful pains of hell,
And know withal, that there they shall
for aye and ever dwell;
And that they are from rest as far
when fifty thousand year,
Twice told, are spent in punishment,
as when they first came there.

This, oh! This makes hell's fiery flakes
much more intolerable;
This makes frail wights and damned
sprites
to bear their plagues unable.
This makes men bite, for fell despite,
their very tongues in twain;
This makes them roar for great horror,
and trebleth all their pain.

✦ MICHAEL WIGGLESWORTH
"A Short Discourse on Eternity,"
last two stanzas, *Day of Doom,* 92

HERESY

We are they, my friends, upon whom the very ends of the world are come; in which not only *homo homini lupus* (one man is a wolf to another), preying upon the body, name, and estate; but *homo homini daemon* (one man is a devil to another), laboring to ensnare and betray the souls, the precious souls one of another. It is very necessary then that we take heed unto ourselves, that we be not slightly carried on to our own destruction. What caution the apostle gave his Colossians, the same do I give to you: "Let no man spoil you through philosophy and vain deceit." And further give me leave to say, let no man spoil you through divinity and vain deceit. For no doubt but the serpent hath his poison in his head as well as his tail, and the devil hath his baits as cunningly set on and as covertly laid in the depths of divinity as in the shallows of philosophy.

✦ NICHOLAS CHEWNEY
Anti-Socinianism, xii–xiii

Adamites, so called from one Adam, the author of their sect; or from the first man, Adam, whose nakedness they imitate in their stoves [i.e., heated chambers] and conventicles, after the example of Adam and Eve in Paradise.

✦ DAVID DICKSON
Truth's Victory over Error, 303

Hemerobaptists, so called from two Greek words, *hemera* (day) and *baptidso* (to baptize), because they maintained that men and women, according to their faults committed every day, ought every day to be baptized.

✦ DAVID DICKSON
Truth's Victory over Error, 306

[All manner of heretics] preach, print, and practice their heretical opinions openly; for books [*The Bloody Tenet* by Roger Williams], witness a tractate of divorce in which the bonds are let loose to inordinate lust, a pamphlet also in which the soul is laid asleep from the hour of death unto the hour of judgment, with many others. Yea, since the suspension of our church government, everyone that listeth turns preacher, as shoemakers, cobblers, button makers, hostlers, and such like take upon them to expound the Holy Scriptures, intrude into our pulpits, and vent

strange doctrine, tending to faction, sedition, and blasphemy.

✦ EPHRAIM PAGITT
Heresiography, iv

Lovers grieve together. Thus, if we love Christ, we shall grieve for those things that grieve Him: "I beheld the transgressors, and was grieved" (Ps. 119:158). We shall grieve to see truth bleeding, heretics increasing. We shall grieve to see toleration setting up its mast and topsail and multitudes sailing in this ship to hell. Toleration is the grave of reformation. It was a charge drawn up against the angel of Pergamos that he had them there, nestling and brooding, who held the doctrine of Baalam (Rev. 2:14). By toleration we adopt other men's sins and make them our own. I pray God this doth not hasten England's funerals. He who loves Christ will lay these things to heart.

✦ THOMAS WATSON
"Christ's Loveliness," in
Discourses, 1:321

HISTORY, STUDY OF

Nestor, who lived three ages, was accounted the wisest man in the world. But the historian may make himself wise by living as many ages as have passed since the beginning of the world. His books enable him to maintain discourse, who, besides the stock of his own experience, may spend on the common purse of his reading. This directs him in his life so that he makes the shipwrecks of others seamarks to himself; yea, accidents which others start from for their strangeness he welcomes as his wonted acquaintance, having found precedents for them formerly. Without history a man's soul is purblind, seeing only the things which almost touch his eyes.

✦ THOMAS FULLER
Holy and Profane States, 113

HOLINESS

He that is resolved to bring us to glory is as much resolved to bring us to it by perseverance in holiness and diligent obedience, for He never decreed the one without the other, and He will never save us by any other way. Indeed, when we are converted, we have escaped many and grievous dangers, but yet there are many more before us which we must by care and diligence escape. We are translated from death to life, but not from earth to heaven. We have the life of grace, but we are short of the life of glory. And why have we the life of grace but to use it and live by it? Why came we into the vineyard but to work? And why came we into the army of Christ but to fight? Why came we into the race but to run for the prize? Or why turned we into the right way but to travel in it?

✦ RICHARD BAXTER
Baxteriana, 125

If you are contented with that measure of holiness that you have, you have none at all, but a shadow and conceit of it. Let those men think of this that stint themselves in holiness and plead for a moderation in it, as if it were intemperance or fury to love God or fear Him

or seek Him or obey Him any more than they do — or as if we were in danger of excess in these. If ever these men had feelingly and by experience known what holiness is, they would never have been possessed with such conceits as these.

✦ RICHARD BAXTER
Baxteriana, 221

The life of grace lieth (1) in the preferring of God and heaven and holiness in the estimation of our minds before all worldly things; (2) in the choosing them and resolving for them with our wills, before all others; (3) in the seeking of them in the bent and drift of our endeavors. These three make up a state of holiness.

✦ RICHARD BAXTER
A Christian Directory, in
Practical Works, 2:514

Holiness is the very picture of God, and certainly no hand can carve that excellent picture but the Spirit of God. Holiness is the divine nature, and none can impart that to man but the Spirit; the Spirit is the great principle of holiness.

✦ THOMAS BROOKS
Cabinet of Choice Jewels, 365

The holiness and happiness of the saints are the shame and torment of the devil and of his children.

✦ JOSEPH CARYL
Directory for the Afflicted, 11

He could not be Lord of any man as a happy creature if He did not, by His power, make them happy; and He could not make them happy unless, by His grace, He made them holy.

✦ STEPHEN CHARNOCK
Discourses upon the Existence and Attributes of God, 699

Holiness can no more approve of sin than it can commit it. To be delighted with the evil in another's act contracts a guilt, as well as the commission of it; for approbation of a thing is a consent to it.

✦ STEPHEN CHARNOCK
Selections, 132–33

Holiness hath in it a natural tendency to life and peace: it "is a tree of life" (Prov. 3:18). Grace and glory grow from the same root; salvation is the end of faith, the flower that grows upon it (1 Peter 1:9).

✦ ELISHA COLES
Practical Discourse, 50

Holiness is the seed of glory, and holy persons are in glory, as to its kind and the certainty of their obtainment. Albeit it has no glory at present in comparison of that which shall be, as the seed of the rose or lily, compared with the flowers they will grow into and which are virtually in them.

✦ ELISHA COLES
Practical Discourse, 251

As holiness is the soul's best evidence for heaven, so it is a continual spring of comfort to it in the way thither. The purest and sweetest pleasures in this world are the results of holiness. Till we come to live holily, we never live comfortably. Heaven is epitomized in holiness.

✦ JOHN FLAVEL
Fountain of Life, 388

Evangelical holiness rather makes the creature willing than able to give full obedience. The saint's heart leaps when his legs do but creep in the way of God's commandments. Mary asked where they had laid Christ, meaning, it seems, to carry Him away on her shoulders, which she was not able for to do; her affections were stronger than her back.

✦ WILLIAM GURNALL
Christian in Complete Armour, 293

[The one seeking to be holy] must as endeavor to mortify corruption so to grow and advance in the contrary grace. Every sin hath its opposite grace, as every poison hath its antidote; he that will walk in the power of holiness must not only labor to make avoidance of sin but to get possession for the contrary grace.... God will not ask us what we were not but what we were; not to swear and curse will not serve our turn, but thou wilt be asked, "Didst thou bless and sanctify God's name?" And he [is] the true Christian that doth not content himself with a bare laying aside evil customs and practices but labors to walk in the exercise of the contrary graces. Art thou discomposed with impatience, haunted with a discontented spirit under any affliction? Think it not enough to silence thy heart from quarreling with God but leave not till thou canst bring it sweetly to rely on God.

✦ WILLIAM GURNALL
Christian in Complete Armour, 308

They that will not love thee because thou art holy cannot choose but fear and reverence thee at the same time for what they hate thee. Let a saint comply with the wicked and remit a little of his holiness to correspond with them, he loses by the hand as to his interest, I mean, in them; for by gaining a little false love, he loses that true honor which inwardly their consciences paid to his holiness. A Christian walking in the power of holiness is like Samson in his strength; the wicked fear him. But when he shews an impotent spirit by any indecency in his course to his holy profession, then presently he is taken prisoner by them and falls under both the lash of their tongue and scorn of their hearts.

✦ WILLIAM GURNALL
Christian in Complete Armour, 334

Pray not only against the power of sin but for the power of holiness. A wicked man may pray against his sins not out of any inward enmity to them or love to holiness but because they are troublesome guests to his conscience. His zeal is false that seems hot against sin but is cold to holiness. A city is rebellious that keeps its rightful prince out, though it receives not his enemy in.

✦ WILLIAM GURNALL
Christian in Complete Armour, 725

You easily persuade yourselves that Christ hath died for you and redeemed you from hell, but you consider not that, if it be so, He hath likewise redeemed you from your vain conversation and hath set you free from the service of sin. Certainly, while you find not that,

you can have no assurance of the other. If the chains of sin continue still upon you, for anything you can know, these chains do bind you over to the other chains of darkness the apostle speaks of (2 Peter 2:4). Let us not delude ourselves: if we find the love of sin and of the world work stronger in our hearts than the love of Christ, we are not as yet partakers of His redemption.

✦ ROBERT LEIGHTON
A Commentary upon the First Epistle of Peter, in *Whole Works*, 1:134

It is really the Spirit of Christ in a believer that crucifies the world and purges out sin and forms the soul to His likeness. It is impossible to be holy not being in Him, and being truly in Him, it is as impossible not to be holy.

✦ ROBERT LEIGHTON
Spiritual Truths, 161

In our desires for heaven, if they are regular, we consider not so much our freedom from trouble as from sin; nor is our aim in the first place so much at complete happiness as perfect holiness.

✦ JOHN OWEN
Golden Book, 215

Men may be in the performance of outward duties, they may hear the word with some delight, and do many things gladly; they may escape the pollutions that are in the world through lust and not run out into the same compass of excess and riot with other men, yet may they be strangers unto inward thoughts of God with delight and complacency. I cannot understand how it can be otherwise with them whose minds are over and over filled with earthly things, however they may satisfy themselves with pretences of their callings and lawful enjoyments or their not being any way inordinately set on the pleasures or profits of the world. To walk with God, to live unto Him, is not merely to be found in an abstinence from outward sins and in the performance of outward duties, though with diligence in the multiplication of them. All this may be done upon such principles for such ends with such a frame of heart as to find no acceptance with God. It is our hearts that He requires, and we can no way give them unto Him but by our affections and holy thoughts of Him with delight.

✦ JOHN OWEN
On Being Spiritually Minded,
in *Oweniana,* 134–35

The thing here engraven on the priest in the law and required of the preacher of the gospel is especially and above all holiness. Not outward riches and greatness: they [are] to us but like wings to the ostrich, which she cannot fly with but only flutter and get the faster away. By these we only get to outgo other men, but by themselves they do not help us to fly up to heaven ourselves or to carry others along with us. No nor so much inward gifts of learning and such like abilities, though such polishing necessary to the priest, yet it's not it but holiness that's here engraven in his crown. Knowledge without grace, learning in the head without holiness in the forehead, is but like a precious stone in a toad's head or like flowers stuck about a dead body, which will not fully keep it from smelling.

✦ ANTHONY TUCKNEY
Sermon 24, in *Forty Sermons,* 428

Holiness is glory in the seed, and glory is holiness in the flower.

✦ THOMAS WATSON
Puritan Gems, 80

Those who are in a state of nature, under the power of sin, unpardoned and unsanctified, are dead in trespasses and sins. Those who are recovered from the fall and brought into a state of grace by the gospel are said to be dead also: dead to sin and dead to the world. But they have a new life, and that of a different kind.... Let this hidden life be the matter of my meditations, and let me inquire into its nature. It is that whereby a man becomes a new creature, a Christian indeed; his spiritual life wherein he is devoted to God and lives to the purposes of heaven and eternity. The Scripture calls this life eternal, for the life of grace survives the grave and is fulfilled in heaven. It is a life of faith, holiness, and peace; a life of faith, or dependence upon God for all we want; a life of holiness, rendering back again to God, in a way of honor and service, whatsoever we receive from Him in a way of mercy; and a life of peace in the comfortable sense of the favor of God and our acceptance with Him through Jesus Christ.

✦ ISAAC WATTS
Devout Meditations, 25–26

THE HOLY SPIRIT

[The Holy Spirit] is as the spring to all your spiritual motions, as the wind to your sails. You can do nothing without it. Therefore, reverence and regard its help, and pray for it, and obey it, and neglect it not. When you are sure it is the Spirit of God, indeed, that is knocking at the door, behave not yourselves as if you heard not. (1) Obey Him speedily: delay is a present, unthankful refusal and a kind of denial. (2) Obey Him thoroughly; a half obedience is disobedience. Put Him not off with Ananias and Sapphira's gift, the half of that which He requires of you. (3) Obey Him constantly—not sometime hearkening to Him and more frequently neglecting Him, but attending Him in a learning, obediential course of life.

♦ RICHARD BAXTER
A Christian Directory, in
Practical Works, 2:197

God the Spirit is our friend:

1. In the illumination of our understandings (Eph. 1:17–18).

2. Conviction of our sins (John 16:8).

3. Mortification of our corruptions (Rom. 8:13).

4. Sanctification of our natures (Ezek. 36:25).

5. Direction of us in duty and helping us (Rom. 8:14, 26).

6. Consolation of our hearts (John 14:16).

♦ WILLIAM BEVERIDGE
Thesaurus Theologious, 4:27

Now he that hath this tree of life, he hath also the fruit that grows upon this tree. "But the fruit of the Spirit is love, joy, peace, longsuffering, gentleness, goodness, faith, meekness, temperance" (Gal. 5:22–23). Now grace is called not the works of the Spirit, but the fruits of the Spirit (1) because all grace is derived from the Spirit, as the fruit is derived from the root; and (2) to note the pleasantness and delightfulness of grace, for what is more pleasant and delightful than sweet and wholesome fruits; (3) to note the profit and advantage that redounds to them that have the Spirit, for as many grow rich by the fruits of their gardens and orchards, so many grow rich in grace, in holiness, in comfort, and in spiritual experiences by the fruits of the Spirit. Now why hath God given thee His Spirit, and why hath He laid in thy soul a stock of supernatural graces? But that thou mayest be every way qualified, disposed, and fitted for private prayer and to maintain secret communion with God.

♦ THOMAS BROOKS
Privy Key of Heaven, 82

The Spirit teacheth the saints in all things; that is, (1) He teacheth them all things needful for the salvation of their souls, all things necessary to bring them to heaven. (2) All things needful to life and godliness (2 Peter 1:3). (3) All things needful to their places, callings, sexes, ages, and conditions. (4) All things needful for you to know to preserve you in the truth and to preserve you from being deluded and seduced by those false teachers.

✦ THOMAS BROOKS
Privy Key of Heaven, 113

It nothing repents me that I have often said, we do now as much need to have the Spirit of God live in us as ever we did need the Son of God to die for us. And as the purchase of reconciliation did require a divine person, the proof of it doth require no less.

✦ DANIEL BURGESS
Man's Whole Duty, 16

It is very tedious to the Spirit of God when we make...ill interpretations of His ways toward us. If God deals with us otherwise than we would have Him, if there can be any sense worse than other made of it, we will be sure to make it, as thus: when an affliction doth befall you, there may be many good senses made of God's works toward you. You should think thus: It may be God intends only to try me by this; it may be God saw my heart too much set upon the creature and so intends to show me what there is in my heart. It may be that God saw that if my estate did continue, I should fall into sin, that the better my estate were, the worse my soul would be; it may be God intended only to exercise some grace; it may be God intends to prepare me for some great work which He hath for me.

✦ JEREMIAH BURROUGHS
Rare Jewel, 82

Observe and comply with the Spirit's motions and methods when under affliction, which is a special season of the Spirit's teaching and working. Afflictions use to be seals to God's instruction (Job 33:16). Seals give weight and authority to writings. The Spirit now sets instructions home; therefore, consider what sin thou hast most need to mortify and what the Lord especially aims at in afflicting thee.... And when the Spirit's work tends to the stirring up of grace, in all the actings of grace have an eye upon the sin that has most endangered thee and comply with the Spirit, especially when thou art moved to the acting of that grace that is most contrary to thy strongest corruption. It is a token of a sanctified affliction when thy sin is discovered in its sinfulness, when there are fixed purposes of heart raised against it, and when there is some notable acting of the grace that is most opposite to it excited.

✦ ALEXANDER CARMICHAEL
Believer's Mortification of Sin, 169–70

Whensoever we give our attendance on the ordinances of God to hearken unto what He shall speak and to receive the law from His mouth, let our chief care be that our souls be duly prepared and disposed for the teachings of the Holy Ghost. Now our preparation for this lies principally in these three things: (1) in a humble sense of our ignorance and great need of His instructions; (2) a thorough willingness and unfeigned desire to be taught by Him and withal a readiness of mind to receive whatever truths He shall impart to us, how contrary soever to our former apprehensions; (3) a real and full purpose of heart to practice according to our knowledge and to live up to those truths which shall be made known to us. If we could ever bring these holy dispositions along with us when we come hither to wait on God in the way of His ordinances, we should then find what it is to have the Holy Ghost for our teacher.

✦ JOHN CONANT
Sermon 2 on John 14:25–26,
in Sermons, 71–72

All the doctrine of the Scriptures may be briefly referred to these two heads: first, how we may be prepared to receive the Spirit of God; secondly, how the Spirit may be retained when we have once received it.

✦ RICHARD GREENHAM
Paramuthion, 141

The Spirit exactly knows the heart of God to the creature, with all His counsels and purposes concerning Him: the Spirit searches all things, the deep things of God (1 Cor. 2:10). And what are those deep things of God the apostle means but the counsels of love which lie deep in His heart, till the Spirit draws them forth and acquaints the creature with them, as appears by verse 9? And also He knows the whole frame of man's heart. It were strange if He that made the cabinet should not know every secret box in it.

✦ WILLIAM GURNALL
Christian in Complete Armour, 378

Look thou attend the motions of the Holy Spirit. The Christian shall find Him as his remembrancer to remind him of the more solemn performance of this duty of prayer; so his monitor to suggest many occasional meditations to his thoughts, as a hint, that now it is a fit time to give God a visit in some holy ejaculation (by thus setting the door, as it were, open for him in God's presence). Sometimes He will be recalling a truth thou hast heard or read, a mercy thou hast received, or a sin thou hast committed, and what means He by all these but to do thee a friendly office, thy affections being stirred, so that thou mayest be invited to dart thy soul up to God in some ejaculation. Now, take the hint He gives, and thou shalt have more of His company and help in this kind.

✦ WILLIAM GURNALL
Christian in Complete Armour, 680

How happy is the condition of God's people that have the word and the Spirit to guide them! The word without the Spirit cannot, the Spirit without the word will not guide us. The word is a light without us; the Spirit is a light within us. The word propounds the way to walk in; the Spirit enables the soul to walk in that way.

✦ MATTHEW MEAD
"The Power of Grace," in
Name in Heaven, 101

What is "waiting"? Waiting is a permanent continuance in the performance of duties against all difficulties and discouragements. It is a permanent abiding, a continuance in duty, whereby we seek for the return of God unto us against all discouragements, difficulties, temptations whatsoever.

✦ JOHN OWEN
Golden Book, 181

But may not men pray in the Spirit and use a form too? It is not denied but that good men may pray by a form and yet in some sense pray in the Spirit too, but since that it is the proper work of the Spirit to help the infirmities of the saints as well in matter and expressions as sighs and groans (Rom. 8:26), what need they use stinted forms, or how can they tie up themselves strictly to those forms without limiting, stinting, and quenching the Spirit?

✦ VAVASOR POWELL
Common Prayer Book No Divine Service, 4

If we cannot endure the Spirit going up and down with a candle and lantern to search our hearts, how can we abide the day of Christ's coming and stand when the Sun of Righteousness shall appear, for He is like refiner's fire and like fuller's soap? Justice, humility, repentance, though now they be but poor and low things with man, yet when the judge shall take the bench more visibly, how high will they be with God? Sincerity, though it be a silent grace at this time and dwells in obscurity, ere long, I hope, will carry the day and bear away the bell.

✦ FRANCIS RAWORTH
On Jacob's Ladder, ii

If we would have the Spirit of Christ, let us labor to subject ourselves unto it. When we have any good motion by the ministry of the word or by conference or by reading of good things (as holy things have a savor in them, the Spirit breathes in holy exercises), oh give way to the motions of God's Spirit. We shall not have them again perhaps. Turn not back those blessed messengers; let us entertain them, let the Spirit dwell and rule in us. It is the most blessed lodger that ever we entertained in all our lives. If we let the Spirit guide and rule us, it will lead us and govern and support us in life and death and never leave us till it have raised our bodies (the Spirit of Christ in us at length will quicken our dead bodies, Rom. 8:11); it will never leave us till it have brought us to heaven. This is the state of those that belong to God, that give way to the motions of God's Spirit to rule and guide them. Therefore, if we would have the Spirit of Christ, let us take heed of rebelling against it.

✦ RICHARD SIBBES
"A Description of Christ," in
Complete Works, 1:25

If we desire the Spirit, we must wait in the way of duty, as the apostles waited many days before the Comforter came. We must also empty our souls of self-love and the love of the world and willingly entertain those crosses that bring our souls out of love with it. The children of Israel in the wilderness had not the manna till they had spent their onions and garlic; so this world must be out of request with us before we can be truly spiritual. Through grace, labor to see the excellency of spiritual things. How despicable then must all the glory of the world appear! These things, duly considered, will raise our desires more and more toward spiritual and heavenly objects.

✦ RICHARD SIBBES
Divine Meditations and Holy Contemplations, 54–55

But how shall I know the witness of the Spirit from a delusion? Answer: The Spirit of God always witnesses according to the word, as the echo answers the voice. Enthusiasts speak much of the Spirit, but they leave the word. That inspiration which is either without the word or against it is an imposture. The Spirit of God did indite the word (2 Peter 1:21). Now if the Spirit should witness otherwise than according to the word, the Spirit should be divided against itself; it should be a spirit of contradiction, witnessing one thing for a truth in the word and another thing different from it in a man's conscience.

✦ THOMAS WATSON
The Beatitudes, in *Discourses*, 2:307–8

HOLY SPIRIT: GRACES OF THE

We should mind [the Holy Spirit] as the root of all good fruits growing in us or sprouting from us, the producer of all good habits formed in us, the assister of all good works performed by us, the spring of all true content that we enjoy; to whom our embracing the faith, our continuing in hope, our working in charity, the purification of our hearts, the mortification of our lusts, the sanctification of our lives, the

salvation of our souls are principally due, are most justly ascribed. As the author and preserver of so inestimable benefits unto us, let us mind Him; and withal let us consider Him as condescending to be a loving friend and constant guest to so mean and unworthy creatures, vouchsafing to attend over us, to converse with us, to dwell in us, rendering our souls holy temples of His divinity, royal thrones of His majesty, bright orbs of His heavenly light, pleasant paradises of His blissful presence.

✦ ISAAC BARROW
"A Defence of the Blessed Trinity," in *Sermons*, 444–45

The soul is dead and cold by nature, but if a quality of the fire of the Spirit be added unto it, then it will be able to do more than it naturally can do. Therefore, examine what new habits and qualities be in you, whether you have a new habit of patience, love, hope, and experience; that is, as patience begets experience, and experience hope, so where the Spirit is, it doth beget new habits and qualities in the soul by which it is able to do more than naturally it can do…. It first builds the house and sweeps the rooms, and then it fits and furnishes the rooms with new habits and qualities of grace.

✦ JOHN PRESTON
"The Saints' Spiritual Strength," in *Remaines*, 128–29

The graces of the Spirit are like a row of pearls which hang together upon the string of religion and serve to adorn Christ's bride. This I note to show you a difference between a hypocrite and a true child of God: the hypocrite flatters himself with a pretense of grace, but in the meantime he hath not an habit of all the graces—he hath not poverty of spirit nor purity of heart; whereas a child of God hath all the graces in his heart, at least radically, though not gradually.

✦ THOMAS WATSON
The Beatitudes, in *Discourses,* 2:58

HOLY SPIRIT, GRIEVING THE

Your work, Christians, is to be tender of the Spirit, to take heed you be not unkind to His person, that you do not undervalue His gracious communications or resist His internal operations. Take heed of unthankfulness for His kindnesses, of slighting His counsels, of unsuitable walking to His rules and mercies if you would not grieve Him and so deprive yourselves of His quickening influences on your spirits.

✦ BARTHOLOMEW ASHWOOD
Heavenly Trade, 139–40

You see [the Holy Spirit] is God, the Rock of Israel. God omnipotent, for He created all things (Gen. 1:31). God omnipresent, filling all things (Ps. 139:7). God omniscient who knows your hearts (Rom. 8:27). Beware therefore of grieving Him, for in so doing you grieve God.

✦ JOHN FLAVEL
Fountain of Life, 415

Wrong Christ, and you grieve His Spirit.

✦ WILLIAM GURNALL
Christian in Complete Armour, 762

Objection: But there is no healing for me? I fear I have sinned the sin against the Holy Ghost. *Answer:*... The fear of sinning it is a sign thou hast not sinned it....

Let me ask, "Why dost thou think thou hast sinned the sin against the Holy Ghost?"

"I have grieved the Spirit of God."

Answer: Every grieving the Spirit of God is not that fatal sin. We grieve the Spirit when we sin against the illumination of it; the Spirit being grieved may depart for a time and carry away all its honey out of the hive, leaving the soul in darkness (Isa. 50:10). But every grieving the Spirit is not the sin against the Holy Ghost. A child of God, when he hath sinned, his heart smites him; and he whose heart smites him for sin hath not committed the unpardonable sin.

✦ THOMAS WATSON
The Beatitudes, in *Discourses,*
2:449–50

HOLY SPIRIT, OPERATION OF THE

The operation of the Spirit appears in spiritual graces and spiritual duties. The kinds of graces are these: faith, hope, joy, love, fear, obedience, repentance, humility, meekness, patience, zeal, and perseverance, concerning which the Lord has made gracious promises to give them and to reward them.

✦ ISAAC AMBROSE
"The Practice of Sanctification,"
in *Works,* 118

We should…meditate upon the blessed Spirit of God with equal goodness, conspiring and cooperating with all the purposes to all the effects of grace which conduce to our everlasting happiness, more especially as the repairer of our decayed frames; the enlivener of our dead souls; the infuser of spiritual light into our dark minds; the kindler of spiritual warmth into our cold hearts; the raiser of spiritual appetite to righteousness and the relish of goodness in our stupid senses; the imparter of spiritual strength and vigor to our feeble powers; the author of all liberty, loosing us from captivity under the tyranny of Satan, from vassalage unto our own carnal lusts and passions, from subjection to a hard and imperious law, from bondage to the terrors of a guilty conscience.

✦ ISAAC BARROW
"A Defence of the Blessed
Trinity," in *Sermons*, 444

The same Spirit doth by this word (heard or read) renew and sanctify the souls of the elect, illuminating their minds; opening and quickening their hearts; prevailing with, changing, and resolving their wills, thus writing God's word and imprinting His image by His word upon their hearts, making it powerful to conquer and cast out their strongest, sweetest, dearest sins and bringing them to the saving knowledge, love, and obedience of God in Jesus Christ. The same Holy Spirit assisteth the sanctified in the exercise of this grace to the increase of it by blessing and concurring with the means appointed by Him to that end and helpeth them to use those means; perform their duties; conquer temptations, oppositions, and difficulties; and so confirmeth and preserveth them to the end. The same Spirit helpeth believers in the exercise of grace to feel it and discern the sincerity of it in themselves in that measure as they are meet for and in these seasons when it is fittest for them. The same Spirit helpeth them, hereupon, to conclude that they are justified and reconciled to God and have right to all the benefits of His covenant.

✦ RICHARD BAXTER
A Christian Directory, in
Practical Works, 2:191

The Holy Spirit who is given to work grace in us, He is also given to witness grace unto us and to make us "know the things that are freely given to us of God" (1 Cor. 2:12). He is a free and sovereign agent indeed, and He works and witnesses in them in whom He worketh as He pleases. He giveth assurance of peace with God as much as He pleases and as soon, and no more and no sooner, than He pleases (1 Cor. 12:11).

✦ DANIEL BURGESS
Man's Whole Duty, 27

It may be thy inward corruption is not stronger than it was, but spiritual light and gracious tenderness may be growing—the Spirit now may be opening up the depths of thy corruption, and this the Lord usually does by degrees, as he dealt with Ezekiel in a like case (Ezek. 8:6–7, 9, 12–13, 15). He is showed greater and greater abominations where mark that they had put a wall between God and them. The secret chambers of sin are opened up, and thou seest that which makes thee tremble and abhor thyself more than ever, for the first saving conviction does not convince to the utmost. The first saving light shines not into every corner, or at least not so brightly that the man can dive into all the mystery of sin within, but leaves room for after discoveries.

✦ ALEXANDER CARMICHAEL
Believer's Mortification of Sin, 202

The Holy Spirit is often moving in the consciences and affections of carnal creatures, counseling, rebuking, and exciting them, so that upon His suggestions, some warm affections are raised in them to that which is good, but presently all is quashed and comes to nothing and the Spirit driven away by the entertainment He finds. Again, you cannot know by the common gifts of the Spirit—illumination, conviction, restraining grace, and assistance to perform the external part of religious duties; these are gifts of the Spirit, but such as do not prove he hath the Spirit that hath them. These gifts are beamed from the Spirit of God and show that the kingdom of God is come nigh such an one, but they do not demonstrate that God is come into that soul and hath taken possession of it for His temple.

✦ WILLIAM GURNALL
Christian in Complete Armour, 758

There is what is called influence, or breathing, of the Spirit. This gracious influence (for of such only do I now speak) is either ordinary; and this is the operations of the Holy Spirit on the soul and the habits of grace there whereby they are still kept alive and in some exercise and acting, although not very discernible. This influence, I conceive, always attends believers and is that "keeping and watering night and day and every moment." Or this influence is more singular and special and is the same to a gracious, although a withered soul, as the "wind and breath to the dry bones," putting them in good case, and "as the dew or rain to the grass," or newly mown field and parched ground. Such influence is meant by the "blowing of the south wind, making the spices to flow out." When the Spirit moves thus, there is an edge put upon the graces of God in the soul, and they are made to act more vigorously. This is the "enlarging of the heart," by which a "man doth run in the ways of God." This influence is more discernible than the former and not so ordinarily communicated.

✦ WILLIAM GUTHRIE
Christian's Great Interest, 189

There is not anything that is good in us, nothing that is well done by us in the way of obedience, but the Scripture expressly and frequently assigns it unto the immediate operations of the Holy Spirit in us. It doth so in general as to all gracious actings whatever, and not content therewith, it proposes every grace and every holy duty, distinctly affirming the Holy Ghost to be the immediate author of them. And when it comes to make mention of us, it positively, indeed, prescribes our duty to us but as plainly lets us know that we have no power in or from ourselves to perform it. But some men speak and preach and write utterly to another purpose: the freedom, liberty, power, and ability of our own wills; the light, guidance, and direction of our own minds or reasons; and from all our own performance of all the duties of faith and obedience are the subjects of their discourses; and that in opposition unto what is ascribed in the Scriptures unto the immediate operations of the Holy Ghost.

✦ JOHN OWEN
On the Holy Spirit, in
Oweniana, 127–28

The operation of the Spirit in believers, the communion of the Holy Ghost, is a great mystery. He works more on them than they feel and know; and they feel more than they can express in words; and they express more than any that have not received "the same spirit of faith" (2 Cor. 4:13) can understand. But this we know, that whenever the Spirit of Christ applies His grace and power to the heart of a sinner, there is something wrought that day which shall last to eternity. There is, by this finger of God, that impression made upon the soul and that mark left upon it that shall never wear out and that sin and Satan shall never be able to blot

out again, but it shall remain and grow and be seen at the coming of Christ at the last day (Phil. 1:6).

✦ ROBERT TRAILL
Sermon 3, in *Sixteen Sermons on the
Lord's Prayer, for His People*, 50

HOLY SPIRIT, QUENCHING THE

Quench not the Spirit. Observe and obey His motions. When He excites, get thee on; when He checks, get thee back. Know the Holy [Spirit] from the evil spirit by its according or differing with the Scriptures; reject that spirit in the heart that is not the same with the Spirit in the word. Try the wind, what and whence it is, by the card and compass; to the law and to the testimony. And when thou perceive it is from above, hoist up thy sails and get thee on. Quench not the Spirit. Grieve not the Holy Spirit of God whereby thou art sealed to the day of redemption.

✦ RICHARD ALLEINE
Heaven Opened, 335

Cherish heavenly motions in your hearts and be tender of all the breathings of the Spirit upon you. It may be the Lord comes in upon the heart with some spiritual light or life in a sermon or in a duty or when alone, stirring up thy desires and warming thy affections, making some offers of grace and help to thy dull and languishing soul. Take heed now how thou slightest or stiflest these. This is one step to the quenching of the Spirit and impeding its gracious assistance and vital operations on thy soul: "Quench not the Spirit" (1 Thess. 5:19). He that will kindle a fire gathers up every little coal and makes the most of the least spark.

✦ BARTHOLOMEW ASHWOOD
Heavenly Trade, 143

The apostle saith unto [children of God], "Quench not the Spirit." And not without cause, for though the Spirit itself can never be utterly taken from them, yet doubtless if pride, security, or any other sin begin to take place in them, the graces of the Spirit may decay and their clear understanding and comfortable feelings may be gone, so that in their own and others' judgments, the Spirit may seem to be quite extinguished. Neither must this seem strange, for if the image of God which was more perfectly placed in Adam might be quite lost, then no marvel if the graces of the Spirit be drowned in us for a time.

✦ JOHN DOD
"Of Extinguishing the Spirit," in
Seven Godly and Fruitful Sermons, 202

Take heed of quenching the Spirit. Let your ears be open to hear what He says to the churches (Rev. 2:29). Deliver up yourselves wholly to the Spirit's conduct and guidance: be led by Him from what ways and in what ways He pleases, or else He will be grieved and withdraw; and if He does so, alas, your helper will be gone and your infirmities will hinder your perseverance in prayer.

✦ NATHANIEL VINCENT
Spirit of Prayer, 123

HOLY SPIRIT, SEALING OF THE

The people of God, first or last, are sealed by the Spirit: "In whom also after that ye believed, ye were sealed with that holy Spirit of promise" (Eph. 1:13). The nature of sealing consists in the imparting of the image or character of the seal to the thing sealed. To seal a thing is to stamp the character of the seal upon it. Now the Spirit of God doth really and effectually communicate the image of God to us, which image consists in righteousness and true holiness. Then are we truly sealed by the Spirit of God when the Holy Ghost stamps the image of grace and holiness so obviously, so evidently upon the soul as that the soul sees it, feels it, and can run and read it; then the soul is sealed by the Holy Spirit. So Ephesians 4:30: "And grieve not the holy Spirit of God, whereby ye are sealed unto the day of redemption."

✦ THOMAS BROOKS
Privy Key of Heaven, 116

Sin-mortifying, sin-subduing times are the Spirit's sealing times.

✦ THOMAS BROOKS
Privy Key of Heaven, 119

Get your interest in Christ sealed to you by the Spirit, else you cannot have the comfort of Christ's being sealed for you. Now the Spirit seals two ways, objectively and effectually. The first is by working those graces in us which are the conditions of the promises. The latter is by shining upon His own work and helping the soul to discern it, which follows the other, both in order of nature and of time. And these sealings of the Spirit are to be distinguished…by the matter of which that comfort is made, which if it be of the Spirit is ever consonant to the written word (Isa. 8:20). And partly by its effects, for it commonly produces in the sealed soul great care and caution to avoid sin (Eph. 4:30); great love to God (1 John 2:5); readiness to suffer anything for Christ (Rom. 5:3–5); confidence in addresses to God (1 John 5:13–14); and great humility and self-abasement, as in Abraham, who lay on his face when God sealed the covenant to him (Gen. 17:1–3). This, oh, this brings home the sweet and good of all when this seal is superadded to that.

✦ JOHN FLAVEL
Fountain of Life, 50–51

Query: What is the Spirit's sealing work, and how is it performed?

Answer: The sealing of the Spirit is His giving a sure and certain testimony to the reality of that work of grace He hath wrought in our souls and to our interest in Christ and the promises, thereby satisfying our fears and doubts about our estate and condition.

✦ JOHN FLAVEL
Sacramental Meditations, 60–61

In sealing the believer, [the Holy Spirit] doth not make use of an audible voice nor the ministry of angels nor immediate and extraordinary revelations, but He makes use of His own graces implanted in our hearts and His own promises written in the Scriptures. And in this method He usually brings the doubting, trembling heart of the believer to rest and comfort.

✦ JOHN FLAVEL
Sacramental Meditations, 63

Query: We will inquire, What are the effects of the Spirit's sealing upon our souls, by which we may distinguish and clearly discern it from all delusions of Satan and ill impostures whatsoever? *Answer*: The genuine and proper effects and fruits of sealing are (1) inflamed love; (2) renewed care; (3) deep abasements; (4) increase of strength; (5) a desire to be with the Lord; (6) improved mortification to the world. Wheresoever these are found consequent to our communion with God and His manifestations of Himself to us therein, they put it beyond all doubt that it was the seal of His own blessed Spirit, and no delusion.

✦ JOHN FLAVEL
Sacramental Meditations, 75

THE HOLY SPIRIT AND THE PREACHED WORD

God is the grand teacher. This is the reason the word preached works so differently upon men: two in a pew — the one is wrought upon effectually, the other lies at the ordinances as a dead child at the breast and gets no nourishment. What is the reason? Because the heavenly gale of the Spirit blows upon one and not upon the other. One hath the anointing of God, which teacheth him all things (1 John 2:27); the other hath it not. God's Spirit speaks sweetly and often irresistibly.

✦ SIMEON ASHE
Primitive Divinity, 26

Plant thyself under the word preached; this is the Spirit's chariot in which He rides, called therefore the "ministration of the Spirit." The serpent, that evil spirit, got into Eve's heart by her ear, and the Holy Spirit ordinarily enters at the same door. He is received "by the hearing of faith" (Gal. 3:2). They that leave off hearing the word to meet with the Spirit do as if a man should turn his back on the sun that it may shine on his face.

✦ WILLIAM GURNALL
Christian in Complete Armour, 760

HONOR

The more you serve God contrary to your own disposition and reach the services of God over the head of your own dispositions, the more you honor God. And the more that you do prefer the things of God in time of competition above other things, the more you honor God. And the more you part with your much for God's lesser, the more you honor God. What is honor? Honor is a testimony of another's excellency. Now when I can part with my much for God's little, His little truths and things, I do testify an excellency in God. I say, the more you can part with your much for God's little, the more you honor God.

✦ WILLIAM BRIDGE
Christ and the Covenant, in
Works, 3:58

HOPE

Hope is a virgin of a fair and clear countenance; her proper seat is upon earth, her proper object is in heaven; of a quick and piercing eye that can see the glory of God, the mercy of Christ, the society of saints and angels, the joys of paradise through all the clouds and orbs, as Stephen saw heaven opened and Jesus standing in the holy place. Her eye is so fixed on the blessedness above that nothing in the world can remove it. Faith is her attorney general, prayer her solicitor, patience her physician, charity her almoner, thankfulness her treasurer, confidence her vice admiral, the promise of God her anchor, peace her chair of state, and eternal glory her crown.

✦ THOMAS ADAMS
Exposition upon…Second…Peter, 437

A Christian's motto always is or always should be *Spero meliora*, I hope for better things. I hope for better things than any the world can give to me or than any that Satan can take from me. A Christian is always rich in hope, though he has not always a penny in hand.

✦ THOMAS BROOKS
Great Gain, 152

Hope is the handkerchief that God puts into His people's hands to wipe the tears from their eyes, which their present troubles and long stay of expected mercies draw from them: "Refrain thy voice from weeping, and thine eyes from tears: for thy work shall be rewarded, saith the LORD; and they shall come again from the land of the enemy. And there is hope in thine end" (Jer. 31:16–17).

✦ WILLIAM GURNALL
Christian in Complete Armour, 153

Hope is a supernatural grace of God whereby the believer, through Christ, expects and waits for all those good things of the promise which at present he hath not fully received.

✦ WILLIAM GURNALL
Christian in Complete Armour, 515

True hope is a jewel that no one wears but Christ's bride, a grace with which no one is graced but the believer's soul. Christless and hopeless are joined together (Eph. 2:12), and here it is not amiss to observe the order in which hope stands to faith. In regard of time they are not one before another, but in order of nature and operation faith hath the precedency of hope. Faith closes with the promise as a true and faithful word, then hope lifts up the soul to wait for the performance of it. Who goes out to meet him whom he believes will not come? The promise is, as it were, God's love letter to His church and spouse in which He opens His very heart and tells all He means to do for her. Faith reads and embraces it with joy, whereupon the believing soul, by hope, looks out at this window with a longing expectation to see her husband's chariot come in the accomplishment thereof.

✦ WILLIAM GURNALL
Christian in Complete Armour, 515

The helmet [of salvation] is of continual use. We shall need it as long as our war with sin and Satan lasts. The Christian is not beneath hope so long as above ground nor above hope so long as he is beneath heaven. Indeed, when once he enters the gates of that glorious city, then farewell hope, and welcome love forever.

✦ WILLIAM GURNALL
Christian in Complete Armour, 517

Hope is a prying grace; it is able to look beyond the exterior transactions of providence. It can, by the help of the promise, peep into the very bosom of God and read what thoughts and purposes are written there concerning the Christian's particular estate, and this it imparts to him, bidding him not to be at all troubled to hear God speaking roughly to him in the language of His providence. "For," saith hope, "I can assure thee He means thee well, whatever He saith that sounds otherwise."

✦ WILLIAM GURNALL
Christian in Complete Armour, 525

Let thy hope of heaven moderate thy affections to earth. "Be sober, and hope," saith the apostle (1 Peter 1:13). You that look for so much in another world may be very well content with a little in this. Nothing more becomes a heavenly hope than an earthly heart. You would think it an unseeming thing to see some rich man that hath a vast estate among the poor gleaners in harvest time, as busy to pick up the ears of corn that are left in the field as the most miserable beggar in the company. Oh, how all the world would cry shame of such a sordid man! Well, Christian, be not angry if I tell thee that thou dost a more shameful thing by far if thou, who pretends to hope for heaven, be as eager in the pursuit of this world's trash as the poor, carnal wretch is who expects no portion but what God hath left him to pick up in the field of this world.

◆ WILLIAM GURNALL
Christian in Complete Armour, 542

Can a bird fly when one of its wings is broken? Faith and a good conscience are hope's two wings; if, therefore, thou hast wounded thy conscience by any sin, renew thy repentance, that so thou mayest exercise faith for the pardon of it and redeem thy hope.

◆ WILLIAM GURNALL
Christian in Complete Armour, 549

The saints are often feeding their hopes on the carcass of their slain fears.

◆ WILLIAM GURNALL
Christian in Complete Armour, 555

[The apostle Paul] exhorts the Corinthians to be "abounding in the work of the Lord," knowing that their labor shall not be in vain in the Lord (1 Cor. 15:58). As worldly hope keeps the world at work in their various employments, so God giveth His people the hope of His glory to keep them close to His service (Heb. 6:11–12; 1 John 3:3). And it is such a sure hope as shall never make them ashamed (Rom. 5:5). Those that think it below the excellency of their love to work from a hope of the heavenly reward do thereby advance their love beyond the love of the apostles and primitive saints, and even of Christ Himself.

◆ WALTER MARSHALL
Gospel Mystery of Sanctification, 55

Hope in general is but an uncertain expectation of a future good which we desire, but as it is a gospel grace, all uncertainty is removed from it which would hinder us of the advantages intended in it. It is an earnest expectation proceeding from faith, trust, and confidence, accompanied with longing desires of enjoyment. From a mistake of its nature, it is that few Christians labor after it, exercise themselves unto it, or have the benefit of it; for to live by hope, they suppose, infers a state not only beneath the life of faith and all assurance in believing but also exclusive of them. They think to hope to be saved is a condition of men who have no faith or assurance. But this is to turn a blessed fruit of the Spirit into a common affection of nature. Gospel hope is a fruit of faith, trust, and confidence; yea, the height of the actings of all grace issues in a well-grounded hope, nor can it rise any higher (Rom. 5:2–5).

◆ JOHN OWEN
On Being Spiritually Minded,
in *Oweniana*, 148–49

This anchor [i.e., hope] is cast upward and fastened not in the depth of the sea but in the height of heaven, whereof it gets firm hold and sure possession. Now that ship, saith one, may be tossed, not shipwrecked, whereof Christ is the pilot, the Scripture the compass, the promises the tackling, hope the anchor, faith the cable, the Holy Ghost the winds, and holy

affections the sails, which are filled with the graces of the Spirit.
✦ JOHN TRAPP
A Commentary...upon...the New Testament, 876

Hope is an active grace; it is called a "lively hope" (1 Peter 1:3). Hope is like the spring in the watch—it sets all the wheels of the soul a-running; hope of a crop makes the husbandman sow his seed; hope of victory makes the soldier fight; and a true hope of glory makes a Christian vigorously pursue glory. Here is a spiritual touchstone to try our grace by: if we have the anointing of the Spirit, it will oil the wheels of our endeavor and make us lively in our pursuit after the heavenly kingdom.
✦ THOMAS WATSON
Body of Practical Divinity, 474

HOSPITALITY

Hospitality is threefold: for one's family, this of necessity; for strangers, this of courtesy; for the poor, this is charity.
✦ THOMAS FULLER
Holy and Profane States, 182

HUMAN RESPONSIBILITY

No one loses God but he that is willing to part with Him.
✦ WILLIAM GURNALL
Christian in Complete Armour, 557

HUMILITY

The first step to humility is to see one's pride; the first step to self-denial is to be convinced of one's desire after self-exalting, self-admiring, self-advancing—O what a proud heart have I! What a self-advancing heart have I! There is no believer till he is fully renewed but what has something of self. We had need therefore to be jealous of ourselves; and if at any time self break out, if at any time the soul begins to be advanced in regard of duty or spiritual things, let us fall down before God and humble ourselves for the pride of our hearts.
✦ ISAAC AMBROSE
"The Practice of Sanctification," in *Works*, 104

Let not great men put too much trust in their greatness; the longer the robe is, the more soil it contracts. Great power may prove the mother of great damnation.
✦ ISAAC BARGRAVE
Sermon Preached, 109

Carefully notice all your humbling circumstances and overlook none of them. Observe your imperfections, inferiority in relations, contradictions you meet with, your afflictions, uncertainty of all things about you, and your sinfulness. Look through them designedly and consider the steps of the conduct of providence toward you in these, that ye may know yourselves and may not be strangers at home, blind to your own real state and case.

Observe what these circumstances require of you, as suitable to them; bend your endeavors toward it to bring your spirits into that temper of humiliation that, as your lot is really low in all these respects, so your spirits may be low too, as under the mighty hand of God. Let this be your great aim through your whole life and your exercise every day.

✦ THOMAS BOSTON
Crook in the Lot, 121–22

Seek not great things for yourselves in this world, for if your garments be too long, they will make you stumble; and one staff helps a man in his journey when many in his hands at once hinders him.

✦ WILLIAM BRIDGE
in Thomas, *Puritan Golden Treasury,* 314

Humility is a grace hardly attained unto. Many, saith Augustine, can more easily give all they have to the poor than themselves become poor in spirit.

✦ THOMAS BROOKS
Cabinet of Choice Jewels, 304

Humility will keep the soul free from many darts cast by Satan and from many erroneous snares spread by him. As low trees and shrubs are free from many violent blasts of wind which shake and rend the taller ones, so humble souls are free from those blasts of error which rend and tear proud, lofty souls. Satan and the world have greater difficulty to fasten errors upon humble souls.

✦ THOMAS BROOKS
Precious Remedies, 110

As the emptying of a vessel fits it for being filled with precious liquor, so humility, by emptying the heart of all self-confidence, self-sufficiency, self-righteousness, self-will, fits the soul in prayer for what it does pray for. The

heart of the humble is a prepared heart to pray to God, likewise to receive and improve the mercies which it seeks in prayer; such an one is most flexible and ready both to use the best means to obtain the mercies desired and to walk worthy of them when obtained.

✦ THOMAS COBBET
Gospel Incense, 226

By humility I mean not the abjectness of a base mind, but a prudent care not to overvalue ourselves upon any account.

✦ OBADIAH GREW
in Bertram, *Homiletic Encyclopaedia,* 501

Humility is a necessary veil to all other graces.

✦ WILLIAM GURNALL
Christian in Complete Armour, 139

The deeper sense thou hast of thy own weakness, the more fit thou art for the Spirit's teaching. A proud scholar and a humble master will never agree: Christ is humble and lowly and so resists the proud but giveth grace to the humble. Though He cannot brook him that is proud, yet He can bear with thee who art weak and dull if humble and diligent, as we may see in the disciples, whom our Savior did not disdain to teach the same lesson over and over again till at last they say, "Lo, now speakest thou plainly" (John 16:29). The eunuch was no great scholar when in his chariot he was reading Isaiah's prophecy, yet because he did it with an honest heart, Philip is dispatched to instruct him.

✦ WILLIAM GURNALL
Christian in Complete Armour, 595

They are great admirers of themselves and lovers of some interest of their own more than [Christ's] that cannot endure to see His work done by other hands than theirs. Or that have nothing of that disposition in them which those words express, "Let Him increase and me decrease."

✦ JOHN HOWE
Funeral Sermon, 14

Humility is not only a grace but a capacity to receive more of it.... All other graces grow together with humility. The more humble we are, the more we have of God with us, the more we have of grace in us; and the more we have of these, the more we have of strength in the inner man, and the more we have of preparation for a day of trial.

✦ EDWARD POLHILL
Armatura Dei, 149–50

Humility imports a deep sense of our own weakness with a hearty and affectionate acknowledgment of our owing all that we are to the divine bounty, which is always accompanied with a profound submission to the will of God and great deadness toward the glory of the world and applause of men.

✦ HENRY SCOUGAL
Life of God in the Soul of Man, 23

The thoughts that pass in our heart in the best and most serious day of our life, being exposed unto public view, would render us either hateful or ridiculous. And now, however we conceal our failings from one another, yet sure we are conscious of them ourselves, and some serious reflections upon them would much qualify and allay the vanity of our spirits. Thus, holy men have come really to think worse of themselves than of any other person in the world.

✦ HENRY SCOUGAL
Life of God in the Soul of Man, 119

Humility will make you easy and contented in every condition of life. You will then be ready to be commanded, easy to be pleased, hard to be provoked, and generally beloved. A humble mind thinks every good it receives more than it deserves, and every evil less. It will not think itself too great or too good to stoop to the meanest services of an honest employment nor be wanting in a modest and respectful behavior to others.

✦ RICHARD STEELE
Religious Tradesman, 43

Many are humbled, but not humble; low, but not lowly.

✦ JOHN TRAPP
in Horn, *Puritan Remembrancer*, 30

Humility is both a grace and a vessel to receive grace.

✦ JOHN TRAPP
in Horn, *Puritan Remembrancer*, 145

Height of place gives opportunity of temptation. The longest robe contracts the greatest soil.

✦ JOHN TRAPP
Commentary...upon...the New Testament, 35

He that is little in his own eyes will not be troubled to be little in the eyes of others.

✦ RALPH VENNING
Canaan's Flowing, 102

Humility looks upon another's virtues and its own infirmities.

✦ THOMAS WATSON
The Christian's Charter of Privileges,
in *Discourses,* 1:129

HUMOR, GUIDELINES FOR

Make not a jest of another man's infirmity; remember thine own. Abhor the frothy wit of a filthy nature whose brains having once conceived an odd scoff, his mind travails till he be delivered of it; yea, he had rather lose his best friend than his worst jest. But if thou be disposed to be merry, have a special care to three things (Prov. 23:17; Phil. 4:4): first, that thy mirth be not against religion; second, that it be not against charity; third, that it be not against chastity, and then be as merry as thou canst, only in the Lord.

✦ LEWIS BAYLY
Practice of Piety, 125

Almost twenty years since I heard a profane jest and still remember it. How many pious passages of far later date have I forgotten! It seems my soul is like a filthy pond wherein fish die soon and frogs live long. Lord, raze this profane jest out of my memory. Leave not a letter thereof behind lest my corruption (an apt scholar) guess it out again, and be pleased to write some pious meditation in the place thereof. And grant, Lord, for the time to come (because such bad guests are easier kept out) that I may be careful not to admit what I find so difficult to expel.

✦ THOMAS FULLER
Good Thoughts, 84–85

Wanton jests make fools laugh and wise men frown. Seeing we are civilized Englishmen, let us not be naked savages in our talk. Such rotten speeches are worst in withered age, when men run after that sin in their words which flies from them in the deed. Let not thy jests, like mummy, be made of dead men's flesh. Abuse not any that are departed, for to wrong their memories is to rob their ghosts of their winding-sheets. Scoff not at the natural defects of any which are not in their power to amend. Oh, 'tis cruelty to beat a cripple with his own crutches. Neither flout any for his profession if honest, though poor and painful. Mock not a cobbler for his black thumbs. He that relates another man's wicked jest with delight adopts it to be his own.

✦ THOMAS FULLER
Holy and Profane States, 186

HYPOCRITES/HYPOCRISY

A hypocrite is like the Sicilian Etna, flaming at the mouth when it hath snow at the foot. Their mouths talk hotly, but their feet walk coldly.

✦ THOMAS ADAMS
Exposition upon…Second…Peter, 256

How often have I heard a common drunkard, with tears, cry out against himself for his sin and yet go on in it? And how many gracious persons have I known whose judgments and wills have been groundedly resolved for God and holiness, and their lives have been holy, fruitful, and obedient, and yet could not shed a tear for sin nor feel any great sorrows or joys? If you judge of a man by his earnestness in some good moods and not by the constant tenor of his life, you will think many a hypocrite to be better than most saints.

✦ RICHARD BAXTER
Baxteriana, 210

It is not the presence of hypocrisy but the reign of hypocrisy that damns the soul; that hypocrisy that is discerned, resisted, opposed, and mourned over will never make a Christian miserable. Where the standing frame and general bent of a man's heart is upright, there the presence of hypocrisy cannot denominate a man a hypocrite. All men must stand and fall forever according to the standing frame and general bent of their hearts; if the standing frame and general bent of their hearts be sincere, they are happy forever!

✦ THOMAS BROOKS
Cabinet of Choice Jewels, 87–88

A sincere Christian will endeavor to obey God in suffering commands as well as in doing commands, in losing as well as gaining commands. An unsound Christian loves cheap obedience; he is willing to fall in with those commands that are not chargeable or costly. He loves a cheap gospel, a cheap ministry, a cheap membership, and a cheap communion of saints.

✦ THOMAS BROOKS
Cabinet of Choice Jewels, 141

A hypocrite may offer sacrifice with Cain and fast with Jezebel, and humble himself with Ahab and lament with the tears of Esau, and kiss Christ with Judas and follow Christ with Demas, and offer fair for the Holy Ghost with Simon Magus; and yet for all this, his inside is as bad as any of theirs. A hypocrite is a Cato without and a Nero within, a Jacob without and an Esau within, a David without and a Saul within, a Peter without and a Judas within, a saint without and a Satan within, an angel without and a devil within.

✦ THOMAS BROOKS
Cabinet of Choice Jewels, 282

Hypocrites love to share with Christ in His happiness, but they do not love to share with Christ in His holiness. They are willing to be redeemed by Christ, but they are not cordially willing to submit to the laws and government of Christ. They are willing to be saved by His blood, but they are not willing to submit to His scepter. Hypocrites love the privileges of the gospel, but they do not love the services of the gospel, especially those that are most inward and spiritual.

✦ THOMAS BROOKS
Cabinet of Choice Jewels, 295

All lip labor is but lost labor; when men's hearts are not in their devotion, their devotion is mere dissimulation. These hypocrites sought God and inquired early after God, but it was still with old hearts, which are no hearts in the account of God.

✦ THOMAS BROOKS
Cabinet of Choice Jewels, 310

Self is the only oil that makes the chariot wheels of the hypocrite move in religious concerns.

✦ THOMAS BROOKS
Privy Key of Heaven, 15

Upon the Frog:
The frog by nature is both damp
   and cold.
Her mouth is large, her belly much
   will hold;
She sits somewhat ascending, loves
   to be
Croaking in gardens, tho' unpleasantly.

Comparison:
The hypocrite is like unto this frog;
As like as is the puppy to the dog.
He is of nature cold, his mouth is wide,
To prate, and at true goodness to
   deride.
And tho' the world is that which has
   his love,
He mounts his head, as if he liv'd
   above.
And though he seeks in churches for
   to croak,
He neither loveth Jesus, nor his yoke.
   ✦ JOHN BUNYAN
   "The Hypocrite" (a rhyme for children),
   in *Divine Emblems*, 56–57

To be lip-holy and heart-hollow is a
brief character of a hypocrite.
   ✦ EDMUND CALAMY
   Saints' Memorials, 29

Let us look to the hypocrite's way in
his converse with the saints, for he is
careful to keep some correspondence
with them. (1) He has inward prejudices against such as walk strictly
and convincingly, that have a watchful and observant eye; he haunts not
such, except it be for some design.
(2) He is careful to speak and act
more watchfully and more hand-
somely than ordinarily he uses. (3) He

cannot endure to be freely and faithfully checked by them, and he would
not have others know his distempers.
Whatever he think of himself, he cannot endure others should question
his graces.
   ✦ ALEXANDER CARMICHAEL
   "An Essay on Hypocrisy," in
   Believer's Mortification of Sin, 236

It is a sad thing to be Christians at a
supper, heathens in our shops, and
devils in our closets.
   ✦ STEPHEN CHARNOCK
   in Horn, *Puritan Remembrancer*, 74

Let us hence learn not to be too rigid
or severe, too harsh or peremptory
in censuring men for their failings or
sometimes perhaps their gross miscarriages—I mean in censuring their
spiritual estate. Dislike and abhor their
sins we may and must and declare our
abhorrence and detestation of them
upon all just occasions, but judge their
persons and estates merely upon that
account we must not. Unless a man
were the searcher of the heart, which
is God's sole prerogative, 'tis a hard
thing to say, "Such a man hath done so
and so; therefore, he is a hypocrite, or
a mere dissembler, or a person utterly
void of any true grace." Upon as good
grounds a man might have passed the
like censure upon Noah and Lot and
David and Peter and other good men
whose shameful falls are mentioned
in Scripture. So long as the common
course of men's lives is agreeable to
the rule of the gospel, so long as the
general tenor of their conversation is
spotless and unblameable, we must not

be so critical and severe as for some particular blemishes to brand them for persons unsound and rotten at heart and presently to blot their names out of the catalog of the faithful.

✦ JOHN CONANT
Sermon 11 on 2 Chronicles 32:31,
in *Sermons*, 400–401

This scripture [i.e., John 6:27] is a part of Christ's excellent reply to an earthly-minded multitude who followed Him not for any spiritual excellencies that they saw in Him or soul advantages they expected by Him, but for bread. Instead of making His service their meat and drink, they only served Him that they might eat and drink. Self is a thing that may creep into the best hearts and actions, but it only predominates in the hypocrite.

✦ JOHN FLAVEL
Fountain of Life, 42

The Christian, by his sorrow, shows himself a conqueror of that sin which even now overcame him, while the hypocrite, by his pride, shows himself a slave to a worse lust than that he resists. While the Christian commits a sin, he hates it, whereas the other loves it while he forbears it.

✦ WILLIAM GURNALL
Christian in Complete Armour, 35–36

It is sincere faith that is the strong faith, sincere love that is the mighty love. Hypocrisy is to grace as the worm is to the oak, the rust to the iron—it weakens them because it corrupts them.

✦ WILLIAM GURNALL
Christian in Complete Armour, 226

The Christian, he like a star in the heavens, wades through the cloud that for a time hides his comfort; but the other [i.e., the hypocrite], like a meteor in the air, blazes a little and then drops into some ditch or other where it is quenched. Or, as the Spirit of God distinguishes them: "The light of the righteous rejoiceth: but the lamp [or candle, as in the Hebrew] of the wicked shall be put out" (Prov. 13:9). The sincere Christian's joy and comfort is compared there to the light of the sun that is climbing higher while it is muffled up with the clouds from our eye and by and by, when it breaks out more gloriously, doth rejoice over those mists and clouds that seemed to obscure it. But the joy of the wicked, like a candle, wastes and spends, being fed with gross fuel of outward prosperity which in a short time fails, and the wretch's comfort goes out in a snuff at last, past all hope of being lighted again.

✦ WILLIAM GURNALL
Christian in Complete Armour, 388

A false friend is worse than an open enemy in man's judgment, and a hypocritical Judas more abhorred by God than a bloody Pilate.

✦ WILLIAM GURNALL
Christian in Complete Armour, 442

The hypocrite seems hot in prayer, but you will find him cold enough at work. He prays very fiercely against his sins, as if he desired them to be all slain upon the place. But doth he set himself upon the work of mortification? Does he withdraw the fuel that feeds them?

When temptations come, do they find them in arms, resolved to resist their motion? No, if a few good words in prayer will do, well and good; but as for any more, he is too lazy. Whereas the sincere Christian is not idle after prayer, when it has given heaven the alarm and called God to his help, then he takes the field himself and opposes his lusts with all his might, watching their motions and taking every advantage he possibly can to fall upon them. Every mercy he receives, he beats it out into a weapon to knock down all thoughts of sinning again.

✦ WILLIAM GURNALL
Christian in Complete Armour, 753

Hypocrisy in religion springs from the bitter root of some carnal affection unmortified.... God is in the hypocrite's mouth, but the world is in his heart, which he expects to gain through his good reputation.

✦ WILLIAM GURNALL
Christian in Complete Armour, 754

We may say let hypocrites, reprobates, or atheists have what they can, they want the three great essentials of religion and true Christianity: (1) They are not broken in their hearts and emptied even of their righteousness, the length of self-loathing yet lying open for relief. Such lost ones Christ came to seek and save. (2) They never took up Christ Jesus as the only treasure and jewel that can only enrich and should satisfy and therefore have never cordially agreed to God's device in the covenant and so are not worthy of Him; neither has the kingdom of God savingly entered into their heart: "The kingdom of heaven is like unto a treasure hid in a field; the which when a man hath found, he hideth, and for joy thereof selleth all that he hath, and buyeth that field." (3) They never in earnest close with Christ's whole yoke without exception, judging all His will just and good, holy and spiritual; and therefore no rest followed on them by Christ: "Take my yoke upon you, and ye shall find rest unto your souls." Therefore, whosoever thou art who can lay clear and just claim to these three mentioned things, thou art beyond the reach of all atheists, hypocrites, and reprobates in the world as having answered the great ends and intents of the law and gospel.

✦ WILLIAM GUTHRIE
Christian's Great Interest, 174–75

The peace which the hypocrite has is built upon the sand; he has not one promise that he can rationally lay any claim to. Nay, the whole Word of God assaults him and tells him how vain his confidence is and that if, for all this, he will speak peace to himself, that he must try shortly whether he can make it good when conscience, Scripture, law and gospel, God and man appear in the field against him. In a word, the cause of his peace is ignorance, hardness, deadness. The god of this world hath blinded his eyes; God is author of the saint's peace and the devil of the sinners (Matt. 7:24; Luke 11:21; Rom. 15:4; Phil. 4:7).

✦ JAMES JANEWAY
Saint's Encouragement, 73–74

[Hypocrisy] is seemingly holy but really wicked. He loves the face of holiness but is without the grace of holiness. His greatest care hath been to wash the outside of his platter.

✦ BENJAMIN KEACH
Travels of True Godliness, 120

Hypocrites must be roused with some asperity and sharpness. So the apostle [says], "O vain man"; so Christ [says], "Ye fools and blind"; so John the Baptist [says], "O generation of vipers" (Matt. 3:7). Hypocrites are usually inconsiderate and of a sleepy conscience, so that we must not whisper but cry aloud. An open sinner has a constant torment and bondage upon his spirit which is soon felt and soon awakened, but a hypocrite is able to make defenses and replies. We must, by the warrant of those great examples, deal with him more roughly; mildness only soothes him in his error.

✦ THOMAS MANTON
Practical Exposition on the Epistle of James, 106–7

The hypocrite is the greatest fool and puts the greatest cheat upon himself in the issue; all that he gains by his designs is but the fee of hell. He shall "appoint him his portion with the hypocrites" (Matt. 24:51). Well, then, reckon sincerity as the highest point of wisdom.

✦ THOMAS MANTON
Practical Exposition on the Epistle of James, 142

True religion is bountiful. Duties of worship are to be accompanied with duties of mercy and bounty, so, upon the Christian Sabbath, there should be collections for the poor (1 Cor. 16:2). Hypocrisy divides these; it is willing to serve God, but in the cheapest way. Hypocrites are all for a cheap religion.

✦ SAMUEL MATHER
Figures or Types of the Old Testament, 416

The righteous shall be saved with a "scarcely"—that is, through much difficulty. He shall go to heaven through many sad fears of hell. The hypocrite shall be almost saved—that is, he shall go to hell through many fair hopes of heaven. There are two things arise from hence of very serious meditation. The one is how oft a believer may miscarry, how low he may fall and yet have true grace. The other is how far a hypocrite may go in the way to heaven, how high he may attain and yet have no grace. The saint may be cast down very near to hell and yet shall never come there, and the hypocrite may be lifted up very near to heaven and yet never come there. The saint may almost perish and yet be saved eternally; the hypocrite may almost be saved and yet perish finally. For the saint at worst is really a believer, and the hypocrite at best is really a sinner.

✦ MATTHEW MEAD
Almost Christian Discovered, 8–9

The best man may do some hypocritical and guileful actions, as David did in the matter of Uriah. It is not the having of hypocrisy that denotes a hypocrite but the reigning of it, which is, when it is not seen, confessed, bewailed, and opposed.

A man should judge of his uprightness rather by his will, bent, and the
inclination of his soul and good desires
and true endeavors to well-doing in
the whole course of his life than by
this or that particular act or by his
power to do. David was thus esteemed
"a man according to God's own heart,"
no otherwise, rather by the goodness
of the general course of his life than by
particular actions. For in many things
he offended God and polluted his soul
and blemished his reputation.

✦ HENRY SCUDDER
Christian's Daily Walk, 216

[Hypocrites] are one thing on their
knees, and another on their feet.

✦ JOHN SHOWER
Family Religion, 64

To discern your state in grace, chiefly
look to your affections, for they are
intrinsical and not subject to hypocrisy. Men of great parts [i.e., gifts]
know much, and so doth the devil, but
he wants love. In fire all things may
be painted but the heat. So all good
actions may be done by a hypocrite,
but the sacred fire of a divine love for
offering the sacrifice he hath not. Oh!
Therefore, chiefly examine the truth
and sincerity of your affections toward
God, whose name is love.

✦ RICHARD SIBBES
*Divine Meditations and Holy
Contemplations*, 102

I say, a man may have excellent notions
of Christ and may be able to make an
elegant discourse of Him and yet not
know Him savingly. Though he be not

grossly ignorant of Christ, yet he may
be spiritually ignorant.... The knowledge that hypocrites have of Christ
hath no saving influence upon them;
it doth not make them more holy. It is
one thing to have a notion of Christ,
another thing to fetch virtue from
Christ. The knowledge of hypocrites
is a dead, barren knowledge. It brings
not forth the child of obedience. There
is a great deal of difference between
a scholar that studies physic for the
theory and notion, that he may have
the rules of it lying before him, and one
that studies physic to practice. Hypocrites are not practitioners; they are all
head, no feet.

✦ THOMAS WATSON
"Christ's Loveliness," in *Discourses*, 1:315

To be only comets and make a show of
piety is a vain thing. Hypocrites lose all
they have done.

✦ THOMAS WATSON
Godly Man's Picture, 11

The hypocrite knows God is of purer
eyes than to behold sin, yet for all this
will play a devotion. He will venture to
abuse God that he may delude men.
The hypocrite takes more care to make
a covenant than to keep it and is more
studious to enter into religion than
that religion should enter into him.

✦ THOMAS WATSON
"God's Anatomy upon Man's
Heart," in *Discourses*, 1:163

The hypocrite doth not so much
desire the way of righteousness as the
crown of righteousness. His desire is
not to be made like Christ but to reign

with Christ. This was Balaam's desire: "Let me die the death of the righteous" (Num. 23:10). This is the hypocrite's hunger; a child of God desires Christ for Himself. To a believer, not only heaven is precious but Christ is precious (1 Peter 2:7). Hypocrites' desires are but desires; they are lazy and sluggish. "The desire of the slothful killeth him; for his hands refuse to labour" (Prov. 21:25). But true desire is quickened into endeavor: "With my soul have I desired thee in the night; yea, with my spirit within me will I seek thee early" (Isa. 26:9).

✦ THOMAS WATSON
Gleanings, 30

THE HYPOSTATIC UNION

Consider the distance of the two natures united in the person of Christ: God and man, the Creator and the creature, infinite and finite meet in one person. If a great prince should vouchsafe to be married to a person of the meanest quality, he would thereby do much honor to that person and her family. But what comparison is there of the distance between the greatest prince in the world and a beggar, with the infinite distance that is between God and His creature? Again, what comparison is there with the relative union between the husband and the wife, and the personal union of the two natures in Christ? Though the man and woman be in some sense one flesh, yet how loose is the conjugal knot, the tie between the husband and the wife, if compared with the close and entire conjunction of the divine and human nature in Christ by the personal union! And therefore if a person of mean quality be so dignified and honored by matching with a prince, what honor is it to the human nature to be, as it were, married to the divine nature by the wonderful and ineffable bond of the hypostatical, or personal, union?

✦ JOHN CONANT
Sermon 7 on Romans 9:5, in
Sermons, 266–67

The two natures being thus united in the person of the Mediator, by virtue thereof the properties of each nature are attributed and do truly agree in the whole person, so that it is proper to say the Lord of glory was crucified (1 Cor. 2:8) and the blood of God redeemed the church (Acts 20:28); that Christ was both in heaven and in the earth at the same time (John 3:13). Yet we do not believe that one nature doth transfuse or impart its properties to the other; or that it is proper to say the divine nature suffered, bled, or died; or the human is omniscient, omnipotent, omnipresent; but that the properties of both natures are so ascribed to the person that it is proper to affirm any of them of Him in the concrete, though not abstractly. The right understanding of this would greatly assist in teaching the true sense of the forenamed and many other dark passages in the Scriptures.

✦ JOHN FLAVEL
Fountain of Life, 37

The incarnation of Christ is *catena aurea*, a golden chain made up of several links of miracles. For instance, that the Creator of heaven should become a creature; that eternity should be born; that He whom the heaven of heavens cannot contain should be enclosed in the womb; that He who thunders in the clouds should cry in the cradle; that He who rules the stars should suck the breasts; that He who upholds all things by the word of His power should himself be upheld; that a virgin should conceive; that Christ should be made of a woman, and of that woman which Himself made; that the creature should give a being to the Creator; that the star should give light to the sun; that the branch should bear the vine; that the mother should be younger than the child she bare, and the child in the womb bigger than the mother; that He who is a Spirit should be made flesh; that Christ should be without father and without mother, yet have both; without mother in the Godhead, without father in the manhood; that Christ, being incarnate, should have two natures (the divine and human) and yet but one person; that the divine nature should not be infused into the human nor the human mixed with the divine, yet assumed into the person of the Son of God; the human nature not God, yet one with God. Here is, I say, a chain of miracles.

✦ THOMAS WATSON
The Christian's Charter of Privileges,
in *Discourses,* 1:64–65

IDIOTS (MENTALLY IMPAIRED)

As for such as are natural idiots, in that respect incapable of the knowledge of God, we must leave them to the secret counsel of God, who alone knows what He hath determined concerning them; only thus much He hath declared, that to whom little is given, of them the less shall be required (Luke 12:48).

✦ JOHN CONANT
Sermon 3 on John 17:3, in
Sermons, 98

IDLE/IDLENESS

The good man is weary of doing nothing, for nothing is so laborious as idleness.

✦ THOMAS ADAMS
Exposition upon…Second…Peter, 55

Avoid idleness, for that is the proper soil for these filthy weeds to grow in. Vile thoughts seldom occur when the soul is usefully employed. A man that is diligent in his calling has employment for his thoughts, but if a man be idle, the devil soon employs him. As a standing pool grows filthy of itself and full of toads and vermin, so the heart that is not engaged in something good and useful is a fit place for the devil to breed evil thoughts and filthy passions in. The inhabitants of Sodom were not worse by nature than other men, but they grew rich in a fertile land, lived at ease in luxury, and then gave themselves up to all abominations.

✦ ISAAC AMBROSE
Christian Warrior, 101

Idleness is indeed the nursery of sins which as naturally grow up therein as weeds in a neglected field. Idleness teaches much evil. It is the general trap whereby every tempter assays to catch our soul. For the mind being loose from care, Satan is ready to step in with his suggestions, the world presents its allurements, fleshly desires rise up; proud, froward, wanton cogitations slip in; ill company doth entice, ill example is regarded, every temptation doth object and impress itself with great advantage and force, men in such a case being apt to close and comply with temptations, even to divert their minds and entertain themselves to cure their listlessness, to pass their time, committing sin for want of better occupation.
✦ ISAAC BARROW
"Of Industry in General," in
Sermons, 275

Idleness breeds temptation. Our vacation is the devil's term; when we are least at work for God, then is Satan most at work about us. By doing nothing men learn to do evil. Yea, idleness is the burying of a living man.
✦ WILLIAM BRIDGE
Lifting Up, 215

Idleness is a sin against the law of creation. God creating man to labor, the idle person violates this law, for by his idleness he casts off the authority of his Creator.
✦ THOMAS BROOKS
Privy Key of Heaven, 204

Idleness is a mother sin; 'tis the devil's cushion on which he sits and the devil's anvil on which he frames great sins. As toads and serpents breed most in standing waters, so sin thrives most in idle persons.
✦ THOMAS BROOKS
Privy Key of Heaven, 205

Idleness is hateful in any, but most abominable and intolerable in ministers; and sooner or later none shall pay so dear for it as such. Witness the frequent woes that are denounced in Scripture against them. Where should a soldier die but in the field? And where should a minister die but in the pulpit?
✦ THOMAS BROOKS
Smooth Stones, 181

O the deadly sins, the deadly temptations, the deadly judgments that idle and slothful Christians are given up to; therefore, be active, be diligent, be abundant in the work of the Lord. Idleness is the very source of sin. Standing pools gather mud and nourish and breed venomous creatures, and so do the hearts of idle and slothful Christians.
✦ THOMAS BROOKS
The Unsearchable Riches of Christ,
in Select Works, 1:172

Harbor no idle persons in your family; let your servants have moderate work and meat. If they deserve reproof, let it be without passion; advice, with some natures, may do more than correction.
✦ JOSEPH CARYL
in Calamy et al., Saints'
Memorials, 83

Best trade! which gives least time to sin
Which souls can least be idle in.
Metals, with which we nothing do,
Soon rust; so souls when idle too.
✦ JOHN COLLINGES
Weaver's Pocket-book, 42

Long ease will bring either superstition, profaneness, or heresy through our corruption.
✦ EZEKIEL CULVERWELL
Time Well Spent, 103

[I] am speaking to the private Christian. Thou canst not be holy if thou art not diligent in a particular calling.... An idle man does none good, and himself most hurt.
✦ WILLIAM GURNALL
Christian in Complete Armour, 312

There is nothing more troublesome to a good mind than to do nothing, for besides the furtherance of our estate, the mind doth both delight and better itself with exercise. There is but this difference, then, betwixt labor and idleness: that labor is a profitable and pleasant trouble; idleness, a trouble both unprofitable and comfortless. I will be ever doing something that either God when He cometh or Satan when he tempteth may find me busied.
✦ JOSEPH HALL
Meditations and Vows, 93–94

The idle man is the devil's cushion on which he taketh his free ease, who, as he is incapable of any good, so he is fitly disposed for all evil motions. The standing water soon stinks, whereas the current ever keeps clear and cleanly, conveying down all noisome matter that might infect it by the force of his stream. If I do but little good to others by my endeavors, yet this is great good to me, that by my labor I keep myself from hurt.
✦ JOSEPH HALL
Meditations and Vows, 153

Standing water putrefies, so doth the lazy person; he that loves to do nothing will soon do worse than nothing.
✦ NATHANIEL HARDY
First General Epistle of St. John, 256

Think of ease, but work on.
✦ GEORGE HERBERT
comp., *Witts Recreations*, proverb 78

EUCHEDIDASCALUS: What remedies have you against idleness in your calling?

PHILEUCHES: I must meditate

1. that God commands all men to labor (Gen. 3:18);

2. that Eve fell in Paradise by idleness (Gen. 3:19);

3. that it was one of the sins of Sodom (Ezek. 16:49);

4. that it is a cushion for Satan to sleep on;

5. that labor puts Satan's assaults away (2 Sam. 11:2);

6. that idleness consumes the body standing waters soon putrefy;

7. that a slothful hand makes poor, as a diligent hand makes rich (Prov. 10:5; 24:34);

8. without diligence we cannot provide for a family or the time to come (Proverbs 31);

9. all creatures, even to the pismire, are diligent (Prov. 6:6);

10. God our Father is ever working (John 5:17);

11. by it we may be able to do good to others (Eph. 4:28);

12. all good men have labored in a calling. And why have people hands and wits but to use them, and the more both are used the better they are.

✦ ROBERT HILL
Pathway to Piety, 1:98–99

Idleness, vanity, and neglecting the precious time is the disease of great and rich men, as they say the gout is. These can find time to dally, to court, to be riotous, etc., but not to pray and serve God; therefore, for the most part, they are most poor in the best things.

✦ ELNATHAN PARR
Abba, Father, in *Workes,* 82

Idleness is a moth or canker of the mind, and the fruits thereof are wicked cogitations, evil affections, and worse actions; corrupt trees without fruit, twice dead and plucked up by the roots, engendering in the mind a loathing of God and godliness.

✦ HENRY SMITH
"The Sinful Man's Search," in
Sermons, 224

It is true [Satan] tempts others to idleness, but himself is never idle.

✦ WILLIAM SPURSTOWE
Wiles of Satan, 27

It is hardly possible that a person should continue absolutely unemployed for any long time and he that is not doing what he ought will be doing what he ought not; the destroyer of souls can hardly wish for a fairer mark at which to direct his temptations than an idle person.

✦ RICHARD STEELE
Religious Tradesman, 17

The proud man is Satan's throne, and the idle man is his pillow.

✦ GEORGE SWINNOCK
in Horn, *Puritan Remembrancer,* 59

Spend the greatest part of the day in thy particular calling. He that minds not his closet before his shop is an atheist, and he that minds not his shop after his closet is a hypocrite. The world is God's great family, and He will allow none in it to be idle.

✦ GEORGE SWINNOCK
The Christian Man's Calling, in
Works, 2:499

Idleness is the hour of temptation, and an idle person is the devil's tennis ball, tossed by him at his pleasure.

✦ JOHN TRAPP
*Commentary…upon…the New
Testament,* 835

An idle person is a fit subject for the devil to work upon.

✦ THOMAS WATSON
"The One Thing Necessary,"
in *Discourses,* 1:363

IDOLATRY

The Lord doth absolutely require the reformation of religion at this time [1644], both in doctrine, worship, discipline, and governments in the church. We must out with idols, not only those in wood, stone, or glass that is in walls and windows but those living idols that are in pews and in some pulpits, they must out; I mean all idol shepherds and dumb dogs. While Israel was without a teaching priest, they were without the law. A preacherless people will be a lawless people. In short, the Lord would have you to demolish all high places and not to leave so much as the stump of Dagon remaining—yea, to bury all the relics of Romish Jezebel, even the skull and the feet and the palms of her hands.

✦ JOHN BOND
Salvation in a Mystery, 48

If you desire a general definition of idolatry, which comprehends all kinds, I think this is full of comprehension. It is…a religious worship given to the creature.

✦ EDWARD MARBURY
Commentarie…upon…Habakkuk, 328

When Elijah derided the worshipers of Baal (1 Kings 18:27), the chief part of his derision was he is on a journey. "You have a god that is absent," saith Elijah, and the end of all idolatry in the world is to feign the presence of an absent deity. All images and idols are set up for no other end but to feign the presence of what really is absent.

✦ JOHN OWEN
Discourse 5 on 1 Cor. 11:28, in
Twenty-Five Discourses, 76

O, that I could give up with this clay idol, this masked, painted, overgilded dirt that Adam's sons adore! We make an idol of our will. As many lusts in us, as many gods. We are all god makers;

we are all like to lose Christ, the true God, in the throng of these new and false gods.

✦ SAMUEL RUTHERFORD
Garden of Spices, 91

However men may contrive to cheat themselves, God is not truly great in the soul till all other things become as nothing; neither doth the soul rightly converse with His infinite fullness so long as anything stands in opposition to it or competition with it.

✦ SAMUEL SHAW
Voice of One Crying in the Wilderness, 81

IGNORANCE

There is a supine and careless ignorance when men having means of knowledge care not to make use of them. And this may proceed from several causes: (1) from pure sloth and laziness because they will not be at the pains to get knowledge; (2) from a disregard and light esteem of knowledge and of all heavenly things. They value them not, and so they mind them not; they look not after them; (3) from extreme earthly-mindedness and an inordinate love of the world. Their hearts are set upon, immersed in, and even swallowed up by the world, and so there is no room for the things of heaven. But all these persons, when they shall be called to an account for the neglect of their duty, will have nothing to plead for their excuse.

✦ JOHN CONANT
Sermon 3 on John 17:3, in *Sermons*, 92

There are, as a learned man truly observes, two doors of the soul barred against Christ: the understanding by ignorance and the heart by hardness. Both these are opened by Christ. The former is opened by the preaching of the gospel, the other by the internal operation of the Spirit.

✦ JOHN FLAVEL
Fountain of Life, 84

Ignorance, above other sins, enslaves a soul to Satan; a knowing man may be his slave, but an ignorant one can be no other. Knowledge does not make the heart good, but it is impossible that without knowledge it should be good. There are some sins which an ignorant person cannot commit; there are more which he cannot but commit. Knowledge is the key (Luke 11:52), Christ the door (John 10).

✦ WILLIAM GURNALL
Christian in Complete Armour, 113

I would rather confess my ignorance than falsely profess knowledge. It is no shame not to know all things, but it is a just shame to overreach in anything.

✦ JOSEPH HALL
Meditations and Vows, 49

None wander from [God], prefer the flesh and world before Him, and in their whole lives walk contrary to Him but from their ignorance of Him. "They are alienated from the life of God [i.e., a spiritual heavenly conversation] through the ignorance that is in them, because of the blindness of their heart" (Eph. 4:18). Dark corners of a house are filled with dust, dark cellars with

vermin, and dark hearts with cursed lusts. None are enlarged in desires after God or ravished with delight in God or can cast their souls and all their concerns on God but those that are acquainted with Him.

✦ GEORGE SWINNOCK
The Incomparableness of God,
in *Works*, 4:381

IMPATIENCE

Impatience is the daughter of infidelity. If a patient hath an ill opinion of the physician and conceits that he comes to poison him, he will take none of his receipts [medicinal preparations]. When we have a prejudice against God and conceit that He comes to kill us and undo us, then we storm and cry out through impatience.

✦ SIMEON ASHE
Primitive Divinity, 97

IMPRECATORY PRAYER

To direct you in this case of imprecation, I shall lay down some propositions: (1) There is a great deal of difference between public and private cases; in all private cases it is the glory of our religion to bless them that curse us, to pray for them that despitefully use us. So we learn of the great Author of our profession, "He was numbered with the transgressors... and made intercession for the transgressors" (Isa. 53:12).... We should be ready to forgive all private and personal wrongs, but in public cases, wherein divine or human right is...disturbed, we may desire God to relieve oppressed innocence, to wound the hairy scalp of evildoers, etc. (2) In public cases we must not desire revenge directly and formally, so our prayers must respect the vindication of God's glory and the avenging of our own case only as it collaterally and by consequence follows thereupon. "Not unto us, O LORD, not unto us, but unto thy name give glory" (Ps. 115:1)—that is, not for our revenge or to satisfy our lusts but to repair the esteem of Thy mercy and truth. The main spring and sway upon the spirit should be a zeal for the divine glory.... The vindication of God's honor and ways is the main aim of their requests. (3) God's people do not desire vengeance against particular persons absolutely but in the general against the enemies of the church, and expressly against such as are known to God to be perverse and implacable. (4) Their ordinary prayers are against the plots rather than the persons of their enemies.

✦ THOMAS MANTON
*Practical Exposition on the
Epistle of James*, 212

A...part of prayer is imprecation. Some are such that we are to desire the Lord would fight against them. The evil angels, we may pray that the Lord would rebuke them and pull down that kingdom of darkness under which the most of men are held in bondage. But with respect to men, we are not to wish them evil. David and the other prophets are not examples for us to follow in this matter, for they knew

by a prophetic spirit God's intentions concerning the persons they prayed against. The general rule which we ought to follow is this: "But I say unto you, love your enemies; bless them that curse you, do good to them that hate you."... We are to beg rather the conversion than the confusion of our enemies, and supposing they are implacable and incorrigible, we must desire rather that they may be hindered from doing harm by their designs and power than that harm may come to them, even when we pray against antichrist, whom we find devoted in Scripture to destruction. We must have no private grudge against the persons of any, but our eye must be to Christ's honor.

✦ NATHANIEL VINCENT
Spirit of Prayer, 53

INDIFFERENCE

Christ is styled the finisher of our faith as well as the author of our faith. There is as much necessity for the Spirit to keep up our graces as there is to bring forth our graces. Indifference in religion is the first step to apostasy from religion. Though Christians be not kept altogether from falling, yet they are kept from falling altogether. They may show an indifference toward Christ for a time, but they shall not depart from Christ forever.

✦ WILLIAM SECKER
Nonsuch Professor, 126

INGRATITUDE

Unthankfulness for daily preservation, this is a great evil and that watchfulness will excellently preserve you from. God usually walks by this rule: he that prizes and improves a little, to him He gives more, so he that prizes and improves and thankfully owns the daily preservation and protection of God, such a one is in the way to receive more at the hand of God; but when the daily goodness of God is slighted and passed over without consideration and being carefully heeded and regarded by any soul, such a soul is like to be left to fall under the stroke of God's indignation.

✦ THOMAS BLAKE
Living Truths in Dying Times, 126–27

He who opens his mouth wide in praises shall have his heart filled with graces. Ingratitude stops the ear of God, and shuts the hand of God, and turns away the heart of the God of grace; and therefore you had need be thankful for a little grace. Unthankfulness is the greatest injustice that may be; it is a withholding from the great Landlord of heaven and earth His due, His debt.

✦ THOMAS BROOKS
The Unsearchable Riches of Christ,
in *Select Works,* 1:92

There be three usual causes of ingratitude upon a benefit received: envy, pride, covetousness; envy, looking more at others' benefits than our own; pride, looking more at ourselves than the benefit; covetousness, looking more at what we would have than what we have. In good turns, I will neither respect the giver, nor myself, nor the gift, nor others; but only the intent and goodwill from whence it proceeded. So shall I requite others' great pleasures with equal goodwill and accept of small favors with great thankfulness.

✦ JOSEPH HALL
Meditations and Vows, 67–68

It highly becomes us to beware of displeasing the Lord by unthankfulness for the favors He bestows upon us. Ingratitude is the grave in which many mercies are buried and concealed.

✦ OLIVER HEYWOOD
Life in God's Favour, 157

Ingratitude makes great guilt and great breach; that heart will grow too heavy for the man which cannot be taught to praise God, to sing new songs as God renews His favor. Three incomparable things are spoiled by ingratitude: God's glory, man's peace, and increase of grace. He grows backward that is ungrateful. It turns all man's welfare into a consumption. It is the thief who robs God and man; it is base baseness. It were endless to tell you the evils of ingratitude.

✦ NICHOLAS LOCKYER
Balm for England, 140

Ingratitude is the grave of all God's blessings.

✦ RICHARD SIBBES
in Horn, *Puritan Remembrancer,* 317

INHERITANCE

A believer's inheritance—his glory, his happiness, his blessedness—shall be as fresh and nourishing after he has been many thousand thousands of years in heaven as it was at his first entrance into it. Earthly inheritances are like tennis balls, which are bandied up and down from one to another and in time wear out. The creature is all shadow and vanity; it is *filia noctis*, like Jonah's gourd. Man can sit under its shadow but a little, little while: it soon decays and dies; it quickly fades and withers. There is a worm at the root of all earthly inheritances that will consume them in time.

✦ THOMAS BROOKS
Great Gain, 31

A man may leave that estate to his children which he hath gotten by wisdom, but he cannot leave them wisdom to guide that estate when they have it.

✦ SAMUEL CLARK
Saint's Nosegay, 165

INTENTION

He that intends what he does is most like to do what he intends.

✦ RALPH VENNING
Canaan's Flowings, 108

IRRESISTIBLE GRACE

Efficacious grace does not at all destroy natural liberty.

✦ THOMAS JACOMB
in Horn, *Puritan Remembrancer*, 206

ISLAM

The Mahometan delusion is so gross that it seems vain to say any more against it than it saith itself, unless it be to those who are bred up in such darkness as to hear of nothing else and never to see the sun which shineth on the Christian world and withal are under the terror of the sword, which is the strongest reason of that barbarous sect.

✦ RICHARD BAXTER
Baxteriana, 41–42

Suppose your lot had fallen among Mahometans, who, next to pagans, spread over the greatest tract of the earth. For though Arabia bred that unclean bird, yet it was not that cage that could long contain him, for not only the Arabians but the Persians, Turks, and Tartars do all bow down their backs under that grand impostor. This poison hath dispersed itself through the veins of Asia, over a great part of Africa, even the circumference of seven thousand miles, and stops not there but hath tainted a considerable part of Europe also.

✦ JOHN FLAVEL
Divine Conduct, 47

Who can count the thousands, or rather myriads, that are held under the power of this delusion of the devil? May we not ask the most of those who busy themselves in seeking a state of happiness, "Why do you lay out your money for that which is not bread? Or why are you as those who build in the fire, where the structure consumes as fast as it is raised?" Let us look abroad a little and see if it be not a truth. And shall we need to take a view of that strange and sudden spread of Mahumetanism, where the seductions of a brutish impostor have prevailed to the deluding of nations and kingdom who have subjected themselves to his laws and are drunk with the expectation of his carnal promises?

✦ WILLIAM SPURSTOWE
Wiles of Satan, 59–60

JESUS *(See CHRIST/JESUS)*

JEWS

I look upon these and such like particular converts among the Jews to be only as firstfruits; we Christians expect ere long a full harvest in the conversion of your whole nation. We believe as well as you that there are many promises and prophecies concerning the Jewish nation that have not yet had their final accomplishment. Give me leave to read some of them (Isa. 11:11–13).

✦ RICHARD MAYO
Conference Betwixt, 31

JOURNALING

This covenant I advise you to make not only in heart but in word; not only in word but in writing. And that you would, with all possible reverence, spread the writing before the Lord, as if you would present it to Him as your act and deed. And when you have done this, set your hand to it; keep it as a memorial of the solemn transactions that have passed between God and you, that you may have recourse to it on doubts and temptations.

✦ JOSEPH ALLEINE
Alarm to the Unconverted, 182

Many of the saints of God have reaped no small benefit by recording the dealings of God with their own souls and looking over them in times of distress. Dr. Calamy speaks of a very good woman that had for many years written down her evidences for heaven. Before she died, she was for a time suffered to sink into darkness and despondency. By reading over her own diary and observing the past lovingkindness of the Lord and the sweet communion she had often enjoyed with Christ her God and Savior, her gloomy fears vanished, and her soul began to triumph in her great deliverer.

✦ ISAAC AMBROSE
Christian Warrior, 154

Keep a diary of all your closet experiences. Carefully record and book down all your closet mercies. Be often reading over and meditating upon your closet experiences. There is no way like this to inflame and engage your hearts in this secret trade of private prayer.

✦ THOMAS BROOKS
Privy Key of Heaven, 226

When good motions are stirred up in us, it's good as soon as may be to draw them to practice, lest either we forget them or want opportunity to do them, and for help of memory to set them down in writing.

✦ EZEKIEL CULVERWELL
Time Well Spent, 231

The thankful person must faithfully record his mercies, else God cannot have His due praise for them. "Bless the Lord, O my soul, and forget not all his benefits" (Ps. 103:2). Forgotten mercies bear no fruit; a bad memory in this case makes a barren heart and life. I confess, the mercies of God are such a multitude that a memory of brass cannot retain them. "I will come before thee in the multitude of thy mercies," saith David (Ps. 5:7). They are called showers of blessings (Ezek. 34:26), and as impossible it is distinctly to recount all our mercies as to number the drops of rain that fall in a shower. Nevertheless, it hath been the pious care and endeavor of the people of God to preserve and perpetuate His mercies by using all the helps to memory they could.

✦ JOHN FLAVEL
"The Seaman's Return," in
Navigation Spiritualized, 338–39

Preserve thy experiences of past mercies, and thy hope will grow stronger for the future. Experience worketh hope (Rom. 5:4). He is the best Christian who keeps the history of God's gracious dealings with him most carefully so that he may read it in his past experiences when at any time his thoughts trouble him and his spiritual rest is broken with distracting fears for the future.

✦ WILLIAM GURNALL
Christian in Complete Armour, 552

Keep a diary of thy family sins and mercies, that neither the one may escape thy confession and humiliation nor the other thy grateful recognition. If this were observed, we should not come with such barren hearts to the work, as now most do.

✦ WILLIAM GURNALL
Christian in Complete Armour, 692

It is of great use for each of us to write down what we observe as most affecting and edifying to us out of the Scriptures and good books and the sermons we hear.

✦ MATTHEW HENRY
Gems, 35

Does anything fall in that doth peculiarly affect your spirits as to that regard which you have to God? Set it down. Most Christians are poor in experience. They have no stock. They have not laid up anything for a dear year or a hard time. Though they may have had many tokens for good, yet they have forgot them. When your hearts are raised by intercourse between God and yourselves in the performance of this duty, be at pains to set them down for your own use. If anything do immediately affect your spirits, you will be no loser by it. It is as easy a way to grow rich in spiritual experiences as any I know.

✦ JOHN OWEN
Discourse 6 on 1 Cor. 11:28, in
Twenty-Five Discourses, 108

JOY

Godly sorrow is not an enemy but a friend to holy joy. I have read of a holy man who, lying upon his sickbed and being asked which were his joyfulest days that ever he had, cried out, "O give me my mourning days, give me my mourning days again, for they were the joyfulest days that ever I had." The higher the springs of godly sorrow rise, the higher the tides of holy joy rise; his graces will flourish most who evangelically mourns most. Grace always thrives best in that garden (that heart) that is watered most with the tears of godly sorrow. He that grieves most for sin will rejoice most in God, and he that rejoices most in God will grieve most for sin.

✦ THOMAS BROOKS
Cabinet of Choice Jewels, 225

There are three expressions of a great joy in Scripture: the joy of a woman after her travail, the joy of harvest, and the joy of him that divides the spoil. The exultation of all these is wrought upon a sad ground; many a pain and tear it costs the travailing woman, many a fear the husbandman, perils and wounds the soldier before they come at their joy, but at last are paid for all, the remembrance of their past sorrows feeding their present joys.

✦ WILLIAM GURNALL
Christian in Complete Armour, 92

Joy is the highest testimony that can be given to our complacency in any thing or person. Love is to joy as fuel to the fire. If love lay little fuel of desires on the heart, then the flame of joy that comes thence will not be great.

✦ WILLIAM GURNALL
Christian in Complete Armour, 364

Holy joy is the oil to the wheels of our obedience.

✦ MATTHEW HENRY
in Horn, *Puritan Remembrancer*, 273

True believers rejoice in what God is in Himself. Whatever is good, amiable, or desirable; whatever is holy, just, and powerful; whatever is gracious, wise, and merciful, and all that is so, they see and apprehend in God. That God is what He is, is the matter of their chiefest joy. Whatever befalls them in this world, whatever troubles and disquietment they are exercised withal, the remembrance of God is a satisfactory refreshment unto them. For therein they behold all that is good and excellent, the infinite center of all perfections. When we can thus think of God and what He is with delight, it is, I say, an evidence that we have a gracious covenant interest even in what God is in Himself, which none have but those who are spiritually minded.

✦ JOHN OWEN
On Being Spiritually Minded,
in *Oweniana*, 104

Joy is the heart's complacency, or taking delight and content in a present good, or the leaping and dancing of the heart in the fruition of good.

✦ EDWARD REYNER
Precepts for Christian Practice, 386

Sorrow is apt to contract the heart and destroy the large and cheerful temper of it, and joy dilates and enlarges it and is ready to make it forget its grief. But though it be hard, yet it is possible. These two may well consist in the same soul, according to that in Psalm 2:11: "Rejoice with trembling."

✦ SAMUEL SHAW
Voice of One Crying in the Wilderness, 75

JUDAS

Judas's profession, [the devil] knew, did not put him a step out of his way to hell; the devil can show a man a way to damnation through duties and ordinances of God's worship. That covetous, traitorous heart which Judas carried with him to hear Christ's sermon and preach his own held him fast enough to the devil; and therefore he gives him line enough, liberty enough to keep his credit awhile with his fellow apostles. [The devil] cares not though others think him a disciple of Christ, so he knows him to be his own slave.

✦ WILLIAM GURNALL
Christian in Complete Armour, 300

The greatness of this sin of despair appears in this: that the least sin envenomed by it is unpardonable, and without this, the greatest is pardonable. That must needs of all sins be most abominable which makes the creature incapable of mercy. Judas was not damned merely for his treason and murder, for others who had their hands deep in the same horrid fact obtained

a pardon by faith in that blood which through cruelty they shed; but for these, heightened into the greatest malignity possible by the despair and final impenitency with which his wretched heart was filled, which he died so miserably of and now is infinitely more miserably damned for.

✦ WILLIAM GURNALL
Christian in Complete Armour, 511

When Judas began to play the thief, I question whether he meant to turn traitor. No, his treason was a punishment for his thievery. He allowed himself in a secret sin, and God gave him up to one more open and horrid.

✦ WILLIAM GURNALL
Christian in Complete Armour, 608

Many have gone laden with gifts to hell. No doubt Judas had great gifts, for he was a preacher of the gospel, and our Lord Jesus Christ would not set him in the work and not fit him for the work; yet Judas is gone to his own place.

✦ MATTHEW MEAD
Almost Christian Discovered, 32

What a goodly profession had Judas! He followed Christ, left all for Christ, he preached the gospel of Christ, he cast out devils in the name of Christ, he ate and drank at the table of Christ, and yet Judas was but a hypocrite.

✦ MATTHEW MEAD
Almost Christian Discovered, 35

Judas confessed himself to a priest and yet went and hanged himself.

✦ JOHN TRAPP
in Horn, *Puritan Remembrancer*, 234

Judas may have the sop, the outward privilege of baptism, the Supper, the church fellowship, etc., but John leaned on Christ's bosom (John 13:23). That is the gospel ordinance posture in which we shall pray and hear and perform all duties. Nothing but lying in that bosom will dissolve hardness of heart.

✦ THOMAS WILCOX
Choice Drop of Honey, 31

JUDGMENT

God not only keeps an account of thy sins but of the mercies thou hast received, and thou must be answerable for both.

✦ WILLIAM GURNALL
Christian in Complete Armour, 741

The judgments of God are audible sermons. They have a voice. The Lord's voice crieth to the city, "Hear ye the rod, and who hath appointed it" (Mic. 6:9). Divine judgments are loudly audible; they have a crying voice, and it is strange that the voice of such a cry should be forgotten that so dreadful an event of providence [the Great Fire of London] should be but as a nine-days' wonder!

✦ JOHN HOWE
"Jerusalem Rebuilt in Troublous Times," in *Works*, 736

We say the personal sins of men are the primary, internal, antecedent dispositive cause of God's judgments, but the sins of other men, they may be the external irritating, exitating cause

of God's judgments, for these are the terms of the Schoolmen.

✦ JOSIAS SHUTE
Judgement and Mercy, 29

My observation is this: that in that a man is most proud of and bears himself most on and is confident in, in that usually God sends His judgment.

✦ JOSIAS SHUTE
Judgement and Mercy, 35

When God brings into a land a people of another language and religion of a fierce countenance and cruel disposition and gives them power to prevail and bring the land under their feet so that the mighty men are cut off by them and the men of valor crushed in the gate, the young men fly and fall before them, and there is none to make any resistance. When they break in upon cities; plunder houses; ravish women and maids; strip and spoil; and put all to the sword, the young with the gray head; cruelly rip up women with child and without any pity on little infants, dash them against the stones. God speaks more terribly by such a judgment than by plague or fire.

✦ THOMAS VINCENT
God's Terrible Voice in the City, 17–18

JUDGMENT DAY

The day of judgment will be to many *dies deceptionis*, a day of deceit; not that it will deceive any but make it appear that many have deceived themselves with vain hopes of heaven, of which they will be disappointed. Many that have passed man's day of approbation may in that day meet with God's reprobation; many that have been looked upon and have looked like gold here may be found dross then—yea, reprobate silver will He call them.

✦ RALPH VENNING
Canaan's Flowings, 110

At midnight breaks forth a light,
    which turns the night to day,
And speedily an hideous cry
    doth all the world dismay.
Sinners awake, their hearts do ache,
    trembling their loins surpriseth;
Amaz'd with fear, by what they hear,
    each one of them ariseth.

They rush from beds with giddy heads,
    and to their windows run,
Viewing this light, which shines more bright
    than doth the noonday sun.
Straightway appears (they see't with tears)
    the Son of God most dread,
Who with His train comes on amain
    to judge both quick and dead.

✦ MICHAEL WIGGLESWORTH
Day of Doom, 22–23, stanzas 5–6

JUSTIFICATION

Out of the point of justification works cannot be sufficiently commended; into the cause of justification they must not be admitted.

✦ THOMAS ADAMS
Exposition upon…Second…Peter, 64

Sanctification and justification are both of them benefits of the covenant of grace, and therefore to evidence the one by the other can be no turning aside to the covenant of works (Jer. 33:8–9; Heb. 8:10, 12). You may run and read in the covenant of grace that he that is justified is also sanctified, and he that is sanctified is also justified; and therefore, why may not he that knows himself to be really sanctified upon that very ground safely and boldly conclude that he is certainly justified. O sirs! The same Spirit that witnesses to a Christian in his justification can shine upon his graces and witness to him his sanctification as well as his justification, and without all controversy, it is as much the office of the Spirit to witness to a man his sanctification as it is to witness to him his justification (1 Cor. 2:12; 1 John 4:13–14).

✦ THOMAS BROOKS
Cabinet of Choice Jewels, 327–28

That we may understand all the essential ingredients to this glorious privilege of our justification, we may take this large and popular description of it: justification is a gracious and just act of God whereby through Christ our Mediator and Surety, a sinner but repenting and believing is pronounced just and hereby put into a state of reconciliation and favor with God, to the praise of God's glorious attributes and to the believer's eternal salvation. I shall not examine this description by accurate logical rules; it's enough that it is comprehensive of everything requisite to the knowledge of justification. And first, we call it an action, for so God as a just and merciful judge is considered in this matter, pronouncing of such as are free from all curses and also just and righteous. Justification is not properly the sentence or judgment whereby we are pronounced righteous, but it's God's action. Now whether it be an immanent action, and so from all eternity, or transient, accomplished in time, I have elsewhere discussed (Treatise of Justification) and there concluded that it's not immanent nor from eternity, but passing upon a believer in time.

✦ ANTHONY BURGESS
*True Doctrine of Justification
Asserted*, 88–89

The work of God's mercy in justifying a soul is to take him off from himself, to unbottom him, and to make him see and be sensible of his own unrighteousness and uncleanness. This is a great and mighty work of God's mercy.

✦ JEREMIAH BURROUGHS
Saints Treasury, 44

It is a righteousness wrought by Jesus Christ, resulting from His active and passive obedience; it consists both of His active conformity and obedience to the law and also of His suffering the curse and penalty which the law required. For in that He did voluntarily take our nature and submit Himself and put Himself under the obligation of the law, His active obedience becomes meritorious.

✦ SAMUEL CRADOCK
Knowledge and Practice, part 2, 53

The first [effect of justification] is a joy most unspeakable and glorious, wherewith our hearts must needs be wholly taken up and ravished when we see ourselves by the righteousness of Christ of the free mercy and grace of God, redeemed from death, delivered from hell, and freed from the fearful condemnation of the wicked. The second [effect of justification] is the peace of conscience, which indeed passes all understanding. While sin and the guilt of sin remained there was no peace nor rest nor quietness to be found, but fear within, terrors without, and troubles on every side. But when once sin is nailed to the cross of Christ, when the guilt thereof is taken out of our consciences and the punishment thereof far removed, then must needs ensue great peace because God is at one with us; and for this we have the warrant and testimony of the Spirit, for flesh and blood cannot work in us this holy and heavenly assurance.

✦ JOHN DOD
"Of Extinguishing the Spirit," in
Seven Godly and Fruitful Sermons, 189

Having thus revealed unto us both our own miserable estate in ourselves and the infinite mercies of God in Christ and moved us truly to assent thereto…[the Holy Spirit] touches our hearts with a sense of our misery and with a hatred of sin which hath brought us into that miserable estate, and by the ministry of the word, which is His power to our salvation and His arm to draw us unto Him, He turns our will and affections from darkness unto light, not only working in us hearty desires to come out of that damnable estate and to be made partakers of Christ but also inspiring into us a settled resolution, that for as much as liberty and salvation is promised to all that receive Christ by faith, we will therefore resolve undoubtedly to acknowledge Him to be our only Savior and to rest upon Him alone for salvation. Thus, by working (1) in our minds an effectual assent to the promise of the gospel; (2) in our hearts an earnest desire to be made partakers of Christ's merits; and (3) in our will a settled resolution to acknowledge Him to be the Messiah and to rely upon the mercies of God and the merits of Christ for justification and salvation (by which three we do receive Christ), the Spirit of God begets the grace of justifying faith in us.

◆ GEORGE DOWNAME
Christian's Freedom, 33–34

There is a twofold evil in sin, the guilt of it and the pollution of it. Justification properly cures the former, sanctification the latter; but both justification and sanctification flow unto sinners out of the death of Christ. And though it is proper to say the Spirit sanctifies, yet, it is certain, it was the blood of Christ that procured for us the Spirit of sanctification. Had not Christ died, the Spirit had never come down from heaven upon any such design.

◆ JOHN FLAVEL
Fountain of Life, 387

We call *justification*, first, the action of God because it is He only which justifies. Secondly, we call it the action of His dispensation to distinguish it from the action of predestination or of God's decree in itself. Thirdly, we call it the second action of His dispensation to distinguish it from the first action, which is our calling preceding it. Fourthly, we call it a gracious and free action because it is dispensed for no merit or deserving of those which receive it, neither for anything given by them to God before whereof it should be the recompense, but is given freely of His grace. Fifthly, we call it the work of God in Christ to distinguish it from the decree of God, which is a work of God in Himself, and to show justification to be a work of external dispensation which wholly is performed by God in Christ, in whom all the blessings of grace are comprehended as our filiation, or justification, and glorification in whom and through whom only God makes us His sons righteous and glorious, He, being made of God unto us wisdom, righteousness, sanctification, and redemption. And these five points are to be considered in the nature of this action.

◆ JOHN FORBES
Treatise Tending to Clear the Doctrine of Justification, 184

Faith itself, as an inherent quality, justifies not. A man is not justified for faith but by it. Not for it as a cause of, but by it as an instrument in justification. Wherever faith is spoken of in reference to justification, it is said we are justified by faith or through faith, never for faith. Faith doth not justify, as it is a grace, but as it hath an office which no other grace hath to apprehend and apply that righteousness which doth justify us. And therefore, whereas it is said that Abraham believed and it was accounted to him for righteousness, you must understand it relatively— that is, in respect of the object of his believing Christ in the promise or else exclusively, as that faith only is that in us which God makes use of in our justification, not as meritorious of it but as instrumental in it. And this also is to be understood not of the habit of faith but the act as it acts on Christ.

> ✦ OBADIAH GREW
> *Sinner's Justification*, 23–24

Justification finds men ungodly, though it do not leave them so.

> ✦ OBADIAH GREW
> *Sinner's Justification*, 53

Many who are clear in the doctrinal part of justification fail in the practical part. They acknowledge justification not to be of works but by grace, yet live as if they were to be justified by works. They do this…when they think that according to the steadiness or unsteadiness of their walking they are more or less justified. It is true, as to the manifestation of our justification to our own souls, that it clouded or cleared according to the frame of our hearts and the course of our lives, but in itself it is still the same. And though we are to be humbled for our own unsteady walking and should make

it our study to walk holily and live fruitfully, yet we should consider that neither the goodness of our works can add anything to our justification nor the defects thereof impair it because our works are not concerned therein. Our righteousness is out of ourselves and in another whose righteousness is everlastingly the same. If therefore you acknowledge justification to be of grace, see that you neither set up works in the room of Christ nor in conjunction with Him. "If by grace, then it is no more of works" (Rom. 11:6).

> ✦ T. S.
> *Aids to the Divine Life*, 42–44

Though faith alone justifies the soul, yet that faith which justifies the soul is not alone. Whatsoever trees are without their fruits, that also is faith without good works. In proof of sanctification, good works cannot be sufficiently magnified, but in point of justification, good works cannot be sufficiently nullified.

> ✦ WILLIAM SECKER
> *Nonsuch Professor*, 167–68

Some affirm that the very act of believing without reference to the merits of Christ justifies, to which I shall say but this: (1) Faith cannot justify, as it is an act, for it must have an object. We cannot (if we make good sense) separate between the act and the object. What is faith if it do not fix upon Christ, but fancy? It was not the people of Israel's looking up that cured them, but the fixing their eye upon the brazen serpent. (2) Faith doth not justify, as it is a grace. This were to substitute faith in Christ's room, it were to make a Christ of faith. Faith is a good grace but a bad Christ. (3) Not as a work, which must needs be if the stress and virtue of faith lie only in the act, and then we should be justified by works, contrary to that, where the apostle saith expressly, "Not of works" (Eph. 2:9). So that it is clear, faith's excellency lies in the apprehending and applying the object Christ; therefore in Scripture we are said to be justified through faith as an instrument deputed, not for faith as a formal cause.

✦ THOMAS WATSON
The Christian's Charter of Privileges,
in *Discourses,* 1:110–11

JUSTIFICATION AND SANCTIFICATION DISTINGUISHED

Justification and sanctification are inseparable companions; distinguished they must be, but divided they can never be. Where sin is pardoned, the gift of sanctity is still conferred. It is weakness, it is wickedness, for a man to conclude that he is in an elected and justified state when he has nothing, when he has not the least thing to evidence himself to be in a sanctified state. Both justification and sanctification have had a necessary respect to the salvation of all those that shall go to heaven.

✦ THOMAS BROOKS
Cabinet of Choice Jewels, 368

A believer is to do nothing for justification, only believe and be saved; though the law be a rule for everyone that believes to walk by, it is not for justification. But if you do not put a difference between justification wrought by the man Christ without and sanctification wrought by the Spirit of Christ within, teaching believers their duty to their God for His love in giving Christ, you are not able to divide the word aright; but contrariwise, you corrupt the word of God and cast stumbling blocks before the people and will certainly one day most deeply smart for your folly, except you repent.

✦ JOHN BUNYAN
Riches, 140

Justification is by a righteousness imputed, sanctification infused; the former is first in order of nature. They commence together in point of time, even as light in the air at the sun's approach, or as the reversing an outlawry instantly reinstates the party in his former privileges, or as the canceling a bill of attainder restores the blood. Sanctification is the divine nature communicated by which the old man is expelled with his deeds or rather subdued and brought under, for they are not totally nulled in this life. Only proud flesh is put down from its seat, and that is a great matter; its dominion is taken away and the seed of God enthroned in its stead, and so we are said to be translated out of Satan's kingdom or government into Christ's (Col. 1:13). It is sometimes called "regeneration," or a being "born again" (John 3:3); the separating a man from his wild stock and grafting him into the true (Rom. 11:17); the forming of Christ in us (Gal. 4:19); and the law written in the heart (Heb. 8:10)—that is, dispositions according to God or a heart after His own. It is also termed the passing away of old things and a becoming new of all (2 Cor. 5:17); there is a change of principles, scope, and end of a man's life.

✦ ELISHA COLES
Practical Discourse, 182–83

In justification…we have communion with Christ in respect of His merits imputed unto us to free us from the guilt of sin and fear of damnation and to entitle us to the kingdom of heaven. In sanctification we have communion with Christ in respect of His graces, which being in Him without measure are by His Spirit derived to us in measure and communicated by infusion to free us from the corruption and dominion of sin and to prepare and fit us for the kingdom of heaven.

✦ GEORGE DOWNAME
Christian's Freedom, 40

"He that is righteous and holy." I must couple them because though there be great distinction, yet is there not any separation between them. As great distinction as there is between justification and sanctification, the obedience of Christ and the obedience of man, the righteousness of God by faith imputed and the righteousness of man by works inherent; as there is between perfection with equality and imperfection with inequality, a good

tree which is first and good fruits which follow after, inward peace of conscience and the outward manifestation of the same.

✦ HANNIBAL GAMMON
God's Just Desertion of the Unjust, 22

Justification and sanctification are inseparable concomitants. Indeed, they are not to be confounded, but withal they ought not to be severed. Distinguished they must be, divided they cannot; and therefore they are fitly called twins in the womb of free grace.

✦ NATHANIEL HARDY
First General Epistle of St. John, 104

God does not only take off sin from His people, which is justification, but does also take His people from off sin, which is sanctification.

✦ RALPH VENNING
Canaan's Flowings, 116

KINGDOM OF GOD

Why is my remove by death my terror? My trouble? This remove will transmit me into a station not more permanent than glorious. I am removing to a better house—yea, to possess a kingdom—a kingdom not like the kingdoms of this world; not a narrow, empty, envied, distracted, divided, shaken, sinful, transient, and temporal kingdom; not a kingdom subject to wars, tumults, fire, famine, pestilence, ruin, and desolation. And yet with ambition men do seek, with joy they remove into, with difficulty and danger they obtain these miserable earthly kingdoms. But my kingdom to which

I shall pass is a spiritual, heavenly, unshaken, united, ample, abundant, undefiled, undisturbed, peaceable, and everlasting kingdom, not subject to any invasion or usurpation; to any confusion or commotions; to any mutations or violent revolution; to any alteration or danger.

✦ ZACHARY CROFTON
Defence against the Dread of
Death, 79–80

The kingdom of grace and of glory is but one and the same kingdom distinguished into two parts, which differ in six circumstances. (1) In time: The kingdom of grace is now present while here we live. The kingdom of glory is to come. (2) In place: This of grace is on earth; that of glory in heaven. (3) In condition: This is continually warfaring against many enemies, in which respect it is styled the church militant; that triumphed over all the enemies, in which respect it is called the church triumphant. (4) In order of entering into them: This is to be entered into and passed through before we can enter into that. The priest was to enter through the sanctuary into the sanctum sanctorum. (5) In the manner of government: This is governed and ordered by many subordinate means, as magistrates, ministers, and sundry ordinances; that immediately by God Himself. (6) In continuance: This hath a date and is to come to an end. That is everlasting without end.

✦ WILLIAM GOUGE
Guide to Goe to God, 50–51

O, sirs, we have many that are running and riding, that are up early and late, that are toiling and moiling all the day long, and of whose labor there is no end. But what is all this about? What is it for? Why, alas, seen things—these are the matters they are seeking; and as for unseen things, they either look not at them or only so coldly and remissly as if they cared not which end goes forward. But, sirs, it concerns you and me to be up and doing about unseen things, to be looking—that is, taking great care and seeking by all means, early and late, to get a sure title to and to assure our interest in the unseen things of heaven and glory. O, these are the great matters that men and women should be stirring about, striving about, laboring for, and pressing after in this world. This is another; unseen things are the things we should look at—that is, seek for and pursue.

✦ HENRY PENDLEBURY
Invisible Realities, 51

KNOWLEDGE

The knowledge of God comprehends in it and is involved in and spirits and animates every grace and duty.... And one says that as feeling is inseparable to all the organs of sense—the eye feels and sees, the ear feels and hears, the palate feels and tastes, the nostrils feel and smell—so knowledge is involved in every grace. Faith knows and believes, charity knows and loves, temperance knows and abstains, patience knows and suffers, humility knows and stoops, repentance knows and mourns, obedience knows and does, compassion knows and pities, hope knows and expects, confidence knows and rejoices; and therefore we believe and love and obey and hope and rejoice because we know. God gives us this knowledge as the eye of our souls, and by that eye He enters with all His power and glory. "That ye…may…know the love of Christ, which passeth knowledge, that ye might be filled with all the fulness of God" (Eph. 3:19).

✦ RICHARD ALLEINE
Heaven Opened, 93–94

True faith carries knowledge with it. Faith is not hoodwinked and blind but hath his discerning. By faith we come to understand. Hence the gospel is to be preached to every creature. What is the gospel but the opening of Jesus Christ, His sufficiency and willingness to save sinners? While persons lie in a state of ignorance they cannot come to have a true title to Jesus Christ.

✦ BARTHOLOMEW ASHWOOD
Best Treasure, 394

Remember that as it is Christ's work to teach, it is yours to hear and read and study and pray and practice what you hear. Do your part, then, if you expect the benefit. You come not to the school of Christ to be idle. Knowledge drops not into the sleepy dreamer's mouth. Dig for it, as for silver, and search for it in the Scriptures as for a hidden treasure.

✦ RICHARD BAXTER
A Christian Directory, in
Practical Works, 2:223

This chief constable [of the Isle of Man] is Illuminated Understanding. This is one that hath both his eyes to see with, of nature and of grace. He is well read both in the excellency common law, the law moral; and the statute law, the law of liberty, the gospel of Christ. He hath been a long practitioner in both and is called the spiritual man who can discern and judge of all things.

✦ RICHARD BERNARD
Isle of Man, 83

Some would fain have more light and knowledge of Christ, but they are afraid of the cold and so dare not open their windows to receive the light. But pray, friends, why should we be afraid of new lights? For why should there not be new lights found out in the firmament of the Scripture, as well as the astrologers [i.e., astronomers] find out new stars in heaven? Be not afraid to set open your windows for any light that God shall make known unto you.

✦ WILLIAM BRIDGE
Christ and the Covenant, in
Works, 3:37

They that have the best knowledge are the most willing to learn more.

✦ ROBERT CLEAVER
AND JOHN DOD
Plain and Familiar Exposition, 21

Logic alone may speak natural reason but seldom good divinity. Therefore, after all disputes about the polemical part of divinity, give me the sincere, unlearned man's religion, who hath no more in his head than he hath in his heart; whose reason doth not outrun his faith and experience. He lives in what he believes and knows more of the nature of faith by one act of faith than others do by reading of a hundred books and discourses of men about it. A downright, plain-hearted Christian who hath but one notion of things (I mean of any one truth), but that is a right one, he keeps to it without any variation in his conceptions about it and walks evenly and uprightly with God all his days according to His light. What a great place in heaven will such a one have who is faithful over a little and is what he is by the grace of God. Whereas others of larger heads, abounding too much in their own sense, keep not their hearts so close to the plain fundamentals of the gospel; their reason outruns their faith and insensibly winds them off from the power of the gospel into many labyrinths of error, or at least into empty airy speculations.

✦ THOMAS COLE
Old Apostolical Way of Preaching, 13

The mind is to the heart as the door to the house; what comes into the heart comes in at the understanding, which is introductive to it.

✦ JOHN FLAVEL
Fountain of Life, 83

The Spirit makes His approach to the understanding, and on it He puts forth an act of illumination. The Spirit will not work in a dark shop; the first thing He does…is to beat out a window in the soul and let in some light from heaven into it. Hence, believers are said to be "renewed in the spirit of [their] mind" (Eph. 4:23), which the same apostle calls being "renewed in knowledge" (Col. 3:10). By nature we know little of God and nothing of Christ or the way of salvation by Him.

✦ WILLIAM GURNALL
Christian in Complete Armour, 444

"A good understanding have all they that do His commandments," says the psalmist (Ps. 111:10). As one said well, "The best way to understand the mysterious and high discourse in the beginning of St. Paul's Epistles is to begin at the practice of those rules and precepts that are in the latter end of them." The way to attain to know more is to receive the truth in the love of it and to obey what you know.

✦ ROBERT LEIGHTON
A Commentary upon the First Epistle of Peter, in *Whole Works*, 1:302

The greatest difficulty is to begin; as one said of his growing rich that he came hardly by a little riches, and easily by great riches. Having once got a stock, he grew rich apace. So once taking be it but the first lessons of this wisdom, learning these well shall facilitate thy knowledge exceedingly. The wise increases learning. Wouldst thou but receive and hearken to the easiest things represented by God, these would enlighten and enlarge thy soul to receive more, especially while walking by the light thou hast, be it ever so little, that invites and draws in more. Be diligent in the practice of what you know if you would know more. Believe it, this is the way to grow.

✦ ROBERT LEIGHTON
"The Observation of Providence,"
in *Sermons*, 226

A man may have much knowledge, much light; he may know much of God and His will, much of Christ and His ways and yet be but almost a Christian. For though there can be no grace without knowledge, yet there may be much knowledge where there is no grace; illumination often goes before when conversion never follows after. The subject of knowledge is the understanding; the subject of holiness is the will. Now a man may have his understanding enlightened and yet his will not at all sanctified. He may have an understanding to know God and yet want a will to obey God. The apostle tells us of some that when they knew God, yet they glorified him not as God. To make a man altogether a Christian, there must be light in the head and heat in the heart, knowledge in the understanding and zeal in the affections. Some have zeal and no knowledge; that is blind devotion. Some have knowledge and no zeal; that is fruitless speculation. But where knowledge is joined with zeal, that makes a true Christian.

✦ MATTHEW MEAD
Almost Christian Discovered, 24–25

Some know but to know. Some know to be known. Some know to practice what they know. Now to know but to know, that is curiosity. To know

to be known, that is vainglory. But to know to practice what we know, that is gospel duty. This makes a man a complete Christian; the other without this makes a man almost, and yet but almost a Christian.

✦ MATTHEW MEAD
Almost Christian Discovered, 27–28

There are four ways by which at this day the great God conveys the knowledge of Himself and His mind unto sinful man: (1) His works of creation and providence (Ps. 19:2); (2) the suggest of conscience, even the remainder of God's image in us; (3) the word or law of God written, expounded, or applied in ordinary preaching; (4) the church, which is the ground and pillar of truth. The knowledge of God and His mind is more especially there held forth by the gifts given and offices therein appointed by Christ. These are distinct ways and methods of God by which He is pleased to make known Himself, and we are obliged even by the law of nature to attend when God doth speak; it is therefore an undoubted moral duty to attend the speaking of God in whatsoever way by providence brought unto us.

✦ PHILIP NYE
Case of Great and Present Use, 1–2

Empty vessels are most receptive; so are self-emptying minds. It is a great help to knowledge not to be ignorant of our ignorance, for sense of want spurs on endeavors after enjoyment. The fructifying showers quickly glide away from the lofty hills, but they stay and soak into the low valleys.

✦ FRANCIS ROBERTS
Great Worth of Scripture
Knowledge, 17

The knowledge of the sense of the Scriptures is the first step to profit. In the law, Aaron was first to light the lamps and then to burn the incense; the lamp of the understanding must be first lighted before the affections can be inflamed. Get what knowledge you can by comparing scriptures, by conferring with others, by using the best annotators. Without knowledge the Scripture is a sealed book; every line is too high for us, and if the word shoot above our head, it can never hit our heart.

✦ THOMAS WATSON
Bible and the Closet, 21–22

Antecedent [to faith] is knowledge. Faith is an intelligent grace; though there can be knowledge without faith, yet there can be no faith without knowledge: "They that know thy name will put their trust in thee" (Ps. 9:10); one calls it quick-sighted faith. Knowledge must carry the torch before faith: "For I know whom I have believed" (2 Tim. 1:12). As in Paul's conversion, a light from heaven shined round about him (Acts 9:3). So before faith be wrought, God shines in with a light upon the understanding. A blind faith is as bad as a dead faith; that eye may as well be said to be a good eye which is without sight, as that faith is good which is without knowledge. Devout ignorance damns, which condemns

the Church of Rome that think it a piece of their religion to be kept in ignorance; these set up an altar to an unknown God.

✦ THOMAS WATSON
The Christian's Charter of Privileges,
in Discourses, 1:102

The knowledge of a godly man is growing. True knowledge is like the light of the morning, which increases in the horizon till it comes to the full meridian. So sweet is spiritual knowledge that the more a saint knows, the more thirsty he is of knowledge.

✦ THOMAS WATSON
Godly Man's Picture, 17

The knowledge of a godly man is self-emptying; carnal knowledge makes the head giddy with pride (1 Cor. 8:2). True knowledge brings a man out of love with himself; the more he knows, the more he blushes at his own ignorance.

✦ THOMAS WATSON
Godly Man's Picture, 17

We may have excellent notions in divinity, but the Holy Ghost must enable us to know them after a spiritual manner; a man may see the figures upon a dial, but he cannot tell how the day goes unless the sun shine. We may read many truths in the Bible, but we cannot know them savingly till God's Spirit does shine upon us (1 Cor. 2:10).

✦ THOMAS WATSON
Godly Man's Picture, 21

Knowledge is the eye which must direct the foot of obedience.

✦ THOMAS WATSON
Lord's Prayer, 151

LAMENT

Certainly, the very soul of prayer lies in the pouring out of a man's soul before the Lord, though it be but in sighs, groans, and tears (1 Sam. 1:13–19). One sigh and groan from a broken heart is better pleasing to God than all human eloquence.

✦ THOMAS BROOKS
Privy Key of Heaven, 102

I...read a little in [*The Morning Exercise at Cripplegate*], and I found my spirit much out of order. O, my soul, where have I been all this while? So dead in duties. So endless in my studies. So unprofitable in company. So unedifying in my family. So negligent of meditation. So formal in preaching. O, my soul, where hast thou been? The Lord put some life into me.

✦ HENRY NEWCOME
Diary, 29 (December 9, 1661)

THE LAW

"For I testify again to every man that is circumcised, that he is a debtor to do the whole law" (Gal. 5:3). The apostle's meaning is he is a debtor in regard of duty because he that thinks himself bound to keep one part of the ceremonial law doth thereby bind himself to keep it all, for all the parts are inseparably united. And he that is a debtor

in duty to keep the whole law quickly becomes a debtor in regard of penalty, not being able to keep any part of it.

✦ JOHN FLAVEL
Fountain of Life, 171

THE LAW AND THE GOSPEL

The law gave menaces; the gospel gives promises. It was the condition of the law, "Do this and live"; it is the promise of the gospel, "Believe and thou shalt be saved.".... The law may express sin, but it cannot suppress sin, for that were to invade the office of the promise. The office of the law is to kill, the office of the promise to give life.

✦ THOMAS ADAMS
Exposition upon...Second...Peter, 34

But we are freed by Christ from the law? I answer, there is a double obligation of the law: the obligation of penalty and the obligation of duty. We are freed from the obligation of penalty but not from the obligation of duty. "Let every one that nameth the name of Christ depart from iniquity" (2 Tim. 2:19). He has taken from the law all power to condemn us but not all power to rule us. We must still serve God according to His law or He will not save us according to His gospel. Our faith in the Lord Jesus and our obedience to the law must be joined together, as Moses and Christ met upon the mountain. "The law was given by Moses, but grace and truth came by Jesus Christ" (John 1:17).

✦ THOMAS ADAMS
Exposition upon...Second...Peter, 184

Tell me, you that desire to mingle the law and the gospel together and to make of both one and the same gospel of Christ, did you ever see yourselves undone and lost unless the righteousness, blood, death, resurrection, and intercession of that man Christ Jesus in His own person were imputed to you and until you could by faith own it as done for you and counted yours by imputation? Yea or no? Nay, rather, have you not set up your consciences and the law and counted your obedience to them better and of more value than the obedience of the Son of Mary without you to be imputed to you? And if so, it is because you have not been savingly convinced by the Spirit of Christ of the sin of unbelief.

✦ JOHN BUNYAN
Riches, 70

Here thou mayst say, "O law, thou mayst roar against sin, but thou canst not reach me; thou mayst curse and condemn, but not my soul, for I have a righteous Jesus, a holy Jesus, a soul-saving Jesus, and He hath delivered me from thy threats, thy curses, thy condemnations. I am out of thy reach and out of thy bounds; I am brought into another covenant under better promises of life and salvation, free promises to comfort me without my merit, even through the blood of Jesus, the satisfaction given to God for me by Him.

✦ JOHN BUNYAN
Riches, 73

The commands of the gospel require the obedience of the creature. There is not one precept in the gospel which interferes with any rule in the law, but strengthens it and represents it in its true exactness; the heat to scorch us is allayed, but the light to direct us is not extinguished. Not the least allowance to any sin is granted; not the least affection to any sin is indulged. The law is tempered by the gospel but not nulled and cast out of doors by it. It enacts that none but those that are sanctified shall be glorified; that there must be grace here if we expect glory hereafter; that we must not presume to expect an admittance to the vision of God's face unless our souls be clothed with a robe of holiness (Heb. 12:14). It requires an obedience to the whole law in our intention and purpose and an endeavor to observe it in our actions; it promotes the honor of God and ordains a universal charity among men; it reveals the whole counsel of God and furnishes men with the holiest laws.

✦ STEPHEN CHARNOCK
Selections, 119–20

For the law is nothing else but a dark gospel, and the gospel nothing else but a clear law. The law was hid and veiled under dark shadows and ceremonies, but the gospel was clear and evident.

✦ CHRISTOPHER LOVE
Zealous Christian, 5

The doctrine of the law, indeed, humbles the soul for Christ, but it is the doctrine of the gospel that humbles the soul in Christ.

✦ JOHN OWEN
Golden Book, 225

LEGALISM

LEGALIST: What, do I not know True Godliness? This is strange! Do not you and I converse together every day?

GODLINESS: Sir, I am not the person you take me for; there is one or two more who go sometimes by my name, and it is very probable you may be acquainted with them. Pray, what are his manners? What doctrine, I mean, doth he teach you? For by that I shall know who it is.

LEGALIST: Why, sir, he teaches me to keep the commandments of God, to lead a righteous life, to do unto all men as I would they should do unto me.

GODLINESS: O, sir, that is my friend and honest neighbor Morality, one that I love very well, and I am sure it is your great ignorance to take him for me. He will not say his name is True Godliness, for though in some things we are a little alike, I teaching the same doctrine you mention, yet we differ exceedingly in many things. First, we herein agree: he says you must keep God's commandments—I say so too. Secondly, he says you must be righteous—I say the like. And thirdly that you must do unto all men as you would they should do to you—I say the very same, it being my Master's own doctrine.

LEGALIST: Why wherein then, sir, pray do you differ?

GODLINESS: He teaches you to seek justification by doing, but I only by

believing. He by keeping the law or by living a sober and honest life; I by God's free grace, through the merits of Christ.

✦ BENJAMIN KEACH
Travels of True Godliness, 98–99

LIES (See *FALSEHOOD*)

LIMITED ATONEMENT
(See *REDEMPTION*)

LISTENING

When you are in the company of those that are above you in wisdom and grace, be more swift to hear than to speak. The emptiest vessels make the greatest sound, and I have often observed in company such as have most need to hear and learn, being self-conceitedly wise, will take up most of the discourse; and instead of drawing waters from deeper wells to fill their empty vessels, they will be pumping out that little they have. This surely doth not bespeak the modesty of such and less becomes their profit.

✦ BARTHOLOMEW ASHWOOD
Heavenly Trade, 302

LITERATURE

The particular end of literature is none other but to remove some part of that curse which is come upon us by sin. Learning is the product of the soul's struggling with the curse for sin. To disentangle the mind in its reasonings, to recover an acquaintance with the works of God—is the aim and tendance of literature.

✦ JOHN OWEN
Golden Book, 225

LOGIC

Logic is the art of using reason well in our inquiries after truth and the communication of it to others. Reason is the glory of human nature and one of the chief eminencies whereby we are raised above our fellow creatures, the brutes, in this lower world. Reason, as to the power and principles of it, is the common gift of God to all men, though all are not favored with it by nature in an equal degree. But the acquired improvements of it in different men make a much greater distinction between them than nature had made. I could even venture to say that the improvement of reason hath raised the learned and the prudent in the European world almost as much above the Hottentots and other savages of Africa as those savages are by nature superior to the birds, the beasts, and the fishes.

✦ ISAAC WATTS
Logic, 1

LONDON

Dear Ned…

Be careful to improve your time. I know London is a bewitching place.

✦ BRILLIANA HARLEY
to her son Ned, November 14, 1640,
in *Letters*, 101

Dear Brother,

I have now exchanged the sweet country air and sports for the dirt, fogs, and trouble of the city [i.e., London]. The employment there is to chase the poor hare or crafty fox; here, to pursue one another. The forest whence I came hath not beasts more savage as we meet every day. The lustful goat, fawning dog, greedy wolf range freely, and what is worst, every one abounds with these wild inhabitants, and want sagacity to pursue and courage to destroy them. If every private person would be an honest hunter, we should not complain of so many Nimrods.

✦ EDWARD HARLEY
to Thomas Harley, 1650/1651, in
Brilliana Harley, *Letters*, 216

LONG LIFE

Old age may be good three ways. Naturally, when it is accompanied with sense and not overtaken with decay of those necessary organs…. Morally, when it is led by the line of virtue; when justice has balanced it, fortitude quickened it, temperance dieted it, and charity quieted it. Constitution and country may make it naturally good, but it is then morally good when a man likes it so well that he would not wish it to begin again. Spiritually good, and this is best when a man can look both ways: backward with comfort to his life past, forward with joy to his reward to come.

✦ THOMAS ADAMS
Exposition upon…Second…Peter, 150–51

The people of God desire long life. (1) Sometimes for the making of their peace with God more fully before they finish this earthly pilgrimage. (2) Sometimes they may also glorify God with their bodies, which by death are disabled to do God any service. (3) Sometimes that they may among men celebrate and praise God for His blessings and favors bestowed upon them, that they may be an encouragement to God's people, an ornament to God's truth, a terror to the adversaries of it here upon earth. (4) Sometimes that they may perfect some good work which they have begun, do good to others in their places and callings.

✦ ALEXANDER GROSSE
Deaths Deliverance, 31

THE LORD'S DAY/SABBATH

Is the weekday unfit for this work of meditation? No, the Sabbath day is our market day, and then after we have bought our market on the Sabbath, we should roast it by meditation on the week. We do not go to the market on the market day to buy meat into the house only for the market day but for all the time until the market day comes about again. Indeed, Solomon says of the sluggard that he is so sluggish and slothful that "he doth not roast what he hath taken in hunting." The Sabbath day is the hunting day for souls wherein the venison is taken; on the weekday we are to roast it and to live upon it by meditation and otherwise. And what is the reason that many do not live upon their venison that they

have taken on the Lord's Day? But because they do not roast it by meditation on the weekday.

✦ WILLIAM BRIDGE
Christ and the Covenant, in
Works, 3:147

Make the Lord's Day the market for thy soul. Let the whole day be spent in prayer, repetitions, or meditations. Lay aside the affairs of the other parts of the week. Let the sermon thou hast heard be converted into prayer. Shall God allow thee six days, and wilt not thou afford Him one?

✦ JOHN BUNYAN
"Mr. John Bunyan's Dying Sayings,"
in *Complete Works*, 80

It is the market day of our souls, wherein we come to God's house, the marketplace, to buy the wine and milk of the word without money.

✦ HENRY BURTON
Law and the Gospel Reconciled, 64

Make the Sabbath the market day for the soul. Lose not one hour, but be either praying, conferring, or meditating. Think not thy own thoughts. Let every day have its duties. Turn the sermon heard into matter of prayer, instruction into petition, reproof into confession, consolation into thanksgiving. Think much of the sermon heard, and make something of it all the week long.

✦ JOHN DOD
Worthy Sayings, n.p.

In the house of God spiritual provision is obtained for the support and nourishment of the soul. The Sabbath is the market and fair day for the soul. A Christian's care lies about the matter of God's ordinances, for the business of the soul should be most looked after. There is small hope of getting our hearts up in our callings when they are down at God's ordinances.

✦ HENRY NEWCOME
"The House of God Remembered in Sickness," in Slate, ed., *Select Nonconformists' Remains*, 331

THE LORD'S SUPPER

They were wont of old at the making of covenants to offer sacrifice, the covenantees passing between the parts thereof and then to feast upon things so offered for the further ratification of their agreement. The covenant we speak of was not established without a sacrifice, even that of Jesus Christ, who through the eternal Spirit offered Himself without spot to God. Who hath also, in further conformity to the custom of those eastern parts, ordained the Lord's Supper, a seal of this covenant, as a feast upon a sacrifice; that by eating and drinking at His Table, as by a sacred federal rite, we might profess our having entered into league with the Most High.

✦ JOHN ARROWSMITH
Covenant Avenging Sword Brandished, 22

The Lord's Supper is called a sacrifice by the learned ancient doctors in four respects. First, because it is a representation and memorial of Christ's sacrifice on the cross: "As often as ye eat this bread, and drink this cup, ye do shew the Lord's death till he come" (1 Cor. 11:26). So, St. Ambrose, Christ is daily sacrificed in the minds of believers, as upon an altar.... Secondly, because in this action we offer praise and thanksgiving unto God for the redemption of the world, and this is the sacrifice of our lips (Heb. 13:15). Thirdly, because every communicant doth offer and present himself body and soul a living, holy, acceptable sacrifice to the Lord (Rom. 12:1); the which excels the sacrifices of the priests in old time, for they did offer dead sacrifices, but we present ourselves a lively sacrifice to God. Fourthly, because it was a custom in the primitive church at the receiving of this blessed sacrament to give large contribution unto the poor, a sacrifice well accepted of God (Heb. 13:16).

✦ JOHN BOYS
Offices for Public Worship, in *Works*, 72

There is...great reason for believers to eat the Lord's Supper, as appears by the agreements betwixt them in these particulars:... In the properties of the Paschal Lamb, which are in Christ our Passover.

1. That was to be without blemish; so was Christ (Isa. 53:9; 1 Peter 1:19–20; Heb. 7:26).

2. That must be a male; so Christ for sex and strength, a mighty Savior (Jer. 31:32).

3. That must be of a year old, in perfect age; Christ about thirty-four years, in the prime of His age.

4. That must be taken out of the flock; Christ must be taken from among mankind that was partaker of flesh and blood (Deut. 18:18; Heb. 2:11).

5. That must be separated from the flock; Christ was separated from sinners (Heb. 7:26).

6. That roast with fire; Christ with the heat of God's wrath.

7. That must be eaten; Christ must be received by faith. That must be eaten.

✦ THOMAS DOOLITTLE
Treatise concerning the Lord's Supper, 20

The properties of the Paschal Lamb... are in Christ our Passover.... [The Paschal Lamb] must be eaten...

1. By every family; Christ is to be received by every person.

2. With unleavened bread; Christ and this sacrament is to be received in sincerity and truth (1 Cor. 5:7–8).

3. With bitter herbs; Christ and this ordinance, with bitter repentings.

4. Wholly; all of it must be eaten whole. Christ must be received in all His offices—prophet, priest, and king; Christ as the Paschal Lamb must be received with all His appurtenances.

5. In haste; Christ must be received presently, without delay.

✦ THOMAS DOOLITTLE
Treatise concerning the Lord's Supper, 21

Remembrance, properly, is the return of the mind to an object about which it hath been formerly conversant, and it may so return to a thing it hath conversed with before two ways: speculatively and transiently, or affectionately and permanently. A speculative remembrance is only to call to mind the history of such a person and His sufferings, that Christ was once put to death in the flesh. An affectionate remembrance is when we so call Christ and His death to our minds as to feel the powerful impressions thereof upon our hearts.

✦ JOHN FLAVEL
Fountain of Life, 194

The sacrament of the Lord's Supper and the very point of death require equal seriousness. A man's spirit should be as deeply solemn and composed at the Lord's Table as upon a deathbed. We should go to that ordinance as if we were then going into another world.

✦ JOHN FLAVEL
Sacramental Meditations, 6

[Christ] was so ready that before His enemies laid hands on Him, He, as it were, laid hands on Himself in the instituting of the Lord's Supper; and there did sacramentally rend the flesh of His own body and broach His own heart to fill that cup with His precious blood, which with His own hand He gave them that they might not look upon His death now at hand as a mere butchery from the hand of man's violence, but rather as a sacrifice wherein

He did freely offer up Himself to God for them and all believers.

✦ WILLIAM GURNALL
Christian in Complete Armour, 405

I may be glad of [Christ] now at a sacrament. Mr. Heyricke preached on Proverbs 14:9, and at the sacrament I was much deadened and distracted by my affliction. Yet the Lord Jesus had a broken body as well as a broken heart when He was crucified for me, and if I could have my heart kindly broken for sin and it is overloaden by affliction, it would greatly tend to my comfort.

✦ HENRY NEWCOME
Diary, 26 (Dec. 1, 1661)

There are three ways whereby God represents Christ to the faith of believers. The one is by the word of the gospel itself, as written; the second is by the ministry of the gospel and preaching of the word; and the third by this sacrament, wherein we represent the Lord's death to the faith of our own souls.

✦ JOHN OWEN
Discourse 4 on 1 Cor. 11:26, in
Twenty-Five Discourses, 52

There is in this ordinance [i.e., the Lord's Supper] a special profession of Christ. There is a profession of Him against the shame of the world, a profession of Him against the curse of the law, and a profession of Him against the power of the devil. All our profession doth much center in a due celebration of this ordinance.

✦ JOHN OWEN
Discourse 4 on 1 Cor. 11:26, in
Twenty-Five Discourses, 62

Remember in particular the love of Jesus Christ, as God-man, in giving Himself for us. This love is frequently proposed to us with what He did for us, and it is represented peculiarly in this ordinance: "Who loved me and gave Himself for me," says the apostle. Faith will never be able to live upon the last expression "gave Himself for me" unless it can rise up to the first, "who loved me." Who "loved us, and washed us from our sins in his own blood," etc. (Rev. 1:5–6).

✦ JOHN OWEN
Discourse 13, in *Twenty-Five Discourses*, 172

Let [believers] look inward and see how great need they have of many and often confirmations of their faith, renovations of their repentance, of stirring up the graces of God in the soul to add an edge and eagerness even to all spiritual affections after holiness to get unto themselves the most powerful provocations unto obedience. Everyone that hath grace knows how frequently the power thereof is impaired by temptations, weakened by worldly distractions even of our lawful employments, and overmastered by the force of sinful lusts so that they must needs discover a great deal of ignorance in their spiritual estate that feel not in their souls a proneness to affamishment [starvation], as well as in their bodies; at least they bewray intolerable carelessness, that finding the emptiness and leanness of their souls yet neglect to repair often unto this holy Table, whereon is set forth the Bread of Life, whereof when they have eaten, their spirit may come again, their hearts may be strengthened, their souls may be replenished as with marrow and fatness.

✦ WILLIAM PEMBLE
Introduction to the Worthy Receiving the Sacrament, 4

Upon what particulars are we chiefly to examine ourselves? We are principally to examine ourselves touching these three particulars, namely, (1) what right we have to the Lord's Supper; (2) what need we have of it; (3) what actual fitness we have for it. If we have no right, we shall but usurp it; if we feel no need, we shall but despise it; if we be not fit, we shall but abuse it.

✦ FRANCIS ROBERTS
Communicant Instructed, 3

We were given up to Thee, O Lord, in baptism; oh, break our hearts for our unfruitfulness and help us now to be steadfast in Thy covenant. We have been baptized with water; oh that we may be washed and sanctified and justified in the name of the Lord Jesus Christ and by the Spirit of our God. Let the ordinance of the Supper be earnestly desired; let not Thy table be contemptible. Oh that we may prize that Bread of God which comes down from heaven and gives life unto the world; let us not labor for the meat that perishes. Wherefore should we spend our money for that which is not bread and our labor for that which cannot satisfy. Let us look unto Christ, whom we have pierced, and mourn. Let us

eternally fall out with sin, beholding it besmeared with the blood of Jesus. Help us to believe that Christ was made sin and bore the curse that was due to us and to conclude that the Lord Jesus is as really given to us as the outward elements. Make us eager to receive a whole Christ and all His benefits and to give up ourselves wholly and immediately to Him.

✦ NATHANIEL VINCENT
Spirit of Prayer, 154–55

The ordinances are the chariot in which Christ rides, the lattice through which He looks forth and shows His smiling face; here Christ displays the banner of love (Song 2:4). The Lord's Supper is nothing else but a pledge and earnest of that eternal communion the saints shall have with Christ in heaven. Then He will take the spouse into His bosom. If Christ be so sweet in an ordinance, when we have but short glances and dark glimpses of Him by faith, oh then how delightful and ravishing will His presence be in heaven when we shall see Him face-to-face and be forever in His loving embraces?

✦ THOMAS WATSON
Godly Man's Picture, 220–21

This ordinance [i.e., the Lord's Supper], when partaken of in faith, hath glorious effects on the hearts of God's children: it quickens their affections, strengthens their faith, mortifies their sin, revives their hopes, increases their joy, and gives a rich foretaste of heaven.

✦ THOMAS WATSON
Puritan Gems, 84

The Lord's Supper is the most spiritual ordinance ever instituted. Here we have to do more immediately with Christ. In prayer we draw near through Christ; in this ordinance we become one with Him. In the word preached we hear of Christ; in the Supper we feed on Him.

◆ THOMAS WATSON
Puritan Gems, 85

THE LORD'S SUPPER AND PREACHING

There are two ways whereby there is a representation made of Christ being lifted up to draw men unto Him. (1) By the preaching of the word. So, the apostle tells us [in] Galatians 3:1 that Jesus Christ was evidently crucified before their eyes. The great end of preaching the word is to represent evidently Christ crucified; it is to lift up Christ that He may draw sinners unto Him. And, (2) it is represented in this ordinance of the Lord's Supper, wherein we show forth His death. Christ is peculiarly and eminently lifted up in this ordinance because it is a peculiar and eminent representation of His death.

◆ JOHN OWEN
Discourse 16 on John 12:32, in
Twenty-Five Discourses, 195–96

LOVE

We must love our own good because we most love ourselves. Our love to God is heightened from our due self-love; there is a sinful self-love when either we love that for a self which is not ourself, when we love our flesh and fleshly interest, or when we love ourselves inordinately more than God, and God only for ourselves. And there is a lawful self-love when we love ourselves in the Lord and for the Lord. And the more we thus love ourselves, the more is the Lord loved by us; and the more He is our own, the more love He hath. Now in Christ the Lord is our God.

◆ RICHARD ALLEINE
Heaven Opened, 155

By love we are one with God, and He with us. It is the soul's willing of God, as I may so speak. Willing of God to itself, and willing itself and all to God.... The heart thus opened to the Lord, when God is come in, will close upon Him. Abide with me; Thou hast entered upon Thy habitation. O let this be Thy dwelling forever. Only this must be further added, that with God it takes in all things of God: His word, His ordinances, His ways, and all His dispensations. With His love, His laws; with His comforts, His counsels; with His counsels, His corrections. With Thee, I accept of all that is Thine: both Thy yoke and Thy cross; Thyself, Lord; Thy love, Lord; and what Thou wilt with Thee.

◆ RICHARD ALLEINE
Heaven Opened, 161–63

Love is to a saint what malice is to Satan: that which gives force to all his actings.

◆ RICHARD ALLEINE
Heaven Opened, 166

Walk in love as Christ has loved you. This is the life of heaven and beginning of that excellent glory which shall never be removed. There is nothing does make thee more like to God, more near and dear to Him, and more fit for His use than this grace of love. Let your affections be extended as large as the objects of them: unto God, His word, ways, and people. Love God to obey Him; His ways to walk in them; His people to delight in them, to sympathize with them, to mourn over them in their sufferings, to help them in their necessities, to rejoice with them in their consolations, counting their mercies your own, which is no easy part of your duty.

✦ BARTHOLOMEW ASHWOOD
Heavenly Trade, xxix–xxx

Love is the commander of the soul, and therefore God knows that if He has our hearts, He has all, for all the rest are at His command; for it is, as it were, the nature of the will, which is the commanding faculty, and its object is the ultimate end which is the commanding object. Love sets the mind on thinking, the tongue on speaking, the hands on working, the feet on going, and every faculty obeys its command.

✦ RICHARD BAXTER
A Christian Directory, in
Practical Works, 2:358

The odious vices contrary to the love of God are (1) privative: not loving Him; (2) positive: hating Him; (3) opposite: loving His creatures in His stead. All these concur in every unsanctified soul.

That they are all void of the true love of God and taken up with creature love is past all doubt, but whether they are all haters of God may seem more questionable. But it is as certain as the other; only the hatred of God in most doth not break out into that open opposition, persecution, or blasphemy as it doth with some that are given up to desperate wickedness; nor do they think that they hate Him.

✦ RICHARD BAXTER
A Christian Directory, in
Practical Works, 2:359

All other graces must do their part in assisting love, and all be exercised in subservience to it and with an intention, directly or remotely, to promote it. Fear and watchfulness must keep away the sin that would extinguish it and preserve you from that guilt which would frighten away the soul from God. Repentance and mortification must keep away diverting and deceiving objects which would steal away our love from God. Faith must show us God as present in all His blessed attributes and perfections. Hope must depend on Him for nearer access and the promised felicity. Prudence must choose the fittest season and means and helps from our special approaches to Him and teach us how to avoid impediments. And obedience must keep us in a fit capacity for communion with Him.

✦ RICHARD BAXTER
A Christian Directory, in
Practical Works, 2:366

When thou seest or feelest what love a parent hath to children and a husband to a wife, or a wife to a husband or faithful friends to one another, think then, "What love do I owe to God!" O how inconsiderable is the loveliness of a child, a wife, a friend, the best of creatures in comparison of the loveliness of God!... How much greater is the love of God!... He gave thee thy being, thy daily safety, and all the mercies of thy life. He gave thee His Son, His Spirit, and His grace. He pardoned thy sins and took thee into His favor and adopted thee for His son and an heir of heaven! He will glorify thee with angels in the presence of His glory! How should such a friend as this be loved! How far above all mortal friends! Their love and friendship is but a token and message of His love. Because He loveth thee, He sendeth thee kindness and mercy by thy friend. And when their kindness ceaseth or can do thee no good, His kindness will continue and comfort thee forever. Love them therefore as the messengers of His love, but love Him in them, and love them for Him, and love Him much more.

♦ RICHARD BAXTER
A Christian Directory, in
Practical Works, 2:390

Love is a commanding affection, a uniting grace; it draws all the faculties of the soul to one center. The soul that loves God, when it hath to do with Him, is bound to the beloved object; it can mind nothing else during such impressions. When the affection is set to the worship of God, everything the soul hath will be bestowed upon it.

♦ STEPHEN CHARNOCK
Discourses upon the Existence and Attributes of God, 170

Love is the great conqueror of the world. Thus will thy soul, being inflamed with love to Christ, set all thy worldly interest adrift rather than put His honor to the least hazard.... Love is compared to fire, the nature of which is to assimilate to itself all that comes near it or to consume them; it turns all into fire or ashes. Nothing that is heterogeneous can dwell with its own simple, pure nature. Thus, love to Christ will not suffer the near neighborhood of anything in its bosom that is derogatory to Christ.

♦ WILLIAM GURNALL
Christian in Complete Armour, 267

I am swallowed up, O God; I am willingly swallowed up in this bottomless abyss of Thine infinite love. And there let me dwell in a perpetual ravishment of spirit till, being freed from this clog of earth and filled with the fullness of Christ, I shall be admitted to enjoy that which I cannot now reach to wonder at, Thine incomprehensible bliss and glory which Thou hast laid up in the highest heavens for them that love Thee in the blessed communion of all Thy saints and angels, Thy cherubim and seraphim, thrones, dominions, and principalities, and powers; in the beatifical presence of Thee, the ever-living God; the eternal Father of spirits; Father, Son, Holy Ghost; one infinite deity in three coessentially, coeternally, coequally glorious persons, to whom be blessing, honor, glory, and power, forever and ever. Amen. Hallelujah.

✦ JOSEPH HALL
"A Meditation on the Love of Christ," in *Select Tracts*, 224

Endeared Sweetheart,

For such a privileged title God's good providence, friends' consent, and my mutual love admits of. When I was last with you there fell into my bosom such a spark of love that nothing will quench it but yourself. The nature of this love is, I hope, sincere; the measure of it great; and, as far as I know my own heart, it is right and genuine. The very bare probability of success ravished my heart with joy and made me rest those words of Elizabeth upon the sight of Mary, that these things are too good to prove true.... [God] has beautified your body; very pleasant are you to me. You are in my heart to live and die in waiting on you, and I extremely please myself in loving you, and I like my affections the better because they tell me they are only placed upon you. But here I stop lest I be suspected of flattery; it is indeed contrary to my natural inclination but more to my grave calling, as I am a minister of the gospel, to speak beyond the truth. I rather beg pardon for my purposed plainness, but sweet Mrs. Betty, as I have given my heart to you, you ought in return to give me yours, and you cannot in equity deny it me. I have been very urgent at the throne of grace, and that which is won by prayer may be worn with praise; but I fear now I shall tire your patience and beg leave to conclude, who am by a thousand links and chains of pure affections

Your devoted servant till death,
Oliver Heywood

✦ OLIVER HEYWOOD
Autobiography, Diaries, 131–32

To relent of our right unto God for His glory is no work of supererogation which we are not bound unto, as the Church of Rome has taught, but due debt. For we do owe love unto God from the ground of our heart, and love seeks not all her own but oftentimes frankly and freely gives of her right unto God. Herein also we may discern that love has great things in it, that it mightily carries the affections to that which it loves and keeps them occupied there, even oftentimes to the neglect of itself.

✦ JOHN KNEWSTUB
Lectures, 197

If you ask, "How shall I do to love?" I answer, "Believe." If you ask, "How shall I believe?" I answer, "Love. Believe and you shall love; believe much and you shall love much. Labor for strong and deep persuasions of the glorious things that are spoken of Christ, and this will command love. Seek to believe Christ's excellency in Himself and His love to us and our interest in Him, and this will kindle such a fire in the heart as will make it ascend in a sacrifice of love to Him." The soul that is possessed with this love of Jesus Christ, the soul which hath its eye much upon

Him, often thinking on His former sufferings and present glory, the more it looks upon Christ, the more it loves; and still the more it loves, the more it delights to look upon Him.

✦ ROBERT LEIGHTON
Spiritual Truths, 87–88

Take but this one word to discover to you whether you walk in your obedience under a sense of the constraining power of Christ; it comprehends all others: "His commandments are not grievous" (1 John 5:3). When a soul works out of love, what it does is not grievous. And the inward and outward commands of Christ will be grievous to all that are not under the constraining power and efficacy of His love.

✦ JOHN OWEN
Discourse 20 on Rom. 5:5–6, in
Twenty-Five Discourses, 233

He that loves not God for Himself— that is, for what He is in Himself and what from Himself alone He is and will be to us in Christ (which considerations are inseparable)—hath no true affection for any spiritual thing whatever.

✦ JOHN OWEN
Golden Book, 243

They that love [God] would have Him be all that He is—as He is and nothing else—and would be themselves like Him.

✦ JOHN OWEN
Golden Book, 244

If the understanding apprehends a thing to be good, whether it be real or apparent only, then the affection that is stirred up by it and to it is love. Love is the opening of the heart to let in a person or thing under the notion of a good that seems to be needful or profitable, comfortable and suitable to you, or the heart's embracing or embosoming thereof.

✦ EDWARD REYNER
Precepts for Christian Practice, 385

Love is that powerful and prevalent passion by which all the faculties and inclinations of the soul are determined and on which both its perfection and happiness depend. The worth and excellency of a soul is to be measured by the object of its love. He who loveth mean and sordid things doth thereby become base and vile, but a noble and well-placed affection doth advance and improve the spirit into a conformity with the perfections which it loves.

✦ HENRY SCOUGAL
Life of God in the Soul of Man, 40

Perfect love is a kind of self-dereliction, a wandering out of ourselves; it is a kind of voluntary death wherein the lover dies to himself and all his own interest, not thinking of them nor caring for them anymore, and minding nothing but how he may please and gratify the party whom he loves.

✦ HENRY SCOUGAL
Life of God in the Soul of Man, 47

Happy the heart where graces reign,
Where love inspires the breast;
Love is the brightest of the train,
And quickens all the rest.

Knowledge, alas! 'Tis all in vain,
And all in vain our fear;
Our stubborn sins will fight and reign,
If love be absent there.

'Tis love that makes our cheerful feet
In swift obedience move;
The devils know, and tremble too,
But Satan cannot love.

Before we quite forsake this clay,
Or leave this dark abode:
The wings of love bear us away,
To see our smiling God.

This is the grace that lives and sings,
When faith and hope shall cease,
'Tis this shall strike our joyful strings,
In the sweet realms of bliss.
✦ ISAAC WATTS
Devout Meditations, 240

The whole duty of man, both unto
God and unto man, requires no more
for both, but true and perfect love to
both. He that loves one perfectly loves
both truly. And he that loves not both
truly loves neither of both perfectly.
✦ EDWARD WILLAN
"An Exhortation to Christian
Charity," in *Six Sermons*, 6

LOVE OF LIFE, SINFUL

I count him the most perfect man in the
world who loves not his own life with
an inordinate, sinful love; who loves it

only in God and not with a creature-
love distinct from God. There are two
ways whereby this natural and lawful
love of life becomes sinful—namely,
immoderateness and inordinateness.
Immoderateness is when men love
their lives at that rate that they are
filled with unreasonable and distracting fears, cares, and thoughts about
them, when the whole business of life is
almost nothing else but a studiousness
to preserve the being of life. Inordinateness is when men, though they do
not love their lives at that excessive rate,
yet do love life as a creature good, not
in God nor in order to Him, but love
it for itself, as something out of God.
Every carnal man in the world is guilty
of the latter, and I fear but few saints
are altogether free from the guilt of it.
✦ SAMUEL SHAW
*Voice of One Crying in the
Wilderness*, 150

LOVE OF THE WORLD

The love of the world plucks the heart
downward, and the lusts of the flesh
are so many weights upon the believer
that he cannot mount up in a spiritual cloud of divine affection to Jesus
Christ; but the pure and spiritual heart
is now more refined and delivered from
these impediments, and it is like a pure
lamp of oil burning upward. When a
man's heart is engaged to anything of
this world, love cannot be perfect, for
love is a man's master, and "no man can
serve two masters."
✦ HUGH BINNING
"An Essay upon Christian Love,"
in *Several Sermons*, 231

[The love of the world] is a fit root for hypocrisy to grow upon if the heart be violently set on anything the world has and it comes to vote peremptorily for having it. "I must be worth so much a year, have such honor"; and the creature begins with Ahab to be sick with longing after them. Then the man is in great danger to take the first ill counsel that Satan or the flesh gives him for the attaining his ends, though prejudicial to his uprightness. Hunters mind not the way they go in; over hedge and ditch they leap so they may have the hare.

♦ WILLIAM GURNALL
Christian in Complete Armour, 271

The love of the world and the love of God are like the scales of a balance; as the one falls, the other does rise. When our natural inclinations prosper and the creature is exalted in our soul, religion is faint and does languish; but when earthly objects wither away and lose their beauty and the soul begins to cool and flag in its prosecution of them, then the seeds of grace take root, and the divine life begins to flourish and prevail.

♦ HENRY SCOUGAL
Life of God in the Soul of Man, 95

LUST

Sin is as a great king, and these are its three princes that command all men under it. They are universal lusts. Some call them sin's or the world's trinity, and these admit many subdivisions. Some of these may more properly be called the lusts of the flesh that have the sensual and brutish part of men only or mostly for them, at least engage only men's corrupted affections; some of them are more subtle and refined and are called the lusts of the mind when they gain not only our affections but our judgment to be for them.

♦ ALEXANDER CARMICHAEL
Believer's Mortification of Sin, 18

My soul's the sea wherein from day
   to day,
Sins, like leviathans, do sport and play,
Great master lusts with all the lesser
   fry,
Therein increase and strangely
   multiply.
Yet strange it is not sin so fast should
   breed,
Since with this nature I receiv'd the
   seed
And spawn of every species; which
   was shed
Into its caverns first, then nourished
By its own native warmth; which, like
   the sun,
Hath quickened them, and now
   abroad they come;
And like the frogs of Egypt, creep
   and crawl
Into the closest rooms within the soul.
My fancy swarms, for there they frisk
   and play,
In dreams by night and foolish toys
   by day.
My judgment's clouded by them,
   and my will
Perverted, every corner they do fill.
As locusts seize on all that's fresh
   and green,

Unclothe the beauteous spring, and
    make it seem
Like drooping autumn; so my soul,
    that first
As Eden seem'd, now's like a ground
    that's cursed.
Lord, purge my streams and kill those
    lusts that lie
Within them; if they do not, I must
    die.
                ✦ JOHN FLAVEL
Navigation Spiritualized, 32

Lust is nothing else but the corrupt appetite of the creature to some sinful object, and therefore look as it is with the appetite with respect to food; so it is with the vitiated appetites of souls to sin. One man loves this food best, and another that; there is endless variety in that, and so in this.
                ✦ JOHN FLAVEL
"A Sober Consideration of the
Sin of Drunkenness," in *Navigation
Spiritualized*, 145–46

Lusts: this is in Scripture the usual name of all the irregular and sinful desires of the heart, both the polluted habits of them and their corrupt streams, both as they exist within and as they outwardly vent themselves in the lives of men. The apostle St. John calls it the lust of the world (1 John 2:17) and love of the world (v. 15) and then branches it into those three, which are indeed the base anti-trinity that the world worships: the lust of the eyes, the lust of the flesh, and the pride of life (v. 16).
          ✦ ROBERT LEIGHTON
*A Commentary upon the First Epistle
of Peter*, in *Whole Works*, 1:114–15

All those three which St. John speaks of (1 John 2:16), the world's accursed trinity, are included under this name here of fleshly lusts. A crew of base, imperious masters they are, to which the natural man is a slave, serving diverse lusts (Titus 3:3). Some are more addicted to the service of one kind of lust, some to that of another; but all are in this unhappy, that they are strangers — yea, enemies — to God, and, as the brute creatures, servants to their flesh; either covetous, like the beasts of the field, with their eye still upon the earth, or voluptuous, swimming in pleasures as fishes in the sea, or, like the fowls of the air, soaring in vain ambition.
          ✦ ROBERT LEIGHTON
*A Commentary upon the First Epistle
of Peter*, in *Whole Works*, 1:270

Lust, which is but the last end and consummation of all pleasures, sucks the bones, and, like a cannibal, eats your own flesh (Prov. 11:5).
          ✦ THOMAS MANTON
*Practical Exposition on the
Epistle of James*, 186

MALICE

Malice and envy are but two branches growing out of the same bitter root; self-love and evil speakings are the fruit they bear. Malice is properly the procuring or wishing another's evil, envy the repining at his good; and both these vent themselves by evil speaking. This infernal fire within smokes and flashes out by the tongue, which St. James says is set on fire of hell (3:6) and fires all about it, censuring the actions of those they hate or envy, aggravating their failings, and detracting from their virtues, taking all things by the left ear; for, as Epictetus says, everything hath two handles. The art of taking things by the better side, which charity always does, would save much of those janglings and heartburnings that so abound in the world.

✦ ROBERT LEIGHTON
A Commentary upon the First Epistle of Peter, in *Whole Works*, 1:174

See the devilish reach of malice that will spoil willfully what it can make no use of.

✦ ADAM MARTINDALE
Life, 44

Malice cares not how true the charge is, but how cutting.

✦ JOHN TRAPP
in Horn, *Puritan Remembrancer*, 104

Meekness is opposed to malice; malice is the devil's picture (John 8:44). Malice is mental murder (1 John 3:15). It unfits for duty.

✦ THOMAS WATSON
The Beatitudes, in *Discourses*, 2:146

MANKIND

[God] gave [Adam] a power soberly to use and dispose of the creatures in the earth, sea, and air. Thus, man was God's deputy governor in the lower world, and this his dominion was an image of God's sovereignty. This was common to the man and to the woman. But the man had one thing peculiar to him—

to wit, that he had dominion over the woman also (1 Cor. 11:7). Behold how the creatures came unto him to own their subjection and to do him homage as their lord and quietly stood before him till he put names on them as his own (Gen. 2:19). Man's face struck an awe upon them; the stoutest creatures stood astonished, tamely and quietly owning him as their lord and ruler.

✦ THOMAS BOSTON
Human Nature in Its Fourfold State, 16

'Tis marvelous to see that Man, so wise
And noble by creation, as is he,
Should in this manner let sin blind his eyes,
That neither heaven nor hell he well can see.

But like one blind or mad or worse he runs
At Satan's beck, to his perpetual shame:
Till into ruin headlong down he comes,
Into the fearful fire and endless flame.

When Man doth study of things here below,
What pretty arts will he invent in time?
He'll find out much, and do it neatly too;
But yet he doth not see the gospel shine.

Oh, 'tis a shame for thee, who know'st so much
Of God, by creatures, Scriptures, mercies great;

To let thy conversation be such,
That God must with His stripes thee
    soundly beat.

The ox is wiser in his kind than thee,
For he doth make his Master's crib his
    choice:
Condemned by him therefore thou
    may'st be,
For he, not thee, obeys his Master's
    voice.
        ✦ JOHN BUNYAN
        Profitable Meditations, 8

Man is nothing but soul and soil, or
breath and body; a puff of wind the
one, and a pile of dust the other.
        ✦ SAMUEL CLARK
        Saint's Nosegay, 142

Our captain counts the image of God;
nevertheless, His image cut in ebony
as if done in ivory. And in the black-
est Moors he sees the representation of
the King of heaven.
        ✦ THOMAS FULLER
        Wise Words and Quaint
        Counsels, 183

Man is made after God's own image:
"Let us make man in our image, after
our likeness" (Gen. 1:26). In other
creatures there are *vestigia*. We may
track God by His works, but man is
His very image and likeness. I shall
not be large in this argument. This
image of God consists in three things:
(1) In his nature, which was intellectual. God gave him a rational
soul, spiritual, simple, immortal, free
in its choice; yea, in the body there
were some rays and strictures of the
divine glory and majesty. (2) In those

qualities of knowledge (Col. 3:10),
uprightness (Eccl. 7:29), "in righteousness and true holiness" (Eph. 4:24).
(3) In his state—in a happy confluence
of all inward and outward blessings, as
the enjoyment of God, power over the
creatures, etc. But now this image is in
a great part defaced and lost and can
only be restored in Christ. Well, then,
this was the great privilege of our creation, to be made like God; the more
we resemble Him, the more happy.
        ✦ THOMAS MANTON
        Practical Exposition on the
        Epistle of James, 131

Of living creatures, new to sight, and
    strange
Two of far nobler shape, erect and tall,
Godlike erect, with native honor clad
In naked majesty seemed lords of all:
And worthy seemed; for in their looks
    divine
The image of their glorious Maker
    shone,
Truth, wisdom, sanctitude severe
    and pure,
(Severe, but in true filial freedom
    placed),
Whence true authority in men;
    though both
Not equal, as their sex not equal
    seemed;
For contemplation he and valor
    formed;
For softness she and sweet attractive
    grace;
He for God only, she for God in him.
        ✦ JOHN MILTON
        Paradise Lost, book 4, ll. 285–97,
        in *Complete Poetical Works*, 107

MARRIAGE

As God by creation made two of one, so again by marriage he made one of two.

✦ THOMAS ADAMS
Exposition upon…Second…Peter, 84

Marriage is called a yoke, too heavy for one alone to bear; therefore, each had a mutual help, a wife. In the participation of good, compassion of evil, in health the best delight, in sickness the best comfort; the sole companion to whom we may communicate our joys and into whose bosom we unload our sorrows. Thus are our griefs lessened, our joys enlarged, our hearts solaced.

✦ THOMAS ADAMS
Exposition upon…Second…Peter, 326

He that is free from a wife may frame his choice to his mind, but he that hath chosen must frame his mind to his choice. Before, he might conform his actions to his affections; now he must endeavor to frame his affection according to his action.

✦ SAMUEL CLARK
Saint's Nosegay, 132

It is not evil to marry but good to be wary.

✦ THOMAS GATAKER
in Thomas, *Puritan Golden Treasury*, 179

I would commend this rule to married persons: to beware of both being angry together, but rather let one be to the other like David's harp to appease Saul's fury.

✦ THOMAS GOUGE
Christian Directions, in *Works*, 229

This duty [of husbands and wives helping each other forward their growth in grace] may be the better effected by these means following. (1) By taking notice of the beginning and least measure of grace and approving the same. (2) By frequent conference about such things as concern the same; mutually propounding questions one to another thereabouts and answering the same. (3) By their mutual practice and example, making themselves each to other a pattern of piety. (4) By performing exercises of religion as praying, singing psalms, reading the Word, and the like together. (5) By maintaining holy and religious exercises in the family. Though this duty especially appertain to the husband, yet the wife must put her husband in mind thereof if he forget it, and stir him up if he be backward. Thus did the good Shunammite (2 Kings 4:9–10). No man's persuasion in this kind can so much prevail with a man as his wife's. (6) By stirring up one another to go to the house of God, to hear the word, partake of the sacrament, and conscionably perform all the parts of God's public worship.

✦ WILLIAM GOUGE
Of Domestical Duties, 243

Dear Pair,
Whom God hath now of two made
  one
Suffer a father's exhortation.
In the first place see that with joint
  endeavor
You set yourselves to serve the Lord
  together,

You are yoked to work, but for work
  wages write,
His yoke is easy and His burden light,
Love one another, pray oft together,
  and see
You never both together angry be—
If one speak fire t'other with water
  come,
Is one provok'd be t'other soft or
  dumb—
Walk low but aim high, spotless be
  your life;
You are a minister and a minister's
  wife.
Therefore as beacons set upon a hill—
To angels and to men a spectacle—
Your slips will falls be called, your
  falls each one
Will be a blemish to religion—
Do good to all, be affable and meek.
Your converse must be preaching all
  the week—
Your garb and dress must not be
  vain or gay,
Reckon good works your richest,
  best array—
Your house must be a Bethel and
  your door
Alway stand open to relieve the poor.
Call your estate God's, not your own,
  engrave
Holiness to the Lord on all you have,
Count upon suffering, or you count
  amiss,
Sufficient to each day its evil is,
All are born once to trouble, but
  saints twice,
And as experience shews [ministers]
  thrice,

But if you suffer with and for your
  Lord,
You'll reign with Him according to
  His word.
  ◆ PHILIP HENRY
  Diaries and Letters, 359–60

[Philip Henry] would commonly say
to his children with reference to their
choice in marriage, "Please God and
please yourselves, and you will never
displease me."
  ◆ PHILIP HENRY
  Life and Sayings, 9

As for the qualifications of a husband or wife, I would advise all to
look at true religion in the first place,
that those that marry may be said to
marry in the Lord. Next to religion, I
should commend a suitable disposition and a conformity in manners, that
man and wife may delight in the society and converse one of another. And
as I would not have a man or woman
marry merely or chiefly by their eyes
or fancies, so neither would I advise a
marriage betwixt those that have an
averseness or antipathy at first sight
each to other.
  ◆ THOMAS HODGES
  Treatise of Marriage, 29–30

Marry neither only or chiefly for
beauty, by the eye; nor for honor, by
the ear; nor for money or wealth, by
the hand; but find out a meet helper,
a suitable yoke fellow, one whom you
are sure you shall love because you do
love her, and that too for her virtues
and qualifications, so decently lodged,
that you cannot but be pleased to dwell

with them. To conclude this particular about the choice of a wife and conversation with a wife, let me mind you what wisdom itself advises—namely, to marry in the Lord.

✦ THOMAS HODGES
Treatise of Marriage, 33

Hast thou a soft heart? It is of God's breaking. Hast thou a sweet wife? She is of God's making. Let me draw up this expression with a double application. When thou layest out for such a good on earth, look up to the God of heaven. Let Him make thy choice for thee who hath made His choice of thee. Look above you before you look about you. Nothing makes up the happiness of a married condition like the holiness of a mortified disposition. Account not those the most worthy that are the most wealthy. Art thou matched to the Lord? Match in the Lord. How happy are such marriages where Christ is at the wedding! Let none but those who have found favor in God's eyes find favor in yours.

✦ WILLIAM SECKER
"A Wedding-Ring for the Finger,"
in *Nonsuch Professor,* 255–56

She must be so much, and no less; and so much, and no more. Our ribs were not ordained to be our rulers. They are not made of the head to claim superiority but out of the side to be content with equality. They desert the Author of nature that invert the order of nature. The woman was made for the man's comfort, but the man was not made for the woman's command.

Those shoulders aspire too high that content not themselves with a room below their head. It is between a man and his wife in the house as it is between the sun and the moon in the heavens. When the greater light goes down, the lesser light gets up; when the one ends in setting, the other begins in shining. The wife may be a sovereign in her husband's absence, but she must be subject in her husband's presence. As Pharaoh said to Joseph, so should the husband say to his wife: "Thou shalt be over my house, and according to thy word shall all my people be ruled: only in the throne will I be greater than thou" (Gen. 41:40). The body of that household can never make any good motion whose bones are out of place.

✦ WILLIAM SECKER
"A Wedding-Ring for the Finger,"
in *Nonsuch Professor,* 256–57

A wife takes sanctuary not only in her husband's house but in his heart. The tree of love should grow up in the family as the tree of life grew up in the garden. They that choose their love should love their choice. They that marry where they affect not will affect where they marry not. Two joined together without love are but two tied together to make one another miserable.

✦ WILLIAM SECKER
"A Wedding-Ring for the Finger,"
in *Nonsuch Professor,* 263

Before man had any other calling, he was called to be a husband.

✦ HENRY SMITH
in Horn, *Puritan Remembrancer,* 185

Marry not where you love not, lest you are tempted to love where you marry not.

✦ RALPH VENNING
Saints' Memorials, 144

Marriage has scarce more that use it than that accuse it. Most men enter into this estate and, being entered, complain thereof. They should rather complain of themselves. It is an unjust thing and a fruit of ignorant pride to cast the blame of our grievances upon God's ordinances. "I had been happy," says one, "had I not been married." Then was thou foolish both before and since thy marriage. Use it well; it shall add to thine happiness. We make bitter sauce and cry out that the meat is bitter.

✦ WILLIAM WHATELY
Bride-Bush, iii

Love is the life and soul of marriage, without which, it differs as much from itself as a carcass from a living body; yea, verily, it is a most uncomfortable society and no better than a living death. This makes all things easy; the want of it makes all things hard. Love seasons and sweetens all estates; love composes all controversies; love overrules all passions; it squares all actions. It is, in a word, the king of the heart, which, in whom it prevails, to them marriage is what it should be, a pleasing combination of two persons into one home, one purse, one heart, and one flesh.

✦ WILLIAM WHATELY
Bride-Bush, 16

Prayer will prevent most discontentments and compose all; for when [a husband and wife] shall appear before God in prayer, instead of blaming each other only or chiefly (which is the evil humor of pride that makes these sores to rankle), they shall each blame themselves and take the greatest fault upon themselves, which being once done, all contentions will cease and all quarrels will come to an end.

✦ WILLIAM WHATELY
Bride-Bush, 24

MARRIAGE: HUSBAND

He must love her at all times, he must love her in all things; love must season and sweeten his speech, carriage, actions toward her; love must show itself in his commands, reproofs, admonitions, instructions, authority, familiarity with her. The rise of which love must not be from her beauty or nobility, but especially because she is his sister in the Christian religion and an inheritor with him of the kingdom of heaven; because of her graces and virtues; because she bears him children, the heirs of his name and substance; and because of the union and conjunction of marriage. Love growing on beauty, riches, lust, or any other slight grounds soon vanishes, but if grounded on these considerations, and especially on this union of marriage, it is lasting and true. The want hereof is the fountain of strife, quarreling, and debate, which converts the paradise of marriage into a hell.

✦ ISAAC AMBROSE
"The Practice of Sanctification,"
in *Works*, 131

Overcome them with love, and then whatever they are in themselves, they will be loving to you, and consequently lovely. Love will cause love as fire kindles fire. A good husband is the best means to make a good and loving wife.

✦ RICHARD BAXTER
A Christian Directory, in
Practical Works, 4:119

He is careful that the wounds betwixt them take not air and be not publicly known. Jars concealed are half reconciled, which, if generally known, it is a double task to stop the breach at home and men's mouths abroad. To this end he never publicly reproves her. An open reproof puts her to do penance before all that are present, after which many rather study revenge than reformation.

✦ THOMAS FULLER
Holy and Profane States, 38

If he cannot reform his wife without beating, he is worthy to be beaten for choosing no better; when he hath used all means that he may and yet she is like herself, he must take her for his cross and say with Jeremiah, "This is my cross, and I will bear it." But if he strike her, he takes away his hand from her, which was the first part he gave her to join them together; and she may put her complaint against him that he hath taken away part of her goods. Her cheeks are made for thy lips, and not for thy fists.

✦ HENRY SMITH
"A Preparative to Marriage,"
in *Works*, 1:26

MARRIAGE: WIFE

Wives must be helpers to their husbands. Now this helpfulness consists in these things: (1) That she be careful to preserve his person in sickness or health, in adversity or prosperity, in youth or old age. (2) That she learn and labor to forecast, contrive, and manage household affairs, for which see a glorious pattern in Proverbs 31:13, that she may help her husband in erecting and establishing Christ's glorious kingdom in their house, and especially in their own hearts. This is that one necessary thing, without which their family is but Satan's seminary and a nursery for hell. This will marvelously sweeten all reproaches cast upon them by envenomed tongues; this will sweetly seal unto them their assurance of meeting together in heaven.

✦ ISAAC AMBROSE
"The Practice of Sanctification,"
in *Works*, 133

She commands her husband in any equal matter by constant obeying him.

✦ THOMAS FULLER
Holy and Profane States, 33

When Livia the empress was asked how had she got such a power over her husband that she could do anything with him she answered, "By my much modesty." A prudent wife commands her husband by obeying.

✦ JOHN TRAPP
Commentary...upon...the
New Testament, 924

MARTYRDOM

It is the cause, not the pain, makes the martyr, or malefactor; my soul, be not troubled at the kind or clamored cause of my death, were I indeed really guilty.
✦ ZACHARY CROFTON
Defence against the Dread of Death, 49

Christ calls not all to martyrdom, no more than He doth to ministry. The one is a gift as well as the other. To you it's given to suffer (Phil. 1:29). As preaching, so likewise suffering without a call will have little comfort. I am persuaded both the reason why some have been in the pulpit without success by Christ and others have been in the prison without sweetness hath been this, want of call.
✦ JOHN DURANT
Sips of Sweetness, 195

Martyrdom came into the world early; the first man that died, died for religion.
✦ WILLIAM JENKYN
in Horn, *Puritan Remembrancer*, 12; and
in Thomas, *Puritan Golden Treasury*, 52

Religion is that phoenix which has always flourished in its own ashes. While magistrates defend the truth with their sword, martyrs defend it with their blood.
✦ WILLIAM SECKER
Nonsuch Professor, 44

MASS (ROMAN CATHOLIC)

Whereas there is no example in all the Scripture of a sign being turned into the thing signified, yet it is very ordinary in Scripture similitudes to give a thing the name of that whereunto it is likened: "I am the rose of Sharon, and the lily of the valleys" (Song 2:1); "I am the living bread" (John 6:51); "I am the door" (John 10:7); "I am the true vine" (John 15:1). All these saith Christ of Himself, but is He therefore turned into a rose or lily or bread or door or vine? No...the meaning is He is like these.... So the Scripture ordinarily gives to signs the names of the things signified: "The three branches are three days" (Gen. 40:12); "The three baskets are three days" (v. 18).... And thus the Holy Ghost gives to sacramental signs the names of the things signified by them. Circumcision is called the "covenant," whereof it was a sign and seal (Gen. 17:13). The lamb is called the "passover" (Ex. 12:11). And so in the text the bread is called Christ's "body" and the wine His "blood" because they are signs and a seal to signify and convey Christ, with the benefits of His body broken and of His blood shed for us.
✦ EDWARD LAWRENCE
"There Is No Transubstantiation in the Lord's Supper," in Annesley, ed.,
Morning Exercises at Cripplegate, 469

[In the Roman Catholic Mass], the priest, with a few words, turned the bread into the body of Christ, and the people have no more to do but to put it into their mouths, and so Christ is partaken of. It was the loss of the mystery of faith in the real participation of Christ that put them on that invention.

✦ JOHN OWEN
Discourse 7, in *Twenty-Five Discourses*, 114

One of the greatest engines that ever the devil made use of to overthrow the faith of the church was by forging such a presence of Christ as is not truly in this ordinance to drive us off from looking after that presence which is true. I look upon it as one of the greatest engines that ever hell set on work. It is not a corporeal presence; there are innumerable arguments against that. Everything that is in sense, reason, and the faith of a man overthrows that corporeal presence.

✦ JOHN OWEN
Discourse 10 on Matt. 28:20, in
Twenty-Five Discourses, 136

The bread and wine themselves away
    are gone,
Shewes of them tarry still,
    but substance none.
They make their god, and then they
    eat him up.
They swallow down his flesh and
    blood up sup.
They'll taste no flesh on Fridays—
    that's not good—
But of their newmade god, and of his
    blood.
And as the whale did Jonas, so they
    eat
Him up alive, body and soule, as meat.
As men eat oysters, so on him they
    feed;

Whole, and alive, and raw, and yet
    not bleed.
This cookery, void of humanity,
Is held in Rome for sound divinity.

✦ THOMAS TUKE
Concerning the Holy Eucharist, 16

MEANS OF GRACE

Be constant in every appointment of God, public and private—of prayer, reading, hearing, holy conference—that you may get nourishment thereby administered to your souls. Get under all the dews and showers of grace for your fruitfulness. Be spiritual as well as frequent in exercising grace under the means of grace. Without this you cannot serve God acceptably (Heb. 12:28) or receive from Him who is the head nourishment to your souls, but by these bands and joints of faith and love (Col. 2:19).

✦ BARTHOLOMEW ASHWOOD
Heavenly Trade, 242

Engage thyself in the cheerful, constant use of the means and helps appointed by God for thy confirmation and salvation. He can never expect to attain the end that will not be persuaded to use the means. Of yourselves you can do nothing. God giveth His help by the means which He hath appointed and fitted to your help.

✦ RICHARD BAXTER
A Christian Directory, in
Practical Works, 2:48

A man, for the health and growth of the body, will use all means: labor in health, physic in sickness, recreation for the whetting of the faculty. In a word, he will use everything that he may strengthen the body. Thus you must do for the strengthening of the inward man; you must use all means as hearing the word, receiving the sacrament, prayer, meditation, conference, the communion of saints, particular resolutions to good, or else the inward man will not grow strong. These are the food that the inward man feeds upon. It is with the inward man as it is with a plant. If you would have a plant to grow, then you must set it in a good soil, you must dig about it and dung it; but if you be careless where you set it, it will not prosper and thrive. Even so, if you do not add fatness of soil unto the beginnings of grace; if you do not use all the means, as the communion of saints and prayer, the inward man will not grow strong, but wither and die. You will be dwarves in grace and holiness.

✦ JOHN PRESTON
"The Saints' Spiritual Strength,"
in *Remaines*, 112

Know that the means without God is but as a pen without ink, a pipe without water, or a scabbard without a sword. They will not strengthen the inward man without God, for it is the Spirit that puts life in the means, and yet you must not cut off the pipe from the wellhead. You must not depend upon God without the use of the means, but you must use both—that is, first seek to God and depend upon Him for

the strengthening of the inward man, and withal use the means constantly, because as water is carried from the wellhead unto the pipe and so from the pipe unto many places, so the means are as pipes to carry grace into the soul. Therefore, use them and cut them not off by carelessness; if you do, you will cut off the strength of the inward man.

✦ JOHN PRESTON
"The Saints' Spiritual Strength,"
in *Remaines*, 113–14

MEDITATION

Meditation is a calling in the thoughts from its stragglings and undue employments, fixing them on, and holding them to their peculiar work. 'Tis the travel of the mind in the search of some spiritual good; from such things as duty and providence lay before it. It weighs things and actions in the balance of truth; it turns things upside down and looks on both sides and through them, that it may take a right estimate of them.

✦ BARTHOLOMEW ASHWOOD
Heavenly Trade, 276

Be much in after-prayer for the Comforter's help to keep the word for you and bring it to your remembrance. Prayer opens the heart to take in the word, and prayer shuts the heart to keep in the word. Keep up meditation of the word (Ps. 119:11). This chews the cud and gets out the sweetness and nutritive virtue of it unto the heart and life. This way the godly come to be as trees planted by the water's side, that bring forth much fruit in their season (Ps. 1:3).

✦ BARTHOLOMEW ASHWOOD
Heavenly Trade, 291

The word of God we are to meditate on, to meditate on God and the things of God upon this account. Now here are four things that will lead you out to meditation: the exactness of the commandment; the faithfulness of the promise; the terror of the threatening; and the weightiness of the examples, all which meet in the Scriptures and in the word of God. And accordingly we are to meditate on the word of God upon this account.

✦ WILLIAM BRIDGE
Christ and the Covenant,
in *Works*, 3:146

In all your settled meditation, begin with reading or hearing. Go on with meditation; end in prayer. For as Mr. Greenham saith well: "Reading without meditation is unfruitful; meditation without reading is hurtful; to meditate and to read without prayer upon both is without blessing."

✦ WILLIAM BRIDGE
Christ and the Covenant,
in *Works*, 3:154

Friends, the more acquaintance you have with this work of meditation, the more time you will get and the less you will lose. A man that has the skill on it need never lose an hour. Who knows the worth of time? This little spot of time does our eternity depend upon, yet, Lord, how many are there that lose their precious hours and time! But what is the reason? They have no hand at this work of meditation. When their business is over they might, otherwise, turn their hand to this work and lose no time. The more acquaintance you have with this work of meditation, the more time you will get and the less you will lose.

✦ WILLIAM BRIDGE
Christ and the Covenant,
in *Works*, 3:157

Meditation fills the vessel of a gracious heart, and prayer opens the heart and pours out the precious things therein. By meditation we beat the spices and cut the offering to pieces and lay them in order, fit to be offered, and then we are the fitter to offer the same up in prayer. Meditation digs and searches and finds out the precious metals and materials, which, being ready at hand, are the sooner and the better coined in prayer.

✦ THOMAS COBBET
Gospel Incense, 176

To read and not to meditate is unfruitful; to meditate and not read is dangerous for error; to read and meditate without prayer is hurtful.

✦ EZEKIEL CULVERWELL
Time Well Spent, 218

Meditation is to the sermon what the harrow is to the seed; it covers those truths which else might have been picked or washed away.

✦ WILLIAM GURNALL
Christian in Complete Armour, 124

Meditation is like the lawyer's studying the case in order to his pleading at the bar. When, therefore, thou hast viewed the promise and affected thy heart with the riches of it, then ply thee to the throne of grace and spread it before the Lord.

✦ WILLIAM GURNALL
Christian in Complete Armour, 619

Meditation is prayer in bullion, prayer in the ore, soon melted and run into holy desires.

✦ WILLIAM GURNALL
Christian in Complete Armour, 679

Meditation is prayer's handmaid, to wait on it both before and after the performance. It is as the plough before the sower to prepare the heart for the duty of prayer, and as the harrow to cover the seed when it is sown.

✦ WILLIAM GURNALL
Christian in Complete Armour, 714

The best ground untilled soonest runs out into rank weeds. Such are God's children: overgrown with security ere they are aware, unless they be well exercised both with God's plough of affliction and their own industry in meditation. A man of knowledge that is either negligent or uncorrected cannot but grow wild and godless.

✦ JOSEPH HALL
Holy Observations, in
Select Tracts, 328

The church in her soul desires the Lord in the night, and then in the morning she seeks Him early. Desires blown by meditation are the sparks that set prayer in a light flame.

✦ SAMUEL LEE
Most Spiritual Profit, 64

The following excellent rules of meditation I propound unto thee, as I find them set down by Victorinus Strigelius, a learned divine: (1) We must not fall away from God for any creature. (2) Infinite eternity is far to be preferred before the short race of this mortal life. (3) We must hold fast the promise of grace, though we lose all temporal blessings and they also in death must needs be left. (4) Let the love of God in Christ and the love of the church for Christ be stronger in thee and prevail against all other affections. (5) It is the principal art of a Christian to believe things invisible, to hope for things deferred, to love God when He shows Him[self] to be an enemy, and thus to persevere unto the end. (6) It is most effectual remedy for any grief to quiet ourselves in a confidence of the presence and help of God and to ask of Him and withal to wait either for some easement or deliverance. (7) All the works of God are done in contrary means.

✦ WILLIAM PERKINS
Grain of Mustard Seed, 24

[Meditation is] a spirited and lively work. There must be a firm and strong purpose and intendment for a vigorous and spirited, a lively and warm work. "Fervent in spirit; serving the Lord" (Rom. 12:11). In every duty we must have a purpose of striking fire, of making the heart burning hot. It must not be lukewarm, in an indifferency—that is but lazy; nor blood warm—that is but low. But the soul's purpose and design must be for highest heat and fervency, greatest vigor and activity, as artists in some high operations seek for the hottest fire; as warmest preaching and warmest hearing, as the disciples' hearts burned within them when Christ opened the Scriptures (Luke 24:32). And so warmest reading and warmest meditating. In David's heart, while he mused, "the fire burned" (Ps. 39:3). So when we meditate, we should intend a warm work, to be very warm at the heart.

♦ NATHANAEL RANEW
Solitude Improved by Divine Meditation, 20

Meditation is not a hasty hurry of thoughts; that is…not meditation. It is not gathering half-ripe fruit, that which hath not its time for the influence of heaven to come down upon it and its own internal principle and power of its nature to produce a kindly maturation, a kindly ripening. We will not have (for want of time) our bread dough-baked or meat raw-roasted, knowing that what is not rightly prepared for the body may breed distempers, if it bring

not death. It is not the way to thrive, look well, and be strong, lively, and cheerful. Why should we gather our soul's precious fruits half-ripe? Feed our souls with dough-baked bread for want of a little time?

♦ NATHANAEL RANEW
Solitude Improved by Divine Meditation, 42

Meditation we described to be an institution of Christ and duty of a Christian, wherein the mind acts upon spiritual things or other things in a spiritual manner by a due considering of them, and this to holy ends or spiritual uses only.

♦ NATHANAEL RANEW
Solitude Improved by Divine Meditation, 57

There are various ends of meditation respecting ourselves. I shall mention, among others, these seven, relating to our own spiritual advantage: (1) as a principal improver of saving knowledge; (2) to make our knowledge clear and distinct; (3) to found a rich treasury of truths and make them sure; (4) to be an introducer of habitual wisdom, an acquired habit of wisdom, to the first given wisdom in heart renovation; (5) for a kindler of heavenly fire and flame in the heart; (6) for a mighty corroborator of holy purpose; (7) to be a constant quickener of the Christian course.

♦ NATHANAEL RANEW
Solitude Improved by Divine Meditation, 65

Meditation is a mighty engine to kindle cooling hearts and make them flame in fervency.

✦ NATHANAEL RANEW
Solitude Improved by Divine Meditation, 73

The Spirit comes, inhabits, sweeps, and cleanses; furnishes the heart with light that was darkness; with truth that was error and deceitfulness; with power that was weakness; life-warmth and qualifications of heavenly graces that was cold, dead, and altogether sinful; and draws the glorious image of Christ upon the soul. He enlivens, establishes, enlarges, and encourages and fills the spirit with peace and joy unspeakable. We act from His blowings on the gardens of our hearts, then the spices of graces flow (Song 4:16). The wheels mentioned in Ezekiel 10:17 moved from the spirit in them; so a Christian moves or not, as the Spirit moves or not. Every day and for every duty in the day there is need of a new blowing of the Spirit, that the spices may flow; new moving, that the wheels may move us. We must neither grieve, quench, nor resist the Holy Spirit (Eph. 4:30; 1 Thess. 5:19; Acts 7:51), the Spirit who is our helper and applier further of Christ and receiving of His fullness. If we would act wisely, the eye of the soul by meditation must daily be pondering the necessity of the Holy Spirit's influences, stirrings-up, strengthenings, and enlargements.

✦ NATHANAEL RANEW
Solitude Improved by Divine Meditation, 98–99

Meditation is the proper service of God in or with the mind. It is the soul's discourse with God or the soul's talking with Him, as a man doth familiarly with his friend (Ex. 33:1). It is like the child sucking of the mother's breasts, like the stomach's drawing nourishment to it, like the beasts chewing of the cud, and like the body's breathing in air, expiring and inspiring. All which things are done daily.

✦ EDWARD REYNER
Precepts for Christian Practice, 100

When you want water, your pump being dry, you, by pouring in a little water and much labor in pumping, can fetch water; so, by much laboring the heart in preparation and by prayer, you may recover the gift of prayer. And as when your fire is out, by laying on fuel and by blowing the spark remaining, you kindle it again — so, by meditation, you stir up the grace that is in you and by the breath of prayer may revive and inflame the spirit of grace and prayer in you.

✦ HENRY SCUDDER
Christian's Daily Walk, 74

The great usefulness of meditation appears in that (1) it doth digest, ingraft, and turn the spiritual knowledge gained in God's word and ordinances into the very life and substance of the soul, changing and fashioning you according to it, so that God's will in His word and your will become one, choosing and delighting in the same things. (2) Meditation fits for prayer, nothing more. (3) Meditation also promotes the practice of godliness, nothing more. (4) Nothing doth perfect and make a man an understanding Christian more than this. (5) Nothing doth make a man more know and enjoy himself with inward comfort nor is a clearer evidence that he is in a state of happiness than this.

✦ HENRY SCUDDER
Christian's Daily Walk, 154–55

Solemn meditation is a serious applying the mind to some sacred subject till the affections be warmed and quickened, and the resolution heightened and strengthened thereby against what is evil and for that which is good.

✦ GEORGE SWINNOCK
The Christian Man's Calling,
in *Works*, 2:425

Meditation without reading is erroneous; reading without meditation is barren. The bee sucks the flower and then works it into the hive and so turns it into honey. By reading we suck the flower of the word; by meditation we work it into the hive of our mind, and so it turns to profit. Meditation is the bellows of the affection.

✦ THOMAS WATSON
Bible and the Closet, 24–25

If it be inquired what meditation is, I answer, meditation is the soul's retiring of itself, that by a serious and solemn thinking upon God the heart may be raised up to heavenly affections.

✦ THOMAS WATSON
"A Christian on the Mount,"
in *Discourses*, 1:199

Meditation is the wing of the soul.

✦ THOMAS WATSON
"A Christian on the Mount,"
in *Discourses*, 1:199

The student's life looks like meditation but doth vary from it. Meditation and study differ three ways. (1) They differ in their nature. Study is a work of the brain, meditation of the heart. Study sets the invention on work; meditation sets the affection on work. (2) They differ in their design. The design of study is notion; the design of meditation is piety. The design of study is the finding out of a truth; the design of meditation is the spiritual improvement of a truth. The one searches for the vein of gold; the other digs out the gold. (3) They differ in the issue and result. Study leaves a man never a whit the better; it is like a winter sun that hath little warmth and influence. Meditation leaves one in a holy frame: it melts the heart when it is frozen and makes it drop into tears of love.

✦ THOMAS WATSON
"A Christian on the Mount,"
in *Discourses*, 1:203

How can the word be in the heart unless it be wrought in by meditation? As a hammer drives a nail to the head, so meditation drives a truth to the heart.

✦ THOMAS WATSON
"A Christian on the Mount,"
in *Discourses*, 1:239

Meditation is the life of religion, and practice is the life of meditation.

✦ THOMAS WATSON
"A Christian on the Mount,"
in *Discourses*, 1:270

In meditation there are two things: (1) A Christian's retiring of himself, a locking himself up from the world. Meditation is a work which cannot be done in a crowd. (2) It is a serious thinking on God. It is not a few transient thoughts that are quickly gone, but a fixing and staying the mind upon heavenly objects. This cannot be done without exciting all the powers of our souls.

✦ THOMAS WATSON
Christian Soldier, 43

Directions for meditation: Read before you meditate. "Give attendance to reading" (1 Tim. 4:13). Then it follows, "meditate upon these things" (v. 15). Reading doth furnish with matter; it is the oil that feeds the lamp of meditation. Be sure your meditations are founded upon Scripture. Reading without meditation is unfruitful; meditation without reading is dangerous.

✦ THOMAS WATSON
Gleanings, 112–13

MEEKNESS

Learn meekness from [Christ's] gentleness, as the elephant does from the lamb; when the elephant is in his greatest fury, set but a lamb before him and his wrath will presently be allayed. Learn of Christ to bear injuries, to restrain your anger, not to be angry but when duty and the cause of God calls you to it. 'Tis only sin should be the object of a Christian's anger. Moses was calm at his own reproaches but could not be still when God was dishonored.

✦ BARTHOLOMEW ASHWOOD
Best Treasure, 187

The meek person above all others is most fit for the service of God. If I would convey a reproof or a reprehension into the heart of a man, a meek and sweet disposition is the most fit for to do it with. If I would convey a comfort or consolation into a man's heart, a meek disposition is most fit for that. Christ gave the gospel, and He was meek; Moses gave the law, and he the meekest man upon earth in his time. So that whether law or gospel, it is best handed into the heart by meekness. I may with a soft breath blow a feather further than with strength of arm I can throw it.

✦ WILLIAM BRIDGE
"The Saints' Hiding-Place in the Time
of God's Anger," in *Works,* 4:369

Wrath is a special friend of Satan's; many of his counsels and designs are effected by it. The more of this humor, the more service has hell; the less of it, the more serviceable for heaven. Moses was the meekest man upon the earth, and he did most work for heaven. Christ was meeker than all other, and He did work the righteousness of God effectually; He did work for heaven and earth.

✦ WILLIAM GREENHILL
Exposition of the Prophet Ezekiel, 108

It were good strife among Christians, one to labor to give no offense and the other to labor to take none.

✦ RICHARD SIBBES
in Horn, *Puritan Remembrancer,* 135

The Christian's meekness must be mixed with wisdom. The apostle calls it meekness of wisdom; meekness opposes the fury in our own quarrel, not zeal in God's cause. The same Spirit that appeared in the form of a dove appeared also in the form of fiery tongues. It may be my duty to be silent when I am wronged, but it is sinful not to speak when God is reproached.... It is a singular mark of a saint to be wet tinder when men strike fire at himself, and touchwood when men strike at God. The meekest man upon the face of the earth was the fullest of fury in the cause of heaven (Ex. 32; Num. 12:2).

✦ GEORGE SWINNOCK
The Christian Man's Calling, in
Works, 2:214

A meek person will part with much of his right to buy his peace. Where he may not wrong his family too much nor dishonor his God, he will yield far to preserve or purchase a friend. Though his privilege be superior, yet he can be contented to hold the stirrup to others and give them place. Abraham was the elder and the nobler man, yet he offered Lot his choice of the country and was willing to take what he would leave.

✦ GEORGE SWINNOCK
The Christian Man's Calling, in
Works, 2:215

Meekness is a grace whereby we are enabled by the Spirit of God to moderate our passion.

✦ THOMAS WATSON
The Beatitudes, in *Discourses*, 2:144

Meekness towards God…implies two things: (1) submission to His will; (2) flexibleness to His word. (1) Submission to God's will: When we carry ourselves calmly without swelling or murmuring under the dispensations of providence: "It is the LORD: let him do what seemeth him good" (1 Sam. 3:18). The meek-spirited Christian saith thus, "Let God do what He will with me; let Him carve out what condition He pleases, I will submit. God sees what is best for me, whether a fertile soil or a barren; let Him checker His work as He pleases, it suffices God hath done it. It was an unmeek spirit in the prophet to struggle with God: "I do well to be angry, even unto death" (Jonah 4:9). (2) Flexibleness to God's word: When we are willing to let the word bear sway in our souls and become pliable to all its laws and maxims; he is spiritually meek who conforms himself to the mind of God and doth not quarrel with the instructions of the word, but the corruptions of his heart.

✦ THOMAS WATSON
The Beatitudes, in *Discourses*, 2:144

MEMORY

The more weight is laid on the seal, the deeper impression is made on the wax. The memory is that faculty which carries the images of things. It holds fast what we receive and is that treasury where we lay up what we desire afterward to use and converse with. Now, the more clear and certain our knowledge of anything is, the deeper it sinks, and surer it is held by the memory.

✦ WILLIAM GURNALL
Christian in Complete Armour, 211

The head may remember what the heart forgets, but the head will never forget what the heart remembers.

✦ RALPH VENNING
Canaan's Flowings, 136

It is with a good Christian's memory as it is with a lamp; though the lamp be not full of oil, yet it hath so much oil as makes the lamp burn. Though thy memory be not full of Scripture, yet thou retain so much as makes thy love to God to burn.

✦ THOMAS WATSON
Bible and the Closet, 46

The memory is diseased. The memory at first was like a golden cabinet in which divine truths were locked up safe, but now it is like a colander or leaking vessel which lets all that is good run out. The memory is like a searcer which sifts out the flour but keeps the bran. So the memory lets saving truths go and holds nothing but froth and vanity. Many a man can remember a story when he hath forgot his creed.

✦ THOMAS WATSON
The Beatitudes, in *Discourses,* 2:417

Oh, let truths be written on your hearts as with the point of a diamond, never to be razed out. A stony heart is a grievous plague, but an iron memory is a great mercy.

✦ JOHN WILKINSON
Sermon 2 on Rev. 3:3, in
England's Remembrancer, 21

MERCY

He that demands mercy and shows none ruins the bridge over which himself is to pass.

✦ THOMAS ADAMS
Exposition upon…Second…Peter, 498

Alas! How will you answer conscience now when that book is opened and the Lord Jesus brings in His bill of so many mercies expended, with skill and capacity to improve them and such a charge of debt issuing thence. So much due for such goods and for other wares: for sermons, sacraments, graces, comforts, frames, prayer returns, gracious providences and protections, so many personal mercies, so many family mercies, so many bodily mercies, so many soul mercies, so many church mercies, so many national mercies, sickbed mercies, health mercies, journey mercies, habitation mercies, caring mercies, sparing mercies, giving mercies, forgiving mercies, seen mercies, unseen mercies, and little or no return yet made for all these. How can the conscience stand up under such a charge or lift up his face without spot when it sees its guilt in all and cannot answer one of a thousand?

✦ BARTHOLOMEW ASHWOOD
Heavenly Trade, 68

Delight yourselves in the particular discoveries of [God's] common mercies to the world, and His special mercies to His saints, and His personal mercies to yourselves from your birth to this moment—both upon your souls and bodies and friends and name and estates and affairs in all relations.

✦ RICHARD BAXTER
Baxteriana, 155

There is nothing in the world renders a man more unlike a saint and more like Satan than to argue from mercy to sinful liberty; from divine goodness to licentiousness. This is the devil's logic.

✦ THOMAS BROOKS
Precious Remedies, 50

Mercies make a humble soul glad but not proud. A humble soul is lowest when his mercies are highest. He is least when he is greatest. He is lowest when he is highest. He is most poor when he is most rich. Nothing melts like mercy; nothing draws like mercy; nothing humbles like mercy.

✦ THOMAS BROOKS
The Unsearchable Riches of Christ,
in *Select Works*, 1:6

To argue from the riches of mercy to sinful liberty is the devil's logic. A soul that thus reasons is a soul left of God, a soul that is upon the last step of the ladder, a soul that Satan has by the hand, and the eternal God knows whither he will lead him.

✦ THOMAS BROOKS
The Unsearchable Riches of Christ,
in *Select Works*, 1:250

This is certainly greater than any affliction, that you have the day of grace and salvation, that you are not now in hell. This is a greater mercy, that you have the sound of the gospel yet in your ears, that you have the use of your reason. This is a greater mercy than your afflictions, that you have the use of your limbs, your senses; that you have the health of your bodies. Health of body is a greater mercy than poverty is an affliction; there is no man that is rich but if he be wise, if he hath a sickly body, he would part with all his riches that he might have his health. Therefore thy mercies are more than thy afflictions.

✦ JEREMIAH BURROUGHS
Rare Jewel, 65

Compare thy mercies and afflictions together. Have not mercies flowed in upon thee like a flood, whereas afflictions have fallen upon thee but like drops? For one affliction, thou hast had an hundred mercies.

✦ SAMUEL CRADOCK
Knowledge and Practice, part 2,
chap. 5, 27

There is a threefold mercy in God: preventing mercy, which steps between us and trouble; delivering mercy, which takes us out of the hand of trouble; and sparing mercy, which though it do not prevent nor deliver, yet it mitigates, allays, and graciously moderates our troubles. And though sparing mercy be desirable and sweet, yet it is the least and lowest sort of mercy that God exercises toward any.

✦ JOHN FLAVEL
Sacramental Meditations, 106

It was a great mercy that Hannah had after her many prayers and long waiting, a son; but a greater that she had a heart to give up her son again to God, who gave him to her. To have estate, health, or any other enjoyment upon waiting on God for the same is mercy, but not to be compared with that blessing which sanctifies the heart to use them for God's glory.

✦ WILLIAM GURNALL
Christian in Complete Armour, 535–36

He is the most thankful man that treasures up the mercies of God in his memory and can feed his faith with what God hath done for him, so as to walk in the strength thereof in present straits. When Job was on the dunghill, he forgot not God's old kindnesses, but durst trust Him with a knife at his throat: "Though He kill me, yet will I trust in Him." He that distrusts God after former experience is like the foolish builder (Matt. 7:26); he rears his monument for past mercies on the sand, which the next tide of affliction washes away.

✦ WILLIAM GURNALL
Christian in Complete Armour, 739

Mercies come from God as returns of prayer, when they make you more to rejoice in the God that hears your prayers and gives you the mercy than in the mercy you receive from God.

✦ CHRISTOPHER LOVE
Zealous Christian, 89

It must be considered that God many times gets glory by the denials of His people; yea, He gets more glory by denying than by the granting of a mercy. And if the denying of a mercy to thee be the way to advance God's glory, it is better that God should have His glory and thou be without the mercy than that thou should have the mercy and God want His glory.

✦ CHRISTOPHER LOVE
Zealous Christian, 93

Mercy in us is a sign of our interest in God's mercy.

✦ THOMAS MANTON
Practical Exposition on the
Epistle of James, 100

Many love their deliverance, but not their deliverer; God is to be loved more than His mercies.

✦ THOMAS WATSON
Godly Man's Picture, 119

MINISTRY

The work [of ministry] is so high and miscarrying in it is of such dreadful consequence that no one should be resolvedly devoted to the ministry who hath not the following endowments. (1) A good natural capacity. It should be somewhat above the ordinary degree. Grace supposes nature, and by sanctifying it turns it the right way but does not use to make wise teachers of natural drones or weak-headed lads who have not sense enough to learn. (2) A competent readiness of speech. One who cannot readily speak his mind in common things is not likely to have that fluent delivery which is necessary to a preacher. (3) He must be hopeful for godliness. He must be captivated by no gross sin. He must not only have a love to learning but religion; to the word of God and good company; to prayer and good books. He must show that he has a serious concern about his soul and the life to come; that his conscience is under some effectual convictions of the evil of sin and the excellence and necessity of a godly life. The youth that hath not these qualifications should not be devoted to the ministry.

✦ RICHARD BAXTER
Appendix: "Hints of Advice to Students,"
in *Reformed Pastor*, 224–25

A man may be a fit minister of Christ yet not meet for every congregation. Few so qualified: a mild and a soft spirit to a meek company; a low voice to a little auditory, else some few hear and the rest must stand and gaze; an undauntable mind to stubborn persons; a loud voice to a great assembly; to a more learned church a better clerk, and one of less understanding to a ruder sort. Join like unto like, that pastor and flock may fit together for their best good. The congregation reaps small benefit where the preacher's gifts fit not for the place. Therefore, as we must have conscience to enter into the ministry rightly, so must we be very respective to settle ourselves with a people conveniently for our best comfort and their more edification.

✦ RICHARD BERNARD
Faithful Shepherd, 7

Consider we that to be wanting to our duty in reference to the souls of men committed to our care is to betray a trust. To murder a man though a stranger, though an enemy, for the preserving of whose life no other obligation lay upon you but what is common to all men, even this were a horrid sin. But if the person were committed to your care and protection, if you were by your superiors required to safeguard and preserve him, and if you had also freely taken upon you this trust and promised to use your best endeavors to secure him from danger, and yet after all this you should be the man that should lay violent hands on him and murder him or betray him to be murdered by another, this were such an aggravation of the sin as greater could not be. This is our very case: if souls committed to our care and charge shall perish and everlastingly miscarry through our unfaithfulness, we contract to ourselves not only the guilt of soul murder but also of treachery and of the violation of a trust.... But alas! How little do some of our calling [i.e., the ministry] mind them or take them to heart!

✦ JOHN CONANT
Sermon 1 on 2 Cor. 5:1, in
Sermons, 24–26

Build in God's way. Expect not to see the happiness of the church by man-pleasing or flattery; this fabric will not stand if it be daubed with untempered mortar. Be faithful to the souls of men, though in so doing you displease them. Still aim at holiness; be always pressing forward toward perfection. So shall the counsel of peace at last be established.

✦ RICHARD GILPIN
Temple Rebuilt, 40

MIRACLES

A miracle is an operation above the order appointed whence true miracles do always give evidence of the omnipotency of the doer. Hence God only is the author of true miracles.

✦ WILLIAM AMES
Marrow of Sacred Divinity, 47

Those who know the infinite sovereignty, power, and wisdom of God will not tie Him to means, much less dictate as to any particular means. But on the other hand, they that understand God's usual and ordinary way of acting, governing, and upholding the world will not tie Him up from means, no, nor expect that He should appear for their relief immediately and miraculously. Though if anyone have a miraculous faith, truly grounded upon some special and particular promise, I will not contend with him; only I would desire to see his miraculous faith justified by some miraculous works, which I conceive always attend it.

✦ SAMUEL SHAW
Voice of One Crying in the Wilderness, 87

God does not always bind miracles to faith nor faith to miracles; He will sometimes be believed without them and sometimes spends them upon unbelievers.

✦ RALPH VENNING
Canaan's Flowings, 140

MISSIONS/MISSIONARIES

No part of my prayers are so deeply serious as that for the conversion of the infidel and ungodly world, that God's name may be sanctified and His kingdom come and His will be done on earth as it is in heaven; nor was I ever before so sensible what a plague the division of languages was, which hinders our speaking to them for their conversion; nor what a great sin tyranny is, which keeps out the gospel from most of the nations of the world. Could we but go among Tartarians, Turks, and heathens and speak their language, I should be but little troubled for the silencing of eighteen hundred ministers at once in England, nor for all the rest that were cast out here and in Scotland and Ireland, there being no employment in the world so desirable in my eyes as to labor for the winning of such miserable souls.

✦ RICHARD BAXTER
Baxteriana, 57

A selfish, private, narrow soul brings little honor to the cause of God. It is always taken up about itself or imprisoned in a corner in the dark, to the interest of some sect or party and seeth not how things go in the world; its desires and prayers and endeavors go no further than they can see or travel. But a larger soul beholds all the earth and is desirous to know how it goes with the cause and servants of the Lord and how the gospel gets ground upon the unbelieving nations, and such are affected with the state of the church a thousand miles off, almost as if it were at hand, as being members of the whole body of Christ and not only of a sect. They pray for the hallowing of God's name, and the coming of His kingdom, and the doing of His will throughout the earth, as it is in heaven before they come to their own necessities, at least in order of esteem and desire. The prosperity of themselves or their party or country satisfies them not while the church abroad is in distress.

✦ RICHARD BAXTER
A Christian Directory, in
Practical Works, 2:456–57

MODERATION

God grant we may hit the golden mean and endeavor to avoid all extremes — the fanatic Anabaptist on the one side and the fiery zeal of the Jesuit on the other, that so we may be true Protestants, or, which is a far better name, real Christians indeed.

✦ THOMAS FULLER
Good Thoughts, 355

Use a moderation in (the use of) meat, drink, and apparel for the quantity, the quality, and the fashionableness; that it be not too much, too rich or costly, nor too conformable to the world and garish, but always within the bounds of religion, reason, your estate, calling, degree, and condition of life — never beyond. But alas! The devil, pride, and self have so blinded all sorts and ranks of men and women and almost all of all sorts that our eyes are almost out, that

we cannot see wood for trees but take one for another, vice for virtue.

✦ THOMAS MOCKET
Christian Advice, 107

We should moderate our desires here and use the world as if we used it not (1 Cor. 7:31). We may as Jonathan dip the end of the rod in honey, but not thrust it in too far; in this sense moderation is good. But moderation in matters of practical piety is sinful; it is contrary to offering violence. Moderation, in the world's sense, is for one not to be too zealous, not to be too fierce for heaven. Moderation is not to venture further in religion than may stand with self-preservation.

✦ THOMAS WATSON
Christian Soldier, 87

MODESTY

As any man is more worthful, he is more modest. Full vessels yield no such sound as empty casks do.

✦ JOHN TRAPP
*Commentary ... upon ... the
New Testament*, 728

MONASTICISM

There is a generation of men that under a pretense of watching and praying always betake themselves to their cloisters and renounce all secular employment, as if it were as easy to put off the world as to change their clothes; but the world hath found those places commonly to have proved not houses to pray in but dens to draw their prey into. It is more likely that those who are pampered with sloth and fullness of bread should be eaten up with luxury and sensuality than with zeal and devotion.

✦ WILLIAM GURNALL
Christian in Complete Armour, 766–67

While the hands of the pious tradesman are employed in the common business of life, his heart will be aspiring to God and delighting itself in His perfections, word, and works. As no ship is so laden but it will contain many jewels more, so no business can so constantly fill up our minds as not to allow of serious intervening thoughts. There is no need to retire to a cloister in order to preserve a religious disposition of mind or lead a virtuous life.

✦ RICHARD STEELE
Religious Tradesman, 206–7

MORALISM

There is a specific difference between moral virtues and divine, or holiness of truth. True holiness has all morality in it, but all that is called moral may be without true holiness, nor will ever rise to it.

✦ ELISHA COLES
Practical Discourse, 229

Moral virtues arise from the soil of nature. There have been eminent moralists among the heathen. Some parts of the earth bring forth not only weeds but vines and mines, and so the nature of man may bring forth with vices, virtues too. There are some sparkles, since Adam, of the law in the conscience of natural men about…what's just and good. They have a natural divinity. And moral virtues are good and very good in their kind, but not so good as to have any place in the reason of a man's justification before God. Neither is this a disparagement to morality to say it cannot justify any more than it is to brass to say it is not current coin and can pay no debts; for though it be not good for this, yet it is good in its kind. Moral virtues are lovely in their sphere. Our blessed Savior loved that young man for his ingenuousness. But yet justification is not the orb where moral virtues move, and therefore know that good works done by the light of nature, or common grace, though good in their matter, they may be very bad in their manner and ends.

✦ OBADIAH GREW
Sinner's Justification, 18–19

They [i.e., mere moralists] are by this moral honesty profitable to those that have civil commerce with them, but it doth not render themselves acceptable to God. Indeed, had not God left some authority of conscience to awe and keep them that have no grace within some bounds of honesty, this world would have been no more habitable for the saints than the forest of wild beasts is now for man. Such is the uprightness of men void of sanctifying grace, that they are rather rid by an overpowering light of conscience that scares them than sweetly led by any inward principle inclining them to take complacency in that which is good.

✦ WILLIAM GURNALL
Christian in Complete Armour, 227

[A] word of caution is to those that are morally upright, and no more. Take heed this uprightness proves not a snare to thee and keeps thee from getting evangelical uprightness. I am sure it was so to the young man in the gospel [the rich young ruler, Matt. 19:16–22]. In all likelihood he might have been better had he not been so good.

◆ WILLIAM GURNALL
Christian in Complete Armour, 229

Holiness enlightens a man to look on the same sins which morality and civility discover with another and a clearer aspect, since while the civil person only abhors them as enemies to his good name, and the moralist as repugnant to reason, the holy man loathes them as breaches of God's law and offenses to His majesty; for so repenting David (Ps. 51:4) and the returning prodigal (Luke 15:21) looked upon their sins as against and before God.

◆ NATHANIEL HARDY
First General Epistle of St. John, 67

It's possible that a man may outwardly reform some things and yet be in a very sick condition still. A man may be better than he was, and yet far short of a good condition. A man may be less wicked than he was, and yet not at all truly good in the sight of God....

A man may part with some one sin to make more sea room for some other sin. Though all lusts are from the devil and lead to the devil and all are contrary to holiness, yet there is some opposition between one lust and another so that one cannot act vigorously unless another which opposes it be brought under. Prodigality is contrary to covetousness, etc....

A man may leave some sins because he hath not ability or opportunity to commit them as before. The prodigal man hath so far wasted his estate that he hath not ability to be so wasteful as before. The adulterer hath so impaired his health and strength that he is not able to act his sin as he did before. A thief may have reformed his thievery because he hath not that opportunity to purloin as he had before; he is better watched than he was.

◆ RALPH ROBINSON
Christ All and in All, 118–19

Morality and Christianity differ especially. The moralist works from nature, a little refined by study or education; the Christian from nature thoroughly renewed by the Holy Ghost. Where this spring is wanting, no motion can be true; be the fruit never so fair to the eye, if the root whence it grows be not good, it will be unpleasant and distasteful. Laban at the last was just in his agreement with Jacob, but shame, not conscience, was the curb that held him in. Such dealings, like fruits which are ripened by art and force, are not kindly, neither be they acceptable to the heavenly taste. Indeed, all such righteousness is unrighteousness, and all such persons, though they are just to men and do them no wrong, yet are unjust to God and deprive Him of His right.

◆ GEORGE SWINNOCK
The Christian Man's Calling,
in *Works*, 2:216

The heart is apt to deceive about this work of salvation two ways. First, it will often make a man take morality for grace. Alas, morality is but nature refined, old Adam put in a better dress. A moralized man is but a tame devil. There may be a fair stream of civility running, and yet much vermin of pride and atheism lie at the bottom; the garnishment of moral excellency is but the setting a garland of flowers upon a dead man.

✦ THOMAS WATSON
"The One Thing Necessary,"
in *Discourses*, 1:353

MORTIFICATION

Christians! How doth it concern you to stand upon your watchtower! You have enemies within you. If a city was besieged by foreign armies, would the citizens harbor traitors within their walls? Nay, would they not put them to death for their own safety? You have within you a host of treacherous enemies, and these seek all occasions to betray you into the devil's hands. Is it not high time for us all to mortify the flesh with its affections and lusts and to implore the aid and assistance of God's Spirit, to mortify our bosom traitors and murderers? These are in some respects more dangerous than the devil himself because they are within us. They open the door to let the enemy in. Satan can do nothing till your bosom sins betray you into his hands. He can never force you to sin but must first gain your consent. Oh, then, how

carefully should you watch over your own hearts and live in prayer!

✦ ISAAC AMBROSE
Christian Warrior, 4

Use sin, as it will use you. Spare it not, for it will not spare you. It is your murderer and the murderer of the world; use it therefore as a murderer should be used. Kill it before it kills you, and then though it kill your bodies, it shall not be able to kill your souls. And though it bring you to the grave, as it did your head, it shall not be able to keep you there.

✦ RICHARD BAXTER
Baxteriana, 39

It is an argument of a spirit not brought down to the lot [i.e., not humbled by affliction] when men are damped and sunk under the hardships of it, as if their condition in the world were the point whereon their happiness turned. It is want of mortification that makes men's comforts to wax and wane, ebb and flow according to the various appearances of their lot in the world.

✦ THOMAS BOSTON
Crook in the Lot, 94

Look upon a rabbit's skin, how well it comes off till it comes to the head, but then what hauling and pulling is there before it stirs! So it is in the mortifying, in the crucifying of sin. A man may easily subdue and mortify such and such sins, but when it comes to the head sin, to the master sin, to the bosom sin, O what tugging and pulling is there, what striving and struggling is there, to get off that sin, to get down that sin!

✦ THOMAS BROOKS
Great Gain, 100

It is sad to consider how few professors in these days have attained the right way of mortifying sin. They usually go out against their sins in the strength of their own purposes, prayers, and resolutions and scarcely look so high as a crucified Christ. They mind not the exercise of their faith upon Christ, and therefore it is a righteous thing with Christ that after all they should be carried away captive by their sins. Nothing eats out sin like the actings of grace; nothing weakens and wastes the strength of sin like the exercise of grace. O did men believe more in Christ, sin would die more. Did they believe the threatenings more, sin would die more. Did they believe the promises more, sin would die more. Did they believe in reigning with Christ more, sin would die more.

✦ THOMAS BROOKS
The Unsearchable Riches of Christ,
in *Select Works*, 1:160

Of all Christians, none so mortified as those in whom grace is most exercised. Sin is a viper that must be killed or it will kill you forever, and there is no way to kill it but by the exercise of grace.

✦ THOMAS BROOKS
The Unsearchable Riches of Christ,
in *Select Works*, 1:179

The original word [*mortify*] signifies to slay, to pursue to death. Sin is not at once slain—it gets a death stroke by the first saving work of grace. It never recovers that, but yet it dies but lingeringly, therefore called a crucifixion, and it is a great part of the Christian's exercise to follow it to death, to be driving nails into it, and keep it bleeding till it expire.

✦ ALEXANDER CARMICHAEL
Believer's Mortification of Sin, 4

A...false way [of mortification] is the letting of sin die alone or of itself, as youthful lusts, vanity, prodigality, and revenge. Either sin kills thee or thou must kill it; but when it dies alone, it is an evidence that it has undone thee—and now, like a victorious champion, it dies in peace on its bed and is not vanquished by thee. O sinner, shall thine enemy die in peace? Wilt thou not pursue it to death and be avenged on it for thy two eyes, for thy two hands—for all the miseries, sorrows, and woes that it has wrought thee?

✦ ALEXANDER CARMICHAEL
Believer's Mortification of Sin, 10–11

Mortification may be either actively or passively considered. Considered actively, it is a work of the Spirit whereby the soul strives not only to beat down the motions and stirrings of every sin but endeavors to destroy the body of it and to slay it in the root thereof, which in some measure every believer effects. Mortification passively considered lies in a deadness of the whole man toward things forbidden and in some sense also to things lawful. The soul is taken off from sinful objects and from inordinate appetite of lawful objects.... Mortification actively considered lies not in unconstant, uneven, and flashy fits of indignation and opposition against some sin, as some take vengeance upon some sins and spare their prime lust, as Saul did the king of the Amalekites; but it is a constant and daily warring of the soul against great and small, especially against our idol lusts, wherein the man not only endeavors to destroy the love of sin and delight in it but the very being of it.

✦ ALEXANDER CARMICHAEL
Believer's Mortification of Sin, 13

They deserve reproof who think to mortify sin by their own endeavors or by mere mortal means. No endeavors, no duties, no consideration of sin's opposition to and inconsistency with our happiness, without the influence of the Spirit, can mortify any one sin. The apostle's manner of urging this great duty deserves a remark. On the one hand, he will not have people think that the Spirit was to do all and they nothing or that they are to be merely passive in the business of mortification: "If ye through the Spirit do mortify the deeds of the body, ye shall live." And on the other hand, he will not have them think that there is any power in them to mortify sin but that it is through the Spirit; it is the Spirit's special work.

✦ ALEXANDER CARMICHAEL
Believer's Mortification of Sin, 85

I mentioned the serious consideration of your own death as a mean to help on mortification. It were good for us were we oftener among the tombs and laying ourselves in our graves. The rich man's skull is not gilded there, nor has the delicate person any better color or smell, nor has the proud man any precedency there. Their dust and skulls and dead bones are not distinguished, yet what is the business and labor of most unmortified souls but to adorn or pamper or honor this corruptible, sinful, and burdensome flesh? We never live like Christians till we can trample upon it, and it be under our soul's feet, and till we live as if we were next moment to die, and till we deal with sin as we would do when a-dying.

✦ ALEXANDER CARMICHAEL
Believer's Mortification of Sin, 116–17

Watchfulness is of singular use to such as would be successful in this business of mortification. You must fight with sin ere ye can mortify it, for sin is not so tame as to make no resistance.

✦ ALEXANDER CARMICHAEL
Believer's Mortification of Sin, 117

To return when the Spirit makes intercession in thee or helps thee to make intercession with groans which cannot be uttered, let these groans be against sin rather than for divine comforts; groan rather for redemption from sin than from any other misery.

✦ ALEXANDER CARMICHAEL
Believer's Mortification of Sin, 166

If any ask, then, "How shall we purpose and engage against sin so as we may be disentangled from it and effectually get it mortified?" Answer: (1) Be sure ye be sincere in them. (2) Be sure your affections concur with your judgment, else they will entangle you. Yet, (3) see that ye be also deliberate and that your resolutions and engagements against such a lust be not only from the present heat of affections. (4) Strive to keep such a frame as ye had when ye engaged, that fear of God and hatred of sin ye then had; and be often thinking on your engagements, humbling yourselves for the least breaches of them. (5) Take in the Spirit's assistance in your purposes and endeavors. (6) If one engagement bind not strongly enough, we must renew and multiply them. "If one knot hold not," says one, "we must cast more that we may never want some bond over our head."

✦ ALEXANDER CARMICHAEL
Believer's Mortification of Sin, 207

Mortify your inordinate affections to earthly things. This makes providences that deprive and cross us so heavy. Mortify your opinion and affection, and you sensibly lighten your affliction. It is a strong affection that makes strong affliction. Dwell much upon the meditation of the Lord's near approach, and then all these things will seem but trifles to you. "Let your moderation be known unto all men; the Lord is at hand." Exercise heavenly-mindedness and keep your hearts upon things eternal under all the providences with which the Lord exercises you in this world.

✦ JOHN FLAVEL
Divine Conduct, 145

Severity to sin is mercy to the soul.

✦ WILLIAM JENKYN
Exposition upon the Epistle of Jude, 353

One great point of our mortification lies in this: to have our wills melted into God's. And it is a great token of spiritual growth when we are not only content but joyful to see our wills crossed that His may be done. When our wills are [the] sacrifice of holy prayer, we many times receive choicer things than we ask expressly.

✦ SAMUEL LEE
Most Spiritual Profit, 77

To mortify... "If ye put to death": A metaphorical expression taken from the putting of any living thing to death. To kill a man or any other living thing is to take away the principle of all his strength, vigor, and power so that he cannot act or exert or put forth any proper actings of his own; so it is in this case. Indwelling sin is compared to a person, a living person, called the old man, with his faculties and properties; his wisdom, craft, subtlety, strength. This, says the apostle, must be killed, put to death, mortified— that is, have its power, life, vigor, and strength to produce its effects taken away by the Spirit.

✦ JOHN OWEN
Of the Mortification of Sin in Believers, in *Works*, 6:8

The choicest believers who are assuredly freed from the condemning power of sin ought yet to make it their business all their days to mortify the indwelling power of sin. So the apostle: "Mortify therefore your members which are upon the earth" (Col. 3:5). Whom speaks he to? Such as were "risen with Christ" (v. 1); such as were "dead" with Him (v. 3); such as whose life Christ was and who should "appear with him in glory" (v. 4). Do you mortify. Do you make it your daily work. Be always at it while you live. Cease not a day from this work. Be killing sin, or it will be killing you.

✦ JOHN OWEN
Of the Mortification of Sin in
Believers, in Works, 6:9

Sin does not only still abide in us but is still acting, still laboring to bring forth the deeds of the flesh. When sin lets us alone we may let sin alone, but as sin is never less quiet than when it seems to be most quiet, and its waters are for the most part deep when they are still, so ought our contrivances against it to be vigorous at all times and in all conditions, even where there is least suspicion.

✦ JOHN OWEN
Of the Mortification of Sin in
Believers, in Works, 6:11

[A] means of mortification is detestation, or utter hatred, of sin as it is sin.... "Ye that love the Lord hate evil," saith the psalmist, for hatred is a stabbing, murdering affection. It pursues sin with a hot heart to death, as an avenger of blood, of the blood of the soul which sin would spill and of the blood of Christ which sin hath shed. Hate sin perfectly and perpetually, then you will not spare it; but kill it presently. Till sin be hated it cannot be mortified; you will not cry against it as the Jews did against Christ, "Crucify it, Crucify it"; but show indulgence to it, as David did to Absalom, and say, "Deal gently with the young man, with this or that lust, for my sake." Mercy to sin is cruelty to the soul.

✦ EDWARD REYNER
Precepts for Christian Practice, 17

God is forced to mortify our sin by afflictions because we will not mortify them by the Spirit in the use of holy means. A gracious God gives us favors from His own tenderest love, but corrections are always forced, though very necessary for our soul's good.

✦ RICHARD SIBBES
Divine Meditations and Holy
Contemplations, 67

MOURNING

Such [believers growing in grace] will mourn for wicked men's sins as well as their own. O the tears, the sighs, the groans that others' sins fetch from these men's hearts (Ps. 119:136; Jer. 9:1–2; 2 Peter 2:7–9)!

✦ THOMAS BROOKS
The Unsearchable Riches of Christ,
in Select Works, 1:190

The more holy any is, the more he is grieved and afflicted for the sin of others; and the more tender any man is, he is pierced with beholding the miseries that lie upon others.

✦ JOHN FLAVEL
Fountain of Life, 175

It is not hard to observe that the more holy any person is, the more he is afflicted with others' sin. Lot vexed his righteous soul with the unclean conversation of the Sodomites; David's eyes gushed out rivers of water because men kept not the law. Those who can look with dry and undispleased eyes upon another's sin never truly mourned for their own.

✦ JOSEPH HALL
Select Thoughts, in *Select Tracts*, 364

There is a habitual mourning frame of spirit required in us, and we may do well to search ourselves about it, whether it is maintained and kept up or no. Whether worldly security and carnal joys do not devour it. For spiritual joys will not do it. Spiritual joys will take off nothing from spiritual mourning, but worldly security and carnal joy and pleasures will devour that frame of spirit.

✦ JOHN OWEN
Discourse 6 on 1 Cor. 11:28,
in *Twenty-Five Discourses*, 109

There is a diabolical mourning, and that is twofold: (1) When a man mourns that he cannot satisfy his impure lust; this is like the devil, whose great torture is that he can be no more wicked. Thus Amnon mourned and was sick till he had defiled his sister Tamar (2 Sam. 13:2). Thus Ahab mourned for Naboth's vineyard: "He laid him down upon his bed, and turned away his face, and would eat no bread" (1 Kings 21:4); this was a devilish mourning. (2) When men are sorry for the good that they have done. Pharaoh grieved that he had let the children of Israel go (Ex. 14:5). Many are so devilish that they are troubled they have prayed so much and have heard so many sermons; they repent of their repentance. But if we repent of the good which is past, God will not repent of the evil which is to come.

✦ THOMAS WATSON
The Beatitudes, in *Discourses*, 2:85

Gospel mourning is spiritual—that is, when we mourn for sin more than suffering. Pharaoh said, "Take away the plague"; he never thought of the plague of his heart. A sinner mourns because judgment follows at the heel of sin, but David cries out, "My sin is ever before me" (Ps. 51[:3]). God had threatened that the sword should ride in circuit in his family, but David doth not say, "The sword is ever before me," but "My sin is ever before me." The offense against God troubled him; he grieved more for the treason than the bloody axe. Thus the penitent prodigal [says in] Luke 15:21, "I have sinned against heaven, and in thy sight." He doth not say, "I am almost starved among the husks, but I have offended my father. In particular, our mourning for sin, if it be spiritual, must be under this threefold notion. (1) We must mourn for sin, as

it is an act of hostility and enmity....
(2) We must mourn for sin, as it is a
piece of the highest ingratitude; it is a
kicking against the breasts of mercy....
(3) We must mourn for sin, as it is a
privation; it keeps good things from us.
It hinders our communion with God.

✦ THOMAS WATSON
The Beatitudes, in *Discourses,* 2:89–90

MURMURING

Murmuring is no better than mutiny in
the heart; it is a rising up against God.
When the sea is rough and unquiet, it
casts forth nothing but foam. When
the heart is discontented, it casts
forth the foam of anger, impatience,
and sometimes little better than blasphemy. Murmuring is nothing else but
the scum which boils off from a discontented heart.

✦ SIMEON ASHE
Primitive Divinity, 35–36

Our murmuring is the devil's music;
this is that sin which God cannot bear:
"How long shall I bear with this people
that murmur against me?" ([see] Num.
14:11). It is a sin which whets the
sword against a people.

✦ SIMEON ASHE
Primitive Divinity, 99

Ah, what murmuring is there against
God! What murmuring against instruments and what murmuring against
providences is to be found among us?
Some murmur at what they have lost,
others murmur at what they fear they
shall lose; some murmur that they are
no higher, others murmur because they
are so low; some murmur because such
a party rules, and others mutter because
themselves are not in the saddle; some
murmur because their mercies are not
so many as others, and others murmur
because their mercies are not so as others are; some murmur because they are
afflicted, and others murmur because
such and such are not afflicted as well
as they. Ah, England! England! Hadst
thou no more sins upon thee, thy murmuring were enough to undo thee did
not God exercise much pity and compassion toward thee.

✦ THOMAS BROOKS
Mute Christian, 75

Murmuring is but as the smoke of the
fire; there is first a smoke and smother
before the flame breaks forth, and so
before open rebellion in a kingdom
there is first a smoke of murmuring,
and then it breaks forth into open
rebellion; but because it hath rebellion in the seeds of it, therefore it
is accounted before the Lord to be
rebellion.

✦ JEREMIAH BURROUGHS
Rare Jewel, 54

Murmuring is a sin betwixt secret
backbiting and open railing, a smoth-
ered malice which can neither utterly
be concealed nor dare openly be vented.

✦ NEHEMIAH ROGERS
"The Watchful Shepherd," in
True Convert, 85

Men murmur at God's providences
because they distrust His promises.

✦ THOMAS WATSON
Lord's Prayer, 167

Murmuring is the scum which boils off from a discontented heart.

✦ THOMAS WATSON
Mischief of Sin, 41

THE NATION

Peace [within the nation] is the mother of prosperity, but prosperity is too often the murderer of peace. For peace breeds wealth, wealth breeds pride, pride breeds contention, and contention kills peace.

✦ THOMAS ADAMS
"The City of Peace," in *Sermons*, 20

Can you say when you come into the presence of God in secret, not only your own but others' sins affect your heart? You know God is as eminently dishonored in this nation [i.e., England] as He has been in most nations of the world; as notorious, desperate sinning against light and against the goodness of God as almost any people have been guilty of; greater breach of covenant, sinning against light, despight [i.e., uncountable things] done to the Spirit of grace. Slighting of and neglecting of the gospel of Christ has scarce been found among a people for many years.

✦ THOMAS BLAKE
Living Truths in Dying Times, 90

There are no such blessings in the world to parishes, cities, and nations as those souls are that are rich in grace. O, they are great blessings to all places where they come. They are persons who are fit for the highest and noblest employments. There is not the highest work that is too high for a man that is rich in grace, not the hottest work that is too hot for a man rich in grace, nor the lowest work below a man rich in grace. Such a man will not say, "I would do it, but that it is below my place, my blood, my parts, my education." "May Christ have honor? May others have good? If so, I will do it," says the soul that is rich in grace, "whatever comes of it, and bless God for the opportunity."

✦ THOMAS BROOKS
The Unsearchable Riches of Christ,
in *Select Works*, 1:218

Generally active nations are strongest abroad and weakest at home.

✦ SAMUEL CLARK
Saint's Nosegay, 139

I confess, beloved, I discern there are very many with whom you shall never talk but they are complaining of the miserableness of our days. Oh, the times are miserable! What glorious times had we three or four years or five or seven years ago, for then they had trading, plenty, and ease, and everyone could sit under his own vine and his fig tree, no adversary nor evil occurrent; and now they hear of nothing but war and blood and exhausting of treasure and loss of their children and kindred and plundering their good everywhere, so that there is nothing but complaining among a world of people, as if our days were most miserable. Now, beloved, give me leave to speak my thoughts freely: I will set aside my text and the matter I am in hand with, and yet I will confidently affirm that our days now are better than they were seven years ago because it is better to see the Lord executing judgment than to see men working wickedness, and to behold a people lie wallowing in their blood rather than [apostatizing] from God and embracing of idolatry and superstition and banishing of the Lord Christ from among them.

✦ STEPHEN MARSHALL
Sacred Panegyrick, 18

I beseech you, make England a happy nation, and though many have deserted you, be not dismayed. I tell you their names shall be written in the dust when yours shall be written in letters of gold, and the generations to come shall say that these glorious walls of Jerusalem were built in a troublesome time, these foundations of God's house were laid and the building reared up in times of calamity, but blessed be God for such Lords, for such Commons, which would not be taken off. Carry on the work still, leave not a rag that belongs to popery, lay not a bit of the Lord's building with anything that belongs to antichrist or antichrist's stuff; but away with all of it—root and branch, head and tail—throw it out of the kingdom. And resolve not to leave till you can say, "Now Christ is set upon His throne and England is subdued to Him," and the good Lord carry you on to do so.

✦ STEPHEN MARSHALL
Sacred Panegyrick, 21

Mourn for the pride of the nation; our condition is low, but our hearts are high. Mourn for the profaneness of the land; Britain is like that man in the gospel who had "a spirit of an unclean devil" (Luke 4:33). Mourn for the removing of landmarks. Mourn for the contempt offered to magistracy, the spitting in the face of authority. Mourn that there are so few mourners; surely if we mourn not for the sin of others, it is to be feared we are not sensible of our own sins. God looks upon us as guilty of those sins in others which we do not lament; our tears may help to quench God's wrath.

✦ THOMAS WATSON
The Beatitudes, in *Discourses*, 2:97–98

NATURAL/GENERAL REVELATION

By natural theology, that all may understand, I mean that knowledge of God and our duty to Him which the light of nature may lead man up to and which is concreat [i.e., perceptible to his senses] with his soul. The image of God upon man in his first creation consisted in knowledge as well as holiness; and the knowledge Adam had of his Creator was partly by the character of His being engraven upon his soul, which is by some styled *verbum*, an implanted word, and partly by what the large power of his intellectual faculty might gather from the works of creation, by both which he was led to God as his ultimate end. Now the light of nature, as it is now found in man, is…the dark and weak remainders of this image still, which the apostle saith the heathens had, who had nothing of the *verbum*, or the external word, either by writing or any other way of revelation.

✦ MATTHEW BARKER
Natural Theology, 4

It is matter of natural revelation that there is a God; that He is infinite in His immensity and eternity, in His power, wisdom, and goodness; that He is the first cause and ultimate end of all things; that He is the preserver and overruling disposer of all things and the supreme governor of the rational world and the great benefactor of all mankind and the special favorer and rewarder of such as truly love Him, seek Him, and obey Him; also that the soul of man is immortal; and that there is a life of reward or punishment to come, and that this life is but preparatory unto that; that man is bound to love God His maker and serve Him with all his heart and might and to believe that his labor is not vain; that we must do our best to know God's will that we may do it. This, with much more, is of natural revelation, which infidels may know.

✦ RICHARD BAXTER
A Christian Directory, in
Practical Works, 2:172–73

There are three lights which God hath afforded to the heathen: the light of creation (Rom. 1:19–20); the light of righteousness, which the schools call synteresin; the light of a natural conscience (Rom. 2:15). Now although these be true lights, yet they are not sufficient lights. They make a discovery of a Godhead unto men (Rom. 1:19–20); they discover so much to men as to leave them without excuse (v. 20). But they cannot discover a Savior to man.

✦ RALPH ROBINSON
Christ All and in All, 159

NATURE/CREATION, BOOK OF

What an excellent book is the visible world for the daily study of a holy soul! Light is not more visible to the eye in the sun than the goodness of God is in it and all the creatures to the mind. If I love not God when all the world reveals His loveliness and every creature tells me that He is good, what a blind and wicked heart have I! O wonderful wisdom and goodness and power which appears in everything we see, in every tree and plant and flower; in every bird and beast and fish; in every worm and fly and creeping thing; in every part of the body of man or beast, much more in the admirable composure of the whole; in the sun and moon and stars and meteors; in the lightning and thunder, the air and winds, the rain and waters, the heat and cold, the fire and the earth, especially in the composed frame of all so far as we can see them set together; in the admirable order and cooperation of all things; in their times and seasons and the wonderful usefulness of all for man. O how glorious is the power and wisdom and goodness of God in all the frame of nature!

✦ RICHARD BAXTER
A Christian Directory, in
Practical Works, 2:377

As Noah, when the deluge of waters had defaced the great book of nature, had a copy of every kind of creature in that famous library of the ark, out of which all were reprinted to the world, so he that hath God hath the original copy of all blessings, out of which if all were perished all might easily be restored.

♦ SAMUEL CLARK
Saint's Nosegay, 69

The great book of the creation had lain long enough open before the world's eyes, yet they could never come to the saving knowledge of God by all that divine wisdom which is written with the finger of God in every page thereof; therefore, it pleased God to send His servant that by preaching the gospel, poor souls might believe on Christ, and believing might be saved. No doctrine but the gospel can save a soul.

♦ WILLIAM GURNALL
Christian in Complete Armour, 807

We should…make use of natural and apply them to spiritual things. If we see a lily, think of God's promise and our duty, we should grow as lilies. When we see a tall tree, think "I must grow higher in grace," and when we see a vine, think "I must grow in fruitfulness." When we go into our fields, orchards, or gardens, let the eye raise the thoughts higher, unto consideration of what is required and of what is promised in God's holy word.

♦ RICHARD SIBBES
Divine Meditations and Holy Contemplations, 117

God hath given us three books which we ought to be studying while we are living: the book of conscience, the book of Scripture, and the book of the creature; in the book of conscience we may read ourselves, in the book of the creature we may read God, in the book of Scripture we may read both God and ourselves. The great God sets us excellent lectures in the volume of the creation; though this book hath but three leaves in it—heaven, earth, sea—yet it teacheth us many rare lessons.

♦ GEORGE SWINNOCK
The Christian Man's Calling,
in *Works,* 2:417

It was an honest speech of a monk who being asked how he could endure that life without the pleasure of books answered, "The nature of the creatures is my library, wherein, when I please, I can muse upon God's deep oracles."

♦ GEORGE SWINNOCK
The Christian Man's Calling,
in *Works,* 2:421

Study much the works and especially the word of God. The works of God are a book wherein you may read of Him and by which you may hear of Him. "The heavens declare the glory of God" (Ps. 19:1); "The earth is full of the goodness of the LORD" (Ps. 33:5). As the shadow hath some proportion to the body to which it relates, so the works of God are some representation of the wise, powerful, gracious God to whom they belong. "The invisible things of him from the creation of the world are clearly seen, being understood by the things that are made, even his eternal power and Godhead" (Rom. 1:[20]); therefore consider the works of the Lord and the operations of His hands.

✦ GEORGE SWINNOCK
The Incomparableness of God,
in *Works,* 4:489

A godly ancient being asked by a profane philosopher how he could contemplate high things since he had no books wisely answered that he had the whole world for his book, ready open at all times and in all places and that therein he could read things divine and heavenly. A bee can suck honey out of a flower that a fly cannot do.

✦ JOHN TRAPP
Commentary…upon…the
New Testament, 129

NEW BIRTH

Hence appears the difference of the first and second birth—the first birth is of the earth, earthly; the second birth is of the Lord from heaven. The first birth is of nature, full of sin; the second is of grace, full of sanctity. The first birth is originally of flesh and blood; the second birth is originally of the Spirit and water. In a word, the first birth ills, the second gives life; generation lost us, it must be regeneration that recovers us. O blessed birth without which no birth is happy, in comparison of which, though it were to be born heir of the whole world, all is but misery!

✦ ISAAC AMBROSE
The Doctrine of Regeneration,
in *Works,* 18

Meditations upon an Egg

The egg's no chick by falling from the
   hen;
Nor man a Christian 'til he's born
   again.
The egg's at first contained in the shell:
Men afore grace, in sins and darkness
   dwell.
The egg, when laid, by warmth is
   made a chicken.
And Christ by grace the dead in sin
   does quicken.
The chick at first is in the cell confin'd;
So heav'n-born souls are in the flesh
   detain'd.
The shell doth crack, the chick doth
   chirp and peep.
The flesh decays, and men then pray
   and weep.
The shell doth break, the chick's at
   liberty,
The flesh falls off, the soul mounts up
   on high.
But both do not enjoy the self-same
   plight;
The soul is safe, the chick now fears
   the kite.
But chicks from rotten eggs do not
   proceed,
Nor is a hypocrite a saint indeed.
The rotten egg, tho' underneath the
   hen,
If crack'd, stinks, and is loathsome
   unto men.
Nor doth her warmth make what is
   rotten sound;
What's rotten, rotten will at last be
   found.
The hypocrite, sin has him in
   possession,
He is a rotten egg under profession.

✦ JOHN BUNYAN
Divine Emblems, 12–13

That the new creature is the product of divine power alone: a point of great concernment, if duly considered. The evangelist John is clear on our side, touching this original and pedigree of it, both whence it is not and whence it is: "It is born, not of blood"—that is, it belongs not to nor is brought forth in any as they are men made of flesh and blood. Nor as they are Abraham's seed according to the flesh (Rom. 9:7). Nor is it born "of the will of the flesh." The carnal and sensual affections have nothing to do in the spiritual birth. "Nor of the will of man": the rational faculties by which men are set above the rank of other creatures, even these contribute nothing to our divine sonship. "But it is of God" (John 1:13)—that is, it is His work alone, and the natural man has nothing to do in it; he is as perfectly unactive in it as the dry bones in causing themselves to live (Ezek. 37:5, 9, 14) or as Lazarus in reviving himself, of whom it is said, "He that was dead came forth, bound hand and foot" (John 11:44).

✦ ELISHA COLES
Practical Discourse, 190

Let them pretend what they please, the true reason why any despise the new birth is because they hate a new life. He that cannot endure to live to God will as little endure to hear of being born of God.

✦ JOHN OWEN
Golden Book, 216

OBEDIENCE

A heart to obey is our obeying; a heart to do is our doing; a heart to suffer in God's account is our suffering for His name. But here it must be carefully noted that though sincere resolution for obedience be obedience, yet every resolution is not that resolution. Resolution for obedience is then sincere where (1) it flows from an inward and rooted inclination; (2) it is founded on a firm belief of Scripture revelation; (3) it is built on the highest and weightiest reasons; (4) it is the result of the most mature and deep deliberation.

✦ RICHARD ALLEINE
Heaven Opened, 205

Our obedience in all the branches of it [the praise owed to the Lord in light of His providential care] should be bettered. Practical praises are the most acceptable. Our lives must witness the gratitude of our hearts.

✦ SIMEON ASHE
Best Refuge, 43

[True obedience] ought to be:

1. sincere (Ps. 51:6);
2. spiritual (John 4:24);
3. regular;
4. loving (Gal. 5:6);
5. believing (1 Peter 2:5–6);
6. universal (Ps. 119:6; 2 Cor. 2:9);
7. constant.

✦ WILLIAM BEVERIDGE
Thesaurus Theologious, 4:128–29

Though no believer does what he should do, yet doubtless every believer might do more than he does in order to God's glory and his own and others' internal and eternal good. Affection without endeavor is like Rachel, beautiful but barren. They are blessed that do what they can, though they cannot but under-do.

✦ THOMAS BROOKS
The Unsearchable Riches of Christ,
in *Select Works,* 1:171

Every man obeys Christ as he prizes Christ, and no otherwise.

✦ THOMAS BROOKS
The Unsearchable Riches of Christ,
in *Select Works,* 1:253

Opportunity is many times a special means which a man of gifts and place hath to do good above others and above himself at other times. Sometimes things fall out so fitly to a man that they even put him upon some service tending to the glory of God, whereas others have not the like. In such cases the rule is do as thine hand shall find; do as occasion shall serve; do as opportunity shall invite thee. Many are called by the Lord's providence, giving them opportunity to do somewhat for His glory, whereunto others have not the like occasion.

✦ WILLIAM GEARING
Sacred Diary, 96

Consider, what thou doest out of thy place is not acceptable to God because thou canst not do it in faith, "without which it is impossible to please God,"

and it cannot be in faith because thou hast no call. God will not thank thee for doing that which He did not set thee about. Possibly thou hast good intentions; so had Uzzah in staying the ark, yet how well God liked his zeal, see 2 Samuel 6:7.

✦ WILLIAM GURNALL
Christian in Complete Armour, 200

A naked command from God is a sufficient ground of obedience from man.

✦ NATHANIEL HARDY
First General Epistle of St. John, 279

He that is altogether a Christian is universal in his obedience: he doth not obey one command and neglect another; do one duty and cast off another. But he hath respect to all the commands; he endeavors to leave every sin and love every duty. The almost Christian fails in this; his obedience is partial and piecemeal. If he obey one command, he breaks another. The duties that least cross his lust he is much in, but those that do, he lays aside.

✦ MATTHEW MEAD
Almost Christian Discovered, 197–98

A resolution…to serve God is…such as it ought to be. When trusting in God, we purpose to forsake all sin and to observe all God's commandments to the end of our lives, and that with the utmost of self-denial in all worldly pleasure, profit, honor, and safety.

✦ JOHN NORTON
Catechistical Guide, 92–93

He that walketh with God sees, by the eye of faith, God present with him in all his actions; seriously thinking of Him upon all occasions, remembering Him in his ways, setting the Lord always before him as David did; seeing Him that is invisible as Moses did; doing all things as St. Paul did, as of God in the sight of God. Now he who so walketh that he always observeth God's presence and keepeth Him still in his view in the course of his life not only with a general and habitual but, as much as he can, with an actual intention to please and glorify God, this man may be said to walk with God.

✦ HENRY SCUDDER
Christian's Daily Walk, 52

Partial and temporary obedience is not obedience; in easy things that do not oppose our lusts, which are not against our reputation, some will do more for a time than they need; but our obedience must be impartial, universal, and constant because God commands it to be so.

✦ RICHARD SIBBES
Divine Meditations and Holy Contemplations, 74

OPPORTUNITY

Watch…for the opportunity because it is God's season, which without doubt is the best season and time for every purpose. Because Satan watches to spoil by mistiming as well as by corrupting whatever thou shalt do for God. "When I would do good," says Paul, "evil is present"; that is, either to withdraw me from my purpose or else to infect my work. That the opportunity may not slip thee, either for want of care or forecast, (1) sit always loose from an overmuch affecting thine own concernments and believe that thou wast not born for thyself. A brother is born for adversity. (2) Get thy heart tenderly affected with the welfare of all things that bear the stamp and image of God. (3) Study thy own place and capacity that God hath put thee in in this world, for suitable to thy place are thy work and opportunities. (4) Make provision beforehand that when things present themselves, thou mayst come up to a good performance. Be prepared for every good work. (5) Take heed of carnal reasonings; keep the heart tender, but set thy face like a flint for God. (6) And look well to the manner of every duty.

✦ JOHN BUNYAN
Riches, 208

Opportunities for duty which render it beautiful ought diligently to be embraced.

✦ JOHN OWEN
Golden Book, 222

"As we have therefore opportunity, let us do good unto all men" (Gal. 6:10). An opportunity to do good to others is a great mercy to ourselves. The oil of grace, like the widow's (2 Kings 4:6), increases by pouring out; an opportunity is a special season which God affords us for the benefit of our own and others' souls.

✦ GEORGE SWINNOCK
The Christian Man's Calling,
in *Works*, 2:219

Time is in itself of great price and ought to be redeemed, but opportunity is of greater value, and it is infinite pity to cut such a precious commodity to waste. It is ordinary, even with good men when they meet though it relate nothing to their callings or concernments, to be talking chiefly of corn and cattle and markets and fairs and foreign transactions, as if they had not a God, a Christ, a soul, an eternal estate to be minding each other of. Our words are the servants of our reason, and to send more than will perform our business or to send them upon unnecessary and trifling errands argues vanity and folly.

✦ GEORGE SWINNOCK
The Christian Man's Calling,
in *Works,* 2:348

ORDINANCES

Communion is founded on union, and union upon likeness. And how like are God and the devil, holiness and unrighteousness, one to the other? There is a vast difference between conversing with ordinances and having communion with God. A man may have great acquaintance with ordinances and be a great stranger to God at the same time. Everyone that goes to court and hangs about the palace doth not speak with the prince, and what sorry things are ordinances without this communion with God!

✦ WILLIAM GURNALL
Christian in Complete Armour, 302

Make conscience of joining with the church in her public worship. Do not think thou art left to thy liberty whether thou wilt or not, but bind it upon thy conscience as a duty, for so indeed it is. You think it is the minister's duty to dispense ordinances, surely then it is your duty to attend on them. He might as well pray for you at home as come to church and not find you there. Is there a woe to him if he doth not provide food for your souls, and none to you if you come not to partake of it? And think not you are time enough there if you hear the sermon, though you miss the prayers, which should prepare you for the word and sanctify the word to you. It is not the way to profit by one ordinance to neglect another. The minister may preach, but God must teach thee to profit. If God opens not thy understanding to conceive of and thy heart to conceive by the word thou hearest, no fruit will come of it. Now prayer is the key to open God's heart, as His Spirit is the key to open thine.

✦ WILLIAM GURNALL
Christian in Complete Armour, 700

Grace hath a mighty efficacy to establish the heart where it is revealed, and God hath appointed ordinances also on purpose to assure us that we might have strong consolation and that He might have great glory. He hath appointed two sacraments to set forth and confirm His grace to us, and the Holy Spirit is not only a teacher but a witness. The Lord first assures the thing, then the person, and, when it may be for the glory of His grace, we shall have the assurance of it as to ourselves.

+ THOMAS JOLLIE
"The Glory of Divine Grace," in Slate,
Select Nonconformists' Remains, 274

They that have received the word must receive it again. Though it were engrafted in them, yet receive it that it may save your souls. God has deputed it to be a means not only of regeneration but of salvation, and therefore, till we come to heaven, we must use this help. They that live above ordinances do not live at all, spiritually, graciously. Painted fire needs no fuel. The word, though it be an immortal seed, yet needs constant care and watering.

+ THOMAS MANTON
Practical Exposition on the
Epistle of James, 64

A heart filled with love to ordinances is a great preparation for an ordinance. How doth David in the Eighty-Fourth Psalm pant and long and breathe after the ordinances of God! To love prayer, to love the word is a great preparation for both. To love the presence of Christ in the Supper is a great preparation for it. To keep a habitual frame of love in the heart for ordinances.

+ JOHN OWEN
Discourse 5 on 1 Cor. 11:28, in
Twenty-Five Discourses, 85

Remember that the ordinances of Christ are not His grave wherein he lies but the throne whereon He sits as king of His church; that you should never be above ordinances until you are

above temptations; and that they lose not their authority because sometimes we miss their influence; and that they are appointed not only to bring men to but also to build men up in Christ.

+ FRANCIS RAWORTH
On Jacob's Ladder, vi

The ordinances. These are the conduits Jesus Christ hath instituted and appointed His ordinances to be the means of carrying His nourishing virtue to the soul. The ordinances are the dishes of gold upon which this heavenly meat is brought. Prayer, reading, preaching, meditation, holy conference, the sacrament—in these Christ presents Himself to the soul. He that forsakes these can expect no feeding from Christ.

+ RALPH ROBINSON
Christ All and in All, 29

There is a fragrancy in the word of Christ. The breath of Christ's mouth is sweeter than any perfume in the world (Song 5:16). His mouth, or palate, is sweetnesses in the original; all His promises and precepts are very savory. There is a fragrancy in all His ordinances. Prayer, sacraments, preaching, singing of psalms are in themselves and to a gracious heart like a sweet-smelling ointment (see Song 2:3).

+ RALPH ROBINSON
Christ All and in All, 299

The body of a man can as soon labor incessantly without food as the soul of a Christian can live continuously without ordinances.

+ WILLIAM SECKER
in Horn, *Puritan Remembrancer*, 121

Live not upon ordinances. These are God's institutions; love them, cleave unto them, attend upon them, let no temptation cause you to leave them. But live not upon them; place not your hope or your happiness in them, but love them only in God. Attend upon them, yet not so much upon them as upon God in them; lie by the pool, but wait for the angel. Love not, no not a divine ordinance for its own sake. Why, who doth so? Alas! who almost doth not?

✦ SAMUEL SHAW
Voice of One Crying in the Wilderness, 158–59

Ordinances—they are the golden ladder by which the soul climbs up to heaven; they are conduits of the water of life. O how precious should these be to us! They that are against ordinances are against being saved.

✦ THOMAS WATSON
The Beatitudes, in *Discourses*, 2:407–8

The soul that loves Christ desires to be much in His presence. He loves the ordinances; he thinks it is good lying in the way where Christ passes by. Ordinances are the chariots of salvation. Christ rides into the believers' hearts in these chariots. Ordinances are the feast of fat things. The soul feasts with Christ here: "He brought me to the banqueting house" (Song 2:4). In the Hebrew it is "He brought me to the house of wine." Word, prayer, sacraments are to a Christian the house of wine. Here, often Christ turns the water of tears into wine. How lovely is this house of wine! The ordinances are the lattice where Christ looks forth and shows His smiling face to His saints. Christ's parents found Him in the temple (Luke 2:46). The soul that loves Christ desires conference with Him in the temple.

✦ THOMAS WATSON
"Christ's Loveliness," in
Discourses, 1:320–21

Never go to work alone. Samson's strength lay in his hair, and a Christian's strength lies in Christ. When you are to do any duty, to resist any tentation, to subdue any lust, set upon it in the strength of Christ; some go out against sin in the strength of resolutions and vows, and they are soon foiled. Do as Samson: he first cried to heaven for help, and then, having taken hold of the pillars, he pulled down the house upon the lords of the Philistines. When we engage Christ in the work and so take hold upon the pillar of an ordinance, we then bring down the house upon the head of our lusts.

✦ THOMAS WATSON
"The One Thing Necessary,"
in *Discourses*, 1:381

Prayer is a sweet ordinance. The saints have conference with God and feel much sweetness and delight coming in. Therefore, prayer is called incense (Lev. 16:12).

✦ HENRY WILKINSON
"The Pleasant and Peaceable Ways of Wisdom," in *Three Decades of Sermons*, 197

ORIGINAL SIN

Iniquity can plead antiquity. He that commits a new act of murder finds it old in the example of Cain; drunkenness may be fetched from Noah.... There is no sin but has white hairs upon it and is exceeding old. But let us look further back yet, even to Adam; there is the age of sin.

✦ THOMAS ADAMS
Exposition upon...Second...Peter, 107

The heart is never soundly broken till thoroughly convinced of the heinousness of original sin. Here fix thy thoughts. This is that which makes thee backward to all good; prone to all evil (Rom. 7:15); that sheds blindness, pride, prejudice, unbelief into thy mind; enmity, unconstancy, obstinacy into thy will; inordinate heats and colds into thy affections; insensibleness, benumbedness, unfaithfulness into thy conscience; slipperiness into thy memory; and, in a word, hath but every wheel of thy soul out of order and made it of a habitation of holiness to become a very hell of iniquity (James 3:6). This is that which hath defiled, corrupted, perverted all thy members and turned them into weapons of unrighteousness and servants of sin (Rom. 6:19); that hath filled the head with carnal and corrupt designs (Mic. 2:1); the hand with sinful practices (Isa. 1:15); the eyes with wandering and wantonness (2 Peter 2:14); the tongue with deadly poison (James 3:8); that hath opened the ears to tales, flattery, and filthy communication and shut them against the instruction of

life (Zech. 7:11, 13).... And wilt thou yet be in love with thyself and tell us any longer of thy good heart?

✦ JOSEPH ALLEINE
Alarm to the Unconverted, 156–57

Among many, three things have and do most molest the children of God: one is the guilt of sin; another is inbred or original corruption; the last is troubles and affliction.

✦ JOHN BARLOW
Good Man's Privilege, 461

Man fallen is but the anagram of man in innocency; he has the same affections and delights, only they are transposed and misplaced.

✦ THOMAS MANTON
Practical Exposition on the Epistle of James, 28

Man fallen is but man inverted and turned upside down. His love is where his hatred should be, and his hatred where his love should be; his glory where his shame should be, and his shame where his glory should be.

✦ THOMAS MANTON
Practical Exposition on the Epistle of James, 177

Here, as touching the want of justice and inclination unto sin, which were two parts of the matter of original sin, ye must be advertised that there is no faculty of the soul of man which is not infected with both these evils together. We reckon as principal powers of the soul the mind (or understanding), the will, and the affections. These two last the Scripture often understands them in the word *heart* because the will and affections be seated in the heart. The first defect, then, is in the mind, and this is the want of light and knowledge; here is also the want of holiness—that is, of a quality wherewith our very knowledge and light must be affected, and assuredly was affected with, in the first creation.

✦ ROBERT ROLLOCK
A Treatise of God's Effectual Calling,
in *Select Works,* 1:170

Original sin is an apostacy from God, a want of original justice, and a certain positive quality repugning against the law of God.

✦ ROBERT ROLLOCK
A Treatise of God's Effectual Calling,
in *Select Works,* 1:173

Original sin debauched the mind and made it think crooked things straight, and straight things crooked; loathsome things lovely, and lovely things loathsome; perverted the will, and made it, as a diseased stomach, to call for and eat unwholesome meat against his own reason; enthralled his affections to sensuality and brutishness; chained the whole man and delivered it up to the law of sin and laid those strengths of reason and conscience in fetters by which it might be hindered in its vicious inclinations and course of profaneness. Hence it comes to pass that neither the beauty of grace, nor equity of living to God, nor the absolute necessity of man's exercising himself to godliness will prevail with him.

✦ GEORGE SWINNOCK
The Christian Man's Calling,
in *Works,* 2:166

As a smith works in his forge, an artificer in his shop. A natural man, as he is the heir of original and father of actual sin, so his soul and all the powers thereof are but Satan's shop of sins; his body and all the parts thereof tools of sin; his life and all his actions of both soul and body a trade of sin by the same reason.

✦ JOHN TRAPP
Commentary...upon...the
New Testament, 758

PARENTS

Though to see [the rebellious child] undutiful is your grief, yet not always your sin. Hath a parent given the child not only the milk of the breast but the sincere milk of the word (1 Peter 2:2)? Hast thou seasoned his tender years with religious education? Thou canst do no more. Parents can only work knowledge; God must work grace. They can only lay the wood together; it is God must make it burn. A parent can only be a guide to show his child the way to heaven; the Spirit of God must be a lodestone to draw his heart into that way.

✦ SIMEON ASHE
Primitive Divinity, 59–60

[Satan] is exceeding desirous to make parents themselves his instruments for their children's sin and ruin. And, alas! How commonly doth he succeed! He knoweth that parents have them under their hands in the most ductile, malleable age and that they have a concurrence of almost all advantages. They have the purse and the portion of their children in their power. They have the interest of love and reverence and estimation. They are still with them and can be often in their solicitings. They have the rod and can compel them. Many thousands are in hell through the means of their own parents; such cruel monsters will they be to the souls of any others that are first so to their own. If the devil can get the parents to be cursers, swearers, gamesters, drunkards, worldlings, proud, deriders, or railers at a holy life, what a snare is here for the poor children!

✦ RICHARD BAXTER
A Christian Directory, in
Practical Works, 2:270–71

The love of parents toward their children is so natural and ordinary that there is less need to put parents in mind of their duty. But contrariwise children are not usually so dutiful to their parents (as the school speaks). Love descends rather than ascends; the benefactor loves more than the beneficiary. And therefore it was necessary to admonish them of their love. Neither is God content with a bare precept but hath adjoined a promise, "that thy days may be long," for there is no reason he should enjoy long life who dishonors those of whom he received life.

✦ JOHN BOYS
Offices for Public Worship, in
Works, 65

The sum is this, that while we chasten the flesh, we should labor to inform and form the mind and spirit by infusing right principles, pressing and urging upon their tender hearts counsel, reproof, and instruction, as the matter requires. This is the duty of parents, to imitate God, to let instruction expound correction; and with a rod in the hand and a word in the mouth, to train up their children to life eternal. A dumb rod is but a brutish discipline and will certainly leave them more brutish than it found them. Chastisement without teaching may sooner break the bones than the heart; it may mortify the flesh but not corruption; extinguish nature but never beget grace. "But the rod and reproof give wisdom." Instruction added to correction, as it makes excellent Christians, so it makes good children.

✦ THOMAS CASE
Correction, Instruction, 148–49

He that will not use the rod on his child, his child shall be used as a rod on him.

✦ THOMAS FULLER
Holy and Profane States, 40

That example is most dangerous which is most commonly in sight. Now the child looks upon the father and mother almost every day; when they rise up, lie down, go forth, come in, talk, eat, or drink, he is still with them. Other men's courses he sees but now and then, but these always. Now, when unmortified, unrestrained vanity shall break out in every passage of their lives and their children be witnesses of it, is it not likely that they will be followers of it also? The child, perhaps, hears a neighbor swear once in a week or month, but when he hears his father every day dishonor God this way, it is very dangerous.

◆ WILLIAM GEARING
Sacred Diary, 92

If parents would have their children blessed at the church and at the school, let them beware they give their children no corrupt example at home by any carelessness, profaneness, or ungodliness; otherwise, parents will do them more harm at home than both pastor and schoolmaster can do good abroad. For the corrupt example of the one fights with the good doctrine of the other, which is by so much the more dangerous because that corrupt walking is armed with nature and therefore more forcibly inclines the affections of children to that side.

◆ RICHARD GREENHAM
Godlie Exhortation, 11–12

"As is the mother, so is her daughter." The mother is lewd, idolatrous, bloody, rebellious, and the daughter is such; look therefore what befell the mother for her sins, what punishment was inflicted upon her. The like shall befall and be inflicted upon thee. Proverbs suitable unto this are these: "Ill birds lay ill eggs"; "Roses grow not out of shrimps"; "From the wicked proceeds wickedness"; "Ill seed, ill corn"; "By the children you may know the parents." Now these are not always true, but sometimes it falls out that wicked parents have good children, and good parents wicked ones. Noah had a Ham, Isaac an Esau, David an Absalom, Hezekiah a Manasseh. And so contrary, Ahaz, that wicked king, had good Hezekiah for his son.

◆ WILLIAM GREENHILL
Exposition of the Prophet Ezekiel, 384

Parents' prayers may prove their children's best portion, even a treasure laid up in heaven for them which may obtain of God many blessings for the children after the parents are dead and gone. Children of many prayers seldom miscarry.

◆ EDWARD REYNER
Precepts for Christian Practice, 121

How many yet…teach their children the way to hell by inducing them to sin betimes; by instructing them to be proud and revengeful, to backbite and rail, to speak filthily, to curse and swear, to scorn holiness and the word, and ministers, and ways of God. How much worse, says one, are such parents than the devil himself? As it is worse for a mother to dash out the brains of her own child against a wall than for a wolf or a dog or a bear to kill her child. It is in your hands to do them the greatest kindness or cruelty in all the world. And if you saw a burning furnace, much more the flames of hell. What would you think of that parent who could find in his heart to cast the child into it or to put him into the hands of one that would? If therefore you love them, show it in those things wherein their greatest interest is concerned. Do not say you love them and yet be so unmerciful as to damn them.

And what can you possibly do more to damn them than to bring them up in ignorance, and sensuality, and neglect of God?

✦ JOHN SHOWER
Family Religion, 48–49

PASTORS

Take heed to yourselves lest you be strangers to the effectual working of that gospel which you preach, and lest, while you proclaim to the world the necessity of a Savior, your own hearts should neglect Him and you should miss of an interest in Him and His saving benefits. Be that first yourselves which you persuade your hearers to be; believe that which you daily persuade them to believe; and heartily entertain that Christ and Spirit which you offer to them. You have a heaven to win or lose yourselves and souls that must be happy or miserable forever; it therefore concerns you to begin at home and take heed to yourselves.

✦ RICHARD BAXTER
Reformed Pastor, 4

The worst of men are in a dead sleep, and the best of men are too often in a sinful slumber; and therefore faithful ministers have need to cry aloud, they have need to be courageous and zealous, to awaken both sinners and saints, that none may go sleeping to hell. Cowardice in a minister is cruelty; if he fears the faces of men, he is a murderer of the souls of men.

✦ THOMAS BROOKS
Smooth Stones, 159

Vinedressers are rewarded according to their diligence and faithfulness, though some vines never bear nor bring forth fruit at all. As ministers are diligent and faithful, so the reward, the crown shall be given full at last. This is many a faithful minister's grief, that he takes a great deal of pains in rubbing and washing, as it were, to make souls white and clean, pure and holy, and yet they remain, after all, as black as hell; but surely their reward shall never be the less with God. The nurse looks not for her wages from the child, but from the parent.

✦ THOMAS BROOKS
The Unsearchable Riches of Christ,
in *Select Works*, 1:292

I beseech you remember, the righteous must be gathered; let us therefore do with them as we do with books that are borrowed; if a man borrows a book he knows he must keep it but for a day or two, and therefore he will be sure to read it over; whereas if the book be a man's own, he lays it aside because he knows he can read it any time. Remember your ministers are but lent you; they are not your own, and you know not but God may take your Elijahs from you this night. Therefore, make what use you can of them while you have them.

✦ EDMUND CALAMY
"Mr. Calamy's Sermon at the Funeral of Mr. Ashe," in *Farewell Sermons*, 355

It is natural to faithful ministers to endeavor the propagation of the same vital principle of holy living and the same union with the Lord Jesus, the head and fountain of it, which themselves believe and experience. Faithful ministers covet most earnestly to change the very tempers and dispositions of men, from their natural probity to a holy aptitude and sufficiency for gracious and heavenly operations. They rejoice in every advance that is made toward the divine life, but that divine life itself (in sincerity at first, and afterward in the progress and final consummation of it) is what they press after themselves, and above all things, with the most assiduous application, endeavor to promote in their hearers and people. Their business is to illuminate the minds of men, to convince their consciences, to rectify their judgments, and persuade their wills to a sound and deep repentance for their past miscarriages to a present reformation of what is amiss in their hearts and lives and to a fixed resolution of walking with God and their fellow creatures (especially those of the same holy Christian profession) in all purity.

✦ JOHN CHORLTON
Glorious Reward, 5

It's a greater thing in a pastor to deal wisely and comfortably with an afflicted soul and soundly and discreetly to meet with a heretic than to preach learnedly.

✦ EZEKIEL CULVERWELL
Time Well Spent, 229

It were a happy nursery for the church if every grounded pastor would train up in life, learning, doctrine, discipline, some toward scholar to make him more fit for the church as Moses did Joshua; Elijah, Elisha; Jeremiah, Baruch; Christ, His disciples; Paul, Timothy.

✦ EZEKIEL CULVERWELL
Time Well Spent, 240

Let us see that our knowledge of Christ is not a powerless, barren, unpractical knowledge. Oh that in its passage from our understanding to our lips it might powerfully melt, sweeten, and delight our hearts! Remember, brethren, a holy calling never saved any man without a holy heart; if our tongues only be sanctified, our whole man must be condemned. Oh, let the keepers of the vineyard look to and keep their own vineyard! We have a heaven to win or lose as well as others.

✦ JOHN FLAVEL
Fountain of Life, 8–9

Those ministers that give men no rest nor quietness in their sins must expect but little rest or quietness themselves. What is it for ministers to preach home to the consciences of others but to pull down the rage of the world upon their own heads?

✦ JOHN FLAVEL
Golden Gems, 55

My dear flock, I have, according to the grace given me, labored in the course of my ministry among you to feed you with the heart-strengthening bread of practical doctrine; and I do assure you, it is far better you should have the sweet and saving impressions of gospel truths feelingly and powerfully conveyed to your hearts than only to understand them by a bare ratiocination or a dry syllogistical inference.

✦ JOHN FLAVEL
epistolary dedication to
Saint Indeed, 26

Doth Satan deal with men in particular to subvert them? How much more then should we [pastors] deal particularly with them (I mean not to particular men's faults in public) but in love to give private instruction, exhortation, counsel, admonition, which is too little used nowadays; yea, we have run out so far from that anti-Christian auricular confession as that we are fallen into the contrary extremity.

✦ THOMAS GRANGER
Application of Scripture, 17

If a watchman wants eyes and knowledge, how can he discern danger, instruct the ignorant, heal the wounded, reduce the straying, lift up the fallen, feed the hungry, comfort the feeble, resolve conscience, and compare things past with things present and future? A watchman, a minister, should be like Argus, who, the poets say, had a hundred eyes; they should be full of eyes. The beasts about Christ's throne were full of eyes, before and behind (Rev. 4:6). They saw things gone and things to come; they saw every way. Ignorance is blamable in any, but chiefly in a watchman.

✦ WILLIAM GREENHILL
Exposition of the Prophet Ezekiel, 110

The want of knowledge in a minister is such a defect as cannot be supplied by anything else. Be he never so meek, patient, bountiful, unblameable, if he hath not skill to divide the word aright, he is not cut out for a minister. Everything is good as it is good for the end it is appointed to; a knife, though it had a shaft of diamonds yet it will not cut, it is no knife. A bell, if not sound, is no bell. The great work of a minister is to teach others; his lips are to preserve knowledge. He should be as conversant in the things of God as others in their particular trades. Ministers are called lights; if the light then be darkness, how great is the darkness of that people like to be! I know these stars in Christ's hands are not all of the same magnitude. There is a greater glory of gifts and graces shines in some than others, yet so much light is accessory to every minister, as was in the star the wise men saw at Christ's birth, to be able out of the word to direct sinners the safe and true way to Christ and salvation.

✦ WILLIAM GURNALL
Christian in Complete Armour, 117

If thou wouldst, therefore, be preserved from error, make use, as of the sword of the Word in thy own hand, so of the holy skill that God hath given thy faithful minister for thy defense. Wait on his public ministry, praying for divine assistance to be poured down on him and a divine blessing from his labors to fall on thyself. If at any time thou art in the dark concerning his message, resort to him, and I dare promise thee (if he answers to his name—a faithful minister of the gospel) an easy access and hearty welcome to him; only come to learn, not to cavil, to have thy conscience satisfied and not from any vain curiosity.

✦ WILLIAM GURNALL
Christian in Complete Armour, 603

That which may pass for diligence in a private Christian's search into the Scriptures may be charged as negligence upon the minister.

✦ WILLIAM GURNALL
Christian in Complete Armour, 620

Indeed, few or none will speak against learning but those that have not so much of it as to make them understand its use. I dare not bid ministers, as some fanatics have done, burn all their books but the Bible. No, but I would exhort them to prefer it above all their other books and to direct all their other studies to furnish them with Scripture knowledge; as the bee that flies over the whole garden and brings all the honey she gets from every flower therein into her hive, so should the minister run over all his other books and reduce their notions for his help in this, as the Israelites offered up the jewels and earrings borrowed of the Egyptians to the service of the tabernacle.

✦ WILLIAM GURNALL
Christian in Complete Armour, 621

Thus as the poor receive the gospel, so they that publish it are many times poor and low; not that thus it ought to be, as the opinion of too many in our days is, who would have ministers live like beggars, upon benevolence, and account it a prudent policy to keep them poor.

✦ NATHANIEL HARDY
Divinity in Mortality, 18

It is certain that God's grace can bring people to heaven without our preaching. But our preaching can never bring people to heaven without God's grace, and therefore we should be as much in care, as much in earnest to pray for the operations of grace as to propose the offers of grace and may better expect in that way to succeed. If we cannot preach people to Christ, let us endeavor to pray them to Christ.

✦ MATTHEW HENRY
"A Sermon Concerning the Work and Success of the Ministry," in
Miscellaneous Writings, 554

We think that they who savingly know not Christ should not be fit to make other men acquainted with Him. He who can tell men what God hath done for his soul is the likeliest to bring their souls to God. Hardly can he speak to the heart who speaks not from it. Before the cock crows to others, he claps his wings and rouses up himself. How can a frozen-hearted preacher warm his hearers' hearts and enkindle them with the love of God? But he whom the love of Christ constrains, his lively recommendations of Christ and speeches of love shall sweetly constrain others to love Him. Above all loves, it is most true of this, that none can speak sensibly of it but they that have felt it. Our most exquisite pulpit orators—yea, speak they with the tongues of men and angels—without the experience of this love are no fit ambassadors for Christ, for His embassy is a love treaty.

✦ ROBERT LEIGHTON
"A Sermon to the Clergy," in
Sermons, 336–37

Their [i.e., pastors'] chief study should be that of their commission, the Holy Scriptures. The way to speak skillfully from God is often to hear Him speak.

✦ ROBERT LEIGHTON
"A Sermon to the Clergy," in
Sermons, 338

The ministers of the gospel should indeed be as the angels of God, going betwixt Him and His people; not only bringing down useful instructions from God to them but putting up earnest supplications to God for them. In the tenth [chapter] of St. Luke, the disciples are sent forth and appointed to preach. And in the eleventh we have them desiring to be taught to pray: "Lord, teach us to pray." And without this there can be little answer or success in the other; little springing up of this seed, though ministers sow it plentifully in preaching, unless they secretly water it with their prayers and tears.

✦ ROBERT LEIGHTON
Spiritual Truths, 178–79

Afflictions light on all ranks of saints, but especially upon the prophets. The cross is kindly to our order: [Martin Luther said], "To preach is nothing but to bait the world." We are God's ambassadors, but we are often "[ambassadors] in bonds" (Eph. 6:20).

What recompense did the prophets receive for all their pains and expense of spirits, but saws and swords and dungeons? It is almost as necessary a character of a minister to be much in afflictions as to be much in spirit and much in labors. God has reserved us, in these latter days, for all the contempt and scorn that villainy and outrage can heap upon our persons, but it is no matter; it is the badge of our order, and we know where to have better entertainment.

✦ THOMAS MANTON
*Practical Exposition on the
Epistle of James*, 192

The work of the ministry is not to contend with ghosts and opinions antiquated, but the errors and sins of the present time. Look, as it is the duty of Christians to spend the heat of their indignation on the main sin with which they are surprised: "I kept myself from mine iniquity" (Ps. 18:23); so must ministers chiefly bend their zeal and strength against the present guilt.

✦ THOMAS MANTON
*Practical Exposition on the
Epistle of James*, 196

Needless avocations from study are carefully to be avoided by ministers, especially young ones.

✦ ADAM MARTINDALE
Life, 102

You that are engaged in the work of God, seek for a reward of your service in the service itself.

✦ JOHN OWEN
Golden Book, 231

Men may have a multitude of thoughts about the affairs of their callings and the occasions of life which yet may give no due measure of the frame of their hearts. So men whose calling and work it is to study the Scripture, or the things revealed therein, and to preach them unto others cannot but have many thoughts about spiritual things; and yet may be, and oftentimes are, most remote from being spiritually minded. They may be forced by their work and calling to think of them early and late, evening and morning, and yet their minds be no way rendered or proved spiritually thereby. It were well if all of us who are preachers would diligently examine ourselves herein. . . . No persons are in greater danger of walking at a hazard with God than those who live in the exercise of spiritual gifts in duties unto their own satisfaction and others.' For they may countenance themselves with an appearance of everything that should be in them in reality and power, when there is nothing of it in them.

♦ JOHN OWEN
On Being Spiritually Minded,
in *Oweniana*, 144

Our ministry, whether by preaching or suffering, will cast a savor through the world both of life and death. I persuade you, my dear brother, there is nothing out of heaven next to Christ dearer to me than my ministry, and the worth of it in my estimation is increased and pains me exceedingly; yet I am content for the honor of my Lord to surrender it back again to the Lord of the vineyard. Let Him do with it and me both what seems Him good.

♦ SAMUEL RUTHERFORD
Prison Sayings, 82

Jan. 11 [, 1641]. In the morning, the Lord presented to me the sad state of the church, which put me upon a spirit of sorrow for my sins as one cause, and to resolve in season to go visit all families; but first to begin with myself and go to Christ, that He may begin to pour His ointment on me, and then to my wife, and then to my family, and then to my brethren, etc.

♦ THOMAS SHEPARD
Meditations and Spiritual Experiences, 37

June 27 [, 1641]. On Sabbath, when I came home, I saw the hypocrisy of my heart, that in my ministry I sought to comfort others and quicken others that the glory might reflect on me as well as on God. Hereupon I considered how ill the Lord took this and how averse He was from this self-seeking, by the sight of which I labored to be averse from it myself and purposed to carry it in mind as one strong mean to help against it for time to come.

♦ THOMAS SHEPARD
*Meditations and Spiritual
Experiences*, 70

We [pastors] should not rack [young believers'] wits with curious or doubtful disputes (Rom. 14:1), for so we shall distract and tire them and give occasion to make them cast off the care of all. That age of the church which was most fertile in nice questions was most barren in religion, for it makes people think religion to be only a matter of wit, in tying and untying of knots. The brains of men given that way are hotter usually than their hearts.

✦ RICHARD SIBBES
Bruised Reed and Smoking Flax, 53–54

It is an office of love here to take away the stones and to smooth the way to heaven. Therefore, we must take heed that under pretense of avoidance of disputes we do not suffer an adverse party to get ground upon the truth, for thus may we easily betray both the truth of God and souls of men.

✦ RICHARD SIBBES
Bruised Reed and Smoking Flax, 54

John the Baptist doth teach us what kind of ministry is like to do most good—namely, that which works upon the consciences of men. He came hewing and cutting down men's sins and afterward preached Christ to them. He first poured in the vinegar of the law, and then the wine of the gospel. John did not so much preach to please as he did to profit. That preaching is most to be preferred which makes the truest discovery of men's sins and opens to them most faithfully their own hearts. Happy that people who love a soul-searching ministry! "They were pricked in their hearts and said, 'What shall we do?'"

✦ THOMAS WATSON
Puritan Gems, 99–100

God's ministers must have their hearts fired—not with passion but with love—and as they are Christ's ambassadors must come to sinners with an olive branch of peace. The thunderbolt may crush, but the sun melts. It is better to love as a pastor than speak as an angel.

✦ THOMAS WATSON
Puritan Gems, 100

PASTORS AND PRAYER

Prayer must carry on our work as well as preaching. He preaches not heartily to his people who doth not often pray for them. If we prevail not with God to give them faith and repentance, we are unlikely to prevail with them to believe and repent.

✦ RICHARD BAXTER
Reformed Pastor, 203

Love to Christ and souls will make a man willing to spend and be spent; he that prays himself to death, that preaches himself to death, that studies himself to death for the honor of Christ and good of souls shall be no loser in the end.

✦ THOMAS BROOKS
Apples of Gold, 11

Let ministers, whose special calling lies in this also, to give themselves to prayer. Be much in it. How often is Paul described as thus employed? Epaphras, the Colossian minister, is commended for this also. Eusebius tells us of James, called Justus, that his knees were grown hard and brawny with being so much in this way employed. And do not ministers' closet sins—as vanity of mind, vainglorious reasonings of spirit, listlessness sometimes to their holy work—call upon them for closet, study prayers? Does not their weighty closet work call for this? Is not prayer, as once Luther said, the best book in our study? Does not Satan ofttimes come into our studies to assault us in our work, as sometimes he did Joshua the priest in his? And had we not then more need than others to be found oft praying there? The Lord vouchsafes ofttimes to be talking in friendly sort with us in our studies, and it were pity and shame if hereby we should not maintain holy conference with Him. Who are more potent with God in public prayer than such ministers as wrestle it out most with God in secret prayer?

✦ THOMAS COBBET
Gospel Incense, 99

"Father, I thank thee," said our Savior, being ready to raise Lazarus, "that thou hast heard me. And I knew that thou hearest me always: but because of the people which stand by I said it, that they may believe that thou hast sent me" (John 11:41–42). It is lawful for ministers in their public prayers to insert passages for the edifying of their auditors, at the same time petitioning God and informing their hearers. For our Savior, glancing His eyes at the people's instruction, did no whit hinder the steadfastness of His looks lifted up to His Father.

✦ THOMAS FULLER
Good Thoughts, 128

He that is more frequent in his pulpit to his people than he is in his closet for his people is but a sorry watchman. In our prayers for our people, God will teach us what we shall preach unto them. We cannot pray for them but we must think on what it is we pray for, and that is the consideration of their condition…. The apostles gave themselves to prayer and the word (Acts 6:4). Prayer is in the first place.

✦ JOHN OWEN
Golden Book, 133–34

A man may read a long prayer that expresses spiritual things and yet never have had one spiritual thought arise in his mind about them, for there is no exercise of any faculty of his mind required unto such reading, but only to attend unto the words that are to be read. This, I say, may be so; I do not say that it is so or that it must be so. But, in extempore prayer, it is impossible but there must be an exercise of reason by invention, judgment, and memory and consequently thoughts of spiritual things. Yet may they all be merely occasional, from the present external performance of the duty, without any living spring or exercise of grace. In such a course may men of tolerable gifts continue all their days unto the satisfaction of themselves and others, deceiving both them and their own souls.

✦ JOHN OWEN
On Being Spiritually Minded,
in *Oweniana*, 201

As by preaching the minister commends God to his people's acceptation, so by prayer he commends his people to God's benediction.

✦ GEORGE SWINNOCK
"The Pastor's Farewell," in *Works*, 4:68

PASTORS: IMPORTANCE OF GODLY CONDUCT

Take heed to your conduct because the success of all your labors does very much depend upon it. If you unsay by your lives what you say with your lips, you will prove the greatest hinderers of your own work. It greatly prevents our success that other men are all the week contradicting to the people in private what we have been speaking to them from the word of God in public, but it will prevent it much more if we contradict it ourselves—if our actions give our words the lie. This is the way to make men think that the word of God is but an idle tale. Surely he that means as he speaks will do as he speaks. One improper word, one unbecoming action may blast the fruit of many a sermon.

♦ RICHARD BAXTER
Reformed Pastor, 23

All that a preacher does is a kind of preaching.

♦ RICHARD BAXTER
Reformed Pastor, 24

What Caesar once said of his wife, that it was not enough for her to be without fault but she should be without all suspicion of fault, may well be applied to ministers, who of all men in the world should be most free from the very appearances of evil. The lives of ministers oftentimes convince more strongly than their words; their tongues may persuade, but their lives command.

♦ THOMAS BROOKS
The Unsearchable Riches of Christ,
in *Select Works*, 1:279

The minister's life is the life of his ministry, and teachers' sins are the teachers of sins.

♦ SAMUEL CLARK
Saint's Nosegay, 118

[The faithful minister] is strict in ordering his conversation. As for those who cleanse blurs with blotted fingers, they make it the worse. It was said of one who preached very well and lived very ill that when he was out of the pulpit it was pity he should ever go into it, and when he was in the pulpit it was pity he should ever come out of it; but our minister lives sermons. And yet I deny not but dissolute men, like unskillful horsemen which open a gate on the wrong side, may by the virtue of their office open heaven for others and shut themselves out.

♦ THOMAS FULLER
Holy and Profane States, 80–81

Men are very apt to question the truth of that doctrine to which the preacher's practice gives the lie! The way to imprint an instruction upon the hearer's heart as well as ear is to speak by our works as well as words.

♦ NATHANIEL HARDY
First General Epistle of St. John, 180

Let us be very careful that we do not by any irregularity in our conversation hinder the success of our praying and preaching and defeat the ends of them. If we be proud and vain and loose in our walking; if we be intemperate and indulgent of the flesh; if we be covetous, selfish, and worldly; if we be contentious, peevish, and passionate; or if any corrupt communication proceed out of our mouth, we pull down with one hand what we build up with the other and not only tempt people but even force them to think that we ourselves do not believe what we would persuade them to believe.

✦ MATTHEW HENRY
"A Sermon Concerning the Work and Success of the Ministry," in *Miscellaneous Writings*, 561

A minister, in his conversation, ought carefully to avoid all foolish and excessive jesting and immoderate mirth. I could never think it a good character of a clergyman to call him a merry fellow or a notable droll, and yet I do not condemn all cheerfulness and freedom nor the innocent exercise of wit. But it is one thing to make use of these now and then, when they come in our way, and another to search and hunt after them; and those who have the knack of it are ready enough to fall into excess.

✦ HENRY SCOUGAL
"Importance and Difficulty of the Ministerial Function," in *Works*, 221

A pastor must thunder in his doctrine and [lightning] in his life.

✦ GEORGE SWINNOCK
in Horn, *Puritan Remembrancer*, 64

Take heed unto thyself that thou be a lively, thriving Christian. See that all thy religion run not in the channel of thy employment. It is found by experience, that as it fares with a minister in the frame of his heart and thriving of the work of God in his soul, so doth it fare with his ministry, both in its vigor and effects. A carnal frame, a dead heart, and a loose walk make cold and unprofitable preaching. And how common is it for ministers to neglect their own vineyard? When we read the word, we read it as ministers to know what we should teach rather than what we should learn as Christians. Unless there be great heed taken, it will be found that our ministry and labor therein may eat out the life of our Christianity.

✦ ROBERT TRAILL
"By What Means May Ministers Best Win Souls?," in *Select Practical Writings*, 125

Does not always the spirit of the ministers propagate itself among the people? A lively ministry, and lively Christians. Therefore, be serious at heart; believe, and so speak; feel, and so speak; and as you teach, so do. And then people will feel what you say and obey the word of God.

✦ ROBERT TRAILL
"By What Means May Ministers Best Win Souls?," in *Select Practical Writings*, 137

"And He took the cup." Anciently of glass, afterward of wood, and lastly of silver or gold. Whence that saying of a [church] father, "Once there were wooden cups, golden priests: now there are golden cups, but wooden priests."

✦ JOHN TRAPP
Commentary…upon…the New Testament, 312

PATIENCE

All virtue is a widow without patience.... Faith without patience is but precipitancy; zeal without patience is but fury; hope without patience is presumption; humility without patience is dejection; charity without patience fills the vessel with milk from her breasts and then kicks it down with her heels. Patience to the soul is as bread to the body, the staff of either the natural or spiritual life. We eat bread with all our meats both for health and relish; bread with flesh, bread with fish, bread with broths and fruits. Such is patience to every virtue; we must hope with patience, and pray in patience, and love with patience, and whatsoever good thing we do, let it be done in patience.

◆ THOMAS ADAMS
Exposition upon...Second...Peter, 692

Patience must not be an inch shorter than affliction. If the bridge reach but halfway over the brook, we shall have but an ill-favored passage.

◆ THOMAS ADAMS
Exposition upon...Second...Peter, 762

What the grace of patience is. Take it at large—that is, in the full comprehension of it—it is a constant persisting whether to do the will of God without fainting or to suffer the will of God with submission and quietness and cheerfulness, to the end of a man's days. And thus taken, it respects doing as well as suffering.

◆ THOMAS GOODWIN
Patience and Its Perfect Work,
in *Works*, 2:436

[Patience] is a constant, thankful, joyful enduring with perseverance to the end of a man's life all the trials that are grievous, how great, how long, how hopeless soever as to coming out of them; mortifying and compescing the inordinacy of opposite passions as fear, grief, care, anxiety, which will arise upon such afflictions, with submitting to God's will for God's glory and His good pleasure's sake; still blessing and sanctifying God in all, waiting on God, and relieving oneself by faith in what is to be had in God and from God in communion with Him and from His love in this life, in expectation also of that glory which is the reward after this life ended.

◆ THOMAS GOODWIN
Patience and Its Perfect Work,
in *Works*, 2:438

Patience is...that grace which digests all things and turns them into good nourishment.

◆ WILLIAM GURNALL
Christian in Complete Armour, 422

Patience has three things in it: passion subdued; the soul quieted; expectation and waiting for good. A heart planed and made even with its condition, neither higher nor lower; a heart still and taking all well; a heart expecting and waiting for what is needed, and Christ has promised—this is a patient soul.

◆ NICHOLAS LOCKYER
Balm for England, 80

Patience is a grace made and cut out for suffering; patience is a sweet submission to the will of God, whereby we are content to bear anything that

He is pleased to lay upon us. Patience makes a Christian invincible; it is like the anvil that bears all strokes. We cannot be men without patience. Passion does unman a man; it puts him beside the use of reason. We cannot be martyrs without patience; patience makes us endure (James 5:10).

✦ THOMAS WATSON
The Beatitudes, in *Discourses*, 2:384

Patience is a cheerful submission of our will to God.

✦ THOMAS WATSON
Godly Man's Picture, 106

Patience opens the ear but shuts the mouth; it opens the ear to hear the rod but shuts the mouth that it has not a word to say against God.

✦ THOMAS WATSON
Godly Man's Picture, 110

PEACE

The conscience cannot be truly pacified till soundly purified (Heb. 10:22). Cursed is that peace that is maintained in a way of sin (Deut. 29:19–20). Two sorts of peace are more to be dreaded than all the troubles in the world: peace with sin, and peace in sin.

✦ JOSEPH ALLEINE
Alarm to the Unconverted, 80

True peace is the blessing of the gospel, and only of the gospel. This will appear in the several kinds of peace, which may be sorted into those four. First, peace with God, which we may call peace of reconciliation. Secondly, peace with ourselves, or peace of conscience. Thirdly, peace with one another, or peace of love and unity. Fourthly, peace with the other creatures, even the most hurtful, which may be called a peace of indemnity and service.

✦ WILLIAM GURNALL
Christian in Complete Armour, 352

[The gospel] is strengthening and restorative; it makes the Christian strong to fight against sin and Satan. The Christian is revived and finds his strength come upon a little tasting of this honey. But oh, what a slaughter doth he make of his spiritual enemies when he hath a full meal of this honey—a deep draught of this wine! Now he goes like a giant refreshed with wine into the field against them. No lust can stand before him; it makes him strong to work. Oh, how Paul laid about him for Christ! "He labored more abundantly than them all." The good man remembered what a wretch he once was and what mercy he had obtained; the sense of this love of God lay so glowing at his heart that it inspired him with a zeal for God above his fellow apostles.

✦ WILLIAM GURNALL
Christian in Complete Armour, 386

If you would maintain a constant, perpetual calm in your souls, take these rules. (1) Bottom your peace upon your justification, and not upon your sanctification.... Christ's righteousness and merit imputed and applied to us is the ground of our peace, and not any righteousness of our own. (2) Labor to understand and be sure to take heed of that which will break the peace.... We must not turn aside to the ways of sin and folly.... (3) If at any time guilt be upon thy soul, make haste to repent. Delay not for fear of the worst.... (4) If we would keep the peace, we must understand on what terms we are with God. We must look on Him as our Father, reconciled in and through Jesus Christ.... (5) We must take heed of misinterpreting God's providences in our afflictions.... Is there no such thing as afflicting for trial? Yes, sometimes God does it to try the graces of His people.... And when He doth so, is there any reason why we should interpret it to the breaking of our peace?... (6) Do not misinterpret the word of God. Many put far from them that which belongs to them, and take that to themselves which is not spoken to them.

✦ PHILIP HENRY
Remains, 147–50

Consider, civil peace depends much upon church peace. Religion is called *religando* [binding together], it being the greatest bond to link men together; contrary opinions in religion usually cause much alienation of affection and disturbances in the commonwealth.

✦ THOMAS MANTON
Meate Out of the Eater, 45

I shall name these three properties of true peace: (1) It will allow no peace with sin. Carnal security is at amity with sin, at least with some sin, but gracious peace is at enmity with all

sin. The prophet mentions this fruit of it (Ps. 85:8). (2) It raises the heart to enjoy more full communion with God. The heart is made more active in all holiness, whereas carnal security deadens the heart. It's a heart-ruling peace (Col. 3:15), a heart-keeping peace (Phil. 4:7). (3) True peace continues even in outward trouble. Outward troubles dash carnal security, not true peace, unless God hide His face in trouble (John 16:33).

✦ RALPH ROBINSON
Christ All and in All, 123

The ancients made the harp the emblem of peace. How sweet would the sounding of this harp be after the roaring of the cannon! All should study to promote this political peace; the godly man, when he dies, "[enters] into peace" (Isa. 57:2). But while he lives, peace must enter into him.

✦ THOMAS WATSON
The Beatitudes, in *Discourses*, 2:275

If God be our God, He will give us peace in trouble. When there is a storm without, He will make peace within. The world can create trouble in peace, but God can create peace in trouble.

✦ THOMAS WATSON
Gleanings, 63

PEEVISHNESS

Grace makes men of the most froward, sour, crabbed nature to be of a sweet, lovely, amiable, pleasing temper. It turns lions into lambs, wolves into sheep, monsters into men, and men into angels, as you may see in Manasseh, Paul, Mary Magdalene, Zacchaeus, and others.

✦ THOMAS BROOKS
The Unsearchable Riches of Christ,
in *Select Works,* 1:184

PERFECTION/PERFECTIONISM

This life was not intended to be the place of our perfection, but the preparation for it.

✦ RICHARD BAXTER
in Thomas, *Puritan Golden Treasury,* 207

Indwelling sin always abides while we are in this world; therefore, it is always to be mortified. The vain, foolish, and ignorant disputes of men about perfect keeping the commands of God, of perfection in this life, of being wholly and perfectly dead to sin I meddle not now with. It is more than probable that the men of those abominations never knew what belonged to the keeping of any one of God's commands and are so much below perfection of degrees that they never attained to a perfection of parts in obedience or universal obedience in sincerity. And therefore many in our days who have talked of perfection have been wiser and have affirmed it to consist in knowing no difference between good and evil. Not that they are perfect in the things we call good, but that all is alike to them, and the height of wickedness is their perfection.

✦ JOHN OWEN
Of the Mortification of Sin in Believers, in Works, 6:10

In playing over a tune upon an instrument, a single string may jar and slip and yet the main be musical. It would be folly, indeed, to think our fields had no corn in them because there is chaff about the wheat or that the ore had no gold in it because there is dross among it. In heaven there is service alone without any sin; in hell there is sin alone without service. But on earth there is sin and service in the same man, as there is light and shade in the same picture.

✦ WILLIAM SECKER
Nonsuch Professor, 183

PERSECUTION

But how do they [i.e., the wicked] do it [i.e., persecute a believer]? Why, either by reproaching him with his former misconduct or by charging him with hypocrisy, singularity, and Puritanism. They charge him with being a fellow of factious spirit and troublesome conduct. Nor is this on his first entrance into the way of life, but ever after while he keeps the way to heaven. Every faithful Christian knows by experience that so long as he acts in the good cause and stands up against the evil practices of the place where he lives, that he shall have the spirit of profaneness to fly in his face with implacable malice and brutish insolence. "All that live godly in Christ Jesus shall suffer persecution."

✦ ISAAC AMBROSE
Christian Warrior, 84

"May we not fly in a time of persecution? Your pressing upon us that persecution is ordered and managed by God makes us afraid to fly." Thou mayest do in this even as it is in thy heart. If it is in thy heart to fly, fly; if it be in thy heart to stand, stand. Anything but a denial of the truth. He that flies has warrant to do so; he that stands has warrant to do so. Yea, the same man may both fly and stand, as the call and working of God with his heart may be. Moses fled, Moses stood; Jeremiah fled, Jeremiah stood; Christ withdrew Himself, Christ stood; Paul fled, Paul stood. But in flying, fly not from religion; fly not for the sake of a trade; fly not that thou mayest have care for the flesh. This is wicked and will yield neither peace nor profit to thy soul, neither now, nor at death, nor at the day of judgment.

✦ JOHN BUNYAN
Riches, 249

Nor are the afflictions God inflicts upon His servants any violations of His goodness. Sometimes God afflicts men for their temporal and eternal good, for the good of their grace in order to the good of their glory, which is a more excellent good than afflictions can be an evil. The heathens reflected upon Ulysses's hardship as a mark of Jupiter's goodness and love to him, that his virtue might be more conspicuous. By strong persecutions brought upon the church, her lethargy is cured, her chaff purged, the glorious fruit of the gospel brought forth in the lives of her children; the number of her proselytes multiply, and the strength of her weak ones is increased by the testimonies of courage and constancy which the stronger present to them in their sufferings. Do those good effects speak a want of goodness in God, who brings them into this condition? By those He cures His people of their corruptions and promotes their glory by giving them the honor of suffering for the truth and raises their spirits to a divine pitch.

✦ STEPHEN CHARNOCK
Selections, 45–46

God's children are like torches that show dim in the light but burn clear in the dark; so they in prosperity and adversity.... Christians under persecution count that God gives them living enough if He give them their lives.... Persecution is the bellows of the gospel, blowing every spark into a flame; and martyrs' ashes are the best compost to manure the church.

✦ SAMUEL CLARK
Saint's Nosegay, 102

Whosoever resolves to live holily must never expect to live quietly.

✦ JOHN FLAVEL
Fountain of Life, 176

Persecution...does but mow the church, which afterward comes up the thicker for it; it is unholiness that ruins it. Persecutors do but plough God's field for Him while He is sowing it with the blood that they let out. But profaneness, that roots it up and lays all waste, consciences and churches also.

✦ WILLIAM GURNALL
Christian in Complete Armour, 301

And when a man shall come to appear before men and angels at the last day, those that are now the fools of the world that are derided for their godliness, that are mocked in their choice as men that are not able to set themselves in the face of the times so as to be somebody in the present age, but when they shall appear before the Lord Jesus to judge the quick and dead in His kingdom, then these will be esteemed of all others the only wise men. This was the soul that was directed by wisdom from above, that carried him still to the right chief good. If this will not stand by you in your greatest troubles, there is nothing in religion will do it.

✦ WILLIAM STRONG
Heavenly Treasure, 171

What is meant by *persecution*: the Greek word for *persecute* signifies to vex and molest, sometimes to persecute another, to arraign him at the bar, and to pursue him to the death. A persecutor is a pricking briar; therefore the church is described to be a "lily among thorns" (Song 2:2).

✦ THOMAS WATSON
The Beatitudes, in *Discourses*, 2:349

A true saint carries Christ in his heart and the cross on his shoulders. Christ's kingdom on earth is the kingdom of the cross. Christ and His cross are never parted. Persecution is the legacy bequeathed by Christ to His people. "In the world ye shall have tribulation" (John 16:33). We are all for reigning. "When wilt thou restore the kingdom again to Israel?" But the apostle tells

us of suffering before reigning. "If we suffer, we shall also reign with Him" (2 Tim. 2:12). Was His head crowned with thorns, and do we think to be crowned with roses?

✦ THOMAS WATSON
Gleanings, 65

PERSEVERANCE OF THE SAINTS

The perseverance of the saints is founded on the election of God and the immutability of His counsel; the foundation of the Lord standeth sure. "Whom he did predestinate, them he also called: and whom he called, them he also justified: and whom he justified, them he also glorified" (Rom. 8:30). This golden chain will hold; not a link of it shall be broken; on whomsoever the first link, election, hath taken hold, it will infallibly bring him up to the last, glory. God is not a man that He should repent.

✦ RICHARD ALLEINE
Heaven Opened, 229

If Jesus Christ has not purchased perseverance in grace to the end for all His people but leaves their continuance in the truth to their free will, then He leaves them in the same state in which they were under the first covenant. For the standing of Adam in the first covenant was upon his own choice and will, but this cannot be because Christ has taken away the first covenant from believers and established the second, which makes the comers thereunto perfect (Heb. 8:6–11; 10:9–10).

✦ BARTHOLOMEW ASHWOOD
Best Treasure, 248

If the soul is sliding and ready to fall, then that promise supports and upholds it in Psalm 37:24: "Though he fall, he shall not be utterly cast down: for the LORD upholdeth him with his hand"; or, as the Hebrew has it, "The Lord upholding Him with His hand." The Hebrew denotes a continued act of God. God has still His everlasting arms under His people so that they shall never totally nor finally fall. And the root from whence this word is derived signifies to sustain or uphold, as the tender mother does the little babe. The safety and security of the child lies not so much in the child's hanging about the mother's neck as in the mother's holding it fast in her arms. So our safety and security lie not so much in our weak holding upon Christ, but in Christ's holding us fast in His everlasting arms. This is our glory and our safety, that Christ's left hand is always under us and His right hand does always embrace us.

✦ THOMAS BROOKS
The Unsearchable Riches of Christ,
in *Select Works*, 1:133–34

That faith and holiness do inseparably follow election is shown before. Our business now is to show that faith and holiness are of an abiding nature and shall never be lost, and this is that we call *perseverance*, which, being the crown and glory of all the former points and that which secures to us the comforts arising thence; being, also, as much impugned as any of those. The proof and confirmation thereof is apparently necessary and tending to profit.

✦ ELISHA COLES
Practical Discourse, 239

Another argument for believers' invincible perseverance is that all the attributes of God do stand engaged for it. Virtue invincible has undertaken it; therefore, must it needs succeed.

✦ ELISHA COLES
Practical Discourse, 257

It is against the nature of grace not to be in motion, not to increase. Therefore, the Spirit of grace never gives over but perfects His work of regeneration, instruction, testification, consolation, preservation from evil, corroboration in good, intercession for our good. And wilt thou hinder Him (as much as in thee lieth)? Wilt thou be weary of praying with unutterable groans, of crying "Abba Father"? Wilt thou be weary of being strengthened with might in the inward man, of keeping thyself (David-like) from thine iniquity? Wilt thou be weary of rejoicing in the Holy Ghost, of believing the mutual testimony of God's Spirit and thine own spirit? Wilt thou be weary of learning all things, of knowing the joys of heaven? To be short, wilt thou be weary of being regenerate more and more, of being holy still? There is no good in thee but it must increase as the waves of the sea.

✦ HANNIBAL GAMMON
God's Just Desertion of the Unjust, 32–33

O where is our faith, sirs? Let God be wise, and all men and devils fools. What, though thou seest a Babel more likely to go up than a Babylon to be pulled down, yet believe God is making His secret approaches and will clap His ladders on a sudden to the walls thereof. Suppose truth were prisoner with Joseph, and error the courtier to have its head lift up by the favor of the times, yet dost not remember that the way to truth's preferment lies through the prison? Yea, what though the church were like Jonah in the whale's belly, swallowed up to the eye of reason by the fury of men; yet dost not remember the whale had not power to digest the prophet? O be not too quick to bury the church before she be dead.

✦ WILLIAM GURNALL
Christian in Complete Armour, 76

You read in Hebrews 6:4 of some that were once enlightened and have "tasted of the heavenly gift, and were made partakers of the Holy Ghost." What work shall we call this? It could not be a saving work, a true change and conversion of state. For notwithstanding this enlightening and tasting and partaking, yet they are said to "fall away" (v. 6). Had it been a true work of grace, they could never have fallen away from that. A believer may fall, but he cannot fall away; he may fall foully, but he can never fall finally, for "underneath are the everlasting arms." His faith is established in the strength of that prayer of Christ, that our "faith fail not"; nay, He tells us expressly that it is "eternal life" which He gives, from which we "shall

never perish" (John 10:28). This work then, here spoken of, cannot be any saving work because it is not an abiding work; for they that are under it are said to fall away from it.

✦ MATTHEW MEAD
Almost Christian Discovered, 135–36

It is not from anything in us that we stand and are preserved, but from without us; yea, from above us, even from the power of God. So saith the apostle: "[We] are kept by the power of God through faith unto salvation" (1 Peter 1:5). It is, you see, grace held to us that causeth grace to hold out in us. Faith lays hold on God's power to be kept, and we are kept by the power of God through faith.

✦ MATTHEW MEAD
"The Power of Grace," in
Name in Heaven, 93

It is true our persistency in Christ doth not, as to the issue and event, depend absolutely on our own diligence. The unalterableness of our union with Christ, on the account of the faithfulness of the covenant of grace, is that which doth and shall eventually secure it. But yet our own diligent endeavor is such an indispensable means for that end as that without it, it will not be brought about.... Diligence and endeavors in this matter are like Paul's mariners when he was shipwrecked at Melita. God had beforehand given him the lives of all that sailed with him in the ship, and he believed that it should be even as God had told him. So now the preservation of their lives depended absolutely on the faithfulness and power of God. But yet when the mariners began to flee out of the ship, Paul tells the centurion and the soldiers that unless those men stayed they could not be saved. But what need he think of shipmen when God had promised and taken upon Himself the preservation of them all (Acts 27:31)? He knew full well that He would preserve them, but yet that He would do so in and by the use of means. If we are in Christ, God hath given us the lives of our souls and hath taken upon Himself in His covenant the preservation of them; but yet we may say with reference unto the means that He hath appointed, when storms and trials arise, unless we use our own diligent endeavors, "we cannot be saved."

✦ JOHN OWEN
Golden Book, 188–89

For the little strength we receive in regeneration is, in point of perseverance, stronger than the great strength which the first Adam received in his creation. Adam was perfectly but changeably holy; God's children in regeneration are made imperfectly but unchangeably holy. This stability of grace now consists in this, in that all who by faith and by the Holy Spirit are ingrafted and incorporated into Christ, the second Adam, have the spring and root of their grace founded in Him, and not in themselves as the first Adam had. They are established in Christ.

✦ HENRY SCUDDER
Christian's Daily Walk, 396

Though Christians be not kept altogether from falling, yet they are kept from falling altogether.

✦ WILLIAM SECKER
in Horn, *Puritan Remembrancer*, 366

The best trees have a winter wherein they seem to be dead and barren, yet they have their life and sap at that time remaining in the root. Christians under desertions and temptations may be judged by themselves and others to be dead and undone, but even at such seasons their life is hid with Christ in God; though they may fall foully, they cannot fall finally.

✦ GEORGE SWINNOCK
The Christian Man's Calling,
in *Works*, 2:468–69

PIETY

Piety shall have riches without rust, wealth without want, store without sore, beauty without blemish, mirth without mixture.

✦ JOHN TRAPP
in Horn, *Puritan Remembrancer*, 197

PLEASURES

[A] common end which men naturally pursue and which we must deny is pleasure. 'Tis true, some pleasures are lawful and in a sober, moderate, seasonable use of them serve for the refreshing, comforting, and supporting of our frail bodies. Yet we must deny them in these cases: (1) when they are baits to draw us into sin; (2) when they are sin, or the concomitants of sin, or the fruits and wages of sin. The directions of self-denial, in respect of worldly pleasures, are these: (1) Look on pleasures not only as vain but as vanishing. They are soon gone from us.... (2) We are soon gone from them.... It is but awhile, and then we and all our pleasures must together vanish; if death draw the curtain and look in upon us, then we must bid a farewell to them all.... When we are called to eternity, then all our delights will leave us and bid us adieu forever, and how doleful will this be to all the sons and daughters of pleasure!

✦ ISAAC AMBROSE
"The Practice of Sanctification,"
in *Works*, 97

Make use of all that prosperity and lawful pleasure which God giveth you in outward things for the increase and advantage of your delight in God. Though corrupted nature is apter to abuse prosperity and earthly delights than any other state, to the diverting of the heart from God; and almost all the devil's poison is given in sugared or gilded allectives [i.e., allurements], yet the primitive, natural use of prosperity, of health and plenty, and honor and peace is to lead up the mind to God and give us a taste of His spiritual delights!

✦ RICHARD BAXTER
A Christian Directory, in
Practical Works, 2:418

Pleasures are like a substance in the pursuit, but clouds in the enjoyment. Pleasure is a beautiful harlot sitting in her chariot whose four wheels are pride, gluttony, lust, and idleness; the two horses are prosperity and abundance; the two drivers are idleness and security; her attendants and followers are guilt, grief, late repentance (if any), and oft death and ruin.

✦ THOMAS BROOKS
Apples of Gold, 90

Tell the sensualist of his voluptuous, brutish life, and you shall have him sometimes reply, "Solomon was not so precise and scrupulous, who saith, 'A man hath no better thing under the sun than to eat and to drink and to be merry.'" As if Solomon—yea, God Himself that directed his pen—meant to fill the drunkard's quaffing cup for him and were a friend of gluttons and winebibbers. Whereas, to eat and drink and be merry, as Solomon meant there, amounts to no more than to serve God with gladness in the abundance of those good things which God gives us to enjoy, as Moses says (Deut. 28:47). Such is the desperate wickedness of man's heart, that the sweetest portions of Scripture are wrested by many to serve their lusts.

✦ WILLIAM GURNALL
Christian in Complete Armour, 587

Luxury is living in pleasure. God allows us to use pleasures, but not to live in them; to take delights, but not that they should take us. To live always at the full is but a wanton luxury.

✦ THOMAS MANTON
Practical Exposition on the
Epistle of James, 185

Some men do nothing but knit pleasure to pleasure; their lives are nothing else but a diversion from one carnal pleasure to another. There is a time to feast and "a time to mourn" (Eccl. 3:4). Such men disturb the order of seasons. Nature is relieved with changes but clogged with continuance; frequency of pleasures begets a habit. And besides, this puts men upon novel curiosities when ordinary pleasures by common use grow stale; pleasure itself must have pleasure to refresh it, accustomed delights becoming our clog and burden.

✦ THOMAS MANTON
Practical Exposition on the
Epistle of James, 186

He buys his pleasures too dear who pays for them with the loss of his soul.

✦ MATTHEW MEAD
Name in Heaven, 12–13

The earth is big in our hopes but little in our hands.

✦ WILLIAM SECKER
in Horn, *Puritan Remembrancer*, 323

Enjoy all things for God by using all for Him. Those riches, honors, interests, and friends which are clogs upon the heels of others, let them be as springs to you to raise you heavenward. Let your souls be winged with those very enjoyments wherewith the wings of others are pinioned, and that which is fuel to their worldly lusts, let it be as fuel to feed and nourish your spiritual love. To use what we have for God is the only way not to abuse it; this is one way of enjoying all for God, to use all for Him.

✦ SAMUEL SHAW
Voice of One Crying in the
Wilderness, 164

Who are void of the Spirit, but sensual ones (Jude 18–19)? Who say to God, "Depart from us," but those that dance (Job 21:10–11)? Better be preserved in brine than rot in honey.

✦ JOHN TRAPP
Commentary...upon...the
New Testament, 847

POLITICS

In plain English, a hypocrite is neither more nor less than a stage player. We all know that stage players some years since were put down by public authority, and though something may be said for them, more may be brought against them who are rather in an employment than a vocation. But let me safely utter my too just fears; I suspect the fire was quenched in the chimney and, in another respect, scattered about the house. Never more strange stage players than now who wear the vizards of piety and holiness, that under that covert they may more securely commit sacrilege, oppression, and whatnot. In the days of Queen Elizabeth, a person of honor or worship would as patiently have digested the lie as to have been told that they did wear false pendants or any counterfeit pearl or jewels about them, so usual in our age; yet would it were the worst piece of hypocrisy in fashion. Oh, let us all labor for integrity of heart and either appear what we are or be what we appear!

✦ THOMAS FULLER
Good Thoughts, 304–5

Christ, when on earth, cured many a spot, especially of leprosy, but never smoothed any wrinkle—never made any old man young again. But in heaven He will do both (Eph. 5:27). When He shall present it to Himself a glorious church, not having spot or wrinkle or any such thing, but that it should be holy and without blemish. Triumphant perfection is not to be hoped for in the militant church; there will be in it many spots and wrinkles as long as it consists of sinful mortal men, the members thereof. It is Christ's work, not man's work, to make a perfect reformation. Such, therefore, are no good politicians who will make a sore to mend a spot, cause a wound to plain a wrinkle, do a great and certain mischief when a small and uncertain benefit will thereby redound.

> ◆ THOMAS FULLER
> *Good Thoughts*, 338–39

Too many in all ages have turned a common weal into a common woe. They have spun themselves superfine suits out of the nation's fleece. Many noble birds have been deplumed that their wings might be richly feathered. When any springs have been opened, they have laid pipes to convey the water into their own cisterns. Such pretended pilots have steered the ship of plenty into their own haven, but justice will certainly squeeze such sponges and leave them as dry at last as they were at first. All those moths shall be destroyed which eat into other men's garments. For a man to advance his interest out of another's property is to keep all the meat in his mouth and starve all the body beside.

> ◆ WILLIAM SECKER
> *Nonsuch Professor*, 46–47

Men confine their usefulness to their own faction, as if they were indebted to seek the good of none beyond it; nay, as if conscience obliged them against all attempts for benefits more common and extensive. They judge all men out of their herd unworthy of their love, concern, or labor. What's the public to them, further than as things affect their own? Let the ship sink, so their cabin can be saved; they'll obstruct all settlement in church or state if it be any other than a provision for their sect or managed by any besides themselves— yea, scruple not to advance their party upon the ruins of the public, as men see from age to age.

> ◆ DANIEL WILLIAMS
> *Excellency of a Publick Spirit*, 65

THE POOR

As for the poor, it is hard in this case [i.e., their duty to liberality] to give them counsel, for such is the weakness of our nature that when we are brought to any hard pinch, we can hardly bear it, especially when we have not the wherewithal to relieve ourselves. Good counsel will then very hardly take place with us, for the belly hath no ears.

> ◆ WILLIAM CUPPER
> "Tenth Sermon concerning God's
> Late Visitation," in *Certaine
> Sermons*, 355

Despising the poor is a sin not only against the word and written will of God but His mind and intent in His works and dispensations. He opposes their practice to God's dispensations. It is a kind of gigantomachy, a resisting of God.... It is against the mind of God in their creation. "The rich and poor meet together: the LORD is the maker of them all" (Prov. 22:2); that is, they meet in this, that they have but one Maker.

✦ THOMAS MANTON
Practical Exposition on the
Epistle of James, 86

POVERTY

This [i.e., the reality of gospel treasure] reproves those of the people of God who have an interest in these vast treasures of Christ and yet are miserably poor in their own souls. Many complain times be hard, estates waste, trades decay; but the greatest poverty lies in spirituals. Faith, love, humility, self-denial, mortifiedness to the world—persons are destitute of these things chiefly; little grace laid out, little grace laid up. Few workings of Spirit in duty and few works of grace in men's lives; this argues wonderful poverty in men's souls.

✦ BARTHOLOMEW ASHWOOD
Best Treasure, 381

Poverty is no disparagement to the godly nor wealth any preferment to the wicked.

✦ ROBERT CLEAVER
AND JOHN DOD
Plain and Familiar Exposition, 85

Much of the glory of heaven may dwell in a simple cottage, and poor persons, even under rags, may be very like God.

✦ JOHN OWEN
Golden Book, 226

PRAISE

Conceive of this duty of praising God according to its superlative excellencies as being the highest service that the tongue of men or angels can perform. To bless or praise or magnify God is not to make Him greater or better or happier than He is, but to declare and extol His greatness, goodness, and felicity.

✦ RICHARD BAXTER
A Christian Directory, in
Practical Works, 2:438

Joy and praise promote each other. And this it does (1) by keeping the soul near to God and within the warmth of His love and goodness; (2) by the exercise of love and joy, which are the cordial, reviving, strengthening graces; (3) by dissipating distrustful, vexing thoughts and diverting the mind to sweeter things; (4) by keeping off the tempter, who usually is least able to follow us with his molestations when we are highest in the praises of our God; (5) by bringing out the evidences of our sincerity into the light, while the chiefest graces are in exercise; (6) and by way of reward from God, that loveth the praises of His meanest servants.

✦ RICHARD BAXTER
A Christian Directory, in
Practical Works, 2:442

Lip praise is good, but life praise is better.

✦ THOMAS CASE
Correction, Instruction, 130

God's praise is too big for the heart; acknowledge all therefore privately in thy prayers to God, and not only so but also to others. When God had delivered the Israelites, Moses tells Jethro what He had done for them (Ex. 18:8). David bids them come to him, and he would tell them what He had done for his soul. Christ's reward of the leper for healing him was, "Go and tell what is done for thee." Instead of foolish jesting, which our mouths are full of, rather give thanks (Eph. 5:4); and if the heart were full, the mouth would be filled with praise.

✦ THOMAS GOODWIN
A Discourse of Thankfulness,
in *Works,* 9:504–5

Obs[ervation]. 1: Praising God is a work very suitable to saints. Obs. 2: After all exhortations for obtaining any good, God must be acknowledged the author of that good. Obs. 3: It is our duty to praise God for future blessings, for what we have in hope as well as for what we have in hand. Obs. 4: Spiritual blessings principally deserve our praises. Obs. 5: In our addresses to God, we should have such apprehensions and use such expressions concerning Him as may most strengthen our faith. Obs. 6: Our speeches concerning Christ must be with highest honor and reverence.

Obs. 7: Praise should conclude that work which prayer began.

✦ WILLIAM JENKYN
Exposition upon the Epistle of Jude, 360

A drop of praise is an unsuitable acknowledgment for an ocean of mercy.

✦ WILLIAM SECKER
Nonsuch Professor, 9

O, my soul, praise God with the best instrument, the heart, and let the instrument be screwed up to the highest, do it with the whole heart. When God is tuning upon the string of mercy, a Christian should be tuning upon the string of praise.

✦ THOMAS WATSON
The Christian's Charter of Privileges,
in *Discourses,* 1:124

Four sacrifices God is much pleased with: the sacrifice of Christ's blood, the sacrifice of a broken heart, the sacrifice of alms, and the sacrifice of thanksgiving. Praise and thanksgiving, says Mr. Greenham, is the most excellent part of God's worship, for this shall continue in the heavenly choir when all other exercises of religion shall cease.

✦ THOMAS WATSON
Godly Man's Picture, 123

PRAYER

Prayer is a matter more of the heart than the head. In prayer, it is not so much fluency prevails as fervency (James 5:16), nor is God so much taken with elegancy of speech as the efficacy of the Spirit. Humility is better than arrogance. Here the mourner is the orator; sighs and groans are the best rhetoric.

✦ SIMEON ASHE
Primitive Divinity, 83

A man may pray like a saint or an angel and yet not have a jot of the Spirit of prayer. But it is the encouragement of the Spirit to wrestle with God by Christ; the inward suggestions of hope when a soul can go to God as to a father, when the very heart goes out to God in prayer, and when prayer is winged with faith and love. These are the effects of a Spirit of prayer and the fruit of a soul's reception of Christ.

✦ BARTHOLOMEW ASHWOOD
Best Treasure, 399

O most gracious God and loving Father, who feedest all creatures living which depend upon Thy divine providence, we beseech Thee, sanctify these creatures which thou hast ordained for us. Give them virtue to nourish our bodies in life and health, and give us grace to receive them soberly and thankfully as from Thy hands, that so, in the strength of these and Thy other blessings, we may walk in the uprightness of our hearts before Thy face this day and all the days of our lives, through Jesus Christ, our Lord and only Savior. Amen (1 Kings 19:8; Ps. 10:17; 147:9; Joel 1:10; 1 Tim. 4:5).

✦ LEWIS BAYLY
Practice of Piety, 152

It is not convenient [for ministers] to be long in prayer usually, except upon extraordinary occasion sometime. Remember that one may more easily continue praying with devotion than others hearing in silence can religiously give an assent with good attention. Half-hour prayers are too tedious, usual with some men, which is their indiscretion; wearisome to all, liked of none, but such as use them who seem to strive to win God by words or to waste time. It may be thought that such weigh not other men's weakness or that prayer is not held fervent, that it is not stretched out to such a length, when experience shows to every man's feeling that fervency of spirit in prayer is not so enduring, but even in a short space is interrupted with wavering thoughts and by fantasies. The edge of godly fervency of affection is soon blunted. Let everyone in praying consider what he is in hearing, and so measure his time.

✦ RICHARD BERNARD
Faithful Shepherd, 14

What is prayer? We oft speak of going to prayer, but what is praying? Why prayer, it may be thus described: it is the breathing of a gracious soul, in the help of the Spirit of grace, whereby it is enabled to go to God in a promise, in the name of Christ, to beg suitable mercy as the case may require.

✦ THOMAS BLAKE
Living Truths in Dying Times, 100

Prayer is the soul's weapon, and is it not a grief to lack a weapon in our spiritual warfare? Prayer is the soul's ornament, the excellent garment of a Christian; and is it not an affliction to be without this garment and to be found naked? Prayer is the Christian's element, and as the fish lives in the water as in its element and dies when it is out of it, so a Christian lives in prayer as in his element, and his heart dies when he is out of it. Prayer is the soul's provisioner, bringing in provision for the soul and for all its graces.

✦ WILLIAM BRIDGE
Lifting Up, 106–7

What is prayer and the nature of it? Prayer is the pouring out of the soul to God; not the pouring out of words nor the pouring out of expressions, but the pouring out of the soul to God.

✦ WILLIAM BRIDGE
Lifting Up, 115

The word *father* is a sweet word, for it sweetens all our duties. Take the word *father* out of prayer, and how sour it is!

✦ WILLIAM BRIDGE
Lifting Up, 130

Prayer is too hard and too high a work for an unsound heart to hold on in; prayer is heart work, and that proves heavy work to him. The soul of prayer lies in the pouring out of the soul before God, and this is a work that a hypocrite has no skill in.

✦ THOMAS BROOKS
Cabinet of Choice Jewels, 305

Cold prayers bespeak a denial, but fervent prayers offer a sacred violence both to heaven and earth.

✦ THOMAS BROOKS
Privy Key of Heaven, 172

Fervent prayer is the soul's contention, the soul's struggling with God. It is a sweating work; it is the sweat and blood of the soul. It's a laying out to the uttermost all the strength and powers of the soul. He that would gain victory over God in private prayer must strain every string of his heart; he must in beseeching God besiege Him, and so get the better of Him.

✦ THOMAS BROOKS
Privy Key of Heaven, 173–74

He is either a fool or a madman, either very weak or very wicked, that prays, and prays but never looks after his prayers; that shoots many an arrow toward heaven but never minds where his arrows alight: "I will hear what God the LORD will speak: for he will speak peace unto his people, and to his saints" (Ps. 85:8). If David would have God to hearken to his prayers, he must then hearken to what God will speak; and upon this point it seems he was fully resolved.

✦ THOMAS BROOKS
Privy Key of Heaven, 202

Prayer is nothing but the breathing that out before the Lord that was first breathed into us by the Spirit of the Lord.

✦ THOMAS BROOKS
Smooth Stones, 228

Pray often, for prayer is a shield to the soul, a sacrifice to God, and a scourge to Satan.

✦ JOHN BUNYAN
"Mr. John Bunyan's Dying
Sayings," in Works, 80

Prayer is a sincere, sensible, affectionate pouring out of the heart or soul to God, through Christ, in the strength and assistance of the Holy Spirit, for such things as God has promised or, according to His word, for the good of the church with submission in faith to the will of God.

✦ JOHN BUNYAN
Prayer, 13

Before you enter into prayer, ask thy soul these questions: To what end, O my soul, art thou retired into this place? Art thou not come to discourse the Lord in prayer? Is He present? Will He hear thee? Is He merciful? Will He help thee? Is thy business slight? Is it not concerning the welfare of thy soul? What words wilt thou use to move Him to compassion?

✦ JOHN BUNYAN
Riches, 305

There is no stinted order presented for our behaving ourselves in prayer, whether kneeling or standing or walking or lying or sitting, for all these postures have been used by the godly. Paul kneeled down and prayed; Abraham and the publican stood and prayed; David prayed as he walked; Abraham prayed lying upon his face; Moses prayed sitting (Acts 20:36; 2 Sam. 15:30–31; Gen. 17:17–18; Ex. 17:12 [, respectively]). And indeed prayer—

effectual, fervent prayer—may be and often is made unto God under all these circumstances. For God has not tied us up to any of them, and he that shall tie himself or his people to any of these doeth more than he hath warrant for from God. And let such take care of innovating; it is the next way to make men hypocrites and dissemblers in those duties in which they should be sincere.

✦ JOHN BUNYAN
Riches, 322–23

In prosperity we pray heavily and drowsily, but adversity adds wings to our prayers (Isa. 26:16).

✦ EDMUND CALAMY
Godly Man's Ark, 12

We are apt to say of prayer...when answered, it must have been so, I or he was so fervent and enlarged in it. Hence, some pray fervently for a mercy and confidently look for it and yet are disappointed—and why? Because not dead to praying and believing, but lay more weight on faith in God and praying to God than on God Himself or on Jesus Christ. Some believe in their believing and pray to their prayers.

✦ ALEXANDER CARMICHAEL
Believer's Mortification of Sin, 27

We used to say, "He that cannot pray, let him go to sea." Thus, I say, affliction opens dumb lips and untieth the strings of the tongue to call upon God. But whom God teacheth in affliction, they learn to pray in another manner, more frequently, more fervently.

✦ THOMAS CASE
Correction, Instruction, 18

One great use which Christians should make of reading the Scriptures is to learn from thence the language of prayer. O that the professors of this age would in this particular learn what to pray and how to pray for their brethren in tribulation. O that they would censure less and pray more, and instead of speaking one of another, speak more one to another and one for another; that was the good old way—"Then they that feared the Lord spake often one to another." But now the tender, praying, healing, restoring Spirit is departed, and if Christians stir not up themselves to call it back again, it is a sad presage that God is departing too.

✦ THOMAS CASE
Correction, Instruction, 140

Though prayer be the key that opens God's treasures, yet faith is the hand that turns the key, without which it will do no good.

✦ SAMUEL CLARK
Saint's Nosegay, 89

Temporal things granted out of ordinary providence only do increase our lusts and are snares to us, but obtained by prayer, they are sanctified to us.

✦ SAMUEL CLARK
Saint's Nosegay, 96

That ship doth always sail the surest which is driven with the breath of godly men's prayers.

✦ SAMUEL CLARK
Saint's Nosegay, 97

The work of prayer is not to move or remove God—He is in one mind, He is still the same—but to move and remove our hearts near to the Lord; and then have we prayed to purpose when by prayer our hearts and spirits are in a more sublime and celestial frame; when we are more above natural, carnal, and formal self; when more off and above the world and all the encouragements and discouragements of it.

✦ THOMAS COBBET
Gospel Incense, 5

Prayer is a spiritual and faithful opening of the heart to God in the name of Christ with an eye to seasonable help and relief from Him. By *heart*, we mean thoughts, desires, affections; these wants and weaknesses and sins to which the heart is privy and of which it is sensible.

✦ THOMAS COBBET
Gospel Incense, 13–14

Such have little love to others who are little with God in prayer.

✦ THOMAS COBBET
Gospel Incense, 96

Be sensible of our utter destitution of what we are to ask of God and our inability to get it any other way: "Lend me three loaves, for a friend of mine is come and I have nothing to set before him." "I perish for hunger; I will arise and go to my father and say, 'Make me as one of thy hired servants.'" "My heart is desolate within me." "My soul thirsteth after thee." When all other means fail such spiritual beggars and that only door of grace is left for their relief or else they must famish, how earnestly will it cause them to knock there.

✦ THOMAS COBBET
Gospel Incense, 151

Take holy advantages of movings of the Spirit in prayer and of Christ's approaches to us; opportunity helps importunity: "And behold two blind men sitting by the wayside when they heard that Jesus passed by cried out, saying, 'Have mercy on us, O Lord, thou son of David.' And Jesus stood still and called them and said, 'What will you that I do unto you?' They say to him, 'Lord, that our eyes may be opened.'" When Christ by His Spirit calls us to Him, puts us upon asking, and when He stands still waiting to be gracious to us, let Him not go till He bless us.

✦ THOMAS COBBET
Gospel Incense, 152

We must sometimes pray that we may pray, and when as we are apt to judge ourselves that we are most unfit to pray, then to pray that we may become fit to pray; as by speaking, men are fitted to speak; by running to run; by wrestling to wrestle; by laboring to labor.

✦ THOMAS COBBET
Gospel Incense, 162

Let such as would hold up such a blessed frame in their hearts be daily drawing from the flowers of God's providences and promises some spiritual sweetness, and then our spiritual combs will be dropping ripe. Drone-like professors, while they neglect this and live upon an old stock of grace or comfort received, grow altogether

listless to prayer; they have enough already. What need they ask more? But this beelike diligence in the saints will make their lips like the dropping honeycomb. And this is done mostly by daily meditation, whereby we do in a holy manner sit and dwell upon and draw out the sweet and sap which is in God's words and works: "Consider my meditation"—that is, prayer.

✦ THOMAS COBBET
Gospel Incense, 175

When we are most frequent and fervent in secret prayers of all other prayers. What is said of grief is true of prayer. He prays most truly and sincerely that prays most secretly. Hence our Savior does oppose secret prayer to hypocritical praying.

✦ THOMAS COBBET
Gospel Incense, 241

If the instrument of a Christian's spirit be not well tuned in prayer, truly he will make but bad music all the day after in his calling and employments. If we speed not well at heaven's court, we shall not do so well in earth's country. If at this holy mart and port we get not well stored and full lading, we shall make but poor markets elsewhere.

✦ THOMAS COBBET
Gospel Incense, 339

We may be short in prayer (1) in case of bodily sickness, pain, faintness, and death approaching: "How can thy servant talk with this my Lord, there remaining no strength in me?" Sick Hezekiah and Jacob were short in prayer: "Jacob worshiped God leaning on his staff." (2) In case of pressing occasions, unavoidable by ordinary prudence or providence. When the Philistines came suddenly upon Samuel and upon Saul in prayer, they soon dispatch. (3) In case of prevailing indisposedness of heart to pray; after much strivings to pray, yet distempers and hurries of spirit abate not. Better then be short than multiply words in any senseless and tumultuous manner and take God's name in vain. (4) In case a Christian be personally persecuted and may not stay long in one place. (5) In case the prayer to be made be only occasional, above that of our ordinary course. In such a case Hezekiah is short.

♦ THOMAS COBBET
Gospel Incense, 346

What ought to be the matter of our prayers? For answer to that, we shall only observe this in the general, that it ought to be framed and suited according to the several parts of prayer—namely, confession, petition, intercession, and thanksgiving. In particular, this rule ought to be observed, that spiritual blessings and such as appertain to the welfare of the soul ought primarily to be sought, and with greatest earnestness. Temporal blessings and such things as appertain this life ought to be begged, with resignation to God and a humble submission to His infinite wisdom and holy will: "And this is the confidence that we have in him, that, if we ask any thing according to his will, he heareth us" (1 John 5:14).

♦ SAMUEL CRADOCK
Knowledge and Practice,
part 2, chaps. 5, 20

Prayer is as the pulse showing the state of the heart. If the spiritual life be weak, such will our prayers be; and contrarily, whosoever is very godly hath great life in prayer.

♦ EZEKIEL CULVERWELL
Time Well Spent, 253

Prayer is a speaking to God in spirit according to His will, or a crying of the heart to God, which sets out the matter and manner, not cold but fervent.

♦ EZEKIEL CULVERWELL
Time Well Spent, 255

What we win by prayer we shall wear with comfort.

♦ JOHN DOD
Worthy Sayings, n.p.

Those truths that are got by prayer leave an unusual sweetness upon the heart.

♦ JOHN FLAVEL
Fountain of Life, 80

Though we die, our prayers do not die with us. They outlive us, and those we leave behind us in the world may reap the benefit of them when we are turned to dust.

♦ JOHN FLAVEL
Golden Gems, 63

They that part praying may hope to meet again rejoicing, and those designs which are not prefaced with prayer cannot wind up with a blessing.

♦ JOHN FLAVEL
"The Seaman's Farewell," in
Navigation Spiritualized, 231

Those that undertake voyages by sea had need not only pray earnestly themselves but also to engage the prayers of other Christians for them.

✦ JOHN FLAVEL
"The Seaman's Farewell," in
Navigation Spiritualized, 231

It is best every day to begin with God. It is the advice of a reverend man: "If more necessary duties call you not away, let secret prayer by yourself alone, or with your chamberfellow, or both go before the common prayers of the family; and delay it not causelessly but, if possible, let it be first before any other work of the day. Yet be not formal and superstitious to your hours, as if God had absolutely tied you to such a time." That hour is best for one that may not be fit for another. Private prayer is most seasonable unto most as soon as they are up and clothed; to others, some other hour may be freer and fitter.

✦ WILLIAM GEARING
Sacred Diary, 41

God is very tender of this flower of His crown, this part of His name. Indeed, He cannot spell it right and leave out this letter, for that is God's name whereby He is known from all His creatures. Now man may be called wise, merciful, mighty; God, only all-wise, all-merciful, all-mighty. So when we leave out this syllable *all*, we nickname God and call Him by His creature's name, which He will not answer to.

✦ WILLIAM GURNALL
Christian in Complete Armour, 14

God has strength enough to give, but He has no strength to deny. Here the Almighty Himself, with reverence be it spoken, is weak; even a child, the weakest in grace of His family that can but say "Father" is able to overcome Him, and therefore let not the weakness of your faith discourage you.

✦ WILLIAM GURNALL
Christian in Complete Armour, 21

He is the best student in divinity that studies most upon his knees.

✦ WILLIAM GURNALL
Christian in Complete Armour, 121

A weak hand with a sincere heart is able to turn the key in prayer.

✦ WILLIAM GURNALL
Christian in Complete Armour, 236

Engage God from His promise when thou pray against any sin; show God His own hand in such promises as these: "Sin shall not have dominion over you" (Rom. 6:14). "He will subdue our iniquities" (Mic. 7:19). Prayer is nothing but the promise reversed, or God's word formed into an argument and retorted by faith upon God again.

✦ WILLIAM GURNALL
Christian in Complete Armour, 486

What is prayer, but the breathing forth of that grace which is breathed into the soul by the Holy Spirit? When God breathed into man the breath of life, he became a living soul; so when God breathes into the creature the breath of spiritual life, it becomes a praying soul: "Behold, he prayeth," saith God of Paul to Ananias (Acts 9:11). As if he had said, "Be not afraid of him; he is an honest soul. Thou mayest trust him, for he prays." Praying is the same to the new creature as crying is to the natural. The child is not learned by art to cry, but by nature it comes into the world crying. Praying is not a lesson got by forms and rules of art but flowing from principles of new life.

✦ WILLIAM GURNALL
Christian in Complete Armour, 627

The greatness of thy request cannot hinder thy success. They are most welcome that ask most. Who are the persons frowned on at the throne of grace but those who lay out the strength of their desires and bestow their greatest importunity for mercies of least worth!

✦ WILLIAM GURNALL
Christian in Complete Armour, 643

There are three privileges purchased for every believer, and none of them can be lost by us without dishonor to [God]. First, He hath purchased a liberty to pray. It had been death to come on such an errand to God till He had by His blood paved a way and procured a safe conduct (Heb. 10:27). Secondly, an ability to pray: as He purchased the Spirit for us called, therefore, "the Spirit of promise." Thirdly, the safe return of our prayers: "Whatsoever ye shall ask the Father in my name, he will give it you" (John 16:23). Indeed it is His business in heaven to own our cause and to present His blood, for all His saints beg that no demur be made to their request. So that either thou must

blot this article of Christ's intercession out of thy creed or else put thyself to shame for questioning thy entertainment with God, when thou hast so good a friend at court to speak for thee.

✦ WILLIAM GURNALL
Christian in Complete Armour, 643

Believers' prayers pass a refining before they come into God's hands. Did He indeed read them with their impertinences and take our blotted copy out of our hand, we could not fear too much, but they come under the Corrector's hand. Our Lord Jesus hath the inspection of them, who sets right all our broken requests and misplaced petitions; He washes out our blots with His blood; through His mediation all that is coarse and heterogeneous in our prayers is separated from the pure; what is of His own Spirit's breathing He presents, and what our fleshly part added He hides so that it shall not prejudice us or our prayers.

✦ WILLIAM GURNALL
Christian in Complete Armour, 652

"This is the confidence that we have in him, that, if we ask any thing according to his will, he heareth us" (1 John 5:14). Faith without a promise is like a foot without firm ground to stand upon. Now, the promise contains this will of God. Be sure thou gather all thy flowers of prayer out of this garden, and thou canst not do amiss; but take heed of mingling with them any wild gourd of thy own.

✦ WILLIAM GURNALL
Christian in Complete Armour, 653–54

When shall I know that I aim at God or self in prayer? This will commonly appear by the posture of our heart, when God delays or denies the thing we pray for. A soul that can acquiesce and patiently bear a delay or denial (I speak now of such mercies as are of an inferior nature, not necessary to salvation, and so not absolutely promised) gives a hopeful testimony that the glory of God weighs more in his thoughts than his own private interest. A selfish heart is…hasty; it must have the thing it cries for, and that quickly, or else it…breaks out into murmuring complaints.

✦ WILLIAM GURNALL
Christian in Complete Armour, 655

Our prayer may be hindered two ways: by lying in any sin we commit against God or in wrath, by not forgiving our brother's sin committed against us. Those two in our Lord's prayer cannot be divorced: "Forgive us as we forgive."

✦ WILLIAM GURNALL
Christian in Complete Armour, 656

Positively, to pray in faith is to ask of God, in the name of Christ, what He hath promised, relying on His power and truth for performance without binding Him up to time, manner, or means.

✦ WILLIAM GURNALL
Christian in Complete Armour, 657

How may I know when I thus exercise faith in prayer? First, by the serenity and composure of thy spirit after prayer. Faith may live in a storm, but it will not suffer a storm to live in it. As faith rises, so the blustering wind of discontented, troublesome thoughts go down. In the same proportion that there is faith in the heart there is peace also; they are joined together: "In returning and rest shall ye be saved; in quietness and in confidence shall be your strength" (Isa. 30:15). Secondly, dost thou continue praying even when God continues to deny? An unbelieving heart will be sure to jade in a long journey. Faith will throw in the net of prayer again and again, as long as God commands and the promise encourages…. As faith uses her wings of prayer to fly to heaven, so she uses her feet of duty and obedience with which she walks and bestirs herself on earth. Faith will make thee to be choice of the means thou uses for the obtaining what thou speaks of God in prayer…. Faith is a working grace.

✦ WILLIAM GURNALL
Christian in Complete Armour, 659–60

Pray in prosperity that thou mayest speed when thou prayest in adversity; own God now, that He may acknowledge thee then. Shall that friend be welcome to us who never gives us a visit but when He comes to borrow? This is acting the part of a beggar, not a friend. Secondly, pray in prosperity to prove that thou didst not pray in hypocrisy when thou wert afflicted. One prayer now will be a better evidence for thy sincerity than a whole bundle of duties performed in adversity. Thirdly, pray in prosperity, that thou mayest not be ensnared by it.

✦ WILLIAM GURNALL
Christian in Complete Armour, 671

Prayer must be the key of the morning and lock of the night. We show not ourselves Christians if we do not open our eyes with prayer when we rise and shut them again with the same key when we lie down at night.
✦ WILLIAM GURNALL
Christian in Complete Armour, 673

Ordinary prayer is the saint's food; he can as little miss the constant returns of it as his usual meals. But extraordinary prayer is his physic to clear and discharge the soul of those distempers which it contracts and cannot conquer by the use of ordinary means, as also to advance and heighten the Christian graces unto a farther degree of strength and activity.
✦ WILLIAM GURNALL
Christian in Complete Armour, 707

Pray often rather than very long. It is difficult to remain long in prayer and not slacken in our affections. Those watches which are made to go longer than ordinary at one winding do commonly lose time toward the end.... He who in a long journey lights often to let his beast take breath will get to his journey's end sooner than he that puts him beyond his strength. Especially observe this in social prayers.
✦ WILLIAM GURNALL
Christian in Complete Armour, 714

Resolutions in time of prayer are good when backed with strenuous endeavors; otherwise they are but a blind for a false heart to cover itself. Samson did not only pray he might be avenged on his enemies but set his hands to the pillars of the house.
✦ WILLIAM GURNALL
Christian in Complete Armour, 723

We pray in our spirit when first, when we pray with knowledge; secondly, in fervency; thirdly, in sincerity. By knowledge, the understanding is set on work; by fervency, the affections; and by sincerity, the will. All these are required before you can pray in the spirit. There may be knowledge without fervency, and this is cold and quickens not. There may be heat without knowledge, and this is like courage in a blind horse. There may be knowledge and fervency, and this is like a chariot with swift horses and a skillful driver, but being dishonest, carries it the wrong way. Neither of these—nor both together—avail because sincerity is wanting. He will have little thanks for his zeal that is fervent in spirit, but serving himself with it, not the Lord.
✦ WILLIAM GURNALL
Christian in Complete Armour, 743

Fervency unites the soul and gathers in the thoughts to the work in hand; it will not suffer diversions but answers all foreign thoughts, as Nehemiah did them that would have called him off from building: "I am doing a great work, so that I cannot come down: why should the work cease?" (Neh. 6:3).
✦ WILLIAM GURNALL
Christian in Complete Armour, 748

In order to pray aright, it is necessary that we pray in or by the Spirit of God. Prayer is the creature's act but the Spirit's gift. There is a concurrence both of the Spirit and the soul of the Christian to the performance of it. The Holy Spirit is said to pray in us (Rom. 8:26), and we are said to pray in Him (Jude 20).

✦ WILLIAM GURNALL
Christian in Complete Armour, 754

As it is foolish and evil, so it is of dangerous consequence to ourselves to faint and cease to pray. First, it is the ready way to bring some stinging affliction upon us. Art thou a servant of God, and fliest from His face? Expect a storm to bring thee back to thy work. Art thou a child, and playest the truant? Expect that thy heavenly Father will send thee to school with a rod at thy back. Secondly, cease to pray, and thou wilt begin to sin. Prayer is not only a means to prevail for mercy but also to prevent sin.

✦ WILLIAM GURNALL
Christian in Complete Armour, 774

Love to the brethren is often given as a character of a true saint. Now, there is no act whereby we express our love to saints which stands more clear from insincerity than this of praying for them. Will you say you love the saints because you frequent their company, show kindness to their persons, stand up in their defense against those that reproach them, or because you can suffer with them? All this is excellent, if sincere; yet how easy is it for vainglory or some other carnal end to mingle with those! But if thou canst find thy heart in secret, where none of these

temptations have such an advantage to corrupt thee, pray to God for them with a deep sense and feeling for their sins, wants, and sorrows; this will speak more for the sincerity of thy love than all the former without this.

✦ WILLIAM GURNALL
Christian in Complete Armour, 782

It is uncharitableness not to pray for others and pride not to expect a benefit from the prayers of others.

✦ WILLIAM GURNALL
Christian in Complete Armour, 785

God's word must be the guide of your desires and the ground of your expectations in prayer; nor can you expect that He should give a gracious ear to what you say to Him if you turn a deaf ear to what He saith to you.

✦ MATTHEW HENRY
*Directions for Daily Communion
with God*, 23

God did not leave off granting till Abraham left off asking; such is the power of prayer.

✦ MATTHEW HENRY
Gems, 7

Prayer is the solemn and religious offering of devout acknowledgments and desires to God or a sincere representation of holy affections, with a design to give unto God the glory due unto His name thereby and to obtain from Him promised favors, and both through the Mediator.

✦ MATTHEW HENRY
Method for Prayer, iii

Our errand at the throne of grace is not only to seek the favor of God but to give unto Him the glory due unto His name, and that not only by an awful adoration of His infinite perfections but by a grateful acknowledgment of His goodness to us, which cannot indeed add anything to His glory, but He is pleased to accept of it and to reckon Himself glorified by it if it come from a heart that is humbly sensible of its own unworthiness to receive any favor from God that values the gifts and loves the giver of them.

◆ MATTHEW HENRY
Method for Prayer, 85–86

Our Lord Jesus has taught us to pray not only with but for others. And the apostle has appointed us to make supplication for all saints, and many of his prayers in his epistles are for his friends. And we must not think that when we are in this part of prayer we may let fall our fervency and be more indifferent because we ourselves are not immediately concerned in it, but rather let a holy fire of love, both to God and man here, make our devotions yet more warm and lively.

◆ MATTHEW HENRY
Method for Prayer, 116

Lord our God, in Thee we live and move and have our being, and from Thee receive all supports and comforts of our being. Thou spread our table and fill our cup and comfort us with the gifts of Thy bounty from day to day. We own our dependence upon Thee and our obligations to Thee; pardon our sins, we pray Thee. Sanctify Thy good creatures to our use, and give us grace to receive them soberly and thankfully and to eat and drink not to ourselves, but to Thy glory, through Jesus Christ our blessed Lord and Savior. Amen.

◆ MATTHEW HENRY
Method for Prayer, 224

Endeavorless prayers are likely to be as unsuccessful as prayerless endeavors.

◆ PHILIP HENRY
in Dod and Henry, *Gleanings
of Heavenly Wisdom*, 60

He that will learn to pray, let him go out to sea.

◆ GEORGE HERBERT
Witts Recreations, proverb 84;
also in Thomas, *Puritan Golden
Treasury*, 216

The more we abound in prayer, the more shall we be furnished with matter of praise.

◆ OLIVER HEYWOOD
Life in God's Favour, 19

A great reason why we reap so little benefit by prayer is because we rest too much in generals; and if we have success, it is but dark, so that often we cannot tell what to make of the issues of prayer. Besides, to be particular in our petitions would keep the spirit much from wandering when we are intent upon a weighty case, and the progress of the soul in grace would manifest its gradual success in prayer.

◆ SAMUEL LEE
Most Spiritual Profit, 90

How to keep the heart from wandering thoughts in prayer? Although it be exceedingly difficult to attain so excellent a frame, yet by frequent remembering and reflecting upon the eye of God in secret; by endeavoring to fix the heart with all possible watchfulness upon the main scope of the prayer in hand; by being very sensible of our wants and indigences; by not studying an impertinent length but rather being more frequent and short; considering God is in heaven and we upon the earth; and by the exercise of holy communion we may, through the implored assistance of the Spirit, attain some sweetness and freedom and also more fixedness of spirit in our addresses before the Lord.

✦ SAMUEL LEE
Most Spiritual Profit, 112–13

Prayer is fetching breath when the soul begins to be out of breath and to faint. It is a fetching out heat with heat, fire with fire, bad fire with good. Strong cries will keep the heart patient under strong trials—whilst a praying Jonah, a patient Jonah. He first fetched patience out of prayer, and then prayer fetched him out of the whale.

✦ NICHOLAS LOCKYER
Balm for England, 97

Now there are four enemies that a man must watch against in prayer: (1) Watch against drowsiness of body. This is a great impediment of prayer, and we have great need to watch against it. (2) Watch against a deadness and dullness of spirit, against

a flat and low temper; that is a great hindrance of importunity. (3) Watch against satanical suggestions. Satan is always ready to assault thee; he watches to disturb and molest you in your prayers. You had need watch to counterwork him. (4) You must watch from secular distractions. All these adversaries you must watch against, and that is the way to get this holy importunity into your hearts.

✦ CHRISTOPHER LOVE
Zealous Christian, 74

It is better to have affections without expressions than expressions without affection. God looks more to the desires of the heart then the words of the mouth.

✦ CHRISTOPHER LOVE
Zealous Christian, 83

Prayer is not for God's information but the creature's submission; we pray that we may have His leave.

✦ THOMAS MANTON
Practical Exposition on the Epistle of James, 150

Prayer is the best remedy for sorrows…. We have great cause in afflictions to use the help of prayer (1) that we may ask patience; if God lay on a great burden, cry for a strong back; (2) that we ask constancy, that you may not "put forth [your] hands unto iniquity" (Ps. 125:3); (3) that we may ask hope and trust and wait upon God for His fatherly love and care; (4) that we may ask a gracious improvement; the benefit of the rod is a fruit of divine grace, as well as the benefit of the word; (5) that we may ask deliverance with a submission to God's will: "I sought the LORD, and he heard me, and delivered me from all my fears" (Ps. 34:4).

✦ THOMAS MANTON
Practical Exposition on the
Epistle of James, 199

Prayer is the key by which those mighty ones of God could lock heaven and open it at their pleasure.

✦ THOMAS MANTON
Practical Exposition on the
Epistle of James, 210

He who prays as he ought will endeavor to live as he prays.

✦ JOHN OWEN
Golden Book, 229

Prayer is a holy conference of a godly mind with God, whereby believing, we ask things necessary and give thanks for benefits received.

✦ ELNATHAN PARR
Abba, Father, in *Workes,* 69

What is prayer? A familiar speech with God in the name of Christ in which either we crave things needful or give thanks for things received.

✦ WILLIAM PERKINS
Foundation of Christian Religion, 30

Let prayer be the key to open the morning and the bar to shut in the evening.

✦ WILLIAM PERKINS
in Richard Rogers, *Garden*
of Spirituall Flowers, 22

Prayer is an offering up of our desires to God in the name of Christ, according to His will, for blessings upon ourselves or others, with confession of sins and thankful acknowledgment of His mercies.

✦ FRANCIS ROBERTS
"A Commentary on the Lord's
Prayer," in *Great Worth of*
Scripture Knowledge, 30

Prayer doth not purchase the promise, but helps both to sanctify and ripen it. He will best hold out waiting that holds on praying.

✦ RALPH ROBINSON
Christ All and in All, 332

What aided [Samuel Rutherford in prayer:]

1. I have benefited by riding alone [on] a long journey, in giving that time to prayer.

2. By abstinence, in giving days to God.

3. By praying for others, for by making an errand to God for them I have gotten something for myself.

4. I have been really confirmed, in many particulars, that God heareth prayer; and therefore I used to pray for anything of how little importance soever.

✦ SAMUEL RUTHERFORD
Garden of Spices, 142–43

Prayer is the midwife of the promises. The promises are wells of comfort to the church, and believing prayer is the vessel to draw the water out of the wells.

✦ WILLIAM SECKER
Nonsuch Professor, 177

God is always willing for us to hit the mark when He directs our arrows. When He teaches us to wrestle, He then intends we should prevail. Spiritual breathings are attended with spiritual blessings. Nothing will ascend to heaven but what came down from heaven. That prayer meets with no answer which is not offered up in faith.

♦ WILLIAM SECKER
Nonsuch Professor, 234

God can pick sense out of a confused prayer. These desires cry louder in His ears than thy sins. Sometimes a Christian has such confused thoughts that he can say nothing, but as a child cries, "O Father," not able to show what it needs, as Moses at the Red Sea. These stirrings of spirit touch the bowels of God and melt Him into compassion toward us when they come from the spirit of adoption and from a striving to be better.

♦ RICHARD SIBBES
Bruised Reed and Smoking Flax, 89

By prayer we learn to pray.

♦ RICHARD SIBBES
Bruised Reed and Smoking Flax, 90

Prayer is a venting of our desires to God from the sense of our wants, and he that is sensible of his wants is empty. A poor man, by the Spirit, earnestly pours out supplications in Christ's name and wrestles with God in prayer.

♦ RICHARD SIBBES
Divine Meditations and Holy Contemplations, 59

Prayers be the seeds of praises. I have sown; therefore I will reap. What we receive as a fruit of our prayers is more sweet than what we have by a general providence.

♦ RICHARD SIBBES
Soul's Conflict, 265

We should not presume to exercise our faith, nor our repentance, nor our obedience, without prayer because there is no faith so perfect but it had need of prayer to strengthen it. Also, there is no love so perfect but it had need of prayer to confirm it. There is no repentance so perfect but it had need of prayer to continue it; there is no obedience so perfect but it had need of prayer to direct it. Therefore, he doth sin which presumes to do any good work without prayer because he seems to do it by his own power.

♦ HENRY SMITH
"The Ladder of Peace," in
Sermons, 118

Prayer is one of the great ordinances that batters down the strongholds of the devil; hence he sets his wits at work to divert men from it. It is the soul's armor and Satan's terror.

♦ GEORGE SWINNOCK
The Christian Man's Calling, in *Works*, 2:494

Some men forget to pray, others forget what they have prayed, and others forget that they have prayed. So little of their hearts is in duty and so little impression of duty is in their hearts, that all comes to nothing.

♦ RALPH VENNING
Canaan's Flowings, 152

When thou prayest, rather let thy heart be without words than thy words without a heart.

Prayer will make a man to cease from sin, or sin will entice a man to cease from prayer.

✦ RALPH VENNING
in Calamy et al., *Saints' Memorials*, 117

Prayer is a duty performed unto God by sensible and believing souls in which they ask for things according to His will, in the name of Christ, with thanksgiving for what has already been received.

✦ NATHANIEL VINCENT
Spirit of Prayer, 9

We must pray...in the name of Christ; and there are four things which we are to have an eye to: the satisfaction, purchase, intercession, and assistance of Christ. The satisfaction of Christ: He has been "wounded for our transgressions"; He "bore the curse" so that we may beg with confidence to be delivered from it.

We are to eye the purchase of Christ. He has purchased all the blessings of the new covenant. Heaven itself is called a "purchased possession" (Eph. 1:14). Christ paid a price for it that it might be ours.

We are to eye the intercession of Christ. "He is able also to save them to the uttermost that come unto God by him, seeing he ever liveth to make intercession for them" (Heb. 7:25). How can prayer fail that is backed with the intercession of such a one?

We are to eye the strength and assistance of Christ. Rightly to pray is a matter of difficulty. Christ by His Spirit is ready to help the infirmities of believers, so that notwithstanding all discouragement and opposition from within and from beneath, they shall make something of this duty of prayer and obtain the blessing.

✦ NATHANIEL VINCENT
Spirit of Prayer, 20–21

We are far from attaining all that is attainable by prayer; therefore, we should persevere in it. Clearer discoveries there may be of God, there may be much larger communications of grace, there may be more of peace and joy; therefore, it concerns us to wait on the Lord still and not to grow weary of our attending.

✦ NATHANIEL VINCENT
Spirit of Prayer, 119

Frequency in prayer will promote a readiness therein. As by writing, you learn to write; so by praying, you will learn to pray. Gifts are increased and augmented by the exercise of them, as grace itself also by being exercised grows stronger.

✦ NATHANIEL VINCENT
Spirit of Prayer, 135

Prayer is the bellows that blows up the affections.

✦ THOMAS WATSON
Christian Soldier, 167

Prayer is nothing but the soul's breathing itself into the bosom of its Father.

✦ THOMAS WATSON
The Beatitudes, in *Discourses*, 2:305

Effectual, fervent prayer prevails much (James 5:16). Cold prayers, like cold suitors, never speed. Prayer without fervency is like a sacrifice without a fire. Prayer is called a pouring out of the soul to signify vehemence (1 Sam. 1:15). Formality starves prayer.

✦ THOMAS WATSON
Gleanings, 100

Prayer is a seed sown in God's ears; other seed sown in the ground may be picked up by the birds, but this seed, especially if watered with tears, is too precious to be lost.

✦ THOMAS WATSON
Godly Man's Picture, 83

The tree of the promise will not drop its fruit unless shaken by the hand of prayer.

✦ THOMAS WATSON
Puritan Gems, 109

The true happiness of every Christian does properly consist in his spiritual communion with God. This communion is chiefly exercised in those two acts of religion, prayer and hearing the word. Praying may be considered under a twofold notion, either as a duty or a gift. It is of very great concernment to every man to be rightly acquainted with it in both these respects.

✦ JOHN WILKINS
Discourse Concerning the
Gift of Prayer, 1

It is such a readiness and faculty, proceeding from the Spirit of God, whereby a man is enabled upon all occasions in a fitting manner to express

and to enlarge the desires of his heart in this duty.

✦ JOHN WILKINS
Discourse Concerning the
Gift of Prayer, 2

We are generally deceived about prayer. It is, think we, a work of memory, of a good wit, a ready invention, a voluble tongue. This makes an excellent prayer in the esteem of a man's self and in the account of others. But this is not prayer. Prayer is the work of God's Spirit in a sanctified heart.

✦ HEZEKIAH WOODWARD
Treatise of Prayer, 11–12

PRAYER: IN SECRET

The religion of most men lies in the marketplace and in the view of others; their hearts, their closets are not privy to any secret transactions between God and their souls, and in the praise of men they have their reward. But the thriving trade of Christianity is the secret trade. Christians be most in those duties which men least observe and chiefly excellent in the invisible part of your visible work. Public duties are most honorable, but secret duties the most gainful (Matt. 6:4).

✦ BARTHOLOMEW ASHWOOD
Heavenly Trade, 376

Closet duty speaks out most sincerity. He prays with a witness that prays without a witness. The more sincere the soul is, the more in closet duty the soul will be.

✦ THOMAS BROOKS
Privy Key of Heaven, 16

The reasons why secret prayer is the mark of a sincere heart are as follows: (1) Because a sincere heart busies itself about heart work to mortify sin, to quicken grace, to observe and resist temptation, to secure and advance his evidences, therefore, it is much conversant with secret prayer.... (2) Because a sincere heart aims at the eye of God, he knows that God, being a spirit, loves to converse with our spirits and to speak to the heart more than the outward ear; he labors to walk before God as being always in His sight, but especially when he presents himself at the footstool of mercy. An invisible God is delighted with invisible prayers, when no eye sees but His; He takes most pleasure in the secret glances of a holy heart.

✦ SAMUEL LEE
Most Spiritual Profit, 58–59

The Christian holds intelligence with heaven; he is conversant with closet holiness; while the hypocrite is in the church a saint but in the closet an atheist.

✦ THOMAS WATSON
Puritan Gems, 111

PRAYER: RELATIONSHIP TO FAITH

For prayer, observe this method: (1) Lay open our sorrow before the Lord; pour out our complaints into His bosom. (2) Confess our sins with hatred and godly sorrow; for want of this God threatened the Israelites, "I will go and return to my place till they acknowledge their offenses." (3) Direct we our supplications to our God: "Lord, how long wilt Thou look on? O rescue my soul from their destruction, my darling from the lions." (4) Then press we the Lord with His promises: "Lord, Thou hast said, 'The rod of the wicked shall not rest upon the lot of the righteous'; Thou hast said, 'Yet a little while, and the indignation shall cease.' These are Thy promises; Lord, make them effectual to my poor soul." (5) For conclusion, tell we the Lord, whatever becomes of us we will trust in Him: "Though Thou slay me, yet will I trust in Thee." These are the acts of faith by which it puts forth and exercises itself in time of affliction.

✦ ISAAC AMBROSE
"The Practice of Sanctification,"
in *Works*, 111

There is more of the success of prayer to be believed than to be felt. If God have promised to hear He doth hear, and we must believe it whether we feel it or not. Prayers are often heard long before the thing is sent us that we prayed for; we pray for heaven but shall not be there till death. If Moses's message to Pharaoh ten times seems lost, it is not lost for all that. What work would ever have been done if on the first conceit of unsuccessfulness it had been given off? Be glad that thou hast time to plough and sow, to do thy part, and if God will give thee fruit at last.

✦ RICHARD BAXTER
A Christian Directory, in
Practical Works, 2:312

This believing and trusting upon God for what we pray for is that which gives life and efficacy to our prayers; without which, all our praying is a mere dead and formal exercise that will stand us in no stead at all. But with it, our prayers are both pleasing unto God and profitable to ourselves insomuch that we may thereby be always secure of all and everything that can any way conduce to make us happy. But for this purpose, though that be also necessary, yet it is not sufficient to act our faith and trust in God to answer our prayers by the lump when we have finished them, but all the while that we are praying, at every petition we put up to Him, we are still, in our minds, to believe and trust on God for the granting of it and so to walk by faith from one petition to another through the whole prayer. For this is properly to pray in faith.

✦ WILLIAM BEVERIDGE
Thesaurus Theologious, 4:272–73

Prayer, it is the very natural breath of faith; supplication and thanksgiving, the two parts of prayer. By these, as the body by the double motion of the lungs, doth the Christian suck in mercy from God and breathe back again that mercy in praise to God. But without faith he could do neither; he could not by supplication draw mercy from God, for "he that cometh to God must believe that he is, and that he is a rewarder of them that diligently seek him" (Heb. 11:6). Neither could he return praises to God without faith. David's heart must be fixed before he can sing and give thanks (Psalm 106).

Thanksgiving is an act of self-denial, and it is faith alone that will shew us the way out of our own doors; and as the creature cannot pray, I mean acceptably, without faith, so with faith he cannot but pray.

✦ WILLIAM GURNALL
Christian in Complete Armour, 449

In prayer we tempt God if we ask that which we labor not for. Our faithful endeavors must second our devotion, for to ask maintenance and not put our hands to the work is only to knock at the door, and yet pull the door unto us that it might not open. If we pray for grace and neglect the spring from whence it comes, how can we speed? It was a rule in ancient times (lay thy hand to the plough and then pray). No man should pray without ploughing nor plough without prayer.

✦ RICHARD SIBBES
Divine Meditations and Holy Contemplations, 63

Prayer is the key that opens God's treasury, but faith is the hand which takes out and receives of His infinite bounty. Prayer must have a promise, or else it is a vessel without a bottom; and that promise must have faith, or else the vessel lies still and cannot stir at all. When a full gale of faith fills the sails, then the vessel of prayer launches forth most hopefully and returns with its riches freight.

✦ GEORGE SWINNOCK
"The Pastor's Farewell," in *Works*, 4:71

Prayer sets an edge upon the word and makes it quick and powerful to kill sin and keep off Satan. Prayer works the word into the heart, and, being hid there, it is a mighty preservative against iniquity. There is a spiritual instinct in believers to join prayer with every ordinance of God because they know that ordinances cannot secure or benefit them, except the Lord concur and work along with them.

✦ NATHANIEL VINCENT
Spirit of Prayer, 29

Prayer is the arrow and faith is the bow by which our requests go up to heaven. A faithless prayer is a fruitless prayer: The father of the child cried out and said with tears, "Lord, I believe." When his tear dropped to the earth, his faith reached heaven.

✦ THOMAS WATSON
Puritan Gems, 108

PREACHING

[Vavasor Powell] was an able minister of the New Testament and always in readiness upon all occasions to fulfill his ministry and, like a good householder, brought out of his treasury things new and old; being very indefatigable in his work, speaking and praying sometimes three, four—nay—six and seven hours together. He was very faithful in delivering the word of truth and in explaining it to the meanest capacity, still endeavoring to suit his discourse to the occasion and condition of his hearers. He neither regarded nor feared the frowns or favor of great men, but faithfully and courageously would

warn and reprove them to their faces. He was very affectionate in drawing sinners to Christ, and as sharply would he reprove the profane and rebellious hypocrites and backsliders; and most compassionately did he sympathize with the weak, afflicted, and tempted. He excelled in illustrating the doctrine by familiar comparisons, parables, and similitudes which used to be very profitable to his hearers, tending greatly to imprint the truth upon their minds, and was so much the way pursued by our Savior, so that it is said, "Without a parable he spoke not." He had a ready wit, was well read in history and geography, a good natural philosopher, and was skilled in medicine, but, above all, was very powerful in prayer.

✦ ANONYMOUS
Life, 22–23

Hear, if possible, that minister that first feels what he speaks and so speaks what he feels, as tends most to make you feel.

✦ RICHARD BAXTER
A Christian Directory, in
Practical Works, 2:523

It is most incongruous for any man in his familiar discourse to speak without great seriousness and reverence of things concerning life eternal. But for a preacher to talk of God, of Christ, of heaven and hell as coldly and sleepily as if he were persuading men not to believe him or regard him that no more regards himself is less tolerable. It is a sad thing to hear a man draw out a dreaming, dull discourse about such astonishing, weighty things and to speak as if it were the business of his art to teach men to sleep while the names of heaven and hell are in their ears, and not to be moved while they hear the message of the living God about their life or death everlasting. I know it is not mere noise that will convert a soul; a bawling fervency, which the hearers may discern to be but histrionical and affected and not to come from a serious heart doth harden the auditors worst of all…. Christ raised not Lazarus by the loudness of His voice, but where the natural ears are the passage to the mind, the voice and manner should be suitable to the matter. Noise without seriousness and pertinent matter is like gunpowder without bullet that causeth sound, and no execution.

✦ RICHARD BAXTER
A Christian Directory, in
Practical Works, 2:524

I know not how it is with other persons, but the most reverent preacher who speaks as if he saw the face of God does more affect my heart, though with common words, than an irreverent man with the most accurate preparations, though he bawl it out with ever so much seeming earnestness. If reverence be not equal to fervency, it has but little effect. Of all preaching in the world, I hate that most which tends to make the hearers laugh or to affect their minds with such levity as stage plays do instead of affecting them with a holy reverence of the name of God.

✦ RICHARD BAXTER
Reformed Pastor, 170

Hark, O man of God that goes to the pulpit: preach this sermon as it were the last that thou should make to thy people.

✦ LEWIS BAYLY
Practice of Piety, 94

If the preacher's method be too curious or confused, then labor to remember (1) how many things he taught which thou knew not before, and be thankful; (2) what sins he reproved whereof thy conscience tells thee that thou art guilty and therefore must be amended; (3) what virtues he exhorted unto which are not so perfect in thee, and therefore endeavor to practice them with more zeal and diligence.

✦ LEWIS BAYLY
Practice of Piety, 198

Consider this blow: a saint [i.e., Ralph Venning]—yea, a minister—one of the many, one that excelled most, an able minister of the New Testament; a workman that need not be ashamed. Beloved, whose ears was not taken with his language? That one that but once heard him, but must come again. He begat you in Christ Jesus, though none of his own but Christ's; and you may get one to succeed him but not to exceed him, but I desire that man to tell me where.

✦ WILLIAM BEERMAN
Sorrow upon Sorrow, 18–19

Preaching should not be a labor of the lips or talk of the tongue from a light imagination, but a serious meditation of the heart in grounded knowledge by much study and illumination of the Spirit.

✦ RICHARD BERNARD
Faithful Shepherd, 12–13

The affections here to be stirred up are four: love to the thing, desire to the means, hope in the means, and joy respecting the benefits in the end.

✦ RICHARD BERNARD
Faithful Shepherd, 66

For a minister to make application to his hearers, to do it profitably, he must preach to them from knowledge out of himself, feeling the corruption of nature and being able to decipher out the old man period. Secondly, also from the knowledge of his auditory, what errors are among them; what practice of virtue; what vices generally; or, in particular callings, who comfortless or discouraged and need consolation.

✦ RICHARD BERNARD
Faithful Shepherd, 72

A man not slavishly bound to words brings not all things with him into the pulpit that there is delivered. The Spirit in prayer helps (Romans 8); so doth He in preaching if there be a ready conceit to take it.

✦ RICHARD BERNARD
Faithful Shepherd, 82

I grant it is an easy thing to let in a sermon at one ear and to let it out at the other, but to let a sermon in at the ear and to let it sink down in the heart and thence to spring up in the life, this is a hard thing. It is an easy thing to write down a sermon in your books, and to repeat it at night in your families, and to discourse and talk of it; but to get this sermon written in your hearts and to repeat it over in your lives—to be doers of it and not hearers only—this will require pains and labor.

✦ ROBERT BRAGGE
Cry for Labourers, 9–10

Ministers should preach feelingly, experimentally as well as exemplarily. They must speak from the heart to the heart. They must feel the worth, the weight, the sweet of those things upon their own souls that they give out to others. The highest mystery in divine rhetoric is to feel what a man speaks, and then speak what a man feels.

✦ THOMAS BROOKS
Smooth Stones, 154

Ministers must so preach to the people as if they lived in the very hearts of the people; as if they had been told all their wants and all their ways, all their sins and all their doubts. No preaching equal to this, no preachers equal to these.

✦ THOMAS BROOKS
The Unsearchable Riches of Christ,
in *Select Works*, 1:281–82

When men come with nets in their ears it is good for the preacher to have neither fish nor fowl in his tongue.

✦ THOMAS FULLER
Good Thoughts, 350

Having brought his sermon into his head, [the faithful minister] labors to bring it into his heart before he preaches it to his people. Surely that preaching which comes from the soul most works on the soul. Some have questioned ventriloquy, when men strangely speak out of their bellies, whether it can be done lawfully or no; might I coin the word *cordiloquy*, when men draw the doctrines out of their hearts, sure all would count this lawful and commendable.

✦ THOMAS FULLER
Holy and Profane States, 83

[The Puritan] esteemed the reading of the word an ordinance of God both in private and public, but did not account reading to be preaching. The word read he esteemed of more authority, but the word preached of more efficacy. He accounted preaching as necessary now as in the primitive church, God's pleasure being still by the foolishness of preaching to save those that believe. He esteemed that preaching best wherein was most of God, least of man, when vain flourishes of wit and words were declined and the demonstration of God's Spirit and power studied.

✦ JOHN GEREE
Character of an Old English Puritane, 2

Surely I think we are all near to eternity, and there are some hearing me today whom I defy the world to assure that ever they shall hear another sermon. Therefore, I entreat you all to hear this preaching as if it were the last preaching that ever ye should hear, and O that we would speak it as if it were the last sermon that ever we would preach unto you.

✦ ANDREW GRAY
"A Sermon concerning Death," in *Works*, 100

There is a great necessity lies upon the prophets and ministers of Christ to preach, and to preach home to the conscience. Warn them they must, and so warn them that they may take notice; else it is in vain and shall be before the Lord as no warning. This they must do, and do it oft—and why? Else the blood of the wicked will be required at their hand. Their blood, their lives lie at the stake for sinners' souls. They have a hard task, a dangerous calling, and therefore had need preach and tell them of their sins that, if it be possible, they may save their souls, if not their own. People wonder many times at some preachers; they are so fiery, so particular, so terrible, so long. You may cease to wonder; their lives, their souls go for it if they do it not; the hazard of souls and lives will make dumb men speak.

✦ WILLIAM GREENHILL
Exposition of the Prophet Ezekiel, 115

[Matthias Nicols] was not only diligent in his calling but also profitable in his teaching. It was not chaff, but good wheat which he sowed amongst you; not the sand of human devices, but the firm and sure rock of God's word did he lay as a foundation for you thereon to build. He fought not with human eloquence, vain flashes, idle quirks, fantastical conceits, enticing words of many wisdom to please men, but his labor was to speak and preach in the demonstration of the Spirit and of power, that your faith might not stand in the wisdom of men but in the power of God.

✦ ALEXANDER GROSSE
Deaths Deliverance, 49

To preach truths and notions above the hearers' capacity is like a nurse that should go to feed a child with a spoon too big to go into its mouth.

✦ WILLIAM GURNALL
Christian in Complete Armour, 118

Pride of gifts robs us of God's blessing in the use of them. The humble man may have Satan at his right hand to oppose him, but be sure the proud man shall find God Himself there to resist him whenever he goes about any duty. God proclaims so much and would have the proud man know whenever He meets him He will oppose him. "He resists the proud." Great gifts are beautiful as Rachel, but pride makes them also barren like her. Either we must lay self aside or God will lay us aside.

✦ WILLIAM GURNALL
Christian in Complete Armour, 137

Such preachers are not likely to reach the conscience who hop from one truth to another but dwell on none.... Were I to buy a garment in a shop, I should like him better that lays one good piece or two before me that are for my turn, which I may fully examine, than him who takes down all his shop and heaps piece upon piece merely to show [off] his store, till at last for variety I can look attentively on none, they lie so one upon another.

✦ WILLIAM GURNALL
Christian in Complete Armour, 163

How often doth the sinner find his heart discovered by the word preached, as if the minister had stood at his window and seen what he did, or some had come and told tales of him to the preacher. Such I have known that would not believe to the contrary, but that the minister had been informed of their pranks and so leveled his discourse, particularly at their breasts, when he hath been as ignorant of their doings as of theirs that live in America and only shot his reproofs like him that smote Ahab, who drew his bow at a venture without taking aim at the person of any. From whence can this property come but God, who claims it as His own incommunicable attribute? "I the LORD search the heart" (Jer. 17:10). God is in the word, and therefore it finds the way to get between the joints of the harness, though sent at random out man's bow.

✦ WILLIAM GURNALL
Christian in Complete Armour, 570

God threatens to bring a famine of hearing the word (Amos 8:11). Mark, not a famine of reading the word, but of hearing the word. If the word be not preached, though we have the Bible to read at home, yet it is a famine, and so we ought to judge it. "The word of the LORD was precious in those days; there was no open vision" (1 Sam. 3:1). The strongest Christians would find a want of this ordinance in time. We see in a town besieged, though it be well laid in with corn, yet when put to grind with private handmills what straits they are soon put to. And so will the best grown saints, when they come to have no more from the word for their souls to live on than what they grind with their own private meditation and labor, then they will miss the minister and see it was merry indeed to have one whose office it was to grind all the week for him.

✦ WILLIAM GURNALL
Christian in Complete Armour, 590

A worthy doctor's advice to ministers, as to their preaching, is applicable to Christians as to their praying. He bade them study for their sermons as if they expected no divine assistance in the pulpit, and when they came into the pulpit to cast themselves upon divine assistance as if they had not studied.

✦ WILLIAM GURNALL
Christian in Complete Armour, 713

[Preaching] is a laborious work: "Know them which labour among you…and admonish you" (1 Thess. 5:12)—those who labor in the word and doctrine, who labor to weariness. He that preaches as he should shall find it a work not of an hour while speaking in the pulpit, but a load that lies heavy on his shoulders all the week; a labor that spends the vitals and consumes the oil which should feed the lamp of nature; such a labor, in a word, as makes old age and youth often meet together.

✦ WILLIAM GURNALL
Christian in Complete Armour, 791

Why then do ministers preach the law? If they preach it as they should, they preach it in subservience to the gospel, not in opposition. He that knows how to distinguish well between the law and the gospel, let him bless God and know that he deserves the name of a divine. We must preach it as a rule, not as a covenant of life. Holiness, as to the matter and substance of it, is the same it ever was. The gospel destroys not the law in this sense, but adds a strong enforcement to all its commands. Again, we must preach the law as the necessary means to drive souls out of themselves to Christ in the gospel.

✦ WILLIAM GURNALL
Christian in Complete Armour, 807

A minister without this boldness is like a smooth file, a knife without an edge, or a sentinel who is afraid to let off his gun when he should alarm the city upon a danger approaching. There is nothing more unworthy than to see a people bold to sin and the minister afraid to reprove them.

✦ WILLIAM GURNALL
Christian in Complete Armour, 812

The minister is to reprove the sins of all, but to name none. Paul, being to preach before a lascivious and unrighteous prince, touched him to the quick but did not name him in his sermon. Felix's conscience saved Paul that labor; he trembled, though Paul did not say he meant him. [Preach with] a meek boldness. "The words of wise men are heard in quiet" (Eccl. 9:17). Let the reproof be as sharp as thou wilt, but thy spirit must be meek. Passion raises the blood of him that is reproved, but compassion turns his bowels. We must not denounce wrath in wrath lest sinners think we wish their misery, but rather with such tenderness that they may see it is no pleasing work to us, but do it that we might not by a cruel silence be accessory to their ruin, which we desire to prevent.

✦ WILLIAM GURNALL
Christian in Complete Armour, 812

Unholiness in the preacher's life either will stop his mouth from reproving or the people's ears from receiving. Oh, how harsh a sound does such a cracked bell make in the ears of his auditors!

✦ WILLIAM GURNALL
Christian in Complete Armour, 813

If God will use ambassadors, why not employ some glorious angel from heaven rather than weak and frail man? The apostle gives the reason: "We have this treasure in earthen vessels, that the excellency of the power may be of God, and not of us" (2 Cor. 4:7); or, as in the original, "in vessels of a shell." As the precious pearl is found in a shell, so this precious treasure of the gospel shall be found in frail men that the excellency of the work may be of God. The more contemptible the instrument, the more glorious appears God's power in using it for so high and noble an end. To see a man wound another with a sword would carry no wonder, but to wound him with a feather would appear to be a miracle. To see men fall down and tremble when an angel (a creature of such might and glory) is the speaker is no great wonder, but to behold a Felix quivering on the bench while a man, and he a poor prisoner at the bar, preaches to his judge, this carries a double wonder.

✦ WILLIAM GURNALL
Christian in Complete Armour, 820

Keep close to thy instructions. Ambassadors are bound up by their commission what they are to say; be sure, therefore, to take thy errand right before thou ascends the pulpit to deliver it. "I have received of the Lord that which I delivered to you." God says to the prophet, "Hear the word at my mouth, and give them warning from me" (Ezek. 3:17). It must be from Him, or it is not right. Take heed thou dost not set the royal stamp upon thy own base metal. Come not to thy people with "Thus saith the Lord" when it is the divination of thy own brain. There is no lie so base as that which is told in the pulpit, and as thou must not speak what He never gave thee in commission, so thou must not conceal what thou hast in command to deliver.

✦ WILLIAM GURNALL
Christian in Complete Armour, 822

Do we say he has the gift of preaching that can deliver himself in a flowing manner of speech to his hearers, that can cite scriptures or fathers, that can please his auditory with the flowers of rhetoric; or rather he that can divide the word aright, interpret it soundly, apply it judiciously, put it home to the conscience, speaking in the evidence of the Spirit, powerfully convincing the gainsayers, comforting the dejected, and drawing every soul nearer to heaven?

✦ JOSEPH HALL
Select Devotional Works, 4–5

In all the variety of the holy passages of the sermon, the devout mind is taken up with digesting what it hears and working itself to a secret improvement of all the good counsel that is delivered; neither is it ever more busy than when it sits still at the feet of Christ. I cannot, therefore, approve the practice which yet I see commonly received of those who think it no small argument of their devotion to spend their time of hearing in writing large notes from the mouth of the preacher, which, however, it may be a help for memory in the future yet cannot, as I conceive, but be some prejudice to our present edification; neither can the brain get so much hereby as the heart loses. If it be said that by this means an opportunity is given for a full rumination of wholesome doctrines afterward, I yield it; but withal, I must say that our afterthoughts can never do the work so effectually as when the lively voice sounds in our ears and beats upon our heart. But herein I submit my opinion to better judgments.

◆ JOSEPH HALL
Select Devotional Works, 40–41

In all ages, the devil troubles the church with extremes. In times of popery, there were many lazy lubbers and officers set up in the church, a numberless number of idle drones which Christ never sent—namely, popes, patriarchs, cardinals, abbots, archbishops, bishops, deans, archdeacons, great canons, petty canons, rural deans, monks, friars, priests, subdeacons, readers, singing men, acolytes, exorcists, etc. These flew too high. We are sunk too low and are pestered with Jeroboam's priests, nailers, tailors, tinkers, weavers, shoemakers, soldiers, collar makers, bodice makers, felt makers, men, women, boys, etc.

◆ THOMAS HALL
Pulpit Guarded, 7

When we go to study, let us pray to God to put a word into our mouth that shall suit the case and reach the consciences of those to whom we are to speak; to direct us both in the choice and management of our subjects; to fill our hands (as the Hebrew phrase for *consecration*) that we may fill the peoples' hearts when we go to preach. Still we need help from heaven to deliver our message as become the oracles of God with purity, gravity, and sincerity; with an air of tenderness and humility, as those who know the worth of souls and our own unworthiness; and yet with an air of assurance, as those who are confident of the truth of what we say and who know whom we have trusted.

◆ MATTHEW HENRY
"A Sermon concerning the Work and Success of the Ministry,"
in *Miscellaneous Writings*, 560

In this month I had the remembrance of much guilt set home upon my conscience in refer[ence] to the Sabbath day. I used to lie longer in bed than I ought, which hath been caused by sitting up over-late the night before, and that by neglecting to make preparations for preaching sooner in the week. I am often put to it to slubber over truths. So two sermons were provided, I have not cared how poorly. Lord, I confess it to Thee with shame and beg Thy grace, that it may be so no more. Amen! Blessed Lord Jesus!

✦ PHILIP HENRY
Diaries and Letters, 53
(June 17, 1657)

The Windows

Lord, how can man preach
　Thy eternal word?
He is a brittle crazy glass;
Yet in Thy temple Thou dost him
　afford
This glorious and transcendent place,
To be a window through Thy grace.
But when Thou dost anneal in glass
　Thy story,
Making Thy life to shine within
The holy preachers, then the light
　and glory
More rev'rend grows, and more
　doth win;
Which else shows wat'rish, bleak,
　and thin.
Doctrine and life, colors and light,
　in one
When they combine and mingle, bring
A strong regard and awe; but speech
　alone
Doth vanish like a flaring thing,
And in the ear, not conscience, ring.

✦ GEORGE HERBERT
Poems, 67

There was in [Henry Newcome] a large stock of solid learning and knowledge, always ready for use; for ostentation, never. Conscience the most strict, and steady to itself, and the remotest from censoriousness of other men.

Eloquence without any labor of his own, not imitable by the greatest labor of another. O the strange way he had of insinuating and winding himself into his hearers' bosoms! I have sometimes heard him when the only thing to be regretted was that the sermon must so soon be at an end.

✦ JOHN HOWE
preface to Chorlton,
Glorious Reward, xvi

Our very sermons, when we study to make important things as plain as we can, are lost upon the most. Though here we see the advantage of a people's having a love to their minister, which is a mighty orator within themselves, and will make them endeavor to take in his heart and soul; as on his part, his love to them will make him willing, as we heard from the apostle, to impart with the gospel his own soul [1 Thess. 2:8].

✦ JOHN HOWE
"A Funeral Sermon on the
Death of Dr. William Bates,"
in *Works*, 982

Ministers must labor for the pulpit and in the pulpit; there must be the labor of study before we speak, the labor of zeal and love in speaking, the labor of suffering must be borne after preaching, always the labor of praying before and after. Their plainest performances must be painful. There must be a diligence even in their seeming negligence.... A sleepy preacher cannot expect a waking auditory. It is uncomely to see a minister weary himself in the world, in the family, in the field, in courts of justice. He must take his leave of other employments. He must not leave the word of God to serve tables (Acts 6:2). He is a warrior and must not entangle himself in the affairs of this life (2 Tim. 2:4). They who sweat in worldly employments are commonly but cold in the pulpit.

✦ WILLIAM JENKYN
Exposition upon the Epistle of Jude, 55

I think truly that no man preaches that sermon well to others who does not first preach it to his own heart.

✦ JOHN OWEN
Golden Book, 136

The heart of the matter is this: preach one Christ, by Christ, to the praise of Christ.

✦ WILLIAM PERKINS
Art of Prophesying, 79

Conviction of sin is the first work of the Spirit of God (John 16:8). He is a convincing before He is a comforting Spirit. You must give the ministers of Christ leave to set sin upon the conscience. The fallow ground must be broken up before the seed of comfort is cast in. A sin-convincing ministry is most likely to be a soul-converting ministry. They cannot discover to men their righteousness (Job 33:23) until they have convinced them of their unrighteousness.

✦ RALPH ROBINSON
Christ All and in All, 130

How necessary the preaching of the law is to true conversion. A man will never be taken off from the opinion of his own healthfulness but by the preaching of the law. The law shows men what they are, what they may expect, etc. The fallow ground of the heart will never be broken up without the plough of the law (Jer. 4:3). The plough of the law must go and make deep furrows too, before the seed of comfort be cast in. Though the preaching of the law does not convert, yet it helps forward conversion, in as much as it works that preparatory work without which conversion ordinarily is not; as the needle makes way for the thread, so the law makes way for conversion. The spirit of bondage makes way for the Spirit of adoption, and that is wrought by the preaching of the law.

✦ RALPH ROBINSON
Christ All and in All, 137

Preaching is an exercise that many are ambitious of, and none more than those that are least qualified for it; and, it is probable, the desire of this liberty is no small temptation to some of our giddy people to go over to that sect and party where all ranks and both sexes are allowed the satisfaction to hear themselves talk in public. But it is not so easy a matter to perform this task aright; to stand in the presence of God and to speak to His people in His name with that plainness and simplicity, that seriousness and gravity, that zeal and concern which the business requires; to accommodate ourselves to the capacity of the common people without disgusting our more knowing hearers by the insipid flatness of our discourse; to excite and awaken drowsy souls without terrifying and disturbing more tender consciences; to bear home the convictions of sin without the appearance of some personal reflection; in a word, to approve ourselves unto God as workmen that need not be ashamed, rightly dividing the word of truth.

✦ HENRY SCOUGAL
"Importance and Difficulty of
the Ministerial Function,"
in *Works*, 210

May 30 [, 1641]. On Sabbath day, after sermon, I saw that my sin was (1) to look on my ministry's faults and be discouraged; (2) to look on their good and be puffed up. (3) If all was done well, then to look upon them as if they were Absalom-like, that from the head to the foot of them there was no blemish. But I loathed myself for it and prayed for everlasting blessing on them.

✦ THOMAS SHEPARD
Meditations and Spiritual Experiences, 66

It is a great scandal to religion that men of great learning and parts are often wicked men; hereupon the world comes to think that religion is nothing but an empty name. Without inward special illumination, they can never know spiritual things experimentally; though they profess to believe these things, yet secretly in their hearts they make a scorn of conversion and mortification. Yea, a preacher may speak of these things excellently and to admiration and yet find not the power of them in his own soul.

✦ RICHARD SIBBES
*Divine Meditations and
Holy Contemplations*, 53

Another cometh to gaze about the church; he hath an evil eye which is still looking upon that from which Job did avert his eye. Another cometh to muse; so soon as he is set, he falls into a brown study. Sometimes his mind runs on his market, sometimes on his journey, sometimes of his suit, sometimes of his dinner, sometimes of his sport after dinner, and the sermon is done before the man thinks where he is. Another cometh to hear, but so soon as the preacher hath said his prayer, he falls fast asleep, as though he had been brought in for a corpse and the preacher should preach at his funeral.

✦ HENRY SMITH
"The Art of Hearing," in
Sermons, 94

In mine opinion two things out of every sermon are especially to be noted: that which thou didst not know before, and that which speaketh to thine own sin; for so thou shalt increase thy knowledge and lessen thy vices.

✦ HENRY SMITH
"The Art of Hearing," in
Sermons, 98

[A]…thing which makes prophets and prophesying despised is the lewdness and negligence of them that are able to do well in their ministry and yet do contrary. It is said of Hophni and Phinehas that by their corrupt sacrificing they made the people abhor the sacrifice (1 Sam. 2:17). So many, by their slubbering of the word for want of study and meditation, do make men think that there is no more wisdom in the word of God than they show out of it, and therefore they stay at home and say they know as much as the preacher can teach them.

✦ HENRY SMITH
"The True Trial of the Spirits,"
in *Sermons*, 43–44

You know [Richard Mayo's] preaching among you to have been solid, weighty, and substantial, apt at once to instruct and move. For the matter of it, it was things of the greatest importance: Christ crucified, the necessity of an interest in Him, conformity and obedience to Him; imputed righteousness and inherent too, not putting one into the room or exalting it to the prejudice of the other, both being necessary in their proper places and to distinct ends, which he knew well how to assign and warmly to press. Three great excellencies in his preaching I have often observed—that it was methodical, clear, and genuinely derived from his text, like ripe and fair fruit that drops from the bough whereon it naturally grew. I had rather that your lives than my tongue or pen should show how successful his labors have been among you, yet I have had the opportunity of knowing that here he hath been far from laboring in vain.

✦ NATHANIEL TAYLOR
Funeral Sermon [on 2 Cor. 5:8], 26

The truth of the gospel shines best in its bare proposal, and its beauty in its simple and naked discovery. We may observe from the church history that still as soundness of doctrine and the power of godliness decayed in the church, the vanity of an affected way of speaking and of writing of divine things came in. Quotations from the fathers, Latin, and languages are pitiful ornaments unto preaching if a man design conversion and soul edification. And yet more despicable are all playing on words, jinglings, and cadences, which things are in all the rules of true eloquence justly exploded; and yet some men reckon much on them. But would any man think his friend in earnest with him that would accost him in any affair with such sort of language and gesture?

✦ ROBERT TRAILL
"By What Means May Ministers
Best Win Souls?," in *Select
Practical Writings*, 135

DIOTREPHES: Such choleric fellows as you do mar all, for you cannot deal mildly and so you trouble the conscience and disquiet the mind of the weak.

PAUL: His conscience must be troubled by lancing before that ever his soul can be cured.

DIOTREPHES: Then I perceive you like well of them that preach the law, so much as they do.

PAUL: Yea, or else should I not like of bringing men unto Christ, which can never be until they be humbled by the law and made poor thereby to receive the gospel.

DIOTREPHES: Do you not also like the preaching of predestination?

PAUL: Yea, or else should I dislike of preaching the truth, for it is a part of God's revealed will.

♦ JOHN UDALL
State of the Church of England, 14

Lay aside those dispositions which may render the preached word ineffectual, as curiosity. Some go to hear the word preached not so much to get grace as to enrich themselves with notions, having "itching ears" (2 Tim. 4:3). "Thou art unto them as a very lovely song of one that hath a pleasant voice, and can play well on an instrument" (Ezek. 33:32). Many go to the word to feast their ears only; they like the melody of the voice and the novelty of the opinions (Acts 17:21). This is to love the garnishing of the dish more than the food; it is to desire to be pleased rather than edified. Lay aside prejudice. The Sadducees were prejudiced against the doctrine of the resurrection. Sometimes prejudice is against the truths preached, and sometimes against the person preaching. "There is yet one man, Micaiah… by whom we may enquire of the LORD: but I hate him" (1 Kings 22:8). This hinders the power of the word. If a patient has an ill opinion of his physician, he will not take any of his medicines however good they may be.

♦ THOMAS WATSON
Gleanings, 94

Lay aside partiality. Partiality in hearing is when we like to hear some truths preached, but not all. We love to hear of heaven but not of self-denial; of reigning with Christ but not of suffering with Him. "Speak unto us smooth things" (Isa. 30:10), such as may not grate upon the conscience. Many like the comforts of the word but not its reproofs. Lay aside censoriousness. Some, instead of judging themselves for sin, sit as judges upon the preacher; his sermon had either too much gall in it, or it was too long. They would sooner censure a sermon than practice it. Lay aside disobedience. "All day long I have stretched forth my hands unto a disobedient and gainsaying people" (Rom. 10:21). If, when God speaks to us in His word, we are deaf, when we speak to Him in prayer, He will be dumb.

♦ THOMAS WATSON
Gleanings, 96

That sin which a man does not love to have reproved is the darling sin. Herod could not endure to have his incest spoken against; if the prophet meddles with that sin, it shall cost him his head. Men can be content to have other sins declaimed against, but if the minister put his finger upon the sore and touches this sin, their hearts begin to burn in malice against him.

♦ THOMAS WATSON
Godly Man's Picture, 134

The mind of our author was not fitted for bustle and strife. It being the custom for the presbytery to inquire of the several brethren twice a year whether they preached to the times. Leighton, when thus interrogated, acknowledged his omission and apologized for it, saying, "If all the brethren have preached to the times, may not one poor brother be suffered to preach on eternity?"

✦ W. WILSON
"Life of Archbishop Leighton," in Leighton, *Spiritual Truths*, vii

PREACHING, PLAINNESS IN

Preaching is a work which requires greater skill and especially greater life and zeal than any of us commonly bring to it. It is no trifling matter to stand up in the face of a congregation and deliver a message of salvation or damnation, as from the living God, in the name of the Redeemer. It is no easy thing to speak so plainly that the most ignorant may understand us, so seriously that the deadest heart may feel, and so convincingly that contradicting cavillers may be silenced. Certainly, if our hearts were set upon the work of the Lord as they ought to be, it would be done more vigorously than by the most of us it is. Alas! How few ministers preach with all their might or speak about everlasting joys and torments in such a manner as may make men believe that they are in earnest!

✦ RICHARD BAXTER
Reformed Pastor, 32

All our teaching should be as plain and intelligible as we can make it. This best suits a teacher's ends. He that would be understood must make it his business to be understood by speaking to the capacities of his hearers. Truth loves the light and is most beautiful when most naked. He is an enemy that hides the truth, and he is a hypocrite who does this under a pretense of revealing it. Highly ornamented sermons are like painted glass in windows which keeps out the light and are too often the marks of hypocrisy. If you would not teach men, what do you in the pulpit? If you would, why do you not speak so as to be understood? For a man purposely to cloud his matter in strange words and hide his mind from the people whom he pretends to instruct is the way to make fools admire his profound learning, but wise men his folly, pride, and hypocrisy.

✦ RICHARD BAXTER
Reformed Pastor, 159–60

A strange tongue hinders the conceit of most hearers (except it be used rarely, aptly, and briefly), being ignorant of the same…and, except it be used with discretion, it is a hiding to them what we profess rather than to teach them, an unprofitable misspending of time…. It may be one, two, three, or some few understand hardly the languages, but all others do not. Must we therefore, pleasing ourselves, seek to delight these few to win a little vain praise of learning, while all the rest stand and gaze, admiring what is said without edification? We that stand up in Christ's room must seek not our own commendations; there we must paint out the truth lively and plainly, approving ourselves faithful dispensers of God's secrets to the conscience of every believer, in everything to the utmost of our power. Nevertheless, necessity constraining, as sometime to declare the emphasis of a word often more significant in the original than in the translation…or in a learned auditory, I doubt not of a liberty therein.

✦ RICHARD BERNARD
Faithful Shepherd, 17

It has many a time made my heart sad to think how those men will answer it in the day of Christ, who affect lofty strains, high notions, and cloudy expressions; who make the plain things of the gospel dark and obscure. Many preachers in our days are like Heraclitus, who was called the dark doctor. They affect sublime notions, obscure expressions, uncouth phrases, making plain truths difficult and easy truths hard. "They darken counsel with words without knowledge."…

It is better to present truth in her native plainness than to hang her ears with counterfeit pearls.

✦ THOMAS BROOKS
The Unsearchable Riches of Christ,
in *Select Works*, 1:123–24

Let this guide us in our studies and preaching. He is not the best preacher that makes the loudest noise, nor yet he that makes the finest flourish and garnishes each period with the flowers of rhetoric, nor he that ostentatiously abounds with needless subtleties and strives to show all the learning he has, whether the subject require it or no. Such preach themselves really, while they profess to set forth Jesus Christ to the people. Those that would turn many to righteousness must choose to treat upon subjects which their auditors

most need in a clear, convincing manner, with gravity and seriousness. They must feel the power of those truths upon their own souls which they would impress upon others. Men of high parts must deny themselves, if need be, for the good of others by condescending to the meanest capacities. They must not think it below them to use familiar and plain expressions, where those will serve best to convey a clear idea of the truths of God to the hearers. Those whose gifts are more slender must double their diligence, that they may not fall too much below the dignity of the subjects they treat and thereby render themselves contemptible to the more understanding and able Christians or to the more curious part of the auditory.

✦ JOHN CHORLTON
Glorious Reward, 24

You see the old apostolic way of preaching was in all plainness and simplicity to propound gospel truths in the name of God to the people and to commend them to their belief upon the bare credit of divine testimony, till faith came by hearing.

✦ THOMAS COLE
Old Apostolical Way of
Preaching, 10

Abstruse preachers who do not make the mysteries of the gospel known but make truths, plain in themselves, mysterious by their dark, perplexed discourses upon them. What is said of some commentators—that the places on which they treat were plain till they expounded them—may be said of some preachers: their text was clear till their obscure discourse upon it darkened it. What greater wrong can a preacher do his hearers than this? The preacher is to open scriptures, but these turn the key the wrong way and lock them up from their knowledge. They are to hold up the gospel glass before their people, whereby they may see to dress their souls, like a bride against her husband's coming; but by that time that they have breathed on their text, it is so obscured that they cannot see their faces in it.

✦ WILLIAM GURNALL
Christian in Complete Armour, 809

Christ evidently held forth is divine eloquence, the eloquence of eloquence. God will not have it said of Christ, as Alexander said of Achilles, that he was beholden to the pen of him that published his acts. 'Tis Christ that is preached, not the tongue of the preacher, to whom is due all praise.

✦ JOHN NORTON
Abel Being Dead yet Speaketh, 32

A minister must preach plain, suiting his matter and style to the capacity of his auditory (1 Cor. 14:19). Some ministers, like eagles, love to soar aloft in abstruse metaphysical notions, thinking they are most admired when they are least understood. They who preach in the clouds instead of hitting their peoples' conscience shoot over their heads.

✦ THOMAS WATSON
Godly Man's Picture, 139

PREACHING, PRAYER FOR

Hearers' prayers help ministers to preach and themselves to hear ([2] Thess. 3:1). Souls never thrive better than when ministers and hearers be much in prayer for the word of the Spirit, and Spirit with the word.

✦ BARTHOLOMEW ASHWOOD
Heavenly Trade, 290

Let your sermons be sermons of many prayers.... How will you get a word from God if you do not seek it, and how can you seek it but by earnest prayer?

✦ THOMAS BOSTON
Art of Man-Fishing, 91–92

Consider your own insufficiency and weakness together with the weight of the work. Who is sufficient for these things? Which if you do, you will not dare study without prayer nor yet pray without study, when God allows you time for both. It is a weighty work to bring sinners to Christ.

✦ THOMAS BOSTON
Art of Man-Fishing, 92

A minister need not fear but he shall preach well afterward if the Lord help him to pray well beforehand.

✦ THOMAS COBBET
Gospel Incense, 100

Beware thou come not in the confidence of thy own preparations. God hath declared Himself against this kind of pride: "By strength no man shall prevail" (1 Sam. 2:9). A little bread with God's blessing may make a meal for a multitude, and great

provision may soon shrink to nothing if God help not in the breaking of
it. It is not thy sermon in thy head or
notes in thy book that will enable thee
to preach, except God open thy mouth;
acknowledge, therefore, God in all thy
ways, and lean not to thy own understanding. The swelling of the heart, as
well as of the wall, goes before a fall.
Did the Ephraimites take it so ill that
Gideon should steal a victory without
calling them to his help? How much
more may it provoke God when thou
goest to the pulpit and passes by His
door in the way without calling for His
assistance?

✦ WILLIAM GURNALL
Christian in Complete Armour, 796

In your access to heaven you are to be
led by two virgins, prayer and preaching. By the one you talk with God;
by the other God speaketh unto you.
In your prayer, you are to be frequent
and fervent. Holy David in the evening, morning, and noon did pray unto
the Lord, and that instantly, and the
Lord heard his prayer. He did rise also
at midnight to give thanks unto the
Lord. Our Savior Christ *pernoctabat
in oratione* [i.e., all night continued in
prayer, Luke 6:12]. As for preaching,
when you enter into the house of God,
be ready and attentive in hearing the
word of God, and make it your own by
meditation and practice. Those beasts
only were accounted clean that rumi-
nate and chew the cud.

✦ WILLIAM HIGFORD
Institutions, 56–57

Because Thou of Thine infinite wisdom hast set apart the ministry of Thy
word to fit us for that time [i.e., day
of visitation]: Lord, bless it at all times
and at this time. Enable me that am to
speak it, the most unworthy of all the
sons of Levi. Lord, cover my sins and
manifold imperfections in that mercy
of Thine that hath no measure, and be
pleased so to assist me by Thy more
particular help, that I may deliver
Thy word boldly, truly, feelingly, and
sincerely. Circumcise the hearts and
ears of this people, that they may
hear attentively, treasure it up in
their hearts carefully, and bring forth
the fruit in their lives and conversations conscionably, to Thy glory and
the assurance of their own salvation
in the day of Jesus Christ. To whom
with thee, O Father and Thy blessed
Spirit, be ascribed, as due is, all honor
and glory, both now and forevermore.
Amen.

✦ JOSIAS SHUTE
Judgement and Mercy, xv

A minister should pray for a blessing
on the word, and he should be much
in seeking God, particularly for the
people. It may be this may be the reason why some ministers of meaner
gifts and parts are more successful
than some that are far above them in
abilities — not because they preach
better so much as because they pray
more. Many good sermons are lost for
lack of much prayer in study.

✦ ROBERT TRAILL
"By What Means May Ministers
Best Win Souls?," in *Select
Practical Writings*, 131–32

Let preachers ply the throne of grace if ever they will preach to purpose.... He that will understand God's riddles must plough with his heifer the Spirit, which is not given but to them that ask it.

✦ JOHN TRAPP
Commentary...upon...the
New Testament, 991

[George Trosse] frequently put up these requests in his prayer before sermon: "Lord, dispose of us and all our concerns, living and dying, by Thy wise and gracious providence as shall be for Thy greatest glory by us, for that must be our greatest good from Thee. Let us never have that prosperity, though we ever so earnestly desire it, which will be a temptation to us to sin and an occasion of Thy dishonor. And let us never want that affliction, though we ever so much deprecate it, which may be for Thy glory and our spiritual good, but let our lives be holy and a continual growth in grace. Let our deaths be hopeful, and let us expire in peace, and after death let us be forever with Thee in glory."

✦ GEORGE TROSSE
Life, 37

Pray for thyself and pray for thy brethren; pray that God would warm thy heart that thou mayest warm theirs. Many run from commentator to commentator when as they should be upon their knees. I disallow no good helps but commend the use of them, yet principally thou must study the Scriptures and so preach a sermon as thou mayest apprehend it to be the fruit of thy prayers; then minister and people are likeliest to do most good upon one another when they mutually join in fervent prayer one for another.

✦ HENRY WILKINSON
"The Wisest Preacher," in
Three Decades of Sermons, 66

PREDESTINATION (See also ELECTION AND PREDESTINATION)

Predestination is the decree of God whereby, according to the counsel of His own will, He foreordained some of mankind to eternal life and refused or passed by others for the praise of His glorious mercy and justice.

✦ CHRISTOPHER NESS
Antidote against Arminianism, 9

This divine decree of predestination hath various properties; it is eternal, unchangeable, absolute, free, discriminating, and extensive.

✦ CHRISTOPHER NESS
Antidote against Arminianism, 11

PRESUMPTION

There are two ladders whereby men climb up into heaven and become acquainted with God: the ladder of petition and the ladder of presumption. The saints ascend by the one to their consolation, the wicked by the other to their confusion.

✦ THOMAS ADAMS
Exposition upon...Second...Peter, 270

PRIDE

Pride of heart overlooks and vilifies mercies one is possessed of and fixes the eye on what is wanting in one's condition, making one like the flies, which pass over the sound places and swarm together on the sore.

✦ THOMAS BOSTON
Crook in the Lot, 92

A proud heart will make a cross to itself where a lowly soul would find none.

✦ THOMAS BOSTON
Crook in the Lot, 96

Proud men scorn their own employment and envy that of others.

✦ WILLIAM BRIDGE
Lifting Up, 217

Pride is a sin that will put the soul upon the worst of sins. Pride is a gilded misery, a secret poison, a hidden plague. It is the engineer of deceit, the mother of hypocrisy, the parent of mercy, the moth of holiness, the blinder of hearts, the turner of medicines into maladies and remedies into diseases.

✦ THOMAS BROOKS
The Unsearchable Riches of Christ,
in *Select Works*, 1:46

That assistance [from God] will not long stay which becomes a nurse to your pride.

✦ WILLIAM GURNALL
Christian in Complete Armour, 11

A proud heart and a lofty mountain are never fruitful.

✦ WILLIAM GURNALL
Christian in Complete Armour, 25

A man may be so very zealous in prayer and painstaking in preaching, and all the while pride is the master whom he serves, though in God's livery. It can take sanctuary in the holiest actions and hide itself under the skirt of virtue itself. Thus, while a man is exercising his charity, pride may be the idol in secret for which he lavished out his gold so freely. It is hard starving this sin; there is nothing almost but it can live on.

✦ WILLIAM GURNALL
Christian in Complete Armour, 136

If God's honor be in danger through thy pride, then expect a rod and most likely the affliction shall be in that which will be most grievous to thee, in the thing thou are proud of. Hezekiah boasted of his treasures; God sends the Chaldeans to plunder him. Jonah was fond of his gourd, and that is smitten. And if thy spirit be blown up with the pride of gifts, thou art in danger of having them blasted, at least in the opinion of others, whose breath of applause, possibly, was a means to overset thy unballasted spirit.

✦ WILLIAM GURNALL
Christian in Complete Armour, 139

Be humble when thou art most holy. Which way soever pride works (as thou shalt find it like the wind, sometimes at one door and sometimes at another), resist it. Nothing more baneful to thy holiness. It turns righteousness into hemlock, holiness into sin. Never art thou less holy than when puffed up with the conceit of it.

✦ WILLIAM GURNALL
Christian in Complete Armour, 341

O, this is the way of killing this weed of pride, to break up our hearts and turn the inside outward—I mean humble and abase ourselves for our former abominations. Pride will not easily thrive in a soil where this plough often walks. Pride is a worm that bites and gnaws out the heart of grace.

✦ WILLIAM GURNALL
Christian in Complete Armour, 343

Pride makes a man incapable of receiving counsel. Nebuchadnezzar's mind is said to be "hardened in pride" (Dan. 5:20). There is no reasoning with a proud man; he castles himself in his own opinion of himself and there stands upon his defense against all arguments that are brought.

✦ WILLIAM GURNALL
Christian in Complete Armour, 443

There are none so knowing that God cannot blind; none so blind and ignorant whose eyes His Spirit cannot open.

✦ WILLIAM GURNALL
Christian in Complete Armour, 594

If pride be at the beginning of the duty, shame will be at the end of it.

✦ WILLIAM GURNALL
Christian in Complete Armour, 762

Pride is the most dangerous of all sins, for both it is most insinuative, having crept into heaven and Paradise, and most dangerous where it is. For where all other temptations are about evil, this alone is conversant only about good things, and one dram of it poisons many measures of grace. I will not be more afraid of doing good things amiss than of being proud when I have well performed them.

✦ JOSEPH HALL
Meditations and Vows, 25

Pride cast the first of creatures (angels) out of heaven; the first of men (Adam) out of Paradise; and the first Israelitish king (Saul) out of his throne.

✦ NATHANIEL HARDY
First General Epistle of St. John, 271

Some look upon that only as pride which manifests itself in costly apparel and bodily ornaments beyond the degree and rank of the person. Some look no farther than the carriage of one man toward another. Now favorably consider with me that the greatest pride in the world is man's undue esteem of himself toward God, and this is in the heart of everyone by nature. Everyone by nature doth lift up himself against God, goes about to dethrone God and to crown himself. Everyone takes counsel in his heart against the Lord saying, "Let us break his bands asunder and cast his cords from us." This is the voice of everyone that dares willfully to sin: "We will not have God to rule over us." Yet this is the working of the pride of a man against God, to thrust God out of the throne of His majesty and to set himself in.

✦ JAMES JANEWAY
Heaven upon Earth, 65

Pride sets men in opposition against God; in other sins, men run away from God, but pride is a coming against God.

✦ ANDREW JONES
Morbus Satanicus, 4

Pride makes men like the devil; it is *morbus Satanicus*, the devil's disease, and far worse than the French [disease, i.e., possibly bubonic plague or small-pox] or any other foul disease.

✦ ANDREW JONES
Morbus Satanicus, 5

Poverty and pride are most unsuitable. It was one of Solomon's odd sights to see "servants upon horses, and princes walking as servants upon the earth" (Eccl. 10:7). A poor proud man is a prodigy and wonder of pride. He has less temptation to be proud; he has more reason to be humble.

✦ THOMAS MANTON
Practical Exposition on the Epistle of James, 22

God abhors them worst who adore themselves most. Pride is not a Bethel (that is, a house where God dwells) but a Babel (that is, a noisome dungeon in which Satan abides). It is not only a most hateful evil but it is a radical evil. As all other lusts are found lodging in it, so they are found springing from it.

✦ WILLIAM SECKER
Nonsuch Professor, 72

The bowing reed of a humble mind shall be preserved entire, while the sturdy oak of a proud, lofty mind shall be broken to shivers. A proud person thinks everything too much that is done by him, and everything too little that is done for him.

✦ WILLIAM SECKER
Nonsuch Professor, 84

The more lofty a man's thoughts be, the more base shall be the means of his humiliation be.

✦ JOSIAS SHUTE
Judgement and Mercy, 22

Pride is intolerable to pride.

✦ RICHARD SIBBES
in Horn, *Puritan Remembrancer*, 28

Tyranny in princes, ambition in nobles, rebellion in subjects, disobedience in children, stubbornness in servants; name pride, and thou hast named their mother. Therefore, shall not God resist pride—which hath sowed so many tares in His ground?

✦ HENRY SMITH
"A Dissuasion from Pride,"
in *Sermons*, 55

Pride comprehends all vice. It is a spiritual drunkenness; it flies up as wine into the brain and intoxicates it. It is idolatry; a proud man is a self-worshiper. It is revenge; Haman plots Mordecai's death because he would not bow the knee. How odious is this sin to God (Prov. 16:5). Everyone that is proud in heart is an abomination to the Lord.

✦ THOMAS WATSON
Godly Man's Picture, 73

PRIDE AND ANGER

Pride makes men imperious and impatient, boisterous and stormy against all that offend them. Pride, anger, and revenge, like serpents, twine and wreath about one another. Pride interprets an offense as a high contempt and raises anger, and anger provoked takes proportionable revenge to the conceived injury.

✦ WILLIAM BATES
The Danger of Prosperity, in
Whole Works, 2:218

No wild beast in a toil doth more rave and tear and rend than a proud man when he is reproved.

✦ JOHN OWEN
Golden Book, 207

A proud man sets a high value upon himself and is angry with others because they will not come up to his price.

✦ THOMAS WATSON
Art of Divine Contentment, 77

PRIDE AND HUMILITY

Humility makes a man compare himself with the best, that he may find how bad he himself is; but pride measures by the worst, that it may hide from a man his own imperfections. The one takes a perfect rule and finds itself nothing. The other takes a crooked rule and imagines itself something.

✦ HUGH BINNING
"An Essay upon Christian Love,"
in *Several Sermons,* 221

A proud heart eyes more his seeming worth than his real want. But a soul truly humbled blushes to see his own righteousness and glories in this, that he has the righteousness of Christ to live upon.

✦ THOMAS BROOKS
The Unsearchable Riches of Christ,
in *Select Works,* 1:8

That which will break a proud man's heart will not so much as break a humble man's sleep. In the midst of a storm, a humble soul is still in a calm. When proud hearts are at their wits' ends, stamping, swearing, and swaggering at God and man and providence, a humble soul is quiet and still, like a ship in a harbor.

✦ THOMAS BROOKS
The Unsearchable Riches of Christ,
in *Select Works,* 1:36

Oh, imitate your pattern [i.e., Christ]; work hard for God and let not pride blow upon it when you have done. It is difficult for a man to do much and not value himself for it too much.

✦ JOHN FLAVEL
Fountain of Life, 353

Let us learn, then, to know that this is a mark of such as are in love with Christ. They think less of themselves than they can do of any other. Pride is not a mark of the children of God.

✦ SAMUEL RUTHERFORD
"The Forlorn Son," in *Quaint
Sermons,* 241

This grace [of humility] is accompanied with a great deal of happiness and tranquility. The proud and arrogant person is a trouble to all that converse with him, but most of all unto himself; everything is enough to vex him but scarce anything is sufficient to content and please him. He is ready to quarrel with everything that falls out, as if he himself were such a considerable person that God Almighty should do everything to gratify him, and all the creatures of heaven and earth should wait upon him and obey his will. The leaves of high trees do shake with every blast of wind, and every breath, every evil word will disquiet and torment an arrogant man. But the humble person hath the advantage when he is despised that none can think more meanly of him than he doth of himself, and therefore he is not troubled at the matter but can easily bear those reproaches which wound the other to the soul.

✦ HENRY SCOUGAL
Life of God in the Soul of Man, 62

PRINTING, INVENTION OF

Printing was a rare invention and the gift of God above two hundred years ago. The benefit is sufficiently noted by Mr. Fox: "Hereby tongues are known, knowledge grows, judgment increases, books are dispersed, the Scripture is seen, the doctors be read, stories are opened, times compared, truth discerned, falsehood detected, and with the finger pointed." And by the printing of the Bible, the doctrine of the gospel has sounded to all nations, and that with great expedition. So many printing presses of the Bible, so many blockhouses against the high towers of antichrist; none but Papists

have envied God's people and Christ's preachers a printed Bible. Who were they that obstructed (what they could) the printing of it in English in King Henry VIII's days but the popish prelates and their creatures? The popish vicar of Croyden, Caiaphas-like, prophesied, "Either we must root out printing, or printing will root out us." Every good Christian has been glad of a piece of a printed Bible when it came first out in our mother language.

✦ JOHN STALHAM
Reviler Rebuked, 21

PROFESSION OF FAITH

First, take heed of resting in a form of godliness. Alas, the profession of godliness is but a sandy foundation to build the hope of an immortal soul upon; therefore lay thy foundation, by faith, upon the Rock, Christ Jesus. Secondly, labor to see an excellency in the power of godliness. The life of holiness is the only excellent life. As it is a proof of the evil of sin that sinners seek to cover it, so it is a proof of the excellency of godliness that so many pretend to it. Thirdly, look upon "things to come" as the greatest realities, for consider, eternity is no dream; hell is no melancholy conceit; heaven is no feigned elysium. There is the greatest reality in these things; though they are spiritual and out of the sight of sense, yet they are real and within the view of faith! Fourthly, set a high value upon thy soul. Take heed that thou art not found overvaluing other things and undervaluing thy soul. Wilt thou clothe and pamper thy body and yet take no care of thy soul? Lastly, meditate much on the strictness and suddenness of that judgment day which thou and I must pass through into an everlasting state, wherein God, the impartial Judge, will require an account at our hands of all our talents. And look, as we have sown here, so we shall reap hereafter.

♦ MATTHEW MEAD
Almost Christian Discovered, ii–iii

To profess Christ is to own Him when none deny Him. To confess Christ is to plead for Him and suffer for Him when others oppose Him. Hypocrites may be professors, but the martyrs are the true confessors. Profession is swimming down the stream; confession is swimming against the stream. Now many may swim with the stream, like the dead fish that cannot swim against the stream with the living fish. Many may profess Christ that cannot confess Christ and so, notwithstanding their profession, yet are but "almost Christians."

♦ MATTHEW MEAD
Almost Christian Discovered, 44

This is the first reason why men go no farther in the profession of religion than to be almost Christians. It is because they mistake their state and think it good when it is not, which mistake hath five causes: a deceitful heart, a proud spirit, taking common grace for saving, outward reformation for true regeneration, want of home application of the law of God to the heart and conscience.

♦ MATTHEW MEAD
Almost Christian Discovered, 176

If to be almost a Christian hinders the true work of conversion; if it be easily mistaken for conversion; if it be a degree of blasphemy; if this be that which quiets conscience; if this subjects a man to commit the unpardonable sin; if it lays us liable to apostasy; if it provokes God to give us up to spiritual judgments; and if it be that which exceedingly aggravates our damnation, sure then it is a very dangerous thing to be almost, and but almost, a Christian.

♦ MATTHEW MEAD
Almost Christian Discovered, 215–16

PROMISES OF GOD

When thou canst not speak in conference to edification, but feel thy heart shut up, apply, "He that believeth on me…out of his belly shall flow rivers of living water" [John 7:38]. "The mouth of the just bringeth forth wisdom" [Prov. 10:31]. "A man shall be satisfied with good by the fruit of his mouth" [Prov. 12:14].… The tongue of the dumb [shall] sing" [Isa. 35:6]. When thou art with the people of God, that thou mayest receive good from them, and do them good, apply, "He that walketh with wise men shall be wise" [Prov. 13:20].… Let all this good which is gotten by their fellowship cause thee to delight in them and take heed of forsaking the fellowship of the saints. When thou go into company, apply these promises to thyself, that thou mayest be so to others, and hinder not thyself by unbelief.

♦ JOSEPH ALLEINE
Saint's Pocket Book, 120–21

Mine omnisciency shall be your over-seer. Mine eyes shall be ever open, observing your wants to relieve them and your wrongs to avenge them; Mine ears shall be open to hear the prayers of My poor; the cry of Mine oppressed; the clamors, calumnies, and reproaches of your enemies. Surely I have seen your affliction and know your sorrows, and shall not God avenge His own elect? I will avenge them speedily. I see the secret plots and designs of your enemies against you and will dis-annul their councils. I see your secret integrity and the uprightness of your hearts toward Me, while the carnal and censorious world condemn you as hypocrites. Your secret prayers, fasts, and tears, which the world knows not of, I observe them and record them. Your secret care to please Me, your secret pains with your own hearts, your secret self-searchings and self-denial—I see them all, and your Father which sees in secret shall reward them openly.

✦ JOSEPH ALLEINE
Voice of God in His Promises, 15

Mine omnipresence shall be company for you, shall be your social friend and familiar acquaintance. Surely I will be with you to bless you. No bolts, nor bars, nor bonds, nor banishment shall remove you from My presence; and the influence of heaven is always with you. In your darkest nights, in your deepest dangers, I am at hand with you, a very present help in the time of trouble. I am not a God afar off or asleep or in a journey when you need My counsel,

Mine ear, or Mine aid; I am always nigh unto them that fear Me. No prison shall hinder the presence of My grace from you...and lighten the darkest dungeon where you can be thrust.

✦ JOSEPH ALLEINE
Voice of God in His Promises, 17

Well, on Saturday, about midnight, [Christian and Hopeful] began to pray and continued in prayer till almost break of day. Now a little before it was day, good Christian, as one half amazed, brake out in this passionate speech: "What a fool," quoth he, "am I, thus to lie in a stinking dungeon, when I may as well walk at liberty! I have a key in my bosom called Promise that will, I am persuaded, open any lock in Doubting Castle."

"Then," said Hopeful, "that's good news. Good brother, pluck it out of thy bosom and try." Then Christian pulled it out of his bosom and began to try at the dungeon door, whose bolt, as he turned the key, gave back, and the door flew open with ease, and Christian and Hopeful both came out.

✦ JOHN BUNYAN
Pilgrim's Progress, 109

God's promises to us must be the ground of our prayers to Him. When God makes a promise, we must make a prayer, for all promises are of mercy, not of duty or debt. Therefore, God is not bound to tender them to us till we beg them.

✦ SAMUEL CLARK
Saint's Nosegay, 91

The chief cause I speak of, of our little growth in Christianity is this, that of all matters in the Scriptures, God's promises are least remembered and regarded in our private meditations or conferences.

✦ EZEKIEL CULVERWELL
Time Well Spent, 169

Commands express our duty unto God without conditions. Promises express the good will of God to us upon conditions.

✦ GILES FIRMIN
Real Christian, 3–4

True faith is careful as well to apply God's precepts, as His promises.

✦ THOMAS GATAKER
Christian Constancy, 6

Whenever you read any promise, remember whose bond it is—the word of no other than God; and when you think on God, be sure you do not confine Him within the little compass of your finite apprehensions but conceive of Him always as an infinite being whose center is everywhere and circumference nowhere. When you have raised your thoughts to the highest, then know you are as far—yea, infinitely farther—from reaching His glory and immensity than a man is from touching the body of the sun with his hand when got upon a mountain. This is to ascribe greatness to God, as we are commanded (Deut. 32:3), and it will admirably facilitate the work of believing.

✦ WILLIAM GURNALL
Christian in Complete Armour, 551

Inquire what effect the promises have upon thy soul. All who have a right to the promise are transformed by the promise. As Satan shed his venomous seed into the heart of Eve by a promise, "Ye shall not surely die" (Gen. 3:4), whereupon she presently conceived with sin and was assimilated into the likeness of his diabolical nature—wicked as the devil himself—so God uses the promises of the gospel, called therefore the immortal seed, to beget His own image and likeness in the hearts of His elect: "exceeding great and precious promises: that by these ye might be partakers of the divine nature" (2 Peter 1:4); that is, be partakers of such heavenly, holy qualities and dispositions as will make you like God Himself. The promises of the gospel have in them a fitness and, when by the Spirit of God applied, a virtue to purify the heart, as well as to pacify the conscience. "Now ye are clean," saith Christ to His disciples, "through the word which I have spoken unto you" (John 15:3). Lay, therefore, thy hand upon thy heart and speak freely. Have the promises had a sanctifying, transforming virtue upon thee?

✦ WILLIAM GURNALL
Christian in Complete Armour, 615

What is the matter of God's promises must be the matter of our prayers.

✦ MATTHEW HENRY
Gems, 129

Every promise is built upon four pillars: God's justice or holiness, which will not suffer Him to deceive; His grace or goodness, which will not suffer

Him to forget; His truth, which will not suffer Him to change; His power, which makes him able to accomplish.

✦ THOMAS MANTON
Practical Exposition on the Epistle of James, 31

Every promise of God hath this consideration tacitly annexed to it—"Is anything too hard for the Lord?"

✦ JOHN OWEN
Golden Book, 221

It is the duty of saints to be very thankful for every promise of God. That God that did not owe us anything should so strongly bind Himself to by the cords of a promise is worth your heartiest thankfulness. Grace and glory are both wrapped up in promises. He that is not thankful for a promise deserves justly the edge of the threatening. Now the heart that is too hasty to have the promise fulfilled will never be so thankful as is meet that the promise was made; the anguish of his spirit in being delayed will weaken, if not quite destroy, the thankfulness of his spirit. A tumultuous Christian can never be a thankful one. Discontentment of heart in tarrying for a promise will certainly hinder that thankfulness of heart which should be given to God for a promise.

✦ RALPH ROBINSON
Christ All and in All, 326

I come to the reasons why God hath thus made many promises unto His people. The first reason is this: that His people might have a fit object for their faith to lay hold upon. For if you look upon all the creatures in the world, you shall not find in all of them jointly or any of them apart a fit object for faith to work upon or to be satisfied in. It is with faith as with a poor woman that hath a child and hath nothing in the world to give it; she takes the child at her back and goes from door to door, and what she gets she gives to the child. So faith takes the soul and carries it to promise after promise, and whatever she finds there she gives it to the soul.

✦ THOMAS SHEPARD
"The Saint's Jewel," in *Sincere Convert*, 394

I come to the reasons why God hath thus made many promises unto His people.... The second reason why God hath made many promises unto His people is that they may have a ground of comfort, for as it is the object of their faith, so it is the ground of their comfort. For all other things of this world cannot profit or comfort the believing soul. As suppose we should go to friends for comfort. It may be they want comfort for themselves and so are unfit to comfort us; or it may be they will not comfort us; or it may be they are a great way off and so cannot do it; or perhaps though able and sometimes willing, yet they are mutable in their comforts, so as though at one time they are willing and do comfort us, yet at another time they fail us. But Christ, to whom the soul is led by the promise, not only hath comfort and is able to comfort us but is willing also to give comfort to us, who knows our wants and is near to all that call upon Him in truth (Ps. 145:18), and also, He is immutable in His comforts.

✦ THOMAS SHEPARD
"The Saint's Jewel," in *Sincere Convert*, 394–95

[The promise] is a declaration of God's will, wherein He signifies what particular good things He will freely bestow and the evils that He will remove…it being a kind of middle thing between His purpose and performance, His intendment of good, and the execution of it upon those whom He loves.

✦ WILLIAM SPURSTOWE
Wells of Salvation Opened, 10

Though the promises be absolutely free in the making of them, having no other cause than God's will, no other motive than His love and mercy, yet in their performance they are conditional and have a dependency upon duties in us. They are fulfilled not only in us but by us. To a clear explication of this rule, I shall propound an ordinary but yet a necessary distinction concerning the promises, which is this: there are promises of grace, and there are promises which are made to grace. The one are so absolute as that they do not depend upon any grace in us foregoing or suppose any good qualifications in us to be partakers of them; such are the promises of conversion and regeneration, in which grace makes way for itself and works all the initial preparations, without any concurrence or activity on our part, we being as fully passive in our second birth as we are in our first birth. The other promises made to grace are conditional, not as supposing anything

to be performed by our strength…or as if the conditions were causes meriting the grace promised; but they are conditional in regard of a precedent qualification and the subject that is to partake of them, without which they cannot be fulfilled, grace being made the condition of grace.

✦ WILLIAM SPURSTOWE
Wells of Salvation Opened, 66–67

Thy best life now is to live upon the promise.

✦ ISAAC WATTS
Devout Meditations, 140

PROSPERITY

Adversity sends us to Christ, as the leprosy sent those ten (Luke 17). Prosperity makes us turn our backs upon Christ and leave Him, as health did those nine.

✦ THOMAS ADAMS
"The Soul's Refuge," in *Works*, 3:26

To see the wicked flourish is matter rather of pity than envy; it is all the heaven they will have.

✦ SIMEON ASHE
Primitive Divinity, 74–75

Many who have abundance of all things to enjoy, yet have not so much content and sweetness in their lives as some that go to their hard labor. Sad, solicitous thoughts do often attend a prosperous condition. Care is as an evil spirit which haunts a rich man and will not suffer him to be quiet. When his chest is full of gold, his heart is full of care either how to manage or how to increase or how to secure what he hath gotten. Oh, the troubles and perplexities that do wait upon prosperity. The world's high seats are very uneasy. Sunshine is pleasant, but sometimes it scorches with its heat. The bee gives honey, but sometimes it stings. Prosperity hath its sweetness and also its sting. Competency, with contentment, is far more eligible. Never did Jacob sleep better than when he had the heavens for his canopy and a hard stone for his pillow. A large voluminous estate is but like a long, trailing garment which is more troublesome than useful.

✦ SIMEON ASHE
Primitive Divinity, 135

Pride, security, and rebellion are the three worms of plenty (Deut. 32:15). The pastures of prosperity are rank and surfeiting. How soon are we broken upon the soft pillow of ease!

✦ SIMEON ASHE
Primitive Divinity, 136

Prosperity is a disguised poison, pleasant to the unwary sense but deadly in the operation, and the more pernicious in the effects because less dangerous in the opinions of men.

✦ WILLIAM BATES
The Danger of Prosperity, in
Whole Works, 2:207

Prosperity is the strongest obstacle against the conversion and reformation of sinners. Whilst they are plying their various pleasures, they have neither will nor leisure to advert to the voice of conscience, so reproachful and stinging to them. And many times, prosperity stupefies conscience, that men are

fearless of divine judgments, involved in sensual security. They will not reverence and obey God's authority till they feel His power; they abuse His blessings to pride and vanity, idleness and luxury, and are hardened in their impenitence, died with the deepest tincture of ingratitude. They drive on through a course of sin till death puts a period to their lusts.

✦ WILLIAM BATES
The Danger of Prosperity, in
Whole Works, 2:207

The Spirit produces a sound mind to judge sincerely of things as they are. And from hence the corrupting vanities of the world lose their attractive charms, and eternal things appear in their reality and excellency and are chosen and sought with persevering diligence. But the sensual heart is a perpetual furnace whose smoke darkens the mind, that it cannot discover sublime and heavenly excellencies, and whose impure heat fires the will that 'tis earnest in the pursuit of fleshly pleasures. Briefly, nothing does more quench the Spirit in His illuminating, quickening, and attractive operations than sensuality, and nothing more heightens sensuality and increases the averseness of carnal men to the holy law of God and makes their conversion more difficult than prosperity.

✦ WILLIAM BATES
The Danger of Prosperity, in
Whole Works, 2:229

Prosperity puffs up sinners with pride, for it is very hard to keep a low spirit with a high and prosperous lot. But

God by affliction calls men down from their heights to sit in the dust.... There are various kinds of affliction—some more, some less humbling—but all of them are humbling.

+ THOMAS BOSTON
Crook in the Lot, 117

It is certain that great prosperity and worldly glory are no sure tokens of God's love, and it is as certain that great troubles and afflictions are no sure mark of God's hatred (Ps. 73:5; Prov. 1:32; Eccl. 9:1–2); and yet many poor Christians, when the waters of affliction rise high and are ready to overflow them, how apt are they to conclude that God hates them and will revenge Himself upon them, and that they have nothing of God, or Christ, or the Spirit, or grace in them.

+ THOMAS BROOKS
Cabinet of Choice Jewels, 83

Riches are called "thick clay" in Habakkuk 2:6, which will sooner break the back than lighten the heart. A little will serve nature, less will serve grace, but nothing will serve men's lusts.

+ THOMAS BROOKS
The Unsearchable Riches of Christ,
in *Select Works*, 1:200

Many men...look at the shine and glitter of prosperity, but they little think of the burden; but there is a fourfold burden. (1) There is a burden of trouble. A rose hath its prickles, and so the Scripture saith, "He that will be rich pierces himself through with many sorrows" (1 Tim. 6:10). (2) There is a burden of danger in it. Men that are in

a prosperous condition are in a great deal of danger. Those men that are set upon a pinnacle on high, these men are in greater danger than other men are. Honey, we know, doth invite bees and wasps unto it; and so the sweet of prosperity doth invite the devil and temptation. (3) In a prosperous estate there is the burden of duty. You look only at the...comfort that they have and the honor and respect that they have who are in a prosperous condition, but you must consider of the duty they owe to God. (4) The last is the burden of account in a prosperous estate. There is a great account that they are to give to God who enjoy great estates and a prosperous condition.

+ JEREMIAH BURROUGHS
Rare Jewel, 41–42

Faith is that that doth overcome the world; it is that that makes all the promises of God to be ours. Now when thou tookest upon thee the profession of religion, did God ever promise thee that thou shouldst live at ease, and quiet, and have no trouble? I remember [Augustine] hath such an expression: "What, is this thy faith? 'What did I ever promise thee,' saith He, 'that thou shouldst ever flourish in the world?' Art thou a Christian to that end? And is this thy faith?"

+ JEREMIAH BURROUGHS
Rare Jewel, 57

We find it by experience that when those that are godly live in the greatest dependence upon God and have no settled [income], do exercise faith more and are in a better condition for their souls than before. Oh! Many times it falls out that the worse thy outward estate is, the better thy soul is; and the better thy outward estate is, the worse thy soul is.

✦ JEREMIAH BURROUGHS
Rare Jewel, 74

Did God heretofore give thee more prosperity? It was to prepare thee for afflictions. We should look at all our outward prosperity as a preparation to afflictions; if thou hadst done so, then it would not have been so difficult for thee to have endured affliction now. When thou hadst a great estate, yet if thou hadst made use of this mercy of God to prepare thee for thy afflicted estate, then the change of thy estate would not be so grievous. That every Christian should do. Have I an estate now? I should prepare for poverty. Have I health now? I should prepare for sickness. Have I liberty? Let me prepare myself for imprisonment. What know I what God may call me to? Have I comfort and peace now in my conscience? Doth God shine upon me? While I have this, let me prepare for God's withdrawing from me. Am I delivered from temptations? Let me prepare now for the time of temptations.

✦ JEREMIAH BURROUGHS
Rare Jewel, 75

In our prosperity we are full of our own wills, and usually we give God counsel when He looks for obedience; and so we dispute our cross when we should take it up.

✦ THOMAS CASE
Correction, Instruction, 11

Prosperity is the nurse of atheism.

✦ THOMAS CASE
Correction, Instruction, 46

The sun of prosperity shines upon the dunghill as well as upon the bed of spices, and the rain of adversity falls upon the fruitful garden as well as upon the barren wilderness. He judges truly of his estate that judges by the word, and not by providence.

✦ THOMAS CASE
Correction, Instruction, 99

For though in prosperity we may have experience of our faith and hope and love to God, yet nothing so soundly and thoroughly as in affliction. In prosperity there is place for the devil's objection "Doth Job serve God for nought?" But in affliction it is taken away, and it appears plainly that we love God, serve and obey Him, not as mercenaries for our own profit but even for Himself. Again, though in our prosperity we might have some experience of the sincerity of our graces, yet not of that great measure of them which we have in affliction.

✦ DANIEL DYKE
"The School of Affliction," in
Two Treatises, 350–51

Take heed lest those estates you have gotten as a blessing, attending the gospel, prove a temptation to you to betray the gospel. "Religion," saith one, "brings forth riches, but the daughter devours the mother." How can you expect acceptance with God who have betrayed His truths and dealt perfidiously with Him?

✦ JOHN FLAVEL
Fountain of Life, 364

He indeed is rich in grace whose graces are not hindered by his riches.

✦ JOHN FLAVEL
Golden Gems, 69

Prosperity excites the love and gratitude of the saints to God, the author of their mercies. While it inflames the sinner's lusts, it fills the good man's heart with benevolent and grateful affections. Not that these outward things are the primary reasons, or motives, of his love to God. Far from it—he loves Him when He takes them away as well as when He bestows them. But God sanctifies prosperity to His people, makes it conducive to their spiritual welfare, and subservient to their usefulness in the world.

✦ JOHN FLAVEL
Husbandry Spiritualized, 329

Outward gains are ordinarily attended with inward losses.

✦ JOHN FLAVEL
Saint Indeed, 76

As hills the higher the barrener, so men commonly the wealthier the worse; the more honor the less holiness.

✦ THOMAS FULLER
in Horn, *Puritan Remembrancer*, 188

Alas, the gospel is not accommodated to [the world's] carnal desires. It tells them of no fields and vineyards it hath to give; it lures them not with the gaieties of worldly honors and pleasures. Had Christ in His gospel but gratified the cravings of men's lusts with a few promises for these things, though He had promised less for another world, the news would have gone down better.

✦ WILLIAM GURNALL
Christian in Complete Armour, 347

There is a burden of care in getting riches, fear in keeping them, temptations in using them, guilt in abusing them, sorrow in losing them, and a burden of account at last to be given up concerning them.

✦ MATTHEW HENRY
Gems, 5

By these examples [in Deuteronomy 32:15]…Moses prescribed not without cause this regle, how to use ourselves in prosperity, which rule contains two precepts: the one, to use moderately the gifts of God and not to abuse them; the other, to acknowledge them to come from God and to put no trust in them. The riches of the world abused engenders pride and forgetfulness of God; therefore, Moses admonishes chiefly man in his wealth to beware he forget not God.

✦ JOHN HOOPER
Early Writings, 302

It is a rare thing to find much retirement unto God, much humility and brokenness of spirit, true purity and spirituality of heart in the affluence and great prosperities of the world. It is no easy thing to carry a very full cup even and to digest well the fatness of a great estate and great place. They are not to be envied who have them.

♦ ROBERT LEIGHTON
Spiritual Truths, 143

The unsoundness of a vessel is not seen when it is empty, but when it is filled with water, then we shall see whether it will leak or not.

♦ THOMAS MANTON
in Spurgeon, *Illustrations and Meditations*, 7

"The unsoundness of a vessel is not seen when it is empty, but when it is filled with water. Then we shall see whether it will leak or not."

It is in our prosperity that we are tested. Men are not fully discovered to themselves till they are tried by fullness of success.

C. H. Spurgeon quoting from and commenting on Thomas Manton in Spurgeon, *Illustrations and Meditations*, 7

In abundance, labor to keep thy heart humble and be courteous toward all, even to the meanest. Take heed of being proud, or domineering over the poor, or slighting them, as rich men are apt to do. For who made thee to differ from the meanest and poorest? Even in abundance take heed of trusting in any worldly things, but labor to live in the world above the world, trusting and relying on God alone (1 Tim. 6:17–18). If riches increase, set not your hearts upon them (Ps. 62:10). Take heed of being ensnared by them

(Deut. 8:10–14). Use the world with weaned affections. Sit loose to all worldly things, as friends, children, worldly goods, that you may be ready to part with them whensoever or howsoever God shall please to take them from you, or you from them (1 Cor. 7:29–31).

♦ THOMAS MOCKET
Christian Advice, 76–77

Riches have been kept for men to their hurt. Wisdom and high place have been the ruin of many. Liberty and plenty are to most a snare. Prosperity slays the foolish. It is enough to fill the soul of any man with horror and amazement, to consider the ways and ends of most of them that are entrusted with this world's goods.

♦ JOHN OWEN
Golden Book, 217

Prosperity and temptation go together. Yea, prosperity is a temptation—many temptations—and that because without eminent supplies of grace, it is apt to cast a soul into a frame and temper exposed to any temptation, and it provides it with fuel and food for all. It hath provision for lust and darts for Satan. Without a special assistance, it hath an inconceivably malignant influence on believers themselves. Thou wantest that which should poise and ballast thy heart; formality of religion will be apt to creep upon thee, and that lays the soul open to all temptations in their full power and strength. Satisfaction and delight in creature comforts, the poison of the soul, will be apt to grow upon thee. In such a time, be vigilant, be circumspect, or thou wilt be surprised.

♦ JOHN OWEN
On Temptation, in Oweniana, 63

It is hard to carry a full cup without shedding or to stand under a heavy load without bowing. It is difficult to walk in the clear day of prosperity without wandering or in the dark night of adversity without stumbling. But from whatever point the wind blows, the skillful mariner knows how to meet it with his sails.

♦ WILLIAM SECKER
Nonsuch Professor, 108

Prosperity is a condition which consists in the fruition of outward good things, as health, strength, friends, riches, honors, and the like. As a constellation is a collection of many stars, so a prosperous condition is a confluence of many temporal comforts. God in His wise providence is pleased to give some persons large draughts of these sugared pleasures; their cup runneth over. They are in themselves mercies for which we may pray with humble submission and for which we must praise God with holy affections, but through the corruption of our hearts, they often prove prejudicial to holiness. Those fires which were made to warm us do often black and burn us. Small vessels carrying a great sail are apt to be overturned with every tempest. A prosperous condition is called a slippery place: "Thou didst set them in slippery places" (Ps. 73:18). Those

that walk on ice had need to be wary how they set their feet, lest they slip and fall.

♦ GEORGE SWINNOCK
The Christian Man's Calling,
in *Works,* 2:47

In particular, take heed of pride, carnal confidence, and senselessness of others' sufferings, which three sins prosperous men are prone to.

♦ GEORGE SWINNOCK
The Christian Man's Calling,
in *Works,* 2:55–56

In prosperity, prepare for adversity.

♦ GEORGE SWINNOCK
The Christian Man's Calling,
in *Works,* 2:67

If thou would in prosperity prepare for adversity, get thine affections mortified to all the comforts of this life. Though outward favors cling about thee, yet let thine heart climb above them. He who counts all worldly gains to be small will never count any worldly loss to be great. Excessive love to the creature causeth excessive grief in the loss of creatures. A man may pull off his glove quickly and quietly, but not his skin because this sticks close to his flesh. The closer the world cleaves to us, the harder it will be to part it from us.

♦ GEORGE SWINNOCK
The Christian Man's Calling,
in *Works,* 2:71–72

Their prosperity [i.e., that of the wicked] is not fast. Their riches and honors do but show themselves like a rainbow in all their dainty colors and then vanish away: "Thou didst set them in slippery places" ([Ps. 73:]18). They stand on ice, [and] are as soon off almost as on. How quickly is the beauty of all worldly blessings blasted! "The triumphing of the wicked is short" (Job 20:5). Though their pains shall be forever, yet their pleasures of sin are but for a season. They are rich in this world, not in the other world (1 Tim. 6:17). They live in pleasures on earth (James [5:]5. The place of their pilgrimage is the only place of their pleasures. They have a time of mirth, but they shall have an eternity of mourning.

✦ GEORGE SWINNOCK
The Christian Man's Calling,
in *Works,* 2:108

These spiritual riches [i.e., grace] sanctify other riches. Riches without grace are hurtful; they are golden snares; they are the bellows of pride, the fuel of lust; they set open hell's gates for men; they are unblest blessings. But grace sanctifies our riches. It corrects the poison; it takes away the curse; it makes them beneficial to us; riches shall be certificates of God's love, wings to lift us up to paradise. Thus grace, by a divine chemistry, extracts heaven out of earth and gives us not only venison but the blessing.

✦ THOMAS WATSON
The Beatitudes, in *Discourses,* 2:461

Prosperity often deafens the ear against God. "I spake unto thee in thy prosperity; but thou saidst, I will not hear" (Jer. 22:21). Soft pleasures harden the heart. Prosperity has its honey and also its sting. Anxious care is the evil

spirit that haunts the rich man; when his chests are full of money, his heart is full of care. Sunshine is pleasant, but sometimes it scorches. The spreading of a full table may be the spreading of a snare. Many have been sunk to hell with golden weights. "They that will be rich fall into…many…hurtful lusts, which drown men in…perdition" (1 Tim. 6:9). The world's golden sands are quicksands. What, if we have less food we have less snare; if less dignity, less danger. As we lack the rich provisions of the world, so we lack the temptations.

✦ THOMAS WATSON
Gleanings, 43

To give us Christ is more than if God had given us all the world. He can make more worlds, but He has no more Christs to bestow. If you have but daily bread enough to suffice nature, be content. Consider it is not having abundance that always makes life comfortable. A staff may help the traveler, but a bundle of staves will be a burden to him. The world is but a great inn. If God give you sufficient to pay for your charges in your inn, you may be content; you shall have enough when you come to your own country.

✦ THOMAS WATSON
Gleanings, 44

PROTESTANTS ON ROMAN CATHOLICISM

I remember we are going to the altar: the God of mercy conquer the hearts of these malicious furies, these wily Gibeonites [i.e., Roman Catholics] who, while they dwell among us, labor to deceive us with the pretense of antiquity; the iron shoes of St. Peter; their old garments of their own merit; their old, moldy bread of Transubstantiation, with all which, though put on but yesterday, they endeavor to deceive Joshua and his people. And we find they did it too, but it was because they asked not counsel of the Lord (Josh. 9:14). Let us therefore to prevent the like wiles go on in the name of the Lord whom we come to serve, and David's resolution will infallibly produce David's blessing. So holy means cannot but produce a happy end.

◆ ISAAC BARGRAVE
Sermon Preached, 106

One main difference betwixt us [i.e., Protestants] and them [i.e., Roman Catholics] in all our controversies is this: that we take away from man all manner of glorying in himself and give the glory of all to God. But they rob God to give to man matter of trusting unto himself and unto others like himself and of boasting in himself and others. Instance the controversies we have with them about the authority of the church above the Scriptures, the power of popes and priests, adoration and invocation of angels and saints, their intercession, the inherent virtue of sacraments, man's free will to good, works of satisfaction and supererogation, merit of works, indulgences, pilgrimages, and many other like these.

◆ WILLIAM GOUGE
Guide to Goe to God, 41

In Hariford they have turned the table in the cathedral and taken away the cops and bassons [i.e., cups and basins] and all such things. I hope they begin to see that the Lord is about to purge His church of all such inventions of men.

◆ BRILLIANA HARLEY
February 17, 1641, *Letters*, 148–49

May [the deceitful heart] not put a fair gloss upon popery itself and say, "The papists have the substance of religion, and why should we scruple human rites and ceremonies? They have the sacred Scriptures, and why should we stumble at superfluous traditions? Their images are not the terminative object of worship but the motive only, and why may we not use human inventions to move us to devotion? Transubstantion itself is but a kind of nicety, they say; the body of Christ is in the Eucharist after the manner or spirits; we say that it is there spiritually. And how little doth the difference seem to be? Praying to saints and angels is but a vanity, a void thing. Human merit is a harmless thing if it be grafted upon Christ and the promise. The pope himself is a bishop, and why need we think him antichrist?" The false heart can paint the whore in every part and make her look as if she were not "Mystery, Babylon, the mother of harlots and abominations of the earth." Labor then to know more and more of the deceitfulness of thy heart, that it may not cheat thee in times of persecution. He that trusts in his heart is a fool—nay, a secret idolater; let us carry a holy jealousy over our hearts.

✦ EDWARD POLHILL
Armatura Dei, 40–41

ENGLISH PROTESTANT: Your religion destroys even the principles of morality, which true religion is so far from destroying that it improves and perfects it. I confess, the bloodiness of your religion hath ever made me both suspect and loath it. I find that Christ is a prince of peace; though He whipped some out of the temple, yet He never whipped any into His church; that He drew in His disciples with the cords of a man, of conviction and persuasion, and so did His apostles after Him. But your religion, like Draco's laws, is written in blood. I perceive you answer our arguments with fire and fagot. Besides this, your religion destroys all civil faith and society; your principle is known, and so is your practice of equivocation and keeping no faith with heretics.

POPISH PRIEST: I know where you are. You mean because of John Huss who, after he had the faith of the emperor given him for his safe conduct, was, contrary to that faith, put to death in the Council of Constance.

ENGLISH PROTESTANT: I do so, and what can you say for it?

POPISH PRIEST: This I say, you must not charge upon our church the opinion of some few private doctors since others disown this and have written against it.

✦ MATTHEW POOLE
Dialogue between a Popish Priest and an English Protestant, 106–7

[The Great Fire of London] does smell of a popish design, hatched in the same place where the Gunpowder Plot was contrived, only that this was more successful. The world sufficiently knows how correspondent this is to popish principles and practices; those who could intentionally blow up king and parliament by gunpowder might (without any scruple of their kinds of conscience) actually burn a heretical city, as they count it, into ashes. For besides the dispensations they can have from His Holiness (or rather His Wickedness), the pope, for the most horrid crimes of murder, incest, and the like, it is not unlikely but they count such an action as this meritorious (in their kind of merit), which, in the issue, they will find to merit the flames of eternal fire instead of a crown of glory, which I wonder that in their way they can have the least hopes of. I believe that the people will now take more heed of them and their ways, and instead of promoting their cause, I hope that a contrary effect is produced and that the before indifferency of a generation more newly sprung up who did not know them is now turned into loathing and detestation of such a religion as can allow of such practices.

✦ THOMAS VINCENT
God's Terrible Voice in the City, 56–57

The canon of the Mass, say they [i.e., Roman Catholics], is perfect and absolute, void of all error, and therefore not to be changed or abrogated.... But we [Protestants], on the contrary side, more truly and agreeable to Scripture, doubt not to say that there can be nothing more corrupt, abominable, fuller of all impiety, heresy, lying than is their idolatrous sacrifice of the Mass; as it shall now more particularly appear by the collection of the several errors.

♦ ANDREW WILLET
Synopsis Papismi, 20–21

PROVIDENCE

He upholds "all things by the word of his power" (Heb. 1:3). He is *pater familias* and disposes all things in this universe with greater care and providence than any householder can manage the business of his private family. He leaves it not, as the carpenter having built the frame of a house, to others to perfect it but looks to it Himself. His creation and providence are like the mother and the nurse; the one produces, the other preserves. His creation was a short providence; His providence a perpetual creation. The one sets up the frame of the house; the other keeps it in reparation.

♦ THOMAS ADAMS
"*Semper Idem*, or The Immutable Mercy of Jesus Christ," in *Works*, 3:6

Contentment hath this excellency—it is the best commentator upon providence. It makes a fair interpretation of all God's dealings. Let the providences of God be ever so dark or mysterious, contentment doth ever construe them in the best sense. I may say of it as the apostle of charity—it "thinketh no evil" (1 Cor. 13:5). "Sickness," saith contentment, "is God's furnace to refine His gold and make it sparkle the more. The prison is an oratory, or house of prayer. What if God melts away the creature from me? He saw, perhaps, my heart grew too much in love with it. Had I been long in that fat pasture I should have surfeited, and the better my estate had been, the worse my soul would have been. God is wise; He hath done this either to prevent some sin or to exercise some grace." What a blessed frame of heart is this! A contented Christian is an advocate for God against unbelief and impatience.

♦ SIMEON ASHE
Primitive Divinity, 103–4

Everyone knows what is most pleasant to him, but God alone knows what is most profitable.

♦ THOMAS BOSTON
Crook in the Lot, 43

Providence in this life is the map of changes, the picture of mutability. Who can sum up the strange circumferences and rare circuits and labyrinths of providence? Providence is as a wheel in the midst of a wheel (Ezek. 1:16) whose motion, and work, and end in working is not discerned by every common eye. Three dreadful judgments God hath lately visited us with—namely, sword, pestilence, and fire. But who repents? Who smites upon his thigh? Who finds out the plague of his own heart?

Who says, "What have I done?" Who ceases from doing evil? Who learns to do well? (Isa. 1:16–17).

♦ THOMAS BROOKS
Cabinet of Choice Jewels, 6

As God created the world and all the creatures therein by His almighty power, so the Scriptures teach that He upholds, directs, disposes, and governs them all by His providence. Nothing so casual but He disposes of it; no agent so free as to be exempted from His control. No affliction or evil of punishment but He has a hand in it. But as for sin, He neither is nor possibly can be the author or approver of it.

♦ SAMUEL CRADOCK
Knowledge and Practice, 11

Providence…is nothing else but the performance of God's gracious purposes and promises to His people.

♦ JOHN FLAVEL
Divine Conduct, 13

Providence doth not only undertake but performs and perfects what concerns us. It goes through with its designs and accomplishes what it begins. No difficulty so clogs it, no cross accident so falls in its way, but it carries its design through it. Its motions are irresistible and uncontrollable; He performs it for us. And, which is sweet to consider, all its products and issues are exceedingly beneficial to the saints. It performs all things for them. It is true, we often prejudice its works and unjustly censure its designs, and under many of our straits and troubles we say,

"All these things are against us." But indeed, providence neither doth nor can do anything that is really against the true interest and good of the saints. For what are the works of providence but the execution of God's decree and the fulfilling of His word? And there can be no more in providence than is in them. Now there is nothing but good to the saints in God's purposes and promises, and therefore, whatever providence doth in their concerns, it must be, as the text speaks, the performance of all things for them [Ps. 57:2].

♦ JOHN FLAVEL
Divine Conduct, 14–15

Though our present views and reflections upon providence be so short and imperfect in comparison with that in heaven, yet such as it is, under all its present disadvantages, it hath so much excellency and sweetness in it that I may call it a little heaven or, as Jacob called his Bethel, the gate of heaven. It is certainly a highway of walking with God in this world, and as sweet communion may a soul enjoy with Him in His providences as in any of His ordinances. How often have the hearts of its observers been melted into tears of joy at the beholding of its wise and unexpected productions! How often hath it convinced them, upon a sober recollection of the events of their lives, that if the Lord had left them to their own counsels, they had as often been their own tormentors, if not executioners! Into what and how many fatal mischiefs had they precipitated themselves if providence had been as shortsighted as they.

✦ JOHN FLAVEL
Divine Conduct, 19

If this puzzle us, what shall we say when we see events produced in the world for the good of God's chosen by those very hands and means which were intentionally employed for their ruin. These things are as much beside the intentions of their enemies as they are above their own expectations, yet such things are no rarities in the world. Was not the envy of Joseph's brethren, the cursed plot of Haman, the decree procured by the envy of the princes against Daniel, with many more of the like nature, all turned by a secret and strange hand of providence to their greater advancement and benefit? Their enemies lifted them up to all that honor and preferment they had.

✦ JOHN FLAVEL
Divine Conduct, 24–25

You can learn the voice and errand of the rod only from the word (Ps. 94:12). The word interprets the works of God. Providences in themselves are not a perfect guide; they often puzzle and entangle our thoughts. But bring them to the word, and your duty will be quickly manifested. "Until I went into the sanctuary of God, then understood I their end" (Ps. 73:16–17); and not only their end but his own duty to be quiet in an afflicted condition and not envy their prosperity. Well, then, bring those providences you have passed through or are now under to

the word, and you will find yourselves surrounded with a marvelous light and see the verification of the Scriptures in them.

✦ JOHN FLAVEL
Divine Conduct, 129

Is the eye of providence ever shut? No, "He slumbers not" that keeps you. Or is it one moment off you? No, "the eye of the Lord is upon the righteous"; He has fixed it forever and with infinite delight pleased Himself in the object. When was His ear shut, or His hand either, from receiving your cries or supplying your wants? Nay, does not your condition take up the thoughts of God, and are they any other than thoughts of peace which He entertains? A few drops of this oil will keep the wheel in motion.

✦ WILLIAM GURNALL
Christian in Complete Armour, 45

As God can make a straight line with a crooked stick, be[ing] righteous when He uses wicked instruments; so also gracious when He dispenses harsh providences.

✦ WILLIAM GURNALL
Christian in Complete Armour, 66

We wrestle against providence when incorrigible under the various dispensations of God toward us. Providence has a voice, if we had an ear; mercies should draw, afflictions drive; now, when neither fair means nor foul do us good, but we are impenitent under both, this is to wrestle against God with both hands.

✦ WILLIAM GURNALL
Christian in Complete Armour, 81

Providences are good and evil to us as they find or make us better or worse; nothing is good to him that is evil. As God makes use of all the seasons of the year for the harvest, the frost and cold of winter as well as the heat of the summer, so doth He of fair and foul, pleasing and unpleasing providences for promoting holiness.

✦ WILLIAM GURNALL
Christian in Complete Armour, 299

When the psalmist had exhorted men to be thankful for the mercies of God in creation and providence, his conclusion is worthy of remark: "Whoso is wise, and will observe these things, even they shall understand the lovingkindness of the Lord," as if he had said, "The reason why so little praise is given for such great mercies is because men see not the lovingkindness of God in them, and they see not His lovingkindness nor observe His mercies because they have not wisdom. It is not a library that makes a scholar, but wisdom to observe and gather the choice notions out of its books. None want mercies to bless God for. Divine providence is a large volume written thick and close with mercies from one end of our life to the other. But, few, alas, have a heart to read in it; and fewer have wisdom to collect the choice passages of it for such a holy purpose as this.

✦ WILLIAM GURNALL
Christian in Complete Armour, 734

When I see my Savior hanging in so forlorn a fashion upon the cross; His head drooping down; His temples bleeding with thorns; His hands and feet with the nails and His side with the spear; His enemies round about Him, mocking at His shame and insulting over His impotence. How should I think any otherwise of Him than as Himself complaineth, forsaken of His Father? But when again I turn mine eyes and see the sun darkened, the earth quaking, the rocks rent, the graves opened, the thief confessing to give witness to His deity; and when I see so strong a guard of providence over Him that all His malicious enemies are not able so much as to break one bone of that body which seemed carelessly neglected, I cannot but wonder at His glory and safety. God is ever near, though oft unseen; and if He wink at our distress, He sleepeth not. The sense of others must not be judges of His presence and care, but our faith. What care I if the world give me up for miserable while I am under His secret protection?

✦ JOSEPH HALL
Meditations and Vows, 109–10

God did not consult us in making the world, yet it is well made. Why should we expect then that He should take His measures from us in governing it?

✦ MATTHEW HENRY
Gems, 88

About this time I had a signal deliverance, fire kindled in the thatch of the house by sparks out of the chimney, which was very providentially discovered and presently quenched, else it might shortly in that dry season, on that windy day, have burned down my house and all the adjacent houses.

It was very teaching to take heed of sparks of temptation, and to take notice of common mercies.

✦ THOMAS JOLLY
Note Book, 19–20
(December 1674)

Stung I was with a bee on my nose. I presently plucked out the sting and laid on honey, so that my face swelled not; thus divine providence reaches to the lowest things. Let not sin, oh Lord, that dreadful sting, be able to poison me.

✦ RALPH JOSSELIN
Diary, 18 (September 5, 1643)

There are three sins especially by which you make providence your enemy: (1) When you abuse them [wealth or created things] to serve your lusts. Where there is pride and wantonness, you may look for a burning; certainly, your flowers will be scorched and dried up. Pleasant Sodom, when it was given to "pride, fulness of bread, and abundance of idleness," met with a burning heat indeed (Ezek. 16:49).... (2) When you make them objects of trust. God can brook no rivals.... If you make idols of the creatures [created things], God will make nothing of them. The fire of God's jealousy is a burning heat. God...certainly... shows that riches are but dead helps when they are preferred before the living God (1 Tim. 6:17). (3) When you get them by wrong means.... You think it is a ready way to advance you; no, this is the ready way to ruin all: "Your gold and silver is cankered;

and the rust of them shall be a witness against you, and shall eat your flesh as it were fire" (James 5:3); that is, draw the fire and burning heat of God's wrath upon yourselves.

✦ THOMAS MANTON
*Practical Exposition on the
Epistle of James*, 27

In the evening, in the close, it will be light, so light as to be to us discernible. In the meantime, we are like unskillful men who, going to the house of some eminent artist, so long as he is about his work, despise it as confused; but when it is finished admire it as excellent. Whilst the passages of providence are on us, all is confusion, but when the fabric is reared, glorious.

✦ JOHN OWEN
Golden Book, 205

There is a call, a cry, in every rod of God, in every chastising providence; and therein He makes a declaration of His name, His holiness, His power, His greatness.

✦ JOHN OWEN
On Being Spiritually Minded,
in *Oweniana*, 218

In a clock made by the art and handiwork of man, there be many wheels, and every one hath his several motion; some turn this way, some that way, some go softly, some apace, and they are all ordered by the motion of the watch. Behold here a notable resemblance of God's special providence over mankind, which is the watch of the great world, allotting to every man his motion and calling and in that calling his particular office and function.

✦ WILLIAM PERKINS
Treatise of the Vocations, 903

Providence is usually exercised in contraries; it is the divine method to humble, that He may exalt; to kill, that He may make alive; to bring light out of darkness and hell out of heaven. We wonder oft why God suffers those to reign who make Christ to suffer and will not suffer Christ to reign, little considering that the Lord oft makes the earth to help the woman [i.e., the church] and loves to strike straight strokes with crooked sticks.

✦ FRANCIS RAWORTH
On Jacob's Ladder, 15–16

Providence hath a thousand keys to open a thousand sundry doors for the deliverance of His own, when it is even come to a desperate case. Let us be faithful and care for our own part, which is to do and suffer for Him and lay Christ's part on Himself and leave it there.

✦ SAMUEL RUTHERFORD
Garden of Spices, 165

Christ may act the part of an enemy a little while, as Joseph did, but it is to make way for acting His own part of mercy in a more seasonable time. He cannot restrain His compassion long; He seems to wrestle with us, as with Jacob, but He supplies us with hidden strength at length to get the better. Faith pulls off the vizard from His face and sees a loving heart under contrary appearances.

✦ RICHARD SIBBES
Bruised Reed and Smoking Flax, 108

[The Christian] believes that all things are ordered by providence; yet time and chance happen to all.

✦ RALPH VENNING
Orthodox Paradoxes, 22

God speaks by His merciful providences; by His patience and bounty and goodness He calls men unto repentance (Rom. 2:4). He giveth witness of Himself in giving rain and fruitful seasons (Acts 14:17). God's providing mercies, God's preventing mercies, God's preserving mercies, God's delivering mercies; the number of God's mercies which cannot be reckoned; the order and strange method of God's mercies, which cannot be declared; the greatness of God's mercies in the kinds and strange circumstances which cannot be expressed do all with open mouth call upon men from the Lord to repent of their sins which they have committed against Him and to yield all love, thankfulness, and obedience unto Him.

✦ THOMAS VINCENT
God's Terrible Voice in the City, 9–10

God speaks by His afflictive providences. There is a voice of God in His rod as well as in His word: "Hear ye the rod, and who hath appointed it" (Mic. 6:9); when God chastens, He teaches (Ps. 94:12). When God lifts up His hand and strikes, He opens his mouth also and speaks and sometimes opens men's ears too and seals their instruction (Job 33:16). Sometimes God speaks by rods more mildly, by lesser afflictions; sometimes God speaks by scorpions more terribly, by greater judgments.

◆ THOMAS VINCENT
God's Terrible Voice in the City, 10

Providence is the queen of the world; it is the hand that turns all the wheels in the universe. Chrysostom calls it the pilot that steers the ship of the creation. Providences are often dark; God writes sometimes in shorthand. The characters of providence are so various and strange and our eyes are so dim that we know not what to make of providence. Hence we are ready to censure that which we do not understand. We think that things are very eccentric and disorderly; God's providence is sometimes secret, always wise.

◆ THOMAS WATSON
"The Christian's Charter of Privileges," in *Discourses*, 1:66

There is no such thing as blind fate, but there is a providence that guides and governs the world. "The lot is cast into the lap; but the whole disposing thereof is of the LORD" (Prov. 16:33)…. Providence is God's ordering all issues and events of things after the counsel of His will to His own glory…. The wheels in a clock seem to move contrary one to the other, but they help forward the motion of the clock and make the alarum strike; so the providences of God seem to be cross wheels, but for all that they shall carry on the good of the elect…. God is not like an artificer that builds a house and then leaves it, but like a pilot He steers the ship of the whole creation.

◆ THOMAS WATSON
Gleanings, 33

Another false rule is providence; providence sits at the helm and disposes of all events and contingencies. But providence is not a rule for the upright man to walk by; we are indeed to observe God's providence: "Whoso is wise… will observe these things" (Ps. 107:43), but we are not to be infallibly led by it. Providence is a Christian's diurnal, not his Bible.

◆ THOMAS WATSON
"The Upright Man's Character,"
in *Discourses*, 1:328

Judge not Christ's love by providence, but by promises. Bless God for shaking off false foundations and for any way whereby He keeps the soul awakened and looking after Christ.

◆ THOMAS WILCOX
Choice Drop of Honey, 26

PSALMS, BOOK OF

The Psalms are, as it were, the anatomy of a holy man; they lay the inside of a true, devout man outward, even to the view of others. If the Scriptures be compared to a body, the Psalms may well be the heart; they are so full of sweet and holy affections and passions. In other portions of Scripture, God speaks to us; in the Psalms, holy men (especially David, who was the penman of most of them) speak to God, wherein we have the passages of a broken, humble soul to God.

◆ RICHARD SIBBES
"The Sword of the Wicked,"
in *Complete Works*, 1:105

PURITANS, CONTEMPORARY VIEWS OF

A certain godly woman riding behind her husband, who was a persecutor of Mr. Bolton [probably Robert Bolton (1572–1631)], as they were riding it thundered and lightninged extraordinarily so that he trembled exceedingly. His wife, with a cheerful voice, said, "Husband, what ails you? Why do you tremble thus?"

He answered, "Do you not hear how terribly it thunders?"

She answered, "Yes, I hear it."

"And, said he, do you not tremble also?"

She answered, no, she was not at all afraid, for she knew it was but the voice of her Father. He was amazed at her cheerfulness and answer and began to think with himself, *Surely these Puritans have something within them that they are able to bear up in such storms and that they have peace and are cheerful, while I tremble.* And being not far off, immediately he did ride up to Mr. Bolton, beseeching pardon that he had persecuted him and desired that he would tell him what he should do to be saved.

✦ ISAAC AMBROSE
Ministration of, and Communion with Angels, 90

About that time it pleased God that a poor peddlar came to the door that had ballads and some good books, and my father bought of him Dr. Sibbes's *Bruised Reed*. This also I read and found it suited to my state, and seasonably sent to me, which opened the love of God to me and gave me a livelier apprehension of the mystery of redemption and how much I was beholden to Jesus Christ.

✦ RICHARD BAXTER
as quoted in Sibbes, *Bruised Reed and Smoking Flax*, ii

I have read of a desperate wretch, that when he came to die, gave good portions to all his children but one, and to him he would give but twelve pence; and being asked the reason of it, he made answer he was a Puritan. "I have heard him say," said his wretched father, "that he had a promise to live on; let us now see whether a promise will maintain him or no."

✦ THOMAS BROOKS
Cabinet of Choice Jewels, 177

Profit, gain, riches are great things in men's eyes, and does God deny these likewise to His people? It may be, you will say, few of these Precisians, Puritans, Fanaticks (as now called) thrive in the world; we must not look for riches amongst them in the way they take. And what, I pray, do profit and riches follow all those who are strangers to God and follow after the world, that make mammon their God? Do we not see the contrary? How many of those who have kept close to God has the Lord blessed and given them power to get wealth (Deut. 8:18) when others have sunk and come to nothing?

✦ GILES FIRMIN
Real Christian, 61

Must we pray above all for saints? Woe then to those who instead of praying for them had rather make a prey of them (Isa. 59:15); who, instead of praying for them, can curse them, perhaps not under the plain name of saints but as fanatics, Puritans, or some other name of scorn invented to cover their malice, so they can devour and tear them in pieces. The saints are a sort of people that none love but those that are themselves such.

✦ WILLIAM GURNALL
Christian in Complete Armour, 782

Whoever was zealous for God's glory or worship could not endure blasphemous oaths, ribald conversation, profane scoffs, Sabbath breaking, derision of the word of God, and the like; whoever could endure a sermon, modest habit or conversation, or anything good, all these were Puritans.

✦ LUCY HUTCHINSON
Memoirs of the Life of Colonel Hutchinson, 81

The common practice of some, that instead of loving the godly best of all persons, they can worst away with them. They could love such a kinsman, tenant, servant, etc., but that he is (as they call them) a Puritan, and they cannot abide these precise fellows. Nay, they have loved such and such a one till it pleased God to convert him, and ever since they could never abide him.

✦ JOHN ROGERS
Treatise of Love, 153

In the eighteeth year of his age [1626], from the care of his schoolmaster Mr. Augur, he [i.e., the author's father] was sent to Sidney College in Cambridge and committed to Mr. Dugard, a pious,

learned, and painful tutor. He grew in grace and learning, happily escaping many temptations and frustrating the designs of some superiors who would have debauched a Puritan, as they called him, though he was still sufficiently conformable to the established ecclesiastical orders.

✦ EDMUND TRENCH
Some Remarkable Passages, 7

Do not our lordly bishops and prelates, with many other learned men, not only themselves but cause and move others to hate the dear children of God, showing it by their mocking, taunting, reproaching with scoffs and jeers, and calling them by the names of Puritans, schismatical, seditious, factious, trouble states, traitors that speak against Caesar, with many slanders; taking away all their livings, casting them into prison, whipping of them, perpetual imprisonment, laying great fines on them, and banishment into remote places, separating those that God had joined together, as the husband from the wife, parents from their children. And as they did with Dr. Leighton (whom I know well), so did they with Master Burton, Doctor Bastwick, and Mr. Prynne; set them in the pillory, cut off their ears to the shedding of much blood that, so as the blood of Abel cried for vengeance, so the blood of Master Udall, Master Hildersham, Master Sates, with divers other men's blood together, do all cry for vengeance, vengeance on this land.

✦ NEHEMIAH WALLINGTON
Historical Notices, 61–62

PURPOSE OF MAN

Man's soul is of high—yea, royal—extraction, for God is the Father of spirits; but this child meets his heavenly Father in the dark and knows him not: "He was in the world, and the world was made by him, and the world knew him not" (John 1:10). As the soul is of high birth, so it is intended for a high end—to glorify and enjoy God its maker. Now, for want of the knowledge of Christ, it can do neither, but debaseth itself to the drudgery of sin and sensual embraces of the creature instead of God, for whom it was at first made. O, how should we prize and study this mystery which brings us to the true knowledge of God, and the way how we may enjoy happiness with Him! Man's primitive happiness consisted in God's love to him and his likeness to God. The gospel discovers a way how man may be restored to both.

✦ WILLIAM GURNALL
Christian in Complete Armour, 805

READING

To read much and practice nothing is to hunt much and catch nothing.

✦ THOMAS BROOKS
in Horn, *Puritan Remembrancer*, 192

Reject not hastily anything you read because of the mean opinion you have of the author. Believe not everything you read because of the great opinion you have of him that wrote it.

✦ HENRY SCUDDER
Christian's Daily Walk, 146

REASON

Some seek comfort in a way of reason and think to reason out their temptation and to reason in their comfort, but as one says well, "Dispute not with God lest you be confounded; dispute not with Satan lest you be deceived."

✦ WILLIAM BRIDGE
Lifting Up, 40

Reason is in man the faculty of his mind by which he is enabled to know and judge, to order and direct himself, his own actions, and all other things belonging to his own, or their being toward the ends and uses for which God has fitted both him and them to the enjoyment of the happiness whereof he and they are capable.

✦ JOHN DURY
Seasonable Discourse, 3

The work of salvation cannot be done by the candlelight of a natural understanding, but by the sunlight of the gospel revelation; this sun must rise before man can go forth to this labor.

✦ WILLIAM GURNALL
Christian in Complete Armour, 795

[There are] many who expressly deny not [Christ's] divine person, yet seem to grow weary of any concernment therein. A natural religion or none at all pleaseth them better than faith in God by Jesus Christ. That anything more is necessary in religion but what natural light will discover and conduct us in, with the moral duties of righteousness and honesty which it directs unto, there are too many that will not acknowledge. What is beyond the line of nature and reason is rejected as unintelligible mysteries or follies. The person and grace of Christ are supposed to breed all the disturbance in religion.

✦ JOHN OWEN
The Person of Christ, in
Golden Book, 106

Faith uses reason, though not as a ground, yet as a sanctified instrument to find out God's grounds, that it may rely upon them. He believes best that knows best why he should believe; confidence and love and other affections of the soul, though they have no reason grafted in them, yet thus far they are reasonable, as that they are in a wise man raised up, guided, and laid down with reason. Or else men were neither to be blamed nor praised for ordering their affections aright, whereas not only civil virtue but grace itself is especially conversant in ruling the affections by sanctified reason.

✦ RICHARD SIBBES
Soul's Conflict, 242

REBUKES/REPROOFS

It was well done of Paul to reprove Peter to his face, and it is well done of Peter to praise Paul in his absence. Paul's censure of Peter behind his back had been calumny, and Peter's commendation of Paul to his face had been flattery. Both being done in their due time and place are proofs of their sincerity.

✦ THOMAS ADAMS
Exposition upon…Second…Peter, 771

Come into the light, that your hearts and lives may be thoroughly known to you. Love the most searching, faithful ministry and books, and be thankful to reprovers and plain-dealing friends.

✦ RICHARD BAXTER
A Christian Directory, in
Practical Works, 2:539

Being challenged for telling a lie, no man is more furiously angry. Then he draws his sword and threatens because he thinks that an offer of revenge, to show himself moved at the accusation, does in some sort discharge him of the imputation, as if the condemning of the sin in appearance acquitted him in effect. Or else because he that is called a liar to his face is also called a coward in the same breath if he swallows it, and the party charged does conceive that if he vindicates his valor, his truth will be given him into the bargain.

✦ THOMAS FULLER
Holy and Profane States, 304

Reproofs are good physic, but they have an unpleasant farewell; it is hard for men not to throw them back on the face of him that gives them. Now nothing is more powerful to keep a reproof from thus coming back than the holiness of the person that reproves. "Let the righteous smite me," saith David, "it shall be a kindness: and let him reprove me; it shall be an excellent oil, which shall not break my head" (Ps. 141:5). See how well it is taken from such hand, from the authority that holiness carries with it. None but a vile wretch will smite a righteous man

with reproach for smiting him with a reproof if softly laid on and, like oil, fomented and wrought into him, as it should, with compassion and love to his soul.
✦ WILLIAM GURNALL
Christian in Complete Armour, 304

I see iron first heated red hot in the fire and after, beaten and hardened with cold water. Thus will I deal with an offending friend: first, heat him with deserved praise of his virtue, and then beat upon him with apprehension. So, good nurses, when their children are fallen, first take them up and speak them fair, chide them afterward. Gentle speech is a good preparative for rigor. He shall see that I love him by my approbation and that I love not his faults by my reproof. If he love himself, he will love those that mislike his vices; and if he love not himself, it matters not whether he love me.
✦ JOSEPH HALL
Meditations and Vows, 155

He that would do good this way [i.e., in reproving] must have fidelity, courage, discretion, patience: fidelity, not to bear with; courage, to reprove them; discretion, to reprove them well; patience, to abide the leisure of amendment, making much of good beginnings and putting up many repulses; bearing with many weaknesses; still hoping, still soliciting, as knowing that those who have been long used to fetters cannot but halt awhile when they are taken off.
✦ JOSEPH HALL
Meditations and Vows, 161–62

Friendly reproof is a duty, and we ought both to give it and take it in love.
✦ MATTHEW HENRY
Gems, 25

A clear conscience, as it enables a man to bear reproaches from others with patience, so it gives him an advantage to reprove others with authority. It is a true rule that he who reproves another ought himself to be free from the fault which he reproves, for otherwise the reproof neither comes with freedom from the reprover nor with efficacy to the reproved.
✦ EZEKIEL HOPKINS
"Of the Nature, Corruption, and Renewing of the Conscience," in *Select Works,* 287

Reproof to a gracious soul is like a sword anointed with balsam; it wounds and heals at the same time. So, Hezekiah said, "Good is the word of the LORD which thou hast spoken" (Isa. 39:8). It was a sad word, a heavy threatening; yet the submission of his sanctified judgment called it good.
✦ THOMAS MANTON
Practical Exposition on the Epistle of James, 57

Usually conviction and reproof beget hatred: "Am I therefore become your enemy, because I tell you the truth?" (Gal. 4:16). Truth is a good mother, but it begets a bad daughter, contempt and hatred. Oh, this should not be so. David counted the smiting of the righteous a chief oil; faithful reproof and counsel are like a sword anointed with balsam that wounds and heals at the same time.

✦ THOMAS MANTON
Practical Exposition on the
Epistle of James, 215

In him that shall stay the mind of another [through reproof], there had need to be an excellent temper of many graces, as (1) knowledge of the grievance, together with wisdom to speak a word in season and to conceal that which may set the cure backward; (2) faithfulness with liberty not to conceal anything which may be for his good, though against present liking. The very life and soul of friendship stands in freedom, tempered with wisdom and faithfulness. (3) love with compassion and patience to bear all and hope all and not to be easily provoked by the waywardness of him we deal with. Short-spirited men are not the best comforters.

✦ RICHARD SIBBES
Soul's Conflict, 134

Reader, what love dost thou show to thy neighbor if thou see him wounding and piercing his inestimable soul and thou dost not endeavor, though against his will, to hold his hand? If thou should see him take a knife to stab himself at the heart, thou wouldst not stay to ask his leave or fear his anger, but do thy utmost to hinder him. And canst thou see him destroying his soul and not seek to prevent him? That pity, without question, is the best which relates to the better part.

✦ GEORGE SWINNOCK
The Christian Man's Calling,
in Works, 2:303

Reprove seriously. Reproof is an edged tool and must not be jested with. Cold reproofs are like the noise of cannons a great way off, nothing affrighting us. He that reproves sin merrily, as one that takes a pride to show his wit and make the company laugh, will destroy the sinner instead of the sin. There are those that spit out their friends with their tongues and laugh them into enemies. Sharpness and acuteness doth ill in sportful festivals, but it becomes purging potions. Lightness is commendable in nothing but worst in things that are weighty.

✦ GEORGE SWINNOCK
The Christian Man's Calling,
in Works, 2:304–5

Reprove prudently. A Christian's wisdom in the matter of his reproof will very much further its working: "As an earring of gold, and an ornament of fine gold, so is a wise reprover upon an obedient ear" (Prov. 25:12). A wise reprover is a credit to the reproved; it is an honor to be wounded thus by one that is wise. Some men would receive blows with more patience if they were given them with more prudence.

✦ GEORGE SWINNOCK
The Christian Man's Calling,
in Works, 2:307

Reprove compassionately; soft words and hard arguments do well together. Passion will heat the sinner's blood, but compassion heal his conscience. Our reprehension may be sharp, but our spirits must be meek. The probe that searches the wound will put the patient to less pain and do the more good if covered with soft lint; those who oppose themselves are to be instructed in meekness (2 Tim. 2:25). There is a rigid austerity which is apt to creep into and corrupt our reproofs. Mollifying ointments are often instrumental to abate great swellings. The iron of Napthali's shoes were dipped in oil. Reproofs should be as oils or ointments gently rubbed in by the warm fire of love.

✦ GEORGE SWINNOCK
The Christian Man's Calling,
in *Works,* 2:309

I confess this duty of reproving is a hard and unpleasing task because truth ordinarily begets hatred, but it is far better that men should hate thee for the discharge of thy duty than that God should hate thee for the neglect of it. It is much easier to endure their rage for a short time than the Lord's wrath forever. If the persons reproved have any true love to themselves, they will love thee; and truly that man's love is little worth who hath none for his own soul. Therefore, reader, obey God's precept and leave the event to His providence: "Have no fellowship with the unfruitful works of darkness, but rather reprove them" (Eph. 5:11).

✦ GEORGE SWINNOCK
The Christian Man's Calling,
in *Works,* 2:312

Our reproving others must be seasonable. Reproof is a duty; when we see others walk irregularly, like soldiers that march out of rank and file, we ought mildly yet gravely to tell them of

their sin (Lev. 19:17), but let this fruit be brought forth in its season.

✦ THOMAS WATSON
The Beatitudes, in *Discourses,* 2:476–77

RECONCILIATION

In this reconciliation, each person of the blessed Trinity hath His gracious part. The Father reconciles us, to wit, as the primary cause, purposing of it (2 Cor. 5:19); the Son reconciles us, to wit, as the meritorious purchaser (Eph. 2:16); the blessed Spirit reconciles us as the efficient worker and witnesser of the grace by which we are made partakers of the reconciliation and are assured thereof (John 3:5; Rom. 5:5), so that the kingdom, power, and glory is here illustriously and equally to be ascribed unto the Father, Son, and Spirit. In the meantime, we also have our part left us. We are bid...to reconcile ourselves—that is, to do our part toward it. So "turn ye, turn ye" (Ezek. 33:11)—that is, reconcile, reconcile yourselves. No longer turn your backs on God as enemies; turn about your faces toward Him as friends.

✦ DANIEL BURGESS
Man's Whole Duty, 83–84

Now that I mention that worthy person [i.e., Alderman Ashurst], I call to mind a passage concerning which deserves to be written in letters of gold. When I was once at London laboring to bring Dr. Owen and Mr. Baxter together in order to a better understanding and brotherly accord betwixt them, I moved Mr. Ashurst to lend his house to that purpose; he readily answered not only lend his house but he would give the one-half of his estate upon such a design.

✦ THOMAS JOLLY
Note Book, 28 (October 1675)

RECREATION

We must not let our covetousness have anything to do in our recreations. If we play at any game, let the end of our doing it be merely to recreate ourselves, not to win money. And to that purpose, be sure never to play for any considerable matter, for if thou do, thou wilt bring thyself into two dangers: the one of covetousness and a greedy desire of winning; the other of rage and anger at thy ill fortune, if thou happen to lose, both which will be apt to draw thee into other sins besides themselves.

✦ RICHARD ALLESTREE
Whole Duty of Man, 151

Recreation is a second creation, when weariness hath almost annihilated one's spirits. It is the breathing of the soul, which otherwise would be stifled with continual business. We may trespass in them, if using such as are forbidden by the lawyer as against the statutes; physician, as against health; divine, as against conscience. Be well satisfied in thy conscience of the lawfulness of the recreation thou uses.

✦ THOMAS FULLER
Holy and Profane States, 224

Refresh that part of thyself which is most wearied. If thy life be sedentary, exercise thy body; if stirring and active,

recreate thy mind. But take heed of cozening thy mind in setting it to do a double task under pretense of giving it a play day, as in the labyrinth of chess and other tedious and studious games.

✦ THOMAS FULLER
Holy and Profane States, 226

To walk abroad to take the air, to entertain our companions with pleasant discourses, to play on some instrument, or the like are recreations so good that to use them well needs nothing but discretion; that gives to everything its order, time, place, and measure. But if we employ too much time therein, it is no more a recreation but an occupation that recreates neither the body nor the spirits but rather dulls and distracts them. Take heed of placing your affections on any of them, for be the recreations in themselves ever so good, it is a vice to set your affections on any of them. But you may take recreation in playing for the time you play; otherwise it would be no recreation. But you must not eagerly desire or long after them, nor yet study on them, nor vex yourself about them. And when your recreation withdraws your mind from walking in an honest calling or eats up the time which might be far better spent in doing those things which might tend to the good of yourself or others, either in respect of this life or the life to come, it is a manifest intemperancy and want of moderation.

✦ WILLIAM GEARING
Sacred Diary, 89–90

I accompanied them in killing a buck in their own park. Far from being taken with any great delight or pleasure in the sport, they sent part of him to Broad-Oke after us.

✦ PHILIP HENRY
Diaries and Letters, 240
(July 12, 1672)

Whereas I have given my mind to unseasonable playing at chess, now it run in my thoughts in my illness as if I had been at chess; I shall be very sparing in the use of that recreation and that at more convenient seasons.

✦ RALPH JOSSELIN
Diary, 47 (February 23, 1648)

REDEMPTION

He that will know his own particular redemption before he will believe begins at the wrong end of his work and is very unlikely to come that way to the knowledge of it. The first act of faith is not that Christ died for all or for you in particular. The one is not true; the other not certain to you, nor can, until after you have believed. He that would live must submit to mercy with "Peradventure He will save me alive."

✦ ELISHA COLES
Practical Discourse of God's Sovereignty, 147

This, I say, is the great work wherein all those glorious attributes shine jointly: the wisdom, and power, and goodness, justice, and mercy of God. As in great maps or pictures, you will see the border decorated with meadows and fountains and flowers, etc., represented in it, but in the middle you have the main design; thus is this foreordained redemption among the works of God. All His other works in the world, all the beauty of the creatures, and the succession of ages, and things that come to pass in them are but as the border to this as the main piece. But as a foolish, unskillful beholder, not discerning the excellency of the principal piece in such maps or pictures, gazes only on the fair border and goes no further, thus do the greatest part of us. Our eyes are taken with the goodly show of the world and appearance of earthly things. But as for this great work of God, Christ foreordained and in time sent for our redemption, though it most deserves our attentive regard, yet we do not view and consider it as we ought.

✦ ROBERT LEIGHTON
A Commentary upon the First Epistle of Peter, in *Whole Works*, 1:139–40

Scriptural Redemption:

1. Christ died for the elect only.

2. All those for whom Christ died are certainly saved.

3. Christ, by His death, purchased all saving grace for them for whom He died.

4. Christ sends the means and reveals the ways of life to all them for whom He died.

5. The new covenant of grace was confirmed to all the elect in the blood of Jesus.

6. Christ by His death purchased, upon covenant and compact, an

assured peculiar people, the pleasure of the Lord prospering to the end in His hand.

7. Christ loved His church and gave Himself for it.

8. Christ died for the infidelity of the elect.

✦ JOHN OWEN
*Death of Death in the Death
of Christ,* 309

[God] is incomparable in the work of redemption. And truly this work is His masterpiece, pure workmanship; and indeed, all His works of creation and providence are subordinate to this. All His attributes sparkle most gloriously in this (Ps. 102:16); all His angels in heaven admire and adore Him for this (Rev. 4:10–11). This is the work of all His works, which He is so mightily pleased with and reaps so much glory and praise from (Isa. 42:1; 43:21). No angels, no men—no, not all together—could with all their united worthiness redeem one soul: "None of them can by any means redeem his brother, nor give to God a ransom for him: (for the redemption of their soul is precious, and it ceaseth for ever...)" (Ps. 49:7–8). None beside God had pity enough for man's misery, or wisdom enough to find out a remedy, or power enough for his recovery. None had pity enough for man's misery. Boundless misery called for boundless mercy.... But where is such mercy to be found among the creatures? Man was a child of wrath, had plunged himself into an ocean of evils and fury, and this required an ocean of love and pity....

But the Creator had infinite grace for infinite guilt and infinite mercy for infinite misery.

✦ GEORGE SWINNOCK
The Incomparableness of God,
in *Works,* 4:432

REGENERATION

Repentance is a change of the mind, and regeneration is a change of man. Till the first Adam be changed into the second, there is no hope of entering into heaven.

✦ THOMAS ADAMS
Exposition upon...Second...Peter, 587

A worldly man may speak of heavenly things, but is thy nature heavenly? A man may think of God, but is thy nature godly? Here is the thing: if a man be regenerate, there is grace got into a man's nature. When God regenerates His people, He saith He will write His laws in their inward parts (Jer. 31:33); He doth not only say they shall do these duties but their very hearts shall carry them, their very hearts shall go to a sermon, their very souls shall go about the duties of God.

✦ WILLIAM FENNER
"The New Birth," in *Four Profitable
Treatises,* 133

There is the greater gulf between no grace and grace than between weak grace and strong, between a chaos and nothing than between a chaos and this beautiful frame of heaven and earth. The first day's work of both creations is the greatest.... Consider it as an act of grace; it is a greater mercy to give the first grace of conversion than to crown that with glory. It is more grace and condescent in a prince to marry a poor damsel than, having married her, to clothe her like the princess. He was free to do the first or not, but his relation to her pleads strongly for the other. God might have chosen whether He would have given thee grace or no, but having done this, thy relation to Him and His covenant also do oblige Him to add more and more, till He hath fitted thee as a bride for Himself in glory.

✦ WILLIAM GURNALL
Christian in Complete Armour, 40

Regeneration is a change of the whole man, in every part and faculty thereof, from a state of sinful nature to a state of supernatural grace, whereby the image of God that we defaced and lost by our first transgression is again, in some good measure, restored.

✦ EZEKIEL HOPKINS
"The Nature and Necessity of Regeneration," in *Select Works*, 124

Urge your soul with the necessity of the means: "Faith cometh by hearing, and hearing by the word of God" (Rom. 10:17). Without grace I cannot be saved; without the word I cannot have grace. Reason thus within yourselves, that you may awaken the soul to a greater conscience of waiting upon God in the word. It is true: divine grace does all, He begets us; but remember, it is by "the word of truth." The influences of the heavens make fruitful seasons, but yet ploughing is necessary. It is one of the sophisms of this age to urge the

Spirit's efficacy as a plea for the neglect of the means.

✦ THOMAS MANTON
Practical Exposition on the Epistle of James, 49

Regeneration is a work of God's Spirit whereby He doth, out of His mere good pleasure, for His own glory and the salvation of His elect, at first renew the whole man after His own image by the ministry of the word.

✦ GEORGE SWINNOCK
"The Door of Salvation Opened by the Key of Regeneration," in *Works*, 5:20

Regeneration…is nothing else but the transforming the heart and casting it into a new mold. You have a pregnant place for this: "Be ye transformed by the renewing of your mind" (Rom. 12:2). In the incarnation, Christ did assume our human nature; and in regeneration, we partake of His divine nature.

✦ THOMAS WATSON
The Christian's Charter of Privileges, in *Discourses*, 1:24

A man unregenerate is spiritually illegitimate; the devil is his father: "Ye are of your father the devil." Thus it is till Christ be formed in the heart of a sinner; then his reproach is rolled away from him. Regeneration doth ennoble a person; therefore, such a one is said to be "born of God" (1 John 3:9). O how beautiful is that soul! I may say with Bernard, "O divine soul, invested with the image of God, espoused to him by faith, dignified with the Spirit!" A person regenerate is embroidered with all the graces: he hath the silver spangles of holiness, the angels' glory shining in him; he hath upon him the reflex of Christ's beauty. The new creature is a new paradise set full of the heavenly plants. A heart ennobled with grace (to speak with reverence) is God's lesser heaven.

◆ THOMAS WATSON
*The Christian's Charter of
Privileges*, in *Discourses*, 1:25

RELIGION

Oh, search, and search again; take thy heart solemnly to task. Woe unto thee if, after all thy profession, thou should be found under the power of ignorance, lost in formality, drowned in earthly-mindedness, envenomed with malice, exalted in an opinion of thine own righteousness, leavened with hypocrisy and carnal ends in God's service, embittered against strictness. This would be a sad discovery that all thy religion were in vain.

◆ JOSEPH ALLEINE
Alarm to the Unconverted, 110

Love is as much worth as all religion; it is the soul and the substance of all religion. All the graces, the duties and exercises of it, are only valued according to the love that is in them. What is knowledge, faith, hope, patience without love? What is prayer, fasting, alms without charity? They are worth nothing, shall I say? Nay, they are nothing. If I had all knowledge, and all faith, and were all prayer, and all labor, and all suffering and had not charity, I

were nothing. Love is worth as much as heaven is worth, as Christ, as God is worth to us. God is love, and God is not if love be not in us.

◆ RICHARD ALLEINE
Heaven Opened, 168

True religion is a union of the soul with God, a real participation of the divine nature, the very image of God drawn upon the soul; or, in the apostle's phrase, it is Christ formed within us. Briefly, I know not how the nature of religion can be more fully expressed than by calling it a divine life.

◆ HENRY SCOUGAL
Life of God in the Soul of Man, 6–7

Here let me desire one thing of the reader, and that is to bear in his mind all along where he finds the word *religion*...that I mean thereby "a divine principle implanted in the soul, springing up into everlasting life."

◆ SAMUEL SHAW
Immanuel, xix

Converse with God—with God in Christ, with God in His promises, with God in His attributes; and labor to do it not speculatively or notionally, but really and practically.... Religion is not an empty, airy, notional thing; it is not a matter of thinking nor of talking, but it hath a real existence in the soul and doth as really distinguish, though not specifically, one man from another as reason distinguishes all men from beasts.

◆ SAMUEL SHAW
*Voice of One Crying in the
Wilderness*, 91

We see it is no easy thing to bring God and the heart together. David, here [in Psalm 42:11], as he often checks his heart, so he doth often charge his heart. Doubts and troubles are still gathering upon him, and his faith still gathering upon them. As one striving to get the haven is driven back by the waves, but recovering himself again gets forward still, and after often beating back at length obtains the wished haven and then is at rest, so much ado there is to bring the soul unto God, the harbor of true comfort. It were an easy thing to be a Christian if religion stood only in a few outward works and duties, but to take the soul to task, and to deal roundly with our own hearts, and to let conscience have its full work, and to bring the soul into spiritual subjection unto God—this is not so easy a matter because the soul out of self-love is loath to enter into itself, lest it should have other thoughts of itself than it would have. David must bid his soul trust, and trust, and trust again before it will yield.

✦ RICHARD SIBBES
Soul's Conflict, 148; see also
Complete Works, 1:200

Religion may well be called fear, for there is no religion where fear is wanting. For "the fear of the LORD is the beginning of knowledge" (Prov. 1:7). And this privilege hath God given to those that fear Him, that they need to fear nothing else.

✦ HENRY SMITH
"The Song of Father Simeon,"
in *Sermons*, 177

True religion is of the greatest necessity. All other concerns compared with this are but as the toys of children to the labors of life. This is "the one thing needful," without which the end of man's creation is lost, the glory of God in His works is frustrated, and the whole existence of reasonable beings is vain. It were infinitely better never to have had a being than leave this world with the guilt of sin unpardoned and the power of it unsubdued. And it is also necessary for securing a blessing upon all our temporal concerns.

✦ RICHARD STEELE
Religious Tradesman, 219

REPENTANCE

Conversion at the eleventh hour is a wonder, at the twelfth a miracle. All thieves do not go from the gallows to glory because one did no more than all asses speak because God opened the mouth of one. Flatter not thyself with hope of time. Man's life is compared to a day.

✦ THOMAS ADAMS
"The Cosmopolite," in *Sermons*, 175

Consideration is the first step toward repentance. The prodigal first came to himself before he came to his father. He considered with himself what a starving condition he was in, feeding on husks, when there was plenty of bread in his father's house. "Why then should I perish with hunger?" said he. "I will arise and go to my father." He did so and was kindly received.

✦ ISAAC AMBROSE
Christian Warrior, 27

If the enemy [i.e., Satan] is at first foiled and the soul resolved to go on, the Holy Spirit usually leads him on by these steps: (1) gives him a sight of sin, (2) a sense of misery, (3) sorrow for sin, (4) seeking for comfort, (5) a sight of Christ, (6) desire after Christ, (7) relying on Christ, (8) obedience to Christ. Satan counteracts him in every step and strives to keep the soul in his power.

✦ ISAAC AMBROSE
Christian Warrior, 40

There is nothing more hinders men from repentance and being saved than hoping to be saved without true repentance, for who will ever turn to God that still hopes to be saved in the worldly, ungodly way that he is in? Who will turn back again that hopes he is right and safe already?

✦ RICHARD BAXTER
Baxteriana, 199

Lay all these together now and see what should be the issue. The Holy Scriptures call upon thee to turn; the ministers of Christ do call upon thee to turn; the Spirit cries, "Turn"; thy conscience cries, "Turn"; the godly, by persuasions and examples, cry, "Turn"; the whole world and all the creatures therein that are presented to thy consideration cry, "Turn"; the patient forbearance of God cries, "Turn"; all the mercies which thou receivest cry, "Turn"; the rod of God's chastisement cries, "Turn"; thy reason and the frame of thy nature bespeaks thy turning, and so do all thy promises to God. And yet art thou not resolved to turn?

✦ RICHARD BAXTER
Call to the Unconverted, 76

I am truly angry with my heart that has so often and foolishly offended Thee. Methinks I hate that heart that is so cold and backward in Thy love and almost grudge it a dwelling in my breast. Alas, when love should be the life of prayer, the life of meditation, the life of sermons, and of holy conference, and my soul in them should long to meet Thee and delight to mention Thee, I wander, Lord, I know not whither!

✦ RICHARD BAXTER
Converse with God in Solitude, 124

[True repentance] is a sorrow or grief that is spiritual, that is supernatural; no man is born with godly sorrow in his heart as he is born with a tongue in his mouth. Godly sorrow is a plant of God's own planting, it is a seed of His own sowing, it is a flower of His own setting, it is of a heavenly offspring, it is from God and God alone. The spirit of mourning is from above; it is from a supernatural power and principle. There is nothing that can turn a heart of stone into flesh but the Spirit of God (Ezek. 36:25–26). Godly sorrow is a gift from God.

✦ THOMAS BROOKS
Cabinet of Choice Jewels, 218

True repentance is a turning from all sin without any reservation or exception; he never truly repented of any sin whose heart is not turned against every sin.

✦ THOMAS BROOKS
Cabinet of Choice Jewels, 253

Repentance is a flower that grows not in nature's garden. "Can the Ethiopian change his skin, or the leopard his spots? Then may ye also do good, that are accustomed to do evil" (Jer. 13:23). Repentance is a gift that comes down from above. Men are not born with repentance in their hearts as they are born with tongues in their mouths.

✦ THOMAS BROOKS
Precious Remedies, 52

Consider that repentance is a continued act; the word *repent* implies the continuation of it. True repentance inclines a man's heart to perform God's statutes always, even unto the end. A true penitent must go on from faith to faith, from strength to strength; he must never stand still nor turn back. Repentance is a grace and must have its daily operation, as well as other graces; true repentance is a continued spring where the waters of godly sorrow are always flowing. "My sins are ever before me." A true penitent is often casting his eyes back to the days of his former vanity. "I was a blasphemer, and a persecutor, and injurious," says the apostle. Repentance is a continued act of turning, a repentance never to be repented of, a turning, never to turn again to folly. A true penitent can as easily content himself with one act of faith or one act of love as he can with one act of repentance.

✦ THOMAS BROOKS
Precious Remedies, 58–59

The work of repentance is not the work of an hour, a day, or a year, but the work of a life. A sincere penitent makes as much conscience of repenting daily as he does of believing daily; and he can as easily content himself with one act of faith, or love, or joy as he can content himself with one act of repentance.

✦ THOMAS BROOKS
Smooth Stones, 99

Repentance unto life is an evangelical grace wrought in the soul by the Spirit of God. And the nature of it will best appear to us by considering the parts of it, which are these six: (1) conviction, (2) contrition, (3) hating and loathing of sin, (4) confession of sin and supplication for pardon, (5) forsaking of sin, and (6) conversion and turning unto God.

✦ SAMUEL CRADOCK
Knowledge and Practice, part 2, 10–11

A godly physician having patients grievously tormented willed them first to be reconciled to God before they fought His help, which they, neglecting, and he, knowing them open sinners, dismissed them saying, "The Lord having laid His rod upon you, I dare not take it off you without the show of some fruits of repentance," which they doing were healed.

✦ EZEKIEL CULVERWELL
Time Well Spent, 278–79

That is a true godly sorrow for sin when no outward pleasure can steal it away nor continuance of time waste it, but only Christ.

✦ EZEKIEL CULVERWELL
Time Well Spent, 316

To forsake sin is to leave it without any thought reserved of returning to it again. Every time a man takes a journey from home about business, we do not say he hath forsaken his house, because he meant when he went out to come to it again. No, but when we see a man leave his house, carry all his stuff away with him, lock up his doors, and take up his abode in another never to dwell there more—here is a man who hath, indeed, forsaken his house.

✦ WILLIAM GURNALL
Christian in Complete Armour, 368

[Repentance] is a gift of God and proceeds from God, and not from nature. It is a flower that never grows in nature's garden. Neither art nor learning nor any other sublunary power or qualification is able to beget repentance. Repentance comes from above; every good and perfect gift, saith St. James, cometh from above (James 1:17). Grace does not grow here below but comes down from the Father of lights.

✦ JOHN HART
Christ's First Sermon, 8

It is a woeful thing to put off repentance to a pained body or a sickbed. Pain in its own nature will rather cause us to blaspheme and turn from God than to return to God, and it's very common that sick persons repent not at all or, if

they do, at the best their repentance is but a sickly repentance. Sickness doth only abate and restrain the power of men's lusts; it never destroys the life of sin. Death itself cannot kill sin.

✦ JOHN HART
Christ's First Sermon, 16–17

Many mourn for their sins that do not truly repent of them; weep bitterly for them and yet continue in love and league with them.

✦ MATTHEW HENRY
Gems, 56

Question: And why then do not men repent?

Answer: Because

1. They have gotten a custom of sinning.
2. They escape unpunished here.
3. They ever think on mercy.
4. They fear not judgment.
5. They believe not God's word.
6. They see that most do so.
7. They observe the life of bad ministers.
8. They look upon great men that are bad.
9. They see not the vileness of sin.
10. They meditate not how God hath plagued the impenitent.

✦ ROBERT HILL
Pathway to Piety, 1:182

I do counsel you to repent (Rev. 2:5). And I must tell you, beloved, that our assembling once in four weeks and spending four hours, from eleven to three, in praying and preaching, as we have often done, is not such a fast as will make our voice be heard on high (Isa. 58:3–4). Several things are essentially necessary to evangelical repentance that it may be acceptable unto God by Jesus Christ—namely, godly sorrow, which worketh repentance, never to be repented of (2 Cor. 7:9–10); a broken contrite spirit (Ps. 51:17; Isa. 57:15; 66:2–3; James 4:9–10). Read these scriptures (Zech. 12:10–11). Alas, where are our tears of godly sorrow, our broken hearts, and our afflicted souls? Reformation after humiliation? Repent and do thy first works (Rev. 2:5).

✦ HANSERD KNOLLYS
Life and Death, 48

Question: What follows after this sorrow [i.e., godly sorrow in a believer for falling into sin]?

Answer: Repentance renewed afresh.

Question: By what signs will this repentance appear?

Answer: By seven: (1) a care to leave the sin into which he is fallen; (2) an utter condemning of himself for it, with a craving of pardon; (3) a great anger against himself for his carelessness; (4) a fear lest he should fall into the same sin again; (5) a desire ever after to please God; (6) a zeal of the same; (7) revenge upon himself for his former offense.

✦ WILLIAM PERKINS
Foundation of Christian Religion, 27

Repentance is as vowels in the alphabet, which we have not only need of to spell with while we are babes but to read withal when we are men in Christ.

✦ FRANCIS RAWORTH
On Jacob's Ladder, iv

But what was it that Peter remembered? It is not said, Peter now considered how he stood naked and open to the flames of hell, or how he had exposed himself to the scourges of an inward tormentor; to the scorchings of a bosom hell, his conscience; or to the fearful judgment and revenge of Him whom he had injured by denying. And therefore he went out and wept. It was fear that made him fall; it made him not repent. But it was only the merciful prediction of Christ which he remembered; what slight esteem he had made of that gracious caution which should have armed him against temptations, and this made him go out and weep. The abuse of God's mercy, the grieving of God's Spirit, the undervaluing of God's truth more wounds the soul of a repenting sinner than all the grips of conscience or flames of hell.

✦ EDWARD REYNOLDS
Meditations on the Fall and Rising of St. Peter, 60–61

We shall now consider how the Spirit works repentance unto life, which is principally insisted on in this answer. This is said to be done by the word of God; not by the law without the gospel, but by them both, in which one is made subservient to the other. The law shows the soul its sin, and the gospel directs him where he may find a remedy; one wounds and the other heals. The law enters, as the apostle expresses it, that the offense might abound (Rom. 5:20), but the gospel shows him how grace does much more abound and where he may obtain forgiveness, by which means he is kept from sinking under that weight of guilt that lies on his conscience. And it leads him to hate and abstain from sin from those motives that are truly excellent, for which reason it is called evangelical repentance.

✦ THOMAS RIDGLEY
Body of Divinity, 171

Repentance must be a continued work; so long as we have sin to repent of, so long we must be repenting of sin, and by after acts the work of repentance comes to be more distinctly, methodically, and evangelically carried on than it was at the first.... A child of God, from a continued experimental sense of the indwelling and working of sin, comes to be more thoroughly convinced of the root, nature, evil, and aggravation of sin and to feel the weight, load, and pressure of it more burdensome than he did.

✦ T. S.
Aids to the Divine Life, 60

In sin the pleasure passes, the sorrow remains; but in repentance the sorrow passes, the pleasure abideth forever. God soon pours the oil of gladness into broken hearts.

✦ JOHN TRAPP
Commentary...upon...the New Testament, 721

Repentance is a grace of God's Spirit whereby the sinner is inwardly humbled and visibly reformed.

✦ THOMAS WATSON
Doctrine of Repentance, 18

If every slight trouble for sin were true repentance, then Judas and Cain may be lifted into the number of penitents. Evangelical repentance works a change of heart (1 Cor. 6:11). It produces sanctity. But the false penitent, though he has trouble of spirit, yet has no transformation or change. He has a weeping eye but an adulterous heart. Ahab fasts and puts on sackcloth, but after this he puts the prophet Micah in prison (1 Kings 22:27).

✦ THOMAS WATSON
Great Gain of Godliness, 51

REPENTANCE, DELAYING

All delay of repentance increases hardness of heart (Heb. 4:7). It does produce a custom of sinning and makes the work of repentance to be harder and harder (Jer. 13:23). The reason is because thereby evil habits are more strengthened and confirmed, the understanding becomes darker (Eph. 4:18). The will grows more obdurate and addicted to sin (Heb. 4:7). All the faculties are more bound and tied, as it were, with chains and knots (Acts 8:23). A young plant is more easily plucked up than that which hath taken deep root. A nail, the oftener it is beaten with a hammer, the more firmly it is fastened and the more hardly drawn out.

✦ WILLIAM AMES
Conscience, 2:6

Delay is the devil's verb.

✦ THOMAS BROOKS
Apples of Gold, 31

Though true repentance be never so late, yet late repentance is seldom true. Millions are now in hell who have pleased themselves with the thoughts of after-repentance. The Lord has made a promise to late repentance, but where has He made a promise of late repentance?

✦ THOMAS BROOKS
Apples of Gold, 58

Concerning the thief on the cross, I offer these things briefly to your thoughts: that as one was saved to teach sinners not to despair, so another was damned to teach them not to presume. A pardon is sometimes given to one on the gallows, but whoso trusts to that, the rope may be his hire. It is an example without a promise. Here is an example of late repentance, but where is there a promise of late repentance?

✦ THOMAS BROOKS
Apples of Gold, 284–85

Dost [thou] think to do that in thy old age which thou wilt not do in thy youth? Canst thou do that in one hour on thy deathbed which thou art not able sufficiently to do all thy lifetime? And then likewise old men have need of repentance; they have lived a long time in sin and have too long neglected repentance. Young men may die soon, but old men cannot live long; therefore, both old and young have need to repent, that they may receive the remission of their sins (Mark 2:5).

✦ JOHN HART
Christ's First Sermon, 6–7

How sad's the case of frail and mortal
  man,
Whose time is short, its length is but
  a span!
In youth he's proud, ambition then so
  reigns,
That he true grace and godliness
  disdains.
Virtue is then contemned, 'tis vice
  which he
Doth make his choice, but yet does
  hope to be,
When old age comes, another man;
  for know,
He would have heaven, but not let the
  earth go:
But when he's old, sin in him's grown
  so strong,
He's more averse to grace than are the
  young.
Take heed you do not on old age
  depend,
Lest he deals by you like a trait'rous
  friend.

✦ BENJAMIN KEACH
Travels of True Godliness, 80

This [delaying repentance] is as evil and dangerous a posture, or frame of mind, as you can well fall under. If you have learned to put off God and Christ and the word for the present season and yet relieve yourselves in this—that you do not intend, like others, always to reject them but will have a time to hearken to their calls; you are secured and fortified against all convictions and persuasions, all fears; one answer will serve for all; within a little while you will do all that can be required of you. This is that which ruins the souls of multitudes every day. It is better dealing with men openly profligate than with such a trifling promiser.

✦ JOHN OWEN
On the Glory of Christ, in *Oweniana,* 77

Usually, where the devil pleads antiquity, he keeps propriety. As there are none so old as that they should despair of mercy, so there are none so young as that they should presume on mercy. If God's today be too soon for thy repentance, thy tomorrow may be too late for His acceptance.

✦ WILLIAM SECKER
Nonsuch Professor, 122

We have but a day wherein we are called to repent, and therefore should repent while it is called today. He is the deafest adder who stops his ears to the voice of the sweetest charmer. The Lord hath made a promise to late repentance, but He hath not made a promise of late repentance. If the heart of man be not now thawed, it may be forever frozen. A pardon is sometimes given to a thief at the gallows, but he who trusts to that sometimes hath a rope for his wages.

✦ WILLIAM SECKER
Nonsuch Professor, 194

It is an old saying, "Repentance is never too late"; but it is a true saying, "Repentance is never too soon."

✦ HENRY SMITH
"The Young Man's Task,"
in *Sermons,* 63–64

There is a heart that cannot repent; that has lost all passive power of coming out of the snare of the devil; that is become such through long trading in sin, as neither ministry, nor misery, nor miracle, nor mercy can possibly mollify. Upon such you may write, "Lord have mercy upon them." "O!" said a reverend man, "if I must be put to my option, I had rather be in hell with a sensible heart than live on earth with a reprobate mind."

✦ JOHN TRAPP
Commentary…upon…the New Testament, 192

Old age is no good age to repent in. When the fingers are stiff, it is ill learning to play on the lute; when the heart is grown hard and stiff in wickedness, it is but ill tuning the penitential string; a tender plant is easily removed, but it is hard to pluck up an old tree that is rooted. An old sinner that hath been a long time rooting in sin is hardly plucked out of his natural estate. In matters of salvation it is dangerous to adjourn. The longer men go on in sin, the more full possession Satan hath of them; the longer poison stays in the stomach, the more mortal. It is a madness to put off the work of salvation till evening and sunset.

✦ THOMAS WATSON
"The One Thing Necessary,"
in *Discourses,* 1:366

REPUTATION

A good name is always better than a great name, and a name in heaven is infinitely better than a thousand names on earth, and the way to both these is to be much with God in secret.

✦ THOMAS BROOKS
Privy Key of Heaven, 62

The Spanish proverb is too true: "Dead men and absent find no friends." All mouths are boldly opened, with a conceit of impunity. My ear shall be no grave to bury my friend's good name. But as I will be my present friend's self, so will I be my absent friend's deputy to say for him what he would, and cannot, speak for himself.

✦ JOSEPH HALL
Meditations and Vows, 86

It is a great mercy when our names outlive us; it is a great punishment when we outlive our names.

✦ WILLIAM JENKYN
in Horn, *Puritan Remembrancer*, 134

A good man's name is like a milk-white ball which exceedingly gathers soil by tossing, and therefore is to be sparingly talked of. Words reported again have another sound, and many times another sense; besides, one dog sets many others a-barking.

✦ GEORGE SWINNOCK
The Christian Man's Calling,
in *Works*, 2:352

Many live to see their names buried before them.

✦ THOMAS WATSON
Gleanings, 134

RESOLUTIONS

Some things which concerned me: (1) To go about always with preservatives. (2) To be doing or getting good. (3) To look at what [God] is doing within us more than what He is doing without us. (4) Be most in spiritual exercises of religion. (5) Set the highest examples before you. (6) Record special providences and favors. (7) Be good at all times, but especially best in bad times. (8) Choose suffering rather than sin. See thy cause be good, thy call clear, thy spirit meek, and thy end right. (9) It is as much a duty in them that have grace to improve it as it is in them that want grace to get it. (10) Study to walk with Christ in white the only way to keep up reputation in the world.

✦ HENRY NEWCOME
Diary, 150–51

REST

Spiritual rest makes no man idle; spiritual walking makes no man weary.

✦ NATHANIEL HARDY
in Horn, *Puritan Remembrancer*, 210

RESURRECTION OF THE BODY

The doctrine of the resurrection, however questioned by heretics and erroneous persons, yet is such a truth that almost all the holy scriptures of God point at and center in it.

✦ JOHN BUNYAN
Riches, 434

My body is part of my self; it must not, it cannot, be lost. Its separation from my soul makes me cease to be; this separation continued would continue me a nonentity forever. My self is redeemed and related to the Lord, and my soul or my body is related to Him, but as parts of my self; these divided must be reunited, that my self may exist to enjoy my redemption by Him and my relation to Him. Though the Lord's special care is for my soul, as my better and more noble part, He has not excluded, He does not despise, He will not neglect my body. My soul and body are now joint subjects of grace; they must therefore hereafter be joint subjects of glory.

✦ ZACHARY CROFTON
Defence against the Dread of Death, 109

The grave is your long home, but not your last home. Though death strip you of your beauty, yet at the resurrection you shall have it restored again.

✦ THOMAS WATSON
Body of Practical Divinity, 205

At the resurrection every soul shall have its own body; the same body that dies shall arise. Some hold that the soul shall be clothed with a new body, but then it were improper to call it a resurrection of the body—it should be rather a creation. It was a custom in the African churches to say, "I believe the resurrection of this body." I confess, the doctrine of the resurrection is

such that it is too deep for reason to wade. You must let faith swim.

✦ THOMAS WATSON
The Christian's Charter of Privileges,
in *Discourses*, 1:75

RETIREMENT

Tradesmen may allowably leave their callings when a considerable degree of age and estate inclines and capacitates them so to do. It is not only lawful but becoming in those who are advanced in wealth and declining in years to make room for the increase of younger tradesmen and, not like aged trees, stand to obstruct the growth of those below them. An increasing love of wealth in the decline of life is a sight shocking to human nature. But then the retired tradesman should remember that though he is discharged from the fatigues of life, he is not so from the duties of it. His leisure should be employed in preparing his mind for another state in acts of benevolence and kindness to others; in pointing out to younger persons the paths of virtue and prosperity, and not used only as an indulgence to sloth and sensuality, lest he come under the character of the fool who said to his soul, "Thou hast much goods laid up for many years" and knew no other use of them than to "eat, drink, and be merry" instead of being rich toward God.

✦ RICHARD STEELE
Religious Tradesman, 228–29

REVELATION

There are two ways whereby the blessed God condescends to manifest Himself to men—His word and His works. Of the written word, we must say no words like these were ever written since the beginning of time which can, as one speaks, take life and root in the soul; yea, doth it as really as the seed doth in the ground and are fitted to be engrafted and naturalized there, so as no coalition in nature can be more real than this (James 1:21). This is the most transcendent and glorious medium of manifestation: God hath magnified His word above all His name (Ps. 138:2). However, the manifestations of God by His works, whether of creation or providence, have their value and glory; but the prime glory and excellency of His providential works consist in this, that they are the very fulfillings and real accomplishments of His written word.

✦ JOHN FLAVEL
Divine Conduct, 3

REVIVAL AND REFORMATION

But would you that your prayers should be heard? Then arise out of your places and fall every man upon a personal reformation. Down with your sin and out with the world. Lift up Christ in your own hearts if you would have antichrist fall in the earth. Let Christ have a name within you above every name, and let everyone that names the name of Christ depart from iniquity, from his own iniquity. Seek not for corn and for wine or for freedom to sit down every man under his own wine and under his own fig tree, where none shall make them afraid, but seek the Lord, that the Lord God may dwell among you, may delight in you and be exalted by you, that you may indeed become the people of His holiness.

✦ RICHARD ALLEINE
Companion for Prayer, 11

[Some say,] "But there is great opposition, many mighty, stubborn enemies there are against us." This is a good evidence that you are about a choice piece of church work. Show me a reformation—I think there is scarcely one in the book of God or in our Protestant histories that went on without difficulties and obstructions. So that these very crags and bogs which you pass through in the way are not discouragements but waymarks—that is, certain signs that you are right in the old reformation way that hath ever been trodden.

✦ JOHN BOND
Salvation in a Mystery, 43

[One] witness which holds forth the Lord's extraordinary power in the reformation of the church from anti-Christianism is that large measure of the Spirit which convincingly followed the gospel and ministry of the word in these last times. This is God's own seal, which is not put to a falsehood; thus He bears witness to His work in the hearts of His people, and by this also the Lord attests the doctrine of the church and commission of His servants. Yea, at some special seasons, when the truth has least encouragement from without, when men will not receive its testimony, then has this in a more full and large measure been discernible. Thus did the Lord eminently confirm the Christian religion in the days of the apostles and for some following ages by so great a downpouring of the Spirit, by such visible and extraordinary effects as then astonished the world and forced men to confess something above nature. And we have also cause to say that the Lord has borne a very solemn testimony to the work of the Reformation and the doctrine of the Reformed churches.

✦ ROBERT FLEMING
Fulfilling of the Scripture, 298

I remember a worthy Christian told me that sometimes in hearing the word, such an evidence of the Lord's presence was with it that he has been forced to rise and look through the church and see what the people were doing; thinking, from what he felt on his own spirit, that it was a wonder how any could go away without some change upon them. It was then sweet and easy for Christians to come thirty or forty miles to these solemn communions and there continue from the time they came until they returned, without wearying or making use of sleep—yea, but little either of meat or drink; and as some of them professed, they did not feel the need of them but went away most fresh and vigorous, their souls being so filled with a sense of God.

✦ ROBERT FLEMING
Fulfilling of the Scripture, 301

O, my brethren, those golden days of the gospel are over when converts came flying as a cloud, as the doves to their windows in flocks. Now gospel news grows stale; few are taken with it. Though a kingdom hath much treasure and riches in it, yet if trade cease, no new bullion comes in nor merchandise be imported; it spends upon its old stock and must needs in time decay. Our old store of saints, the treasure of their times, wears away apace. What will become of us if no new ones come in their room? Alas! When our burials are more than our births, we must needs be on the losing hand. There is a sad list of holy names taken away from us. But where are they which are born to God? If the good go and those which are left continue bad—yea, become worse and worse—we have reason to fear that God is clearing the ground and making way for a judgment.

✦ WILLIAM GURNALL
Christian in Complete Armour, 349

March 2 [, 1641]. I was cast down with the sight of our unworthiness in this church, deserving to be utterly wasted; but the Lord filled my heart with a spirit of prayer not only to desire small things but with an holy boldness to desire great things for God's people here and for myself—namely, that I might live to see all breaches made up and the glory of the Lord upon us; and that I might not die but live to show forth God's glory to this and the children of the next generation. And so I arose from prayer with some confidence of an answer first, because I saw Christ put it into my heart to ask; second, because He was true to hear all prayer.

✦ THOMAS SHEPARD
Meditations and Spiritual Experiences, 46

RICHES

(See *PROSPERITY; WEALTH*)

RIGHTEOUSNESS

There is a twofold righteousness: (1) Moral, such as Paul had before his conversion. This a man may continue in to the last, and yet not be saved. (2) There is a gospel righteousness: first, imputed; this is the righteousness of Christ by which we are justified. Second, infused; this is the divine nature communicated by the Spirit of Christ whereby we are sanctified. These two go inseparably and can never be lost. But the righteousness spoken of in the place objected [Ezek. 18:24] seems to be of the former sort—namely, moral or outward righteousness; for outward conformity to the law was the condition of their possessing the land of Canaan, with long life and prosperity in it.

✦ ELISHA COLES
Practical Discourse, 281

There is a threefold righteousness: (1) A legal righteousness which the law requires and which consists in personal, perfect, and perpetual obedience. This Adam had in his original, primitive estate but lost it by the fall; since then, no son of his can lay claim

to it. (2) There is a moral, or civil, righteousness, which is made up of truth and honesty in men's dealings one with another. But as the other is too high, so this is too low; for a person may have civil righteousness that is without religion and be a very stranger to grace, Christ, and sanctification. Therefore, (3) there is an evangelical righteousness, which…is twofold. Evangelical righteousness is that righteousness which is imputed to the sinner and is the matter of his justification before God, and this is the righteousness of Christ. Evangelical righteousness includes also that righteousness which is infused or imparted, and this is the matter of the righteous man's sanctification.

✦ HENRY PENDLEBURY
"Light in Darkness," in Slate, *Select Nonconformists' Remains*, 378–79

SACRAMENTS

In all sacraments are two parts and a sacramental union betwixt them. (1) The two parts are [first] the outward signs, or signs signifying, as water and washing with it in baptism; bread and wine, with the actions belonging thereto, in the Lord's Supper. [Second,] the inward mysteries signified by those signs, as the washing away of our sins by the blood and Spirit of Christ in baptism and the nourishing of our souls by the benefits of Christ's death in the Lord's Supper. (2) There is a sacramental union betwixt the signs and the things signified founded in Christ's institution.

Whence the sign is sometimes said to be the thing signified, as…"This is My body; this is My blood; this is the new testament in My blood." And the thing signified is called the sign, as… "Christ our passover is sacrificed." This sacramental union consists in a sacramental relation which the signs have to the things in signifying, sealing, and exhibiting them. Hence flows another union betwixt the worthy communicant and the sacrament, so that he who truly partakes the sign according to Christ's institution partakes also the thing signified. This is to be well observed as a special ground of comfort in communicating.

✦ FRANCIS ROBERTS
Communicant Instructed, 95–96

SAINTS AND SINNERS: CONTRASTED

As different as grief is from joy, as torment from rest, as terror from peace, so different is the state of sinners from that of saints in the world to come.

✦ JOHN BUNYAN
"Mr. John Bunyan's Dying Sayings,"
in *Complete Works*, 81

As the wicked are hurt by the best things, so the godly are bettered by the worst.

✦ WILLIAM JENKYN
in Horn, *Puritan Remembrancer*, 342

A godly man is an agent in opposing his corruption and a patient in enduring of it! Whereas a natural man is a secret agent in and for his corruptions and a patient in regard of any help against them. A good man suffers evil and doth good; a natural man suffers good and doth evil.

✦ RICHARD SIBBES
Soul's Conflict, 50

No man is judged healthy by a flushing color in his face but by a good complexion. God esteems none holy for a particular carriage, but for a general course. A sinner in some few acts may be very good. Judas repents, Cain sacrifices, the scribes pray and fast— and yet all were very false. In the most deadly diseases there may be some intermissions and some good prognostics. A saint in some few acts may be very bad. Noah is drunk, David defiles his neighbor's wife, and Peter denies his best friend—yet these persons were heaven's favorites. The best gold must have some grains of allowance. Sheep may fall into the mire, but swine love night and day to wallow in it. A Christian may stumble—nay, he may fall—but he gets up and walks on in the way of God's commandments. The bent of his heart is right, and the scope of his life is straight, and thence he is deemed sincere.

✦ GEORGE SWINNOCK
The Christian Man's Calling,
in *Works*, 2:186

All the saints are excellent, and some are more excellent than other; yet the highest saint is not so far above the lowest as the lowest saint is above the highest of men.

✦ RALPH VENNING
Canaan's Flowings, 197

SALVATION

In election we behold God the Father in choosing; in vocation, God the Son teaching; in justification, God the Holy Ghost sealing; in salvation, the whole deity crowning. God chooses of His love, Christ calls by His word, the Spirit seals by His grace. Now the fruit of all this, of God's love choosing, of Christ's word calling, of the Spirit's grace sanctifying is our eternal glory and blessedness in heaven.

✦ THOMAS ADAMS
Exposition upon…Second…Peter, 119

They [i.e., carnal professors] lay all the burden upon the shoulders of Christ and meddle no more with the matter, as if God would bring them to heaven even whilst they pursue the way to hell or keep that soul from the body when the body had quite given away the soul. He never promised to save a man against his will. As He doth save us by His Son, so He commands us to work up our "salvation with fear and trembling" (Phil. 2:12). He that lies still in the miry pit of his sin and trusts to heaven for help out, without his own concurring endeavor, may hap to lie there still.

✦ THOMAS ADAMS
"The Soul's Refuge," in *Works*, 3:31

Salvation will never come home to any but such as diligently seek it and labor after it. Heaven will not drop into our mouths, though we open them never so wide, as long as our hands lie folded together. Our duties must prove our hopes legitimate, and our obedience must justify our expectation. He that would sleep in Jesus at death must watch with Him in his life; and, whosoever thinks of dying to the Lord must resolve against living to himself.

✦ TIMOTHY CRUSO
Duty and Support of Believers, 18

Illumination must in order of nature go before conviction, and conviction before compunction, etc., but in order of time they may go together. The Spirit of God at the same time lets in a clear light, convinces and strikes the heart with fears, sorrows, etc. It is not thus, that the soul is one week or one day under the work of illumination, another comes under conviction, the third week or day comes under compunction. I know there may be light and conviction many weeks and years when there is no compunction, but it is not so when the Spirit of the covenant is at work. How often have men come home from one sermon with these works wrought?

✦ GILES FIRMIN
Real Christian, 25

There is an opinion which some have lately taken up that the heathens may spell Christ out of the sun, moon, and stars. These may seem kinder than others have been to them, but I wish it doth not make them more cruel to them in the end; I mean by not praying so heartily for gospel light to arise among them, as those must needs do who believe them under a sad necessity of perishing without it. When a garrison is judged pretty well stored with provision for its defense, it is an occasion that relief and succor come the slower to it; and I wish Satan had not such a design against those forlorn souls in this principle. If such a lesson were to be got by the stars, we should before this have heard of some that had learned it. Indeed, I find a star led the wise men to Christ, but they had a heavenly preacher to open the text to them or else they would never have understood it.

✦ WILLIAM GURNALL
Christian in Complete Armour, 347

The greatest monarch the earth hath will be glad, in a dying hour, to change his crown for thy helmet [i.e., God's salvation]. His crown will not procure him this helmet, but thy helmet will bring thee to a crown—a crown not of gold but of glory, which, once on, shall never be taken off, as his is sure to be.

✦ WILLIAM GURNALL
Christian in Complete Armour, 539

The general offer of Christ to all is a ground of reception to any that will believe in Him. Then the way is open, and Christ is free for me as for any to come to and receive. Christ as a common Savior to Jew and Gentile, to all sorts—yea, even the worst sorts, as Scythians and barbarians are accepted with Christ when they believe in Him. There is no respect of persons with Christ, but everyone that will may receive Him and shall be received of Him.

✦ EDWARD REYNER
Precepts for Christian Practice, 41

Mistaken grace, and somewhat like conversion, which is not conversion, is the saddest and most doleful thing in the world. Make sure of salvation and lay the foundation sure, for many are beguiled. Put a low price upon the world's clay; put a high price upon Christ.

✦ SAMUEL RUTHERFORD
Garden of Spices, 98

I often told you that few are saved and many damned. I pray you to make your poor soul sure of salvation and the seeking of heaven your daily task. If you never had a sick night and a pained soul for sin, you have not yet lighted upon Christ. Look to the right marks of having closed with Christ. If you love Him better than the world and would quit all the world for Him, then that saith the work is sound. O, if you saw the beauty of Jesus and smelled the fragrance of His love, you would run through fire and water to be at Him.

✦ SAMUEL RUTHERFORD
Garden of Spices, 102

[The Christian] cries out, "What must I do to be saved?" And yet he never expects to be saved by doing.

✦ RALPH VENNING
Orthodox Paradoxes, 13

"Now is the accepted time" (2 Cor. 6:2). If we put Christ off with delays and excuses, perhaps He will come no more, He will leave off wooing, His Spirit shall no longer strive. And then, poor sinner, what wilt thou do? When God's wooing ends, thy woes begin.

✦ THOMAS WATSON
Godly Man's Picture, 217

SANCTIFICATION

What are the signs of true sanctification?... (1) A reformation of all the powers and faculties of the whole man (1 Thess. 5:23). (2). A respect to all the commandments of God (Ps. 119:6; James 2:10). (3) A constant care to avoid all sin (Prov. 28:14). (4) A walking before God (Gen. 17:1; Acts 24:16; 1 Cor. 10:31; Col. 3:23). (5) A combat between the flesh and the spirit.

✦ WILLIAM AMES
Conscience, 2:27

Now we shall make a progress in sanctification (1) if we exercise ourselves daily to a more perfect denying of sin, and of the world, and of ourselves and to a more earnest and serious seeking of God and His kingdom; (2) if we have our end always in our eyes; (3) if we keep our hearts with all diligence (Prov. 4:23); (4) if we watch to the holy use of all those means which make to sanctification and join earnest prayer with them.

✦ WILLIAM AMES
Conscience, 2:30

Sanctification is a real change of a man from the filthiness of sin to the purity of God's image (Eph. 4:22–24).

✦ WILLIAM AMES
Marrow of Sacred Divinity, 140

Bad men have their good moods, as good men have their bad moods; a bad man may, under pangs of conscience, a smarting rod, the approaches of death, or the fears of hell, or when he is sermon sick, cry out to the Lord for grace, righteousness, and holiness; but he is the only blessed man that hungers and thirsts after righteousness at all times. Heaven is for that man and that man is for heaven that hungers and thirsts in a right manner after the righteousness of justification and after the righteousness of sanctification.

✦ THOMAS BROOKS
Cabinet of Choice Jewels, 49

I readily grant that you must not trust in your graces nor make a savior of your graces, but yet you ought to look upon your graces as so many signs and testimonies of the love and favor of God to your souls. What certainty can there be of election, remission of sins, justification, or glorification if there be not a certainty of your sanctification or renovation? If that persuasion that is in you about your grace or sanctification be false, then that persuasion that is in you concerning remission of sin, predestination, justification, and eternal salvation is false; this highly concerns all them to consider that would not be miserable in both worlds. I know many cry up revelations, impressions, visions (yea, the visions of their own hearts) and speak lightly and slightly of the graces of the Spirit, of sanctification, of holiness, as evidences of the goodness and happiness of a Christian's condition.

✦ THOMAS BROOKS
Cabinet of Choice Jewels, 326–27

Having so firm and impregnable a rock to found your faith upon, why should the greatest of difficulties, even the power of inbred corruption, discourage any soul from casting itself upon elect-ing love as that which is perfectly able, and the very design of it is, to subdue iniquity as well as to pardon it? It chose us not because we were or would be holy but that we might be so (Eph. 1:4), and to that end undertakes the whole of our work for us.

✦ ELISHA COLES
Practical Discourse, 236

Q.: How expectest thou sanctification?

A.: By the work of His Spirit (1 Cor. 6:11).

Q.: How doth the Spirit effect it?

A.: By applying unto my whole man the power of His death and resurrec-tion (Rom. 6:5–6); by the one, killing by degrees all sin in me; by the other, quickening me unto new obedience.

✦ CLEMENT COTTON
"The Sick Man's A, B, C," in
None but Christ, 94–95

But, O adversary [i.e., advocates of human merit], you are wrong in blam-ing our faith. We condemn nothing in you but your presumption. It is the leaven of pride which displeases us.... As for the rest, we recommend and preach, as much or more than you do, the mortification of the old man, the vivification of the new; diligence, vigi-lance, constancy in prayer, in fasting, in alms; and the continual exercise of works of piety and charity. We only desire that the believer should present these divine fruits to God, crowned with modesty and humility; that he should look to it carefully, lest they become spoiled and tainted by the presumptuous notions which you teach, of having fulfilled the law or deserved paradise. But, my dear breth-ren, it is better to refute calumny with works than with words.

✦ JEAN DAILLÉ
Exposition of...Philippians, 132

In meditation make the resemblance and discourse thus within yourselves: This is my seedtime; heaven is my harvest. Here I must labor and toil, and there rest. I see the husbandman's life is a great toil; no excellent thing can be obtained without labor and an obstinate patience. I see the seed must be hidden in the furrows, rotten and corrupted, ere it can spring forth with any increase. Our hopes are hidden; light is sown for the righteous. All our comforts are buried under the clods, and after all this there must be long waiting. We cannot sow and reap in a day; effects cannot follow till all neces-sary causes have first wrought. It is not in the power of husbandmen to ripen fruits at pleasure; our times are in the hands of God. Therefore it is good to wait; a long-suffering patience will reap the desired fruit.

✦ JOHN FLAVEL
Husbandry Spiritualized, 12

The breastplate is...the righteousness of our sanctification, which I called a righteousness imparted, or a righteous-ness wrought by Christ in the believer. Now this take thus described: it is a supernatural principle of a new life planted in the heart of every child of God by the powerful operation of the Holy Spirit, whereby they endeavor to approve themselves to God and man in performing what the word of God requires to be performed to both.

✦ WILLIAM GURNALL
Christian in Complete Armour, 292

Sanctifying graces are connected in their growth and decay—increase one grace, and you strengthen all; impair one, and you will be a loser in all—and the reason is because they are reciprocally helpful to each other. So that when one grace is wounded, the assistance which it would, if in temper, contribute to the Christian's common stock is either entirely lost or much lessened. When love cools, obedience slackens and goes on heavily because it wants the oil on its wheel which love used to drop; when obedience falters, faith weakens. How can there be great faith where there is little faithfulness? When faith is weak, hope presently wavers, for it is the credit of faith's report that hope goes on to expect good from God. And hope-wavering patience becomes a bankrupt and can keep his shop open no longer, because it trades with the stock which hope lends it. In the body, you observe, there are many members, yet all make but one body; and every member so useful that the others are beholden to it. So, in the Christian there are many graces, but one new creature.

✦ WILLIAM GURNALL
Christian in Complete Armour, 513

One great mystery is that the holy frame and disposition whereby our souls are furnished and enabled for immediate practice of the law must be obtained "by receiving it out of Christ's fulness," as a thing already prepared and brought to an existence for us in Christ and treasured up in Him; and that as we are justified by a righteousness wrought out in Christ and imputed to us, so we are sanctified by such a holy frame and qualifications as are first wrought out and completed in Christ for us and then imparted to us. And as our natural corruption was produced originally in the first Adam and propagated from him to us, so our new nature and holiness is first produced in Christ and derived from Him to us, or, as it were, propagated. So that we are not at all to work together with Christ in making or producing that holy frame in us, but only to take it to ourselves and use it in our holy practice, as made ready to our hands. Thus, we have fellowship with Christ in receiving that holy frame of spirit that was originally in Him, for fellowship is when several persons have the same things in common (1 John 1:1–3).

✦ WALTER MARSHALL
Gospel Mystery of Sanctification, 64–65

The golden chain hath so linked the means to the end, and sanctification in order to salvation, that God doth infallibly stir up the elect to the use of the means, as well as bring them to the end by the means. "Brethren, beloved of the Lord; God hath from the beginning chosen you to salvation, through sanctification of the Spirit, and belief of the truth" (2 Thess. 2:13).... Those in whom the Lord hath put His Spirit, let them live as they list, and I am very sure they will live godly lives.

> ✦ CHRISTOPHER NESS
> *Antidote against Arminianism*, 58–59

I counsel you to study sanctification and to be dead to this world.

> ✦ SAMUEL RUTHERFORD
> *Garden of Spices*, 110

Sanctification and the mortification of our lusts are the hardest part of Christianity. It is, in a manner, as natural for us to leap when we see the new Jerusalem as to laugh when we are tickled. Joy is not under command nor at our nod when it kisseth. But O, how many of us would have Christ divided into two halves, that we might take the half of Him only and take His office—Jesus and salvation! But *Lord* is a cumbersome word, and to obey and work out our salvation and perfect holiness is the cumbersome and stormy north side of Christ and that which we eschew and shift.

> ✦ SAMUEL RUTHERFORD
> *Garden of Spices*, 120

When Christ hideth Himself, wait on and make din till He return; it is not time then to be carelessly patient. I love to be grieved when he hideth His smiles, yet believe His love in a patient on-waiting and believing in the dark. Ye must learn to swim and hold up your head above the water, even when the sense of His presence is not with you to hold up your chin. I trust in God that He will bring your ship safe to land. I counsel you to study sanctification and to be dead to this world.

> ✦ SAMUEL RUTHERFORD
> *Garden of Spices*, 235

Sanctification doth differ from justification and adoption in that justification and adoption are acts of God without us: sanctification is a work of God within us. Justification and adoption do make only a relative change; sanctification doth make in us a real change. Justification and adoption are perfect at first; sanctification is carried on by degrees unto perfection.

> ✦ THOMAS VINCENT
> *Explicatory Catechism*, 91

Sanctification is the work of God's free grace, whereby we are renewed in the whole man after the image of God and are enabled more and more to die unto sin and live unto righteousness.

> ✦ THOMAS VINCENT
> *Explicatory Catechism*, 91

There are two parts of sanctification: (1) mortification, whereby we are enabled to die more and more unto sin: "Reckon ye also yourselves to be dead indeed unto sin" (Rom. 6:11). (2) vivification, whereby we are enabled to live unto righteousness: "Yield yourselves unto God, as those that are alive from the dead, and your members as instruments of righteousness unto God" (Rom. 6:13).

> ✦ THOMAS VINCENT
> *Explicatory Catechism*, 92–93

A sanctified heart is better than a silver tongue. There is as much difference between gifts and grace as between a tulip painted on the wall and one growing in the garden.

✦ THOMAS WATSON
Art of Divine Contentment, 90–91

SATAN

The tempter will make his first and sharpest onset on you [i.e., a pastor]. He bears you the greatest malice who are engaged to do him the greatest mischief. He has found, by experience, that to "smite the shepherd" is the most effectual means to "scatter the flock." You therefore shall have his most subtle insinuations, incessant solicitations, and violent assaults.

✦ RICHARD BAXTER
Reformed Pastor, 15

Satan's masterpiece is first to work Christians to blot and blur their evidences for glory by committing this or that heinous sin, and then his next work is to rob them of their evidences for glory that so, though at the long run they may get safe to heaven, that yet Jacob-like they may go halting and mourning to their graves. Satan knows that whilst a Christian's evidences are bright and shining, a Christian is temptation proof. Satan may tempt him, but he cannot conquer him; he may assault him, but he cannot vanquish him.

✦ THOMAS BROOKS
Cabinet of Choice Jewels, 343

God had but one Son without corruption, but He had none without temptation (Heb. 2:17–18). Pirates make the fiercest assaults upon those vessels that are most richly laden; so doth Satan upon those souls that are most richly laden with treasures of grace, with the riches of glory. Pirates let empty vessels pass and repass without assaulting them; so doth Satan let souls that are empty of God, of Christ, of the Spirit, of grace pass and repass without tempting or assaulting of them.

✦ THOMAS BROOKS
Mute Christian, 179

Watchful and suspicious ought we to be in spiritual concernments. We should study and be acquainted with Satan's wiles and policy. The apostle takes it for granted that Christians are not ignorant of his devices (2 Cor. 2:11). "The serpent's eye," as one saith, "would do well in the dove's head." The devil is a cunning pirate; he puts out false colors and ordinarily comes up to the Christian in the disguise of a friend.

✦ JOHN FLAVEL
Navigation Spiritualized, 36

He that shall consider [Satan's] malice and power must unavoidably conclude him to be cruel. Malice is always so where it has the advantage of a proportionable strength and opportunity for the effecting of its hateful contrivances. It banishes all pity and commiseration and follows only the dictate of its own rage with such fierceness that it is only limited by wanting power to execute.

We may then say of Satan that according to his malice and power, such is his cruelty.

✦ RICHARD GILPIN
Daemonologia Sacra, 35–36

It is written, "They were naked" (Gen. 3:7); that is, poor, weak creatures at the will of Satan, a subdued people disarmed by their proud conqueror and unable to make head against him. Indeed, it cost Satan some dispute to make the first breach, but after that he had once the gates opened to let him in as conqueror into the heart of man, he plays the king. Behold, a troop of other sins crowd in after him without any stroke or strife; instead of confessing their sins, they run their head in a bush and by their goodwill would not come where God is. And when they cannot flee from Him, how do they prevaricate before Him! They accuse one another, shifting the sin rather than suing for mercy. So quickly were their hearts hardened through the deceitfulness of sin. And this is the woeful condition of every son and daughter of Adam; naked he finds us and slaves he makes us, till God, by his effectual call, delivers us from the power of Satan into the kingdom of His dear Son.

✦ WILLIAM GURNALL
Christian in Complete Armour, 27

In handling this point of Satan's subtlety, we shall consider him in his two main designs and therein show you his wiles and policies. His first main design is to draw into sin. The second is to accuse, vex, and trouble the saint for sin.

✦ WILLIAM GURNALL
Christian in Complete Armour, 46

Many have yielded to go a mile with Satan that never intended to go two, but when once on the way have been allured further and further, till at last they know not how to leave his company.

✦ WILLIAM GURNALL
Christian in Complete Armour, 50

The Christian wrestles not with his naked corruptions, but with Satan in them. Were there no devil, yet we should have our hands full in resisting the corruptions of our own hearts, but the access of this enemy makes the battle more terrible because he heads them, who is a captain so skillful and experienced. Our sin is the engine, Satan is the engineer; lust the bait, Satan the angler. When a soul is enticed by his own lusts, he is said to be tempted (James 1:14) because both Satan and our own lusts concur to the completing the sin.

✦ WILLIAM GURNALL
Christian in Complete Armour, 85

[Satan's] design is as much against the saint's holiness as God is for it: he hath ever a nay to God's yea; if God be for holiness, he must needs be against it. And what should be our chief care to defend but that which Satan's thoughts and plots are most laid to assault and storm? There is no creature the devil delights so to lodge and dwell in as man. When he enters into other creatures, it is but on design against man, as when he entered the serpent, it was to deceive Eve.... He possessed [the swine] on a design to dispossess the Gergesenes of the gospel (Matt. 8:32).

But might he choose his own lodging, none pleases him but man, and why? Because man only is capable, by his rational soul, of sin and unrighteousness. And as he prefers man to quarter in above all inferior creatures, so he had rather possess the souls of men than their bodies; none but the best room in the house will nerve this unclean spirit to vomit his blasphemies and eject his malice in against God. And why? But because the soul is the proper seat of holiness and sin.

✦ WILLIAM GURNALL
Christian in Complete Armour, 299

The devil is a great student in divinity and makes no other use of his Scripture knowledge than may serve his turn by sophistry to do the Christian a mischief, either by drawing him into sin or into despair for sinning, like some wrangling barrister who gets what skill he can in the law merely to make him the more able to put honest men to trouble by his vexatious suit.

✦ WILLIAM GURNALL
Christian in Complete Armour, 547

Let us therefore be wise for to look to the baits that the devil casts before us, for he is cunning and subtle, and it's good for us to think so. We usually labor and strive against evil company to abstain from them. Why should we then meddle with the devil or be in his company? Eve was drawn to sin through conference with him, although it may be at the first she

intended it not. Gaze not at all upon these baits of Satan.

✦ JOHN PRESTON
"Judas's Repentance," in *Remaines*, 12

It is a piece of the devil's cunning first to fill a man full of abominable thoughts, and then to be the first that shall put in this accusation and doubt—namely, is it possible for any child of God that is sanctified with God's Holy Spirit to have such thoughts? But consider well that an innocent Benjamin may have Joseph's cup put into his sack's mouth without his knowledge or consent by him who, for his own ends, intended thereby to accuse Benjamin of theft and ingratitude. Was Benjamin anything the more dishonest or ungrateful for this? No! Satan doth not want malice or cunning in this kind to play his feats. Where he cannot corrupt men, yet there he will vex and perplex them.

✦ HENRY SCUDDER
Christian's Daily Walk, 368–69

Some again are haunted with hideous representations to their imaginations and with vile and unworthy thoughts of God, of Christ, of the word, etc., which, as busy flies, disquiet and molest their peace. These are cast in like wildfire by Satan, as may be discerned by the (1) strangeness, (2) strength and violence, (3) horribleness of them even unto corrupt nature. A pious soul is no more guilty of them than Benjamin of Joseph's cup put into his sack. Among other helps prescribed by godly writers to cause abomination of them and diversion from them to other things,

let this be one: to complain unto Christ against them, and to fly under the wings of His protection, and to desire Him to take our part against His and our enemy.
✦ RICHARD SIBBES
Bruised Reed and Smoking Flax, 81

As Satan slanders Christ to us, so he slanders us to ourselves. If thou be not so much as smoking flax, then why dost thou not renounce thy interest in Christ and disclaim the covenant of grace? This thou darest not do. Why dost thou not give up thyself wholly to other enjoyments? This thy spirit will not suffer thee.
✦ RICHARD SIBBES
Bruised Reed and Smoking Flax, 110

When Christ was about a work and many were gathered together to hear Him [Luke 8:19–21], the devil thought with himself…"If I let Him alone thus, all the world will follow Him, and I shall be like Rachel, without children"; therefore, devising the likeliest policy to frustrate and disgrace but one of His sermons…he sendeth Christ's mother and put in the minds of His kinsmen to come unto Him at that instant, when He was in this holy exercise, and call upon Him while He was preaching to come away and go with them. Christ, seeing the serpent's dealing, how he made His mother the tempter that all the auditory might go away empty and say where they came, "We heard the man which is called Jesus, and He began to preach unto us with such words, as though He would carry us to heaven; but in the midst of His sermon came His mother and brethren to Him, that it might be known what a kinsman they had. And so soon as He heard that they were come, suddenly He brake off His sermon and slipped away from us to go and make merry with them." Christ, I say, seeing this train laid by Satan to disgrace Him (as he doth all His ministers), did not leave off speaking as they thought He would; but as if God had appointed all this to credit and renown Him, that which was noised here to interrupt His doctrine He taketh for an occasion to teach another doctrine.
✦ HENRY SMITH
"The Affinity of the Faithful,"
in *Sermons*, 203–4

True it is that Satan, by his voluntary defection from God, hath lost that glorious robe of holiness that made him a peer of heaven and dignified him with the title of a son of God; and hath also (as I conceive) impaired his natural abilities, so as that he is become in power, wisdom, and knowledge inferior to those glorious inhabitants of the sacred palace who have kept their first estate and not departed from that purity that is as ancient as their being. For why should not the sin of angels operate as strongly upon them as the lapse and disobedience of man did upon him, whose spirituals were thereby wholly destroyed and his naturals sorely maimed. But though his fall hath debased his being, yet it hath not totally changed it; he hath still the nature, though not the perfection, of an angel, and though he be inferior to them whose equal original he was in all kind of endowments, yet still he retains so great a superiority over the elementary, sensitive, and intellectual part of the world as that he is not only dreaded for his power, which sometimes he puts forth in wonderful effects, but is also adored for his wisdom and knowledge as a god by many nations in it.

◆ WILLIAM SPURSTOWE
Wiles of Satan, 15

[Satan's] experience animates him with confidence to assault the best and holiest of saints, if not to extinguish their light, yet to eclipse their luster; if not to cause a shipwreck, yet to raise a storm; if not to hinder their happy end, yet to molest them in their way. Such practices he hath found not only to have some success against the strong but to intimidate and discourage the weak, who are apt from the particular foils of renowned Christians in the faith to make sad conclusions against themselves.

◆ WILLIAM SPURSTOWE
Wiles of Satan, 23–24

Whenever Satan is really worsted, sin is wounded. He is never put to flight, but lust receives a mortifying blow, for the fight is both made and maintained by faith and other graces of the Spirit which carry in them more immediate opposition unto sin than unto Satan, it being the great work of everyone that is begotten of God to keep himself that the wicked one touch him not (1 John 5:18). Not that he tempt him not, but that he defile him not by any assimilating touch. And this is the only way by which a believer can be said both to

resist him and also to overcome him; we cannot kill the devil nor weaken in the least his power but as we mortify lusts which are the matter that he works upon, and the less of it he finds in us, the less able he is to hurt us.

◆ WILLIAM SPURSTOWE
Wiles of Satan, 56–57

O how powerful are the arts and effascinations [i.e., bewitchings] of this infernal magician, who can thus make men best pleased with that estate in which they are rebels to God and slaves to lusts; and from which they can expect nothing but amazements, horrors, and distractions of mind, which will at one time or other afflict those who prostitute their consciences to such impieties as have in them the highest mixture both of folly and madness? Have we not need to mind… Christ's counsel? "Judge not according to the appearance, but judge righteous judgment" (John 7:24).

◆ WILLIAM SPURSTOWE
Wiles of Satan, 66

[One of Satan's wiles is] to keep raw and smarting any wounds that the Spirit hath inflicted upon the conscience of any poor soul. True it is, Satan is not able to afflict immediately and really the conscience of a man, no more than he is able to comfort a man's conscience; as it is God's prerogative to know the heart, so it is to afflict and comfort the heart…. But yet Satan may help to keep the wounds raw by disturbing the fancy and filling them with horror and terror; he may shake and rattle the chains, though he cannot put them on upon any poor soul and thereby keep them from comfort which is their portion. And therefore when terrors so affright, as to the prejudice of all medicines, we may suspect the hand of Satan in them.

✦ WILLIAM SPURSTOWE
Wiles of Satan, 87

There is a woe to him that is alone. Such a man shall be sure to have Satan for his companion. He is ever ready to assault when none is near to assist. Eve was tempted with too much success when she was alone, without her husband; Dinah, gadding from her father's house, was defiled; Joseph was then assaulted when the whole family was gone, save the instrument of the assault. How soon are stragglers snapped up when those that march with the body of the army are safe! Pirates lie skulking to find a vessel sailing alone, when those that sail in company are a convoy to each other. They who separate are soon seduced.

✦ GEORGE SWINNOCK
The Christian Man's Calling,
in *Works*, 2:346

The cruel pirate Satan watches for those vessels that sail without a convoy.

✦ GEORGE SWINNOCK
The Christian Man's Calling,
in *Works*, 2:383

Satan may allege and corrupt Scripture, but he cannot answer Scripture. It is Christ's word of mighty authority. Christ foiled Satan with it.

✦ THOMAS WILCOX
Choice Drop of Honey, 14

SATAN, METHODS OF

If Satan pleads that the promises are not made to you and that you have no right to them, tell him to his face that he was a liar from the beginning. Recollect that when you were without God in the world, he told you often enough that all the promises belonged to you, and none of the threatenings. And now when you are in Christ, he would persuade you that all the threatenings and none of the promises belong to you. Let the enemy say what he will, if you depart from all iniquity to serve the living God, every promise in Christ is to you a mine of gold.

✦ ISAAC AMBROSE
Christian Warrior, 75

The skillful fisher[man] has his several baits for several fish, but there is a hook under all; Satan, that great angler, has his sundry baits for sundry tempers of men, which they all catch greedily at, but few perceives the hook till it be too late.

✦ ANNE BRADSTREET
Meditation 23, Works, 53

[Satan's]…device to draw the soul to sin is to present the bait and hide the hook; to present the golden cup and hide the poison; to present the sweet and the pleasure that may flow into the soul by yielding to sin, and hide from the soul the wrath and misery that will certainly follow the committing of sin.

✦ THOMAS BROOKS
Precious Remedies, 16

Subtilty and violence are the chiefest distinctions between the temptations of the devil and of the flesh.

✦ EZEKIEL CULVERWELL
Time Well Spent, 294

Divines observe four steps, or degrees, of Satan's tempting power: First, he can find out the constitution evils of men; he knows to what sin their natures are more especially prone and inclinable. Secondly, he can propound suitable objects to those lusts; he can exactly and fully hit every man's humor, as Agrippina mixed her poison in that meat her husband loved best. Thirdly, he can inject and cast motions into the mind, to close with those tempting objects; as it is said of Judas, the devil put it into his heart (John 13:2). Fourthly, he can solicit, irritate, and provoke the heart, and by those continual, restless solicitations weary it; and hereby he often draws men to commit such things as startled them in the first motion.

✦ JOHN FLAVEL
Navigation Spiritualized, 97–98

The haft of Satan's hatchet with which he lies chopping at the root of the Christian's comfort is commonly made of the Christian's wood.

✦ WILLIAM GURNALL
Christian in Complete Armour, 63

Though the devil throws the stone, yet it is the mud in us that disturbs our comforts.

✦ WILLIAM GURNALL
Christian in Complete Armour, 63

That it should be the care of every Christian to stand orderly in the particular place wherein God hath set him, the devil's method is first to rout, and then to ruin. Order supposes company; one that walks alone cannot go out of his rank.

✦ WILLIAM GURNALL
Christian in Complete Armour, 198

The devil may flatter us, but he cannot force us; he may tempt us to sin, but he cannot compel us to sin. He could never come off a conqueror were he not joined by our forces. The fire is his, but the tinder is ours. He could never enter into our houses if we did not set open our doors. Many complain for want of liberty who thrust their feet in Satan's fetters.

✦ WILLIAM SECKER
Nonsuch Professor, 128

[Observe] the art that Satan mingles with his violence; his urgency is not to a course and way of sin, but to the single act and commission of it. That which is often repeated and said over by him in his pressing of it is, "Do it but once; try this time only. Why not once? Why not now?" Is it not better to ease ourselves of the vexation by yielding once to the motion than to be always under it? He knows that if a sin be once committed it will leave a proneness to do it again, and if the terrors of doing of it, which are commonly greatest at first, be once broken through, it will not be a matter of difficulty to obtain the consent to the doing of it the second and third time because the heart must needs be less bent against it in prayer, and the power of grace and faith less vigorous to resist it when weakened by yielding to sin; conscience also less tender and affected with the sense of it.

✦ WILLIAM SPURSTOWE
Wiles of Satan, 50–51

SATAN: TEMPTS BUT DOES NOT FORCE

The devil can do great mischief in the will of men. Though he cannot command and determine it, yet he can persuade and allure it to a thousand evils. Satan works on the affections and passions of men. He deals much with our imaginations, paints sinful objects as lovely and desirable, and so kindles our affections toward them till the consent of the will is obtained and the soul is led captive.

✦ ISAAC AMBROSE
Christian Warrior, 6

Who is it that is so cruel as to be the cause of such a thing as this [i.e., sins such as murder or arson]? And we can meet with few that will own the guilt. It is indeed confessed by all that Satan is the cause, but that doth not resolve the doubt because he is not the principal cause. He doth not force men to sin but tempts them to it and leaves it to their own wills whether they will do it or not. He doth not carry men to an alehouse and force open their mouths and pour in the drink, nor doth he hold them that they cannot go to God's service, nor doth he force their hearts from holy thoughts.

✦ RICHARD BAXTER
Call to the Unconverted, 12

It is not Satan that thinks or wills in us. He may represent objects, but the acts are ours. He can dart in a temptation, but it is through our sin and corruption that it takes fire in the least.

✦ ALEXANDER CARMICHAEL
Believer's Mortification of Sin, 133

If you hold the stirrup, no wonder if Satan get into the saddle.

✦ WILLIAM SECKER
in Horn, *Puritan Remembrancer*, 25

SCHOLARS/SCHOLARSHIP

Our business is to find truth, the which, even in matters of high importance, is not easily to be discovered, being as a vein of silver encompassed with earth and mixed with dross, deeply laid in the obscurity of things, wrapped up in false appearances, entangled with objections, and perplexed with debates; being therefore not readily discoverable, especially by minds clouded with prejudices, lusts, passions, partial affections, appetites of honor and interest; whence to descry it requires the most curious observation and solicitous circumspection that can be, together with great pains in the preparation and purgation of our minds toward the inquiry of it. Our business is to attain knowledge, not concerning obvious and vulgar matters but about sublime, abstruse, intricate, and knotty subjects remote from common observation and sense; to get sure and exact notions about which will try the best forces of our mind with their utmost endeavors; in firmly settling principles, in strictly deducing consequences, in orderly digesting conclusions, in faithfully retaining what we learn by our contemplation and study.

✦ ISAAC BARROW
"Of Industry in Our Particular Calling,
as Scholars," in *Sermons*, 323

It is a palpable error in those ministers who make such a disproportion between their preaching and their living that they will study hard to preach accurately and study little or not at all to live accurately. They are loath to misplace a word in their sermons, but they make nothing of misplacing their affections, words, or actions in the course of their lives.

✦ RICHARD BAXTER
Reformed Pastor, 19

Art thou a student in any profession or faculty? Then, as Cato said of Scipio, thou must be least idle when thou art most idle. For enjoying a quiet, sedentary life by the gracious indulgences of thy prince and large maintenance of thy parents, free from the troubles of the court, labor of the country, business of the city thou must read diligently, confer often, observe daily. For reading makes a full man, conference a ready man, writing an exact man. All thy fine wit is but vanity, all thy great spirit but impudence, all thy brave flaunt of speech is but a sounding brass, except thou join to these labor and industry, without which Almighty God sells no learning, as heathen writers have told us.... For those sermons are most excellent and those writings and exercises of scholars are most sweet which a little smell of the candle.

✦ JOHN BOYS
*The Official Calendar of the
Church*, in *Works*, 654

In a word, brethren, study, and study thoroughly, the sinfulness of sin, emptiness of the creature, and the fullness of Christ.

✦ THOMAS CASE
Correction, Instruction, 118

The manners of scholars is the chief of all other things to be looked into, the way therefore to exercise them in piety, in justice, in temperance; in faithfulness, truth, and diligence is to be settled, and the inspection over them in these things so regulated that no faults, how wittily soever and cunningly carried or covered should be connived at, without a just search thereinto for discovery, censure, and punishment. For if there be no course taken to root up the impiety, the folly, the injuriousness, violence, excess, falsehood, untruth, and laziness which is in the disposition of every child, he will not only grow strong therein but bold to infect and provoke others thereunto, by which means he may bring not only his own soul unto damnation but even spread the infection throughout a whole nation.

✦ JOHN DURY
Seasonable Discourse, 10

What makes the daring soldier rush into the furious battle, into the very mouth of death itself, but the hope of snatching honor and spoil out of its jaws? Hope in his helmet, shield, and all, which makes him laugh in the face of all danger. In a word, what makes the scholar heat his brains so hard, sometimes with the hazard of breaking them, by overstraining his part with too eager and hot a pursuit of learning, but the hope of commencing some degrees higher in the knowledge of those secrets in nature which are locked up from vulgar understanding? Who, when he hath attained his desire, is paid but little better for all his pains and study, which have worn nature in him to the stumps, than he is that tears the flesh off his hands and knees with creeping up some craggy mountain, which proves but a barren, bleak place to stand in, and wraps himself up in the clouds from the sight of others, leaving him little more to please himself with but this, that he can look over other men's heads and see a little farther than they.

✦ WILLIAM GURNALL
Christian in Complete Armour, 518

Nor did [Richard Fairclough] ever produce in public anything which did not smell of the lamp. And I know that the most eminent for quality and judgment among his hearers valued those morning exercises for elaborateness, accuracy, instructiveness, equally with his Lord's Day's sermons.

✦ JOHN HOWE
Funeral Sermon, 52

If thou wouldst exercise thyself to godliness in solitude, accustom thyself to soliloquies—I mean to conference with thyself. He needs never be idle that hath so much business to do with his own soul. It was a famous answer which Antisthenes gave when he was asked what fruit he reaped by all his studies. "By them," saith he, "I have learned both to live and talk with myself." Soliloquies are the best disputes; every good man is best company for himself of all the creatures. Holy David enjoineth this to others, "Commune with your own heart upon your bed, and be still. Selah" (Ps. 4:4). "Commune with your own heart": When ye have none to speak with, talk to yourselves. Ask yourselves for what end ye were made, what lives ye have led, what times ye have lost, what love ye have abused, what wrath ye have deserved. Call yourselves to a reckoning, how ye have improved your talents, how true or false ye have been to your trust, what provision ye have laid in for an hour of death, what preparation ye have made for a great day of account. "Upon your bed": Secrecy is the best opportunity for this duty.

✦ GEORGE SWINNOCK
The Christian Man's Calling,
in *Works*, 2:450–51

A conceited scholar is no good learner. He that thinks he knows enough already will never be beholden to a master to teach him more: "Seest thou a man wise in his own conceit? there is more hope of a fool than of him" (Prov. 26:12). This is that which locked up the Pharisees in the dark dungeon of ignorance: they are blind; truth itself called them blind (Matt. 23:16–17). But they conceited their eyes were good, and so neglected the means of curing them. "Ye say ye see; I do not say ye see, but ye conceit so, therefore your sin remains" (John 9:40–41); therefore your ignorance continues. When ignorance and confidence, which are often twins, go together, the condition of a man is helpless, partly because such a person will not take that pains in reading, and praying, and conference, and meditation, without which the knowledge of God cannot be had.

✦ GEORGE SWINNOCK
The Incomparableness of God,
in *Works,* 4:488

Attention of body, intention of mind, and retention of memory are indispensably desired of all Wisdom's scholars.

✦ JOHN TRAPP
in Horn, *Puritan Remembrancer,* 85;
Thomas, *Puritan Golden Treasury,* 317

No man is an autodidact in heavenly literature. He that here is scholar to himself has a fool to his master.

✦ JOHN TRAPP
*Commentary…upon…the
New Testament,* 548

SCOFFERS

When a man that makes a forward profession of religion and in the general course of his life makes conscience of his ways doth, through temptation or inadvertency, fall into some sin that becomes notorious, what is

more common in the mouths of profane scoffers than this? "This is one of your godly ones! This is one of the sanctified gang!" Thus, they laugh and sneer at him…. When he sins, say not, "Behold one of the godly"; this is blasphemy against religion. No, it is not the godly man that sins. No, it is the corrupt and unholy part in him. It is that part in him that is most like to thee. In Romans 7:17 says the apostle, "It is no more I that do it, but sin that dwelleth in me."… Why do you accuse them whom the apostle vindicates, telling you plainly that it is not they, but sin in them? Learn, therefore, to put a difference betwixt a saint and a sinner in every child of God. And, if it be the sinner in them that exposeth them to your scorns and flouts, what else do you in upbraiding of them but more upbraid yourselves, that are nothing but sinners throughout?

✦ EZEKIEL HOPKINS
"The Nature of Presumptuous Sins,"
in *Select Works,* 416

THE SCRIPTURES

The Bible, which was before to [the unconverted person] but almost as a common book is now as the law of God, as a letter written to him from heaven and subscribed with the name of the Eternal Majesty; it is the rule of his thoughts and words and deeds. The commands are binding, the threats are dreadful, and the promises of it speak life to his soul.

✦ RICHARD BAXTER
Call to the Unconverted, 33

While God's Word is read in either of the chapters, whether of the Old or New Testament, receive it not as the word of men, but (as it is in truth) the word of God, which effectually worketh in you that believe (1 Thess. 2:13). And therefore hearken to it with the same attention, reverence, and faith as you would have done if you had stood by Mount Sinai when God proclaimed the law and by our Savior's side when He published the gospel.

♦ WILLIAM BEVERIDGE
Great Advantage, 81

When a man's mind is empty, as in temptation and want of comfort, it is empty of Christ and full of fear. Then it grinds itself, as in a quern or mill when empty of corn, one stone grinds another. The more full a man's mind is, the more free from temptations and fears. Now Scripture matter is the most filling matter.

♦ WILLIAM BRIDGE
Lifting Up, 43

Where reading ends, see that practicing begins. As soon as the Bible is laid out of your hand, if alone, then think; if in company, speak; if called to any business, act according to what you have been reading. Let God above, conscience within, and men all round you see that it is your governing rule. The more you practice what you read, the more you will read effectually unto practice and unto comfort.

♦ DANIEL BURGESS
Rules and Directions, 30–31

Nothing more strange to reason than the gospel of salvation by Christ.

♦ EZEKIEL CULVERWELL
Time Well Spent, 158–59

Men that dig in mines for any treasure, even for the hope of gain, labor [much] before they find any vein and many times miss, but when they find the silver vein, with what cheerfulness do they labor; it makes them forget their pain and otherwise tedious [labor]. Now we who study the Scriptures are even in the vein of heavenly treasure, how much [more] then should we be encouraged?

♦ EZEKIEL CULVERWELL
Time Well Spent, 295–96

The reading of the Scriptures with general instructions, admonitions, reprehensions, exhortations, and consolations I grant are most necessary, being the groundwork and matter of the cure. But what sound conversion is wrought thereby in any man, without discreet application, let every man that hath profited anything in the school of Christ be judge.

♦ THOMAS GRANGER
Application of Scripture, 5

The testimony of the church is highly to be reverenced because to it are these oracles of God delivered to be kept as a sacred deposit; yea, it is called "the pillar and ground of the truth" (1 Tim. 3:15) and the candlestick (Rev. 1:12) from whence the light of the Scriptures shines forth into the world. But who will say that the proclamation of a prince hath its authenticity from the pillar it hangs on in the market cross or that the candle hath its light from the candlestick! The office of the church is ministerial, to publish and make known the word of God; but not magisterial and absolute to make it Scripture or unmake it, as she is pleased to allow or deny.

✦ WILLIAM GURNALL
Christian in Complete Armour, 562

The Papist hath his thicket and wood at his back also—antiquity and traditions, to which he flies before the face of the Scripture for sanctuary, as Adam did to a bush when God came to him; as if any antiquity were so authentic as God's own oracles and any traditions of men to be laid in the balance with the Scripture.

✦ WILLIAM GURNALL
Christian in Complete Armour, 580

Can we go against sin and Satan with a better weapon than Christ used to vanquish the tempter with? And certainly, Christ did it to set us an example how we should come armed into the field against them, for Christ could with one beam shot from His deity (if He had pleased to exert it) have as easily laid the bold fiend prostrate at his foot as afterward He did them that came to attack Him. But He chose rather to conceal the majesty of His divinity and let Satan come up closer to Him, that so He might confound him with the word and thereby give a proof of that sword of His saints which He was to

leave them for their defense against the same enemy.

✦ WILLIAM GURNALL
Christian in Complete Armour, 582–83

Bless God for the translation of the Scriptures. The word is our sword; by being translated, this sword is drawn out of its scabbard. What use could a poor Christian that hath but one tongue in his head (that understands but one language, I mean, which his mother taught him) make of this sword when presented to him as it is sheathed in Greek and Hebrew?... Bless God for the ministry of the word, which is the public school He opens to His people, that in it they may learn the use of this their weapon. It is a sad fruit that grows upon the little smattering knowledge that some have got from the word to puff them up with a conceit of their own abilities, so as to despise the ministry of the word as a needless work.... Bless God for the efficacy of the word upon thy soul. Did ever its point prick thy heart—its edge fetch blood of thy lusts? Bless God for it; you would do as much to a surgeon for lancing a sore and severing a putrefied part from thy body, though he put thee to exquisite torture in the doing of it. And I hope thou thinks God hath done thee a greater kindness. Solomon tells us, "Faithful are the wounds of a friend; but the kisses of an enemy are deceitful" (Prov. 27:6).

✦ WILLIAM GURNALL
Christian in Complete Armour, 588–90

Make not thy own reason the rule by which thou measure Scripture truths. Is that fit to try the revelation of the word by which is puzzled with so many secrets in nature? Does not the word reveal such things to us as are not only above sense—for eye hath not seen them, nor ear heard them—but also above reason? Being such as "never have entered into the heart of man" (1 Cor. 2:9). Indeed, the whole system of gospel truths speaks in a foreign tongue to reason; it can make no sense of them, except faith be the interpreter. The Scriptures are like the Red Sea, through which the Israelites by faith passed safely; but the Egyptians attempting to do it, for want of that guide, were drowned. A humble believer passes through the deep mysteries of the word safely, without plunging into any dangerous mistakes, whereas those sons of pride who leave faith and take reason for their guide are drowned in many damnable errors—Arianism, Pelagianism, Socinianism, etc.

✦ WILLIAM GURNALL
Christian in Complete Armour, 599

That book must needs be worth reading which hath God for the author. That mystery deserves our knowledge which is the product of His infinite wisdom and love.

✦ WILLIAM GURNALL
Christian in Complete Armour, 804

The Scriptures, or gospel of the New Testament, is both a constant and a standing miracle of itself; and so often as the gospel comes to any soul not in word only but in power and in the Holy Spirit (1 Thess. 1:5), there is a miracle wrought in them that receive the gospel (Luke 7:22), and they then receive the Holy Spirit with His gifts and graces. And who can forbid such preachers of the gospel to baptize or such believers of the gospel to be baptized (Acts 10:44, 47–48). So then we need not stay for a ministry with miracle, being we have a Word with miracle.

✦ HANSERD KNOLLYS
Shining of a Flaming Fire, 10

[The Scriptures] are the golden mines in which alone the abiding treasures of eternity are to be found, and therefore worthy all the digging and pains we can bestow on them.

✦ ROBERT LEIGHTON
A Commentary upon the First Epistle of Peter, in *Whole Works*, 1:96

Mr. Seaman: The reading of the word in reference to God is an act of worship, but in reference to the congregation it is a means of edification; and in both these references the work belongs to the pastor, but not necessarily to do it himself, yet not to any member of the congregation neither.

Dr. Burgess: (1) Public reading is an ordinance of God (Deut. 31:11; Ezra; Acts 15:21). (2) This public work ought to be by a public person only, and by one that hath commission from God to dispense this public administration (Deut. 31:9–10; 1 Tim. 4:13). (3) That whosoever performeth this must be in commission to deliver the whole word by preaching as well as otherwise.

Mr. Marshal: The reading of the word in public is not an ecclesiastical office.

Mr. Gibbon proposed that the pastor and the reader might be two distinct offices.

Mr. Palmer: This office to be performed by none but by one deputed of God (Jer. 36, Baruch).

Mr. Calamy out of Mr. Hildersham: The public reading is God's ordinance, and to be done by a public officer; and we may expect more a blessing upon it than upon the private reading. Upon this subject we spent the whole day till two o'clock.
✦ JOHN LIGHTFOOT
Journal of the ... Assembly of Divines,
November 2, 1643, in *Whole Works,* 13:37

Jewels do not lie upon the surface; you must get into the caverns and dark receptacles of the earth for them. No more do truths lie in the surface and outside of an expression. The beauty and glory of the Scriptures is within and must be fetched out with much study and prayer.
✦ THOMAS MANTON
*Practical Exposition on the
Epistle of James,* 69

In a word, what is there not in the Holy Scriptures? Are we poor? Here's a treasury of riches. Are we sick? Here are medicines. Are we fainting? Here are cordials. Are we Christless? Here's the star that leads to Christ. Are we Christians? Here's the bands that keep in Christ. Are we afflicted? Here's our solace. Are we persecuted? Here's our protection. Are we deserted? Here's our recovery. Are we tempted? Here's our sword and victory. Are we young? Here's our beauty. Are we old? Here's our wisdom. While we live, here's the rule of our conversation; when we die, here's the hope of our glorification. So that I may say with Tertullian, "I adore the fullness of the Scripture." Oh, blessed Scriptures! Who can know them and not love them?
✦ FRANCIS ROBERTS
Great Worth of Scripture Knowledge, 8

[The Scripture] is the rule of all truth. Other books are true no further than they are agreeable and commensurable to this. All other sayings and writings are to be tried by this touchstone. It is not what sense saith, or what reason saith, or what fathers say, or what general councils say, or what traditions say, or what customs say, but what Scripture saith—that is to be the rule of faith and life. Whatsoever is contrary to Scripture, or beside Scripture, or not rationally deducible from Scripture is to be rejected as spurious and adulterate: "To the law and to the testimony: if they speak not according to this word, it is because there is no light [no truth] in them" (Isa. 8:20).
✦ GEORGE SWINNOCK
The Christian Man's Calling,
in *Works,* 2:440

Glorious things are spoken of thee, O thou word of God. Many books have done virtuously, have acted famously for the overthrow of sin and Satan, for the advancement of Christ and holiness, but thou hast excelled them all. Thou hast changed lions into lambs, ravens into doves, beasts into men, and men into angels. Thou hast subdued headstrong passions, mortified natural and riveted corruptions, tore up old and sturdy lusts by the roots, conquered principalities and powers, led captivity captive, and turned the world upside down.

✦ GEORGE SWINNOCK
The Christian Man's Calling,
in *Works,* 2:445

Another duty that concerns thee in secret is to read some portion of the word of God. The workman must not go abroad without his tools. The Scripture is the carpenter's rule, by which he must square his building; the tradesman's scales, in which he must weigh his commodities; the traveler's staff, which helps him in his journey. There is no acting safely unless we act scripturally.

✦ GEORGE SWINNOCK
The Christian Man's Calling,
in *Works,* 2:494

He that is mighty in Scripture is the man that can hit this unclean bird in the eye and wound it mortally with one blow (Acts 18:28). Even women, that are the weaker sex, with this sword in their hands, having learned from the Spirit how to use it, have encountered with great doctors, disarmed them of all their philosophical weapons, and shamefully foiled them.

✦ GEORGE SWINNOCK
"The Pastor's Farewell," in *Works,* 4:96

The truth is that it hath pleased God to leave some places obscure in the Scriptures, (1) that we might know that the understanding of God's word is the gift of God and therefore might beg it of Him by continual prayer; (2) lest we should flatter our wits too much, if all things could presently be understood by us; (3) that the word, for the high and heavenly mysteries contained therein, might be highly accounted of, which for the plainness might be less esteemed; (4) that profane dogs might be driven away from these holy mysteries, which are pearls prized highly by the elect alone (Matt. 13:45) but would be trodden down by swine (Matt. 7:6); (5) that we might be stirred up to a more diligent search of the same; (6) that we might esteem more of the ministry which God hath placed in the church, that by the means thereof we might profit in the knowledge of these mysteries.

✦ JAMES USSHER
Body of Divinity, 28

The Holy Scripture is, as [Augustine] saith, a golden epistle sent to us from God. This is to be read diligently; ignorance of Scripture is the mother of error, not of devotion: "Ye do err, not knowing the scriptures" (Matt. 22:29). We are commanded to "search the scriptures" (John 5:39). The Greek word signifies to search as for a vein of silver. How diligently does a child read over his father's will and testament! And a citizen peruse his charter! With the like diligence should we read God's word, which is our Magna Carta for heaven.

✦ THOMAS WATSON
Bible and the Closet, 15

If you would profit by reading, remove those things that will hinder your profiting…. There are three obstructions must be removed if you would profit by Scripture. (1) Remove the love of every sin. Let a physician prescribe ever so good recipes, if the patient takes poison it will hinder the virtue and operation of the physic. The Scripture prescribes excellent recipes, but sin lives in, poisons all…. (2) Take heed of those thorns which will choke the word read. These thorns our Savior expounds to be the cares of this world (Matt. 13:22). By "care" is meant covetousness. A covetous man hath such diversity of secular employment that he can scarce find time to read, or if he doth, what solecisms doth he commit in reading? While his eye is upon the Bible, his heart is upon the world…. (3) Take heed of jesting with Scripture; this is playing with fire. Some cannot be merry unless they make bold with God; when they are sad, they bring forth the Scripture as their harp to drive away the evil spirit…. In the fear of God beware of this.

✦ THOMAS WATSON
Bible and the Closet, 18–19

The Scripture is the library of the Holy Ghost; it is a code of divine knowledge, an exact model and platform of religion. The Scripture contains in it the credenda, the things which we are to believe, and the agenda, the things which we are to practice; it is able to make us wise unto salvation (2 Tim. 3:15). The Scripture is the standard of truth, the judge of controversy; it is the pole star to direct us to heaven. The Scripture is the compass by which the rudder of our will is to be steered; it is the field in which Christ, the pearl of price, is hid.

✦ THOMAS WATSON
Bible and the Closet, 28

Let no man talk of a revelation from the Spirit; the Spirit of God acts by the word, and he who pretends to a new light which is above the word, or contrary to it, deceives himself and dishonors the Spirit, his light being borrowed from him who "made himself an angel of light."

✦ THOMAS WATSON
Puritan Gems, 120–21

For good success and proficiency in this employment, pray constantly to Him that hath the key of David to unlock thy understanding and to use such helps as the Lord affords thee. And when thou doubt, go to the master of the assembly (Eccl. 12:11). Seek the law at His mouth, for so thou ought to do. To help a bad memory, do this: read with leisure and intention; meditate with delight (this feeds the soul); confer with others at all opportunities, especially with those whom God hath set near thee or give thee in charge (as Deut. 6:6–9; Ps. 34:11). Apply the promises to thyself with joy.

Consider the threatenings with fear and trembling (Ps. 119:110; Isa. 66:3). But above all helps, if thou would have any profiting appear, indeed, whensoever God has taught thee any duty, fall straightway in hand therewith to practice it thence forward.

✦ JOHN WHITE
"An Explication of the Following Direction for the Reading of the Bible Over in a Year," in *Way to the Tree of Life*, 342

The reading of the Scriptures is nothing else but a kind of holy conference with God, wherein we inquire after and He reveals unto us Himself and His will; we shall manifest more fully hereafter, when we shall show that these holy writings are the Word of God Himself, who speaks unto us in and by them. Wherefore when we take in hand the book of the Scriptures, we cannot otherwise conceive of ourselves then as standing in God's presence to hear what He will say unto us.

✦ JOHN WHITE
Way to the Tree of Life, 1

Search the Scriptures daily, as mines of gold wherein the heart of Christ is laid.

✦ THOMAS WILCOX
Choice Drop of Honey, 25

THE SCRIPTURES, INSPIRATION OF

The Holy Scriptures are the undoubted word of God. By the Scriptures, I mean the Old and New Testaments contained in the Bible, both which are that one foundation whereupon our faith

is built: "built upon the foundation of the apostles and prophets" (Eph. 2:20). That is the doctrine which God by them hath delivered unto His church, for they were under the unerring guidance of the Spirit: "All scripture is given by inspiration of God" (2 Tim. 3:16). Breathed by God, it came as truly and immediately from His very mind and heart as our breath doth from within our bodies; yea, both matter and words were indited by God. For the things which they spoke were "not in the words which man's wisdom teacheth, but which the Holy Ghost teacheth" (1 Cor. 2:13). God did not give them a theme to dilute and enlarge upon with their own parts and abilities, but confined them to what He indited. They were but His amanuenses to write His infallible dictate, or, as so many scribes, to transcribe what the Spirit of God laid before them. This is given as the reason why no scripture is to be understood by our private fancy or conceit.

✦ WILLIAM GURNALL
Christian in Complete Armour, 562

THE SCRIPTURES, INTERPRETING

Many have and many do miserably pervert the Scriptures by turning them into vain and groundless allegories. Some wanton wits have expounded Paradise to be the soul, man to be the mind, the woman to be the sense, the serpent to be delight, the Tree of Knowledge of Good and Evil to be wisdom, and the rest of the trees to be the virtues and endowments of the mind.

O friends! It is dangerous to bring in allegories where the Scripture doth not clearly and plainly warrant them and to take those words figuratively which should be taken properly.

✦ THOMAS BROOKS
Privy Key of Heaven, 3

As the lapidary brightens his hard diamond with the dust shaved from itself, so must we clear hard places of Scripture by parallel texts, which, like glasses set one against another, cast a mutual light.

✦ SAMUEL CLARK
Saint's Nosegay, 112

In the waters of life, the divine Scriptures, there are shallows and there are deeps — shallows where the lamb may wade and deeps where the elephant may swim. If we be not wise to distinguish, we may easily miscarry: he that can wade over the ford cannot swim through the deep, and if he mistake the passage, he drowns. What infinite mischief hath arisen to the church of God from the presumption of ignorant and unlettered men that have taken upon them to interpret the most obscure Scriptures and pertinaciously defended their own sense! How contrary is this to practice in whatsoever vocation!

✦ JOSEPH HALL
Select Thoughts, in *Select Tracts*, 369

SECOND COMING OF CHRIST

What is the best frame the soul can be in, in order to its meeting with Christ with the greatest comfort and boldness? As first, to have the love of Christ witnessed and sealed up unto the soul by the Spirit of God; (2) to be disengaged from this world and all the entanglements and incumbrances thereof; (3) to have grace in its exercise; (4) communion with God and a holy conversation maintained and kept up; (5) raised desires and longing of soul for His appearance.

✦ THOMAS BLAKE
Living Truths in Dying Times, 207–8

God in the great day will declare to men and angels how often His people have been pouring out their souls before Him in such and such corners and secret places, and accordingly He will reward them. And Christians, did you really believe and seriously dwell on this, you would (1) walk more thankfully; (2) work more cheerfully; (3) suffer more patiently; (4) fight against the world, the flesh, and the devil more courageously; (5) lay out yourselves for God, His interest and glory, more freely; (6) live with what providence hath cut out for your portion more quietly and contentedly; and (7) you would be in private prayer more frequently and abundantly.

✦ THOMAS BROOKS
Privy Key of Heaven, 19–20

We are indeed justified by faith at present and abundantly secured from future condemnation, but there will be a judicial declaration of our righteousness at the appearing of our Lord Jesus, which will tend more to the honor of God's grace and to the increase of our everlasting joy. All that we have done shall be so absolutely forgiven that Christ will then audibly say in the general assembly of mankind, "Well done." And will not that be a joyful sound? We cannot conceive what glory will redound hence to God and what triumph of spirit it will cause in us.

✦ TIMOTHY CRUSO
Duty and Support of Believers, 13

"Watch therefore: for ye know not what hour your Lord doth come" (Matt. 24:42). There are, indeed, negative signs concerning His coming to the general judgment of the world, by which we may know He will not yet come, as the fall of Babylon, the calling of the Jews, and other prophecies that must be fulfilled before He comes. But there are none from which we can conclude that His coming to any of us by death and summon us to our judgment before His bar shall not yet be.

✦ WILLIAM GURNALL
Christian in Complete Armour, 767

What is it that makes the appearing of Christ to be so glorious? To which I answer there is a concurrence of these eight particulars that make Christ's appearing to judge the world to be so glorious: (1) the excellency and beauty of Christ's person; (2) the royalty of Christ's attendants; (3) the largeness of Christ's authority; (4) the equity of Christ's proceedings; (5) the acclamations and admirations of the elect; (6) the darkening and eclipsing all the glory of the world; (7) Christ's wonderful celerity in discerning the thoughts of men's hearts; (8) His dexterity in

dispatching this great work of judging the world.

✦ CHRISTOPHER LOVE
Heaven's Glory, 38–39

O beloved, Christ's appearing in glory at the last day will be a dreadful day to you who are loath to profess, loath to embrace Jesus Christ. But you will say, "This belongs not to me. What, I ashamed of Jesus Christ, and God forbid, I love Christ with all my heart, and I wish well to Jesus Christ and I would they were in hell that do not. Shall this condemnation belong to me?" Why, mark the words, the day of judgment will not only be a dreadful day to them that are ashamed of the person of Christ but all them that are ashamed of the ordinances of Christ also. If you are ashamed to pray in your family because your neighbors will laugh at you; if you are ashamed to hear the word, to read a chapter because of being called a Puritan, the day of judgment will be a dreadful day to you.

✦ CHRISTOPHER LOVE
Heaven's Glory, 46

Though I desire as much as I may to decline matters of controversy, yet here comes in a query that I cannot well pass over in silence; it is this—namely, whether the sins of the saints shall be laid open and manifested at this day.... The sins of the godly shall not be opened (1) to their condemnation. Our Savior Himself says, "Verily, verily, I say unto you, He that heareth my word, and believeth on him that sent me, hath everlasting life, and shall not come into condemnation" (John 5:24).

"There is, therefore," says the apostle, "now no condemnation to them which are in Christ Jesus, who walk not after the flesh, but after the Spirit" (Rom. 8:1). Nor yet (2) to their shame and reproach. They shall not be produced to their infamy or disgrace. Sinners rise to everlasting shame and contempt, but saints to glory (Dan. 12:2). They may lift up their face and "have boldness in the day of judgment" (1 John 4:17). Nor (3) to the abatement of their joy in that day. The appearance of their sins in that day of the Lord shall no more abate their joy than the appearing of the dead carcasses of the Egyptians on the seashore did the joy of the delivered Israelites. Neither (4) to the damping or diminishing of their love to the Lord. If the woman to whom many sins were forgiven loved much (Luke 7:47), then the saints shall not love God less when they see how much hath been forgiven them. Now these things being thus premised, I say, I conceive it is probable that the sins of the saints shall be opened at this opening.

✦ HENRY PENDLEBURY
The Books Opened, in *Invisible Realities*, 141–42

SELF-CONFIDENCE

We are proud creatures, full of self-confidence, and therefore God, by strange and unexpected providences doth hedge up our way with thorns and wall up our path with hewn stones, brings to despair even of life, bereaves us of counsel, drives us from all our own shifts and policies, brings us under the very sentence of death that we might not trust in ourselves, but in God which raises the dead. He unbottoms us by despair, convinces us of our impotence and folly, shows us what babies and fools we are in ourselves, that in all our future hazards and fears we might know nothing but God.

✦ THOMAS CASE
Correction, Instruction, 45

Beware of self-confidence. Judas was a very confident man of himself. Last of all Judas said, "Master, is it I?" (Matt. 26:25). But he that was last in the suspicion was first in the transgression. "He that trusteth in his own heart is a fool," saith Solomon (Prov. 28:26). It will be your wisdom to keep a jealous eye upon your own hearts and still suspect their fairest pretenses.

✦ JOHN FLAVEL
Fountain of Life, 220

SELF-CONTROL

Suffer not thy mind to feed itself upon any imagination which is either impossible for thee to do or unprofitable if it be done, but rather think of the world's vanity, to condemn it; of death, to expect it; of judgment, to avoid it; of hell, to escape it; and of heaven, to desire it.

✦ LEWIS BAYLY
Practice of Piety, 119

SELF-DEFENSE

In some cases a private man may himself use violence to restrain men from evil. If a man should come to seduce my wife or child in a matter I know will endanger their souls, if I could have no help by the magistrate, I might if I had power keep him off.

✦ JEREMIAH BURROUGHS
Irenicum, 36

A man may stand up in defense of himself when his life is endangered. Some of the Anabaptists hold it unlawful to take up the sword upon any occasion, though when they get the power, I would be loath to trust them, their river water often turning to blood, but questionless a man may take up the sword for self-preservation, else he comes under the breach of the sixth commandment. He is guilty of self-murder. In taking up the sword, he doth not so much seek another's death as the safeguard of his own life; his intention is not to do hurt, but prevent it. Self-defense is consistent with Christian meekness; the law of nature and religion justify it. That God who bids us put up our sword (Matt. 26:52) yet will allow us a buckler in our own defense, and He that will have us innocent as doves, not to offend others, will have us wise as serpents in preserving ourselves.

✦ THOMAS WATSON
The Beatitudes, in *Discourses*, 2:148

SELF-DENIAL

Self-denial is a total, thorough, utter abnegation of a man's own ends, counsels, affections, and a whole prostration of himself and of all that is his under Christ Jesus. And thus we have the meaning of Christ, "If any man will come after Me, let him deny

himself"—that is, let him lay aside his own wisdom as an empty lamp, his own will as an evil commander, his own imaginations as a false rule, his own affections as corrupt counselors, and his own ends as base and unworthy marks to be aimed at. Let him deny himself—whatsoever is of himself, within himself, or belonging to himself—as a corrupt and carnal man. Let him go out of himself, that he may come to Me; let him empty himself, that he may be capable of Me and that I may reign and rule within him.

✦ ISAAC AMBROSE
"The Practice of Sanctification,"
in *Works*, 87

Restitution, as it is most necessary, so it is one of the hardest parts of self-denial. Unjust gain is like a barbed arrow: it kills if it stays within the body and pulls the flesh away if it be drawn out.

✦ ISAAC AMBROSE
"The Practice of Sanctification,"
in *Works*, 95

If you love your Lord you should love to imitate Him and be glad to find yourselves in the way that He hath gone before you. If He lived a worldly and sensual life, do you do so; if He was an enemy to preaching and praying and holy living, be you so. But if He lived in the greatest contempt of all the wealth and honors and pleasures of the world in a life of holy obedience to His Father, wholly preferring the kingdom of heaven, and seeking the salvation of the souls of others, and patiently bearing persecution, derision, calumnies, and death, then take up your cross and follow Him joyfully to the expected crown.

◆ RICHARD BAXTER
A Christian Directory, in
Practical Works, 2:230

Make self-denial appear as rational and reasonable as thou canst to thy soul; the stronger the understanding is able to reason for the equity and rationality of any work or duty, the more readily and cheerfully (if the heart be honest and sincere) is it done. Suppose, Christian, thy God should call for thy estate, liberty—yea, life and all. Can it seem unreasonable to thee? Especially, first, if thou considers that He bids thee deliver His own, not thy own. He lent thee these, but He never gave away the propriety of them from Himself. Dost thou wrong thy neighbor to call for that money thou lentest him a year or two past? No, sure; thou thinks he hath reason to thank thee for lending it to him, but none to complain for calling it from him.

◆ WILLIAM GURNALL
Christian in Complete Armour, 416

Some commands of God cannot be obeyed without much self-denial because they cross us in that which our own wills are carried forth very strongly to desire, so that we must deny our will before we can do the will of God. Now a temptation comes very forcibly when it runs with the tide of our own wills.

◆ WILLIAM GURNALL
Christian in Complete Armour, 429

They that come unto Christ come not only from the world that lieth in wickedness but out of themselves. Of a great many that seem to come to Christ, it may be said that they are not come to Him because they have not left themselves. This is believing on Him, which is the very resigning of the soul to Christ and living by Him. "Ye will not come to me, that ye might have life," says Christ (John 5:40). He complains of it as a wrong done to Him, but the loss is ours.

◆ ROBERT LEIGHTON
*A Commentary upon the First Epistle
of Peter*, in *Whole Works*, 1:200

Acts of self-denial are the great trial of faith. Such was Rahab's, to prefer the will of God before the safety of her own country; and such was Abraham's in the former instance [i.e., the offering up of Isaac]. Self-denial is the first thing that must be resolved upon in Christianity (Matt. 16:24). A man is not discovered when God's way and his own lie together. Your great inquiry should be, "Wherein have I denied myself for God? Thwarted any lust? Hazarded any interest?"

◆ THOMAS MANTON
*Practical Exposition on the
Epistle of James*, 118

What is it to deny ourselves? I answer it is nothing else but not to make ourselves our aim and end, but to make God our end and aim, and to deny ourselves as we are contrary to Him. To deny that dullness and averseness of nature that the Scripture calls "the old man" (Col. 3:9) and "the flesh"

(Rom. 8:3–9). To give this the denial is to deny a man's self, because this is reckoned a man's self. Flesh and corruption of nature is called a man's self. "We preach not ourselves, but Christ" (2 Cor. 4:5). That is, we preach not for our own credit and ends but for Christ and His glory.

✦ JOHN PRESTON
The Doctrine of Self-Denial, in Four Godly and Learned Treatises, 188

What is the difference between poverty of spirit and self-denial? I answer, in some things they agree; in some things they differ. In some things they agree, for the poor in spirit is an absolute self-denier: he renounces all opinion of himself; he acknowledges his dependence on Christ and free grace. But in some things they differ. The self-denier parts with the world for Christ; the poor in spirit parts with himself for Christ—that is, his own righteousness. The poor in spirit sees himself nothing without Christ; the self-denier will leave himself nothing for Christ.

✦ THOMAS WATSON
The Beatitudes, in Discourses, 2:61

Did you strictly examine your hearts and ways, it would appear most men's unusefulness proceeds from their selfishness. This locks your coffers, that you cannot give; this benumbs your powers, that you will not act; this spies the lion in the way that you dare not go; this feels the burden, counts the charge, and resents the inconveniencies of service as too great to be endured for it; whereas in all eminent usefulness, we do neglect the counsel, counteract

the projects, and offer violence to the inclinations of self (Gal. 1:16). And therein we must act not only as such who are not their own, but as them who have no will of their own to obey, no selfish turn to serve.

✦ DANIEL WILLIAMS
Excellency of a Publick Spirit, 70

SELF-EXAMINATION

Say to thine heart, How is it with me? Does my soul prosper? Are my ways such as please the Lord? What is my expectation and my hope? What is the aim and business of my life? Is it that Christ may be magnified by me and that I may be made partaker of His holiness and show forth His virtues in my generation?

✦ RICHARD ALLEINE
Companion for Prayer, 3

He that loves will please and observe whom he loves. How careful are such to watch themselves, that they grieve not their friend! What study does love put them upon to find out what is grateful and acceptable! Acceptable looks, acceptable language, acceptable entertainment. What wilt Thou, Lord? What wilt Thou have me to be? A servant? A doorkeeper? A servant of servants for Thee? I will be nothing but what Thou wilt, anything that Thou wilt have me. What wilt Thou have me to do, Lord? Let me know Thy will, appoint me my work. O that my ways were so directed, that I might keep thy statutes. What wilt Thou have of me? Wilt Thou have mine idols, mine ease, or my honor, or my pleasure, or my house, or my estate? Wilt thou have mine Isaacs? Is there anything dearer to me than another that might be an offering to the Lord? Wilt thou have my liberty or my life? Behold, all is at Thy feet; I can keep back nothing Thou callest for.

✦ RICHARD ALLEINE
Heaven Opened, 164–65

Six necessary questions that every Christian should ask his own heart: First, am I a saint or a hypocrite, a wise or foolish virgin? Secondly, what are the truest and strongest grounds of my being a saint? Thirdly, whether, if I be a Christian, is my spirit legal or evangelical? Fourthly, with which of the saints mentioned in the Scripture can I most compare myself? Fifthly, what are the reasons, with respect to myself, why I continue without full assurance? Sixthly, what is my master sin, and what power hath it in my soul or over it?

✦ ANONYMOUS
Life, 64

Examination:

1. Dost thou avoid all sin as sin (Job 1:1; Ps. 36:1; Prov. 8:13)? Secret as well as open? Little as well as great?

2. Dost thou frequent the ordinances (Acts 13:16)?

3. Dost thou endeavor the constant and conscientious performance of all duties (Eccl. 12:13)? Prayer, closet, family, and public? Meditation? Reading the Scriptures? Conference (Mal. 3:17)?

4. Dost thou endeavor to exercise suitable graces in all conditions? Patience under afflictions, humility in prosperity, thankfulness for mercies, etc. (Ps. 115:11).

✦ WILLIAM BEVERIDGE
Thesaurus Theologious, 4:4

You are much to study your own hearts; such dealings of God without you do call upon you to be looking within you, to be considering the frame of your souls. It calls upon you loudly to be finding out the plague of your own heart (1 Kings 8:38). Every man is to study his own heart, to labor to know that and see the sinfulness, vileness, and wretchedness of that. I tell you, souls, the judgments of God that are abroad are not things of an empty sound, but they do speak powerfully and plainly and are loud calls of God unto you, that you should make it your business and the design of your souls to be more acquainted with yourselves than ever.

✦ THOMAS BLAKE
Living Truths in Dying Times, 52

This improvement shall the escaping remnant make of their escaping: they shall mourn over their hearts and ways at a greater rate than ever. So Ezekiel 7:16: "But they that escape of them shall escape, and shall be on the mountains like doves of the valleys, all of them mourning, every one for his iniquity." The best of saints, I am persuaded, that God carries through common calamity do there and thence take opportunity of looking into their hearts more thoroughly and bemoaning them in the presence of God: "They shall mourn every one for his iniquity." And is not this a mercy, to have a reserve of time to mourn over their ways in the presence of God?

✦ THOMAS BLAKE
Living Truths in Dying Times, 75–76

It is a rare thing for some Christians to see their graces, but a thing very common for such to see their sins, yea, and to feel them too in their lusts and desires to the shaking of their souls.

Question. But since I have lusts and desires both ways, how shall I know to which my soul adheres?

Answer. This may be known thus: (1) Which wouldest thou have prevail, the desires of the flesh or the lusts of the spirit? Whose side art thou of? Doth thy soul now inwardly say, and that with a strong indignation, "Oh, let God, let grace, let my desires that are good prevail against my flesh, for Jesus Christ's sake"? (2) What kind of secret wishes hast thou in thy soul when thou feelest the lusts of thy flesh to rage? Dost thou not inwardly and with indignation against sin say, "O that I might never, never feel one such motion more. O that my soul were so full of grace that there might be no longer room for even the least lust to come into my thoughts?"

✦ JOHN BUNYAN
Riches, 190–91

Reckon with thy own heart every day before thou lie down to sleep, and cast up what thou hast received from God and done for Him and where thou hast also been wanting. This will beget praise and humility and put thee upon redeeming the day that is past, whereby thou wilt be able, through the continual supplies of grace, in some good measure to drive thy work before thee and to shorten it as thy life doth shorten, and mayst comfortably live in the hope of bringing both ends sweetly together.

✦ JOHN BUNYAN
Riches, 218

In every action we should make the inquiry, What is the rule I observe? Is it God's will or my own? Whether do my intentions tend to set up God or self? As much as we destroy this, we abate the power of sin. These two things are the head of the serpent in us which we must bruise by the power of the cross. Sin is nothing else but a turning from God and centering in self, and most in the inferior part of self. If we bend our force against these two, self-will and self-ends, we shall intercept atheism at the spring head, take away that which doth constitute and animate all sin; the sparks must vanish if the fire be quenched which affords them fuel. They are but two short things to ask in every undertaking: Is God my rule in regard of His will? Is God my end in regard of His glory? All sin lies in the neglect of these; all grace lies in the practice of them.

✦ STEPHEN CHARNOCK
Selections, 242

A Christian who can discourse with his own soul may make good company for himself.
✦ THOMAS FULLER
"The Snare Broken," in
Pulpit Sparks, 306

What do your appetites run after most? Some men, if they can but feed their belly, if but clothe their backs, if they can but maintain trade and gather in their debts, they are made men and fear nothing in the world; if you live only a life of nature, you live thus. Therefore, consider you have lived ten, twenty, forty years. But what do you do to nourish this life of grace? What pains do you take in surveying your spirits that an inroad and incursion of sin break not in upon you? What pains do you take to improve ordinances, that by all your suckings at gospel breasts this spiritual life may grow stronger in you? If you do not thus, you have not the spiritual life in you, nor can you say that Jesus Christ is your life.
✦ CHRISTOPHER LOVE
Heaven's Glory, 11

Good men will always be discovering themselves.
✦ THOMAS MANTON
in Horn, *Puritan Remembrancer*, 321

There is no greater duty incumbent upon a Christian than frequent trials of self and state by the measure of present truths. When the word of the Lord is spoken and truth discovered, then to bring it home to the heart and try our spirits and condition by it, this is a great duty. This is the meaning of that in the second epistle to the Corinthians

13:5: "Examine yourselves, whether ye be in the faith."
✦ MATTHEW MEAD
"The Power of Grace in Weaning the Heart from the World," in
Name in Heaven, 123

[I was] sure it would be of precious use to me seriously to debate these questions in my own soul: (1) What evidences [do] I have for heaven? (2) What am I better or worse than I have been? (3) What sins do most prevail in me? (4) What graces [do] I most want? (5) What mercies I have received? (6) What afflictions would God have done me good by? (7) What have I to bear up my heart with if troubles come?
✦ HENRY NEWCOME
Diary, 30 (December 10, 1661)

It is no small evidence of a gracious soul when it is willing to search itself in this matter and to be helped therein from a word of truth; when it is willing that the word should dive into the secret parts of the heart and rip open whatever of evil and corruption lies therein.
✦ JOHN OWEN
On Indwelling Sin, in
Oweniana, 221

We must be watchful against the breakings forth of corrupt nature; observe the frame and disposition of our spirits and the deceitfulness of sin, which has a tendency to harden us; and avoid all occasions of or incentives to it, "hating even the garment spotted by the flesh" (Jude 23); abstaining from all appearance of evil (1 Thess. 5:22).

And to this we may add that we are frequently to examine ourselves with respect to our behavior in every state of life, whether sin be gaining or losing ground in us; whether we make conscience of performing every duty, both personal and relative. What guilt we contract by sins of omission or the want of that fervency of spirit which has a tendency to beget a formal, dead, and stupid frame and temper of mind, and thereby hinder the progress of the work of sanctification? But that which is the principal, if not the only expedient that will prove effectual for the mortifying of sin is our seeking help against it from Him who is able to give us the victory over it.

✦ THOMAS RIDGLEY
Body of Divinity, 155

Can you endure to have your soul ripped up and your beloved sin smitten by a searching minister, approving that ministry and liking that minister so much the more? And do you, with David, desire that the righteous should reprove you? And would you have an obedient ear to a wise reprover?

✦ HENRY SCUDDER
Christian's Daily Walk, 421

Nothing is more common than for persons to be, in truth, otherwise than they judge. For every man's own spirit, so far as it is sinful, is apt to give a false testimony of itself. David said he was cut off from God when he was not. The Laodiceans thought themselves in a good state when Christ said they were wretched and miserable. Now,

that you may not err in this great point, you must use all good means to have your judgment rightly informed, and then be willing to judge of yourself as you are and of your peace with God as it is. I told you that the Holy Scripture must be your guide in judging what you should be and what you are.

✦ HENRY SCUDDER
Christian's Daily Walk, 423

Self-examination is the beaten path to perfection.

✦ WILLIAM SECKER
in Horn, *Puritan Remembrancer*, 223

Let me live no longer as a stranger to myself, but by self-reflection dwell more at home, reckoning my principle work to be within doors, to keep my own vineyard. Teach me to watch over my senses, to guard the door of my lips, to govern my passions; to be wary in the choice of my company and in the right use of it; to be circumspect in every step of my daily walk, to call myself frequently to a reckoning, to cast up my accounts at the foot of every page (by every day's review of my actions), to live always as in God's presence and be awed everywhere by the thought of His holy eye, to shun the occasions and appearances of evil, etc. By a neglect of this, spiritual distempers will insensibly creep upon us.

✦ JOHN SHOWER
Serious Reflections, 181

Be often putting questions to yourselves in a very serious manner: Am I ready indeed? What if I should die before tomorrow comes? O my soul, art thou in such a posture as thou art willing to be found in when Christ shall appear?

✦ NATHANIEL TAYLOR
Funeral Sermon [on Luke 12:40], 23

We ought seriously to consider two things: the sin of our nature and the nature of our sin.

✦ RALPH VENNING
in Edmund Calamy et al.,
Saints' Memorials, 127

Meditate about three things: (1) About thy debts. See if thy debts be paid or no—that is, thy sins pardoned. See if there be no arrears, no sin in thy soul unrepented of. (2) Meditate about thy will; see if thy will be made yet. Hast thou resigned up all the interest in thyself? Hast thou given up thy love to God? Hast thou given up thy will? This is to make thy will. Meditate about thy will. Make thy spiritual will in the time of health. If thou puttest off the making of thy will till death, it may be invalid; perhaps God will not accept of thy soul then. (3) Meditate about thy evidences. These evidences are the graces of the Spirit; see whether thou hast any evidences. What desires hast thou after Christ? What faith? See whether there be no flaw in thy evidences. Are thy desires true? Dost thou as well desire heavenly principles as heavenly privileges? O meditate seriously upon your evidences.

✦ THOMAS WATSON
"A Christian on the Mount,"
in *Discourses*, 1:221

To meditation join examination. When you have been meditating on any spiritual subject, put a query to thy soul, and though it be short, let it be serious. O my soul, is it thus with thee or no? When thou hast been meditating about the fear of God, that it is the "beginning of wisdom" (Prov. 1:17), put a query: O my soul, is this fear planted in thy heart? Thou art almost come to the end of thy days. Art thou yet come to the beginning of wisdom?

✦ THOMAS WATSON
"A Christian on the Mount,"
in *Discourses*, 1:268

SELFISHNESS

Man has fallen from God to himself, so that self is now the god of this world, and selfishness is the life of sin. It runs like blood and spirit through every sin. Now self is either natural, moral, or religious. We must be dead to all.

✦ ALEXANDER CARMICHAEL
Believer's Mortification of Sin, 20–21

If thou wouldst mortify original sin, thou must be sure to mortify self, for selfishness is the soul of sin—this is the great idol that all others truckle under. Man's first sin was self-exaltation and self-satisfaction, and that depravation of our nature, which is the punishment of the first sin, chiefly appears in our self-opening, self-willing, self-loving, self-seeking, and self-pleasing. The natural man beholds himself, apprehends some excellency in himself, believes himself, loves himself, pleases himself, designs himself, and that as his last end wherein he rests.

Hence, the first step of our recovery to God is self-denying, self-abasing, self-loathing, self-annihilating; and the lower self is, the weaker is the body of sin. The more a man is emptied of self and dead to self, the more he is filled with the fullness of God and alive to God. When Christ is all and grace is all, the old man and indwelling sin are at the lower ebb.

✦ ALEXANDER CARMICHAEL
Believer's Mortification of Sin, 89–90

When men live to themselves and are satisfied that they do no hurt, though they do no good; are secure, selfish, wrathful, angry, peevish, or have their kindness confined to their relations; or otherwise are little useful but in what they are pressed unto and therein come off with difficulty in their own minds; who esteem all lost that is done for the relief of others; and the greatest part of wisdom to be cautious and disbelieve the necessities of men—in a word, that make self and its concernments the end of their lives; whatever otherwise their profession be or their diligence in religious duties, they do very little either to represent or glorify God in the world. If we therefore design to be holy, let us constantly in our families, toward our relations, in churches, in our conversations in the world, and dealings with all men; toward our enemies and persecutors, the worst of them, so far as they are ours only; toward all mankind as we have opportunity, labor after conformity unto God and to express our likeness unto Him in His philanthropy, goodness, benignity, condescension,

readiness to forgive, to help and relieve, without which we neither are nor can be the children of our Father, which is in heaven.

✦ JOHN OWEN
On the Holy Spirit, in
Oweniana, 43

SELF-RELIANCE

He has an ill master that is ruled by himself. A master that is blind and proud and passionate; that will lead you unto precipices and thence deject you; that will effectually ruin you when he thinks he is doing you the greatest good; whose work is bad and his wages no better; that feeds his servants in plenty, but as swine, and in the day of famine denies them the husks. Whatever you may now imagine while you are distracted with sensuality, I dare say if ever God bring you to yourselves, you will consider that it is better to be in your father's house, where the poorest servant hath bread enough, than to be fed with dreams and pictures and to perish with hunger. Reject not God till you have found a better master.

✦ RICHARD BAXTER
Baxteriana, 31–32

Be jealous of thine own weakness. Trust not too much to thine own strength. It was Peter's oversight, and we know how foully he fell. And his example is left upon record to make us the more wary. For this is the ruin of not a few: that they presume too much of their own might and so are bold to offer themselves unto those provocations and temptations that prove many times their utter ruin.

✦ THOMAS GATAKER
Christian Constancy, 18

There is a natural, wretched independency in us, that we would be the authors of our own works and do all without Him, without whom indeed we can do nothing. Let us learn to go more out of ourselves, and we shall find more strength for our duties and against our temptations. Faith's great work is to renounce self-power and to bring in the power of God to be ours. Happy they that are weakest in themselves, sensibly so.

✦ ROBERT LEIGHTON
Spiritual Truths, 61

We can have no power from Christ unless we live in a persuasion that we have none of our own.

✦ JOHN OWEN
Golden Book, 218

SELF-SEEKING

Self-seeking blinds the soul, that it cannot see a beauty in Christ nor an excellency in holiness; it distempers the palate that a man cannot taste sweetness in the word of God, nor in the ways of God, nor in the society of the people of God. It shuts the hand against all the soul-enriching offers of Christ. It hardens the heart against all the knocks and entreaties of Christ. It makes the soul as an empty vine and as a barren wilderness; in a word, there is nothing that bespeaks a man to be

more empty and void of God, Christ, and grace than self-seeking.

✦ THOMAS BROOKS
Smooth Stones, 175

SERMONS

Most men hear sermons as they entertain news out of the Indies—matters unconcerning them. Let us mind these things: if any virtue be commended, to practice it; if any vice be condemned, to avoid it; if any consolation be insinuated, to appropriate it; if any good example be propounded, to follow it. So mind that thou hears as if it were spoken only to thyself. Is it comfort? Repent, and it is thine.

✦ THOMAS ADAMS
Exposition upon…Second…Peter, 603

It is our duty to take heed how we hear. For it stands upon us to regard not only what we hear but how we hear, and to look to the manner as well as to the matter. For we may perish as well by not hearing aright as by hearing that which is not right, and consider that it is not enough to hear the truth, but we must hear truly.

✦ WILLIAM ATTERSOLL
"The Conversion of Nineveh,"
in *Three Treatises*, 30

Directions…before hearing
[a sermon]:

1. Consider what thou art going about and Whom thou art going before.

2. Set aside all worldly thoughts, as Abraham, his servants, and

Nehemiah (Neh. 13:19–20), especially sins (James 1:21).

3. If thou wouldst have God pour forth His blessings upon thee in preaching, do thou pour out thy spirit before Him in prayer (Pss. 10:17; 65:2). [Pray] for the minister (Rom. 15:30) [and] yourselves, that God would put in with the word (Isa. 8:11).

4. Come with an appetite (Job 29:23; Matt. 5:6).

5. Come with large expectations.

6. With strong resolutions to practice.

✦ WILLIAM BEVERIDGE
Thesaurus Theologious, 3:26–27

Directions…after [a] sermon:

1. Meditate upon what thou hast heard with thyself (1 Tim. 4:15).

2. Confer of it with others.

3. Square thyself according to it, that thy life may be as a comment upon the sermon (Matt. 7:24–25; James 1:22).

✦ WILLIAM BEVERIDGE
Thesaurus Theologious, 3:27

Acquaint yourselves well with the ends and uses of the word. Read books, and ask ministers, and know as well as they to what purposes God sendeth His oracles. The four comprehensive ends are to convince of sin, to convert unto Jesus Christ, to confirm in grace, to direct and comfort in obedience. Understand these and muse much on them. Come to sermons for these, and you shall not go from sermons without

them. But God hath not pleasure in fools, and if you come to hear for you know not what, it is no marvel if you come away fools as you went.

✦ DANIEL BURGESS
Rules and Directions, 4–5

Take the most earnest heed that you do not let slip what you have received. Your memories be the great servants of your faith, hope, and obedience; and they are but imperfectly sanctified. They be too much like the grates that let go clean water and hold filthy mud. If you take little pains about them, you will have but sorry service from them. The best ground will never hold the good seed if no care be had to drive off the fowls that will be coming and catching it away and if labor be not bestowed to harrow it in. This labor for the word is labor in the Lord, and it shall not be in vain. Thus do, you shall surely prosper and do well. But if this be too much in your conceits; if you are lame, and will not use crutches; if you cannot otherwise remember, and you will not talk with yourselves and families of a sermon, nor go forth unto a repetition; nor ask the Holy Spirit to be your remembrancer, you must take to your sorrow what you get by your sloth. The devil cannot rob you of a sermon against your will, and God will not keep a sermon in your mind without your will.

✦ DANIEL BURGESS
Rules and Directions, 12–13

[Philip Henry] noted in his diary this saying of a godly man, a hearer of his, as that which affected him: "I find it easier to go six miles to hear a sermon than to spend a quarter of an hour in meditating upon it and praying over it in secret, as I should when I come home."

✦ JOHN DOD AND PHILIP HENRY
Gleanings of Heavenly Wisdom, 45

While the word is preaching, it does so ransack the heart that such as hear it cannot but be persuaded the minister is acquainted with their sins, and that he aims at them.... The bow is drawn...by our hand. It is God that guides the flight into Ahab's bosom; He answers you according to the idols in your hearts (Ezek. 14:4). When you come to a sermon, know you come to a narrow Searcher which will tell you of your adulteries, oppressions, etc.

✦ NEHEMIAH ROGERS
The Penitent Citizen, in
Mirrour of Mercy, 12

After the sermon is ended, say not, as the common manner is, "Now the sermon is done," but consider it is not done till thou hast done it. After reading and hearing, do as men do after dinner: sit a while, concoct it; by pondering of it, digest it, and after draw it out into action.

✦ SAMUEL WARD
"The Happiness of Practice," in
Sermons and Treatises, 172

SERVICE

God hath many servants but little service in the world. We do so trust and thrust His work one upon another, that still it is not done. They say, "Many hands make light work"; but it is usually seen that many hands make slight work.... The sea breaks in; all the borderers contend whose right it is to mend the dam, but whilst they all strive much and do nothing, the sea breaks further in upon them and drowns the whole country.

✦ THOMAS ADAMS
Exposition upon...Second...Peter, 40

Most true believers are weak in faith. Alas! How far do we all fall short of the love and zeal and care and diligence which we should have, if we had but once beheld the things which we do believe? Alas! How dead are our affections? How flat are our duties? How cold, and how slow are our endeavors? How unprofitable are our lives, in comparison of what one hour's sight of heaven and would make them be?

✦ RICHARD BAXTER
Baxteriana, 81

O the horrid drudgery that is in the ways of sin, Satan, or the world. Thy worst day in Christ's service is better than thy best days, if I may so speak; in sin or Satan's service.

✦ THOMAS BROOKS
The Unsearchable Riches of Christ,
in *Select Works*, 1:112

Why are the consolations of God goat's hair and small things with thee? Or dreamest thou that they be talents given thee for thy own comfort, and not for God's use and special service? Or, tell me plainly, canst thou thyself take comfort in them, unless thy God has glory from them?

✦ DANIEL BURGESS
Man's Whole Duty, 58

Nothing better to clear the soul of sloth and listlessness of spirit in the service of God than hope well improved and strengthened. It is the very physic which the apostle prescribes for this disease: "We desire every one of you do shew the same diligence to the full assurance of hope unto the end: that ye be not slothful" (Heb. 6:11–12).

✦ WILLIAM GURNALL
Christian in Complete Armour, 520

We must venture upon men's displeasure rather than neglect our duty.

✦ ADAM MARTINDALE
Life, 120

Faith is an ingenuous grace; as it hath one eye at the reward, so it hath another eye at duty. The time of life is the only time we have to work for God. Heaven is a place of receiving; this, of doing.

✦ THOMAS WATSON
The Christian's Charter of Privileges,
in *Discourses*, 1:143

SICKNESS/THE PLAGUE

Some women and passionate, weak-spirited men, especially in sickness, are so peevish and of such impatient minds that their daily work is to disquiet and torment themselves. One can scarce tell how to speak to them or look at them, but it offends them. And the world is so full of occasions of provocation that such persons are like to have little quietness. It is unlike that these should delight in God, who keep their minds in a continual, ulcerated, galled state, incapable of any delights at all, and cease not their self-tormenting.

✦ RICHARD BAXTER
A Christian Directory, in
Practical Works, 2:417

Will you say, "O, but suppose the plague should come, all my friends would leave me; I shall be left all alone, and what shall become of me then?" Why, says [the psalmist] at the fifteenth verse [of Psalm 91], "He shall call upon me, and I will answer him: I will be with him in trouble," spoken in regard of the plague.

✦ WILLIAM BRIDGE
Righteous Man's Habitation, 56–57

No godly man falls in any common calamity till his glass be run and his work done; so I say of all those dear servants of the Lord that have fallen by the pestilence in the midst of us. Their hour was come and their course was finished. Had God had any further doing work, or suffering work, or bearing work, or witnessing work for them in this world, 'twas not all the angels in heaven nor all the malignant diseases in the world that could ever have cut them off from the land of the living.

✦ THOMAS BROOKS
Heavenly Cordial, 53–54

And as [those who are sick] show their love and thankfulness to God, so let them also show brotherly love toward men, [that] until they be fully recovered, let them abstain from company, lest by their means any be infected;

neither let them take it grievously that their friends at such times do not so often visit them as many do, which through foolishness and want of true love when they are infected themselves care not who be infected with them.

✦ WILLIAM CUPPER
"Tenth Sermon concerning God's Late Visitation," in *Certaine Sermons*, 363

Q. Is it lawful for any man to flee the infection [i.e., the plague]?

A. Yes, for albeit magistrates, necessary officers, and they that are pastors of the visited congregations may not flee, yet they that either are fearful or freed from their ordinary calling (for they are not bound, being in no public and necessary office) may lawfully flee. For first a man may preserve himself by flight, so that he [in] nothing [can] hurt another. A man may shun dangers of the like nature as war, famine, waters, fires, and why not then this judgment?

✦ THOMAS DRAXE
Christian Armory, 39–40

Lord, when Thou shalt visit me with a sharp disease, I fear I shall be impatient, for I am choleric by my nature and tender by my temper and have not been acquainted with sickness all my lifetime. I cannot expect any kind usage from that which hath been a stranger unto me. I fear I shall rave and rage. O whither will my mind sail when distemper shall steer it? Whither will my fancy run when diseases shall ride it? My tongue, which of itself is a fire, sure will be a wildfire when the furnace of my mouth is made seven times hotter with a burning fever. But Lord, though I should talk idly to my own shame, let me not talk wickedly to Thy dishonor. Teach me the art of patience whilst I am well, and give me the use of it when I am sick. In that day either lighten my burden or strengthen my back. Make me, who so often in my health have discovered my weakness presuming on my own strength, to be strong in sickness when I solely rely on Thy assistance.

✦ THOMAS FULLER
Good Thoughts, 2–3

It is usual in providence that they who have God's heart should feel God's hand most heavy. I have observed it, that God's children never question His love so much as in sickness. Our thoughts return upon us in such retirement, and the weakness of the body discomposes the mind and deprives us of the free exercise of spiritual reason; to sense and feeling all is sharp.

✦ THOMAS MANTON
Practical Exposition on the Epistle of James, 203

Men will shun a house infected with the pestilence. [How] much more then is the dwelling place of the harlot to be avoided, who is infinitely more contagious and dangerous than any plague.

✦ PETER MUFFET
Commentary on the Whole Book of Proverbs, 29

The…property of the prudent man is, upon the sight of the plague or evil, to hide himself. The safest and best hiding of a man's self in danger is flying unto

God and reposing of a man's self in His secret place and under His wings by a lively faith (Ps. 91:1; 143:9). But it is also lawful and good not only to hide the heart but the head and to use the outward means whereby we may be preserved from evils.

✦ PETER MUFFET
Commentary on the Whole Book of Proverbs, 118

Sickness brings death. Dorcas was sick and died (Acts 9:37). Long sickness, if not removed, will bring the strongest body to the dust of death. Sickness is indeed *anteambulo mortis*, the forerunner of death. The sickbed is the direct way to the dark bed, the grave. Sin brings death to the soul. One disease of sin, if it be not healed by Christ's blood, will certainly bring the soul to eternal death (Rom. 6:23); it hath brought many to hell, and it will certainly bring all others to the same condition that live and die in it unhealed. He that dies in his sin shall die forever.

✦ RALPH ROBINSON
Christ All and in All, 81

SILENCE

As he cannot be wise who speaks much, so he cannot be known for a fool that says nothing.

✦ THOMAS BROOKS
in Horn, *Puritan Remembrancer*, 2

SIN

Sin is the strength of death and the death of strength; by what means soever the Lord makes that weaker, we grow stronger.

✦ THOMAS ADAMS
Exposition upon...Second...Peter, 763

Sin is the insurrection and rebellion of the heart against God. It turns from Him and turns against Him; it runs over to the camp of the enemy and there takes up arms against God. Sin is a running from God and a fighting against God; it would spoil the Lord of all the jewels of His crown. It opposes the sovereignty of God. A sinful heart would set up itself in God's throne; it would be king in His stead and have the command of all. Sinners would be their own gods: Our tongues are our own, who is Lord over us?

✦ RICHARD ALLEINE
Heaven Opened, 190

With this nature or corrupt inclination, we are all now born into the world, for "who can bring a clean thing out of an unclean?" As a lion hath a fierce and cruel nature before it doth devour, and as an adder hath a venomous nature before she stings, so in our very infancy we have those sinful natures and inclinations before we think or speak or do amiss. And hence springs all the sin of our lives.

✦ RICHARD BAXTER
Call to the Unconverted, 25

[God] would sanctify you by His Spirit, and you resist and quench it. If any man reprove you for your sin you fly in his face with evil words, and if he would draw you to a holy life and tell you of your present danger, you give him little thanks, but either bid him look to himself, he shall not answer for you; or else at best, you put him off with heartless thanks and will not turn when you are persuaded. If ministers would privately instruct and help you, you will not come near them; your unhumbled souls feel but little need of their help. If they would catechize you, you are too old to be catechized, though you are not too old to be ignorant and unholy. Whatever they can say to you for your good, you are so self-conceited and wise in your own eyes, even in the depth of ignorance, that you will regard nothing that agrees not with your present conceits, but contradict your teachers, as if you were wiser than they; you resist all that they can say to you, your ignorance and willfulness, and foolish cavils, and shifting evasions, and unthankful rejections; so that no good which is offered can find any welcome acceptance and entertainment with you.

✦ RICHARD BAXTER
Call to the Unconverted, 123

The condemnation of the whole world by the sin of Adam speaks the evil of sin. If the eating of the apple, committing that one sin, brought condemnation upon all the world, how great must the evil of sin be. The fire of hell speaks the evil of sin, for what is the fuel that the fire of hell feeds upon, but sin. Take sin away, and the fire of hell will die; it will be quenched. The spoil of duties speaks it. One sinful thought is enough to spoil a prayer, to spoil a duty, to spoil a sermon. And if one drop of ink shall blacken a whole glass of milk, how black is that ink. The horror of conscience speaks it, for if but one sin set on upon the soul by God doth put a man into such horror of conscience, how great is the evil of sin…. Sins in the saints are but wasps without their sting, and if the wasps without their sting be so troublesome, how troublesome are the wasps that have their stings in them. How troublesome is sin in itself.

✦ WILLIAM BRIDGE
Christ and the Covenant, in
Works, 3:109

Death puts an end to all other troubles, as poverty, sickness, disgrace, scorn, contempt, crosses, losses. But sin is so great an evil that death itself cannot put an end to it; eternity itself shall never put a stop, a period, to this evil of evils. All outward evils can never make a man the subject of God's wrath and hatred. A man may be poor and yet precious in the eyes of God; he may be greatly abhorred by the world and yet highly honored by God; he may be debased by men and yet exalted by God. But sin is so great an evil that it subjects the sinner's soul to the wrath and hatred of God. All other evils do but strike at a man's present well-being, but sin strikes at a man's eternal well-being.

♦ THOMAS BROOKS
Cabinet of Choice Jewels, 112

True repentance includes a sense of the mischievousness of sin: that it cast angels out of heaven, Adam out of Paradise; that it laid the first cornerstone in hell and brought in all the curses, crosses, and miseries that are in the world; and that it renders men liable to all temporal, spiritual, and eternal wrath; yea, it hath left men without God, Christ, hope, or heaven.

♦ THOMAS BROOKS
Precious Remedies, 56–57

They that name the name of Christ, let them depart from their constitution sin, or, if you will, the sin that their temper most inclines them to. Every man is not alike inclined to the same sin, but some to one and some to another. Now, let the man that professes the name of Christ religiously consider with himself, "Unto what sin or vanity am I most inclined? Is it pride? Is it covetousness? Is it fleshly lust?" and let him labor by all means to leave off and depart from that.

♦ JOHN BUNYAN
Riches, 218

Look upon sin as the greatest of evils—greater than poverty, imprisonment, banishment, or death itself. Choose the greatest affliction rather than commit the least sin. If hell were on one side and sin on the other, choose rather to go into hell than to sin against God. For sin is a greater evil than hell because it is the cause of hell and more opposite to God (who is the chiefest good) than hell is.

♦ EDMUND CALAMY
Godly Man's Ark, xv

Sin is the spawn of the old serpent, the birth of hell, and the vomit of the devil. Sin is more hateful to God than the devil, for He hates the devil for sin's sake, not sin for the devil's sake.

♦ SAMUEL CLARK
Saint's Nosegay, 26

When a man dives under water, he feels not the weight of it, though there be many tons of water over his head; whereas half a tub of it taken out of its place and set upon his head would be burdensome. So, whilst a man is over head and ears in sin, he is not sensible of nor troubled with the weight of it. But when he begins to come out of that state of sin, then sin begins to hang heavy, and he feels the great weight of it.

♦ SAMUEL CLARK
Saint's Nosegay, 27

There is no sin whereof every man hath not the seed in himself, which, without the Lord's mercy, would in time break out.

♦ EZEKIEL CULVERWELL
Time Well Spent, 303

Sin and the creature are never known as they are till God be known in some measure as He is. And proportionable to the knowledge of God, the high and honorable conceptions of God, so is our knowledge and the conceptions we have of the vanity of the creature, the evil of sin, and that misery into which we have brought ourselves.

✦ GILES FIRMIN
Real Christian, 38

Oh the depth of the evil of sin! If ever you wish to see how great and horrid an evil sin is, measure it in your thoughts, either by the infinite holiness and excellency of God, who is wronged by it, or by the infinite sufferings of Christ, who died to satisfy for it, and then you will have deeper apprehensions of the evil of sin.

✦ JOHN FLAVEL
Fountain of Life, 128

Did not God spare His own Son? Then let none of us spare our own sins. Sin was that sword which pierced Christ. O let sorrow for sin pierce your hearts! If you spare sin, God will not spare you (Deut. 29:20). We spare sin when we faintly oppose it; when we excuse, cover, and defend it; when we are impatient under just rebukes and reproofs for it. But all kindness to sin is cruelty to our own souls.

✦ JOHN FLAVEL
Sacramental Meditations, 120

We must look to the root from whence sin springs that is to our aversion from God, for by how much the more a man turns from God, with greatest contempt of God, with greatest delight in sin, with greatest hurt to his neighbor, with greatest knowledge against his conscience, with fullest consent of his will; by so much the more he sins, he deserves the title of an unjust and filthy person.

✦ HANNIBAL GAMMON
God's Just Desertion of the Unjust, 12

God doth not only see the sins of His children but their failings are more distasteful to Him than others' because the persons in which they are found are so dear and stand so near unto Him. A dunghill in a prince's chamber would be more offensive to Him than one afar off from His court.

✦ WILLIAM GURNALL
Christian in Complete Armour, 233

Never think to find honey in the pot when God writes poison on its cover. We may say of every sin in this respect…if God call it folly, there is no wisdom to be found in it. The devil, indeed, teacheth sinners to cover foul practices with fair names— superstition must be styled devotion; covetousness, thrift; pride in apparel, handsomeness; looseness, liberty; and madness, mirth. And truly there is need for sinners to do thus to make this fulsome dish go down with less regret. There are some who have made a hearty meal of horseflesh or the like carrion under a better name whose stomachs would have risen against it if they had known what it was.

✦ WILLIAM GURNALL
Christian in Complete Armour, 605

The nature of sin, as the word defines it. See its description [in] 1 John 3:4: "Sin is the transgression of the law";

a few words, but of weight enough to press the soul that commits it to hell.

> ✦ WILLIAM GURNALL
> *Christian in Complete Armour*, 605

There is a twofold deliberation that makes a sin presumptuous: (1) When a man sins, after he hath deliberated with himself whether he shall sin or not; when, upon debating the case at length, after much pondering and consideration, he consents to sin.... (2) When men do deliberate and contrive, how they may sin to the greatest advantage, how they may make the most of their iniquities. When they plot and contrive with themselves, how they may squeeze and draw out the very utmost of all that pleasure and sweet that they imagine sin carries with it. This makes that sin a presumptuous sin.

> ✦ EZEKIEL HOPKINS
> "The Nature of Presumptuous Sins,"
> in *Select Works*, 382–83

Sin knows no mother but your own hearts.

> ✦ THOMAS MANTON
> *Practical Exposition on the
> Epistle of James*, 38

There is in all a cursed root of bitterness which God mortifies, but not nullifies; it is cast down, but not cast out. Like the wild fig tree or ivy in the wall: cut off stump, body, bough, and branches, yet some strings or other will sprout out again, till the wall be plucked down. God will have it so, till we come to heaven. Well, then, (1) Walk with more caution; you carry a sinning heart about you. As long as there is fuel for

a temptation, we cannot be secure. He that has gunpowder about him will be afraid of sparkles. (2) Censure with the more tenderness; give every action the allowance of human frailty (Gal. 6:1). We all need forgiveness; without grace thou might fall into the same sins. (3) Be the more earnest with God for grace. God will keep you still dependent and beholden to His power. "Who shall deliver me?" (Rom. 7:24). (4) Magnify the love of God with more praise. Paul groans under his corruption at the latter end of Romans 7, and then in the commencement of the following admires the happiness of those who are in Christ; they have many sins and yet are condemned for none.

> ✦ THOMAS MANTON
> *Practical Exposition on the
> Epistle of James*, 122

Though we cannot be altogether without sin, yet we must not altogether leave off to resist sin. Sin reigns where it is not resisted.

> ✦ THOMAS MANTON
> *Practical Exposition on the
> Epistle of James*, 130

A gracious man opposes sin as it crosses God's holiness; a wicked man, as it crosses God's justice. The one saith, "God hates this"; the other saith, "God will punish this." The one works out of a principle of love, the other of fear. The one hates sin as defiling, the other as damning. The one as disabling him for good (Rom. 7:18; Gal. 5:17), the other because of incommodity and sensible inconvenience; otherwise they can brook sin well enough. He does not oppose sin as it interrupts his communion with God. A wicked man cares not to be with God so that he might be securely without Him.

✦ THOMAS MANTON
Practical Exposition on the
Epistle of James, 147

Good God, whither is man fallen! First, we practice sin, then defend it, then boast of it. Sin is first our burden, then our custom, then our delight, then our excellency!

✦ THOMAS MANTON
Practical Exposition on the
Epistle of James, 178

He is no true believer unto whom sin is not the greatest burden, sorrow, and trouble.

✦ JOHN OWEN
The Mortification of Sin in Believers,
in Golden Book, 152

Sin sets up a partition wall, or separates between Christ and the soul, and keeps them at a distance that the soul cannot come nigh Him to take Him. Sin darkens and blinds the eye that should behold Christ; withers the hand that should receive Christ; and shuts the heart that should entertain Him. While you will keep sin, you neither will nor can take Christ nor open your hearts to let the King of glory come in.

✦ EDWARD REYNER
Precepts for Christian Practice, 58

Sickness begets torment and anguish in the body. When sickness is in extremity in the body, how doth a man cry out of pain and head and heart, and every part is under torment. What restless tossings are men under when diseases are violent; hear how Job complains [in] chapter 30:16–18. Sin is the cause of torment and painfulness in the soul. The sin of Felix made him tremble (Acts 24:25). Cain's sin put his spirit into such anguish that he cried out, "My punishment is greater than I can bear" (Gen. 4:13–14). The sin of Judas brought such despairing torment upon his soul that he takes away his life to end his misery (Matthew 27). And even God's own people, when they fall into this spiritual disease, are pained at the very heart till, by pardon and remission, they have obtained a healing from God. How full of pain was David's spirit by reason of his sin. He was as a man upon the rack for a long time; if he did ever recover his former serenity, see Psalms 6 and 38. Many of the dear children of God do, by sin, fill their hearts with such anguish that they are never without much smart to the day of their death.

✦ RALPH ROBINSON
Christ All and in All, 80

Sin is the most loathsome disease in all the world, and the most infectious. The smallpox, the pestilence, the leprosy: these are delightful, pleasant diseases in comparison of sin. Sin doth pollute everything it comes near; it pollutes the conscience, the ordinances, relations, persons, nations. If it were possible that one drop of sin could enter heaven, it would turn heaven into hell. It's compared in Scripture to all loathsome things; 'tis compared to the plague of pestilence and of leprosy (1 Kings 8:38). The leprosy of the law was a type of it. It's compared to poison (Ps. 140:3), to the vomit of a dog (2 Peter 2:22). It's called filthiness, abomination, lewdness. All the things that are loathsome in the world are used in Scripture to shadow out the loathsomeness of sin.

♦ RALPH ROBINSON
Christ All and in All, 83

Small sins serve to make way for greater. Huntsmen first ply the deer with their little beagles, 'til it be heated…then they put on their great buckhounds. Such use the devil makes of little sins. A long thread of iniquity he has let in with a small needle.

♦ NEHEMIAH ROGERS
The Penitent Citizen, in
Mirrour of Mercy, 86

There is more real evil in a particle of corruption than in an ocean of tribulation. In suffering, the offense is offered to us; in sinning, the offense is committed against God. In suffering, there is an infringement of man's liberty; in sinning, there is a denial of God's authority. The evil of suffering is transient, but the evil of sin is permanent. In suffering, we lose the favor of men, but in sinning, we hazard the favor of God.

♦ WILLIAM SECKER
Nonsuch Professor, 61

Sin never ruins but where it reigns.

♦ WILLIAM SECKER
Nonsuch Professor, 183

Sin is a sinking of the soul down to the self and the creature, and redemption from sin is nothing else but a recovery of the soul into a state of favor and fellowship with God.

♦ SAMUEL SHAW
A Welcome to the Plague, in Vint,
Suffering Christian's Companion, 282

There is more mercy in Christ than sin in us; there can be no danger in thorough dealing. It is better to go bruised to heaven than sound to hell. Therefore, let us not take off ourselves too soon nor pull off the plaster before the cure be wrought, but keep ourselves under this work till sin be the sourest and Christ the sweetest of all things. And when God's hand is upon us in any kind, it is good to direct our sorrow for other things to the root of all, which is sin. Let our grief run most in that channel, that as sin bred grief, so grief may consume sin.

♦ RICHARD SIBBES
*Bruised Reed and Smoking
Flax*, 31–32

Insomuch as we give way to our will in sinning, in such a measure of distance we set ourselves from comfort. Sin against conscience is a thief in the candle which wastes our joy and thereby weakens our strength. We must know, therefore, that willful breaches in sanctification will much hinder the sense of our justification.

♦ RICHARD SIBBES
*Bruised Reed and Smoking
Flax*, 104

The more of the will, the more heinous the sin; when we venture upon sinful courses deliberately, it exceedingly wastes our comfort. When we fall into sin against conscience and abuse our Christian liberty, God fetches us back by some severe affliction. There shall be a cloud between God's face and us, and He will suspend His comforts for a long time. Let no man venture upon sin, for God will take a course with him that shall be much to his sorrow.

✦ RICHARD SIBBES
Divine Meditations and Holy
Contemplations, 35–36

All misery calleth sin mother.

✦ GEORGE SWINNOCK
in Horn, *Puritan Remembrancer*, 18

It may be, reader, when thou hear lascivious stories; or sinful, witty jestings; or tales of sly, subtle cheats; or the like, thou dost secretly applaud and approve them. I tell thee, thou art partaker of them. If thou hast a heart in the sin, thou hast a hand in the sin. Thy affecting it makes thee as really guilty as if thou didst act it. Nay, I must tell thee, the greatest guilt arises from the fullest consent of the will. It is possible for the approver to be more guilty than the actor.

✦ GEORGE SWINNOCK
The Christian Man's Calling,
in *Works*, 2:287

Sin, Satan, and war have all one name; evil is the best of them. The best of sin is deformity; of Satan, enmity; of war, misery.

✦ JOHN TRAPP
Commentary…upon…the
New Testament, 296

Sin turns all God's grace into wantonness. Sin is the dare of God's justice, the rape of His mercy, the jeer of His patience, the slight of His power, and the contempt of His love.

✦ RALPH VENNING
in Calamy et al., *Saints' Memorials*, 179

[Sin] goes about to ungod God.

✦ RALPH VENNING
Sinfulness of Sin, 30

[Sin] strives with and fights against God, and if its power were as great as its will is wicked, it would not suffer God to be.

✦ RALPH VENNING
Sinfulness of Sin, 36

Sin has the devil for its father, shame for its companion, and death for its wages.

✦ THOMAS WATSON
in Horn, *Puritan Remembrancer*, 86

I shall name some of the worst of these diseases. Pride is the tympany of the soul; lust is the fever; error, the gangrene; unbelief, the plague of the heart; hypocrisy, the scurvy; hardness of heart, the stone; anger, the frenzy; malice, the wolf in the breast; covetousness, the dropsy; spiritual sloth, the green sickness; apostasy, the epilepsy. Here are eleven soul diseases, and when they come to the full height, they are dangerous and most frequently prove mortal.

✦ THOMAS WATSON
The Beatitudes, in *Discourses*, 2:421

Sin is worse than hell. In hell there is the worm and the fire, but sin is worse. (1) Hell is of God's making, but sin is none of His making; it is a monster of the devil's creating. (2) The torments of hell are a burden only to the sinner, but sin is a burden to God: "I am pressed under you, as a cart is pressed that is full of sheaves" (Amos 2:13). (3) In hell torments there is something that is good. There is the execution of God's justice—there is justice in hell. But sin is the most unjust thing; it would rob God of His glory, Christ of His purchase, the soul of its happiness, so that it is worse than hell.

✦ THOMAS WATSON
Body of Practical Divinity, 590

Fear sin as hell. Sin is hell's fuel; sin, like Samson's foxes, carries devouring fire in the tail of it.

✦ THOMAS WATSON
"A Christian on the Mount,"
in *Discourses,* 1:230

Sin stops the mouth of prayer.

✦ THOMAS WATSON
Godly Man's Picture, 79

Sin clips the wings of prayer so that it will not fly to the throne of grace.

✦ THOMAS WATSON
Mischief of Sin, 58

There is more evil in a drop of sin than in a sea of affliction.

✦ THOMAS WATSON
Puritan Gems, 123

SIN, THE DANGER OF ONE

See that there be no allowed sin in your hearts or practice: "If I regard iniquity in my heart, the Lord will not hear"

my prayer nor help me (Ps. 66:18). An allowed sin is as the dead flesh in the wound; whatever methods or medicines be taken, there will be no healing till the dead flesh be eaten off. You may profess and pray and hear all your life long and yet will never prosper while you are privy to any one indulged sin.

✦ RICHARD ALLEINE
Companion for Prayer, 4

O, remember that as one hole in a ship may sink it, and as one stab at the heart will kill a man, and as one glass of poison will poison a man, and as one act of treason will make a man a traitor, so one sin lived in and allowed will damn a man forever. One wound strikes Goliath dead, as well as three-and-twenty did Caesar; one Delilah will do Samson as much mischief as all the Philistines; one wheel broken spoils all the whole clock; one vein's bleeding will let out all the vitals, as well as more; one bitter herb will spoil the pottage; by eating one apple, Adam lost Paradise; one lick of honey endangered Jonathan's life; one Achan was a trouble to all Israel; one Jonah was a lading too heavy for a whole ship. So one sin lived in and allowed is enough to make a man miserable forever.

✦ THOMAS BROOKS
Cabinet of Choice Jewels, 284

By allowing one sin, we disarm and deprive ourselves of having a conscientious argument to defend ourselves against any other. He that can go against his conscience in one cannot plead conscience against any other, for if the authority of God awes him from one, it will from all.

✦ WILLIAM GURNALL
Christian in Complete Armour, 608

On Saturday (May 8) [, 1641], at night, I saw union to God to be the greatest good, and my sin in not cleaving wholly to Him with all my heart the height of all sin from Hosea 10:1. Hence, in prayer I saw sin my greatest evil (1) because it had separated me from the greatest good; (2) because it kept my heart with a secret love to it from returning again to Him, as my greatest good; (3) nay, I saw that it made me make my death my life—namely, neglect of living and acting for God my very life, and my war with God my peace, and my damnation my salvation. Hence I mourned.

✦ THOMAS SHEPARD
Meditations and Spiritual Experiences, 62

1. One sin gives Satan as much advantage against thee as more. The fowler can hold the bird by one wing. Satan held Judas fast by one sin.

2. One sin lived in argues the heart is not sound. He who hides one rebel in his house is a traitor to the Crown; that person who indulges one sin is a traitorous hypocrite.

3. One sin will make way for more, as a little thief can open the door to more. Sin is linked and chained together. One sin will draw on more. David's adultery made way for murder. One sin never

goes alone; if here be but one nest egg, the devil can brood upon it....

8. One sin allowed will damn as well as more. One disease is enough to kill. If a fence be made never so strong, leave open but one gap; the wild beast may enter and tread down the corn. If there be but one sin allowed in the soul, you set open a gap for the devil to enter.

9. One sin harbored in the soul will unfit for suffering. How soon may an hour of trial come; he who has a hurt in his shoulder cannot carry a heavy burden, and he who hath any guilt in his conscience cannot carry the cross of Christ. Will he deny his life for Christ that cannot deny his lust for Christ? One sin in the soul unmortified will bring forth the bitter fruit of apostacy. Would you then show yourselves godly, give a bill of divorce to every sin. Grace and sin may be together, but grace and the love of sin cannot. Therefore, parley with sin no longer, but with the spear of mortification, let out the heart blood of every sin.

✦ THOMAS WATSON
Godly Man's Picture, 136–38

SIN, NATIONAL

What are those special seasons wherein the Christian is to practice this duty of extraordinary prayer?...

When sin abounds more than ordinary in the times we live in. Sinning times have ever been the saints' praying times. This sent Ezra with a heavy heart to confess the sin of his people and to bewail their abominations before the Lord (chap. 9). And Jeremiah tells the wicked of his degenerate age that his "soul shall weep in secret places for your pride" (Jer. 13:17). Indeed, sometimes sin comes to such a height that this is almost all the godly can do, to get into a corner and bewail the general pollutions of the age. "If the foundations be destroyed, what can the righteous do?" (Ps. 11:3). Such dismal days of national confusion our eyes have seen, when foundations of government were destroyed and all hurled into military confusion. When it is thus with a people, what can the righteous do? Yes, this they may and should do, "fast and pray."

✦ WILLIAM GURNALL
Christian in Complete Armour, 703, 705

Take a farther walk in thy meditations to view the public state of the nation. See what mercies are written with the golden pen of providence upon its forehead, and pay thy humble thanks; observe what prognostics of judgments there are, and get into the gap before the wrath begins. Did Abraham so plead for Sodom, though himself was far enough from the danger of the storm, and not thou for thy own nation, who art likely to be taken in it if it falls in thy days, if the cloud impending be not scattered by the prayers of the faithful?

✦ WILLIAM GURNALL
Christian in Complete Armour, 778

Where the minister hath not liberty to preach the truth, the people will not long have liberty to profess it; nor can that place expect long to enjoy its outward peace. When God removes His gospel, it is to make way for worse company, even all His sore plagues and judgments (Jer. 6:8).

✦ WILLIAM GURNALL
Christian in Complete Armour, 795

If the gospel go, God will go, the gospel being the sign and means of His special presence; and woe be unto us when God shall depart from us (Hos. 9:12). And if God depart with the gospel, farewell, peace and prosperity in England; nothing, I dare be confident, but temporal misery and ruin will be the consequence. If the eclipse bring such misery, what will the quite darkening of the sun do?

✦ THOMAS VINCENT
God's Terrible Voice in the City, 100

SIN, SMALLNESS OF

One sin never goes alone; Cain's anger is seconded with murder (Gen. 4:6, 8). Ahab's covetousness is attended with bloody cruelty, and Jeroboam's rebellion with idolatry (1 Kings 12); and Judas's thievery with treason. I might give instances of this in Adam and Eve and in Lot, Abraham, Noah, Jacob, Joseph, Job, David, Solomon, and Peter. But a touch on this string is enough; one sin commonly disposes the heart to another sin. A small sin many times draws the heart to a greater, and one great sin draws the heart to another great sin, and that to a greater, till at last the soul comes to be drowned in all excess.

✦ THOMAS BROOKS
Cabinet of Choice Jewels, 257

A little hole in a ship sinks it. A small breach in a sea bank carries away all before it. A little stab in the heart kills a man. And a little sin, without a great deal of mercy, will damn him.

✦ THOMAS BROOKS
Precious Remedies, 33

A humble soul knows that little sins (if I may so call any) cost Christ His blood, and that they make way for greater; and that little sins multiplied become great, as a little sum multiplied is great; that they cloud the face of God, wound conscience, grieve the Spirit, rejoice Satan, and make work for repentance. A humble soul knows that little sins (suppose them so) are very dangerous.

✦ THOMAS BROOKS
The Unsearchable Riches of Christ,
in *Select Works*, 1:15

Consider, little sins do usually make way and open a passage into the heart for the greatest and vilest sins. Thus, a little thief that creeps in at the window may unlock the door for others that stand without. And thus it fared with David: while sensual delight crept in by the eye at the sight of Bathsheba, it opened his heart to the temptation, and in rushed those two outrageous sins of adultery and murder. Believe it, there is no sin so small but it tends to the utmost wickedness that can possibly be committed: an irreverent thought of God tends to no less than blasphemy and atheism. A slight grudge at another tends to no less than murder. A lascivious thought tends to no less than impudent and common prostitution. And though at first they seem to play only singly about the heart, yet within a while they will mortally wound it.

✦ EZEKIEL HOPKINS
"The Great Evil and Danger of Little Sins," in *Select Works*, 337–38

A little poison in a cup and one leak in a ship may ruin all.

✦ THOMAS MANTON
Practical Exposition on the Epistle of James, 93–94

The smallness of sin is a poor excuse. It is an aggravation rather than an excuse. It is the more sad that we should stand with God for a trifle. Luke 16:21: He would not give a crumb, and this wonderfully displeased God; he did not receive a drop. God's judgments have been most remarkable when the occasion was least. Adam was cast out of Paradise for an apple; so gathering of sticks on the Sabbath day, looking into the ark, etc. God's command binds in lesser things as well as greater; though the object is different, the command is still the same.

✦ THOMAS MANTON
Practical Exposition on the Epistle of James, 94

SINCERITY

What are the signs of sincerity? First, if a man love the light of the word and come to it that his deeds may be made manifest (John 3:21). Secondly, if he be obedient in the absence as well as in the presence of lookers-on in secret as well—yea, and more—than in public (Matt. 6:6; Phil. 2:12). Not only when

God makes His presence manifest by His judgments, but even when He seems to be absent (Ps. 78:34). Thirdly, if he cleave fast unto God in adversity as well as in prosperity (Job 1:8–11). Fourthly, if he have a care of all God's commandments, even of those which seem to be least (Matt. 5:19). Fifthly, if he abstain from all appearance of evil (1 Thess. 5:22). Sixthly, if he neither cover nor excuse his sins, but confess them and forsake them (Prov. 28:13).

✦ WILLIAM AMES
Conscience, 3:55

A child of God obeys all the commands of God in respect of sincere desires, purposes, resolutions, and endeavors; and this God accepts in Christ for perfect and complete obedience. This is the glory of the covenant of grace: that God accepts and esteems sincere obedience as perfect obedience.

✦ THOMAS BROOKS
Cabinet of Choice Jewels, 140–41

Labor for sincerity. Endeavor to be that inwardly that thou make profession of outwardly, else there is no hope of continuance. For nothing that is counterfeit will last long. Counterfeit pearls may make a fair show for some time, but their luster will not last. And this is one main cause of the apostasy of many: they were never but hollow-hearted; they were never sound at the heart.

✦ THOMAS GATAKER
Christian Constancy, 15

Sincerity, it is the life of all our graces and puts life into all our duties; and as life makes beautiful and keeps the body sweet, so sincerity the soul and all it doth. A prayer breathed from a sincere heart, it is heaven's delight.

✦ WILLIAM GURNALL
Christian in Complete Armour, 240

There is a threefold strength sincerity brings with it which the false, hypocritical heart wants: (1) a preserving strength, (2) a recovering strength, (3) a comforting strength.

✦ WILLIAM GURNALL
Christian in Complete Armour, 278

Sincerity enables the Christian to do two things in this case which the hypocrite cannot—to speak good of God, and to expect good from God. And the soul cannot be uncomfortable, though head and heart ache together, which is able to do these.

✦ WILLIAM GURNALL
Christian in Complete Armour, 284

Nothing makes thee more like God in the simplicity and purity of His nature than sincerity.

✦ WILLIAM GURNALL
Christian in Complete Armour, 289

Who had not rather be sincere with mean gifts than rotten-hearted with great parts? We do not count him the best patriot that is the best orator and makes more rhetorical speeches than others, but he that takes the best side. It is not the rhetoric of the tongue but the hearty amen with which the sincere soul seals every holy request that God values, and this thy honest heart will help thee to do which his head cannot, that wants this sincerity. It is not the fairness of the hand that gives the force to the bond, but the person whose hand and seal it is. Gifts may make a fair appearance, but faith and sincerity make a valid prayer.

✦ WILLIAM GURNALL
Christian in Complete Armour, 636

"Manners make a man," saith the courtier. "Money makes a man," saith the citizen. "Learning makes a man," saith the scholar. "Conduct makes a man," saith the soldier. But "sincerity in religion makes a man," saith the divine.

✦ ROBERT HARRIS
in Clarke, *Aurea Legenda*, 75

Sincerity is a kind of perfection.

✦ THOMAS MANTON
*Practical Exposition on the
Epistle of James*, 88

It is this that commends both the doer and the duty to God. With sincerity, God accepts the least we do; without sincerity, God rejects the most we do, or can do. This is that temper of spirit which God highly delights in (Prov. 11:20). They that are of a froward heart are an abomination to the Lord, but such as are upright in their way are His delight. The apostle calls it in 2 Corinthians 1:12 "godly sincerity"— that is, such a sincerity as is God's special work upon the soul, setting the heart right and upright before Him in all His ways. This is the crown of all our graces and the commendation of all our duties; thousands perish and go to hell in the midst of all their performances and duties, merely for want of

sincerity of heart to God. Where there is not a change of state, a work of grace in the heart, there can be no sincerity toward God, for this is not an herb that grows in nature's garden.

✦ MATTHEW MEAD
Almost Christian Discovered, 168

Sincerity is the perfection of Christians. Let not Satan therefore abuse us. We do all things when we purpose and endeavor to do all things and are grieved when we cannot do better; then, in some measure, we do perform all things through Christ strengthening us.

✦ RICHARD SIBBES
*Divine Meditations and Holy
Contemplations*, 65

A sincere heart is a suspicious heart. The hypocrite suspects others and hath charitable thoughts of himself; the sincere Christian hath charitable thoughts of others and suspects himself. He calls himself often to account, "O my soul, hast thou any evidences for heaven? Are they not to seek when they should be to show? Is there no flaw in thy evidences? Thou mayest mistake common grace for saving. Weeds in the cornfields look like flowers. The foolish virgins' lamps looked as if they had oil in them. O, my soul, is it not so with thee?" The sincere soul, being ever jealous, plays the critic upon himself and doth so traverse things in the court of conscience, as if he were presently to be cited to God's bar. This is to be pure in heart.

✦ THOMAS WATSON
The Beatitudes, in *Discourses*, 2:245
(an error in pagination designates this 445)

Sincerity causes stability. When the apostle exhorts to stand fast in the evil day, among the rest of the Christian armor, he bids them put on the girdle of truth: "Stand therefore, having your loins girt about with truth" (Eph. 6:14). The girdle of truth is nothing else but sincerity.

✦ THOMAS WATSON
Great Gain of Godliness, 10

SLANDER

Slander is a water in great request; every guest of the devil is continually sipping of this vial. It robs man of his good name, which is above all riches. It is the part of vile men to vilify others and to climb up to unmerited praise by the stairs of another's disgrace.

✦ THOMAS ADAMS
"The Fatal Banquet," in *Sermons*, 40

Wherefore speak well of all men always, if it may be done with truth; and when it cannot, then be silent. Or else interrupt evil detraction with other meet and merry communication, as Samson at his marriage feast propounded a riddle to his friends, hereby to stop the mouths of backbiters and to occupy their wits another way. Bernard [says] excellently, "The talebearer hath the devil in his tongue; the receiver, in his ear." The thief does send one only to the devil, the adulterer two. But the slanderer hurts three: himself, the party to whom, and the party of whom he tells the tale.

✦ JOHN BOYS
Offices for Public Worship,
in *Works*, 70

He that willingly takes from my good name unwillingly adds to my reward.

✦ THOMAS BROOKS
in Horn, *Puritan Remembrancer*, 95

To divulge a report before we speak with the party and know the truth of it is unmercifulness and cannot acquit itself of sin. The same word in the Hebrew, to raise a slander, signifies to receive it (Ex. 23:1). The receiver is even as bad as the thief; it is well if none of us have, in this sense, received stolen goods. When others have stolen away the good names of their brethren, have not we received the stolen goods? There would not be so many to broach false rumors, but that they see this liquor pleases other men's taste.

✦ THOMAS WATSON
The Beatitudes, in *Discourses*, 2:200

SLEEP

Let your sleep be no more than nature and necessity require. And remember, as he that starts first is most like to win the race, so he that first offers his petition to Almighty God hath the more early title to a blessing.

Change not day into night, and night into day; be not addicted to idleness and sleep, for that is the way to turn your blessing to a dream.

Let not that imagination seize you that you may lie in bed, having no business immediately to do. For he that hath a soul and would save that soul hath enough to do to make his calling and election sure.

✦ JOSEPH CARYL
in Calamy et al., *Saints' Memorial*, 80

The abuse of lawful things is unlawful and hurtful. Moderate sleep is needful, the word of God allows it, the Lord Himself bestows it, the nature of man requires it; but to delight in it, to exceed in it, to fall into it too often or to continue in it too long—this is sinful, this is dangerous, this engenders corruptions in the heart, this doth breed annoyances to the body, and this doth work the ruin to the estate.

✦ ROBERT CLEAVER
AND JOHN DOD
Plain and Familiar Exposition, 127

A good Christian may go to bed without fear. You shall find many promises in Scripture about this blessing. "When thou liest down, thou shalt not be afraid: yea, thou shalt lie down, and thy sleep shall be sweet" (Prov. 3:24). Thou shalt take thy rest in safety, thou shalt lie down, and none shall make thee afraid ([see] Job 11:18). David says, "I laid me down and slept; I awaked; for the LORD sustained me" (Ps. 3:5). "I will both lay me down in peace, and sleep: for thou, LORD, only makest me dwell in safety" (Ps. 4:8). Every member of Jesus Christ is secure through faith in Him. The shepherd wakes when others are asleep to keep his sheep from the wolf. God is the Keeper of His flock; He is always vigilant to defend them. "Behold, he that keepeth Israel shall neither slumber nor sleep. The LORD is thy keeper" (Ps. 121:4–5).

✦ WILLIAM GEARING
Sacred Diary, 153

SLOTH

Sloth, indeed, does affect ease and quiet, but by affecting them does lose them; it hates labor and trouble, but by hating them does incur them. It is a self-destroying vice, not suffering those who cherish it to be idle but creating much work and multiplying pains unto them; engaging them into diverse necessities and straits which they cannot support with ease; and out of which, without extreme trouble, they cannot extricate themselves.

✦ ISAAC BARROW
"Of Industry in General," in
Sermons, 266

A slothful spirit is an impediment to a heavenly life, and I verily think there is nothing hinders it more than this in men of a good understanding. If it were only the exercise of the body, the moving of the lips, the bending of the knee, men would as commonly step to heaven as they go to visit a friend. But to separate our thoughts and affections from the world, to draw forth all our graces and increase each in its proper object, and to hold them to it till the work prospers in our hands—this, this is the difficulty.

✦ RICHARD BAXTER
The Saints' Everlasting Rest,
in *Baxteriana*, 25

Observe (and this is not peculiar to the weaver's trade, but common to it with any other) that there are two great causes of men's ruin: luxury is one, but slothfulness is the other. And it may admit a dispute which of these ruins most.

✦ JOHN COLLINGES
Weaver's Pocket-book, 113

The house of correction is the fittest hospital for those cripples whose legs are lame through their own laziness.

✦ THOMAS FULLER
Holy and Profane States, 184

Great opportunities for service neglected and great gifts not improved are oftentimes the occasion of plunging the soul into great depths. Gifts are given to trade withal for God; opportunities are the market days for that trade. To napkin up the one and let slip the other will end in trouble and disconsolation. Disquietments and perplexities of heart are worms that will certainly breed in the rust of unexercised gifts. God loses a revenue of glory and honor by such slothful souls, and He will make them sensible of it. I know some at this day whose omissions of opportunities for service are ready to sink them into the grave.

✦ JOHN OWEN
*A Practical Exposition of the
130th Psalm*, in *Oweniana*, 44

To expect that sustenance should drop from the clouds, without labor and care of our own, is an absurdity so obvious and flagrant that none are stupid enough to maintain it; yet their conduct is not much wiser who pretend to live upon providence while they live in sloth and do not exert themselves in some proper business for their own support. But let a person's

circumstances be what they will, the God of nature, who doth nothing in vain, by having given us capacities and powers for action, plainly intimates that it is our duty to employ them in a rational and useful manner.

✦ RICHARD STEELE
Religious Tradesman, 13

My brethren, a man that is slothful, there is no love in that man. Lazy love is pretended love, for where love is and according to the degrees of it, such will a man's labor be. You that find dullness in duties and the ways of God, you do not run the ways of God's commands; strengthen your love, and you will mend your pace—that is certain. Now pray, look to your whole lives and observe what your labor is laid out for.

✦ WILLIAM STRONG
Heavenly Treasure, 357

SODOM

It was in the destruction of Sodom God came with resolution to destroy that place (Gen. 19:12–13). Great provocations call for great desolation; dreadful judgments are the necessary consequents of great preceding iniquities. But Lot, he must be taken care of, and a shelter and refuge must be provided for him.

✦ THOMAS BLAKE
Living Truths in Dying Times, 36

Truly the sins of Sodom are at this day the sins of England, pride and fullness of bread. The Lord grant we have not the judgment of Sodom, fire and brimstone, ere long poured down upon us.

Let England, especially London, seriously remember the sad examples of fire.

✦ ARTHUR DENT
Plain Man's Plain Path-way, 7
(published one year before the
Great Fire of London, 1666)

Had I beheld Sodom in the beauty thereof, and had the angel told me that the same should be suddenly destroyed by a merciless element, I should certainly have concluded that Sodom should have been drowned, led thereunto by these considerations: (1) It was situated in the plain of Jordan, a flat, low, level country. (2) It was well watered everywhere, and where always there is water enough, there may sometimes be too much. (3) Jordan had a quality in the first month to overflow all his banks. (4) But no drop of moisture is spilt on Sodom; it is burnt to ashes. How wide are our conjectures when they guess at God's judgments! How far are His ways above our apprehension! Especially when wicked men with the Sodomites wander in strange sins, out of the road of common corruption, God meets them with strange punishments out of the reach of common conception, not coming within the compass of a rational suspicion.

✦ THOMAS FULLER
Good Thoughts, 134–35

Sodom sinned after a new mode, and God destroys them after a new way, sending hell from above upon them.

✦ WILLIAM GURNALL
Christian in Complete Armour, 126

SOLITUDE

Our solitudes and retirements…give us the most genuine trials whether we are spiritually minded or no. What we are in them, that we are and no more.

✦ JOHN OWEN
Golden Book, 242

Solitude is a release to the soul that was imprisoned in company.

✦ GEORGE SWINNOCK
The Christian Man's Calling,
in *Works*, 2:405

Secret meals are those that make the soul fat.

✦ JOHN TRAPP
in Horn, *Puritan Remembrancer*, 305

Some men are least alone when most alone. When Jacob was left alone, he wrestled with God.

✦ RALPH VENNING
Canaan's Flowings, 218

SORROW

Sorrow commonly comes on horseback but goes away on foot. It runs like Cushi to David with ill news (2 Sam. 18:32), so fast that it is out of breath; but when it is come, it tarries with us; it does not run back again.

✦ THOMAS ADAMS
Exposition upon…Second…Peter, 762

When sorrow is indisposing, it untunes the heart for prayer, meditation, and holy conference; it cloisters up the soul. This is not sorrow but rather sullenness, and doth render a man not so much penitential as sinful.

✦ SIMEON ASHE
Primitive Divinity, 87

Question: But when is a man's trouble or sorrow for sin sinful?

Answer: (1) When it keeps Christ and the soul asunder. (2) When it keeps the soul and the promise asunder. (3) When it unfits a man for the duties of his place and calling wherein the providence of God has placed him. (4) When it unfits a man for the duties of religion, either private or public. (5) When it takes off the sweet and comfort of all outward comforts and enjoyments and renders all our mercies like the white of an egg that has no taste or savor in it. (6) When it weakens, wastes, or destroys the outward man, for all godly sorrow is a friend to the soul and no enemy to the body.

✦ THOMAS BROOKS
Cabinet of Choice Jewels, 97

To be truly sensible of sin is to sorrow for displeasing of God, to be afflicted that He is displeased by us more than that He is displeased with us.

✦ JOHN BUNYAN
"Mr. John Bunyan's Dying Sayings,"
in *Complete Works*, 79

Question: What sign is there of this [godly] sorrow?

Answer: The true sign of it is this, when a man can be grieved for the very disobedience of God in his evil word or deed, though he should never be punished and though there were neither heaven nor hell.

✦ GILES FIRMIN
Real Christian, 303

Godly sorrow will constantly incite the mind unto all duties, acts, and fruits of repentance whatever; it is never barren nor heartless, but being both a grace and a duty, it will stir up the soul unto the exercise of all graces and the performance of all duties that are of the same kind. This the apostle declares fully (2 Cor. 7:11). This therefore is another thing which belongs unto that state of repentance which faith will bring the soul unto and whereby it will evidence itself.... And indeed, if this sorrow be constant and operative, there is no clearer evidence in us of saving faith. They are blessed who thus mourn. I had almost said it is worth all other evidences, as that without which they are none at all. Where this frame is not in some good measure, the soul can have no pregnant evidence of its good estate.

✦ JOHN OWEN
"Grounds of Faith," in
Oweniana, 90–91

THE SOUL

The soul is of a precious nature.... In man's composition there is a shadow of the Trinity, for to make up one man there is an elementary body, a divine soul, and a firmamental spirit. Here is the difference: in God there are three persons in one essence; in us three essences in one person. So in the soul there is a trinity of powers—vegetable, sensitive, rational. The former would only be; the second be, and be well; the third be, be well, and be forever well. O excellent nature in whose cabinet ten thousand forms may sit at once, which gives agitation to the body, without whom it would fall down a dead and inanimate lump of clay! This soul shall be required.

✦ THOMAS ADAMS
"The Cosmopolite," in *Sermons*, 171–72

The soul hath three places of being: in the body from the Lord, in the Lord from the body, in the body with the Lord. The two last are referred to our salvation in heaven, either in part, when the soul is glorified alone, or totally, when both are crowned together. Now, the soul must be even here in the Lord's keeping or else it is lost. If God let go His hold, it sinks. It came from God; it returns to God. It cannot be well one moment without God.

✦ THOMAS ADAMS
"The Soul's Refuge," in *Works*, 3:30

Consider the worth and excellency of souls. A soul is a spiritual, immortal substance. It is capable of the knowledge of God, it is capable of a union with God, of communion with God, and of a blessed and happy fruition of God. Christ left His Father's bosom for the good of souls. He assumed man's nature for the salvation of men's souls. Christ prayed for souls; He wept for them, bled for them, hung on the cross for them; He trod the winepress of His Father's wrath for them; He died; He rose again from death; He ascended; He intercedes for souls; and all the glorious preparations that He has been making in heaven these eighteen hundred years are for souls.

✦ THOMAS BROOKS
Apples of Gold, 132–33

While I was thus afflicted with the fears of my own damnation, there were two things would make me wonder: the one was when I saw old people hunting after the things of this life, as if they should live here always; the other was when I found professors much distressed and cast down when they met with outward losses, as of husband, wife, or child, etc. Lord, thought I, what is seeking after carnal things by some, and what grief in others for the loss of them! If they so much labor after and shed so many tears for the things of this present life, how am I to be bemoaned, pitied, and prayed for! My soul is dying, my soul is damning. Were my soul but in a good condition, and were I but sure of it, ah! how rich should I esteem myself, though blessed but with bread and water! I should count these but small afflictions and should bear them as little burdens. "A wounded spirit who can bear!"

✦ JOHN BUNYAN
Grace Abounding, 37–38

Hath God bestowed such excellent souls upon us? It is then an insufferable and horrible abuse of our excellent souls that we defile and debase them by sin, whereby we make one of the most beautiful and lovely creatures that ever came out of the hands of the Creator the most filthy and loathsome part of His whole creation. God gave us a noble soul, with His own image imprinted on it, and we by sin impress the character of the devil upon it. God gave us an immortal soul, and we, by abusing it to sin, do what we can to destroy it. How ill must God take it at our hands that we thus deface and spoil the masterpiece of His workmanship!

✦ JOHN CONANT
Sermon 1 on 2 Cor. 5:1,
in *Sermons*, 18–19

All this [i.e., the glorious creation that is the human body] is but the enameling of the case or polishing the casket wherein the rare jewel lies. Providence hath not only built the house but brought the inhabitant (I mean the soul) into the possession of it. A glorious piece it is, that bears the very image of God upon it, being all in all, and all in every part. How noble are its faculties and affections! How nimble, various, and indefatigable are its motions! How comprehensive is its capacity! It is a companion for angels—nay, capable of espousals to Christ and eternal communion with God. It is the wonder of earth and the envy of hell.

✦ JOHN FLAVEL
Divine Conduct, 41

The immortality of human souls puts it [i.e., the reality of the future state] beyond all doubt. The soul of man vastly differs from that of a beast, which is but a material form, and so wholly depending on that it must need perish with matter. But it is not so with us: ours are reasonable spirits that can live and act in a separated state from the body. "Who knoweth the spirit of man that goeth upward, and the spirit of the beast that goeth downward to the earth?" (Eccl. 3:21). For if a man dispute whether man be rational, this his very disputing it proves him to

be so. So our disputes, hopes, fears, and apprehensions of eternity prove our souls immortal and capable of that state.

✦ JOHN FLAVEL
Fountain of Life, 317

Love is that powerful and prevalent passion by which all the faculties and inclinations of the soul are determined and on which both its perfection and happiness depend. The worth and excellency of a soul is to be measured by the object of its love. He who loveth mean and sordid things doth thereby become base and vile, but a noble and well-placed affection doth advance and improve the spirit into a conformity with the perfections which it loves.

✦ HENRY SCOUGAL
Life of God in the Soul of Man, 40

A paraphrase upon 1 John 4:16: "Dwelleth in God, and God in him."

My God is all things unto me;
All God is also mine:
I am, O Lord, wholly in Thee,
And also wholly Thine.

God is all things unto me.

The powers of each created good
In God are all contain'd;
In Him my comforts all do bud,
Flourish and are maintain'd.

All God is mine.

He gave me all that He had made;
All which did not suffice
My larger soul; therefore I pray'd,
He gave Himself likewise.

I am wholly in God.

In midst of God I live and breathe,
In him alone I'm bright;
The rays with which I shine beneath
Are borrowed from His light.

I am wholly God's.

O Lord, I'm not at all mine own,
Nor for another free:
Let life be a reflection
Of beams received from Thee.

All things below thee, Lord, I judge
To be below my soul;
O let my nobler mind e'en grudge,
Itself in dust to roll.

Be more myself, O God, to me
Than I myself have been;
Make me, O God, more one with Thee
Than with myself! Amen.

✦ SAMUEL SHAW
"God and the Soul," in *Voice of
One Crying in the Wilderness,*
174–75 (italics original)

Thy sufferings are outward only, in thy
name, or estate, or body. Neither men
nor devils can hurt thy soul or make
a flaw in that diamond, but thy glory
shall be both outward and inward.
Thy body shall shine like the sun in its
noonday dress, but ten thousand suns
will be darkness to thy soul's attire.
Thy soul is the chiefest seat of grace,
and thy soul will be the choicest subject of glory.

✦ GEORGE SWINNOCK
The Christian Man's Calling,
in *Works,* 2:139

Thy soul, reader, is of unconceiv-
able value and excellency: (1) as it is
immediately created by God, without
any preexisting matter; (2) as it is of
an immaterial and spiritual nature;
(3) as it is capable of the image, and
life, and love, and fruition of God
Himself; (4) as it is immortal and of
eternal duration; though years and
ages and generations and time have an
end, the soul hath no end; (5) as it is
the bottom in which the body and its
everlasting good is embarked; (6) as
it is the standard and measure of all
our outward excellencies; as friends,
and health, and food, and life, and
riches, and honor, and ministers, and
ordinances are more or less worth as
they are more or less serviceable to the
soul. Now, grace and godliness is the
honor and elevation and excellency of
the soul.

✦ GEORGE SWINNOCK
The Christian Man's Calling,
in *Works,* 2:174

We must be merciful to the souls of
others; this is spiritual alms. Indeed
soul-mercy is the chief. The soul is
the most precious thing: it is a vessel
of honor; it is a bud of eternity; it is a
spark lighted by the breath of God. It is
a rich diamond set in a ring of clay. The
soul hath the blood of God to redeem
it, the image of God to beautify it. It
being therefore of so high a descent,
sprung from the Ancient of Days, that
mercy which is shown to the soul must
needs be the greatest.

✦ THOMAS WATSON
The Beatitudes, in *Discourses,* 2:193

Consider how unworthy it is for a Christian to have his heart set upon the world. It is unworthy of his soul. The soul is dignified with honor; it is a noble coin that hath a divine impress stamped upon it; it is capable of communion with God and angels. Now it is too far below a man to spend the affections and operations of this heaven-born soul upon drossy things. It is as if one should embroider sackcloth with gold or set a diamond in clay.

✦ THOMAS WATSON
"A Christian on Earth Still in Heaven," in *Discourses*, 1:287

The soul is a divine spark kindled by the breath of God.... It is a bright mirror in which some refracted beams of God's wisdom and holiness do shine forth; the soul is a blossom of eternity.

✦ THOMAS WATSON
"The One Thing Necessary," in *Discourses*, 1:371

The soul is the richest piece of embroidery ever made by the hands of God: the understanding bespangled with light; the will invested with liberty; the affections, like a harp, tuned by the Holy Ghost.

✦ THOMAS WATSON
Puritan Gems, 124

SOVEREIGNTY OF GOD

In prosperity we forget our mortality. Adversity causeth us to know not only that we are but men, but frail men; that God hath us between His hands (as it is, Ezek. 21:17) and can as easily crush us as we do moths; that we are in God's hands as the clay in the hands of the potter; that He hath an absolute sovereignty over us; and that we depend upon Him for our being, well-being, and eternal being. These things we know feelingly and practically in the day of affliction. And it much concerns us to know these things and to know them powerfully, for this will make us stand in awe of God and study to serve and please Him. He that depends upon a man for his livelihood, knowing that he hath him at an advantage and can easily undo him, will certainly endeavor to comply with him and to obtain his favor. The ground of all service and obedience is dependence. And did we really and experimentally know our dependence upon God and the advantages He hath us at, we could not—we would not—but comply with Him and labor above all things to gain His love and favor.

✦ EDMUND CALAMY
Godly Man's Ark, 7

I shall treat...of God's sovereignty.... The sum...lies in this proposition—namely, that the great God, blessed forever, hath an absolute power and right of dominion over His creatures, to dispose and determine of them as seemeth Him good. That there is such a power and that this power belongs to God, no other reason needs be assigned but that "He is God, and there is none besides Him." There can be no more because (1) there can be but one infinite, for such a being fills heaven and earth, and so no place or room for another; (2) there can be but one omnipotent, for He that is such hath all others under His feet; besides, where one can do all, more would be impertinent; (3) there can be but one supreme; supreme power may reside in many (as in mixed monarchies and commonwealths), but as lawmakers and supreme, they are but one; (4) there can be but one first cause from which all beings else derive their original, and that is this blessed One we are speaking of, of whom and for whom are all things (1 Cor. 8:6). And if He be the author of all, He needs must have a sovereign right and power to determine all, both as to their being, order, efficacy, and end.

✦ ELISHA COLES
Practical Discourse, 21–22

Having founded this discourse on the sovereignty of God as the best and most natural ground of satisfaction or captivation to reason touching election, now as a means to qualify our spirits and reconcile them with the doctrine of sovereignty, it seemeth expedient to annex that of His righteousness; and I think there is not a more rational proposition or more obliging to submission than that there is no unrighteousness with God. This is the natural adjunct of divine sovereignty, which, as we are indispensably bound to believe, so to be well grounded in the faith of it, will be of exceeding great usefulness to us in every condition, especially under those darker administrations of which we do not see at present the cause, reason, or tendency; when matters of great importance seem to be confused

or neglected; when all things in view fall out alike to all, and you cannot know either good or evil by all that is before you.

✦ ELISHA COLES
Practical Discourse, 44

Now [Satan] is a prince elect by the unanimous choice of corrupt nature; "Ye are of your father the devil," saith Christ, "and his lusts ye will do." But this also hath a flaw in it, for man by law of creation is God's subject and cannot give away God's right. By sin he loses his right in God as a protector, but God loses not His right as a sovereign. Sin disabled man to keep God's law, but it doth not enfranchise or discharge him that he need not keep it.

✦ WILLIAM GURNALL
Christian in Complete Armour, 91

SPEECH

Provide matter of holy discourse of purpose beforehand. As you will not travel without money in your purses to defray your charges, so you should not go into company without a provision of such matter as may be profitable for the company that you may be cast upon.

✦ RICHARD BAXTER
Baxteriana, 251

Keep thy speech as clean from all obscenity as thou wouldst thy meat from poison, and let thy talk be gracious, that he who hears thee may grow better by thee. And be ever more earnest when thou speakest of religion than when thou talkest of worldly matters. If thou perceivest that thou hast erred, persevere not in thine error; rejoice to find the truth and magnify it. Study, therefore, three things especially—to understand well, to say well, and to do well.

✦ LEWIS BAYLY
Practice of Piety, 124

We know metals by their tinkling and men by their talking.

✦ THOMAS BROOKS
in Horn, *Puritan Remembrancer*, 321

[Philip Henry] had observed concerning himself that he was sometimes the worse for eating, but never for abstinence; sometimes the worse for wearing too few clothes, but never for wearing too many; sometimes the worse for speaking, but never for keeping silence.

✦ JOHN DOD AND PHILIP HENRY
Gleanings of Heavenly Wisdom, 47

Idle words—that is, useless chat, unprofitable talk that is not referred any way to the glory of God. This is a common evil and little regarded by most men, but yet a sin of severer aggravations than the most imagine: light words weigh heavy in God's balance.

✦ JOHN FLAVEL
"The Art of Preserving the Fruit of the Lips," in *Navigation Spiritualized*, 163

The persons to whom you speak are to be considered, for you must not speak everything to everybody. To some it were a folly to do it; to some it were dangerous to do it: it were like

Hezekiah's opening his treasures to his enemy, which was little better in effect than the betraying of his kingdom. Observe the condition and quality of the person, and accordingly learn to speak or to be silent.

✦ WILLIAM GEARING
Sacred Diary, 131

Good words cost nothing but a little self-denial, yet they purchase great things. Gentleness will do what violence will not do.

✦ MATTHEW HENRY
Gems, 74

God's graces, which we are to show forth in our communication, are these: wisdom, truth, reverence, modesty, meekness, sobriety in judgment, urbanity, fidelity, care of others' good name.... Wisdom in our speech is a goodly ornament.

✦ WILLIAM PERKINS
Direction for the Government of the Tongue, 6

Sobriety in judgment is when a man either suspends his opinion of his neighbor's sayings or doings; or else speaks as charitably as he can by saying as little as may be, if the thing be evil; or by interpreting all in better part if the speech or action be doubtful. Therefore, do thus: despise not thy neighbor, but think thyself as bad a sinner and that the like defeats may befall thee. If thou cannot excuse his doing, excuse his intent, which may be good; or if the deed be evil, think it was done of ignorance. If thou can in no way excuse him, think some great temptation befell him and that thou should be worse if the like temptation befell thee, and give God thanks that the like as yet hath not befallen thee. Despise not a man being a sinner, for though he be evil today, he may turn tomorrow.

✦ WILLIAM PERKINS
Direction for the Government of the Tongue, 16

Urbanity is a grace of speech whereby men in seemly manner use pleasantness in talk for recreation or for such delights as is joined with profit to themselves and others.... Now this mirth must be joined with the fear of God.

✦ WILLIAM PERKINS
Direction for the Government of the Tongue, 17

SPIRITUAL GROWTH
(see *MEANS OF GRACE*)

SPIRITUAL MATURITY

An old disciple, an old Christian, is rich in spiritual experiences. Oh, the experiences that he hath of the ways of God, of the workings of God, of the work of God, of the love of God! Oh, the divine stories that old Christians can tell of the power, sweetness, and usefulness of the word, as a light to lead the soul, as a staff to support it, as a spirit to quicken it, as an anchor to stay it, and as a cordial to comfort and strengthen it! Oh, the stories that he can tell you concerning the love of Christ, the blood of Christ, the offices of Christ, the merits of Christ, the righteousness of Christ, and the graces of Christ, and the influences of Christ! Oh, the stories that an old disciple can tell you of the indwellings of the Spirit, of the operations of the Spirit, of the leadings of the Spirit, of the witnessings of the Spirit, and of the comforts and joys of the Spirit! Oh, the stories that an old Christian can tell you of the evil, bitterness, deceitfulness, prevalency of sin, and the happiness of the conquest over it! Oh, the stories that he can tell you of the snares, devices, temptations, rage, watchfulness of Satan, and the ways of triumphing over him!

✦ THOMAS BROOKS
Apples of Gold, 66–67

SPIRITUAL WARFARE

Israel going into Egypt had no opposition, but traveling into Canaan, they were never free.

✦ THOMAS BROOKS
Mute Christian, 180

A humble soul being once in a great conflict with Satan said thus to him: "Satan, reason not with me—I am but weak. If thou hast anything to say, say it to Christ; He is my advocate, my strength, and my Redeemer, and He shall plead for me." A humble soul is good at turning Satan over to the Lord Jesus, and this increases Satan's hell.

✦ THOMAS BROOKS
The Unsearchable Riches of Christ, in Select Works, 1:39

When the sword is in the scabbard, the traveler is easily surprised; and when the guard is asleep, the city is quickly conquered. The strongest creature, the lion, and the wisest creature, the serpent, if they be dormant, are as easily surprised as the weakest worms. So the strongest and wisest saints, if their graces be asleep, if they be only in the habit and not in the exercise, may be as easily surprised and vanquished as the weakest Christians in all the world, as you may see in David, Solomon, Samson, Peter. Every enemy insults over him that has lost the use of his weapons.

✦ THOMAS BROOKS
The Unsearchable Riches of Christ,
in *Select Works,* 1:168

This is ground of consolation to the weak Christian who disputes against the truth of His grace from the inward conflicts and fightings he hath with his lusts and is ready to say, like Gideon, in regard of outward enemies, "If God be with me, why is all this befallen me? Why do I find such strugglings in me, provoking me to sin, pulling me back from that which is good?" Why dost ask? The answer is soon given: because thou art a wrestler, not a conqueror. You mistake the state of a Christian in this life. When one is made a Christian, he is not presently called to triumph over his slain enemies but carried into the field to meet and fight them. The state of grace is the commencing of a war against sin, not the ending of it.

✦ WILLIAM GURNALL
Christian in Complete Armour, 83

[The helmet of salvation] makes the fifth in the apostle's order, and what is observable: this and most of the

pieces…are defensive arms, and all to defend the Christian from sin—none to secure him from suffering. First, they are mostly defensive arms. Indeed, there is but one of all the pieces in the whole panoply for offense: that is the sword. It may be to give us this hint, that this spiritual war of the Christian lies chiefly on the defense and therefore requires arms most of this kind to wage it. God hath deposited a rich treasure of grace in every saint's heart. The devil's greatest spite is against this; to plunder him of which and with it of his happiness, he commences a bloody war against him. So that the Christian overcomes his enemy when himself is not overcome by him, his work being rather to keep what is his own than to get what is his enemy's.

✦ WILLIAM GURNALL
Christian in Complete Armour, 511

All the pieces [of the armor of God] are to defend the Christian from sin—none to secure him from suffering. They are to defend him in suffering, not privilege him from it. He must prepare the more for suffering because he is so well furnished with armor to bear it. Armor is not given for men to wear by the fireside, but in the field. How shall the maker be praised if the metal of his arms be not known? And where shall it be put to the proof, but amidst swords and bullets? He that desires to live all his days in a state of ease and security will never make a good Christian. Resolve for hardship or lay down thy arms.

✦ WILLIAM GURNALL
Christian in Complete Armour, 512

The Christian's armor will rust, except it be furbished with the oil of prayer. What the key is to the watch, prayer is to our graces; it winds them up and sets them going.

◆ WILLIAM GURNALL
Christian in Complete Armour, 624

The... question is whether lusts war in the heart of a godly man.... I answer yes. The life of a Christian is a wrestling, conflicting estate; there is a double nature in the best, flesh and spirit (Gal. 5:17). We carry an enemy in our bosoms; the Canaanite is not wholly cast out. It was a good prayer of him that said, "Lord, deliver me from one evil man, and it shall suffice," meaning himself. Flesh and spirit, like the twins in Rebekah's womb, war and struggle; yea, lusts stir and rage more in a godly heart to sense and feeling than in a wicked. "When a strong man armed keepeth his palace, his goods are in peace" (Luke 11:21). There is no stir; wind and tide go together. Conviction may sometimes awaken drowsy lusts; otherwise, all is still and quiet. But usually there is more trouble with sin after conversion, especially presently upon conversion.

◆ THOMAS MANTON
Practical Exposition on the
Epistle of James, 147

It is not so easy a matter to pray as men think. In regard of the unspiritualness of our nature compared with the duty itself in which we draw near to a holy God, we cannot endure to be separated from our lusts; and there is great rebellion in our hearts against everything that is good; and Satan also is our special enemy.... When we go to God by prayer, the devil knows we go to fetch strength against him, and therefore he opposes us all he can. But though some may mumble over a few prayers, yet (indeed) no man can pray as he ought, or in faith, that is not within the covenant of grace, nor without the Holy Ghost.

◆ RICHARD SIBBES
Divine Meditations and Holy
Contemplations, 59

As we must be sober in tempering our hearts and affections, so we must be watchful, which is a duty required of us as Christians, but indispensably necessary as we are Christian soldiers engaged "*in bello semper, et si non in pralio*," as Livy speaks—always in a war, though not always in battle. A Christian hath no peace but in his conscience and the grave.

◆ WILLIAM SPURSTOWE
Wiles of Satan, 91

The spiritual warfare is the daily exercise of our spiritual strength and armor against all adversaries with assured confidence of victory. For the state of the faithful in this life is such that they are sure in Christ and yet fight against sin, there being joined with repentance a continual fighting and struggling against the assaults of a man's own flesh, against the motions of the devil, and enticements of the world. We shall only overcome these enemies by a lively faith in Christ Jesus, and our principal strength is the powerful assistance of God in Christ (2 Cor. 12:9; Phil. 4:13), who hath loved us, whereby we become more than conquerors (Rom. 8:37).

✦ JAMES USSHER
Body of Divinity, 397

Pray to God to bless you in your work. "The race is not to the swift, nor the battle to the strong" (Eccl. 9:11); nothing prospers without a blessing. And what way to obtain it but by prayer? It is a saying of one of the ancients, "The saints carry the keys of heaven at their girdle." Prayer beats the weapon out of the enemy's hand and gets the blessing out of God's hand.

✦ THOMAS WATSON
"The One Thing Necessary,"
in *Discourses*, 1:382

STEWARDSHIP

A prosperous condition hath in it a greater reckoning; every man must be responsible for his talents. Thou that hast great possessions in the world, dost thou trade thy estate for God's glory? Art thou rich in good works? Grace makes a private person a common good. Dost thou disburse thy money for public uses? It is lawful—in this sense—to put out our money to use. Oh, let us all remember, an estate is a depositum! We are but stewards, and our Lord and Master will ere long say, "Give an account of your stewardship." The greater our estate, the greater our charge; the more our revenues, the more our reckonings.

✦ SIMEON ASHE
Primitive Divinity, 139–40

First or last God will call for an account how His goods have been improved. He has given you a stock to trade up on for Him: light, grace, parts, capacities, gospel privileges and opportunities, liberty, peace, experiences, with many mercies and afflictions, which are all your Lord's goods and must be accounted for, upon the passing of which depends your eternal state or much of your soul's peace. The Lord Jesus has a double audit, or accounting, with His servants: in this life in the court of conscience and in the judgment day at the bar of God.

✦ BARTHOLOMEW ASHWOOD
Heavenly Trade, 67

Whenever you have several ways before you for the laying out of your money or your time, let the question be seriously put to your heart: Which of these ways shall I wish at death and judgment that I had expended it? And let that be chosen as the way.

✦ RICHARD BAXTER
Baxteriana, 258

God doth not expect much where little is bestowed nor accept little where much is received. "Hear this word that the LORD hath spoken against you, O children of Israel.... You only have I known of all the families of the earth" (Amos 3:1–2). God hath exalted you above all others, and therefore you must do more for God than others. It was a great blemish in Hezekiah that his returnings were not answerable to his receivings. O believers, let me beseech you to do much, to love much, to give much, to pray much, seeing you have received much.

✦ WILLIAM DYER
Christ's Famous Titles, 84

It were hard that God should be denied what Himself gave. "I came to my own," saith Christ, "and they would not receive Me; thus here, I came to My own creature, he had his life from Me, and brings a dead heart unto Me." Suppose a friend should give you notice that he will ere long be at your house and send you in beforehand a vessel of rich wine. Would you be unwilling to broach it for his entertainment?

✦ WILLIAM GURNALL
Christian in Complete Armour, 749

It is no small commendation to manage a little well. He is a good wagoner that can turn in a narrow room. To live well in abundance is the praise of the estate, not of the person. I will study more how to give a good account of my little than how to make it more.

✦ JOSEPH HALL
Meditations and Vows, 124

He that lays up his gold may be a good jailer, but he that puts it out is a good steward.

✦ FRANCIS RAWORTH
in Horn, *Puritan Remembrancer*, 111

Certainly there is some atheistical right of property that in some degree or other is apt to steal into the most devout minds. And sure I am, we do not only barely offend but we do ourselves much hurt; we wound our own peace.... We both lessen our creature comforts, and multiply our griefs, and aggravate our sorrows by calling things our own. If we had not taken them to be our own, it would not have troubled us to part with them.

✦ SAMUEL SHAW
A Welcome to the Plague, in Vint,
Suffering Christian's Companion, 305–6

A man may know that he loves the world if he be more careful to get than to use it. We are but stewards, and everyone should consider, "I must be as careful in distributing as in getting riches." For when a person is all in getting and nothing in distributing, this man is a worldling; though moderate in getting wealth without wrong to any man, the world hath gotten his heart. He makes not that use of it [as] he should.

✦ RICHARD SIBBES
Divine Meditations and Holy
Contemplations, 19

The Holy Ghost, when He speaks of all things of this life, saith, "If thou be not faithful in that which is another man's" (Luke 16:11). I warrant there is never a rich man here but thinks your estates are your own. A Nabal may say indeed, "Shall I take my meat and my drink?" And everything is my and my. But the Spirit of God is quite contrary; He saith, "Thou art the steward of it for the present, but 'tis another Man's." And therefore when He speaks of giving to the poor, He saith, "Withhold not from Him to whom it is due." You do not think it is due; it is at your own liberty. Now here is the deceit: men take that to be their own good which is another man's.

✦ WILLIAM STRONG
Heavenly Treasure, 97

Natural men are earthly in the use of heavenly things, but spiritual men are heavenly in the use of earthly things.

✦ RALPH VENNING
Canaan's Flowings, 133

While others fret at the prosperity of the wicked and are envious at the foolish because they abound in goods, my prayer for them shall be this: much good may they do with it, and much good may it do them. The first is the duty, the next is the blessing; if the duty be not done, the blessing will not come. If they do not do good, 'twill do them no good. For not what one has but what one does with what one has makes happy or miserable.

✦ RALPH VENNING
Canaan's Flowings, 170–71

STUBBORNNESS

Though obstinate persons be excluded from good counsel, yet they are not to be exempted from due punishment.

✦ ROBERT CLEAVER
AND JOHN DOD
Plain and Familiar Exposition, 92

SUBMISSION

God's end in all His cross providences is to bring the heart to submit and be content, and, indeed, this pleases God much. He loves to see His children satisfied with what portion He doth carve and allot them.

✦ SIMEON ASHE
Primitive Divinity, 108

There is nothing got by struggling against the will of God, nor anything lost by a quiet submission to it.

✦ RICHARD BAXTER
A Christian Directory, in
Practical Works, 2:408

A lion in God's cause must be a lamb in his own.

✦ MATTHEW HENRY
Gems, 121

Subjection to the will of God is not only a test of our present duty but it is also an evidence of our future glory. To expect to see God in heaven and not to seek Him on earth is as foolish as if a husbandman should throw his plough into the hedge and then look for a rich harvest.

✦ WILLIAM SECKER
Nonsuch Professor, 176

The less any man strives for himself, the more is God his champion.

✦ JOHN TRAPP
in Horn, *Puritan Remembrancer*, 335

Whatever God gives to us He gives freely, and whatever He takes from us He takes justly. Therefore, where God is free to give, let us be just to use; and where God is just to take, let us be free to resign.

✦ RALPH VENNING
Canaan's Flowings, 225–26

SUFFERING

The thought of the many distressing troubles which God's people are exposed unto in this world may serve to abate in our hearts the immoderate desire of long life on earth. Mistake me not, for I know that long life is a desirable blessing. Yet should we all labor to sit loose, both in regard of the means of bodily livelihood and life itself.

◆ SIMEON ASHE
Best Refuge, 12

Like as the armed knight,
Appointed to the field,
With this world will I fight,
And Christ shall be my shield.

"Faith, in the fathers old"
Obtained righteousness;
Which makes me very bold
To fear no world's distress.

"I now rejoice in heart,"
And hope bids me do so;
For Christ will take my part,
And ease me of my woe.

"More enemies now I have"
Than hairs upon my head;
Let them not me deprave,
But fight Thou in my stead.

"On Thee my care I cast,"
For all their cruel spite;
I set not by their haste,
For Thou art my delight.

◆ ANNE ASKEW
in Sharp, *Anne Askew,
Martyr AD 1545*, 11

A man must not run into a suffering without a call, and he must not rush out of it without a call. And therefore you shall find Christ and the apostles, and all the martyrs, that thus they acted. They would hide, and go aside, and avoid their sufferings; but when they were in hold they would not go out though the doors were open. So that that is the next thing: be sure of this, that you do not run into sufferings without a call nor rush out of sufferings without the same call from God.

◆ WILLIAM BRIDGE
Seasonable Truths in Evil Times,
in *Works*, 3:315

These...temporal infirmities which God's people here are subject to, and that more than others, their sufferings in their estates, good names, liberties, by crosses and losses, reproaches, restraints, etc. Here also is the strength of God perfected in their weakness in supporting and delivering them, bearing up their spirits under them and giving them comfortable issue out of them.

◆ JOHN BRINSLEY
Aqua Coelestis, 160

[Christ] shares with you in all sufferings and persecutions, as well as in all your afflictions. "Saul, Saul, why persecutest thou Me?" There is such a near union between the Lord Jesus Christ and the weakest saints that a man cannot strike a saint but he must strike through the very heart of Christ. Their sufferings are held His (Col. 1:24); and their afflictions are His afflictions; and their reproaches are His reproaches (Heb. 13:13); and their provocations are His provocations (Neh. 4:4–5). God is provoked more than Nehemiah.

♦ THOMAS BROOKS
The Unsearchable Riches of Christ,
in *Select Works*, 1:88

That saying (2 Cor. 1:9) was of great use to me: "But we had the sentence of death in ourselves, that we might not trust in ourselves, but in God which raiseth the dead." By this scripture I was made to see that if ever I would suffer rightly, I must first pass a sentence of death upon everything that can properly be called a thing of this life, even to reckon myself, my wife, my children, my health, my enjoyments, and all as dead to me, and myself as dead to them. The second was to live upon God that is invisible, as Paul said in another place; the way not to faint is "to look not on the things that are seen, but at the things that are not seen; for the things that are seen are temporal, but the things that are not seen are eternal." And thus, I reasoned with myself, if I provide only for a prison, then the whip comes at unawares and so doth also the pillory. Again, if I only provide for these, then I am not fit for banishment. Further, if I conclude that banishment is the worst, then if death comes I am surprised. So that I see the best way to go through sufferings is to trust in God through Christ.

♦ JOHN BUNYAN
Grace Abounding, 122–23

It is not every suffering that makes a martyr, but suffering for the word of God after a right manner: that is, not only for righteousness, but for righteousness' sake; not only for truth, but out of love to truth; not only for God's word, but according to it; to wit, in that holy, humble, meek manner as the word of God requires. It is a rare thing to suffer aright and to have thy spirit in suffering bent only against God's enemy, sin: sin in doctrine, sin in worship, sin in life, and sin in conversation.

♦ JOHN BUNYAN
"Mr. John Bunyan's Dying Sayings,"
in *Complete Works*, 80

In a word, suffering time is the time wherein God makes His attributes visible—"The Lord will be a refuge to His people, a refuge in time of trouble." And what follows? "And they that know Thy name will put their trust in Thee." In the school of affliction God reads lectures upon His attributes and expounds Himself unto His people so that many times they come to know more of God or more experimentally by half a year's sufferings than by many years' sermons.

♦ THOMAS CASE
Correction, Instruction, 53

They that are taught of God in affliction can speak experimentally, in one degree or other, of the gains and privileges of a suffering condition. They can speak experimentally of communion with God: "Though I walk through the valley of the shadow of death, I will fear no evil." Why? "For Thou art with me." I have had comfortable experience of Thy upholding, counseling, comforting presence with me in my deepest desertions; so of other fruits of affliction, this I have got by my sufferings. I bless God,

I have learned more patience, humility, and self-denial; to be more sensible of my brethrens' sufferings; to sit looser to the world, to mind duty, and to trust safety with God; to prepare for death and to provide for eternity.

◆ THOMAS CASE
Correction, Instruction, 72–73

The baptism of affliction wherewith you are baptized is Christ's. Count not, call not that yours which is His. Surely He rather suffers in you than you for Him. Or if you will say you suffer for Him, yet know He sympathizes with you in that suffering. Surely this sympathy is sweet. Have you ever a friend that while you fast, refuses to eat; that while you are in the field, neglects his bed; that while you watch, will not sleep; that weeps with you, sighs for you. Tell me, what is this friend's name? What call you this carriage? Christ is this friend; this is His carriage. Sweet is His name, and sweetness is with Him. Is it not apparent in this carriage? The carriage of Christ is sweet unto His suffering members, in that He orders all their sufferings for quality, quantity, and duration. Persecuted saints! Christ is the supervisor of all your sufferings.

◆ JOHN DURANT
Sips of Sweetness, 164–65

Four things are to be wisely heeded by all such as expect Christ's sweetness in their sufferings. If you therefore look to experience the truth of this doctrine in your own souls, mind them. You must look in all your sufferings that

(1) your cause be good, (2) your call be clear, (3) your carriage meek, and (4) your end be right.

◆ JOHN DURANT
Sips of Sweetness, 194

Those people can never be ruined who thrive by their losses; conquer by being conquered; multiply by being diminished.

◆ JOHN FLAVEL
Fountain of Life, 265

When a child, I loved to look on the pictures in the [Foxe's] *Book of Martyrs.* I thought that there the martyrs at the stake seemed like the three children in the fiery furnace, ever since I had known them there, not one hair more of their head was burnt nor any smell of the fire singeing of their clothes. This made me think martyrdom was nothing. But oh, though the lion be painted fiercer than he is, the fire is far fiercer than it is painted. Thus, it is easy for one to endure an affliction, as he limns it out in his own fancy and represents it to himself but in a bare speculation. But when it is brought indeed and laid home to us, there must be the man — yea, there must be God to assist the man to undergo it.

◆ THOMAS FULLER
Good Thoughts, 92

This readiness to suffer…enables the Christian for service. It is a sure truth, so far and no more is the Christian fit to live serviceably than he is prepared to suffer readily because there is no duty but hath the cross attending on it, and he that is offended at the cross will not be long pleased with the service that it brings. Prayer is the daily exercise of a saint; this he cannot do as he should, except he can heartily say, "Thy will be done." And who can do that in truth unless ready to suffer? Praising God is a standing duty; yea, in everything we must give thanks (1 Thessalonians 5). But what if affliction befall us? How shall we tune our hearts to that note if not ready to suffer?

✦ WILLIAM GURNALL
Christian in Complete Armour, 408

The Christian is not to pray for an immunity from all temporal sufferings. There is no foundation for such a prayer in the promise, and what God thinks not fit to promise, we must not be bold to ask. God had one Son without sin, but none in this life without suffering.

✦ WILLIAM GURNALL
Christian in Complete Armour, 725

We are not prepared for our Canaan but by this condition. By war the soldier is fitted for peace; by a storm the traveler is fitted for home; by toil the laborer is fitted for his bed. Yea, we are the better prepared by greater sufferings for a richer heaven, and it will be the sweeter to us when we arrive there: "For our light affliction, which is but for a moment, worketh for us a far more exceeding and eternal weight of glory" (2 Cor. 4:17).

✦ THOMAS JOLLIE
"Heavenly-Mindedness," in Slate,
Select Nonconformists' Remains, 224

A man is not only unknown to others but to himself that hath never met with such difficulties as require faith and Christian fortitude and patience to surmount them. How shall a man know whether his meekness and calmness of spirit be real or not while he meets with no provocation, nothing that contradicts or crosses him?

✦ ROBERT LEIGHTON
A Commentary upon the First Epistle of Peter, in *Whole Works,* 1:54

The integrity of your suffering depends much upon your joy in suffering. Murmuring suffering is sinning; you will suffer for this again. As God calls for the heart in doing, so in suffering. I cannot stand on this, let me conclude all thus—the more backward you are to suffer, the more you will suffer; the more forward, the less. Joy to suffer long for Christ will shorten long suffering.

✦ NICHOLAS LOCKYER
Balm for England, 116

To suffer as a Christian is to suffer for Christ: for the name of Christ, for the truths of Christ, for the ways of Christ, for the worship of Christ.

✦ JOHN OWEN
Discourse 12 on Phil. 3:10, in
Twenty-Five Discourses, 159

Many have the knowledge of Christ in a way of speculation, but we must have the savor of His sweet ointments upon our heart that we may follow Him into suffering. We had need feel the sweetness of His blood in the calms of conscience, that we may shed our own blood for Him. Let us not content ourselves to have Christ only in our Bibles but endeavor to have a proof of Him in our hearts: a proof of His sweet-smelling sacrifice in our inward peace; a proof of His rich anointings in our supplies of grace. The experience of Christ in us is a strong encouragement to suffer for Him. He that hath a Christ only in notion will fall off from Him, but he that hath a tried Christ will hardly leave Him.

◆ EDWARD POLHILL
Armatura Dei, 74

Our sufferings are washed in Christ's blood, as well as our souls, for Christ's merits brought a blessing to the crosses of the sons of God. We are over the water some way already; we are married, and our marriage portion is paid; we are already more than conquerors, "as dying, and behold we live." I never before heard of a living death or a quick death, but ours. Our death is not like the common death; Christ's skill, His handiwork, and a new cast of Christ's admirable act may be seen in our quick death. I bless the Lord that all our troubles come through Christ's fingers, and that He casteth sugar among them, and casteth in some ounce-weights of heaven, and of the spirit of glory that resteth on suffering believers into one cup, in which there is no taste of hell.

◆ SAMUEL RUTHERFORD
Garden of Spices, 84

Losses and crosses are the wheels of Christ's triumphing chariot.

◆ SAMUEL RUTHERFORD
Garden of Spices, 156

God's children usually in their troubles overcome by suffering. Here lambs overcome lions and doves, eagles by suffering, that herein they may be conformable to Christ, who conquered most when He suffered most. Together with Christ's kingdom of patience there was a kingdom of power.

◆ RICHARD SIBBES
Bruised Reed and Smoking Flax, 154

As men cherish young plants at first and fence them with hedges, but when grown, they remove them and leave the trees to the wind and storms, so God sustains His children at first with inward comforts. But afterward they are exposed to storms and winds because better able to bear them. Let no man think himself the better because he is more free from trouble than others; God sees him not fit to bear greater.

◆ RICHARD SIBBES
Divine Meditations and Holy Contemplations, 80

He that rides to be crowned will not think much of a rainy day.

◆ JOHN TRAPP
in Horn, *Puritan Remembrancer*, 27

Christ has been before in suffering. Consider what Christ endured for us. Christ's whole life was a series of sufferings. Christian, what is thy suffering? Art thou poor? So was Christ: "The Son of man hath not where to lay his head" (Matt. 8:20). Art thou surrounded with enemies? So was Christ: "Against thy holy servant Jesus...both

Herod, and Pontius Pilate, with the Gentiles, and the people of Israel, were gathered together" (Acts 4:27). Do our enemies lay claim to religion? So did His: "The chief priests took the silver pieces, and said, It is not lawful for to put them into the treasury, because it is the price of blood" (Matt. 27:6). Godly persecutors! Art thou reproached? So was Christ: "The reproaches of them that reproached thee are fallen upon me" (Ps. 69:9). Art thou slandered? So was Christ: "The Pharisees said, He casteth out devils through the prince of the devils" (Matt. 9:34). Art thou ignominiously used? So was Christ: "Some began to spit on him, and to cover his face, and to buffet him, and say unto him, Prophesy: and the servants did strike Him with the palms of their hands" (Mark 14:65). Art thou betrayed by friends? So was Christ: "Jesus said unto him, Judas, betrayest thou the Son of man with a kiss?" (Luke 22:48). Is thy estate sequestered? And do the wicked cast lots for it? So Christ was dealt with: "They parted my garments among them, and upon my vesture did they cast lots" (Matt. 27:35). Do we suffer unjustly? So did Christ; His very judge did acquit Him: "Then said Pilate to the chief priests and to the people, I find no fault in this man" (Luke 23:4). Art thou barbarously dragged and hauled away to suffering? So was Christ: "And when they had bound him, they led him away" (Matt. 27:2). Dost thou suffer death? So did Christ: "And when they were come to the place, which is called Calvary, there they crucified him" (Luke 23:33).

✦ THOMAS WATSON
Gleanings, 70–72

A Christian is never the worse for reproach.... Reproaches are but... splinters of the cross. How will he endure the stake who cannot bear a scoff? Reproaches for Christ are ensigns of honor, badges of adoption (1 Peter 4:14), the high honors of accusations, says Chrysostom. Let Christians bind these as a crown about their head. Better have men reproach you for being good than have God damn you for being wicked. Be not laughed out of your religion. If a lame man laugh at you for walking upright, will you therefore limp?

✦ THOMAS WATSON
Great Gain of Godliness, 11

Suffering is the way to prevent sufferings; suffering loss of goods, liberty, life for Christ's sake is the way to prevent eternal sufferings.

✦ HENRY WILKINSON
"A Suffering Faith," in *Three Decades of Sermons*, 104

SUICIDE

Does the enemy tempt you with self-murder? Be aware that this is by no means an uncommon temptation from the devil; many of God's people in every age of the world have been harassed and tormented with it. Many that are now in heaven, far out of the reach of temptation, have been exercised with this bitter trial while on the earth. Nay, our Lord and Savior Himself drank of this bitter cup when Satan would persuade Him to cast Himself down from the pinnacle of the temple. What wonder, then, if His servants are made to taste of this bitter cup, as well as their Lord and Master? Nervous people are more harassed than any other with this black temptation of self-murder and blasphemy, but black as the temptation is, they may smile at it when they take shelter in the clefts, the wounds of Christ.

✦ ISAAC AMBROSE
Christian Warrior, 49–50

Some under these terrors [of conscience] have thought hell more tolerable, and by a violent hand have thrust themselves out of the world into it to avoid these gnawings. Yet Jesus Christ can quickly calm these mystical waves also and hush them with a word; yea, He is the physician, and no other.

✦ JOHN FLAVEL
Navigation Spiritualized, 92

He that would not die when he must, and he that would die when he must not are both of them cowards alike.

✦ GEORGE SWINNOCK
in Horn, *Puritan Remembrancer*, 15

SURRENDER

Abraham gave unto the Lord Isaac, his son, which when the Lord did behold, He quickly gave him his son again; and so will He deal with us still. The readiest way to retain life, goods, etc., is to yield them up wholly into God's hands, not with this condition: that He shall give them to us again, for that were to mock the Lord. But without all care to have them, we must give them to Him, being heartily well content for His glory to forgo them, and then if they be good for us, we shall receive them again. If not, we shall receive some spiritual grace which shall better supply the want of them.

✦ JOHN DOD
"Of Murmuring in the Time of Affliction," in *Seven Godly and Fruitful Sermons*, 210–11

A…way to show thanks is to honor God with thy substance (Prov. 3:9); to do good with thy gifts to profit others (1 Cor. 12:7); to spend thy sweetness and thy fatness for the good of God and man; and to consecrate all thy learning, wit, wealth to God to use and call for and command, as if they were His own. This is to be thankful.

✦ THOMAS GOODWIN
"A Discourse of Thankfulness," in *Works*, 9:505

Why should you fear to be stripped of that which you have resigned already to Christ? It is the first lesson you learn, if a Christian, to deny thyself, take up thy cross, and follow thy Master so that the enemy comes too late; thou hast no life to lose because thou hast given it already to Christ.

✦ WILLIAM GURNALL
Christian in Complete Armour, 87

SYMPATHY/COMPASSION/PITY

Three things promote sympathy in Christians: One is the Lord's pity for them; He doth as it were suffer with them: "In all their affliction he was afflicted" (Isa. 63:9). Another is the relation we sustain to God's afflicted people. They are members with us in one body, and the members should have the same care of one another (1 Cor. 12:25). The last is we know not how soon we ourselves may need from others what others now need from us.
✦ JOHN FLAVEL
Fountain of Life, 179

Pity is a debt due to the distressed, and the world shows not a greater distress than this. If ever you have been in troubles of this kind yourselves, you will never slight others in the same case. Nay, one end of God's exercising you with troubles of this nature is to teach you compassion toward others in the same case.
✦ JOHN FLAVEL
Fountain of Life, 332

The Jews would not willingly tread upon the smallest piece of paper in their way but took it up, for possibly, said they, the name of God may be on it. Though there was a little superstition in that, yet truly there is nothing but good religion in it if we apply it to men. Trample not on any; there may be some work of grace there that thou knowest not of. The name of God may be written upon that soul thou treadest on. It may be a soul that Christ thought so much of as to give His precious blood for it; therefore despise it not.
✦ ROBERT LEIGHTON
Spiritual Truths, 294–95

Sympathy is a debt we owe to sufferers.
✦ WILLIAM SECKER
in Horn, *Puritan Remembrancer*, 67

TAKING UP THE CROSS

The covenant hath its cross. The doctrine of the gospel is the doctrine of the cross; the preaching of the gospel is the preaching of the cross (1 Corinthians 1). The mysteries of a crucified Jesus and of His crucified saints do fill up the whole New Testament. The cross is not only imposed upon the saints as their burden but bequeathed unto them as a legacy. It is given unto them as an honor and a privilege.
✦ RICHARD ALLEINE
Heaven Opened, 55

A cross without a Christ never made any man better, but with Christ, saints are much the better for the cross. Hath God put you so many times into the furnace, and yet is not the dross separated? The more afflictions you have been under, the more assistance you have had for this life of holiness.
✦ JOHN FLAVEL
Fountain of Life, 452

Your Lord will not give you painted crosses. He pares not all the bitterness from the cross, neither taketh He the sharp edge quite from it; for in that case it should be of your selecting and not of His, which would have as little reason in it as it would have profit for us.

✦ SAMUEL RUTHERFORD
Garden of Spices, 68

They are blessed who suffer and sin not, for suffering is the badge which Christ hath put upon His followers. Take what we can to heaven, the way is hedged up with crosses; there is no way but to break through them. Wit and wiles, shifts and laws will not find a way around the cross of Christ, but we must through. One thing by experience my Lord hath taught me, that the waters betwixt this and heaven may all be ridden if we be well horsed—I mean if we be in Christ—and not one shall drown by the way but such as love their own destruction.

✦ SAMUEL RUTHERFORD
Garden of Spices, 71

TALENTS

Use your talents for Christ's glory; spend and be spent for Him. Let your heart study for Christ, your hands work for Christ, and your tongue speak for Him. If Christ be our advocate in heaven, we must be factors for Him on earth. Everyone in his sphere must act vigorously for Christ.

✦ THOMAS WATSON
Puritan Gems, 33

TALKATIVENESS

Are you addicted to verbosity or talkativeness, to speak too much or rashly and vainly? Take James, his curb, into your mind and mouth daily: If any man seem to be religious and bridles not his tongue, he deceives his own heart; this man's religion is vain. If I cannot rule my tongue, I spoil my religion; I shall contract much guilt and bewray much folly.... If I do not guide my tongue I shall undo myself utterly, for tongue as well as hand may bring me to hell.

✦ EDWARD REYNER
Precepts for Christian Practice, 25

TEACHABLE, BEING

It is fitter for youth to learn than teach and for age to teach than learn, and yet fitter for an old man to learn than to be ignorant. I know I shall never know so much that I cannot learn more. And I hope I shall never live so long as till I be too old to learn.

✦ JOSEPH HALL
Meditations and Vows, 33

Let us not neglect any help we can receive and ever be ready to catch the gales of God's Spirit. We may sometimes light our candle at the lamp of others, and we should never be above accepting help from even the meanest. All lawful endeavors must be used, and a man must chafe his own hands if he complain of cold. For we must not be too proud to make use of others nor too slothful to bestir ourselves. The influences of the Holy Spirit must be peculiarly prized. How can we pass the seas without His gales?

✦ THOMAS JOLLIE
"Heavenly-Mindedness," in Slate,
Select Nonconformists' Remains, 239

Torches are many times lighted at a candle, and the most glorious saints advantaged by the meanest. Christ would teach His disciples by a child; He took a child "and set him in the midst of them" (Matt. 18:2). It is proud disdain to scorn the meanest gifts. There may be gold in an earthen vessel. There are none too old, none too wise, none too high to be taught. "Let every man be swift to hear."

✦ THOMAS MANTON
*Practical Exposition on the
Epistle of James*, 54

It is much to be desired: There were that love in some men to teach what they know and that humility in others to be instructed in what they know not. God humbles sometimes great persons to learn of others that are mean, and it is our duty and will be our comfort to embrace the truth, whosoever brings it. And often mean persons are the instruments of knowledge and comfort to many that have greater endowment than themselves, as Aquila and Priscilla instructed Apollos (Acts 18:26).

✦ RICHARD SIBBES
*Divine Meditations and Holy
Contemplations*, 94

TEACHING

There is a twofold teaching of God. There is a common teaching which even the heathen, men out of the church, hypocrites, and reprobates within the church may have; there is a special teaching, proper and peculiar only to the children of promise. A covenant teaching: "All thy children shall be taught of God." It is the covenant of God with the Redeemer.

✦ THOMAS CASE
Correction, Instruction, 67

Teaching is the fruit of affliction. It must have a ripening time, and therefore, O thou discouraged soul, say not God doth not teach thee at all if He do not teach thee all at once. "The entrance of thy word giveth light." God lets in light by degrees; usually He teacheth His children as we teach ours—now a little, and then a little; somewhat this week, and more next week; somewhat by this affliction, and more by the next affliction.

✦ THOMAS CASE
Correction, Instruction, 80

He had an admirable faculty in teaching youth, for every boy can teach a man, whereas he must be a man who can teach a boy. It is easy to inform them who are able to understand, but it must be a masterpiece of industry and discretion to descend to the capacity of children.

✦ THOMAS FULLER
Wise Words and Quaint Counsels, 228

TEARS

Sin in the review looks dreadful. Its pleasant flowers quickly turn to thorns; it pricks the heart, how much soever it pleased the eye. It ordinarily enters by the eye and often runs out the same way it came in—runs out in tears. When [David] thought thereon, he wept. At least it warns and makes more watchful after. Thou seest what it is, take heed; take it for a warning, and do no more. The pain of sin, if it do not force a tear, it will set a watch.

✦ RICHARD ALLEINE
Heaven Opened, 133

Prayers and tears are the church's armor.

✦ JOHN BOYS
in Horn, *Puritan Remembrancer,* 76

Tears are a kind of silent prayers which, though they say nothing, yet they obtain pardon, they prevail for mercy, and they carry the day with God, as you may see in that great and clear instance of Peter; he said nothing, he confessed nothing that we read of, but went out and wept bitterly and obtained mercy.

✦ THOMAS BROOKS
Cabinet of Choice Jewels, 245

Penitent tears are undeniable ambassadors that never return from the throne of grace without a gracious answer.

✦ THOMAS BROOKS
Privy Key of Heaven, 32

Godly sorrow breaks the heart of sin. Tears that are squeezed and wrung from a man and that come only from inward compunction and pricking of the heart may fortify and feed sin, but when they are the juice of a broken heart and flow from a contrite heart that is melted down by the heavenly warmth of divine love, they stifle and extinguish sin.

✦ ALEXANDER CARMICHAEL
Believer's Mortification of Sin, 88

First, there may be loads of sorrow upon the heart when there is not one tear in the eye; this is well known, so that tears are not the index of great sorrows always. Secondly, tears that rise from a tender, broken heart are precious, but tears that flow from constitution of the body (as in most they do) signify little; some have tears at command. I have known persons of very unbroken hearts, stout wills, who could pour out tears at their pleasure. I speak of Christians. Thirdly, are tears common with thee for other things? If so, and they be strangers only when you come to sin, this deserves good attendance. Fourthly, a man may have a more soft, tender, broken heart who cannot shed tears (at least not in that measure); he may be a better Christian than he that can shed many tears. Observation has made this good.

✦ GILES FIRMIN
Real Christian, 86

Deep displeasure with thyself for sin, hearty resolutions and desires of the complete mortification of it—these are essential to all spiritual sorrow; but tears are accidental and in some constitutions rarely found. If thou hast the former, trouble not thyself for want of the latter, though it is a mercy when they kindly and undissembledly flow from a heart truly broken.

✦ JOHN FLAVEL
Fountain of Life, 200

Because though the object about which our affections and passions are moved may be spiritual, yet the motives and principles that set them on work may be but carnal and natural ones. When I see a person affected in the hearing of the word or prayer, even unto tears, I cannot presently conclude, surely this is the effect of grace; for it is possible the pathetical nature of the subject matter, the rhetoric of the speaker, the very affecting tone, and modulation of the voice may draw tears as well as faith.

✦ JOHN FLAVEL
Fountain of Life, 240

Some think they do right if they sorrow out of measure for sin and take their pennyworth of themselves. But God seeks no more of you but as much as to toom your souls of pride, that Christ may come in with His full vessel to fill it. Do not think to buy God's kindness with tears, as if sorrow were a fat feast to God.

✦ SAMUEL RUTHERFORD
"The Spouse's Longing for Christ,"
in *Quaint Sermons*, 96

A tear from a bleeding heart is a precious perfume in heaven.

✦ THOMAS WATSON
"God's Anatomy upon Man's Heart,"
in *Discourses*, 1:156

TEMPTATIONS

If Satan knock, it is in our choice to open. A booty lies in our way; we may choose whether we will stoop and take it up. To suggest evil is Satan's blame; to resist evil, this is our praise.

✦ THOMAS ADAMS
Exposition upon…Second…Peter, 386

Till the fire of hell be out in the saints, the devil will not lay down his bellows. Where there is no sin, there is no matter of temptation to work on.… Corruption keeps open the door for Satan. Never look for silence from Satan till you find cessation from sin.

✦ ASHWOOD BARTHOLOMEW
Heavenly Trade, 405–6

Take heed of security and Satan's ambushments. Distinguish between cessation and conquest. You conquer not every time that you have rest and quietness from temptation. Till the sin be hated and the contrary grace or duty in practice, you have not at all overcome. And when that is done, yet trust not the devil or the flesh nor think the war will be shorter than your lives, for one assault will begin where the other ended. Make use of every cessation but to prepare for the next encounter.

✦ RICHARD BAXTER
A Christian Directory, in
Practical Works, 2:308

If God has such an overruling hand of grace upon all the temptations of the saints that He causes them to turn to their good, then they have no reason to be cast down or to be discouraged because of them. Now God would never permit His people to be tempted unless He intended to destroy their temptations by their temptations. Consider the end and the issue of an evil; that was God's design in permitting that evil to come to pass. And this is the end and issue of all the saints' temptations, that thereby they are more enlightened. *Tentatio dat intellectum* (temptation gives understanding); tempting times are teaching times.

✦ WILLIAM BRIDGE
Lifting Up, 156–57

That temptation is not much to be feared when a man fears himself for his temptation. He is to be feared most that does fear least, and he is to be feared least that does fear most. A godly, gracious man or woman is humbled under nothing more than under his temptations; he looks upon his temptations as the greatest afflictions in all the world.

✦ WILLIAM BRIDGE
"On Temptation," in *Works*, 1:140

Pride of heart, pride of apparel, pride of talents; young men are apt to be proud of health, strength, friends, relations, wit, wisdom. Two things are very rare: the one is to see a young man humble and watchful, and the other is to see an old man contented and cheerful.

✦ THOMAS BROOKS
Apples of Gold, 85

Temptation is God's school wherein He gives His people the clearest and sweetest discoveries of His love; a school wherein God teaches His people to be more frequent and fervent in duty—when Paul was buffeted, then he prayed thrice (i.e., frequently and fervently); a school wherein God teaches His people to be more tender, meek, and compassionate to other poor, tempted souls than ever; a school wherein God teaches His people to see a greater evil in sin than ever, and a greater emptiness in the creature than ever, and a greater need of Christ and free grace than ever; a school wherein God will teach His people that all temptations are but His goldsmiths, by which He will try and refine and make His people more bright and glorious.

✦ THOMAS BROOKS
Great Gain, 130

A tempted soul, when it is at worst with him, may safely argue thus: If God were not my friend, Satan would not be so much my enemy; if there were not something of God within me, Satan would never make such attempts to storm me; if the love of God were not set upon me, Satan would never shoot so many fiery darts to wound me; if the heart of God were not toward me, the hand of Satan would not be so strong against me.

✦ THOMAS BROOKS
Mute Christian, 180

By temptations the Lord will make His people more frequent and more abundant in the work of prayer. Every temptation proves a strong alarm to prayer. When Paul was in the school of temptation, he prayed thrice—that is, often. Days of temptation are days of great supplication. Christians usually pray most when they are tempted most; they are most busy with God when Satan is most busy with them. A Christian is most upon his knees when Satan stands most at his elbow.

✦ THOMAS BROOKS
Mute Christian, 188

You can never take a just measure of your own strength till temptation have tried it.

✦ JOHN FLAVEL
Fountain of Life, 278

Alas! You know not what hearts you have till temptations prove them. And what comfort can you take in the success and prosperity of your affairs, be it never so great, if you return with consciences polluted and wounded with sin! He that brings home a pack of fine clothes, infected with the plague, hath no such great bargain of it, how cheap soever he purchased them.

✦ JOHN FLAVEL
"The Seaman's Farewell," in
Navigation Spiritualized, 236

But it is possible thou mayest do it unawares by a less matter than thou dreamest on. A silly child playing with a lighted straw may set a house on fire, which many wise men cannot quench. And truly Satan may use thy folly and carelessness to kindle lust in another's heart. Perhaps an idle, light speech drops from thy mouth and thou meanest no great hurt, but a gust of temptation may carry this spark into thy friend's bosom and kindle a sad fire there. A wanton attire, perhaps naked breasts and shoulders, which we will suppose thou wears with a chaste heart and only because it is the fashion yet may ensnare another's eye. And if he that kept a pit open but to the hurt of a beast sinned, how much more thou, who givest occasion to a soul's sin, which is a worse hurt? Paul would not eat flesh while the world stood if it made his brother to offend (1 Cor. 8:13). And canst thou dote on a foolish dress and immodest fashion, whereby many may offend, still to wear it? "The body," Christ saith, "is better than raiment." The soul then of thy brother is more to be valued surely than an idle fashion of thy raiment.

✦ WILLIAM GURNALL
Christian in Complete Armour, 479

Steadfastness in believing doth not exclude all temptations from without. When we say a tree is firmly rooted, we do not say that the wind never blows upon it.

✦ JOHN OWEN
Golden Book, 204

There are advantages for temptations lying ofttimes in men's natural tempers and constitutions. Some are naturally gentle, facile, easy to be entreated, pliable, which, though it be the noblest temper of nature and the best and choicest ground when well broken up and fallowed for grace to grow in; yet, if not watched over, will be a means of innumerable surprisals and entanglements in temptation. Others are earthly, froward, morose, so that envy, malice, selfishness, peevishness, harsh thoughts of others, repinings lie at the very door of their natures, and they can scarce step out but they are in the snare of one or other of them. Others are passionate and the like. Now he that would watch that he enter not into temptation had need be acquainted with his own natural temper, that he may watch over the treacheries that lie in it continually. Take heed lest you have a Jehu in you that shall make you drive furiously; or a Jonah in you that will make you ready to repine; or a David that will make you hasty in your determinations, as he was often in the warmth and goodness of his natural temper. He who watches not this thoroughly, who is not exactly skilled in the knowledge of himself, will never be disentangled from one temptation or another all his days.

♦ JOHN OWEN
On Temptation, in Oweniana, 57–58

I find it to be most true that the greatest temptation out of hell is to live without temptations. If my waters should stand, they would rot. Faith is the better of the free air and of the sharp winter storm in its face. Grace withers without adversity. The devil is but God's master fencer to teach us to handle our weapons.

♦ SAMUEL RUTHERFORD
Letters, 69

[Satan] has temptations for the old age: covetousness, peevishness.

♦ WILLIAM SPURSTOWE
Wiles of Satan, 69

[Satan] tempts middle ages to a [love of honor]. He stirs up an itch of honor and of being some great ones, of building their families and laying foundations of a name; and in this very snare many are caught who by this very temptation have their thoughts and minds so possessed as that they willfully resist light and put themselves upon courses that turn away their hearts from God. It is the thought and project of many a man that after he hath feathered his nest and done so and so, he will bethink himself of his soul.

♦ WILLIAM SPURSTOWE
Wiles of Satan, 69

If you would not be overcome by temptation, be much in prayer. Prayer is the best antidote against temptation. Christ prescribes this remedy, "Watch ye and pray, lest ye enter into temptation" (Mark 14:38). When Paul had a "messenger of Satan to buffet" him, he betook himself to prayer. "For this thing I besought the Lord thrice, that it might depart from me" (2 Cor. 12:7–8). When Satan assaults furiously, let us pray fervently.

♦ THOMAS WATSON
Gleanings, 83

THANKFULNESS

An unthankful person is but a devourer of mercies and a grave to bury them in, and one that hath not the wit and honesty to know and acknowledge the hand that giveth them.

✦ RICHARD BAXTER
A Christian Directory, in
Practical Works, 2:421

True thankfulness to God is discerned from counterfeit by these qualifications: (1) True thankfulness, having a just estimate of mercies comparatively, prefers spiritual and everlasting mercies before those that are merely corporal and transitory. But carnal thankfulness chiefly values carnal mercies, though notionally it may confess that the spiritual are the greater. (2) True thankfulness inclines the soul to a spiritual rejoicing in God and to a desire after more of His spiritual mercies. But carnal thankfulness is only a delight in the prosperity of the flesh or the delusion and carnal security of the mind, inclining men to carnal, empty mirth and to a desire of more such fleshly pleasure, plenty or content—as a beast that is full fed will skip and play and show that he is pleased with his state or, if he have ease, he would not be molested. (3) True thankfulness kindles in the heart a love to the giver above the gift, or at least a love to God above our carnal prosperity and pleasure, and brings the heart still nearer unto God by all His mercies.... (4) True thankfulness inclines us to obey and please Him that obliges us by His benefits. But carnal thankfulness puts God off with the hypocritical, complimental thanks of the lips and spends the mercy in the pleasing of the flesh and makes it but the fuel of lust and sin. (5) True thankfulness to God is necessarily transcendent...and causes the thankful person to devote and resign himself and all that he has to God, to answer so great an obligation. But carnal thankfulness falls short of this absolute and total dedication and still leaves the sinner in the power of self-love, devoting himself (really) to himself, and using all that he is or has to the pleasing of his fleshly mind.

✦ RICHARD BAXTER
A Christian Directory, in
Practical Works, 2:422–23

A thankful obedience and an obedient thankfulness are a Christian's life.

✦ RICHARD BAXTER
A Christian Directory, in
Practical Works, 2:432

For as the Lord loves a cheerful giver, so likewise a cheerful thanksgiver. God is terrible to the wicked but a God of gladness to such as have seen the light of His countenance. For being reconciled unto God, they have such inward joy and peace that it passes all understanding.

✦ JOHN BOYS
Offices for Public Worship,
in *Works*, 49

Desire not much. He that desires much will expect much; and he that expects much, he will not be content with little, much less thankful for everything. Jacob was a plain-hearted man;

he desired little, he was content with less, he was thankful for everything. So must you be.

♦ WILLIAM BRIDGE
"Thankfulness Required in Every Condition," in *Works*, 4:109

Thanksgiving is a self-denying grace; it is an uncrowning ourselves and the creatures to set the crown upon the head of our Creator; it is the making ourselves a footstool, that God may be lifted up upon His throne and ride in a holy triumph over all.

♦ THOMAS BROOKS
The Unsearchable Riches of Christ,
in *Select Works*, 1:94

Thankfulness is, in a well-explained sense, all our gospel obedience. 'Tis the general duty of the gospel, containing and animating all duties. All without it are impure carcasses. Repentance, if it be not thankful, is rather a legal rack and rage than a gospel repentance. And faith, if it be not a thankful consent unto the gospel covenant, 'tis no saving consent. Nor is the love of God or any service of Him proper or tolerable, unless they be grateful.

♦ DANIEL BURGESS
Man's Whole Duty, 60

As children when they cannot have all they would many times throw away that which they have, so when we seek to God for that which we want, we are so intent upon that, that we forget the mercies we have received and return not thanks for them.

♦ SAMUEL CLARK
Saint's Nosegay, 100

The thankful man must not only observe what mercies he hath and from whom they come but must particularly consider them in their natures, degrees, seasons, and manner of conveyance. There is much of God's glory, and our comfort lost for want of this. "The works of the LORD are great, sought out of all them that have pleasure therein" (Ps. 111:2). And indeed, there is no employment in all the world that yields more pleasure to a gracious soul than the anatomizing of providences doth. How sweet is it to observe the mutual respects, coincidences, and introductive occasions of our mercies. Every minute circumstance hath its weight and value here. He hath little pleasure in his meat that swallows it whole without chewing.

♦ JOHN FLAVEL
"The Seaman's Return," in
Navigation Spiritualized, 338

The thankful person must order his conversation suitably to the engagements that His mercies have put him under. When we have said all, it is the life of the thankful that is the very life of thankfulness. Obedience and service are the only real manifestations of gratitude. "Whoso offereth praise glorifieth me: and to him that ordereth his conversation aright will I shew the salvation of God" (Ps. 50:23). Set down this for an everlasting truth, that God was never praised and honored by an abused mercy.

♦ JOHN FLAVEL
"The Seaman's Return," in
Navigation Spiritualized, 340

He that gives no thanks for one mercy hath little ground to expect another.

◆ JOHN FLAVEL
"The Seaman's Return," in
Navigation Spiritualized, 343

God being so glorious a God, we are to do all to Him and for Him, and obey Him in all, and make Him the end of all, which is called glorifying Him. Suppose we were no way beholden to Him, all this were a due to His excellency and glory, which might challenge it from us, might extort it: "Give unto the LORD the glory due unto his name" (Ps. 29:2); that alone would challenge all the service, all the praise that you do or could make to Him. But now we all are, upon a further ground, to do all to Him and for Him because of all the many mercies we receive from Him. Now to return all in this relation is called thankfulness. To do all out of a sense of His excellency and glory that is in Himself, this is to glorify Him. But to do all out of a sense of His mercies to us and our obligement unto Him, this is thankfulness.

◆ THOMAS GOODWIN
"A Discourse of Thankfulness,"
in *Works*, 9:499–500

What thankfulness is? It is a free rendering to God the glory of His goodness, principally to the end we may glorify it and testify our love to Him.

◆ THOMAS GOODWIN
"A Discourse of Thankfulness,"
in *Works*, 9:500

Thankfulness to God is most profitable…because it is the way to get more, and unthankfulness is the way to lose all we have; therefore, "let your requests be made known" with thanksgiving (Phil. 4:6–7); otherwise, requests alone will not move God. It is not earnestness only for what thou wantest but withal thanks for what thou hast must prevail. As you use to put water into the pump to fetch more, so return thanks to fetch more mercies; whereas the want of thankfulness and returning all to God again forfeits all the blessings you have (Deut. 28:47–48).

◆ THOMAS GOODWIN
"A Discourse of Thankfulness,"
in *Works*, 9:510

[Job] blesses God…because he found that God had blessed him with such things and blessings heavenly which could not be taken away. He found the love of God the same still. It is a sure rule, we never bless God but when we find that God blesses us first, as we do not love God but because God loves us first. Now when the soul finds that in afflictions and tentations God doth bless it, this draws out from the soul a blessing of God again. And then doth the soul say, "It is not only the will of my Father, and therefore shall I not drink the cup He gives me? But it is the blessing of my Father, and shall not I bless Him for it? "In every thing give thanks," saith the holy apostle (1 Thess. 5:18); that is, whatever the condition be, still there is matter of thanks, and so of blessing God.

✦ THOMAS GOODWIN
"Patience and Its Perfect Work,"
in *Works*, 2:454

As God does nothing but He aims at His own glory thereby (Prov. 16:4), so there is no act of God toward His people wherein He intends not their good, and as such becomes the subject of their thanksgiving. Hence, we are bid, "in everything give thanks." O, what a copious theme hath God given His people to enlarge their meditations upon? "In everything." The whole course of divine providence toward the saints is like a music book, in every leaf whereof there is a song ready set for them to learn and sing to the praise of their God; there is no passage in their life of which they can say, "In this we received no mercy for which we should bless our God."

✦ WILLIAM GURNALL
Christian in Complete Armour, 731

The more free God is of His mercy, the more close some are in their thankful returns. When poor, they could be thankful for a short meal of coarse fare, more than now for their varieties. When sick, O how thankful were their hearts for a few broken slumbers in the night! Whereas now they can rise and take little notice of the goodness of God that gives them their full rest night after night. Is it not strange to see a man grow colder in his love to God as the sun of God's mercy rises

higher and shines hotter upon him? O, it is sad to see the heap increase and the heart waste, to find a man grow rich in mercy and poorer in thankfulness.

✦ WILLIAM GURNALL
Christian in Complete Armour, 737

Consider what an ornament a thankful frame of heart is to religion. This commends God to the unbelieving world, who know little more of Him than what your lives preach to them; they read religion in that character you print it and make their report of God and His ways as they see you behave yourselves in the world. If you walk disconsolately or murmur at divine providence, how can they believe that the ways of God are so pleasant as they are said to be?

✦ WILLIAM GURNALL
Christian in Complete Armour, 742

We must retain a thankful remembrance of our benefits. Not write our mercies in the sand, but in marble: "Forget not" (Ps. 103:2). Israel soon forgot. It was presently over with them. And it was their fault. I should much desire a catalog of my sins and of my mercies: the former, to repent of them every day; the latter, to give thanks every day.

✦ PHILIP HENRY
Remains, 137

Thanksgiving is a spirit still upon the wing, rising and ascending to heaven from everything. Never at home but at heaven; it is a very low thing that he cannot rise from as high as heaven.

He eats and looks up, drinks and looks up, looks down and looks up; whatsoever he looks upon he cannot look off God. Whatsoever he sees, hears, tastes, smells he takes wing from and goes bound in spirit for heaven; whether he eats or drinks, or whatsoever he does, he does all to the glory of God. Thankfulness is an eagle-grace whose aim lies all in soaring and mounting toward the sun. It is a soul still traveling from earth to heaven, from the creature to the Creator.

◆ NICHOLAS LOCKYER
Balm for England, 134

He enjoys much who is thankful for a little.

◆ WILLIAM SECKER
in Horn, *Puritan Remembrancer*, 19

The thankful heart shall never want mercies from God to be thankful for.

◆ GEORGE TROSSE
Life, 71

Behold, therefore, I give thee here a register or inventory which I wish thee to keep and use as a table of thanks due to God....

A Thankful Man's Calendar

Public—Consider in what times and places the lot of my life hath fallen: in what king's reign, in what nation, in what town, under what magistracy and ministry.

Domestical—What parents, schoolmasters, and tutors; what wife, children, and servants hath God blessed me withal?

Personal and Privative—What sickness have I been delivered from? What dangers, casualties by sea or land? What suits and vexations by law or otherwise?

Positive, Corporal—What measure of health and strength of body?

External—What talents of wealth, birth, office, authority, repute?

Mental—What faculties of understanding, memory? What helps of arts, sciences, education, etc.?

When and how my conversion to God was wrought? What assurance of God's love in Christ, what peace and joy in the Holy Ghost, etc.? What progress, growth, and increase have I made in grace and in good duties of my place and calling? What victory over tentations and special sins, old and inveterate customs of evil?

◆ SAMUEL WARD
"A Peace-Offering to God," in
Sermons and Treatises, 146–47

A godly man is a thankful man; praise and thanksgiving is the work of heaven, and he begins that work here which he shall be always doing in heaven. The Jews have a saying, "The world subsists by three things: the law, the worship of God, and thankfulness," as if where thankfulness were wanting, one of the pillars of the world were taken away and it were ready to fall.

◆ THOMAS WATSON
Godly Man's Picture, 114

THIEF ON THE CROSS

We find these things remarkable in that business between Christ and the thief: (1) The man falls out with his former companion. (2) He dares not speak a wrong word of God, whose hand is on him, but justifies Him in all that has befallen him. (3) He now sees Jesus Christ persecuted by the world without a cause, and most injuriously. (4) He discovers Christ to be a Lord and a King, whilst His enemies seem to have Him under. (5) He believes a state of glory after death so really that he prefers a portion in it to the present safety of his bodily life, which he knew Christ was able to grant him at that time, that he might have chosen that with the other thief. (6) Although he was much abased in himself and so humbled that he pleaded but that Christ would remember him, yet he was nobly daring to throw himself upon the covenant, on life and death; and he had so much faith of Christ's all-sufficiency that he judged a simple remembrance from Christ would satisfyingly do his business. (7) He acquiesced sweetly in the word which Christ spoke to him for the ground of his comfort. All which are very clear in the case of that poor dying man and prove a very real work of God upon his heart.

✦ WILLIAM GUTHRIE
Christian's Great Interest, 97–98

THINGS INDIFFERENT (*ADIAPHORA*)

Whatsoever is neither forbidden nor commanded in the Word may sometimes be done for maintenance of love, and sometimes be undone for avoiding of superstition.

✦ EZEKIEL CULVERWELL
Time Well Spent, 196

Neutrality in things good or evil is both odious and prejudicial, but in matters of an indifferent nature is safe and commendable. Herein taking of parts maketh sides and breaketh unity. In an unjust cause of separation, he that favoreth both parts may perhaps have least love of either side but hath most charity in himself.

✦ JOSEPH HALL
Holy Observations, in
Select Tracts, 321

When we infringe Christian liberty and condemn others for things merely indifferent, this is to master it indeed and lay snares upon the conscience; a wrong not so much to our brethren as to God's own law, which we judge as if it were an imperfect rule (James 4:11). In habits and meats there is great latitude, and as long as rules of sobriety and modesty are not violated, we cannot censure, but must leave the heart to God. See Romans 14.

✦ THOMAS MANTON
*Practical Exposition on the
Epistle of James*, 120

TIME

Let good fellows sit in a tavern from sun to sun and they think the day very short, confessing (though insensible of the loss) that time is a light-heeled runner. Bind them to the church for two hours, and you put an ache into their bones, the seats be too hard. Now time is held a cripple, and many a weary look is cast up to the glass. It is a man's mind that makes any work pleasant or troublesome.

✦ THOMAS ADAMS
"The Two Sons," in *Sermons*, 196

Time is that space between two eternities, limited by divine pleasure to divine use. "Seeing his days are determined, the number of his months are with thee, thou hast appointed his bounds that he cannot pass" (Job 14:5). And if time be the Lord's, then 'tis fit it should be used for God.

✦ BARTHOLOMEW ASHWOOD
Heavenly Trade, 423

O precious time! How swiftly does it pass away! How soon will it be gone! What are the forty years of my life that are past? Were every day as long as a month, methinks it were too short for the work of a day. Have we not lost time enough in the days of our vanity that we have any now to lose? Never do I come to a dying man who is not utterly stupid but he better sees the worth of time than others generally do. O then, if they could call time back again, how loud would they call! What would they give for it! Can we then afford to trifle it away? Is it possible that a man

of any true compassion and honesty, or any concern about his ministerial duty, or any sense of the strictness of his account should have time to spare for idleness and vanity?

✦ RICHARD BAXTER
Reformed Pastor, 146–47

Is there an eternal state into which souls pass after this life? How precious then is present time upon the improvement whereof that state depends. Oh, what a huge weight hath God hung upon a small wire! God hath set us here in a state of trial. According as we improve these few hours, so will it fare with us to all eternity. Every day, every hour—nay, every moment of your present time—hath an influence upon your eternity.

✦ JOHN FLAVEL
Fountain of Life, 317

Christ often thought upon the shortness of His time and wrought diligently because He knew His working time would be but little. So you find it [in] John 9:4: "I must work the works of him that sent me, while it is day; the night cometh, when no man can work." Oh, in this be like Christ: rouse your hearts to diligence with this consideration. If a man have much to write and he be almost come to the end of his paper, he will write close and thereby put much matter in a little room.

✦ JOHN FLAVEL
Fountain of Life, 353

Take a little breath and return to thy labor, as the seedsman that sits down at the land's end to rest himself awhile and then rises up to go before his plough again. We [pastors] have reason to be more choice of our time than others because it is less our own. There are none in thy parish but have a share in it.

✦ WILLIAM GURNALL
Christian in Complete Armour, 621

Account that day lost in which thou hast not done or learnt some good. Be more careful to keep thy word than thy money. Acquaint thyself with such as are good and virtuous. Look upon everything here below as very uncertain, so shalt thou not rejoice overmuch in thy prosperity nor be oversad or dismayed in adversity.

✦ ANDREW JONES
Dying Man's Last Sermon, 18

Foolish men that are riotous and prodigal of their time, as if it were given them only to sport and play and roar and revel in, pine and whine at last that they are lost because their time is so short. But wise and gracious persons that deny themselves and crucify the flesh, that can redeem time from toys and idle talk and foolish sports, and unnecessary diversions to pray and hear and read and examine their souls and bemoan their sins and provide for heaven—these grow rich in good works and find the days of their pilgrimage sufficient for them.

✦ GEORGE SWINNOCK
The Christian Man's Calling,
in *Works*, 2:506

THE TONGUE

The engine that carries this mischievous burden is the tongue. "It flies lightly, but it injures heavily," says Bernard. It is but a little member, but the nimblest about a man; able to do both body and soul too a mischief. How many on account of free tongues have chained feet!

✦ THOMAS ADAMS
Exposition upon…Second…Peter, 440

[A] good tongue is God's dish, and He will accept it at His own table. But an evil tongue is meat for the devil, according to the Italian proverb: "The devil makes his Christmas pie of lewd tongues." It is his daintiest dish and he makes much of it, whether on earth, to serve his turn as an instrument of mischief; or in hell, to answer his fury in torments. Thus, saith Solomon of the good tongue: "The tongue of the just is as choice silver…. The lips of the righteous feed many" (Prov. 10:20–21). But St. James of the bad one: "It is an unruly evil, full of deadly poison."

✦ THOMAS ADAMS
"The Taming of the Tongue,"
in *Works*, 3:12

God hath given man two ears: one to hear instructions of human knowledge, the other to hearken to His divine precepts; the former to conserve his body, the latter to save his soul. Two eyes, that with the one he might see to his own way; with the other pity and commiserate his distressed brethren. Two hands, that with the one he might work for his own living; with the other give and relieve his brother's wants. Two feet: one to walk on common days to his ordinary labor. "Man goeth forth unto his work and to his labor until the evening" (Ps. 104:23). The other, on sacred days to visit and frequent the temple and the congregation of saints. But among all, he hath given him but one tongue, which may instruct him to hear twice so much as he speaks; to work and walk twice so much as he speaks. "I will praise thee; for I am fearfully and wonderfully made: marvellous are thy works; and that my soul knoweth right well" (Ps. 139:14). Stay and wonder at the wonderful wisdom of God!

✦ THOMAS ADAMS
"The Taming of the Tongue,"
in *Works*, 3:13–14

Because [the tongue] is so unruly, the Lord hath hedged it in, as a man will not trust a wild horse in an open pasture but prison him in a close pound. A double fence hath the Creator given to confine it: the lips and the teeth.

✦ THOMAS ADAMS
"The Taming of the Tongue,"
in *Works*, 3:14

For your tongue: (1) Have I bridled my tongue and forced it in (James 1:26; 3:2–4; Ps. 39:1)? (2) Have I spoke evil of no man (Titus 3:2; James 4:11)? (3) Hath the law of the Lord been in my mouth as I sat in my house, went by the way, was lying down and rising up (Deut. 6:7)? (4) Is there no company I come into but I have dropped

something of God and left some good savor behind (Eph. 4:29; Col. 4:6)?

✦ JOSEPH ALLEINE
"Useful Questions," in *Alarm to the Unconverted*, 239

How have I used my tongue? It was designed to be my glory, but has it not been my shame? Has not much corrupt communication proceeded out of my mouth, and little of that which is good, which might either manifest grace or minister grace? Have not I sometimes spoke unadvisedly and said that in haste which at leisure I could have wished unsaid! Have not I said that by which God's great name has been dishonored, or my brother's good name reproached, or my own exposed? If for every idle word that I speak I must give account to God, I had best call myself to account for them; and I shall find innumerable of these evils compassing me about.

✦ MATTHEW HENRY
The Communicant's Companion, in
Miscellaneous Writings, 207

We should weigh our words before we utter them. When men are swift to speak and much in talk, they bewray some folly which is a stain to them. So, "he that hath knowledge spareth his words" (Prov. 17:27). Empty vessels sound loudest, and men of great parts, like a deep river, glide on with the least noise.

✦ THOMAS MANTON
*Practical Exposition on the
Epistle of James*, 56

An evil tongue has a great influence upon other members. It defiles the whole body. When a man speaks evil, he will commit it; when the tongue has the boldness to talk of sin, the rest of the members have the boldness to act it. "Evil communications corrupt good manners" (1 Cor. 15:33). First we think, then speak, and then do. Men will say it is but talk. Be not deceived; a pestilent tongue will infect other members.

✦ THOMAS MANTON
*Practical Exposition on the
Epistle of James*, 127

The mind is the guide of the tongue. Therefore, men must consider before they speak. The tongue is the messenger of the heart, and therefore as oft as we speak without meditation going before, so oft the messenger runs without his errand. The tongue is placed in the middle of the mouth, and it is compassed in with lips and teeth as with a double trench to show us how we are to use heed and preconsideration before we speak.

✦ WILLIAM PERKINS
*Direction for the Government
of the Tongue*, 5

Set a watch before thy tongue, lest it make thy throat thy sepulcher—a grave to bury thy estate and outward comforts in. It is a sin in many Christians that they know not when to be silent. The wise man tells us, "There is a time to speak, and a time to keep silence" ([see] Eccl. 3:7). This is a great part of Christian prudence, to under stand when to keep silence. It is much harder to learn to be silent than to learn to speak.

✦ GEORGE SWINNOCK
The Christian Man's Calling,
in *Works*, 2:289

TOTAL DEPRAVITY

Man in his natural state is without grace (Eph. 2:12). There are five withouts: (1) without Christ, (2) without the church, (3) without the promise, (4) without hope, (5) without God in the world. Now, every natural man being under these five withouts, how is it possible that he should have any serious desires after grace? Such is the corruption of our nature, that if you propound any divine good to it, it is entertained as fire by water or wet wood with hissing.

✦ THOMAS BROOKS
Cabinet of Choice Jewels, 176

SHERLOCK: If you be unholy, then you must make yourself holy.

SATAN: I, but I doubt that's past my skill. There is a spiritual impotency and inability in a sinner to do any good thing.

SHERLOCK: Who told you so, Sir Satan? John Calvin, I dare say, or John Owen? But I hope you have more wit than to believe them.

SATAN: No, indeed, I was told so by St. Augustine and many a great man of your church, fathers and sons.

✦ THOMAS DANSON
Friendly Debate, 5

There are no holy nor divine habits left in the will of a carnal man whereby he should be able to regenerate and convert himself. For what holy habit can there be in the will of one that is wholly corrupted? If any such be supposed, it may also be supposed that it is true grace. And to affirm that a man in a state of nature hath true grace inherent in him whereby he is able to convert and regenerate himself is double nonsense and a flat contradiction, for it is to affirm that he hath grace before he hath it. A will, totally corrupted, cannot make a holy man, cannot produce grace, nor make a man holy. Grace is beyond and above its sphere. The motions of the will in its fallen estate, what through defect of a right principle from whence they flow and a right end to which they tend, are all evil and sinful. And it is very strange to affirm that a gracious habit may be wrought in us by sinful actions. And besides, the will of man by the fall is a fleshly will, but in regeneration it is made spiritual. Now it were a strange kind of production if fleshly could beget spiritual, nor would it any longer hold true that our Savior saith in John 3:6: "That which is born of the flesh is flesh." So that I think it is very evident that all that a man can do by the power of nature cannot tend efficiently to produce grace in him.

✦ EZEKIEL HOPKINS
"The Almost Christian Discovered,"
in *Select Works*, 217

It is the character of all men in the state of depraved nature and apostasy from God that every imagination of the thoughts of their hearts is only evil continually (Gen. 6:5). All persons in that condition are not swearers, blasphemers, drunkards, adulterers, idolaters, or the like. These are the vices of peculiar persons, the effect of particular constitutions and temptations. But thus it is with them, all and every one of them—all the imaginations of the thoughts of their hearts are evil, and that continually: some, as to the matter of them; some, as to their end; all, as to their principle. For out of the evil treasure of the heart can proceed nothing but what is evil. The man that understands the evil of his own heart, how vile it is, is the only useful, fruitful, solidly believing, and obedient person. Others are fit only to delude themselves, to disquiet families, churches, and all relations whatever.

✦ JOHN OWEN
On Indwelling Sin, in *Oweniana*, 1

TRIALS

The compass of our knowledge of ways and means is very narrow, as, if one is blocked up, oftentimes we cannot see another. But our God knows many ways of relief where we know but one or none at all, and it is very usual for the Lord to bring the lifting up of His people in a way they had no view to after repeated disappointments from those quarters whence they had great expectation.

✦ THOMAS BOSTON
Crook in the Lot, 170

The proud heart dwells and expatiates on the man's sufferings in the trial and casts out all the folds of the trial on that side and views them again and again. But when the Spirit of God comes duly to humble in order to lifting up, He will cause the man to pass, in a sort, the suffering side of the trial and turn his eyes on his own conduct in it, ransack it, judge himself impartially, and condemn himself, so that his mouth will be stopped. This is that humility that goes before the lifting up in time in the way of the promise.

✦ THOMAS BOSTON
Crook in the Lot, 171

It was a good speech, if well understood, of a good man once, that he was as much beholden to God for his infirmities as for his graces. If Peter had not fallen, he had fallen. The saints sometimes fall that when they rise they may stand the faster.

✦ FRANCIS RAWORTH
On Jacob's Ladder, 14

Think not much of a storm upon the sea when Christ is in the ship.

✦ SAMUEL RUTHERFORD
Prison Sayings, 47

Grace tried is more than grace; it is glory in its infancy. Who knows the truth of grace without a trial? Oh, how little Christ gets of us but that which He wins, so to speak, with much toil and pains! And how soon would faith freeze without a cross!

✦ SAMUEL RUTHERFORD
Prison Sayings, 59–60

Those whose houses have fallen by the fire [of London] the Lord could, and confident I am, the Lord has made them greater gainers another way. They have lost, it may be, much in temporal things; but they are, or may be (if they be not wanting to themselves) gainers of spiritual things which are of a higher and more excellent nature. I have known and heard of many of God's people whose houses are burnt and goods spoiled who have taken the loss with so much cheerfulness, humility, meekness, patience, contentment, and thankfulness that anything was saved, if it were only their lives, that it has been my wonder and joy; to gain such a spirit has more of good than the loss of all external enjoyments has of evil.

✦ THOMAS VINCENT
God's Terrible Voice in the City, 79

THE TRINITY

[God the Father] is indeed first, not in priority of nature, for there is but one God, one infinite; nor in priority of time, for there is but one eternal; nor in priority of honor, for none is greater than another; but in respect of order, *prioritate originis*, as being the fountain of the deity, *principium deitatis*. The Father is of none, the Son is of the Father only, the Holy Ghost from them both.

✦ THOMAS ADAMS
Meditations upon the Creed,
in *Works*, 3:99

That there is one divine nature or essence common unto three persons incomprehensibly united and ineffably distinguished, united in essential attributes, distinguished by peculiar idioms and relations, all equally infinite in every divine perfection, each different from other in order and manner of subsistence; that there is a mutual inexistence of one in all and all in one; a communication without any deprivation or diminution in the communicant; an eternal generation and an eternal procession without precedence or succession, without proper causality or dependence; a Father imparting His own, and the Son receiving His Father's life, and a Spirit issuing from both without any division or multiplication of essence. These are notions which may well puzzle our reason in conceiving how they agree but should not stagger our faith in assenting that they are true, upon which we should meditate not with hope to comprehend but with disposition to admire, veiling our faces in the presence and prostrating our reason at the feet of wisdom so far transcending us.

✦ ISAAC BARROW
"A Defence of the Blessed Trinity,"
in *Sermons*, 423

As there are three persons in the Trinity—the Father, the Son, and the Holy Ghost—so each of these persons have their several works which are eminently ascribed to them. The Father's works were to create us to rule us as His rational creatures by the law of nature and judge us thereby and in mercy to provide us a Redeemer when we are lost and to send His Son and accept His ransom.

The works of the Son for us were these: to ransom and redeem us by His sufferings and righteousness; to give out the promise or law of grace and rule and judge the world as their Redeemer on terms of grace and to make intercession for us, that the benefits of His death may be communicated; and to send the Holy Ghost, which the Father also doth by the Son.

The works of the Holy Ghost for us are these: to indite the Holy Scriptures by inspiring and guiding the prophets and apostles and sealing the word by His miraculous gifts and works; and the illuminating and exciting the ordinary ministers of the gospel, and so enabling them and helping them to publish that word; and by the same word illuminating and converting the souls of men.

✦ RICHARD BAXTER
Call to the Unconverted, 26–27

The doctrine of the Trinity! That is the substance, that is the ground and fundamental of all, for by this doctrine and this only the man is made a Christian; and he that has not this doctrine, his profession is not worth a button. You must know that sometimes the church in the wilderness has but little light, but the diminution of her light is not then so much in or as to substantials as it is as to circumstantial things; she has then the substantials with her in her darkest day. The doctrine of the Trinity! You may ask me what that is. I answer, it is that doctrine that showeth us the love of God the Father in giving His Son, the love of God the Son in giving Himself, and the love of the Lord the Spirit in His work of regenerating us, that we may be made able to lay hold of the love of the Father by His Son and so enjoy eternal life by grace.

✦ JOHN BUNYAN
Riches, 38–39

There is a twofold knowledge of God, absolute and relative. The absolute knowledge of the eternal power and Godhead is in part discovered by the works of God, as has been shown... but the relative knowledge of God (I speak of inward relations between the three subsistences) is not—nay, cannot be—attained unto by the light of nature; no example can illustrate, no reason angelic or human comprehend the hidden excellency of this glorious mystery, but it is discovered to us by a divine revelation in the written Word, and therefore our faith must receive and our piety adore what our reason cannot comprehend.

✦ FRANCIS CHEYNELL
Divine Trinunity, 18–19

The distinct subsistences of the persons of the Godhead and blessed Trinity are more brightly discovered in Jesus Christ than ever before. God was but darkly seen before in the distinct subsistences of the persons of the Trinity, but in the gospel, through Jesus Christ, there is a glorious manifestation thereof (2 Cor. 4:6).

✦ PATRICK GILLESPIE
Ark of the Covenant Opened, 171

TRUST

Let thy soul retain the deepest impression of the almightiness, wisdom, goodness, and faithfulness of God and how certainly all persons, things, and events are in His power; and how impotent all the world is to resist Him, and that nothing can hurt thee but by His consent. The principal means for a confirmed confidence in God is to know Him and to know that all things that we can fear are nothing and can do nothing but by His command and motion or permission. I am not afraid of a bird or a worm because I know it is too weak for me. And if I rightly apprehend how much all creatures are too weak for God and how sufficient God is to deliver me, His trust would quiet me.

✦ RICHARD BAXTER
A Christian Directory, in
Practical Works, 2:400

Remember the grounds of confidence and quietness which God hath given you in His Son, His covenant, His Spirit, His sacraments, and your own and others' manifold experiences. I name them all together because I would have you set them all together before your eyes. Will He not give you "all things with Him" that hath "given you His Son"? Is not Christ a sufficient undertaker and encourager? Are not His covenant, promise, and oath sufficient security for you?

✦ RICHARD BAXTER
A Christian Directory, in
Practical Works, 2:401

A person at peace with God becomes then a child of God. And when once the Christian comes to know his relation and the dear love of his heavenly Father to him, afflictions from or sufferings for Him dread him not because he knows it is inconsistent with the love of a father either to hurt his child himself or suffer him to be hurt by another if he can help it. I have wondered at Isaac's patience to submit to be bound for a sacrifice and see the knife so near his throat without any hideous outcries or struggling that we read of; he was old enough to be apprehensive of death and the horror of it, being conceived by some to be above twenty years of age. That he was of good growth is out of doubt by the wood which Abraham caused him to carry for the sacrifice, but such was the authority Abraham had over his son and the confidence that Isaac had in his father that he durst put his life into his hands, which, had the knife been in any other hand, he would hardly have done. Whoever may be the instrument of any trouble to a saint, the rod or sword is at God's disposure; Christ saw the cup in His Father's hand, and that made Him take it willingly.

♦ WILLIAM GURNALL
Christian in Complete Armour, 419

Where faith enables men to live to God, as to their eternal concerns, it will enable them to trust Him in all the difficulties and hazards of this life. To pretend a trust in God as to our souls and in visible things and not resign our temporal affairs with patience and quietness to His disposal is a vain pretense, and we may take hence an eminent trial of our faith. Too many deceive themselves with a presumption of faith in the promises of God as to things future and eternal, but if they are brought into any temporal trial, they seem utter strangers to the life of faith. It was not so with Abraham; his faith acted itself uniformly with respect to the providences as well as the promises of God.

♦ JOHN OWEN
Oweniana, 96–97

The incomparable God must have incomparable trust. The more able and faithful any person is, the more firmly we trust him. Now God is incomparable in power: He hath an almighty arm; incomparable in faithfulness: he "cannot lie" (Titus 1:2); "It is impossible for God to lie" (Heb. 6:18). Therefore God must have our surest love and firmest faith (Rom. 4:20; Heb. 6:18). We must esteem His words as good as deeds and rely on all His promises as if it were already performed.

♦ GEORGE SWINNOCK
The Incomparableness of God,
in *Works*, 4:475

TRUTH

Such is the immutability of truth: the patrons of it make it not greater, the opposers make it not less—as the splendor of the sun is not enlarged by them that bless it nor eclipsed by them that hate it. That thing which may be extended may also be contracted; if it admit addition, it may also suffer diminution. God and His truth are liable to neither.

✦ THOMAS ADAMS
Exposition upon…Second…Peter, 247

In seeking truth, rest not upon any means though it be never so great, nor despise any means though it be never so small…. God…delights to reveal His truths to those that are most unlikely. The great truth of the incarnation, first revealed to shepherds. The great truth of the resurrection, first revealed to Mary, a woman.

✦ WILLIAM BRIDGE
"The Saints' Hiding Place in
the Time of God's Anger,"
in *Works*, 4:366

Truth is like our first parents, most beautiful when naked. It was sin that covered them, and it's ignorance that hides this.

✦ SAMUEL CLARK
Saint's Nosegay, 125

It's just with God, that those who will not have truth their king and willingly obey it should have falsehood their tyrant, to whom their judgments should be captivated and enslaved.

✦ SAMUEL CLARK
Saint's Nosegay, 151

It is a known experiment, that the more spiritual any truth is, the more will carnal reason object against it: "How can these things be?" (John 3:9).

✦ ELISHA COLES
Practical Discourse, 185

Some things we trust God with; some things God trusts us with. The great thing which we put into God's hand to be kept for us, your soul: "He is able to keep that which I have committed unto him against that day" (2 Tim. 1:12). That which God trusts us chiefly with is His truth. It is therefore said to be delivered to them as a charge of money to a friend whom we confide in: "Contend for the faith which was once delivered unto the saints" (Jude 3).

✦ WILLIAM GURNALL
Christian in Complete Armour, 218

It is good to preserve truth, but small distempers will not need a cure; 'tis as if a man should [set] fire [to] a house to destroy the mice in it. Union is good, but rigorous enforcements, especially in trifles and things that lie far from the heart of religion, are not so warrantable.

✦ THOMAS MANTON
Meate out of the Eater, 49

Sometimes truth is lost first in a church, and then holiness; and sometimes the decay or hatred of holiness is the cause of the loss of truth. But when either is rejected, the other will not abide.

✦ JOHN OWEN
Golden Book, 129

Truth and good company will give a modest man a little confidence sometimes.

✦ JOHN OWEN
Golden Book, 233

Let truth have full scope without check or restraint, and let Satan and his instruments do their worst, they shall not prevail; as Jerome said of the Pelagians in his time: "The discovery of your opinions is the vanquishing of them; your blasphemies appear at the first blush."

✦ RICHARD SIBBES
Bruised Reed and Smoking Flax, 140–41

What is spiritual is eternal. Truth is a beam of Christ's Spirit, both in itself and as it is ingrafted into the soul; therefore it and the grace, though little, wrought by it will prevail. A little thing in the hand of a giant will do great matters. A little faith strengthened by Christ will work wonders.

✦ RICHARD SIBBES
Bruised Reed and Smoking Flax, 151

UNBELIEF

Unbelief may be considered the greatest bar to justification, yet pride is the greatest hindrance to sanctification. All sins do homage to pride as their captain and their king. The Lord frequently makes use of other sins to humble the sin of pride in His saints, but pride is not employed to weaken any other sin.

✦ ISAAC AMBROSE
Christian Warrior, 106

There are three great causes of this dark and dangerous state of soul which make the thoughts of heaven uneffectual and uncomfortable to us, which therefore must be overcome with the daily diligence of your whole lives. First, unbelief, which makes you look toward the life to come with doubtings and uncertainty, and this is the most common, radical, powerful, and pernicious impediment to a heavenly life. The second is the love of present things, which being the vanity of a poor, low, fleshly mind, the reviving of reason may do much to overcome it, but it's the sound belief of the life to come that must prevail. The third is the inordinate fear of death, which hath so great advantage in the constitution of our nature that it is commonly the last enemy which we overcome, as death itself is the last enemy which Christ overcomes for us.

✦ RICHARD BAXTER
Baxteriana, 138–39

Unbelief usually argues from one of these two grounds: Can God do this? or Will God do it? It is questioning either His power or His will; but after this [i.e., Christ's incarnation], let it cease forever to cavil against either. His power to save should never be questioned by any that know what sufferings and infinite burdens He supported in our nature, and surely His willingness to save should never be put to a question by any that consider how low He was content to stoop for our sakes.

✦ JOHN FLAVEL
Fountain of Life, 169

Unbelief is the Beelzebub, the prince of sins. As faith is the radical grace, so is unbelief a radical sin, a sinning sin. As of all sinners, those are most infamous who are ringleaders and make others sin, which is the brand that God hath set upon Jeroboam's name—Jeroboam the son of Nebat, who sinned and made Israel to sin (1 Kings 14:16)—so among sins they are most horrid that are most productive of other sins. Such a one is unbelief above any other; it is a ringleading sin, a sin-making sin.

✦ WILLIAM GURNALL
Christian in Complete Armour, 439

There are two sins that claim a pre-eminence in hell—hypocrisy and unbelief; and therefore, other sinners are threatened "to have their portion with hypocrites" (Matt. 24:51) and "with the unbelievers" (Luke 12:46), as if those infernal mansions were taken up principally for these, and all others were but inferior prisoners. But of the two, unbelief is the greatest and that which may with an emphasis be called, above this or any other, the damning sin. "He that believeth not is condemned already" (John 3:18).

✦ WILLIAM GURNALL
Christian in Complete Armour, 440

Most under the gospel know that unbelief is a damning sin and that there is no name to be saved by but the name of Christ, yet how few of those know this convincingly, so as to apply this to their own consciences and to be affected with their own deplorable state. As he is a convicted drunkard in law who in open court or before a lawful authority, upon clear testimony, and deposition of witnesses is found and judged to be such, so he, scripturally, is a convinced sinner who upon the clear evidence of the word brought against him by the Spirit is found by his own conscience (God's officer in his bosom) to be so. Speak now, poor creature, did ever such an act of the Spirit of God pass upon thee as this is?

✦ WILLIAM GURNALL
Christian in Complete Armour, 445

It cannot, indeed, be denied but that an unbeliever sins when he prays, but it is not his praying is his sin but in his praying unbelievingly. And therefore he sins less in praying than in neglecting to pray, because when he prays, his sin lies but in the circumstance and manner. But when he doth not pray, then he stands in a total defiance to the duty God hath commanded him to perform and means God hath appointed him to use for obtaining grace.

✦ WILLIAM GURNALL
Christian in Complete Armour, 459

Now, if faith be the work of God above all other, then unbelief is the work of the devil, and that which he had rather thou should do than any other sin; and despair is unbelief at the worst. Unbelief among sins is as the plague among diseases, the most dangerous; but when it rises to despair, then it is as the plague with the tokens appearing that bring the certain message of death with them. Unbelief is despair in the bud; despair is unbelief at its full growth.

✦ WILLIAM GURNALL
Christian in Complete Armour, 509

Unbelief is a soul-enfeebling sin. It is to prayer as the moth is to the cloth; it wastes the soul's strength so that it cannot look up to God with any hope.

✦ WILLIAM GURNALL
Christian in Complete Armour, 775–76

Men are said to tempt God when they will not rest in that truth concerning God revealed in His word but will needlessly make experiments whether He be so just, wise, faithful, etc. as in His word He is said to be, which may be done, first, by willful sinning, as it were trying whether He be omniscient… (Acts 5:3). Secondly, by needless rushing upon any danger without a calling (Matt. 4:6–7). Thirdly, by requiring a sign needlessly and out of a false, dissembling heart, only to see whether such a miracle can be wrought or no (Matt. 16:1). Fourthly, by prescribing God when and how He shall perform His promises, which limiting of God proceeds from infidelity.

✦ ARTHUR JACKSON
*Help for the Understanding of
Holy Scripture, 466*

Unbelief is itself the grand disobedience. For this is the work of God, that which the gospel mainly commands, that ye believe (John 6:29); therefore, the apostle calls it the obedience of faith (Rom. 1:5). And there is nothing indeed more worthy of the name of obedience than the subjection of the mind to receive and to believe those supernatural truths which the gospel teaches concerning Jesus Christ.

✦ ROBERT LEIGHTON
*A Commentary upon the First Epistle
of Peter, in Whole Works, 1:225*

Unbelief is the root of rebellion and apostasy (Heb. 3:12).

✦ JOHN TRAPP
*Commentary on the Old and
New Testaments, 1:267*

Unbelief is the root and receptacle of sin.

✦ THOMAS WATSON
The Beatitudes, in Discourses, 2:239

Unbelief hardens the heart; these two sins are linked together: "He… upbraided them with their unbelief and hardness of heart." Unbelief breeds the stone of the heart; he that believes not God's threatenings will never fear Him; he that believes not God's promises will never love Him.

✦ THOMAS WATSON
The Beatitudes, in Discourses, 2:240

Of all sins, beware of the rock of unbelief. "Take heed…lest there be in any of you an evil heart of unbelief" (Heb. 3:12). Men think as long as they are not drunkards or swearers it is no great matter to be unbelievers. This is the gospel sin. It disparages Christ's infinite merit as if it would not save; it makes the wound of sin to be broader than the plaster of Christ's blood. This is high contempt offered to Christ and is a deeper spear than that which the Jews thrust into His side.

✦ THOMAS WATSON
Gleanings, 15

UNCERTAINTIES

There are four things which do admit of much uncertainty: (1) One is all our earthly possessions and comforts. "Wilt thou set thine eyes upon that which is not?" saith Solomon (Prov. 23:5).... (2) The second is the gracious motions of the Spirit of God working upon our spirits: "My spirit shall not always strive with man" (Gen. 6:3). The dealings of God's Spirit with us are many times like Peter's vision of the sheet, which was let down but quickly drawn up to heaven again.... (3) The third is the day of grace, our gospel day, wherein Christ reveals Himself and offers Himself and... salvation; this is a day for eternity, but it is not an eternal day. It may quickly be lost, and forever lost. (4) The fourth is all the lives and pains and labors of the prophets and ministers of God.... This day the minister lives and preaches, the next day he is sick and dies; you cannot say of the best minister on earth, he shall be ours forever or long or a week or a day. Such an instability is there not only in the best of our outward comforts but also in the best of our spiritual helps.

✦ OBADIAH SEDGWICK
"Elisha His Lamentation," in Strong,
Heavenly Treasure, 414–17

UNITY

Self-denial and true love are inseparable. Self-love makes a monopoly of all things to its own interest, and this is most opposite to Christian affection and communion, which puts all in one bank. If every one of the members should seek its own things, and not the good of the whole body, what a miserable distemper would it cause in the body?

✦ HUGH BINNING
"An Essay upon Christian Love,"
in *Several Sermons*, 178

Were Christians duly instructed how many lesser differences in mind and judgment and practice are really consistent with the nature, ends, and genuine fruit of the unity that Christ requires among them, it would undoubtedly prevail with them so to manage themselves in their differences by mutual forbearance and condescension in their love, as not to contract the guilt of being disturbers or breakers of it. To speak plainly, among all the churches in the world which are free from idolatry and persecution, it is not different opinions or a difference in judgment about revealed truths; not a different practice in sacred administrations; but pride, self-interest, love of honor, reputation, and dominion, with the influence of civil or political intrigues and considerations that are the true cause of that defect of evangelical unity that is at this day amongst them.

✦ JOHN OWEN
*A Discourse concerning Evangelical
Love, Church Peace, and Unity,*
in *Golden Book*, 104

This is the unity, or rather conspiracy, of the Church of Rome. The spouse only is but one (Song 6:9). Other societies are but as the clay in the toes of Nebuchadnezzar's image. They may cleave together but not incorporate one into another. There is a great deal of seeming unity under antichrist. The Turks also have little dissension in their religion, as any. But well may that garment have no seam that has no shape.

♦ JOHN TRAPP
Commentary...upon...the New Testament, 1012

Christ not only prayed for peace but bled for it. "Having made peace through the blood of his cross" (Col. 1:20), He died not only to make peace between God and man but between man and man. Christ suffered on the cross that He might cement Christians together with His blood; as He prayed for peace, so He paid for peace. Christ was Himself bound to bring us into the bond of peace.

♦ THOMAS WATSON
The Beatitudes, in *Discourses*, 2:285

UNIVERSALISM

The criers up of universal grace say that Christ died intentionally for all. But then why are not all saved? Can Christ be frustrate of His intention? Some are so gross to aver that all shall actually be saved. But hath not our Lord Christ told us that the gate is strait, "and few there be that find it" (Matt. 7:14)? How all can go in at this gate and yet but few find it seems to me a paradox.

♦ THOMAS WATSON
"The One Thing Necessary,"
in *Discourses*, 1:359–60

UNPARDONABLE SIN

The sin against the Holy Ghost is an utter, willful, and spiteful rejection of the gospel of salvation by Christ, together with an advised and absolute falling away from the profession of it so far that, against former knowledge and conscience, a man doth maliciously oppose and blaspheme the Spirit of Christ in the word and ordinances of the gospel and motions of the Spirit in them, having resisted, rejected, and utterly quenched all those common and more inward gifts and motions wrought upon their hearts and affections which sometimes were entertained by them. Insomuch that out of hatred of the Spirit of life in Christ, they crucify to themselves afresh the Son of God and do put Him, both in His ordinances of religion and in His members, to open shame, treading underfoot the Son of God, counting the blood of the covenant, wherewith they were sanctified, an unholy thing; doing despite to the Spirit of grace. If you carefully look into those places of the Scripture which speak of this sin and also observe the opposition which the apostle makes between sinning against the law and sinning against the gospel, you will clearly find out the nature of this sin (Matt. 12:24, 31–32; Mark 3:28–30; Luke 12:10; Heb. 6:4–6; 10:26–29).

♦ HENRY SCUDDER
Christian's Daily Walk, 312–13

I would ask you who think you have committed the sin against the Holy Ghost these questions: Does it grieve you that you have committed it? Could you wish that you had not committed it? If it were to be committed, would you not forbear it, if you could choose? Should you esteem yourself beholden to God if He would make you partaker of the blood and Spirit of His Son, thereby to pardon and purge your sin and to give you grace to repent? Nay, are you troubled that you cannot bring your heart unto a sense of desire of pardon and grace? If you can say yea, then although the sin or sins which trouble you may be some fearful sin of which you must be exhorted speedily to repent, yet certainly it is not the sin against the Holy Ghost. It is not that unpardonable sin, that sin unto death.

♦ HENRY SCUDDER
Christian's Daily Walk, 313

UNREGENERACY

The state of unregeneracy is a state of friendship with sin and Satan. If it be enmity against God (as it is), then friendship with Satan.... Sometimes indeed there appears a scuffle between Satan and a carnal heart, but it is a mere cheat, like the fighting of two fencers on a stage. You would think at first they were in earnest, but observing how wary they are where they hit one another, you may soon know they do not mean to kill; and that which puts all out of doubt, when the prize is done you shall see them making merry together with what they have got of their spectators, which was all they fought for. When a carnal heart makes the greatest bustle against sin by complaining of it or praying against it, follow him but off the stage of duty (where he had gained the reputation of a saint, the prize he fights for), and you shall see them sit as friendly together in a corner as ever.

♦ WILLIAM GURNALL
Christian in Complete Armour, 28

A man in the state of corrupt nature is nothing else but a filthy dunghill of all abominable vices. He is a stinking, rotten carrion, become altogether unprofitable and good for nothing. His heart is the devil's storehouse, a heap of odious lusts; his tongue is a fountain of cursing and bitterness and rotten communication; his hand is a mischievous instrument of filthiness, deceit, and violence; his eyes great thoroughfares of lust, pride, and vanity; his feet are swift engines, moving strongly to revenge, wantonness, and lucre; his life a long chain of sinful actions, every later link being more wicked than the former. Yea, it is but (as it were) one continued web of wickedness, spun out and made up by the hands of the devil and the flesh, an evil spinner, and a worse weaver. He is nothing but a pitcher of earth, filled up to the brim with the poisonous liquor of hell.

♦ WILLIAM WHATELY
New Birth, 7–8

UNTEACHABLE

An unteachable heart is a great judgment. This was Pharaoh's judgment; no counsel, no message, no reproof, no warning, no plague could soften him. When the Lord designs to bring judgment upon a soul, then He gives it up to an unteachable frame.

✦ MATTHEW MEAD
"The Power of Grace," in
Name in Heaven, 88

VISIONS

In this case they [i.e., people suffering from overmuch sorrow] are exceeding prone to think they have revelations, and whatever comes into their minds, they think some revelation brought it thither. They used to say, "This text of Scripture at such a time was set upon my mind, and that text at another time was set on my mind," when oft the sense that they took them in was false or a false application of it made to themselves, and perhaps several texts applied to contrary conclusions, as if one gave them hope and another contradicted it.... And some of them hereupon are very prone to prophesies and verily believe that God hath foretold them this or that, till they see that it comes not to pass, and then they are ashamed.

✦ RICHARD BAXTER
Preservatives against Melancholy, 20–21

So many Christians, when they lie under great agonies and sore perplexities of soul and are encouraged to act faith upon the promises and to rest their weary souls upon the word of grace, are ready to think and say that these things, these means will never heal them nor comfort them nor be a relief or support unto them unless the Lord does from heaven, by extraordinary revelations, visions, signs, miracles confirm His promises to them; and hereupon they make light of the blessed Scriptures, which are the springs of life and the only ground upon which all our comfort, peace, and happiness is to be built. Yea, they relinquish that more sure word of prophecy which shines as a light in a dark place (2 Peter 1:19).

✦ THOMAS BROOKS
Cabinet of Choice Jewels, 37

As to visions of angels, we believe the Christian reader will easily persuade himself that the blessed angels would rather lie down in the flames of hell than come to confirm such wicked, anti-Christian doctrines, but this is an old fetch of the prince of darkness.

✦ CHRISTOPHER FOWLER
Daemonium meridianum,
Satan at Noon, xxix

VIVIFICATION

Vivification is the second part of sanctification, whereby the image or life of God is restored in man (Eph. 4:24; Col. 3:10; Rev. 12:2). Having put on the new man, be ye transformed by the renewing of your mind.

✦ WILLIAM AMES
Marrow of Sacred Divinity, 144

VOCATION

Let the nailer keep to his hammer, the husbandman his plough, the tailor to his shears, the baker to his kneading trough, the miner to his toll, the tanner to his hides, and the soldier to his arms, etc. They must not leap from the shop to the pulpit, from the army to the ministry, from the blue apron to the black gown, etc. But if ever men would have comfort, let them keep the bounds and limits of their particular callings. God hath set every calling its bounds, which none may pass. Superiors must govern; inferiors obey and be governed. Ministers must study and preach; people must hear and obey, etc.

✦ THOMAS HALL
Pulpit Guarded, 25

WAITING UPON GOD

Patience includes and comprehends an act of waiting upon God and His good pleasure. Waiting is an act of faith continued or lengthened out, and where faith would of itself be short-winded, patience ekes it out.

✦ THOMAS GOODWIN
"Patience and Its Perfect Work,"
in *Works*, 2:449

WANDERING THOUGHTS

Our thoughts at best are like wanton spaniels who, though they go with and accompany their master and come to their journey's end with him, yet do run after every bird and wildly pursue every flock of sheep they see.

✦ SAMUEL CLARK
Saint's Nosegay, 33

If we have not mines of precious truths hid in our hearts, no wonder if our thoughts coin nothing but dross. Frothy thoughts, for better

materials which should feed the mint, are wanting.

✦ SAMUEL CLARK
Saint's Nosegay, 34

WATCHFULNESS

If our worst enemies be sometimes our best friends, then what reason is there that we should be discouraged, although we be much opposed? Now so it is many times; as our best friends are our worst enemies by flattering us, so our worst enemies are our best friends by making us more watchful. "So many enemies, so many schoolmasters," said one.

✦ WILLIAM BRIDGE
Lifting Up, 201

The helps of…holy watching are [the following]:

(1) Sobriety, which is joined to prayer watchfulness: "Be sober and watch unto prayer."…

(2) Bodily watchfulness: both are aimed at under that exhortation. "Watch and pray lest ye enter into temptation." The eyes of the mind are hardly watching when the eyes of the body are scarce waking.…

(3) A heavenly frame of spirit. Angels are very vigilant. "Their angels are always beholding the face of my heavenly Father." A godly man's watchtower is a more sublime station and condition than is usual; earthly, sensual, worldly spirits are not fit to keep this holy watch.

(4) A wise and awful frame of heart, apprehensive of the weight and worth of prayer, of the glory and greatness of God....

(5) Composedness of mind and thought, together with earnestness of desires and deep sensibleness of our present pressing necessities....

(6) A holy keeping ourselves in a constant and general watch of spirit in other things and passages of our Christian work and way. Watch unto, in and after hearing the word and reading of it, conference about it, meditation upon it, and practicing of it. "We must observe all the commandments of the Lord."

♦ THOMAS COBBET
Gospel Incense, 272–73

Watchfulness doth include some further business or duty to be done that is not yet performed, for watchfulness is an act to help forward some further act. As, for example, we are bound to remember God in all our ways; the want of this is the reason we so often sin against God. Now if we did remember God, if we did remember His holiness, if we did remember the greatness of His power and the strictness of His justice against sin, if we did remember our death and what account we are to make before Him, this would be a great help to keep us from sin.

♦ WILLIAM FENNER
"The Spiritual Watch," in *Four Profitable Treatises*, 77

The saint's sleeping time is Satan's tempting time; every fly dares venture to creep on a sleeping lion. No temptation so weak but is strong enough to foil a Christian that is napping in security. Samson asleep, and Delilah cut his locks. Saul asleep, and the spear is taken away from his very side, and he never the wiser. Noah asleep, and his graceless son has a fit time to discover his father's nakedness. Eutychus asleep, nods and falls from the third loft and is taken up for dead. Thus, the Christian asleep in security may soon be surprised so as to lose much of his spiritual strength.

♦ WILLIAM GURNALL
Christian in Complete Armour, 203

He that watches his heart all day is most likely to find it in tune for prayer at night, whereas loose walking breeds lazy praying.

♦ WILLIAM GURNALL
Christian in Complete Armour, 674

He that prays and watches not is like him that sows a field with precious seed but leaves the gate open for hogs to come and rout it up.

♦ WILLIAM GURNALL
Christian in Complete Armour, 715

Watching is taken metaphorically for the vigilancy of the soul; this is principally meant here and in other Scriptures where we are commanded to watch (Mark 13:35; 1 Thess. 5:6; 1 Peter 5:8; Rev. 16:15).

♦ WILLIAM GURNALL
Christian in Complete Armour, 763

Dear Ned,

There is so much discourse of wars that it may well put us in mind of our spiritual warfare; in both, there is nothing more requisite than to stand upon the watch. To be surprised is both a shame and great disadvantage to a soldier; therefore, dear Ned, stand, as it were, sentinel and be sure you be not found sleeping. Watch against your enemy, and the Lord of heaven, that never comes so near sleep as to slumber, keep you in all safety.

✦ BRILLIANA HARLEY
to her son Edward, 1639,
in *Letters*, 57

After such gracious manifestations of divine favor, are you excited to watchfulness and circumspection? A person who travels in a strange country, having rich jewels and other valuable articles in his possession, is constantly on his guard, lest he should be robbed of his treasure. Do you proceed with the same caution, lest sin, Satan, or a deluding world should deprive you of your spiritual comforts?

✦ OLIVER HEYWOOD
Life in God's Favour, 183

We ought to watch, but when we do so in obedience to our commander, the Captain of our salvation, yet it is His own watching who sleeps not nor so much as slumbers; it is that preserves us and makes ours not to be in vain (Ps. 121:5; Isa. 27:3). And therefore those two are jointly commanded: watch and pray that ye enter not into temptation. Watch, there is the necessity of our diligence; pray, there is the insufficiency of it and the necessity of His watching, by whose power we are effectually preserved; and that power is our fort.

✦ ROBERT LEIGHTON
A Commentary upon the First Epistle of Peter, in *Whole Works*, 1:49

When once the soul of a believer hath obtained sweet and real communion with Christ, it looks about him, watches all temptations, all ways whereby sin might approach, to disturb him in his enjoyment of his dear Lord and Savior, his rest and desire. How doth it charge itself not to omit anything nor to do anything that may interrupt the communion obtained!… A believer that hath gotten Christ in his arms is like one that hath found great spoils, or a pearl of price. He looks about him every way and fears everything that may deprive him of it. Riches make men watchful, and the actual sensible possession of Him in whom are all the riches and treasure of God will make men look about them for the keeping of Him. The line of choicest communion is a line of the greatest spiritual solicitousness.

✦ JOHN OWEN
On Communion with God, in *Golden Book*, 171

For want of watchfulness, God often gives us up for a time to such a perplexed estate that we shall not know we have any grace; though we have a principle of grace, yet we shall not know it, but may even go out of the world in darkness and fear.

✦ RICHARD SIBBES
Divine Meditations and Holy Contemplations, 40

WEALTH

Wealth is like a bird; it hops all day from man to man, as that doth from tree to tree, and none can say where it will roost or rest at night.

✦ THOMAS ADAMS
"Semper Idem, or The Immutable Mercy of Jesus Christ," in Works, 3:3

Many distrustful fathers are so carking for their posterity that while they live, they starve their bodies and hazard their souls to leave them rich. To such a father it is said justly: *Dives es haeredi, pauper inopsque tibi* (like an overkind hen, he feeds his chickens and famishes himself).... Their folly is ridiculous; they fear lest their children should be miserable yet take the only course to make them miserable, for they leave them not so much heirs to their goods as to their evils. They do as certainly inherit their father's sins as their lands.

✦ THOMAS ADAMS
"Semper Idem, or The Immutable Mercy of Jesus Christ," in Works, 3:8–9

For prayer observe this method: (1) Acknowledge God's mercy both in His promises and performances; say, "Lord, Thou hast promised that no good thing wilt Thou withhold from them that walk uprightly; and surely Thou art true in Thy sayings. I believe by virtue of Thy promise I enjoy this land and those goods. I have nothing, Lord, but merely of free grace and by virtue of a promise." (2) Importune the Lord for sanctification of prosperity and for God's blessing upon the means. The more we prosper, the more earnest should the prayers of faith be; for of ourselves we have no power to wield a good estate well, no ability to preserve or keep it. In greatest wealth we lie open to many temptations, and if we pray not earnestly that God may sanctify all His temporal blessings to us, we shall cool in grace. (3) Praise God for His mercies, and devote ourselves unto Him from whom we have received all.

✦ ISAAC AMBROSE
"The Practice of Sanctification," in Works, 113

God hath taken away your estate, but not your portion. This is a sacred paradox. Honor and estate are not part of a Christian's jointure; they are rather accessories than essentials and are extrinsical and foreign. Therefore, the loss of these cannot denominate a man miserable. Still, the portion remains—"The LORD is my portion, saith my soul" (Lam. 3:24). Suppose one were worth a million of money and he should chance to lose a pin off his sleeve; this is no part of his estate, nor can we say he is undone. The loss of sublunary comforts is not so much to a Christian's portion as the loss of a pin is to a million.

✦ SIMEON ASHE
Primitive Divinity, 55

A crown of gold cannot cure the head-ache nor can a velvet slipper ease the gout; no more can honor or riches quiet or still the conscience.

✦ THOMAS BROOKS
Precious Remedies, 76

These things that are absolutely good are [an] absolute pledge of God's love, and by God bestowed upon His best beloved. They are the blessing of His right hand and belong to those that shall stand at His right hand. But riches and honors are in His left hand, saith Solomon. He fills the bellies of wicked men with this treasure. They are not *bona throni* [a good from the throne], but *bona scabelli* [a good from the footstool]. No man can know love or hatred by them or say, "God gives me riches; therefore He loves me." But of grace we may say, "God gives me faith and charity, and therefore He loves me."

✦ RALPH BROWNRIG
Sermon 3 on Prov. 30:8, in
Forty Sermons, 452

Must men be careless of their states in providing for their salvation? Is all to be done for the soul and nothing for the house? What shall I leave my children? Providence for thy everlast-ing state doth nothing to impair thy present state, and thy liberality doth augment and not diminish thy chil-dren's prosperity. Is the Lord so barren of wisdom or destitute of power as that He cannot enrich the one but He must impoverish the other, or that he cannot help the father without hurting the child?

✦ ROBERT CLEAVER
AND JOHN DOD
Plain and Familiar Exposition, 74

Death taketh me from my outward comforts, but yet I leave them to and for the comfort of my relations and friends which stay behind me. They will have the use of them, they will do them good. Though I leave them, they are not lost; my turn is served by them. Shall I grudge that others have them to serve their turn as they served mine? Hath it not been my care to get goods that I might leave them to my relations? And shall I now be unwilling to leave them that little which I have gotten? And which can now do me no more good?

✦ ZACHARY CROFTON
*Defence against the Dread of
Death, 62–63*

Reader, I advise thee, under all disap-pointments of thy expectations, to bless God for any comfortable enjoy-ment thou hast. If God give thee a smaller estate and a contented heart, it is as well—yea, better—than if thou hadst enjoyed thy desire. The bee makes a sweeter meal upon two or three flowers than the ox that hath so many mountains to graze upon.

✦ JOHN FLAVEL
"The Disappointed Seaman," in
Navigation Spiritualized, 327

The sluggard would fain prosper with-out diligence, and the atheist hopes to prosper by his diligence alone. But

Christians expect their prosperity from God's blessing in the way of honest diligence.

✦ JOHN FLAVEL
"The Successful Seaman," in
Navigation Spiritualized, 300–301

That man is surely rich in grace whose graces suffer no eclipse by his riches. It is as hard to be prosperous and humble as to be afflicted and cheerful.

✦ JOHN FLAVEL
"The Successful Seaman," in
Navigation Spiritualized, 310

Christians have two sorts of goods—the goods of the throne and the goods of the footstool—moveables and immoveables.

✦ JOHN FLAVEL
in Horn, *Puritan Remembrancer*, 5

[The good parent] does not give away his loaf to his children and then come to them for a piece of bread. He holds the reins (though loosely) in his own hands and keeps to reward duty and punish undutifulness, yet on good occasion, for his children's advancement, he will depart from part of his means. Base is their nature who will not have their branches lopped till their body be felled and will let go none of their goods as if it presaged their speedy death, whereas it doth not follow that he that puts off his cloak must presently go to bed.

✦ THOMAS FULLER
Holy and Profane States, 42

The world is to be minded but on the by, and the things of God and of the soul are to be my main business here in the world. Wherefore hath God set me in this world? Is it to get riches and honors and to have my pleasures and to gratify my lusts? No, but to glorify His name and to work out my own salvation; now when I make this my main business, I use the world aright.

✦ WILLIAM GREENHILL
Against Love of the World, in
Sound-Hearted Christian, 284

[Some people] by base practices make haste to be rich. But God makes as much haste to melt their estate as they to gather it. No care and providence of man will keep that estate from God's curse which is got by so sinful a pursuit: "Wealth gotten by vanity"—that is, vain, unwarrantable courses—"shall be diminished" (Prov. 13:11).

✦ WILLIAM GURNALL
Christian in Complete Armour, 534

When the ship is likely to sink, we must not only pray but apply our hands to the pump. Is it temporal subsistence thou prays for? Pray and work, or pray and starve. Dost thou think to set God at work whilst thou sits with thy hand in thy bosom? Those two proverbs are observable—"The hand of the diligent maketh rich" (Prov. 10:4) and verse 22, "The blessing of the LORD, it maketh rich, and he addeth no sorrow with it." He that prays but is not diligent is not likely to be rich; he that is diligent but prays not may be rich, but he cannot be blessed with his riches; but he that obtains his riches by sincere prayer in conjunction with his diligence is rich by the blessing of God and shall escape the sorrow which the worldling lays up with his money. Yea, though he gets not an estate, yet he hath the blessing of God, and that makes him rich when there is no money in his purse.

✦ WILLIAM GURNALL
Christian in Complete Armour, 717

Riches may be well compared unto cisterns or pools which a small stream will easily fill if there be no leaks or wastes, but small wastes and expenses continuing, and not prevented, have deceived and undone many. No man knows how.

✦ WILLIAM HIGFORD
Institutions, 9

If Christ shall thus appear in glory to judge the world, let this doctrine put you upon the practice of this duty, moderately to use all the comforts you enjoy here in this life. This use the Holy Ghost makes: "Let your moderation be known unto all men. The Lord is at hand. Be careful for nothing; but in every thing by prayer and supplication let your requests be made known unto God" (Phil. 4:5–6). If the Lord be at hand, you should not dote too much upon the vanities of this world. You should not look upon your houses as if the foundation were laid in marble, and not in the dust. You should not so look upon the comforts of your life as if your flesh were iron and your bones of brass. Either Christ will come from heaven quickly to judge you, or else you must go from earth quickly to be judged by Him.

✦ CHRISTOPHER LOVE
Heaven's Glory, 58

Riches are not altogether inconsistent with Christianity. Let "the rich"—that is, the rich brother. Usually riches are a great snare. It is a hard matter to enjoy the world without being entangled with the cares and pleasures of it. The moon never suffers an eclipse but when it is at the full.

✦ THOMAS MANTON
Practical Exposition on the Epistle of James, 25

Riches beget pride and pride ends in atheism.

✦ THOMAS MANTON
Practical Exposition on the Epistle of James, 88

Our prosperity is like glass, brittle when shining.

✦ THOMAS MANTON
Practical Exposition on the Epistle of James, 198

As the things of this world are uncertain in the getting, so they are uncertain in the keeping. If men do not ruin us, moths may; if robbery doth not, rust may; if rust doth not, fire may; to which all earthly treasures are incident, as our Lord Christ teacheth us (Matt. 6:19). Solomon limned the world with wings: "Riches take themselves wings and fly as the eagle toward heaven." A man may be rich as Dives today, and yet poor as Lazarus tomorrow. Oh, how uncertain are all worldly affairs! But the true treasure of grace in the heart can never be lost; it is out of the reach both of rust and robber. He that gets the world gets a good he can never keep, but he that gets grace gets a good he shall never lose.

♦ MATTHEW MEAD
Almost Christian Discovered, 224

Riches and honor are but common blessings. They are the good things of the footstool, not of the throne; they are in the left hand of wisdom (Prov. 3:16). Now, no common mercy can argue special love: "No man knoweth either love or hatred by all that is before them" (Eccl. 9:1).

♦ RALPH ROBINSON
Christ All and in All, 113

Reader, why should you be so taken up with your riches when you will be so soon taken from your riches? Why do you dote upon a flower which a day may wither? As you are traveling beyond the world, so also it would be your wisdom to be trading above the world. But, alas, such are not easily awaked who fall so fast asleep on the world's pillow.

♦ WILLIAM SECKER
Nonsuch Professor, 135

Reader, did you never hear a rich man complain of the want of riches? Though he has enough to support him, yet he has not enough to content him. Were it possible for the eye to see all that is to be seen, yet it would not be satisfied with seeing. If there be not enough in the world to satisfy the senses of men, how should there be enough in it to satisfy the souls of men?

♦ WILLIAM SECKER
Nonsuch Professor, 160

[A] principle by which a Christian should walk is this: that there is no judging of the inward conditions of men by the outward dispensations of God. The greatness of our estates is no argument of the goodness of our hearts. To prize ourselves by what we have and not by what we are is to estimate the value of the jewel by the golden frame which contains it. Grace and gold can live together, but the smallest degree of the former in the heart is preferable to a chain of the latter about the neck.

♦ WILLIAM SECKER
Nonsuch Professor, 213

Is it for a heaven-born soul to stand gazing and doting upon or passionately weeping over created friends, carnal liberty, corporeal health, houses made with hands, things below God— yea, and below itself too? Pore not too much upon them; value them only in God and refer them freely to Him. If you can say you have anything of your own, make much of it and spare not; but give unto God the things that are God's. And by that time you have done so, I think you need not dote upon what is left. We ought indeed at all times to enjoy all our creature comforts with hearts loosed from them, but if formerly our hearts have been too much joined to them, it is now time to loosen them.

♦ SAMUEL SHAW
Voice of One Crying in the Wilderness, 85

Can the posterity of such men rise up and call them blessed who make them heirs to nothing but poverty and distress? Or will it excuse them that they have been just to others who are thus cruel to their own flesh? No, limit yourselves in the expenses of dress, diet, and furniture; allow yourselves in no unreasonable or costly pleasures; be diligent in your callings and prudent in your concerns, that you may leave your families above the charity of their friends and enable them to live when your period of life ceases; that your exit may not be like the brutes, who have no concern for the offspring they leave behind them. "A good man leaveth an inheritance to his children's children." "Wealth and riches shall be in his house: and his righteousness endureth forever" (Prov. 13:22; Ps. 112:3).

♦ RICHARD STEELE
Religious Tradesman, 121

This is the way to a quiet conscience and a firm estate; you may then enjoy with pleasure and leave with comfort to your posterity whatever acquisitions a diligent hand and a good God has offered you. To which end: (1) Let the fear of God rule in hearts. Fear of shame may restrain men from many instances of injustice, but nothing less than the religious fear of God will make them universally just and honest. (2) Conquer your undue love to the world. A covetous and selfish temper is the grand spring of all injustice and oppression…. (3) Learn contentment in your present state and trust in God for futurity. His providence overrules and directs all the conditions of His creatures…. (4) Love your neighbor as yourself and place yourself in his

stead in all your dealings with him; it is certain you will then do nothing that is unjust or dishonorable by him. (5) Lastly, as this and every other virtue and grace must be derived from Christ Jesus…so let the practice of it be recommended to God by a true and living faith in Him as the great Mediator. Then, whatever your success is here below, you will not fail of an abundant reward above in the presence and favor of the just and righteous God.

♦ RICHARD STEELE
Religious Tradesman, 130–31

The threatenings of God's law that break poor men's hearts do but harden rich men's, as the sunbeams which soften the wax do nevertheless make the clay harder. We threaten death, and they live. We threaten poverty, and they are rich. We threaten want, and they abound. Long enough may we threaten ere they amend. If we seek by fair means to reclaim them, what care they for promised happiness who think they have attained present felicity?

♦ FRANCIS TAYLOR
God's Glory in Man's Happiness, 73

Riches are a mere uncertainty, an obscurity, a fallacy—one while they appear, and another while they disappear, as meteors in the air, as divedappers [i.e., waterfowl] in the water, as a flock of birds in a man's field. He cannot say they are his because they sit there, for they take unto them wings, saith Solomon, and flee away.

♦ JOHN TRAPP
Marrow of Many Good Authors, 1052

Have you much in the world? Do your riches increase? Set not your heart upon them. Make use of what God hath given you without such pinching and self-denial which the Lord Jesus never commanded in His precepts of that kind. God never gave riches to save but to use; take heed of exceeding the bounds in spending, and do not spare the moderate use of what you have for fear of future wanting; use part of your estates for yourselves in what is needful for the body and suitable to your degree and quality; lay aside part for your posterity; and lay out part in the help of those in necessity for relief of the poor, whereby you will lay up for yourselves "a good foundation against the time to come" and, at last, "lay hold on eternal life" (1 Tim. 6:18–19).

✦ THOMAS VINCENT
God's Terrible Voice in the City, 217

Remember, in every loss there is only a suffering. But in every discontent there is a sin, and one sin is worse than a thousand sufferings.

✦ THOMAS WATSON
Art of Divine Contentment, 58

Distribute your silver and gold to the poor before "the silver cord be loosed, or the golden bowl be broken" (Eccl. 12:6). Make your hands your executors, not as some do who reserve all they give till the term of life is ready to expire. And truly what is then bestowed is not given away but taken away by death. 'Tis not charity but necessity.

✦ THOMAS WATSON
Gleanings, 28

Gain is the golden bait with which Satan fishes for souls.

✦ THOMAS WATSON
Godly Man's Picture, 133

And what is one the better for all his wealth at death? "We brought nothing into this world, and it is certain we can carry nothing out" (1 Tim. 6:7). When the rich miser dies, what scrambling is there? His friends are scrambling for his goods, the worms are scrambling for his body, and the devils are scrambling for his soul.

✦ THOMAS WATSON
Mischief of Sin, 31

Creature confidence is another great bane and ruin of rich men, that certainly they had been happy if they had not been happy and they had been rich forever if they had not been rich for a moment. How many thousand men are undone by their estates? Men commit adultery, secret adultery, with a piece of earth in their affections, all for getting and grasping; and when they grasp it, then commit open idolatry in their hopes and expectations and say to gold, "Thou art my hope," and to a piece of silver, "Thou art my confidence" ([see] Job 31:24). This is that that God's soul abhors and cannot endure in any of His people.

✦ JEREMIAH WHITAKER
Christians Great Design on Earth, 10

THE WICKED

Heaven is given to the poor in spirit. Earth is bequeathed to the meek. What then remains for the proud and scornful wicked men but hell, their proper inheritance? As it is said of Judas, that son or heir of perdition, that he was gone to his own place (Acts 1:25). Now then, if wicked men have anything, they have it for the godly men's sakes because they are mixed together.

✦ DANIEL CAWDREY
Good Man, a Publick Good, 11

The world is a stage: every man an actor and plays his part here, either in a comedy or tragedy. The good man is a comedian which however he begins, ends merrily. But the wicked man acts a tragedy and therefore ever ends in horror. Thou sees a wicked man vaunt himself on his stage, stay till the last act and look to his end, as David did—and see whether that be peace. Thou wouldest make strange tragedies if thou wouldest have but one act. Who sees an ox grazing in a fat and rank pasture and thinks not that he is near to the slaughter? Whereas the lean beast that toils under the yoke is far enough from the shambles. The best wicked man cannot be so envied in his first shews as he is pitiable in the conclusion.

✦ JOSEPH HALL
Meditations and Vows, 70–71

As for the wicked of the world, they measure all their religion by their profit and will do nothing but for gain. They use God that they may enjoy the world, and this indeed is a base and mercenary love, like that love which the prodigal found from them upon whom he had spent his patrimony (Luke 15:30). But the godly use the world that they may enjoy God.

✦ NEHEMIAH ROGERS
The Penitent Citizen, in *Mirrour of Mercy*, 107

Beware we also of their companies; avoid we as much as may be both conversation and conference with the wicked. Their heads are forges of wicked wiles. They are plentifully furnished with store of stratagems and have mischievous fetches to bring their purposes to pass. Of receiving harm, we stand in great peril; of effecting good there is small hope.

✦ NEHEMIAH ROGERS
The Watchful Shepherd, in
True Convert, 101

The wicked first watch for a godly man's fall and then are big with blasphemy against godliness. Like miners, they work hard, though unseen, to blow up a saint's name. The psalmist tells us, "They…compassed us in our steps: they have set their eyes bowing down to the earth" (Ps. 17:11). It is an allusion to hunters, who go poring on the ground to find the print of the hare's claws when their dogs are at a loss in their scent; so Satan's agents go with their eyes bowing down, marking the saints' footsteps to find out if it be possible where they have slipped or stepped awry, that their bloodhounds may follow both their persons and their profession with loud cries and fresh noise.

✦ GEORGE SWINNOCK
The Christian Man's Calling,
in *Works,* 2:192

THE WILL

The will is the man in God's account, and what a man truly would be and have, he is and shall have.

✦ RICHARD BAXTER
Baxteriana, 226

What the foot is to the body, the will is to the soul.

✦ WILLIAM GURNALL
in Horn, *Puritan Remembrancer,* 9

All pains spring from one—that we have so little of God. All pains and cares, therefore, should be turned into one. What have I of God? How might I have more—more of His love, more of His power working in my soul? God gives all might to many and yet remains all might for any. Man has his heaven as he will. He that will have it in the full and all enjoyment of the creature, he has it in this: God fills men's bellies with this treasure. Those who will have their heart in nothing but in the full and all enjoyment of God have it so; He satisfies men's thirst, let it be what it will or how great it will. He satisfies the hungry belly and the hungry soul.

✦ NICHOLAS LOCKYER
Balm for England, 35

Action speaks out affection. To what a man hath a heart, he hath a hand, a head, a foot; his heart commands all. The will is general and orders all to move as she will. Where there is no foot toward heaven, no hand toward heaven, nor bending that way, is the heart toward heaven? From your lives you will be condemned. Ye speak out your hearts, and yet you plead for them. You have set your way which you will go and yet pretend you are bound in spirit for heaven.

✦ NICHOLAS LOCKYER
Balm for England, 190

WILLFULNESS

Willful men are most vexed in their crosses. It is not for those to be willful that have not a great measure of wisdom to guide their wills, for God delights to have His will of those that are wedded to their own wills, as in Pharaoh. No men more subject to discontentments than those who would have all things after their own way.

✦ RICHARD SIBBES
Soul's Conflict, 15

As men are, so are their counselors, for such they will have, and such God lets them have. Men whose wills are stronger than their wits, who are wedded to their own ways, are more pleased to hear that which complies with their inclinations than a harsh truth which crosses them; this presages ruin because they are not counselable.

✦ RICHARD SIBBES
Soul's Conflict, 130

WITCHES

Many are unjustly accused for witches sometimes out of ignorance of natural and misapplying of supernatural causes; sometimes out of their neighbors' mere malice, and the suspicion is increased if the party accused be notoriously ill-favored, whereas deformity alone is no more argument to make her a witch than handsomeness had been evidence to prove her a harlot; sometimes out of their own causeless confession: being brought before a magistrate, they acknowledge themselves to be witches, being themselves rather bewitched with fear or deluded with fancy. But the self-accusing of some is as little to be credited as the self-praising of others if alone without other evidence.

> ✦ THOMAS FULLER
> *Holy and Profane States*, 284

M. B. [the schoolmaster]: Doubtless the devil hath not power until it be given him to touch any creature, to hurt or to destroy the body, but only to tempt and to lead into sin. I am also sure that the witch cannot give him power, but only God above.

DAN. [Daniel]: Lay these two together, then, that the devil only hurts and that none can give him power, neither man nor woman, but only God, and tell me whether the people be not wonderfully carried awry in a rage. For when as they should consider that the devil is the Lord's executioner, and then finding that he hath any power given him to molest, to hurt and vex them in their bodies or goods, to know certainly it cometh from the Lord and then gather from thence (as the truth is) that the Lord is displeased with them for their offenses and so seek unto Him, humbly craving pardon and deliverance from this enemy seeking to be armed with the mighty power of faith, to cast him forth and resist him, as the Lord wills (1 Peter 5).

> ✦ GEORGE GIFFORD
> *Dialogue concerning Witches and Witchcraft*, 31–33

A witch is a magician who, either by open or secret league, wittingly and willingly consenteth to use the aid and assistance of the devil in the working of wonders.

> ✦ WILLIAM PERKINS
> *A Discourse of Witchcraft,*
> in *Works*, 3:636

WITNESS

One eyewitness is better than many ear witnesses.

> ✦ THOMAS ADAMS
> *Exposition upon…Second…Peter*, 168

'Tis the duty of Christians in general to "shine as lights in the world" (Phil. 2:15). When 'tis expected of ministers that they be the best of Christians, should not they be more shining, more exemplary in their lives? We should have a special care that the ministry be not blamed. The sun has most eyes on it when in an eclipse (see Matt. 5:19). If we are seen to live in the breach of any of God's commands, 'tis as a teaching others to break them. We that should

be guides, O let us take great heed that we be not stumbling blocks to others.
✦ JOHN BARRET
Funeral Sermon, 17

The Christian's life should put his minister's sermon in print; he should preach that mystery every day to the eyes of his neighbors which the minister preaches to their ears.
✦ WILLIAM GURNALL
Christian in Complete Armour, 810

Dare to own God in the worst time. He is King of kings and is able to reward all His servants. We may be losers for Him; we shall never be losers by Him.
✦ THOMAS WATSON
Lord's Prayer, 58

WORD OF GOD

This incomprehensible God, who is of Himself and for Himself, cannot be made known to His creatures but by Himself. Men and angels cannot know Him any further than He is pleased to reveal Himself unto them. The word of God is pure and perfect. It does fully discover God's mind and our duty.
✦ FRANCIS CHEYNELL
Divine Trinunity, 11

It is the great design God drives at in His word and ordinances to make His people holy and righteous. The word of God is both seed to beget and food to nourish, holiness begotten in the heart; every part of it contributes to this design abundantly. The preceptive part affords a perfect rule of holiness for the saint to walk by... [not made] as men's laws are, who make their laws as tailors their garments to fit the crooked bodies they are for, so they, the crooked minds of men. The commands of God gratify the lusts of none; they are suited to the holy nature of God, not the unholy hearts of men. The promises present us with admirable encouragements to allure us on in the way of holiness, all of them so warily laid that an unholy heart cannot, without violence to his conscience, lay claim to any one of them, God having set that flaming sword, conscience, in the sinner's bosom to keep him off from touching or tasting the fruit of this tree of life.
✦ WILLIAM GURNALL
Christian in Complete Armour, 298

He that taught Christians to pray for their daily bread did suppose they had need of it; and surely He did not mean only or chiefly corporeal bread who in the same chapter bids them "seek ye first the kingdom of God" (Matt. 6:33). Well, Christian, prize thou the word, feed on the word, whether it be dished up in a sermon at the public or in a conference with some Christian friend in private, or in a more secret duty of reading and meditation by thy solitary self.
✦ WILLIAM GURNALL
Christian in Complete Armour, 464

Promises are like the beams of the sun; they shine as freely in at the window of the poor man's cottage as of the prince's palace. And these hope trades

with, and these animate the Christian at his work.
♦ WILLIAM GURNALL
Christian in Complete Armour, 522

Most nations have some particular weapons proper to themselves, but few or none come into the field without a sword. A pilot without his chart, a scholar without his book, and a soldier without his sword are alike ridiculous. But above all these, how absurd is it for one to think of being a Christian without knowledge of the word of God and some skill to use this weapon!
♦ WILLIAM GURNALL
Christian in Complete Armour, 558–59

There are two secrets that the word discloses. First, what a man's own heart knows, and no creature besides. Thus, Christ told the woman of Samaria what her neighbors could not charge her with, from which she concluded Him to be a prophet—a man of God. And may we not conclude the Scripture to be the word of God that does the same? Secondly, those things which a man's own heart is not privy to: God is said to be "greater than our heart, and knoweth all things" (1 John 3:20). He knows more by us than we by ourselves.
♦ WILLIAM GURNALL
Christian in Complete Armour, 571

This is the great privilege which the poorest believer in the church has by the covenant of grace, such a one as Adam had not in the first covenant. He, when fallen, had a flaming sword to keep him out of Paradise, but had no such sword when innocent to keep him from sinning, and so from being turned out of that happy place and state. No, he was left to stand upon his own defense and, by his vigilance, to be a lifeguard to himself. But now the word of God stands between the saints and all danger.
♦ WILLIAM GURNALL
Christian in Complete Armour, 577

Those that care not for the word are strangers to the Spirit, and they that care not for the Spirit never make a right use of the word. The word is nothing without the Spirit, and only animated and quickened by Him. The Spirit and the word are like the veins and arteries in the body that give life to the whole. And therefore, where the word is most revealed, there is most of the Spirit.
♦ RICHARD SIBBES
Divine Meditations and Holy Contemplations, 48

WORK

The belly is not filled with words or the back clothed with wishes.
♦ THOMAS MANTON
in Horn, *Puritan Remembrancer*, 137

[God] abhors him as an infidel who doth not provide for his own; surely, then, He will take care of His own Himself. Aristotle saith propriety is the ground of all the toil and labor in the world. If all things were [held in] common, everyone would be careless; but because it is their own ground, therefore they dung and plough and sow it because it is their own wealth. Therefore they work hard to increase it.

✦ GEORGE SWINNOCK
"The Pastor's Farewell," in *Works*, 4:72

THE WORLD/WORLDLINESS

The danger of a disease lies in its seizure on the heart. Earthly things under the hand are a duty but in the heart a disease. The heart is Christ's royal fort, to which the devil, the world, and flesh lay siege; and if that be taken, all is gone. Earthly things are briars and thorns and therefore dangerous to come near the heart; the least prick at the heart is mortal. The heart is Christ's nuptial bed, into which Christ retires; the world is the saint's servant. Now to admit a servant into the Lord's bed is adulterous. The heart is God's seat, pavilion, and throne, into which none must come but Himself.

✦ BARTHOLOMEW ASHWOOD
Heavenly Trade, 71

As for the fullness of the earth...it costs a man many times more than its worth. It costs him his time, his precious thoughts, his soul; much is laid out for it—much care to get it, much fear to keep it, and much grief to lose it. Oh! But the fullness of Jesus Christ, it costs him nothing: "Come, buy wine and milk without money" or money's worth (Isa. 55:1). Christ gives much and takes little, takes nothing; it costs you nothing, and having it, you have all.

✦ WILLIAM BRIDGE
"Grace for Grace," in *Works*, 1:217

Where one thousand are destroyed by the world's frowns, ten thousand are destroyed by the world's smiles. The world, siren-like, it sings us and sinks us; it kisses us and betrays us, like Judas; it kisses us and smites us under the fifth rib, like Joab. The honors, splendor, and all the glory of this world are but sweet poisons that will much endanger us if they do not eternally destroy us.

✦ THOMAS BROOKS
Great Gain, 87

Where is the glory of Solomon? The sumptuous buildings of Nebuchadnezzar? The nine hundred chariots of Sisera? The power of Alexander? The authority of Augustus that commanded the whole world to be taxed?

✦ THOMAS BROOKS
Precious Remedies, 123

Should the child that is proclaimed heir of a crown be troubled for want of a rattle? And why then should a Christian that is heir apparent to a heavenly crown be troubled upon the want of worldly toys?

✦ THOMAS BROOKS
The Unsearchable Riches of Christ,
in *Select Works*, 1:151

Now what is it to love the world? First, to love the world is highly to esteem of the world, to have the world in a high account. For Christ saith, "The things that are of high account with men are abomination with God." When we have the world and the things of it in high esteem and in high account—this is to love the world.

✦ WILLIAM GREENHILL
Against Love of the World, in
Sound-Hearted Christian, 257

We are said to love the world when as we do watch all opportunities and occasions to get the things of the world: to buy cheap, and sell dear; to get great estates and houses and lands and things of that nature.

✦ WILLIAM GREENHILL
Against Love of the World, in
Sound-Hearted Christian, 261

To forsake Christ for the world or a lust is to leave a treasure for a trifle; a mountain of gold for a heap of dung; the pure, lasting fountain for the broken cistern; eternity for a moment; reality for a shadow; all things for nothing.

✦ WILLIAM JENKYN
*Exposition upon the Epistle of
Jude*, 104–5

The treasures of most men are perishing—earthly treasures, cankered and moth-eaten treasures, treasures of vanity. Christians! Where is your treasure? Is it in this world or the next? Is it in present vanities or future glory? Is it in present contentments or in the everlasting inheritance? Is it in corn and wine and oil, or is it in the light of God's countenance? Is it in profits, pleasures, and honors, or is it in grace and glory? Do ye build and plant and sow in the other world that hereafter ye may reap in an eternal harvest of blessedness? If so, then are your names written in heaven.

✦ MATTHEW MEAD
Name in Heaven, 60

Believers build their tombs where others build their tabernacles. The men of the world fix upon the things of the world; that is the cabinet wherein they lock up all their jewels. Though God has given the earth to beasts, yet such beasts are men as to give themselves to the earth.

✦ WILLIAM SECKER
Nonsuch Professor, 133

Are the empty sounds of popular applause, the breaking bubbles of secular greatness, the shallow streams of sensual pleasures, the smiles and lisping eloquence of wives and children, the flying shadows of creature refreshments, the momentary flourishes of worldly beauty and bravery—are these food for a soul? Are these the proper object or the main happiness of such a divine thing as an immortal soul? Why are we not rather weary of this body that makes us so weary of heavenly employment? Why do we not rather long to part with that life that parts us from our life?

✦ SAMUEL SHAW
*Voice of One Crying in the
Wilderness*, 120

We are members of two worlds. While we live here, we must use this world. How many things doth this poor body need in our passage! We must have necessaries, but yet should use the world as if we used it not; for there is great danger lest our affections cleave to things of this present life and we forget heaven, our home.

✦ RICHARD SIBBES
*Divine Meditations and Holy
Contemplations*, 16

Here's a true character of carnal wisdom: the world is a pearl in its eyes; it cannot see God. Earthly, it is called, as managing the lusts of the eyes unto the ends of gain; sensual, managing the lusts of the flesh unto the ends of pleasure; and devilish, managing the pride of life unto the ends of power.

✦ JOHN TRAPP
*Commentary...upon...the New
Testament*, 909

Pleasure, profit, preferment: the worldling's trinity, as one says. Compare here with Christ's threefold temptation and St. James his character [i.e., characterization] of worldly wisdom (James 3:15). It is his pleasure, his profit, and his honor (faith a divine) that is the natural man's trinity, and his carnal self that is these in unity.

✦ JOHN TRAPP
*Commentary...upon...the New
Testament*, 948

Carnal men love the God that they make and hate the God that made them.

✦ RALPH VENNING
Canaan's Flowings, 21

Christians must stave off the world, that it gets not into their heart (Ps. 62:10). For as the water is useful to the ship and helps it to sail better to the haven, but let the water get into the ship, if it be not pumped out at the leak, it drowns the ship; so riches are useful and convenient for our passage. We sail more comfortably with them through the troubles of this world. But if the water get into the ship, if the love of riches get into the heart, then we are drowned with them (1 Tim. 6:9).

✦ THOMAS WATSON
"A Christian on Earth Still in Heaven,"
in *Discourses*, 1:285

WORRY

Whatsoever business ye have upon your hands, how great and difficult soever it may seem, do not stretch your thoughts, be not careful about it, but do what you think at present to be best; and apply yourselves to God, believing and trusting on Him for His direction and assistance, and then ye will find that all will be well, far better than your solicitude and thoughtfulness can make it. For then God Himself will take the business into His own hands. As ye depend upon Him for it, He will concern himself in it. He will direct your thoughts to the best means and assist and bless you in the use of them. He will keep off everything that may any way impede or hinder it. He will order all things relating to it, so as to make them concur to the effecting of it. And if you thus always cast your care upon Him, He will always take care of you. He will instruct you by His wisdom, He will guide you by His counsel, He will assist you by His grace, He will sanctify and comfort you by His Holy

Spirit, He will strengthen and protect you by His almighty power, and at last receive you to Himself in glory.

✦ WILLIAM BEVERIDGE
Sinfulness and Mischief of Worldly Anxiety, 68–70

Lawful care is an act of wisdom, whereby after a person hath rightly judged what he ought to do, what not, what good he is to pursue, and what evil is to be shunned or removed, he, accordingly with more or less intention and eagerness of mind as the things to be obtained or avoided are greater or less, is careful to find out and diligent to use lawful and fit means for the good and against the evil, and that with all circumspection. That he may omit nothing which may assist him nor commit anything that may hinder him in his lawful designs, which, when he hath done, he rests quiet and cares no farther, casting all care of success upon God, to whom it belongs, expecting a good issue upon the use of good means, yet resolving to submit his will to God's will, whatever the success shall be. Sinful care is an act of fear and distrust exercising not only the head but chiefly the heart to the disquietude and disturbance thereof, causing a person inordinately and anxiously to pursue his desires, perplexing himself with doubtful and fearful thoughts about success.

✦ HENRY SCUDDER
Christian's Daily Walk, 242–43

WORSHIP

Oh, for one dram of this reverence! But indeed, it is in vain to bend the knees with unbended souls; it is a poor worship to move our hats, not our hearts. But he does best that expresses before men his zeal by his reverence and commends before God his reverence by his zeal.

✦ THOMAS ADAMS
Exposition upon…Second…Peter, 82

God is a spirit infinitely happy; therefore we must approach to Him with cheerfulness. He is a spirit of infinite majesty; therefore we must come before Him with reverence. He is a spirit infinitely high; therefore we must offer up our sacrifices with the deepest humility. He is a spirit infinitely holy; therefore we must address Him with purity. He is a spirit infinitely glorious; we must therefore acknowledge His excellency in all that we do and in our measures contribute to His glory by having the highest aims in His worship. He is a spirit infinitely provoked by us; therefore we must offer up our worship in the name of a pacifying mediator and intercessor.

✦ STEPHEN CHARNOCK
Selections, 267

There is nothing more equal and just than to worship and serve Him whose we are; to love and to live to Him from whom we have our life and breath, especially considering that "his commandments are our life" (Deut. 26:16–20; 32:47).

✦ ELISHA COLES
Practical Discourse, 47

WRATH OF GOD

That we may see the difference between the wrath of God falling on His people and on His enemies, we must distinguish between His paternal and His judicial wrath. One is the stroke of vindictive justice, aiming at satisfaction for sin, exacting on the sinner a debt of punishment which he can never repay. The other is, with a design, to humble and bring the soul to a true repentance for sin and make him, for the future, watchful against it.

✦ THOMAS RIDGLEY
Funeral Sermon, 12–13

WRITERS

How easy is pen-and-paper piety for one to write religiously! I will not say it costs nothing, but it is far cheaper to work one's head than one's heart to goodness. Some, perchance, may guess me to be good by my writings, and so I shall deceive my reader. But if I do not desire to be good, I most of all deceive myself. I can make a hundred meditations sooner than subdue the least sin in my soul.

✦ THOMAS FULLER
Good Thoughts, 95

Herein I observe a singular providence: I have my book about heart treasures to finish, but at home I had not liberty to write any for visits, studying sermons, and preaching, but at those gentlemen's houses I have a chamber to myself and write it all the day long, so as I could not do at my own house.

✦ OLIVER HEYWOOD
Autobiography, Diaries, 224 (April 4, 1666)

He that puts forth a book sentences his reason to the gantelope: everyone will strive to have a lash at it in its course, and he must be content to bear it.

✦ JOHN OWEN
Golden Book, 204

ZEAL

Labor we to get more heat, to burn more; as one says, "Zeal is as proper in the ministry as fire was upon the altar." Indeed, it cannot but be a great defect in a minister to want that which no Christian should be without. John was burning in zeal; he came in the spirit and power of Elias, who was very jealous for the Lord. Ministers, as they are devoted to the Lord to serve Him in a special manner, no doubt they ought to be fervent in spirit…. Without zeal, what danger of their perverting that text [Rom. 12:11], as to be mere time servers…. True zeal would carry a minister through difficulties and discouragements.

✦ JOHN BARRET
Funeral Sermon, 15

Are you zealous for God and truth and holiness, and against the sins and errors of others? Take heed lest you lose it while you think it doth increase in you. Nothing is more apt to degenerate than zeal. In how many thousands hath it turned from an innocent, charitable, peaceable, tractable, healing, profitable, heavenly zeal into a partial zeal for some party or opinions of their own? And into a fierce, censorious, uncharitable, scandalous, turbulent, disobedient, unruly, hurting, and destroying zeal, ready to wish for fire from heaven and kindling contention, confusion, and every evil work.

✦ RICHARD BAXTER
A Christian Directory, in
Practical Works, 2:159

This [the apostle Paul] calls then zeal, or that fervency of spirit which is opposed to lukewarmness or indifferency for the Christian religion, which is now too manifest in most of those who profess it.

✦ WILLIAM BEVERIDGE
Duty of Zeal, 7

True zeal for God will not only put us upon reproving, correcting, and preventing, as much as in us lies, any dishonor that may be cast upon Him by those among whom we live, but likewise upon promoting His honor and glory as far as we can in all other places. And seeing His glory…shines forth most gloriously in the way that He has made for the salvation of mankind and revealed in His glorious gospel, therefore if we have any zeal for His glory, it will appear in striving all we can to spread and propagate His said gospel, that His way may be known upon earth and His saving health among all nations. That all nations may know Him and serve Him and worship Him and give Him thanks for His great glory manifested in their redemption and so partake of it themselves to their eternal happiness and salvation, which will itself also be an addition to His glory; for the more are saved by Him,

the more there will be to serve and glorify Him forever.

✦ WILLIAM BEVERIDGE
Duty of Zeal, 12–13

Zeal is an extreme heat of all the affections set against sin and working strongly toward God.

✦ THOMAS BROOKS
Cabinet of Choice Jewels, 230

Zeal is like fire: in the chimney it is one of the best servants, but out of the chimney it is one of the worst masters. Zeal, kept by knowledge and wisdom in its proper place, is a choice servant to Christ and the saints; but zeal not bounded by wisdom and knowledge is the highway to undo all and to make a hell for many at once.

✦ THOMAS BROOKS
Smooth Stones, 22; *The Unsearchable
Riches of Christ*, in *Select Works*, 1:64

Zeal ordered by wisdom feeds upon the faults of offenders, not on their persons.

✦ THOMAS BROOKS
The Unsearchable Riches of Christ,
in *Select Works*, 1:64

Zeal without knowledge is like a mettled horse without eyes or like a sword in a madman's hand, and there is no knowledge where there is not the word.

✦ JOHN BUNYAN
Riches, 303

Another jewel was [Simeon Ashe's] prudence and spiritual wisdom; he was not only a pious and godly but a wise and prudent minister that had

zeal for God, but knew how to mingle his zeal with discretion. Discretion indeed without zeal is nothing but carnal policy, but zeal without discretion is nothing but frantic fury. Discretion without zeal will quickly eat out the heart of religion and eat religion out of the heart. Zeal without discretion is not a coal from the altar, but a coal kindled by the wildfire of passion that is able to set a nation on fire; but this reverend minister had zeal sweetly tempered with discretion.
✦ EDMUND CALAMY
"Mr. Calamy's Sermon at the
Funeral of Mr. Ashe," in Calamy
et al., *Farewell Sermons*, 361

We are to take heed that the love of men's persons slack not our zeal in rebuking sin in them, and that our zeal against sin slack not our love to the person.
✦ EZEKIEL CULVERWELL
Time Well Spent, 350

A man may love God in a lukewarm measure, hate sin in a lukewarm measure, grieve for his corruptions, desire faith and repentance, delight in good duties, pity the miseries of others, fear to transgress God's commandment. A man may have all these affections thus in a lukewarm measure. As this is displeasing to God, so it is not zeal. Zeal is a high measure, the highest strain of all the affections.
✦ WILLIAM FENNER
A Treatise of the Affections,
in *Works*, 62

Zeal is the running of the soul.... As the affections are the feet of the soul, so zeal is the swift running pace of these feet.
✦ WILLIAM FENNER
A Treatise of the Affections,
in *Works*, 69

The faster a man rides, if he be in a wrong road, the farther he goes out of his way. Zeal is the best or worst thing in a duty; if the end be right, it is excellent, but if wrong, it is worthless. And it is no easy thing to propound a right end.
✦ WILLIAM GURNALL
Christian in Complete Armour, 709

[Holy zeal] is a full and vehement bent of a man's desires, affections, and endeavors after Jesus Christ in the gospel, so that no difficulties or discouragements whatsoever shall take him off from his pursuit after Christ in the way of His ordinances.
✦ CHRISTOPHER LOVE
Zealous Christian, 9

A zealous minister will be faithful and fervent in the reproving of sin, though others prove dumb dogs or flatterers that sow pillows under men's elbows.
✦ CHRISTOPHER LOVE
Zealous Christian, 23

Heady violence is accompanied with stoutness of heart both toward God and men; it proceeds from a natural rashness. But holy violence is accompanied with humiliation. The church of Laodicea is commanded to be zealous and repent (Rev. 3:19). Their zeal for God must be joined with the breaking of their own hearts.

✦ CHRISTOPHER LOVE
Zealous Christian, 25

Meekness without zeal is nothing else but lukewarmness and cowardice. Zeal without meekness degenerates into sinful passion. We should be meek in our own cause but zealous in the cause of God.

✦ SAMUEL MATHER
*Figures or Types of the Old
Testament*, 96

There is a blind zeal—a zeal without knowledge. "They have a zeal," saith the apostle, "but not according to knowledge" (Rom. 10:2). Now as knowledge without zeal is fruitless, so zeal without knowledge is dangerous; it is like wildfire in the hand of a fool or like the devil in the man possessed that threw him sometimes in the fire, sometimes into the water (Matt. 17:15).

✦ MATTHEW MEAD
Almost Christian Discovered, 85

Zeal in the heart is like boiling water that wastes in the seething. Just so the Lord Jesus: "The zeal of Thine house hath eaten Me up." It makes a man overlook all interests concerning himself in the world and be intent only upon the interest of the person beloved.

✦ WILLIAM STRONG
Heavenly Treasure, 363

Discretion without zeal is slow-paced, and zeal without discretion is heady; let, therefore, zeal spur on discretion and discretion rein in zeal.

✦ GEORGE SWINNOCK
in Horn, *Puritan Remembrancer*, 14

He that hath a good mixture of zeal and prudence is like a fire on the hearth, of much use and service; but zeal without discretion is like fire on the top of the chimney, which often doth much mischief. Zeal to a Christian is like a high wind filling the sails of a ship, which, unless it be ballasted with discretion, doth but the sooner overturn it.... Zeal in a man is like wings to a bird or mettle to a horse, but the bridle of discretion is requisite, as the poets fable that Minerva put a golden bridle on Pegasus lest he should fly too fast. Bernard hath a good saying, "Discretion without zeal is slow-paced, and zeal without discretion is heady; let therefore zeal spur on discretion, and discretion rein in zeal."

✦ GEORGE SWINNOCK
*The Christian Man's Calling,
in Works*, 2:290

Zeal is the heat or intension of the affections; it is a holy warmth whereby our love and anger are drawn out to the utmost for God and His glory. Now, our love to God and His ways and our hatred of wickedness should be increased because of ungodly men.

✦ GEORGE SWINNOCK
*The Christian Man's Calling,
in Works*, 2:296

These are the special notes and symptoms of strange fires. The kinds, also, are many and might be distributed into many heads, but I will reduce them into three, which are known by their names: (1) counterfeit zeal, false fire; (2) blind zeal, smoky fire, or fool's fire (*ignis fatuus*); (3) turbulent zeal, wildfire. The first, wanting truth and sincerity, propounds sinister ends. The second, knowledge and discretion, takes wrong ways. The third, love and humility, exceeds measure. The first abounds amongst subtle and crafty professors and is to be abhorred and detected. The second, among simple and devout, is to be pitied and directed. The third, amongst passionate and affectionate, and is to be moderated and corrected.

✦ SAMUEL WARD
"A Coal from the Altar," in
Sermons and Treatises, 75

Zeal is the richest evidence of faith and the clearest demonstration of the Spirit. The baptism of water is but a cold proof of man's Christendom, being common to all comers; but if any be baptized with fire, the same is sealed up till the day of redemption.

✦ SAMUEL WARD
"A Coal from the Altar," in
Sermons and Treatises, 78

Do we [preachers] love Christ more than ordinary? Would we give proof of our treble love to Him? Let us, then, feed His flock with a treble zeal, expressed in our prayer, preaching, and living. Let us make it appear to the consciences of all that the top of our ambition is God's glory and that we prefer the winning of souls to the winning of the world.

✦ SAMUEL WARD
"A Coal from the Altar," in
Sermons and Treatises, 89

Of all others, let ministers be impatient when God's glory is impeached and eclipsed. A minister without zeal is like salt that hath lost its savor. Zeal will make men take injuries done to God as done to themselves. It is reported of Chrysostom that he reproved any sin against God, as if he himself had received a personal wrong. Let not ministers be either shaken with fear or seduced with flattery; God never made ministers to be as false glasses, to make bad faces look fair; for want of this fire of zeal, they are in danger of another fire, even the burning lake (Rev. 21:8), into which the fearful shall be cast.

✦ THOMAS WATSON
The Beatitudes, in *Discourses*, 2:308–9

Consider then, seriously, the more violent we are for heaven and the more work we do for God, the greater will be our reward. The hotter our zeal, the brighter our crown. Could we hear the blessed souls departed speaking to us from heaven, sure thus they would say, "Were we to leave heaven a while and to dwell on the earth again, we would do God a thousand times more service than ever we have done. We would pray with more life, act with more zeal; for now we see, the more hath been our labor, the more astonishing is our joy and the more flourishing our crown."

✦ THOMAS WATSON
Christian Soldier, or, Heaven Taken by Storm, 138–39

Remember, you have that corruption within you which is ready to abate this blessed violence. The brightest coal has those ashes growing on it as is apt to choke the fire. You have those inbred corruptions that, like ashes, are ready to choke the fire of your zeal. How was Peter's grace cooled when he denied Christ! The church of Ephesus lost her keen edge of religion (Rev. 2:4). Take heed of declining in your affections.

✦ THOMAS WATSON
Christian Soldier, or, Heaven Taken by Storm, 172–73

Zeal is a mixed affection; it is a compound of love and anger. It boils up the spirits to the height and makes them run over. Zeal is a fire kindled from heaven; blessed be its anger, for it is without sin, and its wrath, for it is against sin. When Paul saw their idolatry at Athens, "his spirit was stirred in him" (Acts 17:16). He was in a burning fit of zeal.

✦ THOMAS WATSON
"The Upright Man's Character,"
in *Discourses,* 1:335

ANNOTATED BIBLIOGRAPHY

Adams, Thomas. *An Exposition upon the Second Epistle General of St. Peter*. London: Henry G. Bohn, 1848.

——. *The Sermons of Thomas Adams: The Shakespeare of Puritan Theologians*. Edited by John Brown. Cambridge: Cambridge University Press, 1909.

——. *The Works of Thomas Adams*. Vol. 1. Edinburgh: James Nichol, 1861.

——. *The Works of Thomas Adams*. Vol. 3. Edinburgh: James Nichol, 1862.

Alleine, Joseph. *An Alarm to the Unconverted*. 1671. Reprint, Hanover, N.H.: printed by Charles Spear, 1816.

——. *A Call to Archippus; or, An Humble and Earnest Motion to Some Ejected Ministers…to Take Heed to Their Ministry, that They Fulfil It*. 1664. Reprint, London: sold by Ann Baldwin, 1703.

——. *Christian Letters Full of Spiritual Instructions*. n.p.: published by J. Darby, 1672.

——. *The Saint's Pocket Book*. 1766. Reprint, London: William Tegg, 1866.

——. *The Voice of God in His Promises; or, Strong Consolation for True Christians*. 1766. Reprint, Leeds: printed for A. Newsom, 1797.

Alleine, Richard. *A Companion for Prayer: or, Directions for Improvement in Grace, and Practical Godliness in Time of Extraordinary Danger*. London: printed by J. R. for T., 1684.

——. *Heaven Opened; or, A Brief and Plain Discovery of the Riches of God's Covenant of Grace*. 1665. Reprint, London: Religious Tract Society, 1836.

Allestree, Richard. *The Whole Duty of Man*. London: C. & J. Rivington, 1828.

Ambrose, Isaac. *The Christian Warrior Wrestling with Sin, Satan, the World and the Flesh*. London: R. B. Seeley and W. Burnside, 1837.

——. *Looking unto Jesus: A View of the Everlasting Gospel*. 1658. Reprint, Pittsburgh: Luke Loomis, 1832.

————. *Ministration of, and Communion with Angels*. 1674. Reprint, Berwick: printed by W. Phorson, 1797.

————. *Works of Isaac Ambrose*. London: Thomas Tegg and Son, 1835.

Ames, William. *Conscience, with the Power and Cases Thereof*. Vols. 2 and 3. n.p., 1639.

————. *The Marrow of Sacred Divinity*. London: printed by Edward Griffin, 1642. Also known as *The Marrow of Theology*.

Annesley, Samuel, ed. *The Morning Exercises at Cripplegate, St. Giles in the Fields, and in Southwark: Sermons Preached A.D. 1659–1689, by Several Ministers of the Gospel*. 6 vols. London: Thomas Tegg, 1844–1845.

Arrowsmith, John. *The Covenant Avenging Sword Brandished: In a Sermon before the Honorable House of Commons, at their Solemn Fast, January 25, 1642*. 1643. Reprint, Dumfries: C. M'Lachlan, 1797.

Ashe, Simeon. *The Best Refuge for the Most Oppressed, in a Sermon Preached to the Honourable House of Commons at Their Solemn Fast, March 30, 1642*. London: Edward Brewster and John Burroughs, 1642.

————. *Primitive Divinity, a Treatise on Divine Contentment*. 1653. Reprint, Philadelphia: Stavely and Bringhurst, 1824.

Ashwood, Bartholomew. *The Best Treasure, or, The Way to Be Truly Rich*. London: printed for William Marshal, 1681.

————. *The Heavenly Trade, or The Best Merchandizing: The Only Way to Live Well in Impoverishing Times*. London: printed for Samuel Lee, 1679.

Attersol, William. *Three Treatises*. London: T. Cotes, 1633.

Austin, William. *Certain Devout, Godly, and Learned Meditations*. London: printed for J. L. and Ralph Mab, 1635.

Bakewell, Thomas. *A Short View of the Antinomian Errours: With a Brief and Plain Answer to Them*. London: printed by T. B., 1643.

Bargrave, Isaac. *A Sermon Preached Before the Honorable Assembly of Knights, Citizens, and Burgesses, of the Lower House of Parliament, February the Last, 1623*. London: printed by G. P., 1624.

Barker, Matthew. *Natural Theology*. London: printed for Nathaniel Ranew, 1674.

Barlow, John. *The Good Man's Privilege*. London: imprinted by F. K. for Nathanael Newbery, 1618.

Barret, John. *A Funeral Sermon, Preached at Nottingham, Occasioned by the Death of That Faithful Servant of Christ, Mr. John Whitlock, Sen., Dec. 8, 1708*. London: printed by T. W. for Nath. Cliffe, 1709.

Barrow, Isaac. *Sermons Selected from the Works of the Rev. Isaac Barrow*. Vol. 1. Oxford: Clarendon Press, 1812.

Bates, William. *The Danger of Prosperity: Discovered in Several Sermons upon Prov. 1:27.* London: printed for Brabazon Aylmer, 1685.

———. *The Whole Works of the Reverend W. Bates.* Vol. 2. London: printed for James Black, 1815.

Baxter, Richard. *Baxteriana: Containing a Selection from the Works of Baxter.* Collected by Arthur Young. London: printed for J. Hatchard, 1815.

———. *A Call to the Unconverted to Turn and Live.* Glasgow: Porteous and Hislop, 1863.

———. *Converse with God in Solitude.* London: James Nisbet, 1829.

———. *The Practical Works of the Rev. Richard Baxter.* 23 vols. London: James Duncan, 1830.

———. *Preservatives against Melancholy and Overmuch Sorrow.* London: printed by W. R. for William Hill, 1713.

———. *The Reformed Pastor.* London: printed by Couchman for William Baynes, 1808.

———. *The Saint's Everlasting Rest.* Philadelphia: Stoddart & Atherton, 1830.

Bayly, Lewis. *The Practice of Piety.* London: Hamilton, Adams, 1842.

Baynes, Paul. *An Entire Commentary upon the Whole Epistle of St. Paul to the Ephesians.* 1643. Reprint, Edinburgh: James Nichol, 1866.
Baynes is sometimes referred to as Bayne.

Beerman, William. *Sorrow upon Sorrow: or, The Much Lamented Death of the Worthy Mr. Ralph Venning, Being a Sermon Preached upon the Sad Occasion of His Death Before His Burial, from Acts 20.38.* London: printed for Francis Smith, 1674.

Bernard, Richard. *The Faithful Shepherd, or, The Shepherd's Faithfulness.* London: printed by Arnold Hatfield, 1607.

———. *The Isle of Man: or, The Legal Proceedings in Manshire against Sin.* 1627. Reprint, Bristol: printed by and for Richard Edwards, 1803.

Bertram, Robert Aitkin. *A Homiletic Encyclopaedia of Illustrations in Theology and Morals.* New York: Funk & Wagnalls, 1885.

Beveridge, William. *The Duty of Zeal.* Oxford: printed by D. A. Talboys, 1838.

———. *The Great Advantage and Necessity of Public Prayer and Frequent Communion.* 7th ed. London: printed for William Taylor, 1721.

———. *The Sinfulness and Mischief of Worldly Anxiety.* Edinburgh: James Hogg and Sons, 1858.

———. *Thesaurus Theologious, or, A Complete System of Divinity.* London: printed for R. Smith, 1711.

Binning, Hugh. *Several Sermons upon the Most Important Subjects of Practical Religion*. Glasgow: William Duncan, Sen., 1760.

———. *The Works of the Rev. Hugh Binning*. Vol. 1. Edinburgh: William Whyte, 1839.

Blake, Thomas. *Living Truths in Dying Times: Some Meditations (upon Luke 21:30) Occasioned by the Present Judgement of the Plague*. London, 1665.

Bond, John. *Salvation in a Mystery, or, A Prospective Glasse for England's Case*. London: printed by L. N. for Francis Eglesfeild, 1644.

Boston, Thomas. *The Art of Man-Fishing*. 1773. Reprint, Scotland: Christian Focus, 1998.

———. *The Crook in the Lot*. 1737. Reprint, New York: Robert Carter and Brothers, 1852.

———. *Human Nature in Its Fourfold State*. 1720. Reprint, London: Thomas Tegg, 1824.

Bownd, Nicholas. *The Doctrine of the Sabbath*. London: printed by Widdow Orwin for John Porter and Thomas Man, 1595.

Boys, John. *The Works of John Boys: An Exposition of the Several Offices Adapted for Various Occasions of Public Worship*. 1622. Reprint, New York: Stanford and Swords, 1851.

Bradford, John. *John Bradford*. Edited by Charles Bradley. Select British Divines, vol. 22. London: printed for L. B. Seeley and Son, 1825.

Bradshaw, William. *A Meditation of Mans Mortalitie*. London: Iohn Dawson for Fulke Clifton, 1621.

Bradstreet, Anne. *The Works of Anne Bradstreet in Prose and Verse*. Edited by John Harvard Ellis. Charlestown, Mass.: Abram E. Cutter, 1867.

Bragge, Robert. *A Cry for Labourers in God's Harvest, Being a Sermon Preached upon the Sad Occasion of the Late Funeral of the Eminent Servant of Christ, Mr. Ralph Venning*. London: printed by John Hancock Sr. and Jr., 1674.

Bridge, William. *A Lifting Up for the Downcast*. 1649. Reprint, Edinburgh: Banner of Truth, 1995.

———. *The Righteous Man's Habitation in the Time of Plague and Pestilence; Being a Brief Exposition of the 91st Psalm*. 1665. Reprint, London: Simpkin and Marshall, 1835.

———. *The Works of the Rev. William Bridge*. Vols. 1–5. London: Thomas Tegg, 1845.

Brinsley, John (the Younger). *Aqua Coelestis, or A Sovereign Cordial*. London: printed for George Sawbridge, 1663.
Brinsley's father, John Brinsley (the Elder), also authored several works.

Brook, Benjamin. *The Lives of the Puritans, Containing a Biographical Account of*

Those Divines Who Distinguished Themselves in the Cause of Religious Liberty, from the Reformation under Queen Elizabeth to the Act of Uniformity in 1662. London: printed for James Black, 1813.

Brooks, Thomas. *Apples of Gold, or A Word in Season to Young Men and Women*. 1660. Reprint, Philadelphia: Presbyterian Board of Publication, 1857.

————. *A Cabinet of Choice Jewels*. 1669. Reprint, Huntly: Duncan Matheson, 1861.

————. *Great Gain Gleaned from the Writings of Thomas Brooks*. Edinburgh: Alexander Hislop, 1869.

————. *A Heavenly Cordial*. London: printed for John Hancock, 1666.

————. *London's Lamentations, or, A Serious Discourse Concerning That Late Fiery Dispensation that Turned Our (Once Renowned) City into a Ruinous Heap*. London: printed for John Hancock and Nathaniel Ponder, 1670.

————. *The Mute Christian under the Smarting Rod*. 1658. Reprint, London: printed by W. Nicholson, 1806.

————. *Precious Remedies against Satan's Devices*. 1652. Reprint, Philadelphia: Jonathan Pounder, 1810.

————. *The Privy Key of Heaven, or, Twenty Arguments for Closet Prayer*. 1665. Reprint, Llanfyllin: printed by Robert Pugh, 1820.

————. *The Select Works of Thomas Brooks*. Vol. 1. Edited by C. Bradley. Select British Divines, vol. 16. London: printed for L. B. Seeley and Son, 1824.

————. *Smooth Stones Taken from Ancient Brooks*. Compiled by Charles H. Spurgeon. New York: Sheldon & Company, 1860.

Brownrig, Ralph. *Forty Sermons*. London: printed by Tho. Roycroft, 1661.

Bunyan, John. *The Complete Works of John Bunyan*. Philadelphia: Bradley, Garretson, 1872.

————. *Divine Emblems: or, Temporal Things Spiritualized. Fitted for the Use of Boys and Girls*. London: printed for J. Mawman, 1802.

————. *Grace Abounding to the Chief of Sinners, Heart's Ease in Heart Trouble, The World to Come, or Visions of Heaven and Hell, and the Barren Fig-Tree*. 1660. Reprint, Philadelphia: J. J. Woodward, 1828.

————. *The Pilgrim's Progress*. Edited by Charles Sears Baldwin. Longmans' English Classics. 1678. Reprint, New York: Longmans, Green, 1909.

————. *Prayer*. Edinburgh: Banner of Truth Trust, 1991.
This edition combines *Praying in the Spirit* (1662) and *The Throne of Grace* (1692).

————. *Profitable Meditations; A Poem*. Introduction and notes by George Offor. 1661. Reprint, London: John Camden Hotten, 1860.

————. *The Riches of John Bunyan: Selected from His Works*. Compiled by Jeremiah Chaplin. New York: American Tract Society, 1850.

Burgess, Anthony. *CXLV Expository Sermons upon the Whole 17th Chapter of the Gospel according to St. John: or Christ's Prayer Before His Passion Explicated, and Both Practically and Polemically Improved*. London: Abraham Miller, 1656.

————. *The True Doctrine of Justification Asserted & Vindicated from the Errours of Many, and More Especially Papists and Socinians; or, A Treatise of the Natural Righteousness of God, and Imputed Righteousness of Christ*. London: printed for Thomas Underhill, 1654.

Burgess, Daniel. *Man's Whole Duty, and God's Wonderful Intreaty of Him Thereunto*. London: printed by J. Richardson for Thomas Parkhurst, 1690.

————. *Rules and Directions for Hearing and Reading the Word of God with Certain and Saving Benefit*. 1693. Reprint, London, 1788.

Burroughs, Jeremiah. *The Evil of Evils*. 1654. Reprint, Grand Rapids: Soli Deo Gloria, 2008.

————. *Irenicum, to the Lovers of Truth and Peace*. London: printed for Robert Dawlman, 1653.

————. *The Rare Jewel of Christian Contentment*. 1655. Reprint, London: Thomas Ward, 1840.

————. *The Saints Treasury…Being Sundry Sermons Preached in London*. London: printed by T. C., 1654.

Burton, Henry. *The Law and the Gospel Reconciled*. London: printed for Michael Sparkes, 1631.

Byfield, Nicholas. *The Cure of the Fear of Death*. London: printed by G. P. for Ralph Rounthwaite, 1618.

Calamy, Edmund. *The Godly Man's Ark*. 1659. Reprint, London: Tho. Parkhurst, 1709.

Calamy, Edmund, Joseph Caryl, Ralph Venning, James Janeway. *Saints' Memorials, or, Words Fitly Spoken, Like Apples of Gold in Pictures of Silver. Being a Collection of Divine Sentences*. London, 1674.

Calamy, [Edmund], [Thomas] Manton, [Joseph] Caryl, [Thomas] Case, [William] Jenkins, [Richard] Baxter, [Thomas] Jacomb, et al. *The Farewell Sermons of the Late London Ministers, Preached August 17th, 1662*. London, 1662.

Carmichael, Alexander. *The Believer's Mortification of Sin, by the Spirit, to Which Is Added, An Essay on Hypocrisy*. 1677. Reprint, Edinburgh: W. P. Kennedy, 1846.

Cary, Philip. *A Solemn Call unto All That Would Be Owned as Christ's Faithful*

Witnesses...or, A Discourse Concerning Baptism. London: printed for John Harris, 1690.

Caryl, Joseph. *A Directory for the Afflicted; Select Extracts from the First Fourteen Chapters of the Rev. Joseph Caryl's Commentary on the Book of Job*. Edited by John Berrie. Edinburgh: printed for David Brown, W. M. Oliphant, John Wardlaw, 1824.

Case, Thomas. *Correction, Instruction: or The Rod and the Word. A Treatise on Afflictions*. 1652 or 1671. Reprint, London: printed by W. Smith, 1802.

Cawdrey, Daniel. *The Good Man, a Publick Good*. London: printed by Tho. Harper, 1643.

Author's last name also spelled Cawdry.

Charnock, Stephen. *The Choice Works of the Rev. Stephen Charnock with His Life and Character*. New York: Robert G. Carter, 1847.

———. *Discourses upon the Existence and Attributes of God*. 1681–1682. London: Tegg, 1840.

———. *Selections from the Discourses of Stephen Charnock*. London: Religious Tract Society, 1878.

Chewney, Nicholas. *Anti-Socinianism*. London: printed by J. M. for H. Twifford, 1656.

Cheynell, Francis. *The Divine Trinunity of the Father, Son, and Holy Spirit; or, the Blessed Doctrine of the Three Coessentiall Subsistents in the Eternall Godhead without Any Confusion or Division of the Distinct Subsistences, or Multiplication of the Most Single and Entire Godhead*. London: printed by T. R. and E. M., 1650.

Chorlton, John. *The Glorious Reward of Faithful Ministers Declared and Improved. In a Sermon upon the Occasion of the Funeral of That Excellent Minister of Jesus Christ Henry Newcome, Etc.* Preface by John Howe. London: printed for T. P., 1696.

Clark, Samuel. *Aurea Legenda, or Apothegms, Sentences, and Sayings of Many Wise and Learned Men, Useful for All Sorts of Persons*. London: printed for Nathanael Ranew, 1682.

———. *The Saint's Nosegay*. 1642. Reprint, London: privately printed by Wyman and Sons, 1881.

This 1881 reprint includes a memoir of Samuel Clark—or, more commonly in the seventeenth century, Clarke—by his descendant G. T. C.

Clarkson, David. *The Practical Works of David Clarkson*. Vol. 3. Edinburgh: James Nichol, 1865.

Cleaver, Robert, and John Dod. *A Plain and Familiar Exposition of the Eighteenth, Nineteenth, and Twentieth Chapters of the Proverbs of Salomon*. London: printed for Roger Jackson, 1611.

Cobbet, Thomas. *Gospel Incense, or A Practical Treatise on Prayer.* 1657. Reprint, Boston: Congregational Board of Publication, 1856.

Cole, Thomas. *The Old Apostolical Way of Preaching, or Peter's Last Legacy to All His True Successors in the Ministry and Faith of the Gospel, Being an Awakening Word.* London: printed for Thomas Cockeril, 1676.

Coles, Elisha. *A Practical Discourse of God's Sovereignty.* 1673. Reprint, Philadelphia: Smith and English, 1854.

Collinges, John. *The Weaver's Pocket-book.* 1675. Reprint, Edinburgh: printed by John Mosman, 1723.

Conant, John. *Sermons on Several Subjects.* Oxford: printed by L. Lichfield, 1736.

Cotton, Clement. *None but Christ, None but Christ…(with "The Sicke Man's A.B.C.").* 1561 [?]. London: printed by T. B. for Samuel Enderby, 1644.

Cradock, Samuel. *Knowledge and Practice.* London: William Grantham, Henry Mortlock, and William Miller, 1673.

Crisp, Tobias. *Christ Alone Exalted.* Vol. 1. London: printed by R. Noble, 1791.

Crofton, Zachary. *A Defence against the Dread of Death.* n.p., 1665.

Cruso, Timothy. *The Duty and Support of Believers in Life and Death. A Funeral Sermon on the Death of Mrs. Mary Smith.* London: printed for Tho. Cockerill and John Smith, 1688.

Culverwell, Ezekiel. *Time Well Spent in Sacred Meditations, Divine Observations, Heavenly Exhortations.* London: printed by T. Cotes for Tho. Payne, 1635.

Cupper, William. *Certaine Sermons concerning God's Late Visitation in the Citie of London and Other Parts of the Land, Teaching All Men to Make Use Thereof That Meane to Profit by Gods Fatherly Chastisements.* London: imprinted for Robert Dexter, 1592.

Daillé, Jean. *An Exposition of the Epistle of Saint Paul to the Philippians.* London: Henry G. Bohn, 1843.
Includes the author's commentary on Colossians. The author was a French Protestant, and this work was first translated and published in English in this edition.

Danson, Thomas. *A Friendly Debate between Satan and Sherlock.* n.p., 1676.

Dent, Arthur. *The Plain Man's Plain Path-way to Heaven.* London: printed for Eliz. Andrews, 1665.

Dickson, David. *Truth's Victory over Error.* 1684. Reprint, Glasgow: printed by John Bryce, 1772.

Dod, John. *A Sermon on Malt.* Manchester: Temperance Union, 1899.

———. *Seven Godly and Fruitful Sermons.* London: imprinted by Felix Kyngston for William Welby, 1614.

———. *The Worthy Sayings of the Late Reverend John Dod*. Kettering, England: Dash Printers, n. d.
"A sheet of 'Sayings,' attributed to him were very popular, and in the last century was often hung upon the walls instead of a picture, for the admonition of the household." Dod, *Sermon on Malt*, 5.

Dod, John, and Philip Henry. *Gleanings of Heavenly Wisdom, or The Sayings of John Dod and Philip Henry*. London: T. Nelson and Sons, 1851.

Doe, Charles. *A Collection of Experience of the Work of Grace*. London: printed for Chas. Doe, 1700.

Doolittle, Thomas. *A Treatise concerning the Lord's Supper*. 1667. Reprint, Aberdeen: George and Robert King, 1844.

Downame, George. *The Christian's Freedom*. 1635. Reprint, London: E. Couchman, 1836.

Downame, John. *The Christian Warfare*. London: printed by William Stansby, 1634.

Draxe, Thomas. *The Christian Armory*. London: William Hall, 1611.

Durant, John. *Sips of Sweetness, or, Consolation for Weak Believers*. London: printed by M. S. for Hanna Allen, 1649.
Author's name sometimes appears as Durance.

Durham, James. *A Treatise concerning Scandal*. 1659. Reprint, Glasgow: printed by Robert Urie and Company, 1740.

Dury, John. *A Seasonable Discourse… 1. What the Grounds and Method of Our Reformation Ought to Be in Religion and Learning. 2. How Even in These Times of Distraction, the Worke May Be Advanced. By the Knowledge of Orientall Tongues and Jewish Mysteries. By an Agency for Advancement of Universall Learning*. London: Samuel Hartlib, 1649.

Dyer, William. *Christ's Famous Titles*. 1665 [?]. Reprint, Glasgow: Porteous and Hislop, 1863.

Dyke, Daniel. *The Two Treatises*. London: printed by G. P. for Robert Mylbourne, 1618.

England's Remembrancer: Being a Collection of Farewell Sermons, Preached by Divers Non-Conformists in the Country. London, 1663.

Estey, George. *Certain Godly and Learned Expositions upon Diverse Parts of Scripture*. London: printed by I. R. for Richard Banckworth, 1603.
Author's name also spelled Estye.

Featley, Daniel. *The Dippers Dipt: or, The Anabaptists Duck'd and Plung'd Over Head and Eares at a Disputation in Southwark*. London: printed for Nicholas Bourn and Richard Royston, 1646.

Fenner, William. *Four Profitable Treatises*. London: printed by A. Maxey, 1657.

———. *The Works of W. Fenner*. London: printed for William Gilbertson, 1657.

Firmin, Giles. *The Real Christian, or A Treatise of Effectual Calling.* London: printed for Dorman Newman, 1670.

———. *A Sober Reply to the Sober Answer of Rev. Mr. Daniel Cawdrey.* London: printed by J. G., 1653.

[Fisher, Edward?]. *The Marrow of Modern Divinity.* 1645. Reprint, Edinburgh: John Boyd, 1828.
> While the author of this volume wrote under the pseudonym E. F., he is generally considered to be Edward Fisher. Notes in the text are by Thomas Boston.

Flavel, John. *Divine Conduct, or, The Mystery of Providence.* 1678. Reprint, Philadelphia: Presbyterian Board of Publication, 1840.

———. *The Fountain of Life Opened or, A Display of Christ in His Essential and Mediatorial Glory.* 1671. Reprint, London: Religious Tract Society, 1836.

———. *Golden Gems for the Christian, Selected from the Writings of Rev. John Flavel.* Edited by Joseph Banvard. Boston: Gould, Kendall & Lincoln, 1848.

———. *Husbandry Spiritualized, or The Heavenly Use of Earthly Things, in which Husbandmen are Directed to an Excellent Improvement of Their Common Employment.* Middletown: J. A. Boswell, 1824.

———. *Navigation Spiritualized, or, A New Compass for Seamen, Consisting of Thirty-Two Points.* Plymouth: J. Bennett, 1822 [?].

———. *Sacramental Meditations upon Divers Select Places of Scripture, wherein, Believers Are Assisted...in That Most Awful and Solemn Ordinance of the Lord's Supper.* London: printed for Nath. Crouch, 1690.

———. *A Saint Indeed.* Richmond: Joseph Martin, 1826.

Fleming, Robert. *The Fulfilling of the Scripture, for Confirming Believers and Convincing Unbelievers.* 1681. Reprint, Philadelphia: Presbyterian Board of Publication, 1840.

Forbes, John. *A Treatise Tending to Clear the Doctrine of Justification.* Middelburgh: printed by Richard Schilders, 1616.

Ford, Simon. *The Conflagration of London: Poetically Delineated.* London: Sa. Gellibrand, 1667.

Fowler, Christopher. Daemonium meridianum, *Satan at Noon or, Antichristian Blasphemies.* London: printed for Francis Eglesfeild, 1655.

Fuller, Thomas. *Good Thoughts in Bad Times.* London: William Pickering, 1830.
> The contents of this work contain three separate but similar works that were printed in 1647, 1649, and 1660.

———. *The Holy and Profane States.* Boston: Little, Brown, 1864.

———. *Pulpit Sparks, Being XIX Sermons of that Godly and Popular Divine Thomas Fuller.* London: S. Sonnenschein, Le Bas and Lowrey, 1886.

————. *Wise Words and Quaint Counsels of Thomas Fuller*. Selected and arranged by Augustus Jessopp. Oxford: Clarendon Press, 1892.

Gale, Theophilus. *Theophilie: or a Discourse of the Saints Amitie with God in Christ*. n.p.: printed by R. W. for Giles Widdows, 1671.

Gammon, Hannibal. *God's Just Desertion of the Unjust: And His Persevering Grace to the Righteous. In a Sermon Preached at the Assizes at Launston, the 18. of July, 1621*. London: printed by G. Eld, 1622.

Gataker, Thomas. *Christian Constancy Crowned by Christ, A Funerall Sermon… Preached at the Buriall of M. William Winter*. London: printed by John Haviland, 1624.

Gearing, William. *The Sacred Diary; or, Select Meditations for Every Part of the Day, and the Employments Thereof*. London: Religious Tract Society, 1838.

Geree, John. *The Character of an Old English Puritane, or Non-Conformist*. London: printed by A. Miller, 1649.

Gifford, George. *A Dialogue concerning Witches and Witchcraft*. 1603. Reprint, London: printed for the Percy Society, 1842.

Gillespie, Patrick. *The Ark of the Covenant Opened*. London: printed for the Parkhurst, 1677.

Gilpin, Richard. *Daemonologia Sacra; or, A Treatise of Satan's Temptations*. 1677. Reprint, Edinburgh: James Nichol, 1867.

————. *The Temple Rebuilt*. London: printed by E. T. for Luke Fawne, 1658.

Goodwin, Thomas. *The Heart of Christ in Heaven, Towards Sinners on Earth. Or, A Treatise Demonstrating the Gracious Disposition and Tender Affection of Christ in His Humane Nature Now in Glory*. London: printed for R. Dawlman, 1642.

————. *The Works of Thomas Goodwin*. 12 vols. Edinburgh: James Nichol, 1861–1866.

Gouge, Thomas. *Riches Increased by Giving to the Poor*. London: Partridge, 1856.

————. *The Works of Thomas Gouge, in Six Parts*. Albany: George Lindsay, 1815.

Gouge, William. *A Guide to Goe to God*. London: printed by G. M. and R. B. for Edward Brewster, 1626.

————. *Of Domestical Duties*. London: printed by John Haviland, 1622.

Granger, Thomas. *The Application of Scripture, or, The Maner How to Use the Word to Most Edifying*. London: printed by T. S., 1616.

Gray, Andrew. *The Works of the Reverend and Pious Andrew Gray*. Aberdeen: George King, 1839.

Greenham, Richard. *A Godlie Exhortation, and Fruitfull Admonition to Vertuous Parents and Modest Matrons*. London: imprinted for Nicholas Ling, 1584.

————. Paramuthion, *Two Treatises of the Comforting of an Afflicted Conscience.* London: printed by Richard Bradocke for Robert Dexter, 1598.

Greenhill, William. *An Exposition of the Prophet Ezekiel.* London: Samuel Holdsworth, 1839.

————. *The Sound-Hearted Christian, or A Treatise of Soundness of Heart.* London: printed for Nath. Crouch, 1670.

Grew, Obadiah. *A Sinner's Justification.* 1670. Reprint, Cornwall: H. A. Simcoe, 1835.

Grosse, Alexander. *Deaths Deliverance, and Eliahs Fiery Charet, or the Holy Mans Tryumph after Death.* London: I. D. for James Boler, 1632.
   This text is incomplete and contains only *Elijah's Fiery Chariot.*

Gurnall, William. *The Christian in Complete Armour.* Originally published in three parts: 1655, 1658, 1662. Reprint, London: William Tegg, 1862.

————. *Gleanings from William Gurnall.* Morgan, Pa.: Soli Deo Gloria, 1996. This is a reprint of *Gleanings from the Past: Extracts from the Writings of William Gurnall.* Compiled by Hamilton Smith. London: Central Bible Truth Depot, 1914.

Guthrie, William. *The Christian's Great Interest.* 1658. Reprint, Philadelphia: Presbyterian Board of Publication, 1840.

Hakewill, George. *King David's Vow for Reformation.* London: printed for Mathew Lownes, 1621.

Hall, Joseph. *Meditations and Vows.* 1606, 1607, 1609. Reprint, London: for William Pickering, 1851.

————. *Select Devotional Works of Joseph Hall.* London: Religious Tract Society, 1850.

————. *Select Tracts from the Writings of the Right Rev. Joseph Hall.* Edited by C. Bradley. London: L. B. Seeley and Son, 1824.

Hall, Thomas. *The Pulpit Guarded with XVII Arguments.* London: printed by J. Cottrel for E. Blackmore, 1651.

Hardy, Nathaniel. *Divinity in Mortality, or, The Gospel's Excellency and the Preacher's Frailty.* London: printed by A. M. for Nathanael Webb and William Grantham, 1653.

————. *The First General Epistle of St. John the Apostle Unfolded and Applied.* 1656. Reprint, Edinburgh: James Nichol, 1865.

Harley, Brilliana. *Letters of the Lady Brilliana Harley.* Introduction and notes by Thomas Taylor Lewis. London: printed for the Camden Society, 1854.

Harris, Robert. *David's Comfort at Ziklag: A Plain Sermon Made in Time of Dearth and Scarcity.* London: printed for John Bartlet, 1628.

———. *The Drunkard's Cup*. London: printed by Bernard Alsop for Thomas Man, 1622.

Hart, John. *Christ's First Sermon: or, The Absolute Necessity of Gospel Duty and Christian Repentance Opened and Applied*. 26th ed. n.p., 1690.

———. *Christ's Last Sermon: or, The Everlasting Estate and Condition of All Men in the World to Come*. 23rd ed. London: printed by William Dicey, 1720.

Henderson, Alexander. *A Sermon Preached to the Honourable House of Commons, at Their Late Solemn Fast, Wednesday, December 27, 1643*. London: printed for Robert Bostock, 1644.

Henry, Matthew. *Directions for Daily Communion with God*. New York: Robert Carter, 1848.

———. *Gems from Matthew Henry*. Compiled by H. A. London: James Nisbet, 1875.

———. *A Method for Prayer*. Edinburgh: T. Maccliesh, 1803.

———. *The Miscellaneous Writings of Matthew Henry*. London: printed for Samuel Bagster, 1811.

Henry, Philip. *Diaries and Letters of Philip Henry, M.A., of Broad Oak, Flintshire, A.D. 1631–1696*. Edited by Matthew Henry Lee. London: Kegan Paul, Trench, 1882.

———. *The Life and Sayings of the Rev. Philip Henry*. London: printed by T. Cordeux for T. Blanshard, 1819.

———. *Remains of the Rev. Philip Henry, A. M., Extracted from Unpublished Manuscripts*. Edited by John Bickerton Williams. London: Religious Tract Society, 1848.

Herbert, George. *The Poems of George Herbert*. 1633. Reprint, London: Oxford University Press, 1913.

———, comp. *Witts Recreations Selected from the Finest Fancies of Modern Muses with a Thousand Outlandish Proverbs*. London: printed for Humph. Blunden, 1640.

Heywood, Oliver. *Heart Treasure*. Vol. 2 of *The Works of Oliver Heywood*. Morgan, Pa.: Soli Deo Gloria, 1997. Reprint of *The Works of Oliver Heywood*. London: John Vint, 1825.

———. *Life in God's Favour, A Seasonable Discourse in Death-Threatening Times*. Luddendenfoot: printed at Brearley Hall, 1796.

———. *The Rev. Oliver Heywood, 1603–1702; His Autobiography, Diaries, Anecdote and Event Books*. Vol. 1. Edited by J. Horsfall Turner. Brighouse: A. B. Bayes, 1882.

Higford, William. *Institutions: or, Advice to His Grandson, in Three Parts*. 1658. London: W. Bulmer, 1818.

Hildersham, Arthur. *The Canticles; or, Song of Solomon Paraphrased*. London: printed by T. Milbourn for Robert Clavel, 1672.
> Includes Song of Solomon, Song of Moses, and Song of Deborah in meter.

Hill, Robert. *The Pathway to Piety*. Vol. 1. 1629. Reprint, London: William Pickering, 1847.
> The work is a catechism featuring the teacher Euchedidascalus, "a teacher of prayer," and the pupil Phileuches, "a lover of prayer."

Hodges, Thomas. *A Glimpse of God's Glory*. London: printed for John Bartlet, 1642.

———. *A Treatise of Marriage*. London: printed by J. D., 1673.
> The text is signed by T. H., and Hodges's authorship is assumed.

Hooper, John. *Early Writings of John Hooper, D. D., Lord Bishop of Gloucester and Worcester*. Cambridge: printed at the University Press, 1843.

Hopkins, Ezekiel. *Select Works of Ezekiel Hopkins*. 1701, 1712. Reprint, London: L. B. Seeley and Son, 1826.

Horn, H. J., comp. *The Puritan Remembrancer*. London: Stanley Martin, 1928.
> This work is a collection of Puritan quotes not available through Google Books. Horn does not provide a full citation for the quotes. This work has been republished as *The Puritans Day by Day* (Edinburgh: Banner of Truth, 2016).

Howe, John. *A Funeral Sermon for That Faithful and Laborious Servant of Christ, Mr. Richard Fairclough*. London: printed for John Dunton, 1682.

———. *A Treatise of Delighting in God*. 1674. Reprint, London: James Nisbet, 1839.

———. *The Works of the Rev. John Howe*. Edited by Edmund Calamy. 1724. Reprint, London: Henry G. Bohn, 1846.

Hutchinson, Lucy. *Memoirs of the Life of Colonel Hutchinson*. 1806. Reprint, London: Henry G. Bohn, 1848.

Jackson, Arthur. *A Help for the Understanding of the Holy Scripture*. Cambridge: Roger Daniel, 1643.

Janeway, James. *Heaven upon Earth, or, Jesus the Best Friend of Man*. 1670. Reprint, New York: Robert Carter, 1848.

———. *The Saint's Encouragement to Diligence in Christ's Service*. 1673. Reprint, Philadelphia: Presbyterian Board of Publication, 1840.

Jenkyn, William. *An Exposition upon the Epistle of Jude*. 1652–1654. Reprint, London: Samuel Holdsworth, 1839.

Jolly, Thomas. *The Note Book of the Rev. Thomas Jolly, A.D. 1671–1693. Extracts from the Church Books of Altham and Wymondhouses, 1649–1725. And*

an Account of the Jolly Family of Standish, Gorton, and Altham. Edited by Henry Fishwick. Manchester: printed for the Chetham Society, 1895.
The author's name is also spelled Jollie.

Jones, Andrew. *The Black Book of Conscience.* 1658. Reprint, Greenfield: printed for Timothy Frary, 1811.

———. *The Dying Man's Last Sermon: or the Father's Last Blessing. Left and Bequeathed as a Legacy unto His Children, Immediately Before His Death. Being Comfortable Meditations and Preparations for the Day of Death.* 12th ed. London: printed for Elizabeth Andrews, 1665.
The author known as Andrew Jones may have also authored tracts under the name John Hart.

———. Morbus Satanicus. *The Devil's Disease: or, The Sin of Pride Arraigned and Condemned.* 10th ed. London: printed for Elizabeth Andrews, 1662.

Josselin, Ralph. *The Diary of the Rev. Ralph Josselin 1616–1683.* Edited by E. Hockliffe. London: Offices of the Society, 1908.

Keach, Benjamin. *Light Broke Forth in Wales, Expelling Darkness; or The Englishman's Love to the Antient Britains.* London: printed for John Marshall, 1705.
The interior title page reads *Believer's Baptism: or, Love to the Antient Britains Displayed,* i.

———. *The Travels of True Godliness.* 1684. Reprint, London: printed for W. Baynes, 1817.
Keach explores the theme allegorically.

———. *War with the Devil: or, The Young Man's Conflict with the Powers of Darkness.* 1673. Reprint, Leeds: printed by John Binns, 1795.

Keach, Benjamin, and Thomas Delaune. Tropologia; *A Key to Open Scripture Metaphors.* 1681. Reprint, London: William Hill Collingridge City Press, 1856.

Knewstub, John. *The Lectures of John Knewstub, upon the Twentieth Chapter of Exodus, and Certeine Other Places of Scripture.* 1577. Reprint, London: imprinted for Thomas Woodcocke, 1584.
The author's name also appears as Knewstubs.

Knollys, Hanserd. *The Life and Death of That Old Disciple of Jesus Christ, and Eminent Minister of the Gospel, Mr. Hanserd Knollys.* London: printed for John Harris, 1692.

———. *The Shining of a Flaming Fire in Zion: or, A Clear Answer unto 13. Exceptions, against the Grounds of New Baptism (So Called) in Mr. Saltmarsh His Book.* London: printed by Jane Coe, 1646.

Lee, Samuel. *The Most Spiritual Profit and Secret Prayer Successfully Managed.* With *The Bible and the Closet: or, How We May Read the Scriptures with The Most Spiritual Profit* by Thomas Watson. Edited by John Overton Choules. Boston: Gould, Kendall & Lincoln, 1842.

Leighton, Robert. *Sermons*. Edited by C. Bradley. Select British Divines, vol. 4. London: printed by A. J. Valpy, 1821.

———. *Spiritual Truths, Extracted from the Writings of Archbishop Leighton*. Compiled by W. Wilson. London: B. Wertheim, Aldine Chambers, 1847.

———. *The Whole Works of Robert Leighton*. Vol. 1. London: James Duncan, 1825.

Life of the Rev. Vavasor Powell. London: Religious Tract Society, 1832.

Lightfoot, John. *The Journal of the Proceedings of the Assembly of Divines from January 1, 1643 to December 31, 1644 and Letters to and from Dr. Lightfoot*. Edited by John Rogers Pitman. Vol. 13 of *The Whole Works*. London: printed by J. F. Dove, 1824.

Lockyer, Nicholas. *Balm for England; or, Useful Instructions for Evil Times*. 1643. Reprint, London: printed for the Religious Tract Society, 1831.

Love, Christopher. *Heaven's Glory; Hell's Terror*. 1653. Reprint, Glasgow: printed by Alexander Miller, 1738.

———. *The Zealous Christian Taking Heaven by Holy Violence: In Several Sermons*. London: printed for John Rothwell, 1654.

Lye, Thomas. *The Assemblies Shorter Catechism*. London, 1674.

Lyford, William. *The Plain Man's Senses Exercised to Discern Both Good and Evil*. London: printed for Richard Royston, 1655.

Manton, Thomas. *Meate Out of the Eater*. London: printed by M. S. for Hanna Allen, 1647.

———. *A Practical Exposition on the Epistle of James*. 1693. Reprint, London: Samuel Holdsworth, 1840.

Marbury, Edward. *A Commentarie or Exposition upon the Prophecie of Habakkuk*. London: printed by T. R. and E. M. for Octavian Pullen, 1650.

Marshall, Stephen. *A Sacred Panegyrick, or A Sermon of Thanksgiving*. London: printed for Stephen Bowtell, 1644.

Marshall, Walter. *The Gospel Mystery of Sanctification*. 1692. Reprint, Edinburgh: James Taylor, 1873.

Martindale, Adam. *The Life of Adam Martindale, Written by Himself*. Edited by Richard Parkinson. Manchester: printed for the Chetham Society, 1845.

Mather, Samuel. *The Figures or Types of the Old Testament*. 1683. Reprint, London: printed for Nath. Hillier, 1705.

Mayo, Richard. *A Conference Betwixt a Protestant and a Jew: or A Second Letter from a Merchant in London to His Correspondent in Amsterdam*. London: printed for Tho. Parkhurst, 1678.

Mead, Matthew. *The Almost Christian Discovered*. 1662. Reprint, London: printed for L. B. Seeley and Son, 1825.

————. *A Name in Heaven the Truest Ground of Joy*. London: printed for Edmund Parker and Daniel Mead, 1707.

Milton, John. *The Complete Poetical Works of John Milton*. 1892. Reprint, New York: T. Y. Crowell, 1920.

Mitchel, Jonathan. *A Discourse of the Glory by Which God Hath Called Believers by Jesus Christ*. With a preface by Increase Mather. 2nd ed. 1677. Reprint, Boston: B. Green, 1721.

Mocket, Thomas. *Christian Advice Both to Old and Young, Rich and Poor...Under XXVII General Useful Heads*. London: printed for Edw. Brewster, 1671.

Muffet, Peter. *A Commentary on the Whole Book of Proverbs*. Edinburgh: James Nichol, 1868.

Ness, Christopher. *An Antidote against Arminianism*. 1700. Reprint, London: J. Bennett, 1836.

Newcome, Henry. *The Diary of the Rev. Henry Newcome, from September 30, 1661, to September 29, 1663*. Edited by Thomas Heywood. Manchester: printed for the Chetham Society, 1849.

Newcomen, Matthew. *The Best Acquaintance and Highest Honour of Christians*. London: printed for Peter Parker, 1668.

Norton, John. *Abel Being Dead yet Speaketh, or Memoir of John Cotton*. 1658. Reprint, New York: Saxton & Miles, 1842.

————. *A Catechistical Guide to Sinners, and to Such Converts That Are Babes in Christ*. London: printed by J. D., 1680.

Nye, Philip. *A Case of Great and Present Use, Whether We May Lawfully Hear the Now Conforming Ministers, Who Are Re-Ordained, and Have Renounced the Covenant, and Some of Them Supposed to Be Scandalous in Their Lives?* London: printed for Jonathan Robinson, 1677.

Owen, John. *The Death of Death in the Death of Christ*. 1647. Reprint, Carlisle, Pa.: George Kline, 1792.

————. *The Golden Book of John Owen*. Edited by James Moffatt. London: Hodder and Stoughton, 1904.

————. *Oweniana: or, Select Passages from the Works of Owen*. Arranged by Arthur Young. London: printed for J. Hatchard, 1817.

————. *Twenty-Five Discourses Adapted (Suitable) to the Lord's Supper*. Leeds: printed by George Wilson, 1806.

————. *The Works of John Owen*. Edited by William H. Goold. Vol. 6. Edinburgh: T&T Clark, 1862.

Pagitt, Ephraim. *Heresiography: or, A Description of the Heretickes and Sectaries of These Latter Times*. 1645. Reprint, London: printed for William Lee, 1654.

Parr, Elnathan. *The Workes of That Faithfull and Painfull Preacher, Mr. Elnathan Parr*. London: printed by Ed Griffin and Wil. Hunt, 1651.

Pearse, Edward. *The Great Concern, or A Serious Warning to a Timely and Thorough Preparation for Death*. 1671. Reprint, Edinburgh: printed by the heirs and successors of Andrew Anderson, 1715.

Pemble, William. *An Introduction to the Worthy Receiving the Sacrament of the Lord's Supper*. London: printed by H. L. for James Boler, 1629.

Pendlebury, Henry. *The Books Opened*. In *Invisible Realities the Christian's Great Concern*. Bury: printed by B. Crompton, 1816.

————. *Invisible Realities the Christian's Great Concern; to Which Is added The Books Opened. With a Memoir of the Author*. Bury: printed by B. Crompton, 1816.

Penry, John. *A Defence of That Which Hath Bin Written in the Questions of the Ignorant Ministerie, and the Communicating with Them*. n.p., 1588.

Perkins, William. *The Art of Prophesying* with *The Calling of the Ministry*. Edinburgh: Banner of Truth, 1996.
  The Art of Prophesying was first published in 1606. *The Calling of the Ministry* was first published in 1605.

————. *A Direction for the Government of the Tongue according to God's Word*. Cambridge: printed by John Legat, 1597.

————. *The Foundation of Christian Religion, Gathered into Six Principles*. London, 1723.

————. *A Grain of Mustard Seed*. Newcastle: printed by John White, 1760.

————. *A Treatise of the Vocations*. Cambridge: John Legat, printer to the University of Cambridge, 1605.

————. *The Works of That Famous and Worthy Minister of Christ, W. Perkins*. Vol. 3. London: printed by John Haviland, 1631.

Polhill, Edward. *Armatura Dei: or, A Preparation for Suffering in an Evil Day*. 1682. Reprint, London: for Messrs. Hatchard and Son, 1824.

Poole, Matthew. *Dialogue between a Popish Priest and an English Protestant*. 1667. Reprint, Philadelphia: Presbyterian Board of Publication, 1843.

Powell, Vavasor. *Common Prayer Book No Divine Service*. London: printed for Livewell Chapman, 1660.

————. *Spirituall Experiences of Sundry Beleevers*. London: printed for Robert Ibbitson, 1653.

Preston, John. *Four Godly and Learned Treatises*. London: printed by T. C., 1633.

————. *Remaines of that Reverend and Learned Divine, John Preston*. London: printed for Andrew Crooke, 1634.

Ranew, Nathanael. *Solitude Improved by Divine Meditation.* 1670. Reprint, London: Religious Tract Society, 1839.

Raworth, Francis. *On Jacob's Ladder, or, The Protectorship of Sion, Being the Substance of a Discourse on Gen. Xxviii, 12, 13.* 1654. Reprint, London: G. Keith, 1762.

Reyner, Edward. *Precepts for Christian Practice.* London: printed for John Clark, 1662.

Reynolds, Edward. *Meditations on the Fall and Rising of St. Peter.* 1677. Reprint, London: printed for C. Brown, 1819.

Ridgley, Thomas. *A Body of Divinity in Four Volumes.* Vol. 3. 1731. Reprint, Philadelphia: printed by and for William W. Woodward, 1815.

———. *A Funeral Sermon Preached on the Death of Mrs. Elizabeth Bankes.* London: printed for J. Clark, 1711.

Roberts, Francis. *A Communicant Instructed: or Practical Directions for Worthy Receiving of the Lord's Supper.* 1648. Reprint, London: printed by F. L. for George Calvert, 1676.

———. *The Great Worth of Scripture Knowledge.* Burton-upon-Trent: printed by T. Wayte, 1794.
This work is abridged by John Tift. From the preface: "The substance of the following pages were published by Dr. Roberts, 1675, at the beginning of a folio volume, called *The Key of the Bible.*"

Robinson, Ralph. *Christ All and in All.* 1660. Reprint, Woolwich: printed for T. Sharp (the editor), 1827.

Rogers, John. *A Treatise of Love.* London: printed by John Dawson for Nathanael Newbery, 1632.

Rogers, Nehemiah. *A Mirrour of Mercy.* London: printed by G. M. for Edward Brewster, 1640.

———. *The True Convert: or, An Exposition upon the Fifteenth Chapter of St. Luke's Gospel.* London: printed by George Miller for Edward Brewster, 1632.

Rogers, Richard. *A Garden of Spirituall Flowers Planted by Ri. Ro(gers), Will. Per(kins), Ri. Gree(nham), M. M. and Geo. Web(be).* London: printed by T. S. for T. Panier, 1612.

———. *Holy Helps for a Godly Life.* Puritan Treasures for Today. Grand Rapids: Reformation Heritage Books, 2018.

Rollock, Robert. *Select Works, in Two Volumes.* Edinburgh: printed for the Wodrow Society, 1849 (vol. 1), 1844 (vol. 2).
The first volume was printed after the second volume.

Rutherford, Samuel. *A Garden of Spices: Extracts from the Religious Letters of*

Samuel Rutherford. Compiled by Lewis R. Dunn. Cincinnati: Hitchcock & Walden, 1869.
The letters extracted in this volume are from 1628 to 1661 with most of them written in the 1630s.

―――. *Letters of Samuel Rutherford: A Selection.* Edinburgh: Banner of Truth, 2015.
The first edition of Rutherford's letters was published in 1664.

―――. *The Prison Sayings of Samuel Rutherford, A.D. 1637.* London: James Nisbet, 1854.

―――. *Quaint Sermons of Samuel Rutherford, Hitherto Unpublished.* London: Hodder and Stoughton, 1885.

Sclater, William. *An Exposition with Notes, on the Whole Fourth Chapter to the Romanes. Wherein the Grand Question of Justification by Faith Alone without Works, Is Controverted, Stated, Cleared, and Fully Resolved.* London: printed by J. L. for Christopher Meredith, 1650.

Scougal, Henry. *The Life of God in the Soul of Man.* 1677. Reprint, Boston: Nichols and Noyes, 1868.

―――. *The Works of the Rev. Scougal, Containing the Life of God in the Soul of Man. With Nine Other Discourses on Important Subjects. To which Is Added a Sermon Preached at the Author's Funeral by George Gairden.* New York: Jonathan Leavitt, 1833.

Scudder, Henry. *The Christian's Daily Walk in Holy Security and Peace.* Glasgow: William Collins, 1826.

Secker, William. *The Nonsuch Professor in His Meridian Splendour, or The Singular Actions of Sanctified Christians Laid Open in Seven Sermons.* London: Richard D. Dickinson, 1867.

Sedgwick, Obadiah. *The Shepherd of Israel or God's Pastoral Care over His People.* London: D. Maxwell, 1658.

Sharp, Benjamin Oswald. *Anne Askew, Martyr A.D. 1545 (A Sermon on Mark 14:3).* London: S. W. Partridge, 1869.

Shaw, Samuel. *Immanuel: or, A Discovery of True Religion.* Vol. 1. 1667. Reprint, Leeds: printed by George Wilson, 1804.

―――. *The Voice of One Crying in the Wilderness; or, the Business of a Christian Both Antecedaneous to, Concomitant of, and Consequent upon, a Sore and Heavy Visitation, Represented in Several Sermons.* 1667 [?]. London: printed for Religious Tract Society, 1830.

Shepard, Thomas. *Meditations and Spiritual Experiences.* Glasgow: David Bryce, 1847.

————. *The Sincere Convert; and The Sound Believer.* Paisley: printed by Stephen and Andrew Young, 1812.

Shower, John. *Family Religion, in Three Letters to a Friend.* London: printed by J. D. for John Lawrence, 1694.

————. *Serious Reflections on Time and Eternity.* Glasgow: printed for William Collins, 1828.
Includes *On the Consideration of Our Latter End, and Other Contemplations* by Matthew Hale.

Shute, Josias. *Judgement and Mercy, or, The Plague of Frogges Inflicted, Removed, Delivered in Nine Sermons.* London: printed for Charles Greene, 1645.

Sibbes, Richard. *The Bruised Reed and Smoking Flax.* 1620. Reprint, Philadelphia: Presbyterian Board of Publication, n.d.

————. *The Complete Works of Richard Sibbes.* Vol. 1. Edinburgh: James Nichol, 1862.

————. *Divine Meditations and Holy Contemplations.* 1638 [?]. London: printed for J. Buckland, Paternoster-Row; G. Keith, Gracechurch-Street; E. and C. Dilly, Poultry; and W. Harris, St. Paul's Church-Yard, 1775.

————. *The Soul's Conflict and Victory over Itself by Faith.* 1635. Reprint, London: Pickering, 1837.

Simpson, Sydrach. *Two Books of Mr. Sydrach Simpson.* London: printed by Peter Cole, 1658.

Slate, Richard, ed. *Select Nonconformists' Remains: Being Original Sermons of Oliver Heywood, Thomas Jollie, Henry Newcome, and Henry Pendlebury.* London: printed for Longman, Hurst, Rees, Orme, and Brown, 1814.

Smith, Henry. *The Sermons of Henry Smith, the Silver-Tongued Preacher.* Edited by John Brown. Cambridge: Cambridge University Press, 1908.

————. *Three Sermons Made by Master Henry Smith.* London: imprinted by F. K. for Nicholas Ling, 1604.

————. *The Works of Henry Smith.* Vol. 1. Edinburgh: James Nichol, 1866.

Spurgeon, Charles H. *Illustrations and Meditations or Flowers from a Puritan's Garden.* London: Passmore and Alabaster, 1883.

Spurstowe, William. *The Wells of Salvation Opened, or, A Treatise Discovering the Nature, Preciousness, Usefulness of Gospel-Promises, and Rules for the Right Application of Them.* London: printed by T. R. and E. M., 1655.

————. *The Wiles of Satan.* London, 1666.

Stalham, John. *The Reviler Rebuked: or, A Re-Inforcement of the Charge against the Quakers, So Called for Their Contradictions to the Scriptures of God, and to Their Own Scriblings.* London: printed by Henry Hills and John Field, 1657.

Stated Christian Conference Asserted to Be a Christian Duty. London: printed for and sold by Will. Marshal, 1697.

Steele, Richard. *The Religious Tradesman*. 1684. Reprint, Charlestown: printed by Samuel Etheridge, 1804.

Sterry, Peter. *The Rise, Race, and Royalty of the Kingdom of God in the Soul of Man, Opened in Several Sermons upon Matthew 18:3, as Also the Loveliness & Love of Christ Set Forth in Several Other Sermons upon Psal. 45:1–2, Together with an Account of the State of a Saint's Soul and Body in Death*. London: printed for Thomas Cockerill, 1683.

Strong, William. *Heavenly Treasure, or Man's Chiefest Good*. London: printed by R. W. for Francis Tyton, 1656.
Also contains the appended work "Elisha His Lamentation" by Obadiah Sedgwick, which is the funeral sermon he preached at William Strong's funeral.

Swinnock, George. *The Works of George Swinnock*. Vols. 2, 4, and 5. 1665. Reprint, Edinburgh: James Nichol, 1868.

Symonds, Joseph. *The Case and Cure of a Deserted Soul*. 1639 [?]. Reprint, Edinburgh: printed by John Mosman, 1721.

T. S. *Aids to the Divine Life as a Series of Practical Christian Contemplations*. Liverpool: Edward Howell, 1865. This work was originally titled *Divine Breathings: or, a Manual of Practical Contemplations, in One Century; Tending to Promote Gospel Principles, and a Good Conversation in Christ* (London: Nathaniel Ponder, Poultry, 1680).
The author's identity is unknown.

Taylor, Francis. *God's Glory in Man's Happiness*. London: printed by E. C., 1654.

Taylor, Nathaniel. *A Funeral Sermon [on Luke 12:40], Occasioned by the Sudden Death of the Reverend Mr. Nathanael Vincent*. London: printed for John Lawrence, 1697.

———. *A Funeral Sermon [on 2 Cor. (5):8] on the Decease of the Reverend Mr. Richard Mayo*. London: printed for Thomas Cockerill, 1695.

Taylor, Thomas. *The Pilgrims Profession. Or a Sermon [on Ps. Xxxix. 12] Preached at the Funeral of Mrs. M. Gunter*. London: printed by I. D., 1622.

Thomas, I. D. E., ed. *A Puritan Golden Treasury*. Edinburgh: Banner of Truth, 1989. Isaac David Ellis Thomas (d. 2013) assembled this excellent collection of Puritan quotes that is still published by Banner of Truth as part of their Puritan Paperback series.

Traill, Robert. *Select Practical Writings of Robert Traill*. Edinburgh: printed for the Assembly's Committee, 1845.

———. *Sixteen Sermons on the Lord's Prayer, for His People in John 17:24*. 1705. Reprint, London: Religious Tract Society, 1799.

Trapp, John. *A Commentary on the Old and New Testaments.*Vol. 1. London: Richard D. Dickinson, 1867.

———. *A Commentary or Exposition upon all the Books of the New Testament.* London: printed by R. W., 1656.

———. *The Marrow of Many Good Authors.* London: printed for Nathaniel Eakins, 1655.

Trench, Edmund. *Some Remarkable Passages in the Holy Life and Death of the Late Reverend Mr. Edmund Trench, Most of Them Drawn Out of His Own Diary.* London: printed by T. Warren for Tho. Parkhurst, 1693.

Trosse, George. *Life of the Rev. George Trosse, of Exeter.* 1714. Reprint, London: Religious Tract Society, 1832.

Tuckney, Anthony. *Forty Sermons upon Several Occasions.* London: printed by J. M., 1676.

Tuke, Thomas. *Concerning the Holy Eucharist and the Popish Breaden God.* 1625. Reprint, n.p., 1872.

Udall, John. *The State of the Church of England Laid Open in a Conference between Diotrephes a Bishop, Tertullus a Papist, Demetrius a Usurer, Pandochus an Innkeeper, and Paul a Preacher of the Word of God.* 1588. Reprint, Westminster: Archibald Constable, 1895.

Ussher, James. *A Body of Divinity.* London: R. B. Seeley and W. Burnside, 1841. This work has been collected and compiled by Ussher. Some of the material is his, and some forms a kind of commonplace book.

Venning, Ralph. *Canaan's Flowings. Or, Milk and Honey. Being a Collation of… Christian Experiences, Sayings, Sentences, etc.* London: printed by T. C. for John Rothwel, 1658.

———. *Mysteries and Revelations.* London: printed for John Rothwell, 1652.

———. *Orthodox Paradoxes.* London: J. Rothwell Printer, 1654.

———. *The Sinfulness of Sin.* Edinburgh: Banner of Truth, 1993. First published in 1669 as *The Plague of Plagues.*

Vincent, Nathaniel. *The Spirit of Prayer.* London: printed for and sold by G. Youngman, 1815. The author is the younger brother of Thomas Vincent.

Vincent, Thomas. *Christ's Sudden and Certain Appearance to Judgment.* Wheeling, Va.: Davis & McCarty, 1823.

———. *An Explicatory Catechism or An Explanation of the Assembly's Shorter Catechism.* 1674. Reprint, Edinburgh: printed for J. Dickson and J. Fairbairn, 1799.

———. *God's Terrible Voice in the City.* 1667. Reprint, London: James Nisbet, 1832.

Vint, William, ed. *The Suffering Christian's Companion*. Idle: printed by John Vint, 1830.

Wales, Elkanah. *Mount Ebal Levelled, or Redemption from the Curse*. 1659. London: reprinted for G. Offor, 1823.

Wallington, Nehemiah. *Historical Notices of Events Occurring Chiefly in the Reign of Charles I*. Vol. 1. London: Richard Bentley, 1869.

Ward, Samuel. *Sermons and Treatises*. 1636. Reprint, Edinburgh: James Nichol, 1862.

Watson, Thomas. *The Art of Divine Contentment*. 1653. Reprint, London: L. B. Seeley and Sons, 1839.

———. *The Bible and the Closet: or, How We May Read the Scriptures; with The Most Spiritual Profit* and *Secret Prayer Successfully Managed* by Samuel Lee. Edited by John Overton Choules. Boston: Gould, Kendall & Lincoln, 1842.

———. *A Body of Practical Divinity*. 1692. Reprint, Philadelphia: printed by James Kay, Jun., 1833.

———. *The Christian Soldier, or, Heaven Taken by Storm, Shewing the Holy Violence a Christian Is to Put Forth in the Pursuit After Glory. To Which Is Added: The Happiness of Drawing Near to God, and The Saint's Desire to Be with Christ*. New York: Robert Moore, 1816.

———. *Discourses on Important and Interesting Subjects, Being the Select Works of Thomas Watson*. Vols. 1 and 2. Glasgow: Blackie, Fullarton, 1829.

———. *The Doctrine of Repentance*. 1668. Reprint, Edinburgh: Banner of Truth, 1999.

———. *Gleanings from Thomas Watson*. Compiled by Hamilton Smith. Morgan, Pa.: Soli Deo Gloria, 1995.
This is a reprint of *Gleanings from the Past: Extracts from the Writings of Thomas Watson* (London: Central Bible Truth Depot, 1915).

———. *The Godly Man's Picture Drawn with a Scripture-Pensil*. Glasgow: printed by John Robertson, 1758.

———. *The Great Gain of Godliness*. Edinburgh: Banner of Truth, 2008.
First published as *Religion Our True Interest*. London, 1682.

———. *The Lord's Prayer*. 1692. Reprint, Edinburgh: Banner of Truth, 1993.
First published as part of *A Body of Practical Divinity* (1692).

———. *The Mischief of Sin*. 1671. Reprint, Morgan, Pa.: Soli Deo Gloria, 1994.

———. *Puritan Gems, or Wise and Holy Sayings of Thomas Watson*. London: J. Snow, and Ward, Paternoster Row; Nisbet, Berners Street; E. F. Gooch, King William Street, 1850.

Watts, Isaac. *Devout Meditations: From, Dr. Watts.* London [?]: reprinted by Darton and Harvey, 1791.

———. *Logic, or, The Right Use of Reason, in the Enquiry after Truth.* 1724. Reprint, London: John Bumpus, 1822.

Whately, William. *A Bride-Bush; or, A Direction for Married Persons.* 1619. Reprint, Bristol: printed by William Pine, 1768.

———. *The New Birth: or, A Treatise of Regeneration, Delivered in Certain Sermons.* London: imprinted by Felix Kyngston for Thomas Man, 1619.

Whitaker, Jeremiah. *The Christians Great Design on Earth, Is, to Attain Assurance for Heaven, or, How Is This Life Hee May Lay Bold on Eternall Life.* London: printed by G. Miller for John Bellamie, 1645.

White, John. *A Way to the Tree of Life: Discovered in Sundry Directions for the Profitable Reading of the Scriptures, etc.* London: printed by M. F. for R. Royston, 1647.

Wigglesworth, Michael. *The Day of Doom, or, A Poetical Description of the Great and Last Judgment: With Other Poems.* 1662. Reprint, New York: American News Company, 1867.

Wilcox, Thomas. *A Choice Drop of Honey from the Rock Christ.* London: J. Nisbet, 1823.
The author's last name is sometime spelled Wilcocks.

Wilkins, John. *A Discourse concerning the Gift of Prayer.* London: J. Lawrence, 1690.

Wilkinson, Henry. *Three Decades of Sermons.* Oxford: printed for T. Robinson, 1660.

Willan, Edward. *Six Sermons, 1. Of Christian Charity, 2. Of True Felicity, 3. Of the Worlds Vanity, and Soules Excellency, 4. Of an Humble Conversion, and an Holy Conversation, 5. & 6. Of St. Paul's Concrucifixion.* London: printed for R. Royston, 1651.

Willet, Andrew. *Synopsis Papismi, or, a General View of the Papacy, with General Confutations of Romish Errors from the Scriptures, Fathers, Councils, etc.* Vol. 6. 1592. Reprint, London: published at the Society's Office, 1852.

Williams, Daniel. *The Excellency of a Publick Spirit; Set Forth in a Sermon Preached at the Funeral of Samuel Annesley.* London: printed for John Dunton, 1697.

Woodward, Hezekiah. *A Treatise of Prayer, Two Queries Resolved Touching Formes of Prayer. And Six Queries Relating Specially to the Lord's Prayer.* London: printed by M. S. for Henry Cripps, 1656.

BIBLIOGRAPHY OF WORKS RECOMMENDED

Allen, Lewis, and Tim Chester. *The Glory of Grace: An Introduction to the Puritans in Their Own Words*. Edinburgh: Banner of Truth, 2018.

Beeke, Joel R. "Reading the Best in Puritan Literature: A Modern Bibliography." *Reformation and Revival Journal* 5, no. 2 (Winter 1996): 117–58.

———. *Reformed Preaching*. Wheaton, Ill.: Crossway, 2018.

Beeke, Joel R., and Mark Jones. *A Puritan Theology: Doctrine for Life*. Grand Rapids: Reformation Heritage Books, 2012.

———. *A Puritan Theology Study Guide*. Grand Rapids: Reformation Heritage Books, 2016.

Beeke, Joel R., and Randall J. Pederson. *Meet the Puritans with a Guide to Modern Reprints*. Grand Rapids: Reformation Heritage Books, 2006.

Bremer, Francis J. *Puritanism: A Very Short Introduction*. Oxford: Oxford University Press, 2009.

Brook, Benjamin. *The Lives of the Puritans, Containing a Biographical Account of Those Divines Who Distinguished Themselves in the Cause of Religious Liberty, from the Reformation under Queen Elizabeth to the Act of Uniformity in 1662*. 3 vols. London: printed for James Black, 1813.

Cosby, Brian H. *Suffering and Sovereignty: John Flavel and the Puritans on Afflictive Providence*. Grand Rapids: Reformation Heritage Books, 2012.

Davies, Horton. *The Worship of the English Puritans*. Morgan, Pa.: Soli Deo Gloria, 1997.

Dever, Mark. *The Affectionate Theology of Richard Sibbes*. Orlando, Fla.: Reformation Trust, 2018.

Di Gangi, Mariano. *A Golden Treasury of Puritan Devotion*. Phillipsburg, N.J.: P&R, 1999.

Elmer, Robert, ed. *Piercing Heaven: Prayers of the Puritans*. Bellingham, Wash.: Lexham Press, 2019.

Hall, Edwin. *The Puritans and Their Principles*. New York: Baker and Scribner, 1846.

Haller, William. *The Rise of Puritanism*. New York: Columbia University Press, 1938.

Hambrick-Stowe, Charles E. *The Practice of Piety: Puritan Devotional Disciplines in Seventeenth-Century New England*. Chapel Hill: University of North Carolina Press, 1982.

Hedges, Brian G. *Watchfulness: Recovering a Lost Spiritual Discipline*. Grand Rapids: Reformation Heritage Books, 2018.

Hill, Christopher. *The Century of Revolution 1603–1714*. New York: W. W. Norton, 1961.

———. *Society and Puritanism in Pre-Revolutionary England*. 2nd ed. New York: Schocken Books, 1967.

Hulse, Erroll. *Who Are the Puritans?…and What Do They Teach?* Darlington, England: Evangelical Press, 2000.

Jung, Joanne J. *Godly Conversation: Rediscovering the Puritan Practice of Conference*. Grand Rapids: Reformation Heritage Books, 2011.

———. *The Lost Discipline of Conversation*. Grand Rapids: Zondervan, 2018.

Kapic, Kelly M., and Randall C. Gleason, eds. *The Devoted Life: An Invitation to the Puritan Classics*. Downers Grove, Ill.: InterVarsity Press, 2004.

Knappen, M. M. *Tudor Puritanism: A Chapter in the History of Idealism*. 1939. Reprint, Chicago: University of Chicago Press, 1965.

Lloyd-Jones, D. M., ed. *Puritan Papers*. Vol. 1, *1956–1959*. Philadelphia: P&R, 2000.

———. *The Puritans: Their Origins and Successors*. 1987. Reprint, Edinburgh: Banner of Truth, 1991.

Martin, Robert P. *A Guide to the Puritans: A Topical and Textual Index to Writings of the Puritans and Some of their Successors Recently in Print*. Edinburgh: Banner of Truth, 1997.

McMahon, C. Matthew, and Therese B. McMahon, eds. *Light from Old Paths: An Anthology of Puritan Quotations*. Vol. 1. Coconut Creek, Fla.: Puritan Publications, 2014.

Miller, Perry. *Errand into the Wilderness*. Cambridge: Belknap Press, 1956.

Nuttall, Geoffrey F. *The Puritan Spirit: Essays and Addresses*. London: Epworth Press, 1967.

Packer, J. I. *A Quest for Godliness: The Puritan Vision of the Christian Life*. Wheaton, Ill.: Crossway, 1990.

Rushing, Richard, ed. *Voices from the Past: Puritan Devotional Readings*. Edinburgh: Banner of Truth, 2015.

Ryken, Leland. *Worldly Saints: The Puritans as They Really Were*. Grand Rapids: Zondervan, 1986.

Saxton, David W. *God's Battle Plan for the Mind: The Puritan Practice of Biblical Meditation*. Grand Rapids: Reformation Heritage Books, 2015.

Simpson, Alan. *Puritanism in Old and New England*. Chicago: University of Chicago Press, 1955.

Toon, Peter. *God's Statesman: The Life and Work of John Owen*. Grand Rapids: Zondervan, 1971.

———. *Puritans and Calvinism*. Swengel, Pa.: Reiner, 1973.

Wallace, Dewey D., Jr., ed. *The Spirituality of the Later English Puritans: An Anthology*. Macon, Ga.: Mercer University Press, 1987.

INDEX OF AUTHORS

222, 223, 250, 297, 343, 357, 383,
462, 478, 483, 544, 582, 608
Collinges, John, 46, 91, 213, 219, 280,
537
Conant, John, 32, 112, 201, 255, 273,
277, 278, 282, 340, 541
Cotton, Clement, 103, 483
Cradock, Samuel, 175, 191, 293, 338,
396, 448, 468
Crisp, Tobias, 14
Crofton, Zachary, 115, 119, 298, 327,
475, 596
Cruso, Timothy, 480, 505
Culverwell, Ezekiel, 26, 46, 84, 121, 139,
140, 169, 171, 227, 234, 280, 288,
330, 368, 396, 435, 468, 469, 492,
497, 523, 572, 611
Cupper, William, 388, 520

Daillé, Jean, 483
Danson, Thomas, 576
Delaune, Thomas, 65, 66
Dent, Arthur, 163, 244, 538
Dod, John, 21, 77, 123, 143, 193, 216,
221, 262, 293, 299, 307, 389, 396,
518, 536, 545, 551, 558, 594
Doolittle, Thomas, 309
Downame, George, 69, 150, 179, 294,
297
Downame, John, 85
Draxe, Thomas, 520
Durance/Durant, John, 11, 327, 554
Durham, James, 181
Dury, John, 456, 494
Dyer, William, 19, 28, 54, 62, 64, 70, 91,
127, 161, 201, 227, 234, 239, 550
Dyke, Daniel, 17, 21, 123, 440

Estey/Estye, George, 90

Featley, Daniel, 36
Fenner, William, 8, 9, 150, 463, 591,
611
Firmin, Giles, 71, 103, 104, 106, 108,

163, 171, 435, 454, 480, 524, 539,
562
Fisher, Edward, 107
Flavel, John, 7, 20, 22, 25, 32, 35, 39,
41, 47, 50, 54, 55, 63, 64, 65, 67,
69, 92, 100, 115, 116, 119, 123,
125, 127, 131, 133, 143, 157, 162,
163, 168, 171, 182, 189, 190, 204,
210, 217, 223, 227, 238, 240, 244,
250, 258, 263, 273, 277, 283, 286,
288, 294, 300, 303, 309, 319, 338,
348, 350, 368, 369, 381, 396, 397,
431, 441, 448, 449, 476, 483, 486,
492, 506, 524, 541, 545, 554, 558,
559, 563, 565, 568, 569, 573, 583,
594, 595
Fleming, Robert, 477
Forbes, John, 294
Ford, Simon, 231
Fowler, Christopher, 589
Fuller, Thomas, 39, 43, 50, 72, 78, 100,
116, 135, 161, 181, 249, 267, 270,
321, 326, 342, 365, 374, 387, 388,
412, 413, 441, 457, 461, 512, 520,
537, 538, 554, 561, 595, 602, 609

Gale, Theophilus, 193
Gammon, Hannibal, 158, 297, 383, 524
Gataker, Thomas, 322, 435, 516, 533
Gearing, William, 183, 358, 366, 397,
461, 536, 545
Geree, John, 413
Gifford, George, 602
Gillespie, Patrick, 205, 214, 580
Gilpin, Richard, 11, 72, 341, 487
Goodwin, Thomas, 60, 61, 63, 67, 155,
166, 377, 390, 558, 569, 570, 590
Gouge, Thomas, 25, 165, 195, 196, 197,
322
Gouge, William, 201, 298, 322, 445
Granger, Thomas, 369, 497
Gray, Andrew, 17, 37, 100, 217, 413
Greenham, Richard, 92, 255, 366
Greenhill, William, 104, 125, 185, 201,
206, 335, 366, 369, 413, 595, 606

INDEX OF TOPICS